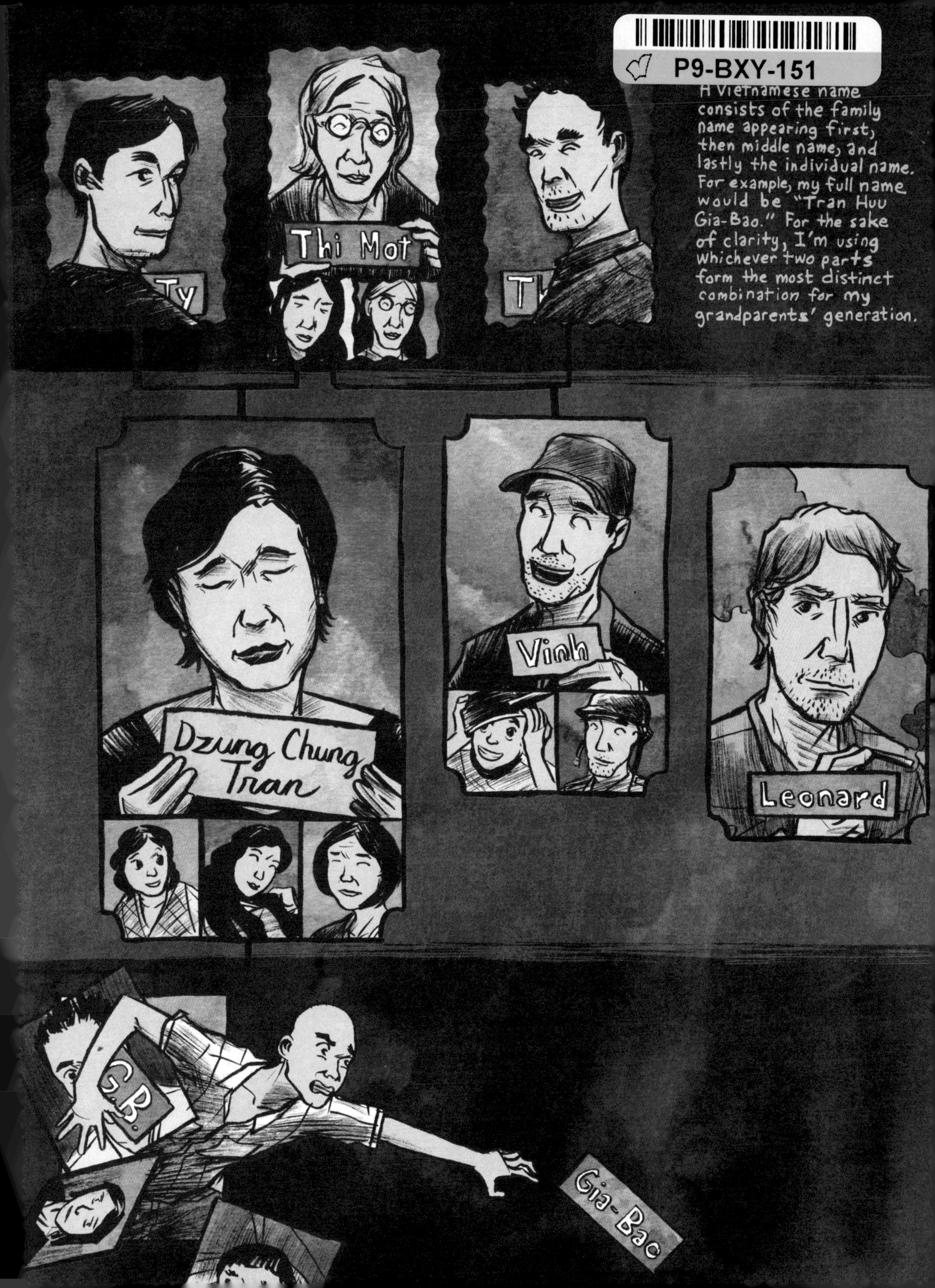
A Vietnamese name consists of the family name appearing first, then middle name, and lastly the individual name. For example, my full name would be "Tran Huu Gia-Bao." For the sake of clarity, I'm using whichever two parts form the most distinct combination for my grandparents' generation.
Ty
Thi Mot
Dzung Chung Tran
Vinh
Leonard
G.B.
Gia-Bao

VIETNAMERICA

A FAMILY'S JOURNEY

VIETNAMERICA

A FAMILY'S JOURNEY
Written and Illustrated by GB TRAN

VILLARD · NEW YORK

Published in the United States by Villard Books,
an imprint of the Random House Publishing Group,
a division of Random House, Inc., New York.

Villard Books and Villard & "V" Circled Design are
registered trademarks of Random House, Inc.

ISBN 978-0-345-50872-0

Printed in China

www.villard.com

2 4 6 8 9 7 5 3 1

For Mom and Dad

VIETNAMERICA

A FAMILY'S JOURNEY

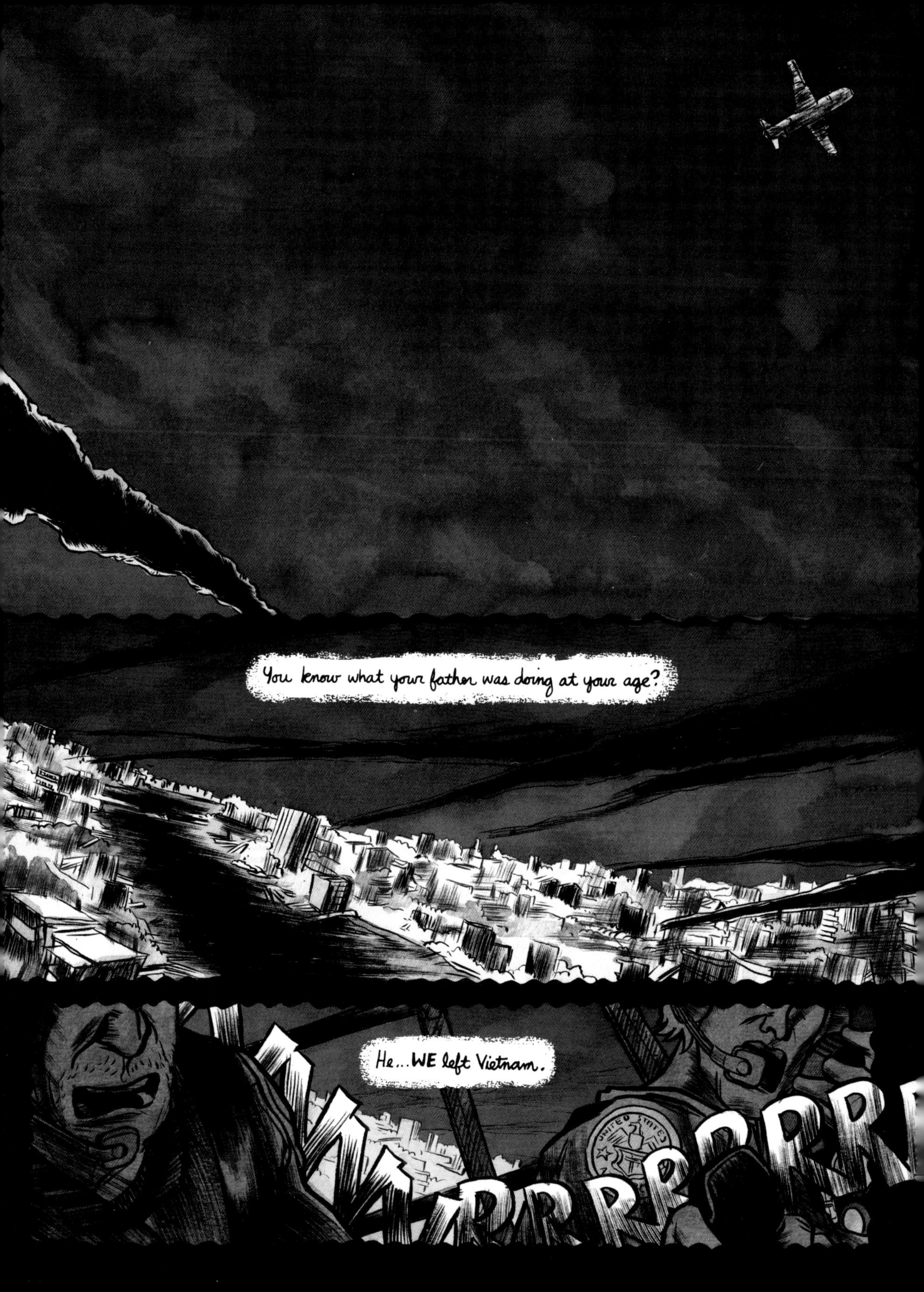
You know what your father was doing at your age?
He... WE left Vietnam.
WRRRRRR

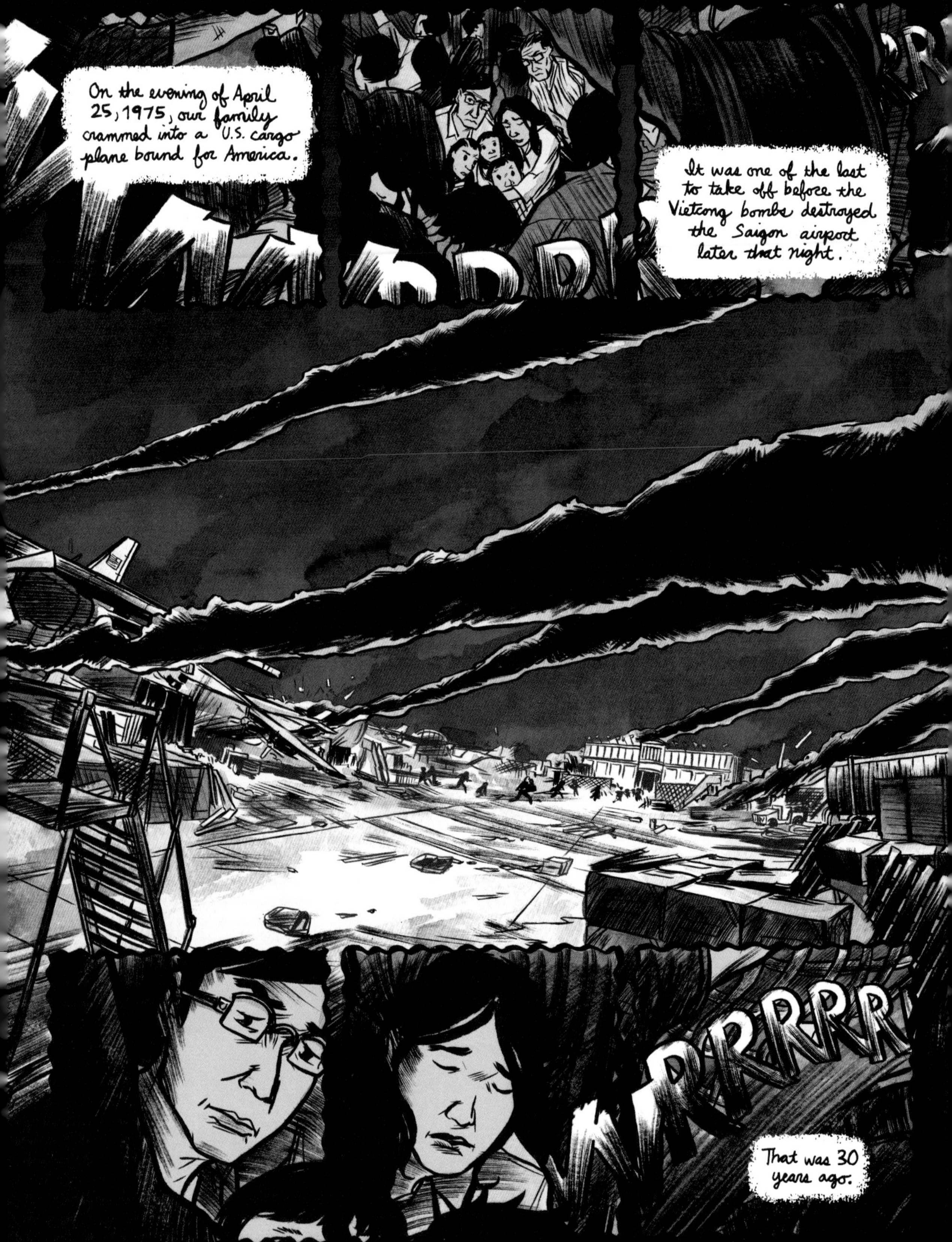
On the evening of April 25, 1975, our family crammed into a U.S. cargo plane bound for America.
It was one of the last to take off before the Vietcong bombs destroyed the Saigon airport later that night.
WRRRRR
That was 30 years ago.

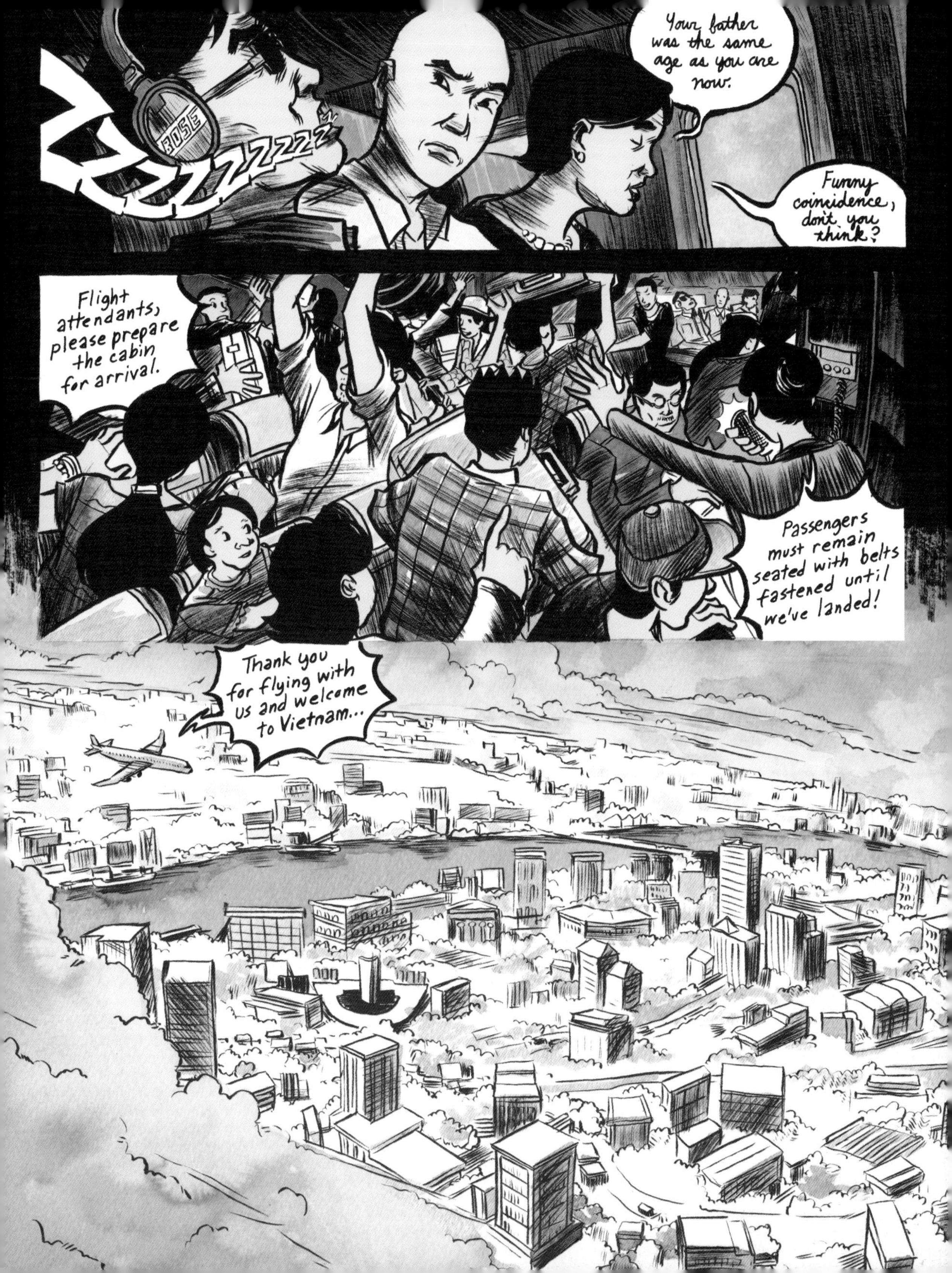
ZZZZZZZZZZ
BOSE
Your father was the same age as you are now.
Funny coincidence, don't you think?
Flight attendants, please prepare the cabin for arrival.
Passengers must remain seated with belts fastened until we've landed!
Thank you for flying with us and welcome to Vietnam...

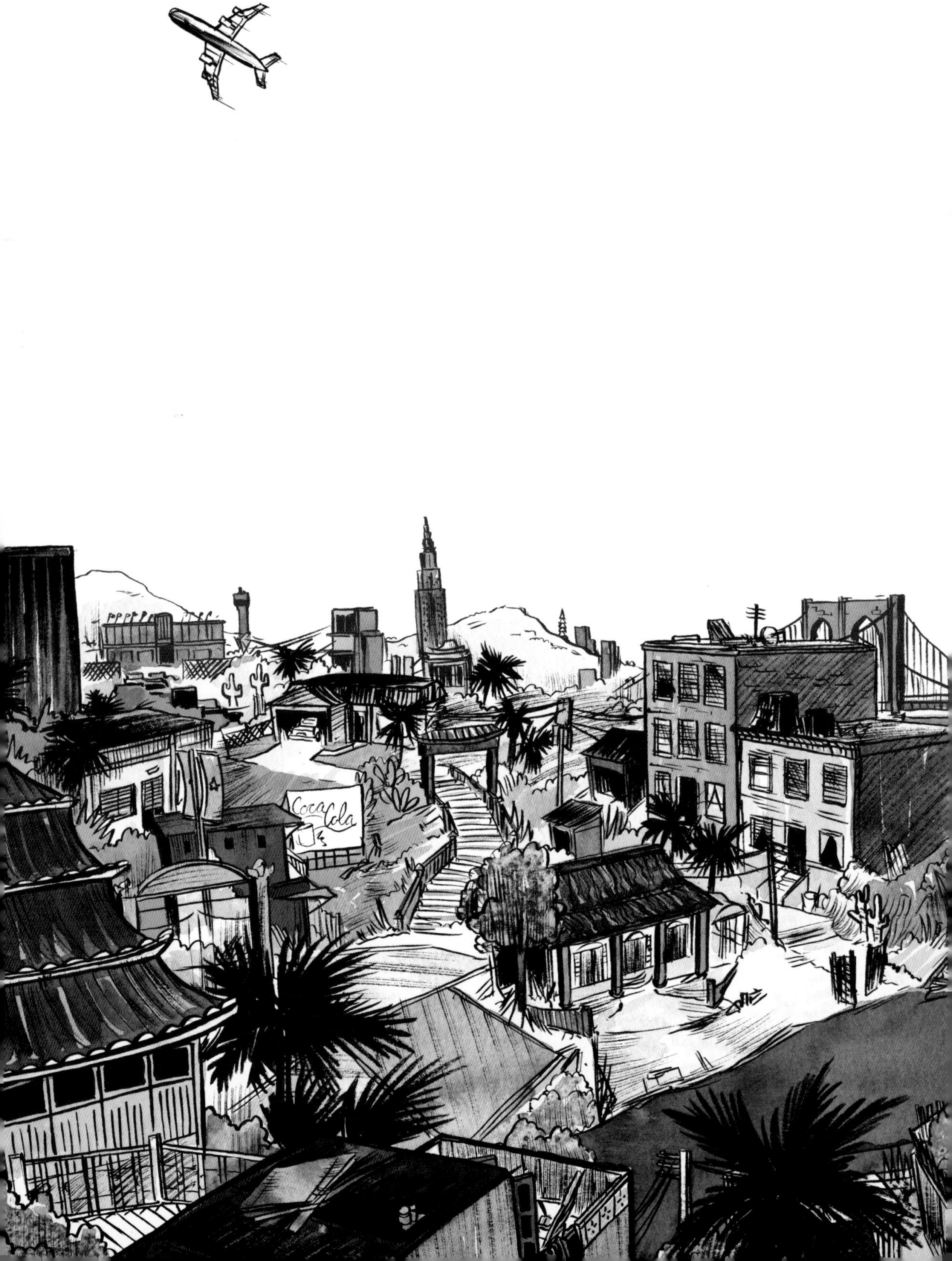
Coca Cola

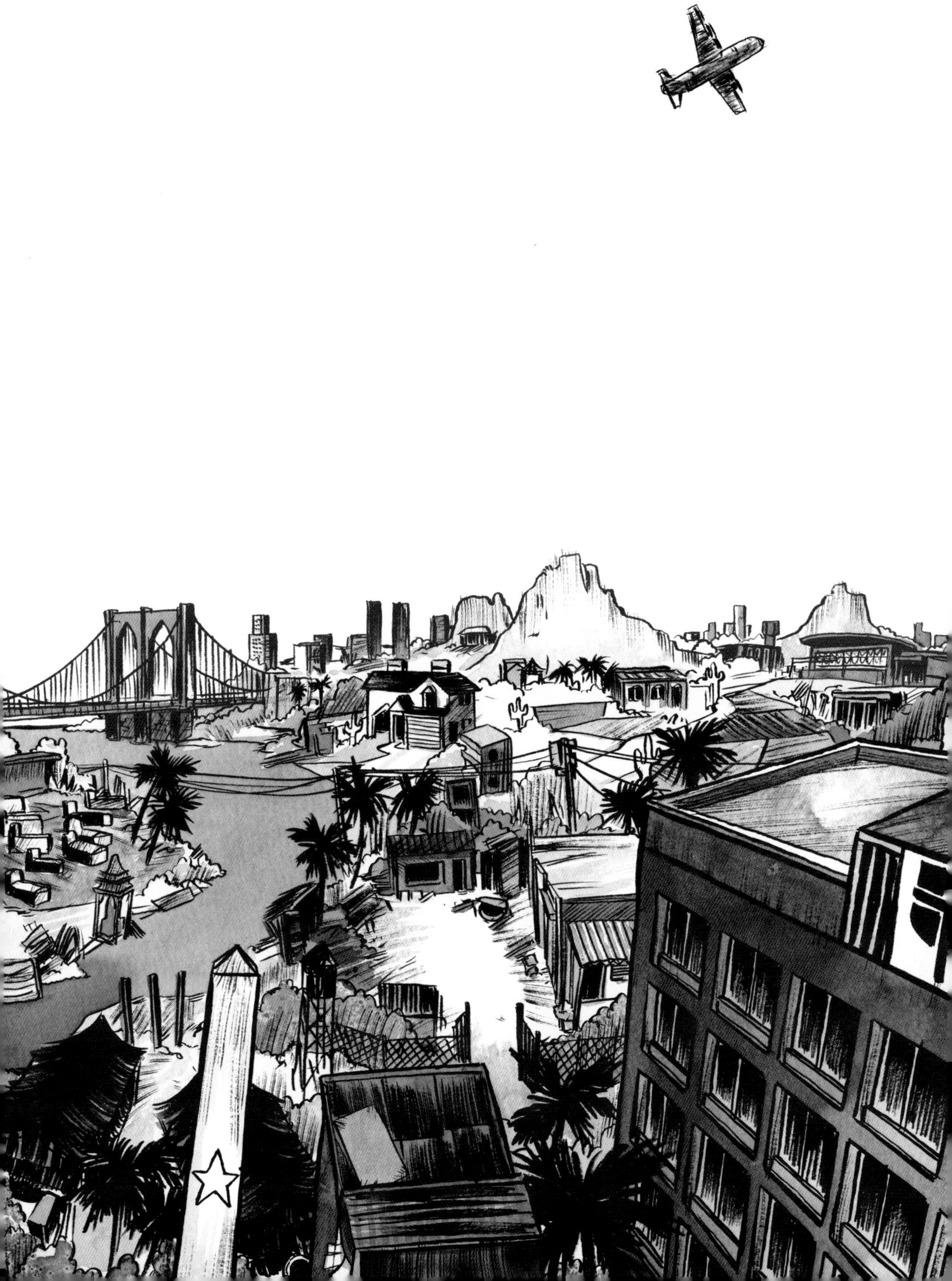

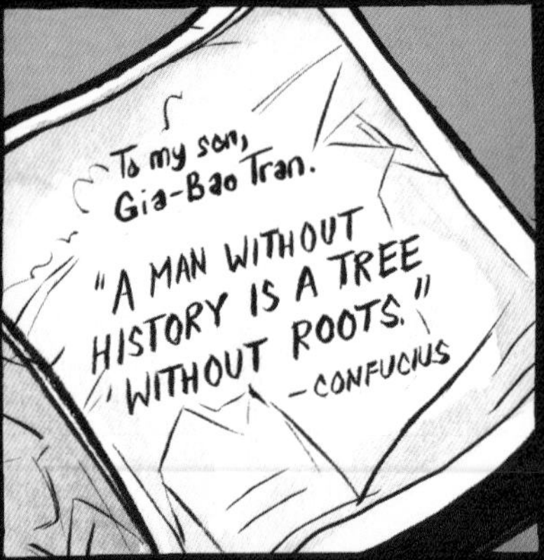
To my son,
Gia-Bao Tran.
"A MAN WITHOUT HISTORY IS A TREE WITHOUT ROOTS."
-CONFUCIUS

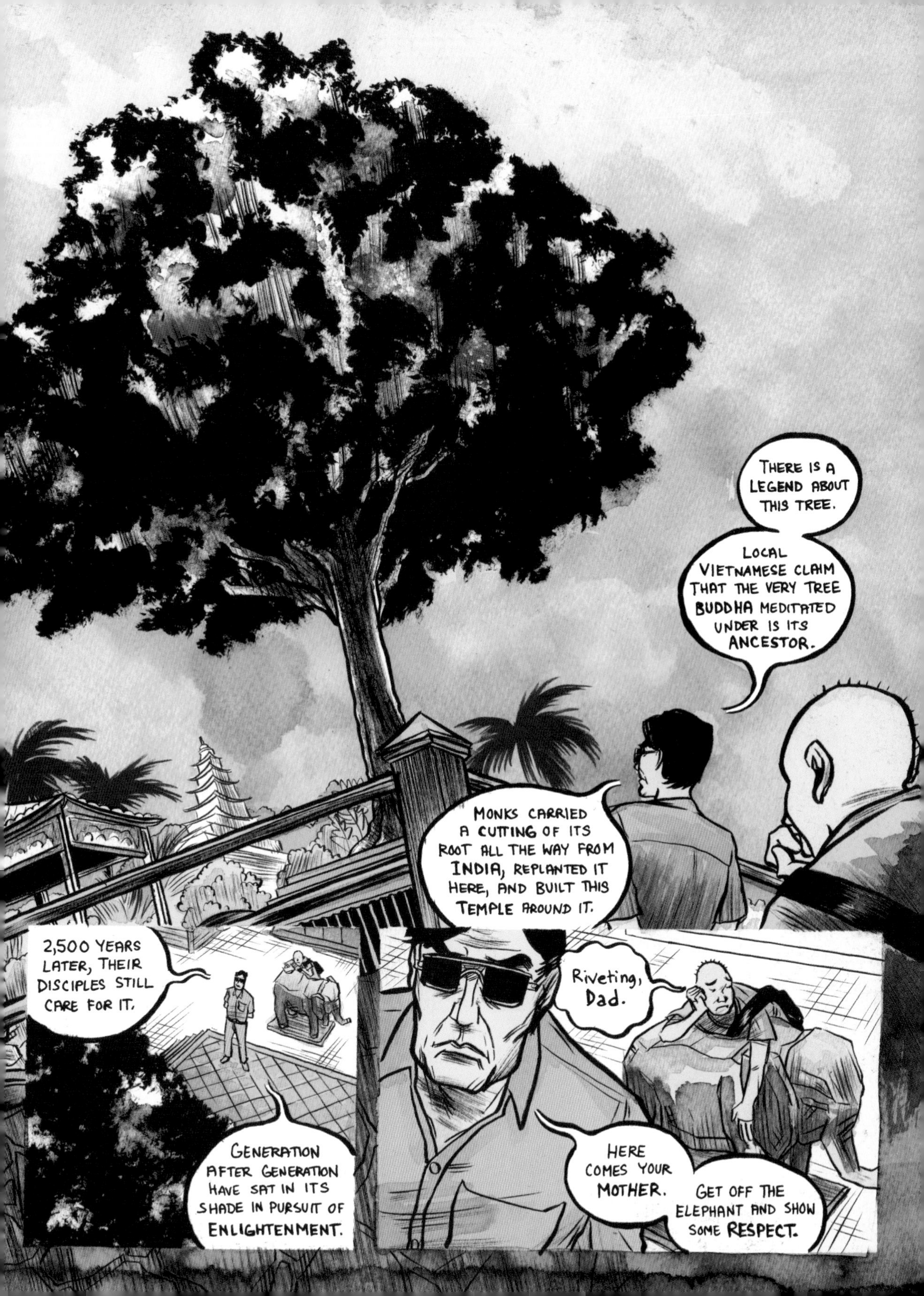
THERE IS A LEGEND ABOUT THIS TREE.
LOCAL VIETNAMESE CLAIM THAT THE VERY TREE BUDDHA MEDITATED UNDER IS ITS ANCESTOR.
MONKS CARRIED A CUTTING OF ITS ROOT ALL THE WAY FROM INDIA, REPLANTED IT HERE, AND BUILT THIS TEMPLE AROUND IT.
2,500 YEARS LATER, THEIR DISCIPLES STILL CARE FOR IT.
GENERATION AFTER GENERATION HAVE SAT IN ITS SHADE IN PURSUIT OF ENLIGHTENMENT.
Riveting, Dad.
HERE COMES YOUR MOTHER.
GET OFF THE ELEPHANT AND SHOW SOME RESPECT.

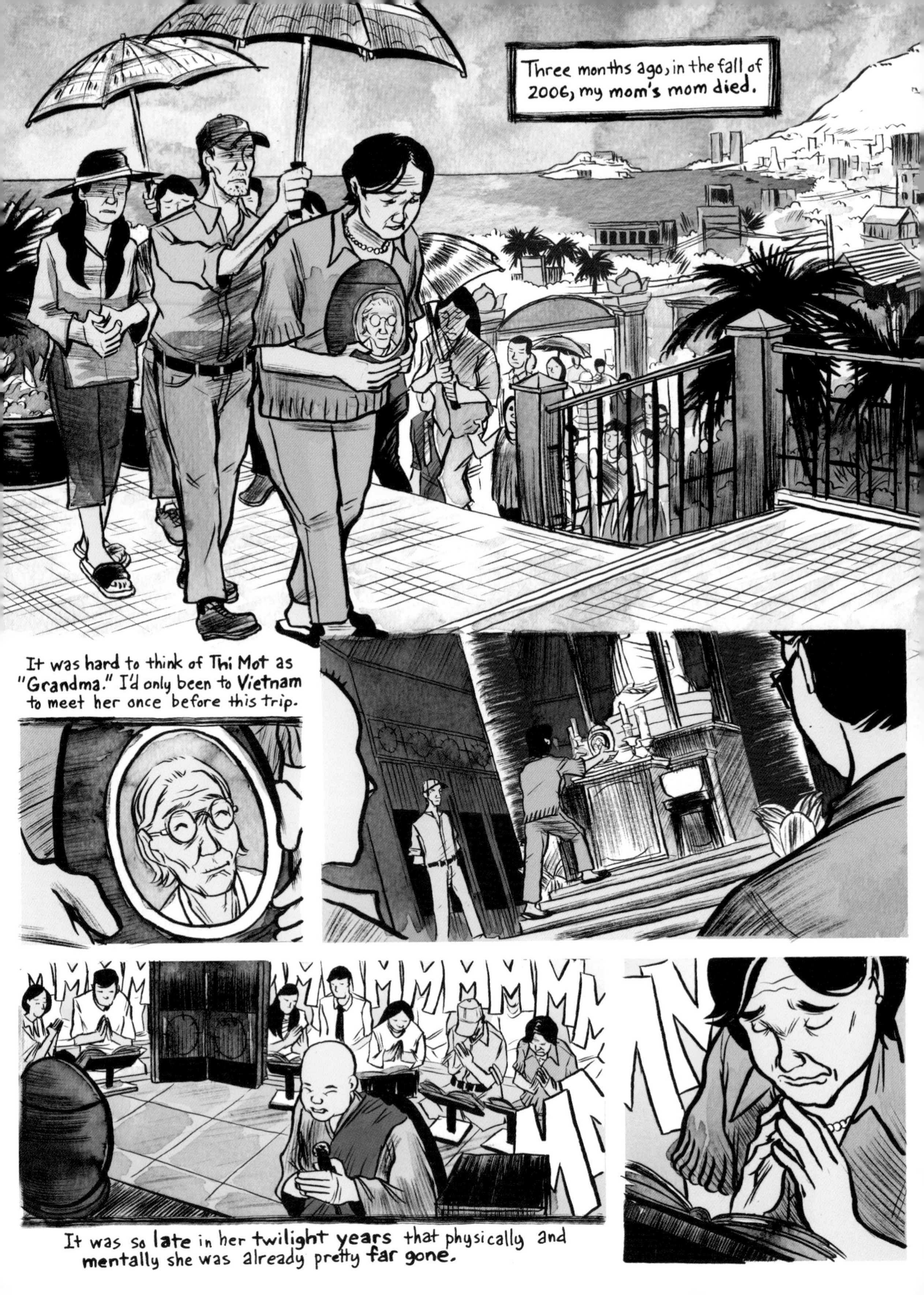
Three months ago, in the fall of 2006, my mom's mom died.
It was hard to think of Thi Mot as "Grandma." I'd only been to Vietnam to meet her once before this trip.
It was so late in her twilight years that physically and mentally she was already pretty far gone.

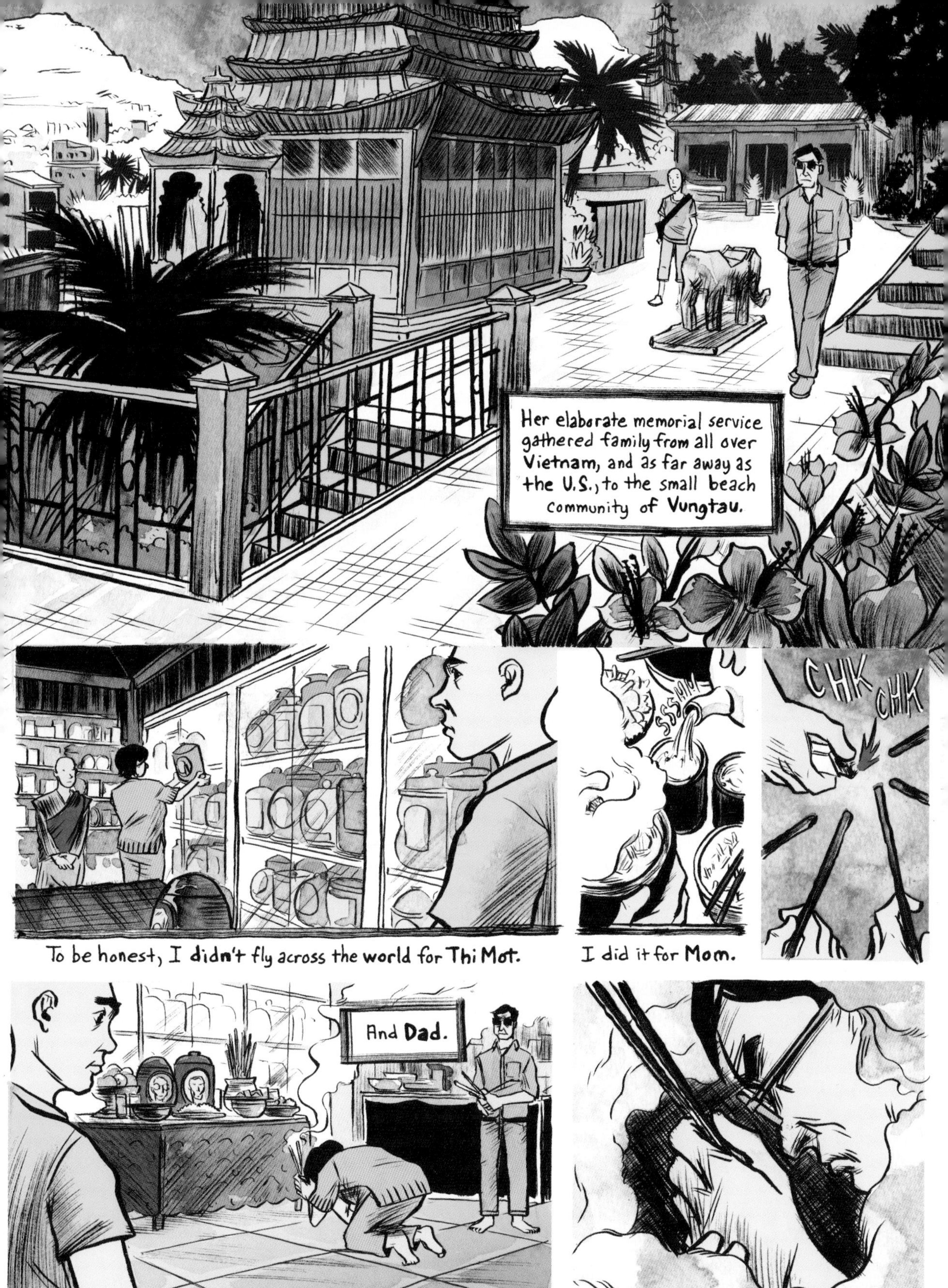
Her elaborate memorial service gathered family from all over Vietnam, and as far away as the U.S., to the small beach community of Vungtau.
To be honest, I didn't fly across the world for Thi Mot.
I did it for Mom.
CHK CHK
And Dad.

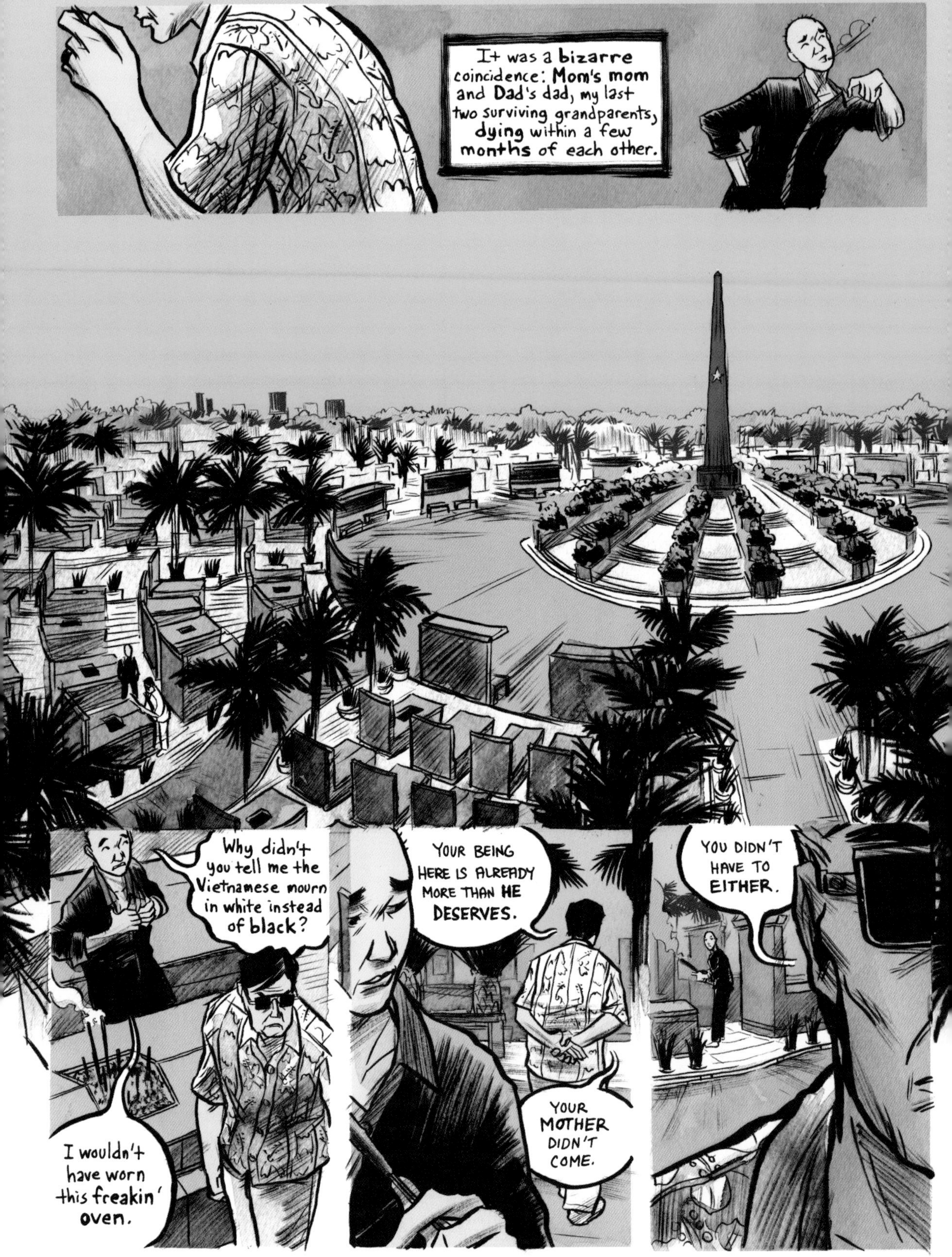
It was a bizarre coincidence: Mom's mom and Dad's dad, my last two surviving grandparents, dying within a few months of each other.
Why didn't you tell me the Vietnamese mourn in white instead of black?
I wouldn't have worn this freakin' oven.
YOUR BEING HERE IS ALREADY MORE THAN HE DESERVES.
YOUR MOTHER DIDN'T COME.
YOU DIDN'T HAVE TO EITHER.

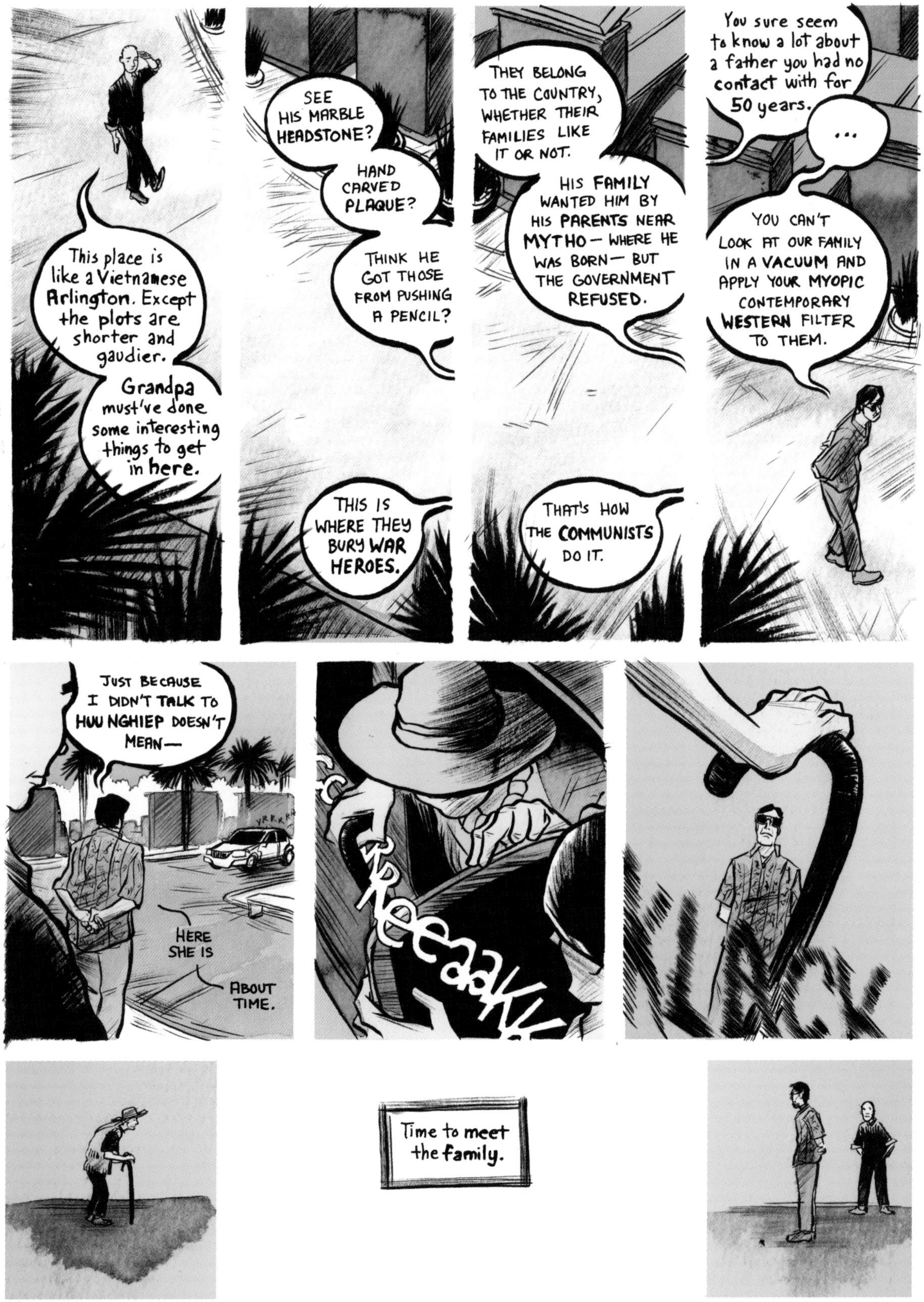

This place is like a Vietnamese Arlington. Except the plots are shorter and gaudier.
Grandpa must've done some interesting things to get in here.
SEE HIS MARBLE HEADSTONE?
HAND CARVED PLAQUE?
THINK HE GOT THOSE FROM PUSHING A PENCIL?
THIS IS WHERE THEY BURY WAR HEROES.
THEY BELONG TO THE COUNTRY, WHETHER THEIR FAMILIES LIKE IT OR NOT.
HIS FAMILY WANTED HIM BY HIS PARENTS NEAR MYTHO— WHERE HE WAS BORN— BUT THE GOVERNMENT REFUSED.
THAT'S HOW THE COMMUNISTS DO IT.
You sure seem to know a lot about a father you had no contact with for 50 years.
...
YOU CAN'T LOOK AT OUR FAMILY IN A VACUUM AND APPLY YOUR MYOPIC CONTEMPORARY WESTERN FILTER TO THEM.
JUST BECAUSE I DIDN'T TALK TO HUU NGHIEP DOESN'T MEAN—
YRRRRR
HERE SHE IS
ABOUT TIME.
KREEAAKK
Time to meet the family.

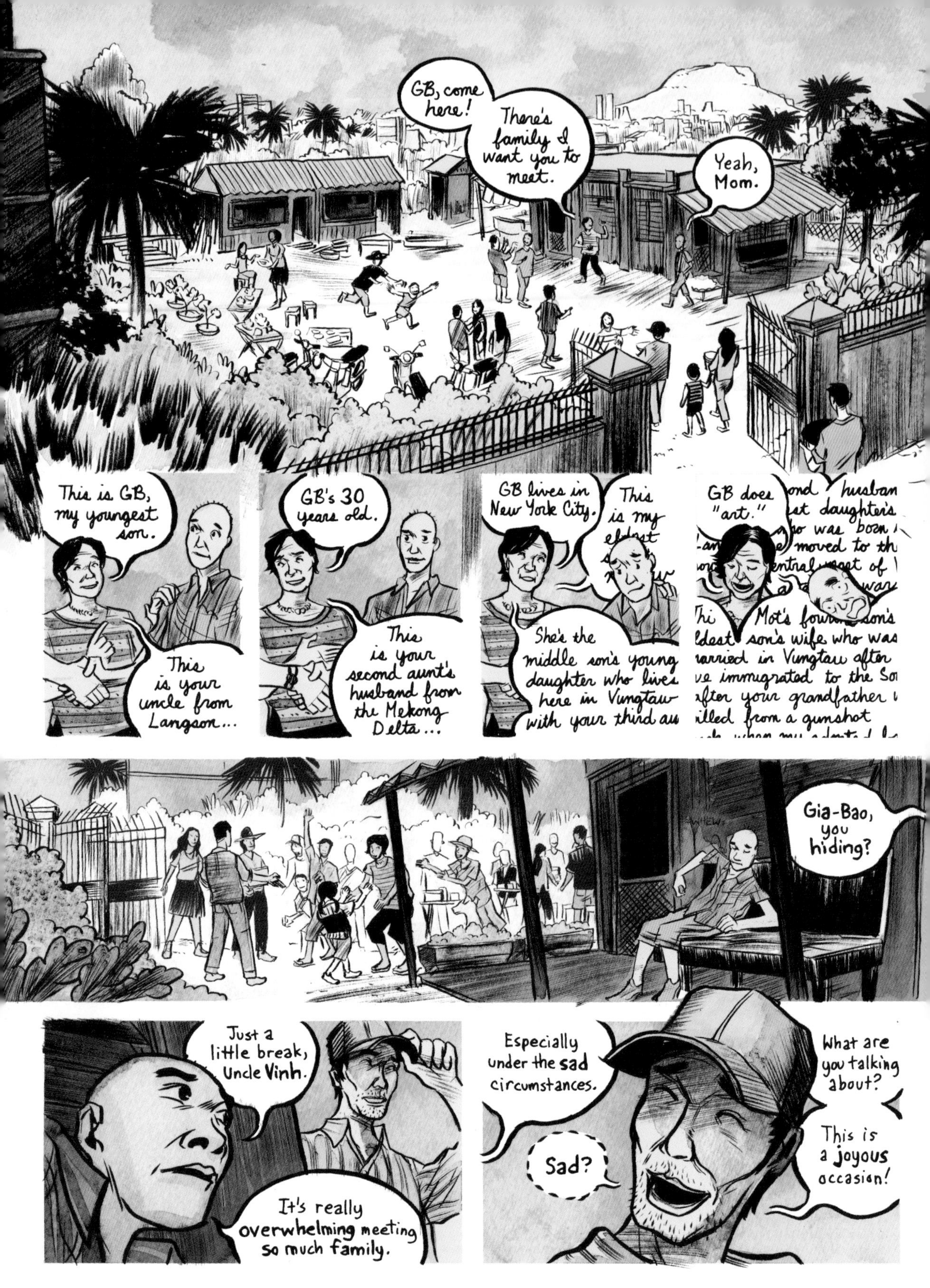
GB, come here!
There's family I want you to meet.
Yeah, Mom.
This is GB, my youngest son.
This is your uncle from Langson...
GB's 30 years old.
This is your second aunt's husband from the Mekong Delta...
GB lives in New York City.
This is my
She's the middle son's young daughter who lives here in Vungtau with your third au
GB does "art."
ldest son's wife who was
arried in Vungtau after
ve immigrated to the So
fter your grandfather
illed from a gunshot
Gia-Bao, you hiding?
Just a little break, Uncle Vinh.
It's really overwhelming meeting so much family.
Especially under the sad circumstances.
Sad?
What are you talking about?
This is a joyous occasion!

Family and friends have traveled from all over Vietnam— all over the **WORLD**—to celebrate your grandmother's life.

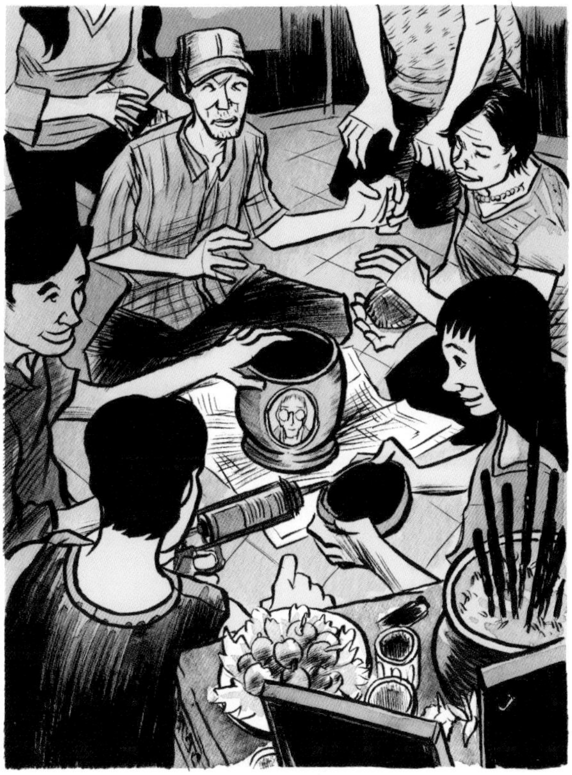

I'm reunited with my big sis—your mom—again! Most of these people haven't seen her since she fled over 30 years ago!

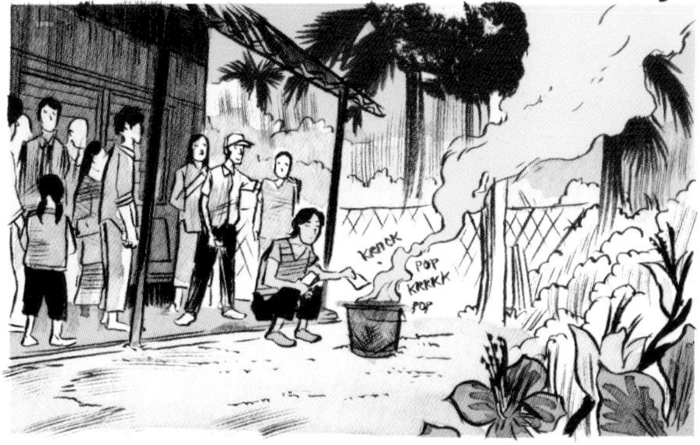
KRRCK
POP
KRRKK
POP

Sad? Gia-Bao, you've been in America too long. Just **look** around—this is happiness! All Thi Mot's children together!

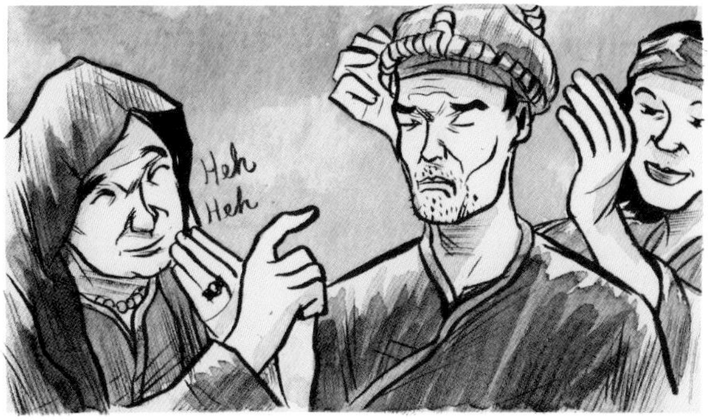
Heh
Heh

Despite war and three decades of seperation, we're a family again!

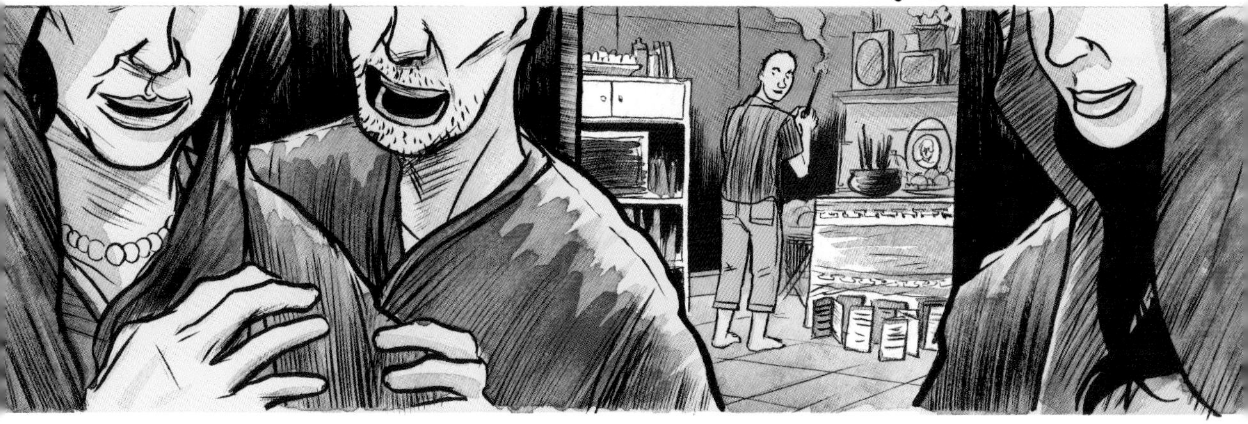

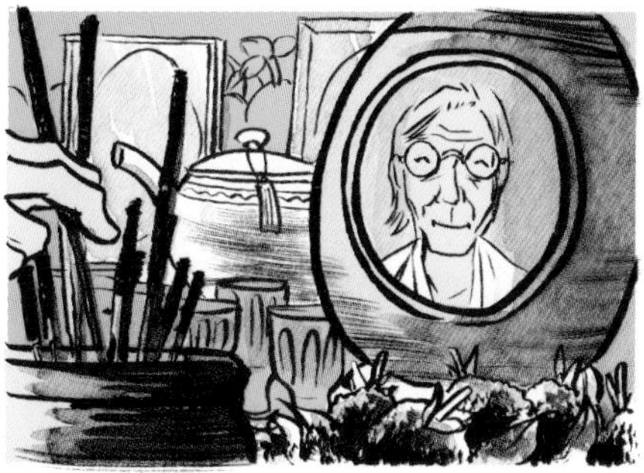

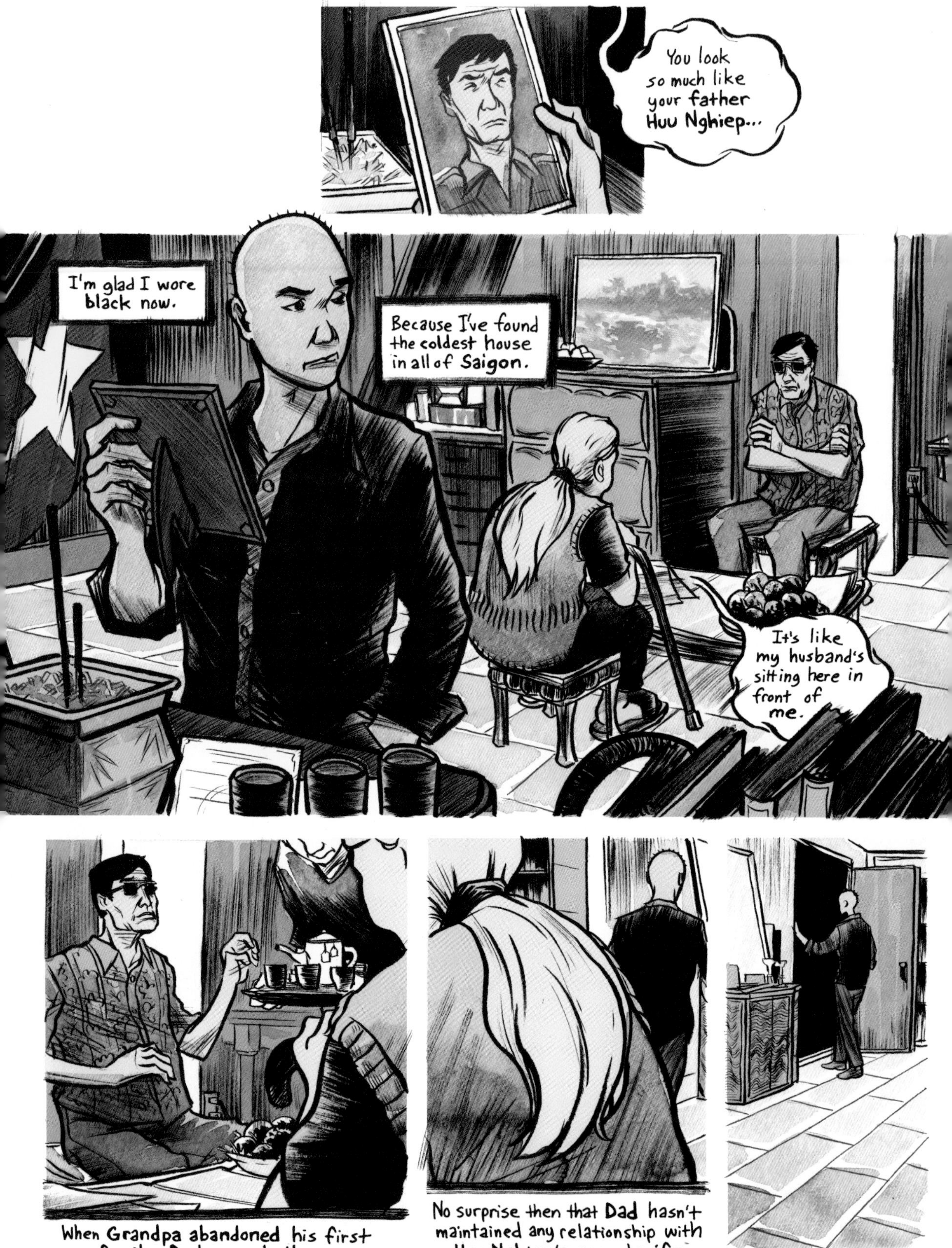
You look so much like your father Huu Nghiep...
I'm glad I wore black now.
Because I've found the coldest house in all of Saigon.
It's like my husband's sitting here in front of me.
When Grandpa abandoned his first family, Dad was only three.
No surprise then that Dad hasn't maintained any relationship with Huu Nghiep's second wife.

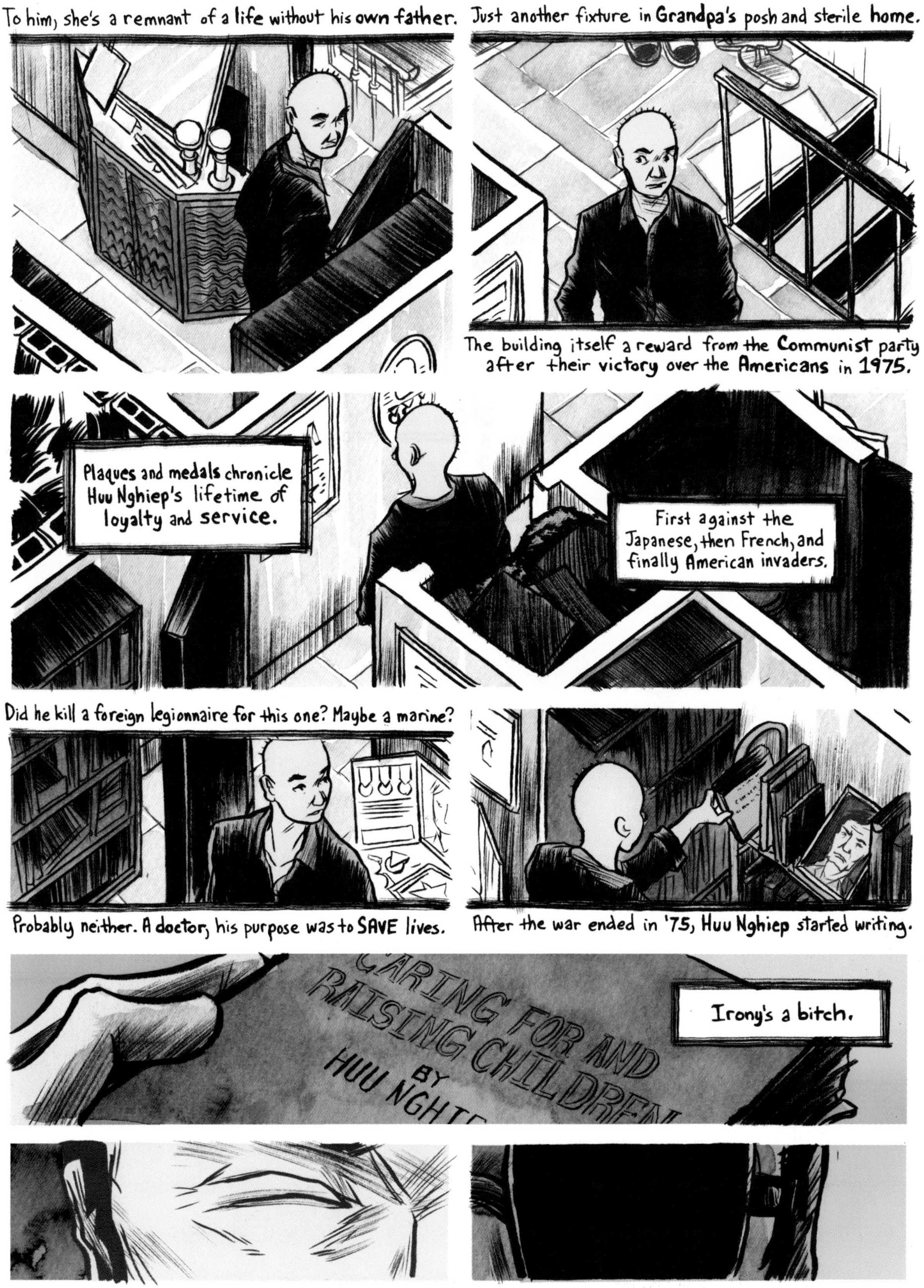

To him, she's a remnant of a life without his own father.
Just another fixture in Grandpa's posh and sterile home.
The building itself a reward from the Communist party after their victory over the Americans in 1975.
Plaques and medals chronicle Huu Nghiep's lifetime of loyalty and service.
First against the Japanese, then French, and finally American invaders.
Did he kill a foreign legionnaire for this one? Maybe a marine?
Probably neither. A doctor, his purpose was to SAVE lives.
After the war ended in '75, Huu Nghiep started writing.
CARING FOR AND RAISING CHILDREN BY HUU NGHIE
Irony's a bitch.

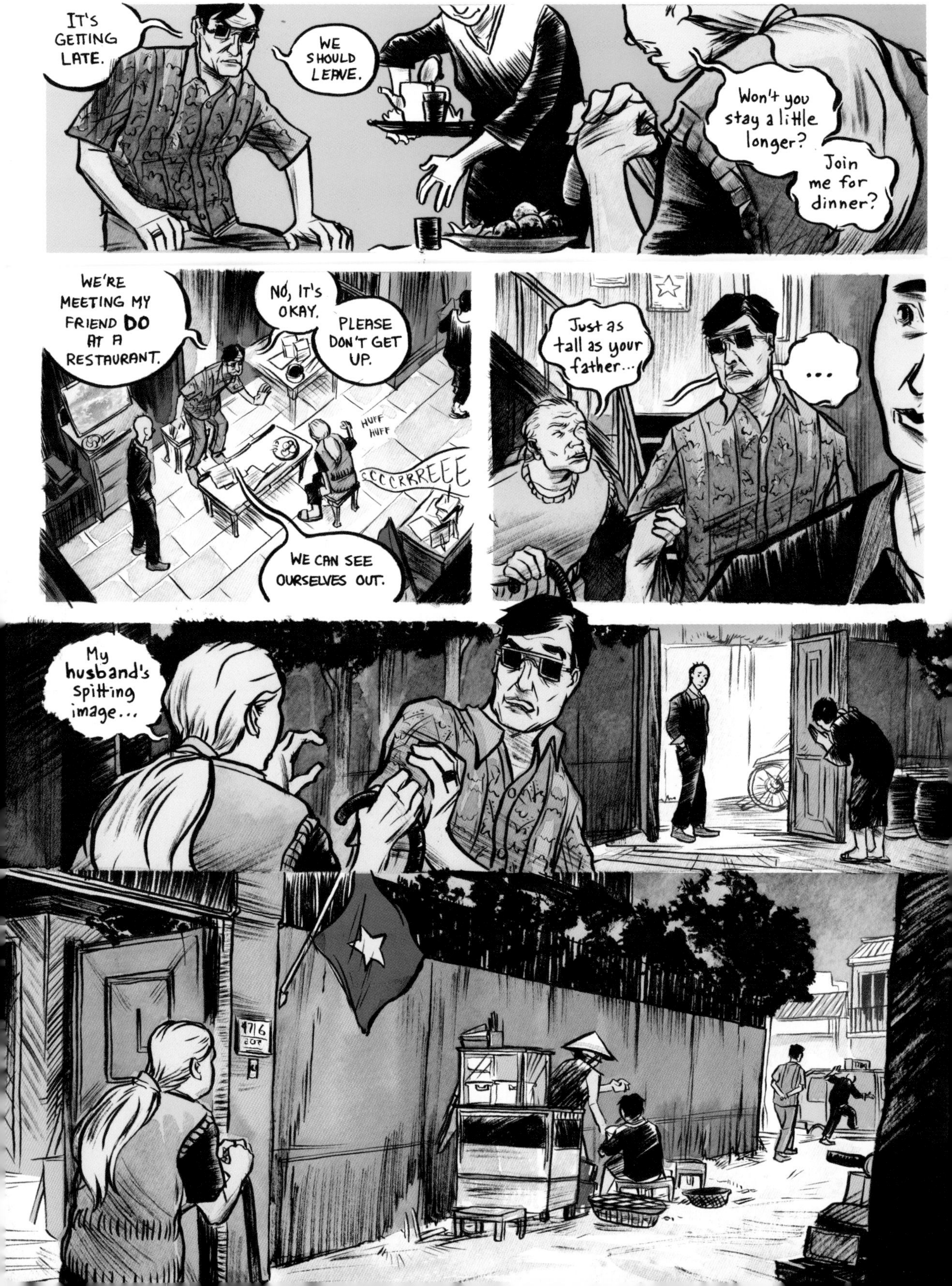

IT'S GETTING LATE.
WE SHOULD LEAVE.
Won't you stay a little longer?
Join me for dinner?
WE'RE MEETING MY FRIEND DO AT A RESTAURANT.
NO, IT'S OKAY.
PLEASE DON'T GET UP.
HUFF HUFF
CCCCRRREEE
WE CAN SEE OURSELVES OUT.
Just as tall as your father...
...
My husband's spitting image...

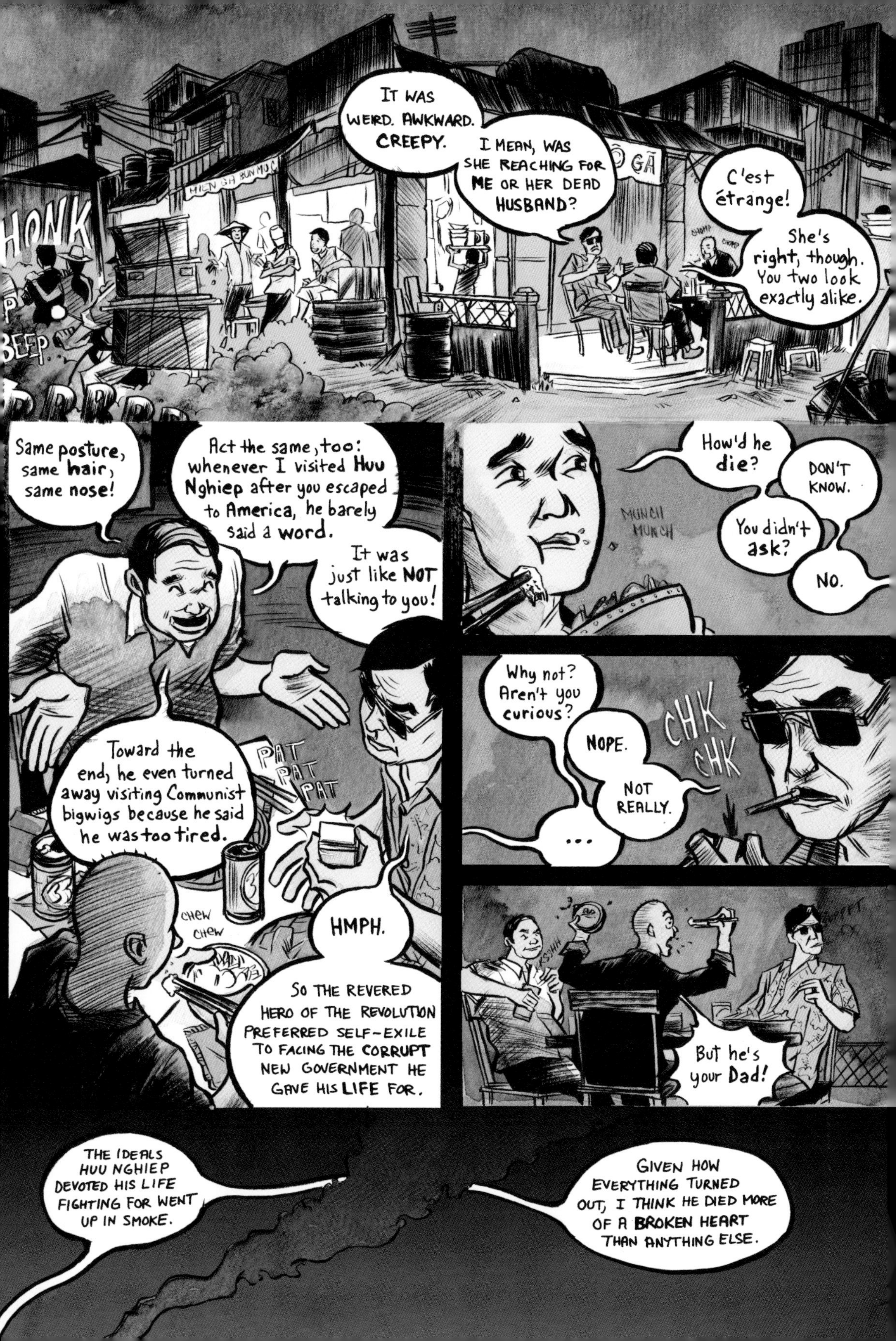
HONK
BEEP
It was weird. Awkward. Creepy.
I mean, was she reaching for me or her dead husband?
C'est étrange!
She's right, though. You two look exactly alike.
Same posture, same hair, same nose!
Act the same, too: whenever I visited Huu Nghiep after you escaped to America, he barely said a word.
It was just like NOT talking to you!
How'd he die?
DON'T KNOW.
MUNCH MUNCH
You didn't ask?
NO.
Toward the end, he even turned away visiting Communist bigwigs because he said he was too tired.
PAT PAT PAT
Why not? Aren't you curious?
NOPE.
CHK CHK
NOT REALLY.
...
CHEW CHEW
HMPH.
SO THE REVERED HERO OF THE REVOLUTION PREFERRED SELF-EXILE TO FACING THE CORRUPT NEW GOVERNMENT HE GAVE HIS LIFE FOR.
But he's your Dad!
THE IDEALS HUU NGHIEP DEVOTED HIS LIFE FIGHTING FOR WENT UP IN SMOKE.
GIVEN HOW EVERYTHING TURNED OUT, I THINK HE DIED MORE OF A BROKEN HEART THAN ANYTHING ELSE.

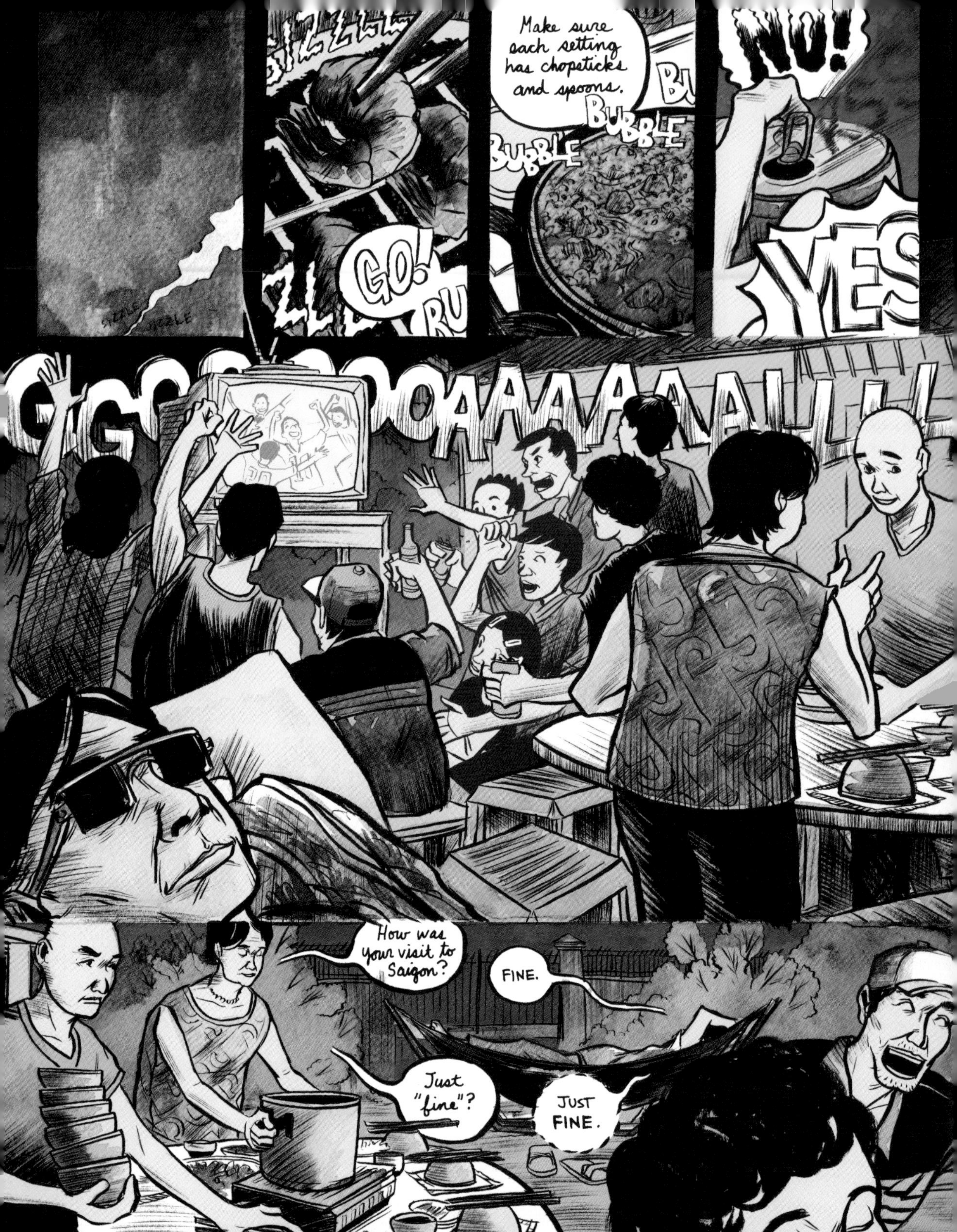
SIZZLE SIZZLE
SIZZLE
GO!
RU
Make sure each setting has chopsticks and spoons.
BU
BUBBLE
BUBBLE
NO!
YES
GOOOOOAAAAAAALLL!
How was your visit to Saigon?
FINE.
Just "fine"?
JUST FINE.

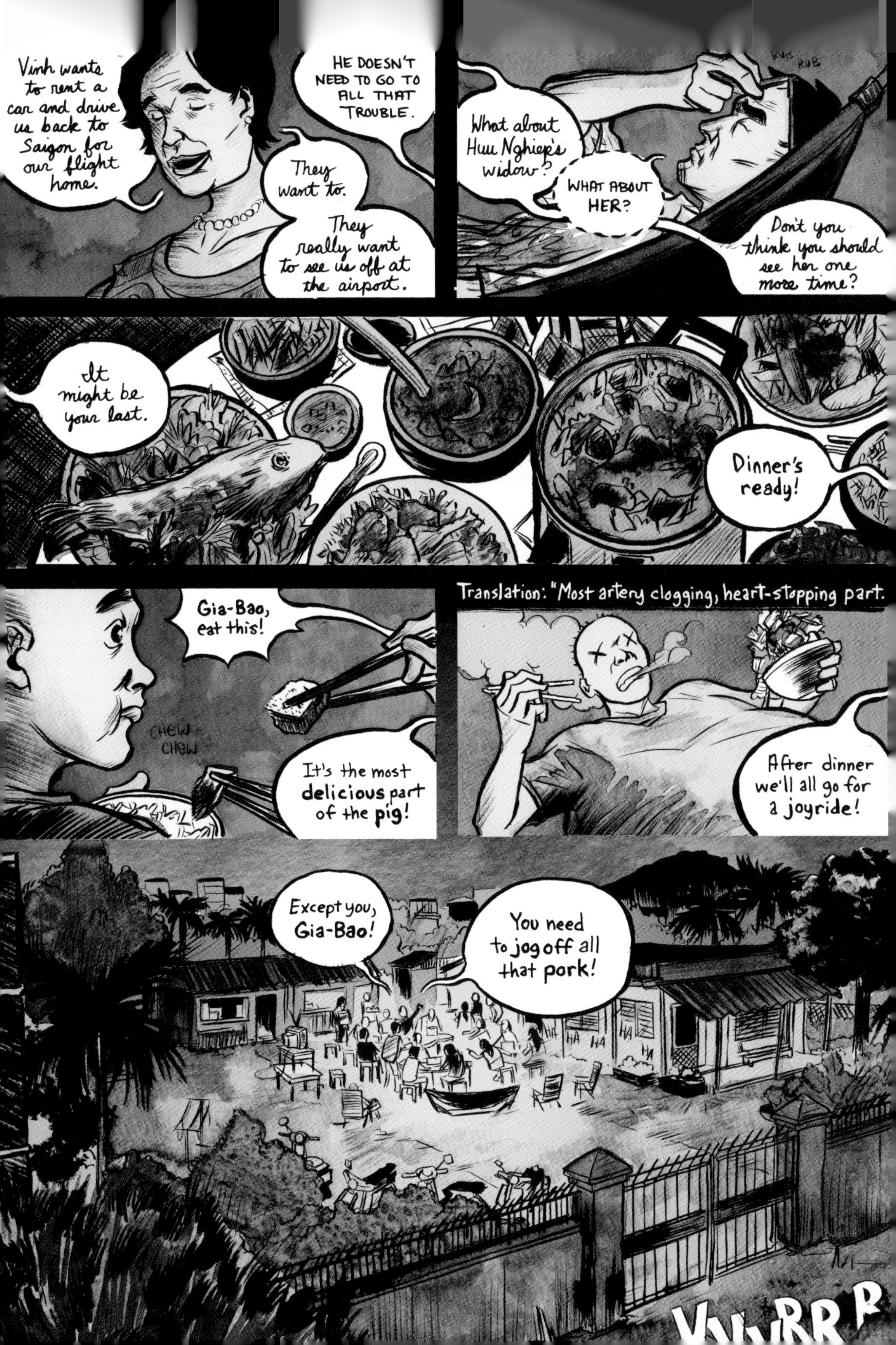
Vinh wants to rent a car and drive us back to Saigon for our flight home.
HE DOESN'T NEED TO GO TO ALL THAT TROUBLE.
They want to.
They really want to see us off at the airport.
RUB RUB
What about Huu Nghiep's widow?
WHAT ABOUT HER?
Don't you think you should see her one more time?
It might be your last.
Dinner's ready!
Gia-Bao, eat this!
CHEW CHEW
It's the most delicious part of the pig!
Translation: "Most artery clogging, heart-stopping part."
After dinner we'll all go for a joyride!
Except you, Gia-Bao!
You need to jog off all that pork!
HA HA HA HA
VVVVRRR R

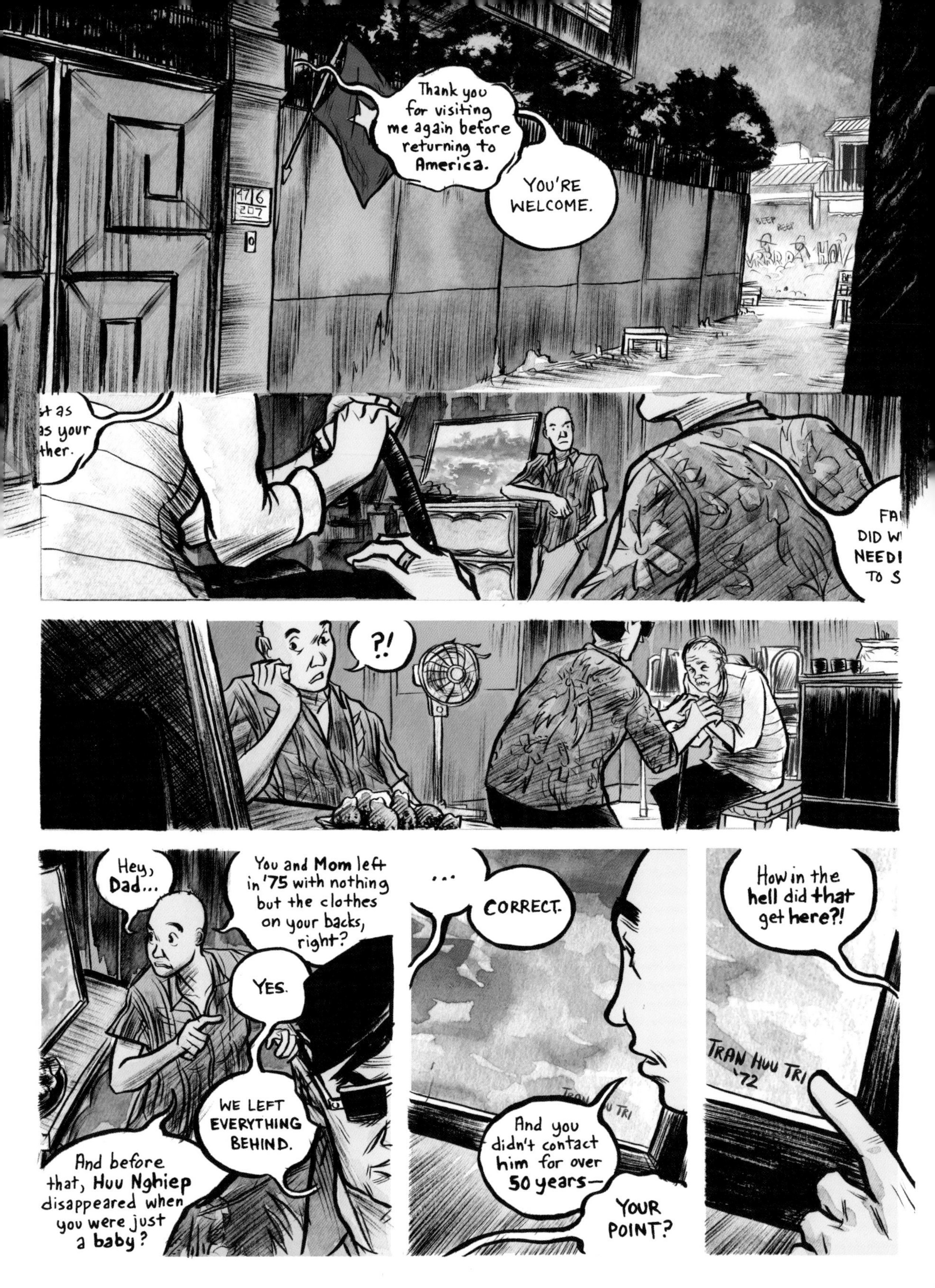
Thank you for visiting me again before returning to America.
YOU'RE WELCOME.
st as
as your
ther.
FA
DID W
NEED
TO S
?!
Hey, Dad...
You and Mom left in '75 with nothing but the clothes on your backs, right?
YES.
WE LEFT EVERYTHING BEHIND.
And before that, Huu Nghiep disappeared when you were just a baby?
...
CORRECT.
And you didn't contact him for over 50 years—
YOUR POINT?
How in the hell did that get here?!
TRAN HUU TRI '72

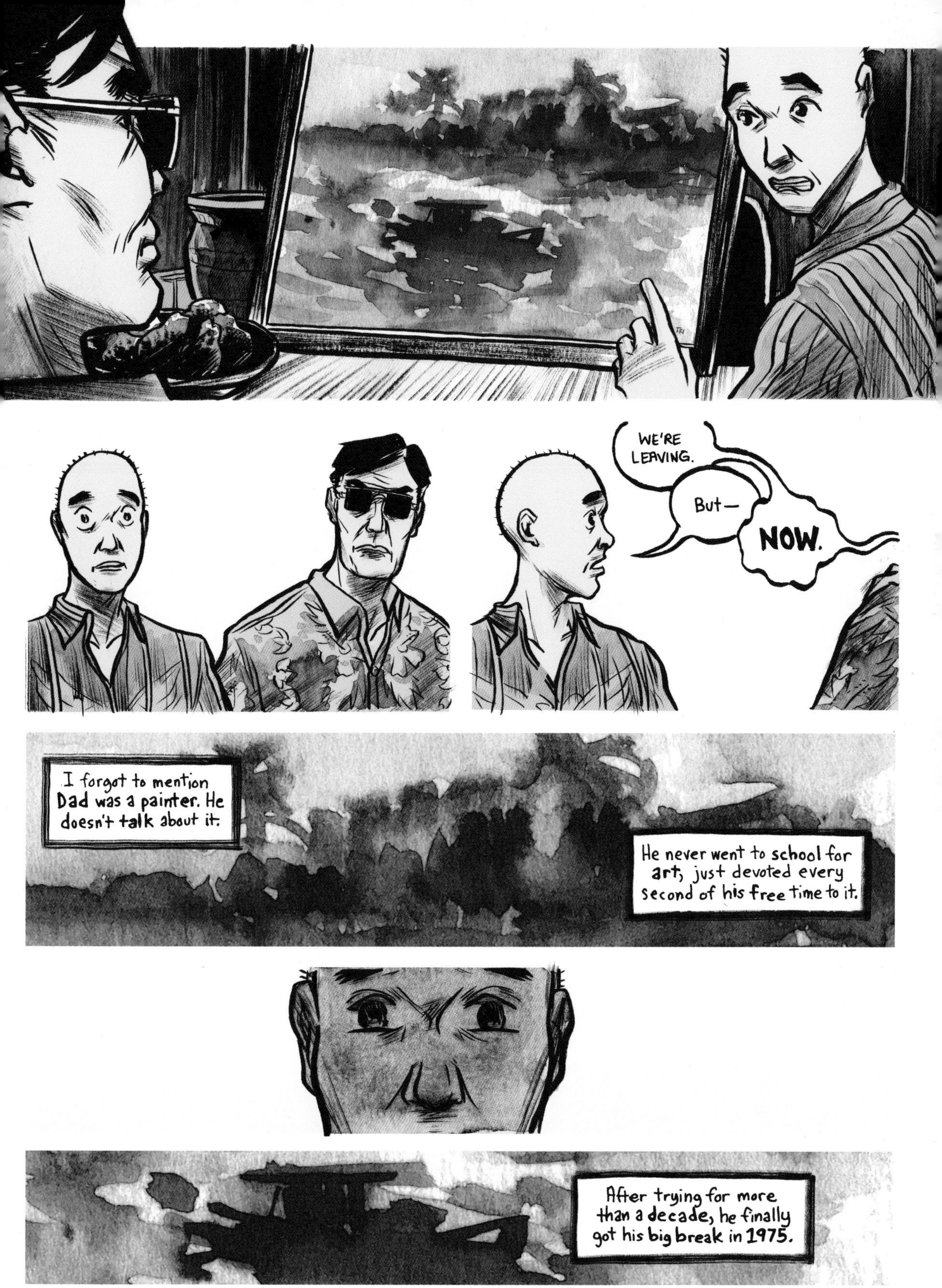
WE'RE LEAVING.
But—
NOW.
I forgot to mention Dad was a painter. He doesn't talk about it.
He never went to school for art, just devoted every second of his free time to it.
After trying for more than a decade, he finally got his big break in 1975.

A huge gallery show of his French impressionist styled, romanticized **Vietnamese** landscapes.

It was met by an enthusiastic audience and foreign buyers.

He quickly became a rising star in **Vietnam's** art scene.

CLAP
CLAP
CLAP
CLAP
CLA

Only a few months later, all his paintings were lost and destroyed.

POP
SNAP
KKR
POP

Dad abandoned them when he and Mom fled **Vietnam.**

Sometimes doing what's right means leaving things behind.

There's an old **Vietnamese** saying:

"Our parents care for us as our teeth sharpen..."

"Some care for them as their..."

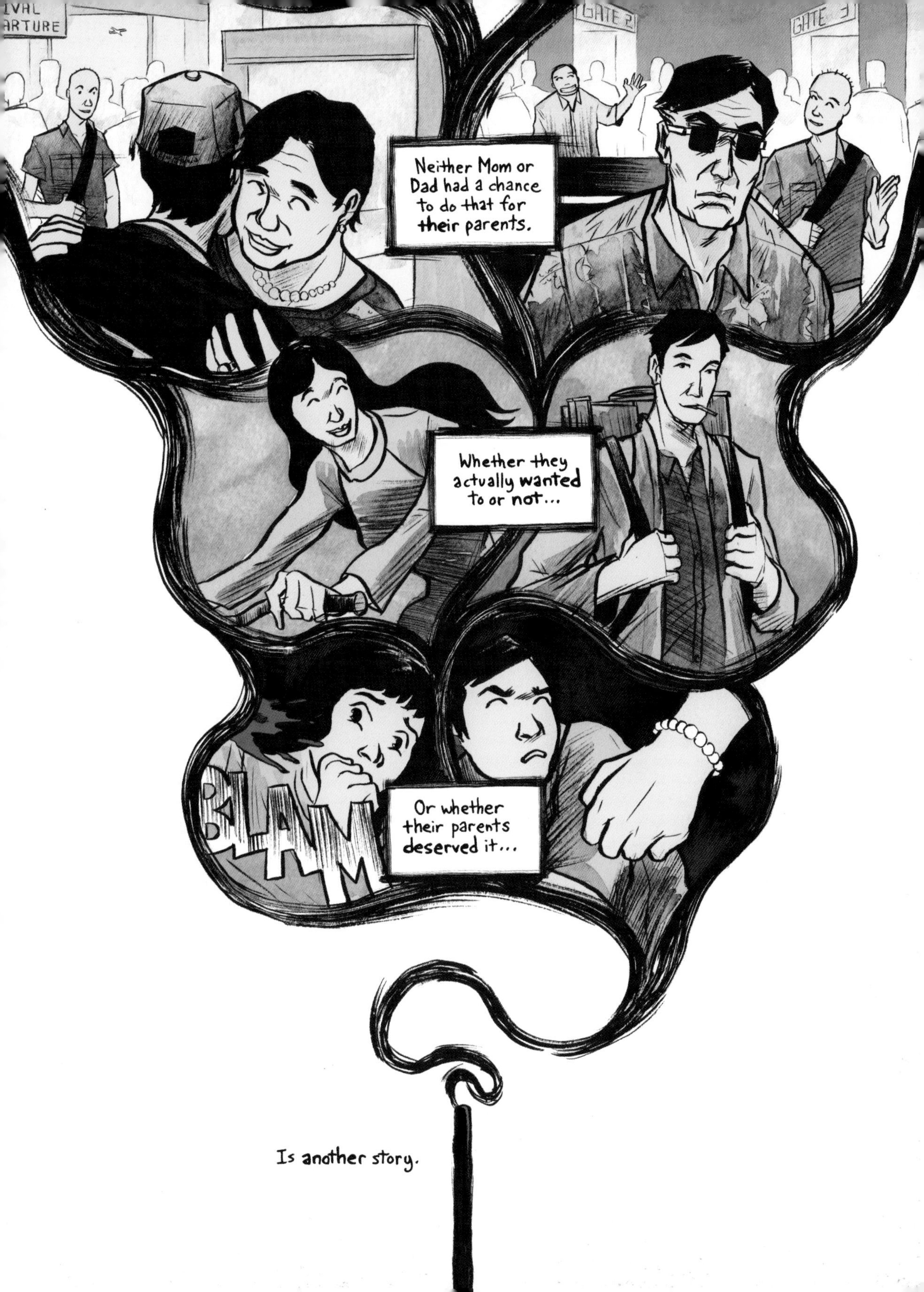
IVAL
ARTURE
GATE 2
GATE 3
Neither Mom or Dad had a chance to do that for their parents.
Whether they actually wanted to or not...
BLAM
Or whether their parents deserved it...
Is another story.

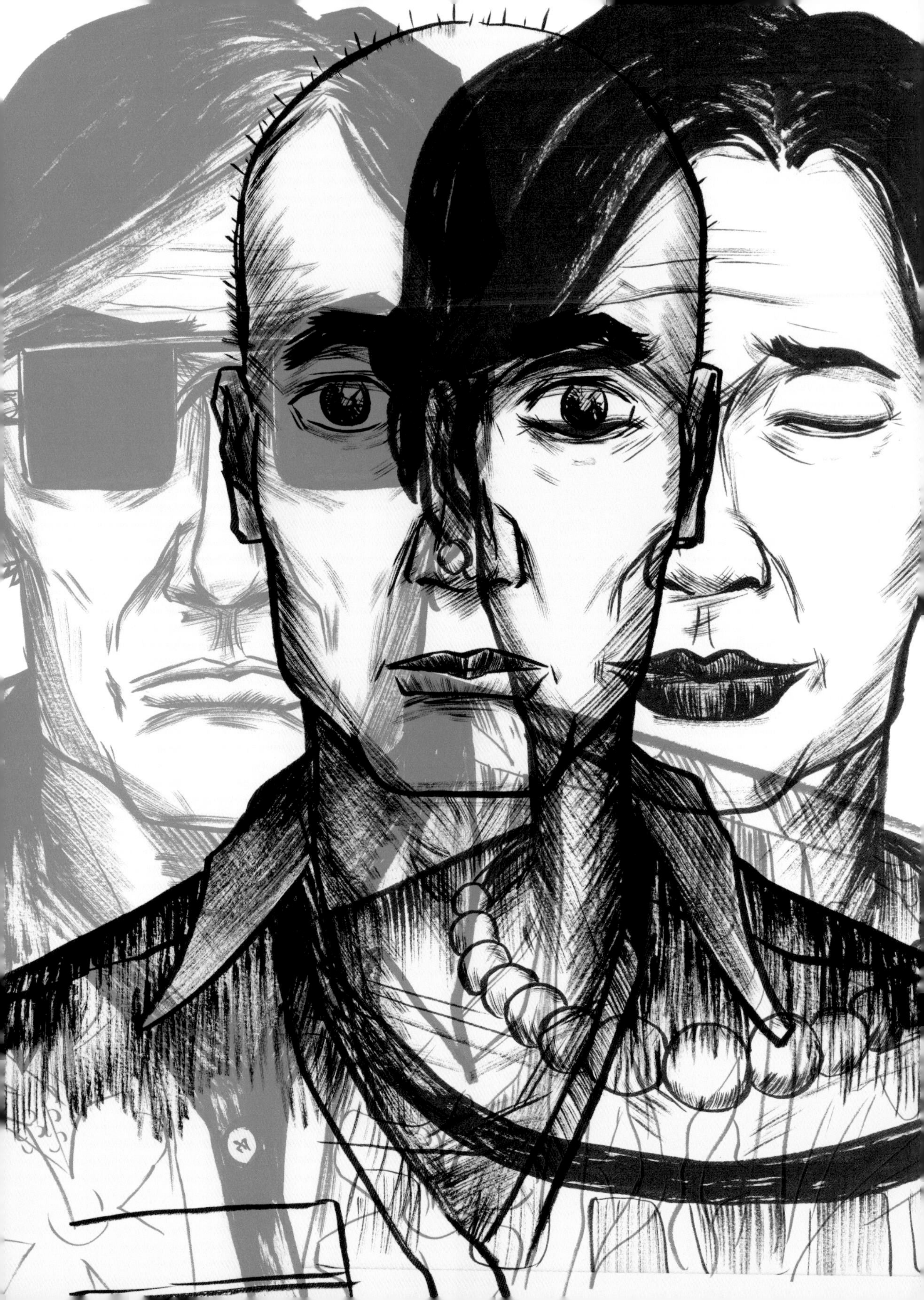

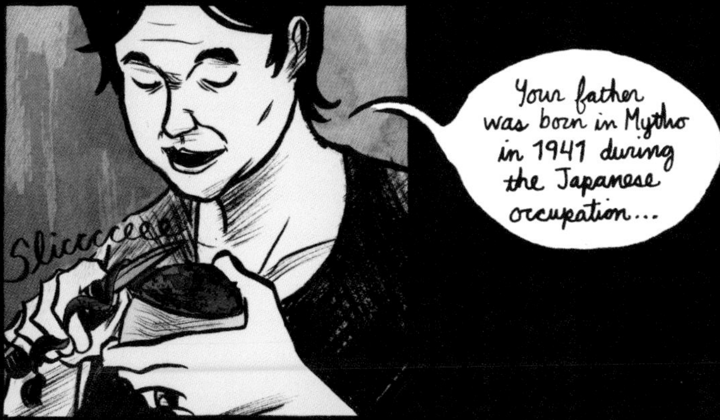
Slicccce
Your father was born in Mytho in 1947 during the Japanese occupation...

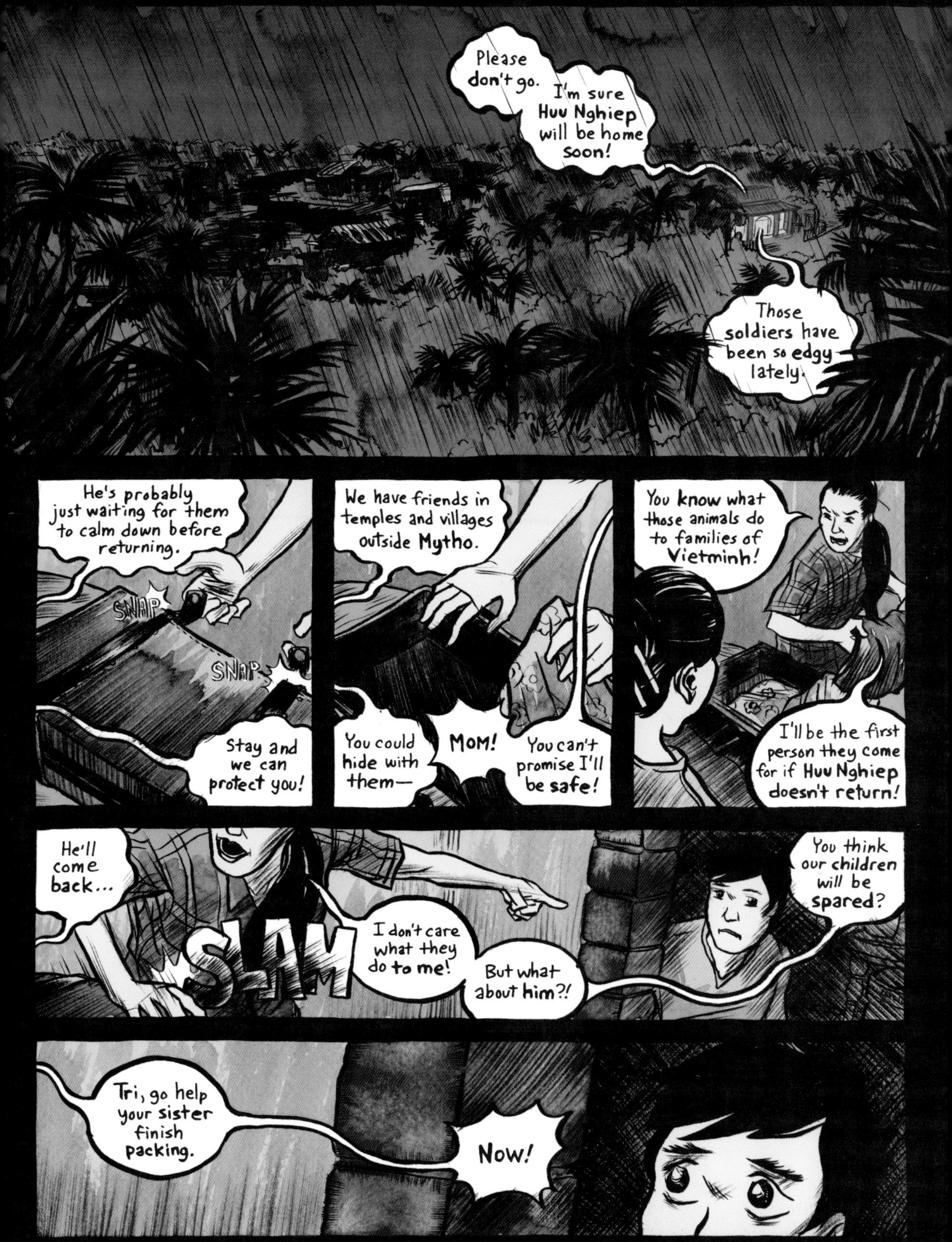
Please don't go.
I'm sure Huu Nghiep will be home soon!
Those soldiers have been so edgy lately.
He's probably just waiting for them to calm down before returning.
SNAP
SNAP
Stay and we can protect you!
We have friends in temples and villages outside Mytho.
You could hide with them—
MOM!
You can't promise I'll be safe!
You know what those animals do to families of Vietminh!
I'll be the first person they come for if Huu Nghiep doesn't return!
He'll come back...
SLAM
I don't care what they do to me!
But what about him?!
You think our children will be spared?
Tri, go help your sister finish packing.
Now!

Your Dad was too young to remember when his mother Le Nhi took him and his siblings to hide in the jungles of South Vietnam.

World War II had ended and the Allies were forcing the Japanese out of the country.

Before they left, they hunted down Vietminh like your grandfather Huu Nghiep.

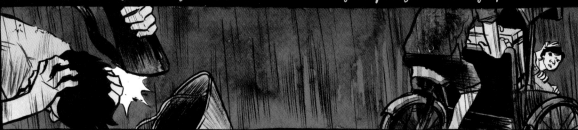

Of course, no one thought life would improve just because one occupier was being replaced by another.

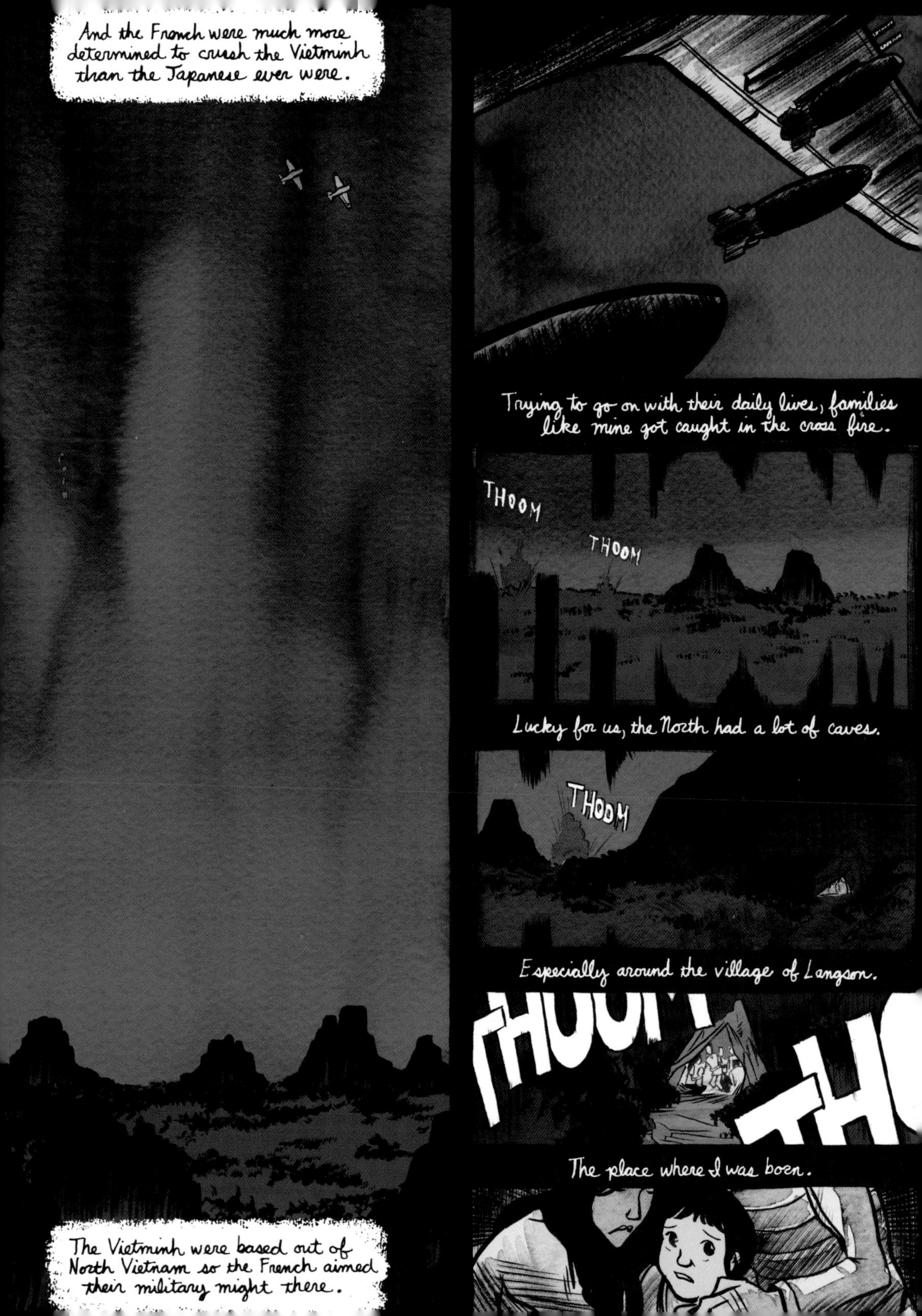
And the French were much more determined to crush the Vietminh than the Japanese ever were.
The Vietminh were based out of North Vietnam so the French aimed their military might there.
Trying to go on with their daily lives, families like mine got caught in the cross fire.
THOOM
THOOM
Lucky for us, the North had a lot of caves.
THOOM
Especially around the village of Langson.
The place where I was born.

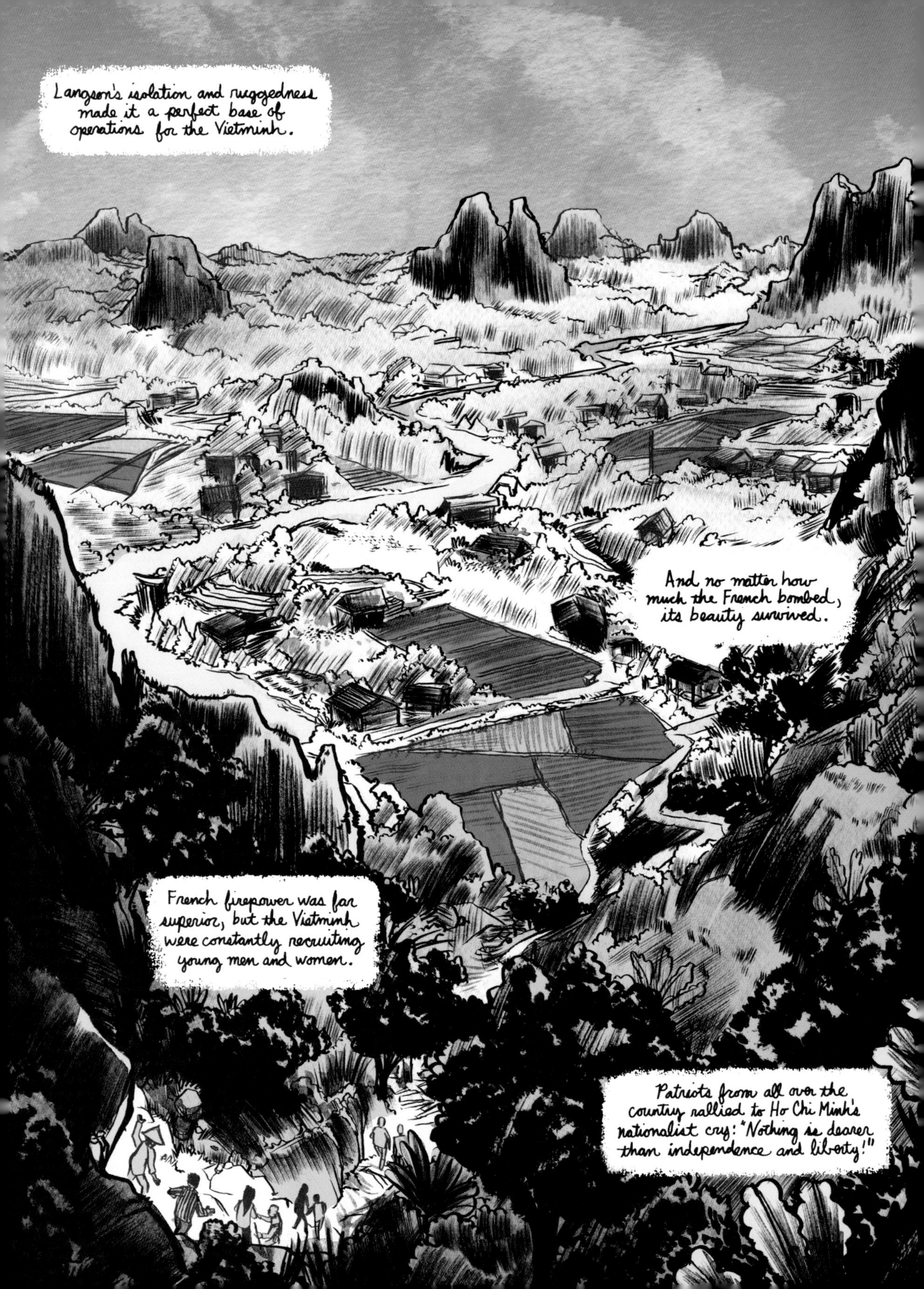
Langson's isolation and ruggedness made it a perfect base of operations for the Vietminh.
And no matter how much the French bombed, its beauty survived.
French firepower was far superior, but the Vietminh were constantly recruiting young men and women.
Patriots from all over the country rallied to Ho Chi Minh's nationalist cry: "Nothing is dearer than independence and liberty!"

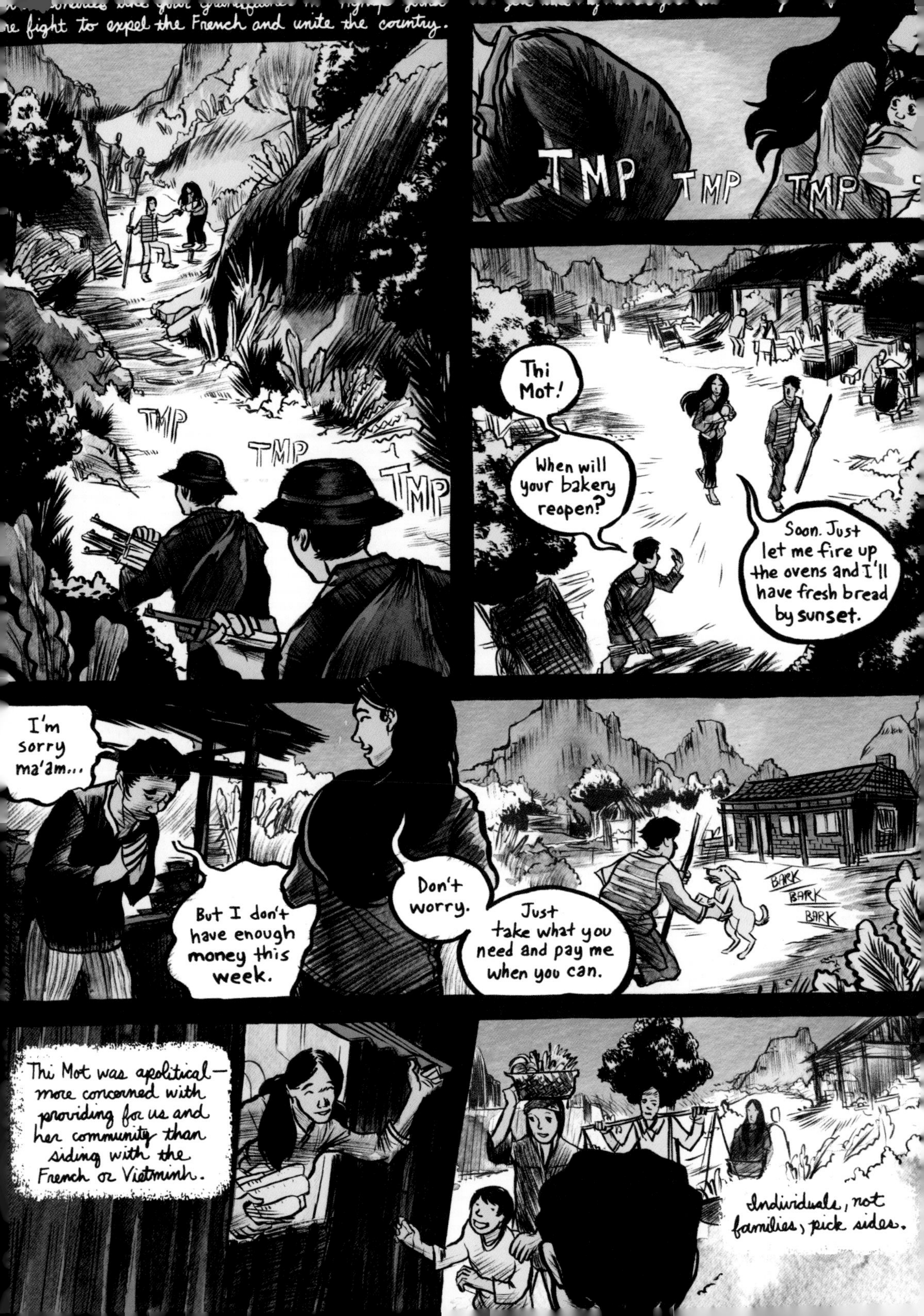
fight to expel the French and unite the country.
TMP
TMP
TMP
TMP TMP TMP
Thi Mot!
When will your bakery reopen?
Soon. Just let me fire up the ovens and I'll have fresh bread by sunset.
I'm sorry ma'am...
But I don't have enough money this week.
Don't worry.
Just take what you need and pay me when you can.
BARK
BARK
BARK
Thi Mot was apolitical—more concerned with providing for us and her community than siding with the French or Vietminh.
Individuals, not families, pick sides.

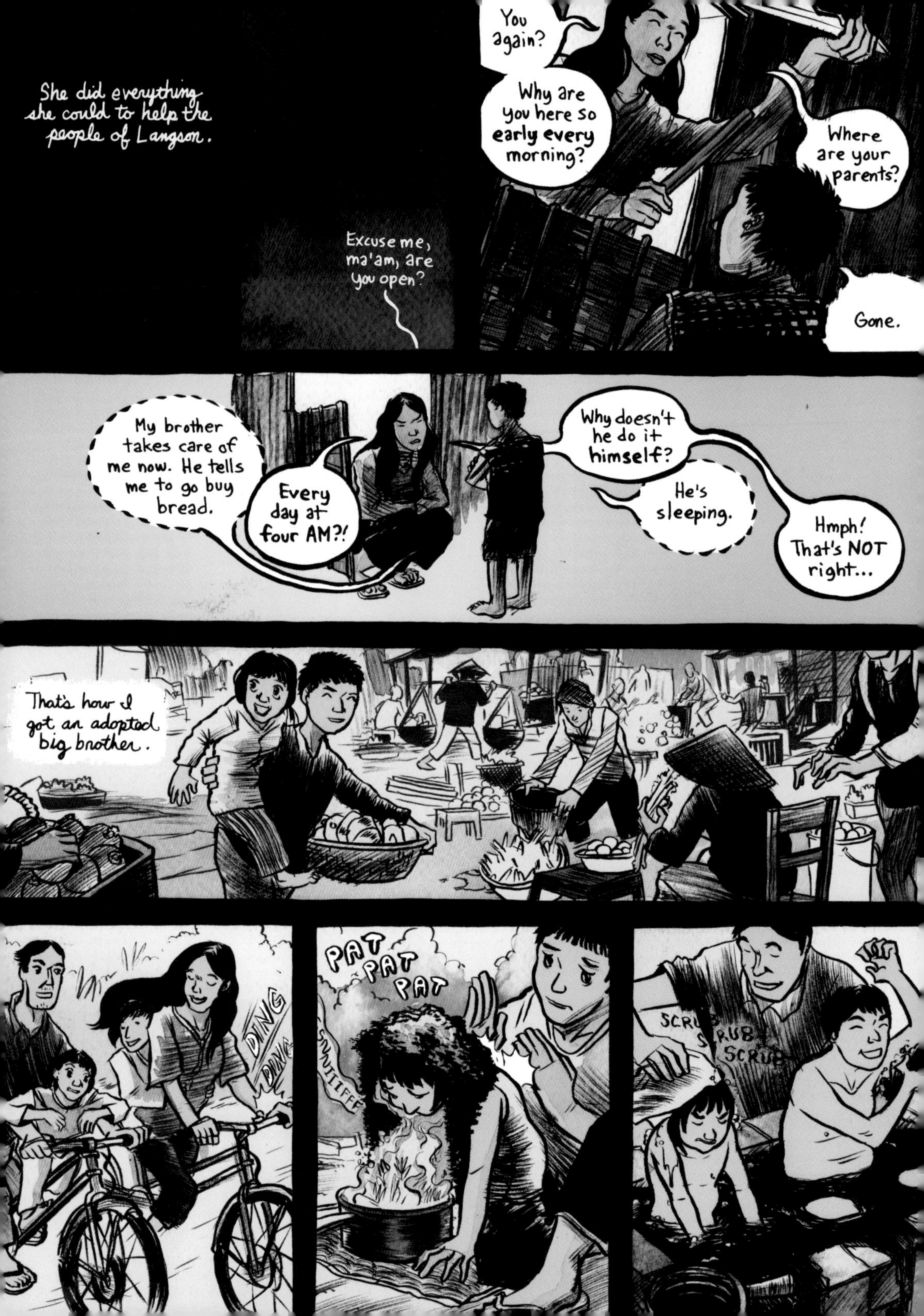

She did everything she could to help the people of Langson.
Excuse me, ma'am, are you open?
You again?
Why are you here so early every morning?
Where are your parents?
Gone.
My brother takes care of me now. He tells me to go buy bread.
Every day at four AM?!
Why doesn't he do it himself?
He's sleeping.
Hmph! That's NOT right...
That's how I got an adopted big brother.
DING DING
PAT PAT PAT
SNIIIIFF
SCRUB SCRUB SCRUB

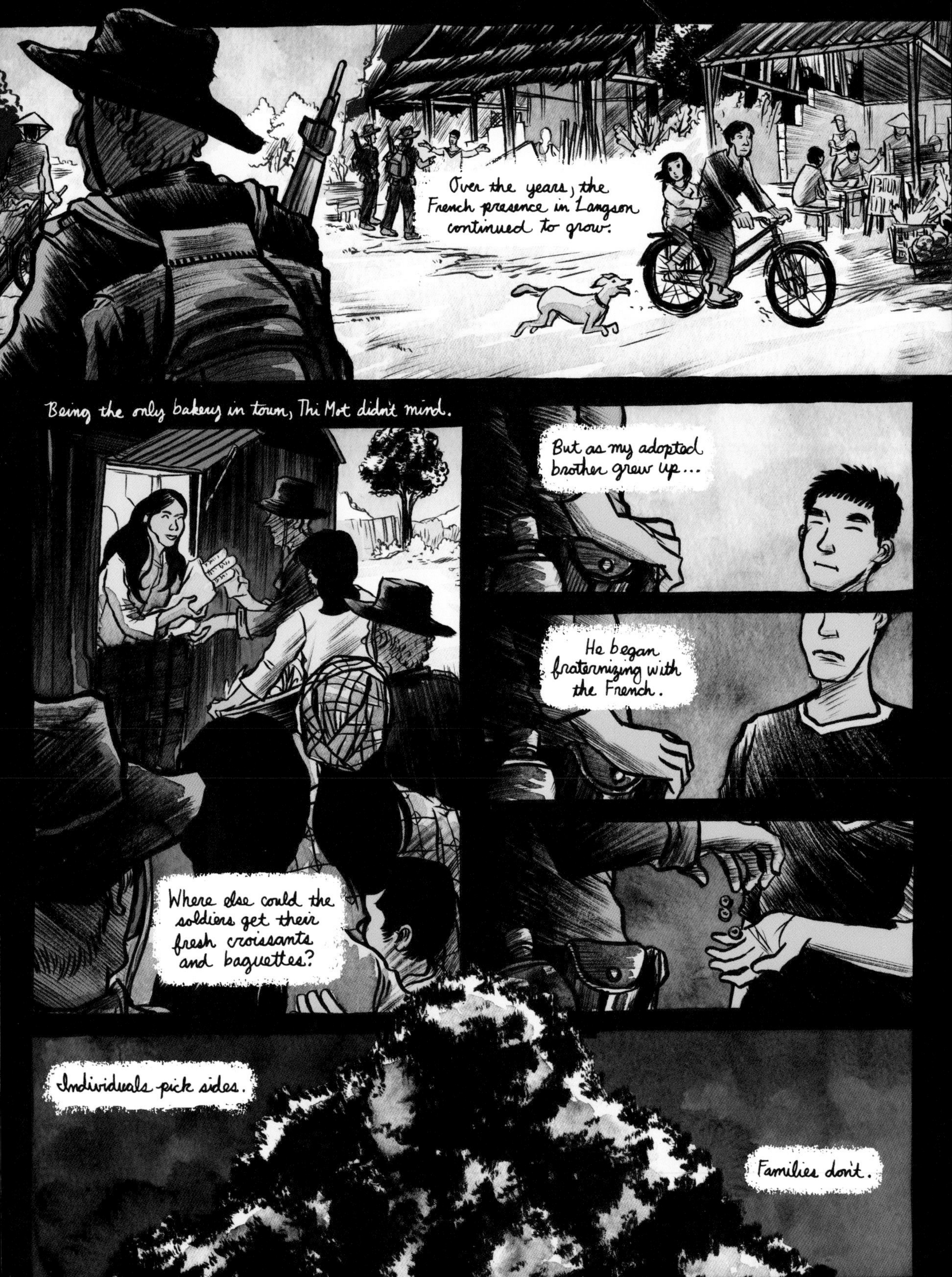

Over the years, the French presence in Langson continued to grow.
Being the only bakery in town, Thi Mot didn't mind.
Where else could the soldiers get their fresh croissants and baguettes?
But as my adopted brother grew up...
He began fraternizing with the French.
Individuals pick sides.
Families don't.

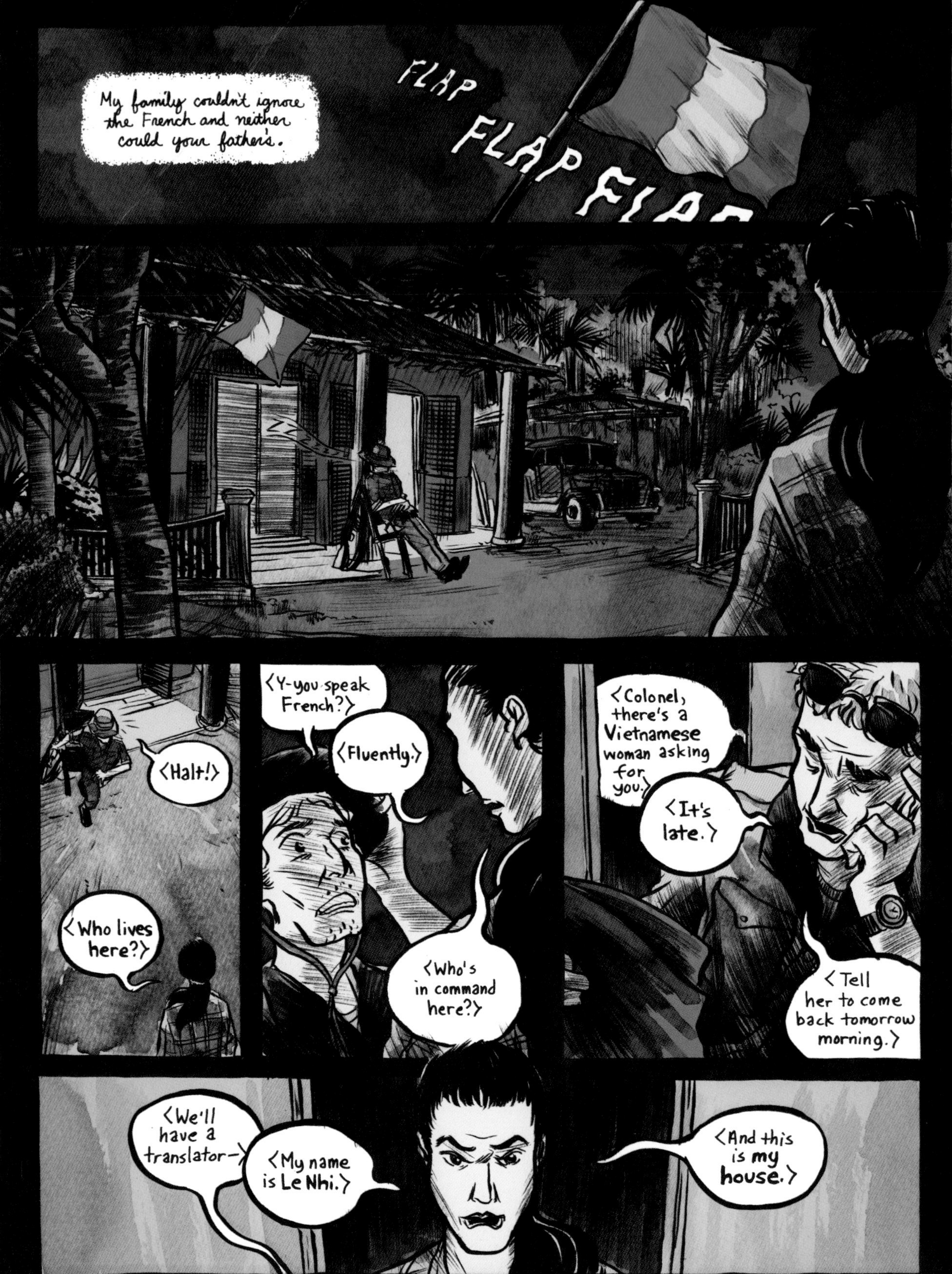
My family couldn't ignore the French and neither could your father's.
FLAP
FLAP
FLAP
FLAP
<Halt!>
<Who lives here?>
<Y-you speak French?>
<Fluently.>
<Who's in command here?>
<Colonel, there's a Vietnamese woman asking for you.>
<It's late.>
<Tell her to come back tomorrow morning.>
<We'll have a translator—>
<My name is Le Nhi.>
<And this is my house.>

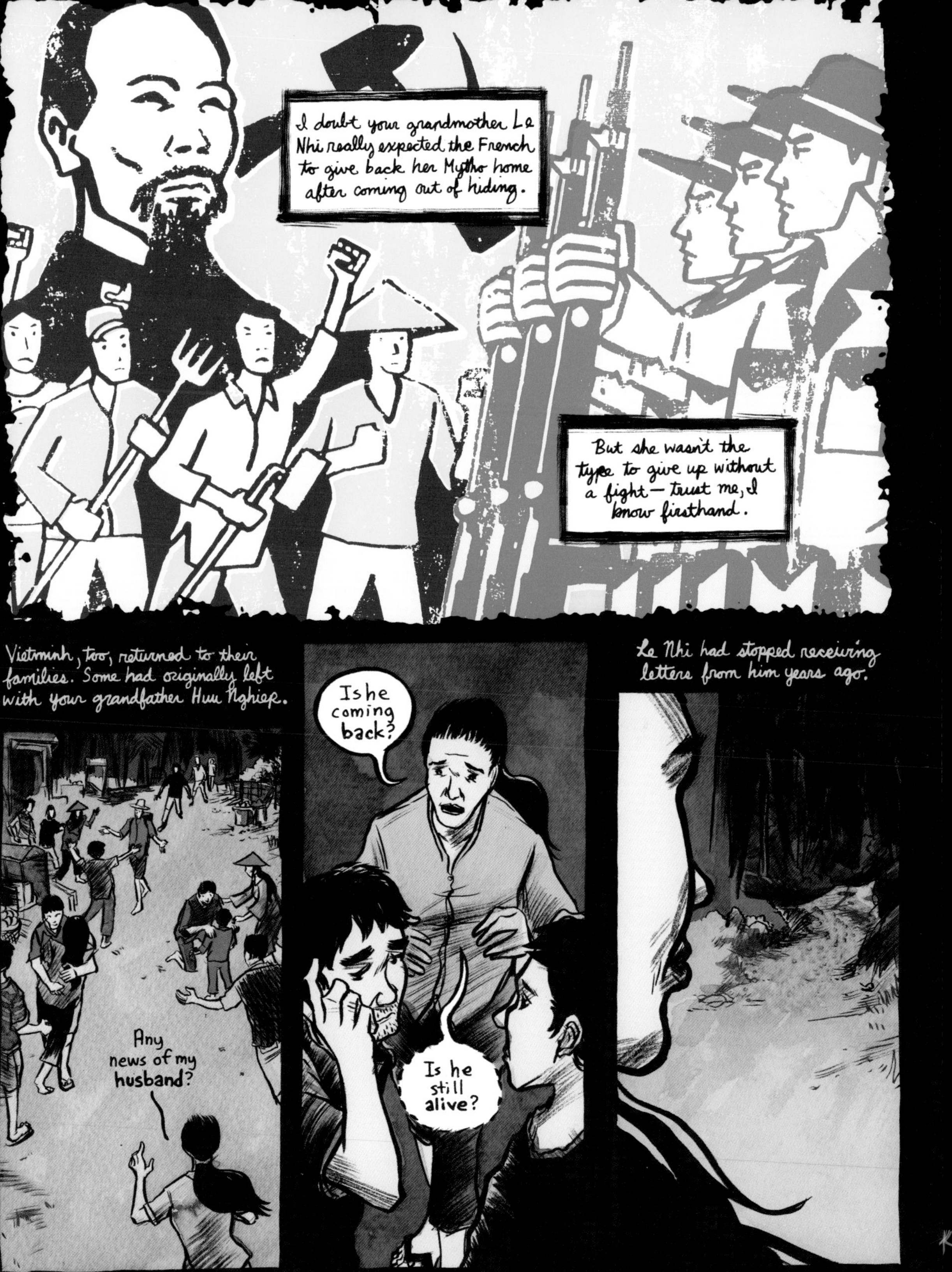
I doubt your grandmother Le Nhi really expected the French to give back her Mytho home after coming out of hiding.
But she wasn't the type to give up without a fight—trust me, I know firsthand.
Vietminh, too, returned to their families. Some had originally left with your grandfather Huu Nghiep.
Any news of my husband?
Is he coming back?
Is he still alive?
Le Nhi had stopped receiving letters from him years ago.

Thankfully, she found another home to raise your father and his siblings.

Husbandless, Le Nhi was both mother and father to them.

I think your dad got the "father" half more often.

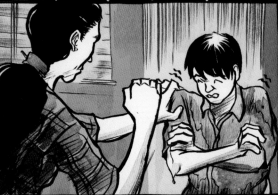

Le Nhi's parents supported her, their only child, as much as possible. They were respected and powerful community leaders so that turned out to be quite helpful.

Thanks to them, Le Nhi was very well educated.

She was also very beautiful and suddenly found herself single.

BEEP BEEEP

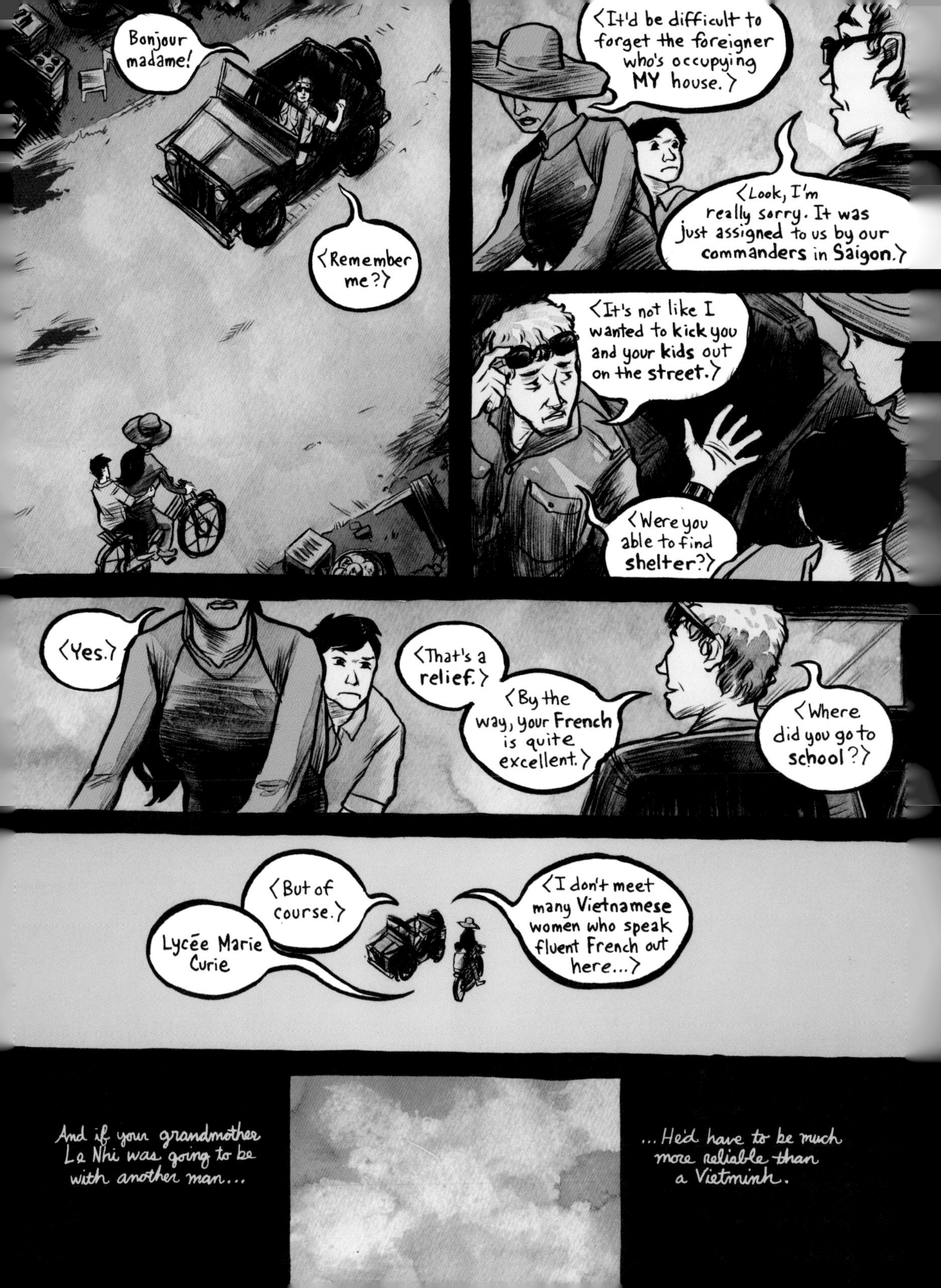
Bonjour madame!
<Remember me?>
<It'd be difficult to forget the foreigner who's occupying MY house.>
<Look, I'm really sorry. It was just assigned to us by our commanders in Saigon.>
<It's not like I wanted to kick you and your kids out on the street.>
<Were you able to find shelter?>
<Yes.>
<That's a relief.>
<By the way, your French is quite excellent.>
<Where did you go to school?>
<But of course.>
Lycée Marie Curie
<I don't meet many Vietnamese women who speak fluent French out here...>
And if your grandmother Le Nhi was going to be with another man...
...He'd have to be much more reliable than a Vietminh.

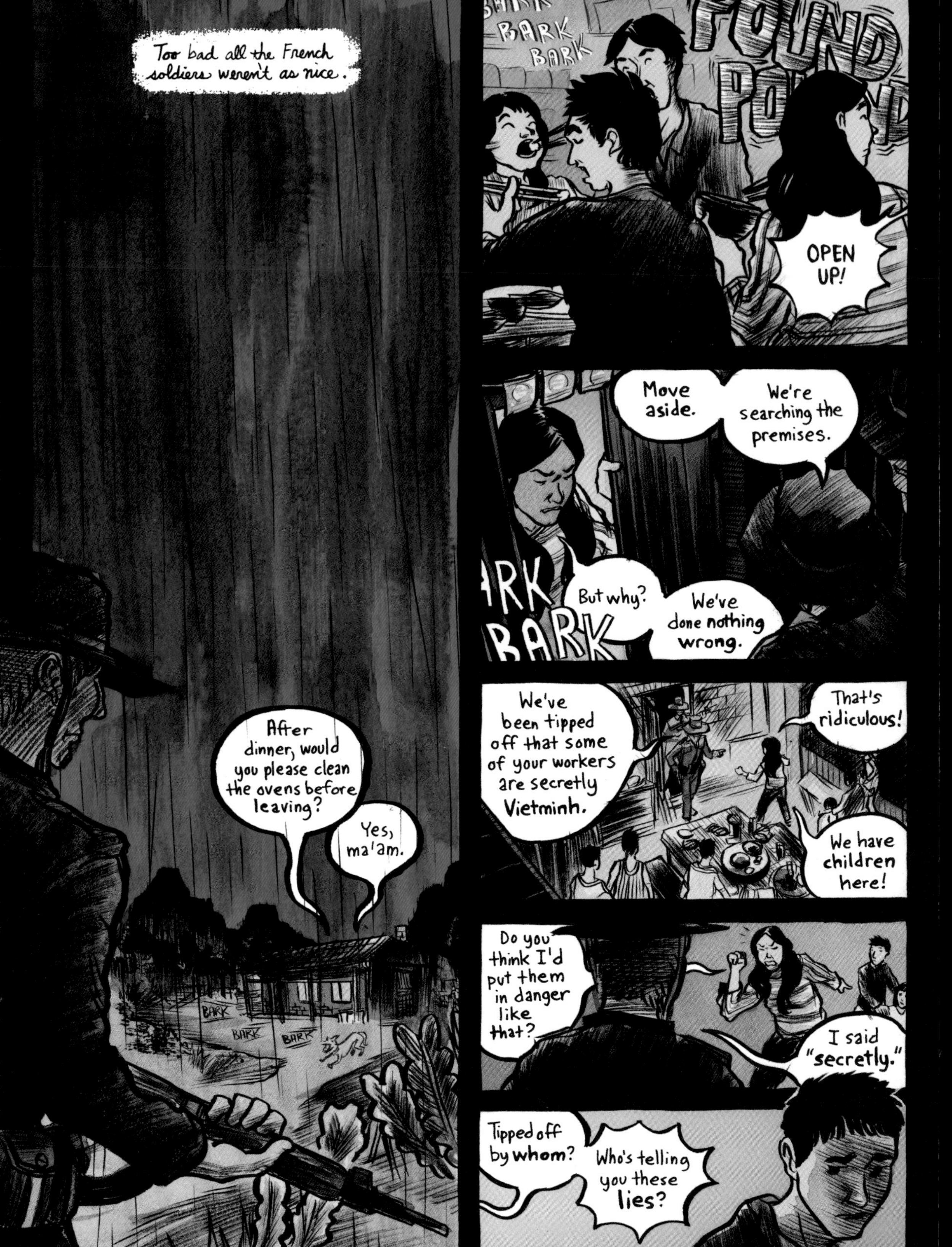

Too bad all the French soldiers weren't as nice.
After dinner, would you please clean the ovens before leaving?
Yes, ma'am.
BARK
BARK
BARK
BARK
BARK
POUND POUND
OPEN UP!
Move aside.
We're searching the premises.
But why?
We've done nothing wrong.
We've been tipped off that some of your workers are secretly Vietminh.
That's ridiculous!
We have children here!
Do you think I'd put them in danger like that?
I said "secretly."
Tipped off by whom?
Who's telling you these lies?

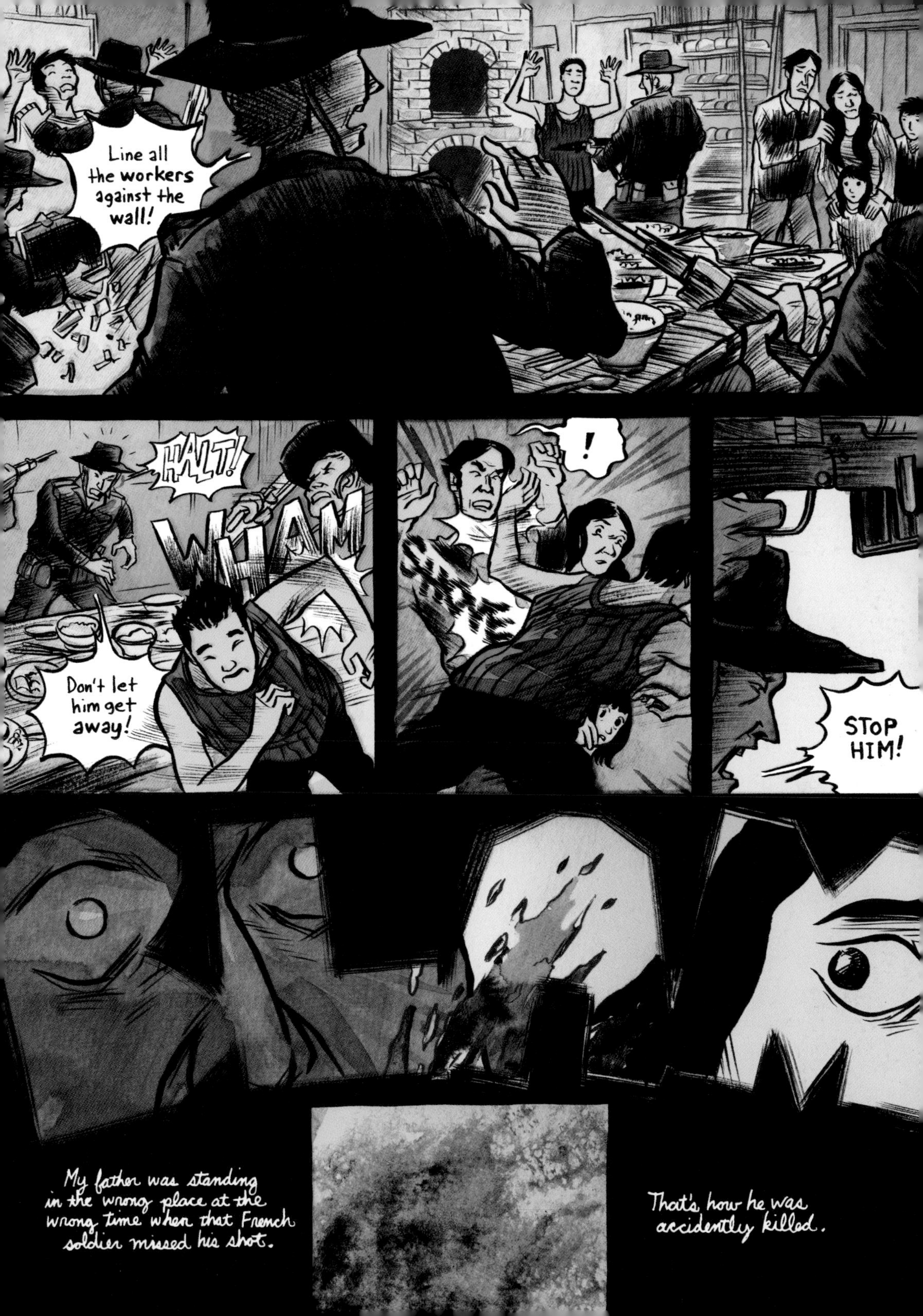
Line all the workers against the wall!
HALT!
WHAM
Don't let him get away!
!
SHOVE
STOP HIM!
My father was standing in the wrong place at the wrong time when that French soldier missed his shot.
That's how he was accidently killed.

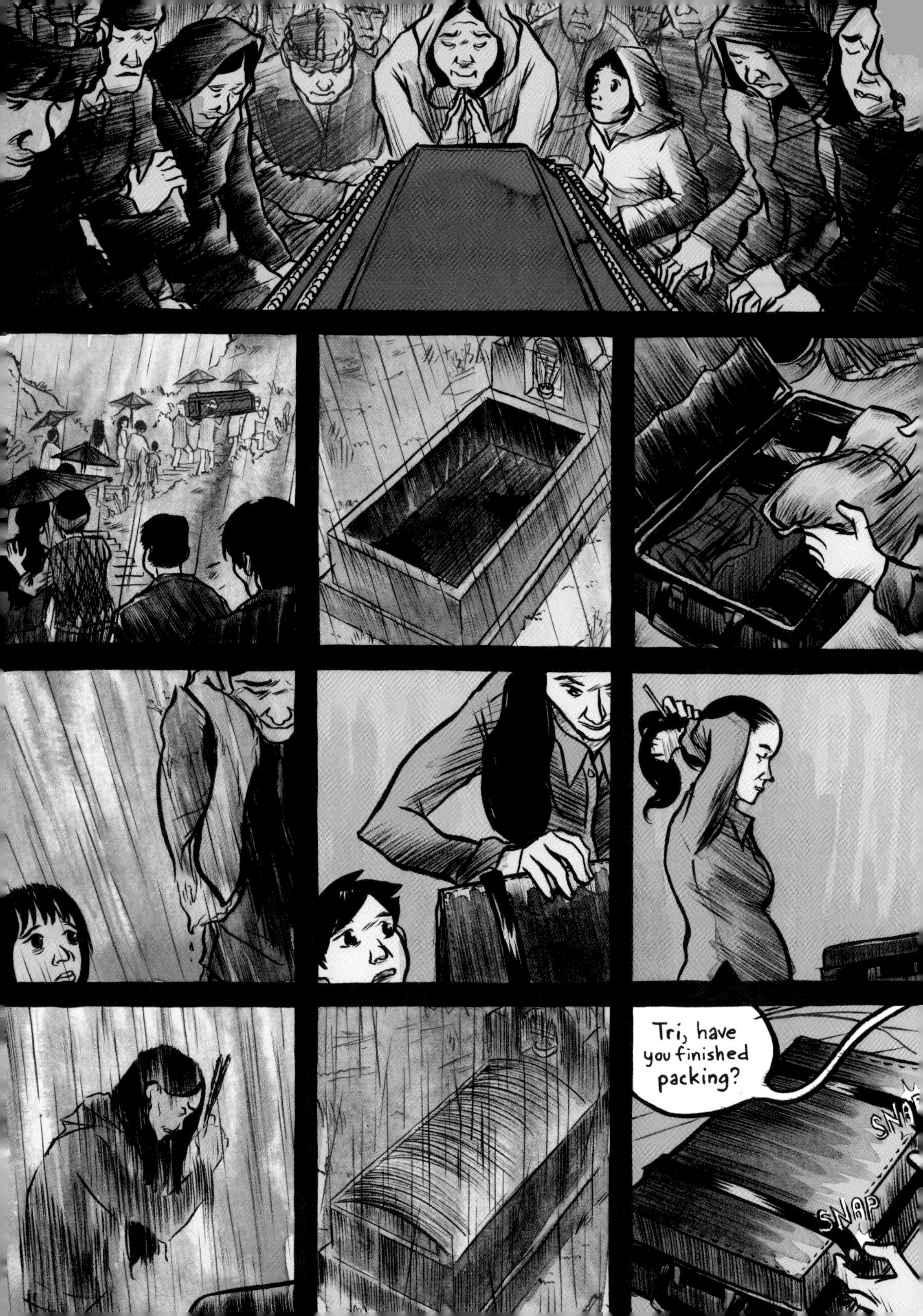
Tri, have you finished packing?
SNAP
SNAP

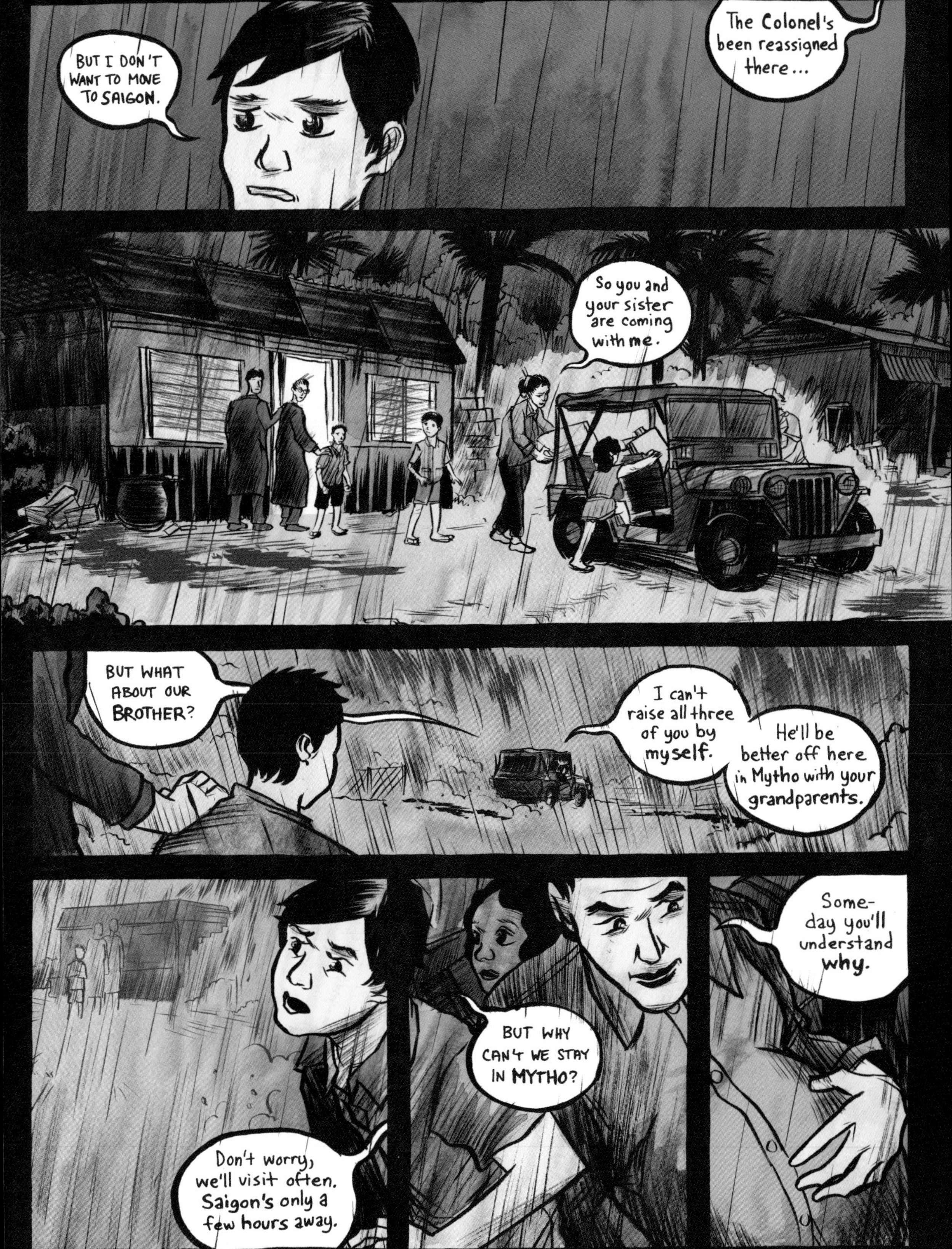
BUT I DON'T WANT TO MOVE TO SAIGON.
The Colonel's been reassigned there...
So you and your sister are coming with me.
BUT WHAT ABOUT OUR BROTHER?
I can't raise all three of you by myself.
He'll be better off here in Mytho with your grandparents.
BUT WHY CAN'T WE STAY IN MYTHO?
Don't worry, we'll visit often. Saigon's only a few hours away.
Some-day you'll understand why.

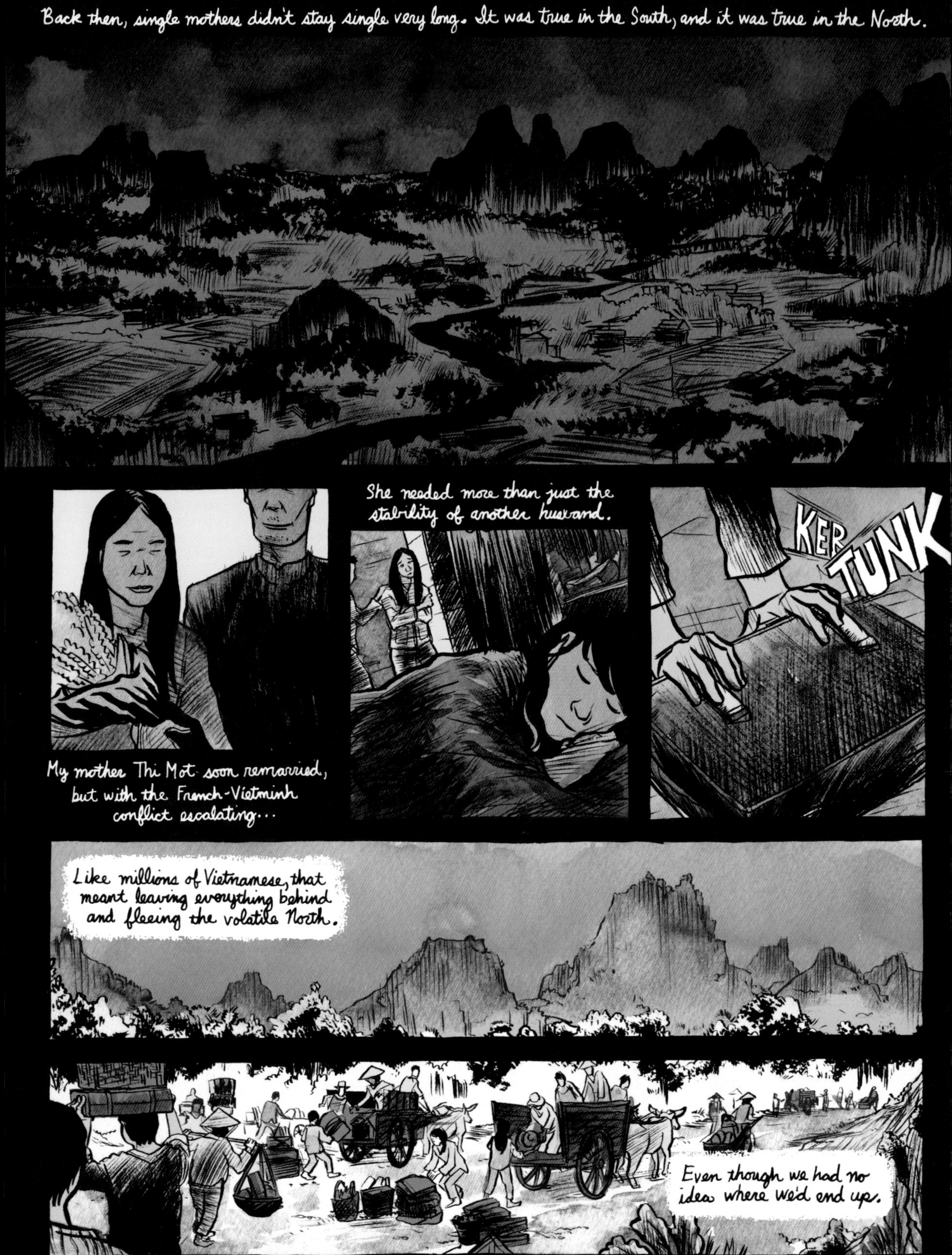

Back then, single mothers didn't stay single very long. It was true in the South, and it was true in the North.
My mother Thi Mot soon remarried, but with the French-Vietminh conflict escalating...
She needed more than just the stability of another husband.
KER TUNK
Like millions of Vietnamese, that meant leaving everything behind and fleeing the volatile North.
Even though we had no idea where we'd end up.

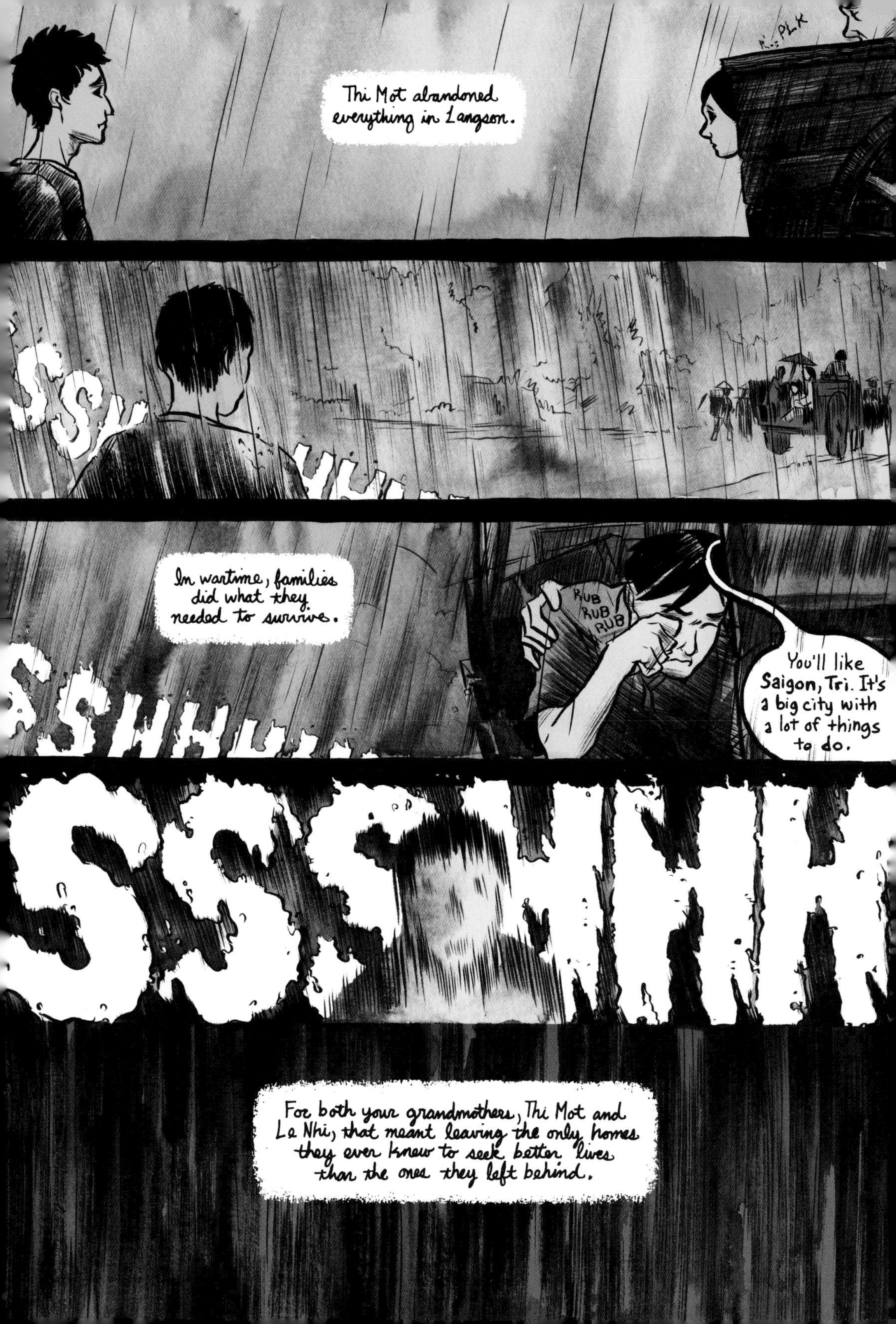
Thi Mot abandoned everything in Langson.
In wartime, families did what they needed to survive.
RUB RUB RUB
You'll like Saigon, Tri. It's a big city with a lot of things to do.
SSHH
For both your grandmothers, Thi Mot and Le Nhi, that meant leaving the only homes they ever knew to seek better lives than the ones they left behind.

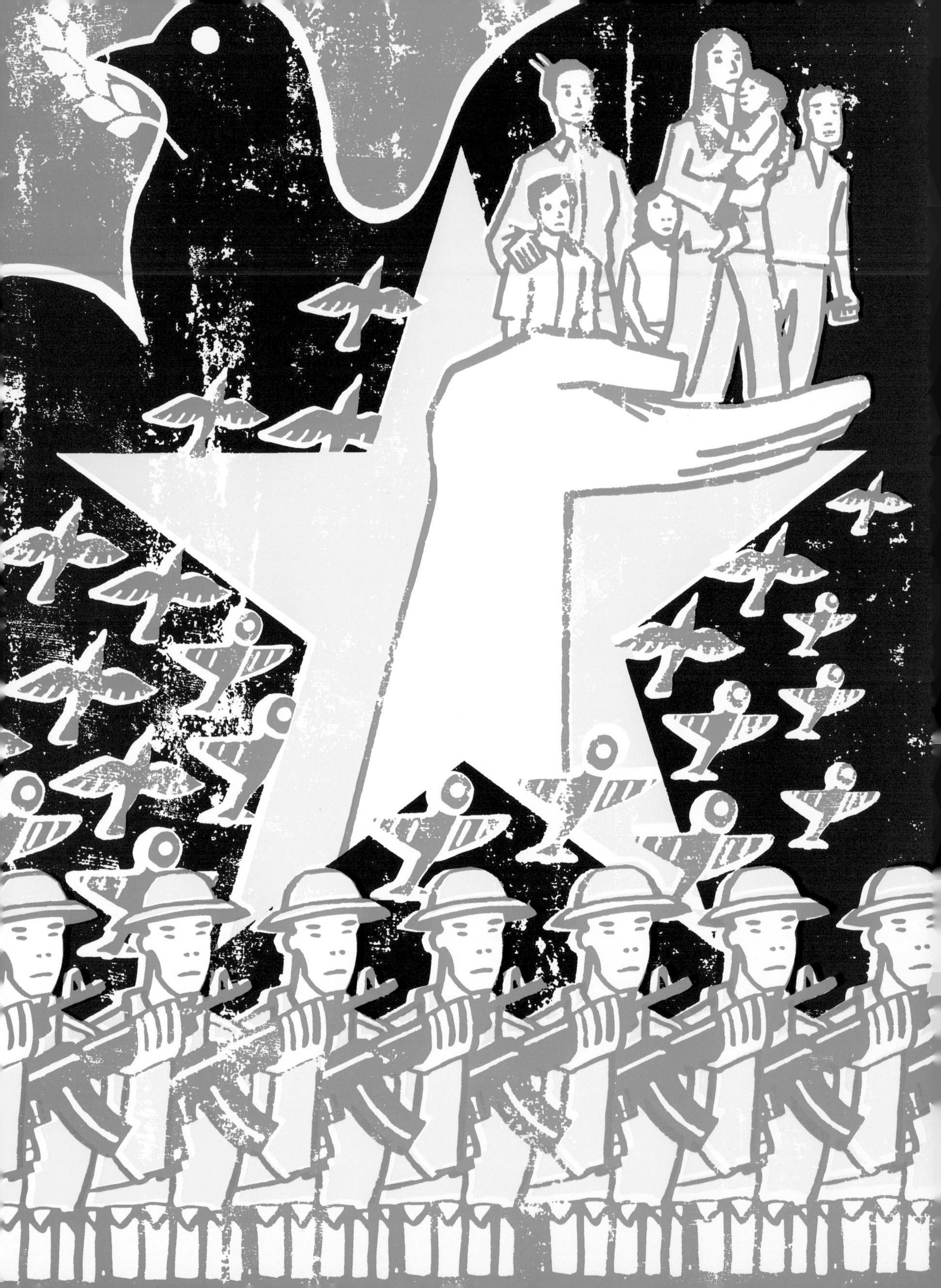

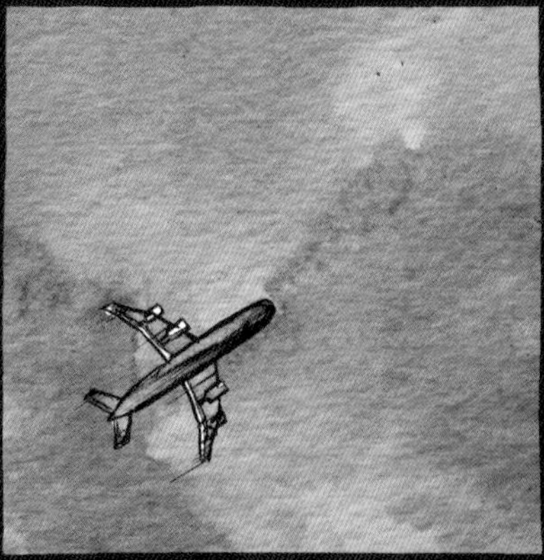

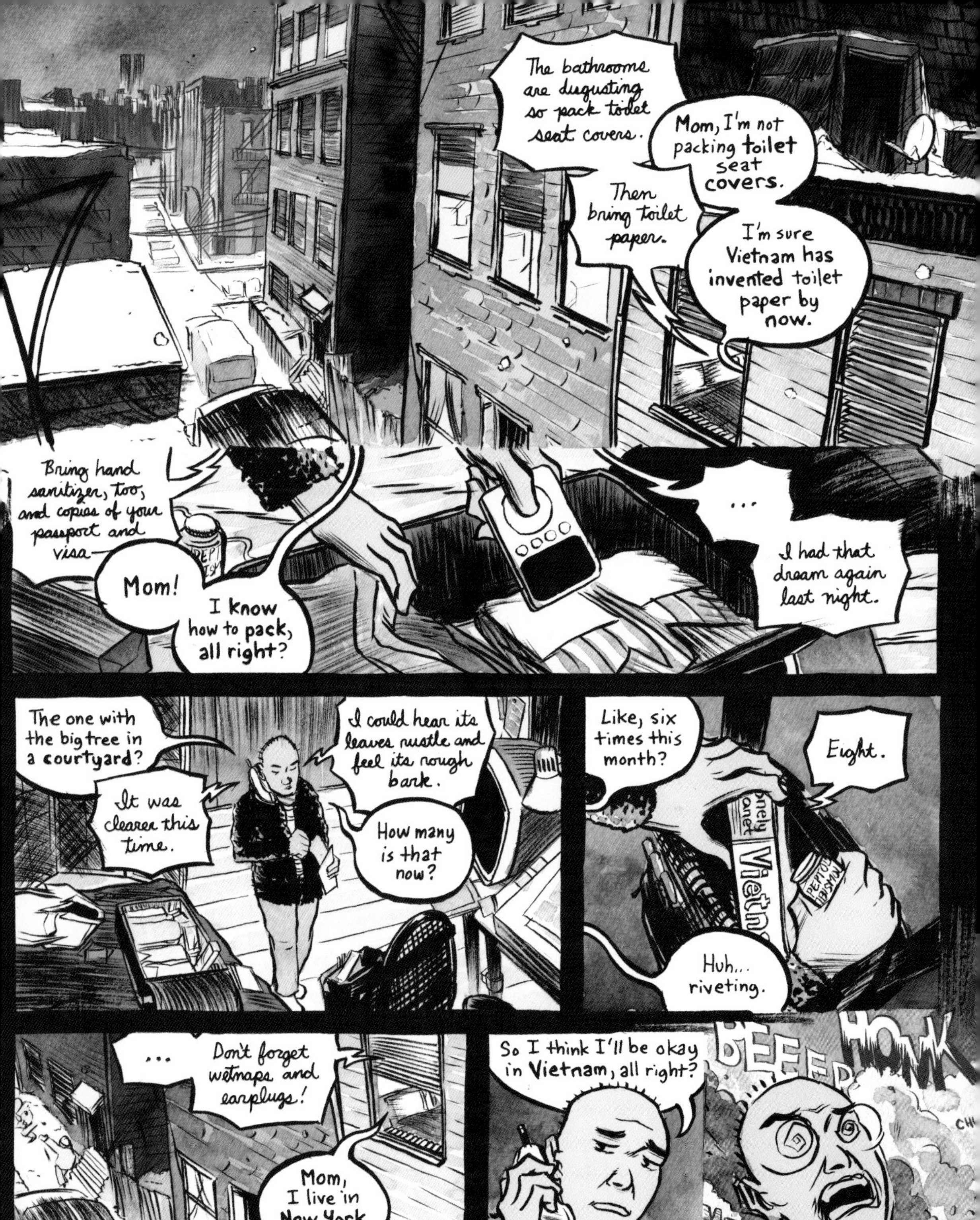
The bathrooms are dugusting so pack toilet seat covers.
Mom, I'm not packing toilet seat covers.
Then bring toilet paper.
I'm sure Vietnam has invented toilet paper by now.
Bring hand sanitizer, too, and copies of your passport and visa—
Mom!
I know how to pack, all right?
...
I had that dream again last night.
The one with the big tree in a courtyard?
It was clearer this time.
I could hear its leaves rustle and feel its rough bark.
How many is that now?
Like, six times this month?
Eight.
Huh... riveting.
...
Don't forget wetnaps and earplugs!
Mom, I live in New York City. It's not exactly the cleanest or quietest place on Earth!
So I think I'll be okay in Vietnam, all right?
Whatever you say, Mr. World Traveler.
HONK

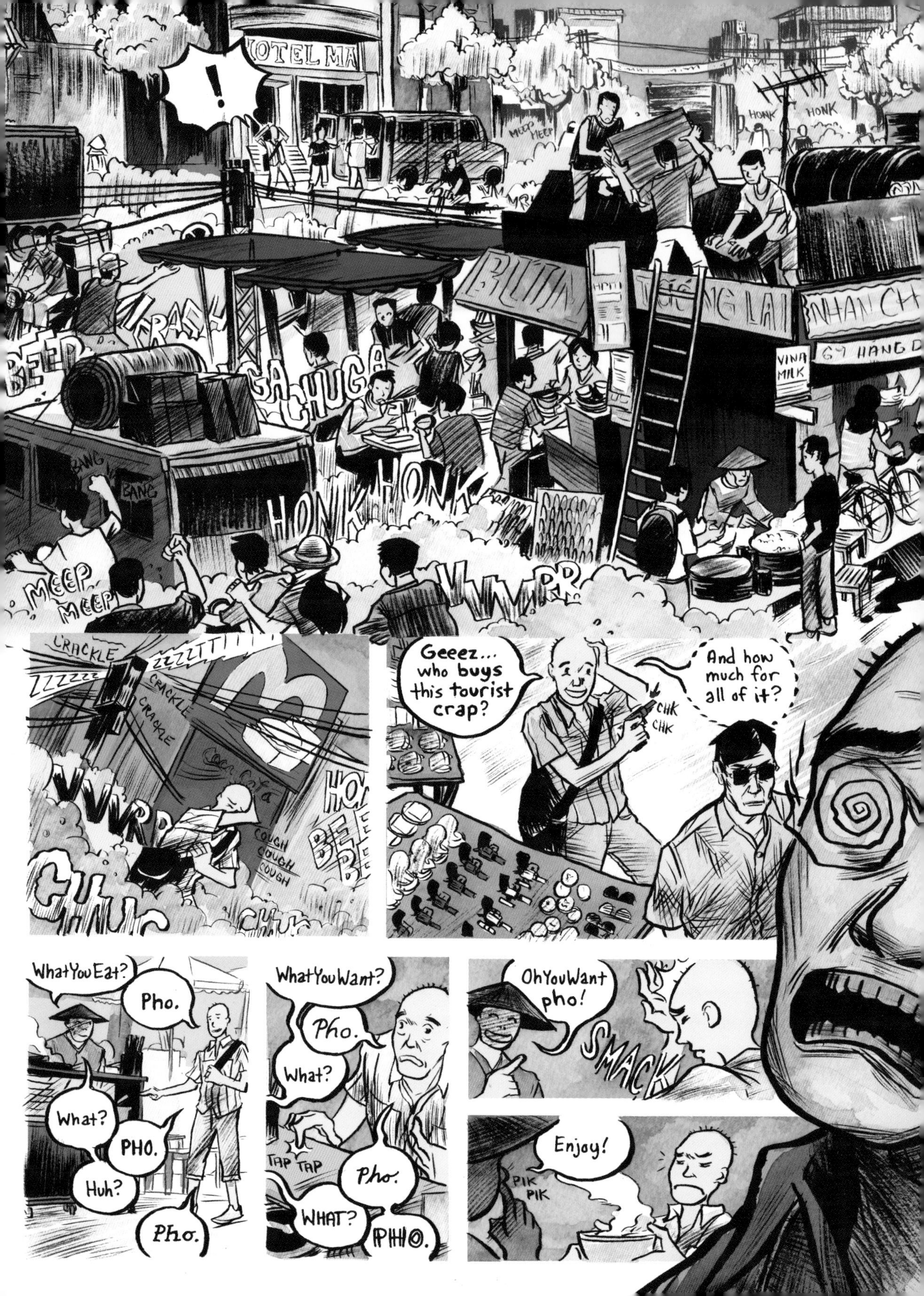

!
HOTEL MA
MEEP MEEP
HONK
HONK
CRASH
BEEP
CHUGA
CHUGA
BUN
NHAN CH
67 HANG D
VINA MILK
BANG
BANG
HONK HONK
MEEP MEEP
VVVVRR
CRACKLE
ZZZZTT
ZZZZZZ
CRACKLE
CRACKLE
VVVRR
COUGH COUGH COUGH
Geeez... who buys this tourist crap?
CHK CHK
And how much for all of it?
WhatYouEat?
Pho.
What?
PHO.
Huh?
Pho.
WhatYouWant?
Pho.
What?
TAP TAP
Pho.
WHAT?
PHO.
OhYouWant pho!
SMACK
Enjoy!
PIK PIK

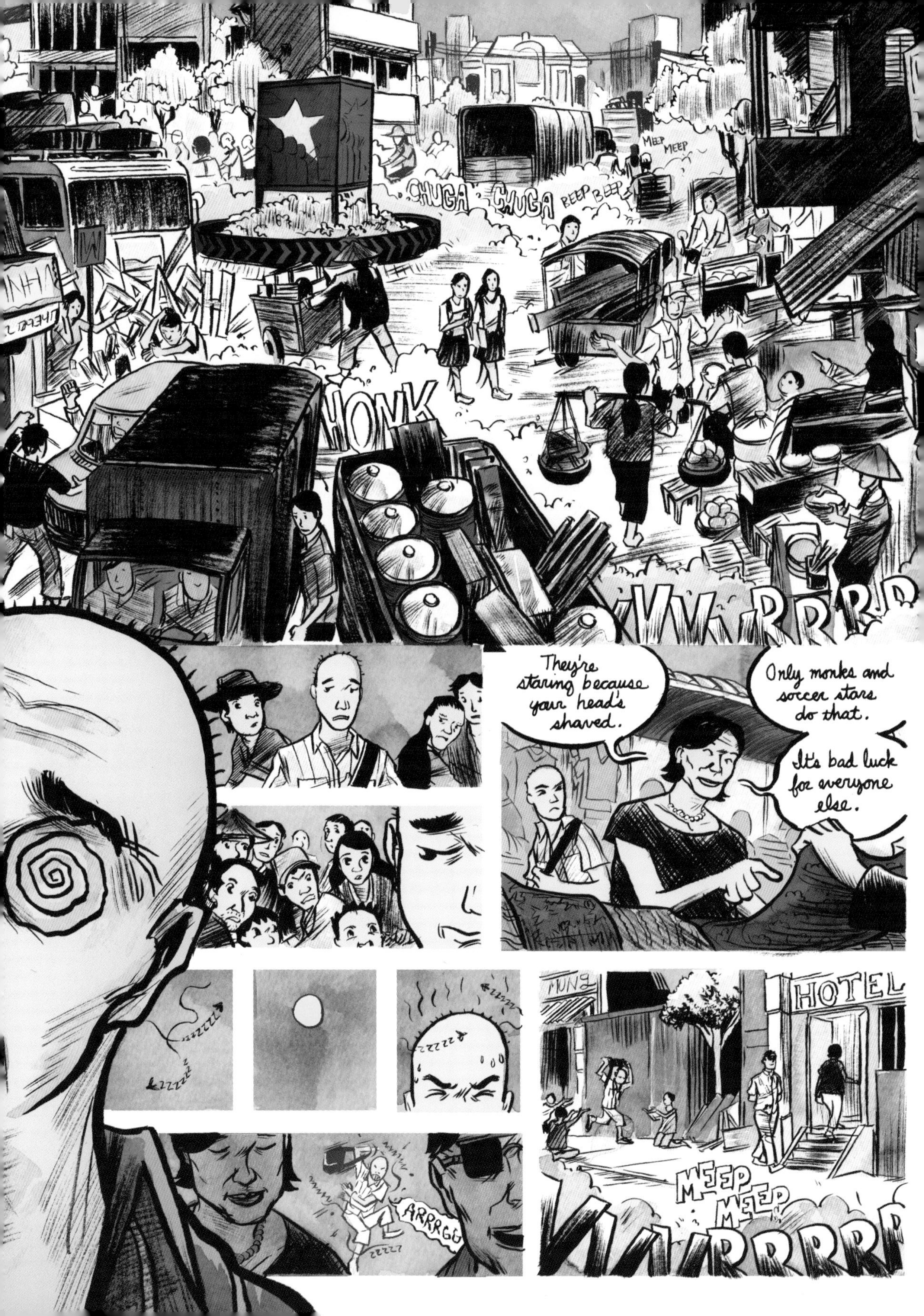
CHUGA CHUGA BEEP BEEP
MEEP MEEP
HONK
VVVRRRR
They're staring because your head's shaved.
Only monks and soccer stars do that.
It's bad luck for everyone else.
HOTEL
ARRRGG
MEEP MEEP
VVVRRRRR

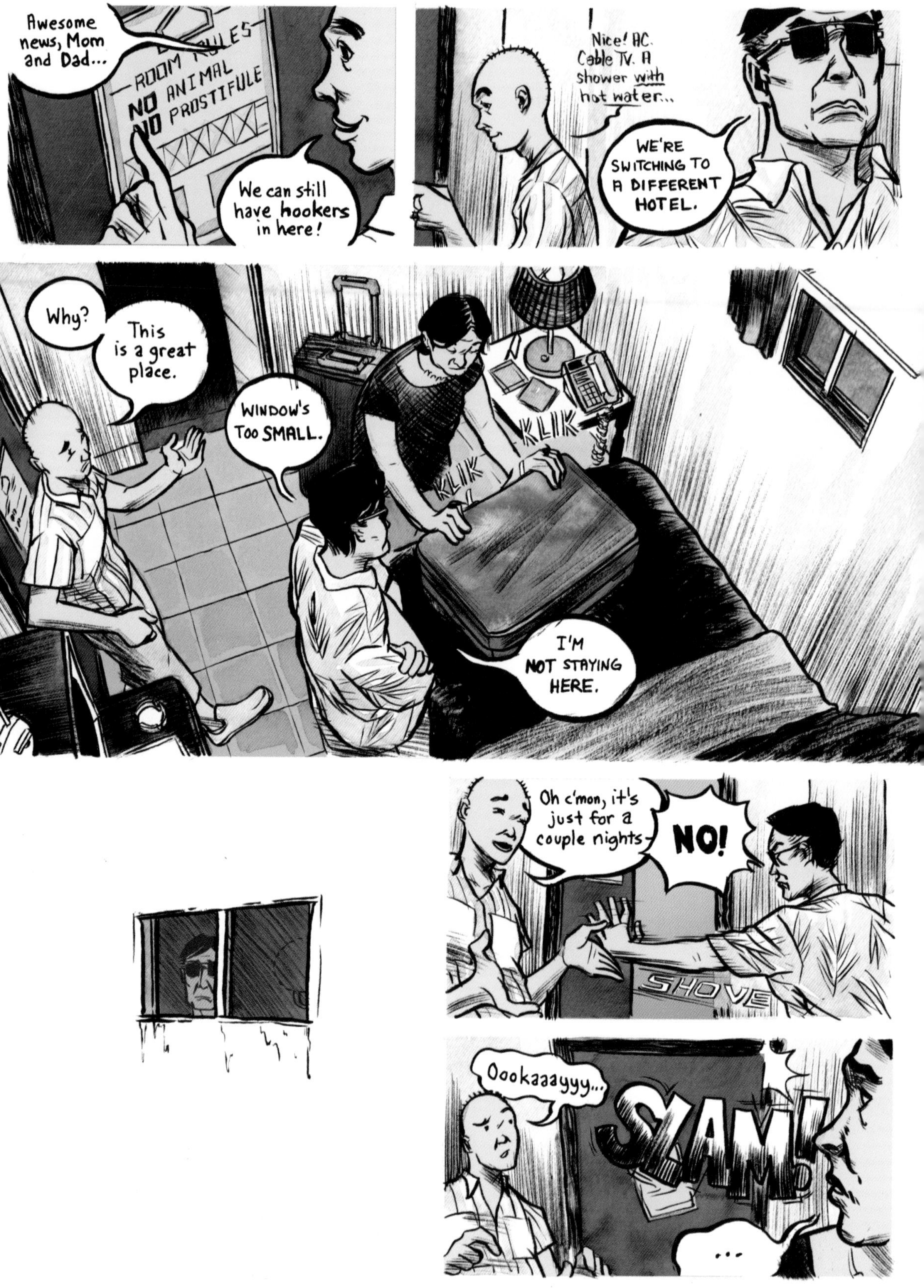

ROOM RULES
NO ANIMAL
NO PROSTIFULE
Awesome news, Mom and Dad...
We can still have hookers in here!
Nice! AC. Cable TV. A shower with hot water...
WE'RE SWITCHING TO A DIFFERENT HOTEL.
Why?
This is a great place.
WINDOW'S TOO SMALL.
KLIK
KLIK
I'M NOT STAYING HERE.
Oh c'mon, it's just for a couple nights-
NO!
SHOVE
Oookaaayyy...
SLAM!
...

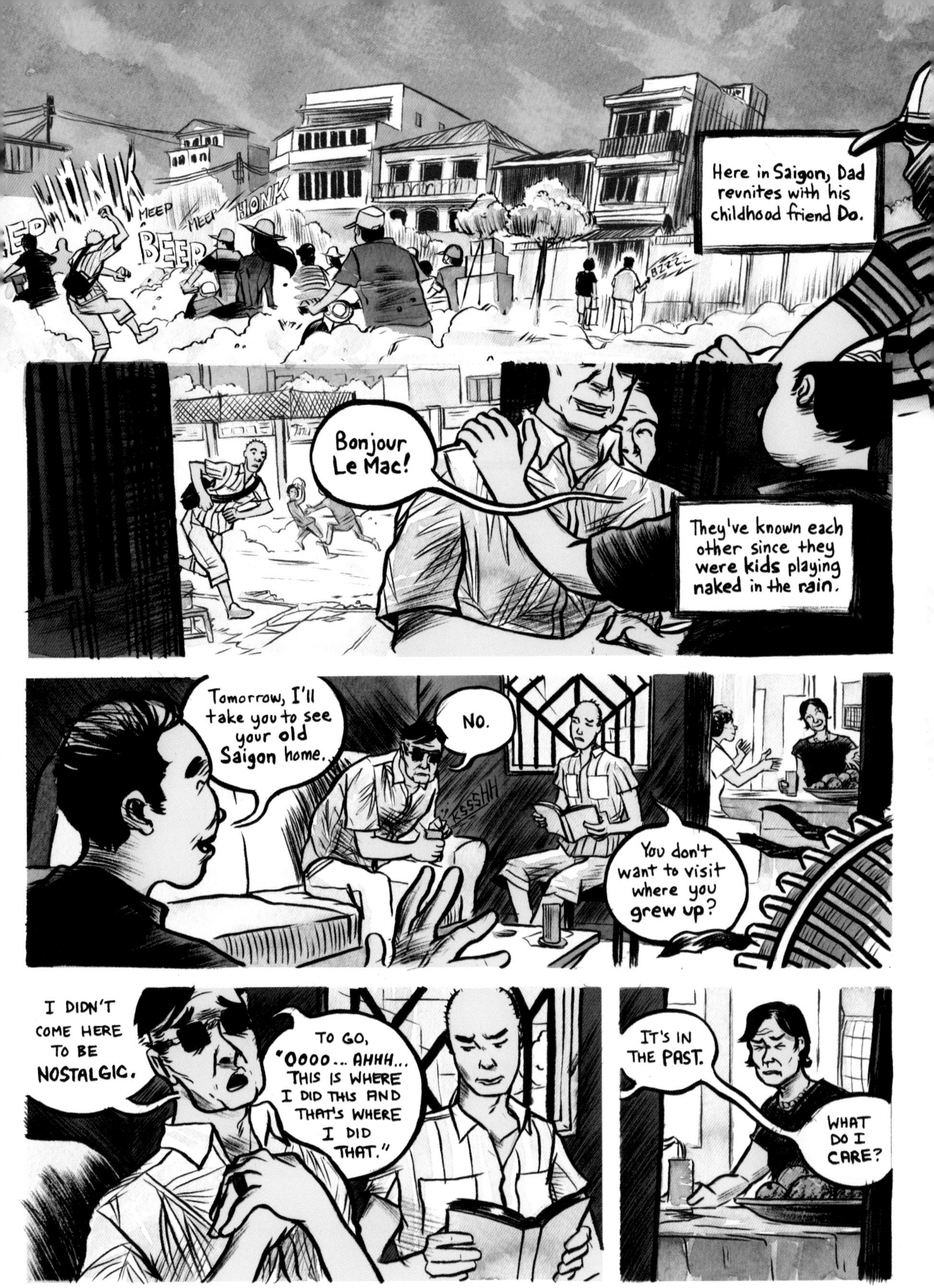
HONK
MEEP
MEEP
HONK
BEEP
Here in Saigon, Dad reunites with his childhood friend Do.
BZZZ
Bonjour Le Mac!
They've known each other since they were kids playing naked in the rain.
Tomorrow, I'll take you to see your old Saigon home.
No.
KSSSHH
You don't want to visit where you grew up?
I DIDN'T COME HERE TO BE NOSTALGIC.
TO GO, "OOOO... AHHH... THIS IS WHERE I DID THIS AND THAT'S WHERE I DID THAT."
IT'S IN THE PAST.
WHAT DO I CARE?

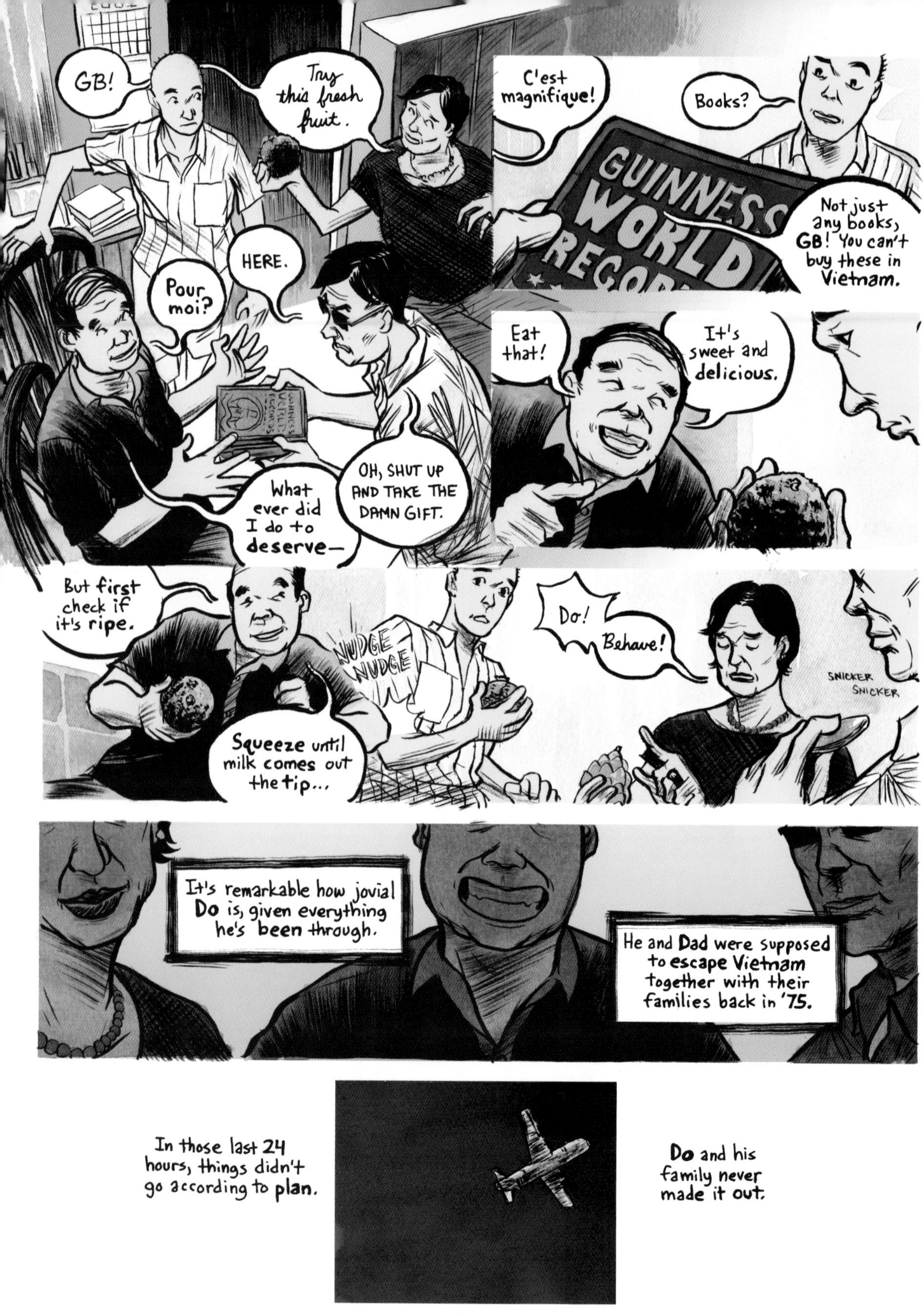
GB!
Try this fresh fruit.
C'est magnifique!
Books?
GUINNESS WORLD RECORDS
Not just any books, GB! You can't buy these in Vietnam.
HERE.
Pour moi?
What ever did I do to deserve—
OH, SHUT UP AND TAKE THE DAMN GIFT.
Eat that!
It's sweet and delicious.
But first check if it's ripe.
NUDGE NUDGE
Squeeze until milk comes out the tip...
Do!
Behave!
SNICKER SNICKER
It's remarkable how jovial Do is, given everything he's been through.
He and Dad were supposed to escape Vietnam together with their families back in '75.
In those last 24 hours, things didn't go according to plan.
Do and his family never made it out.

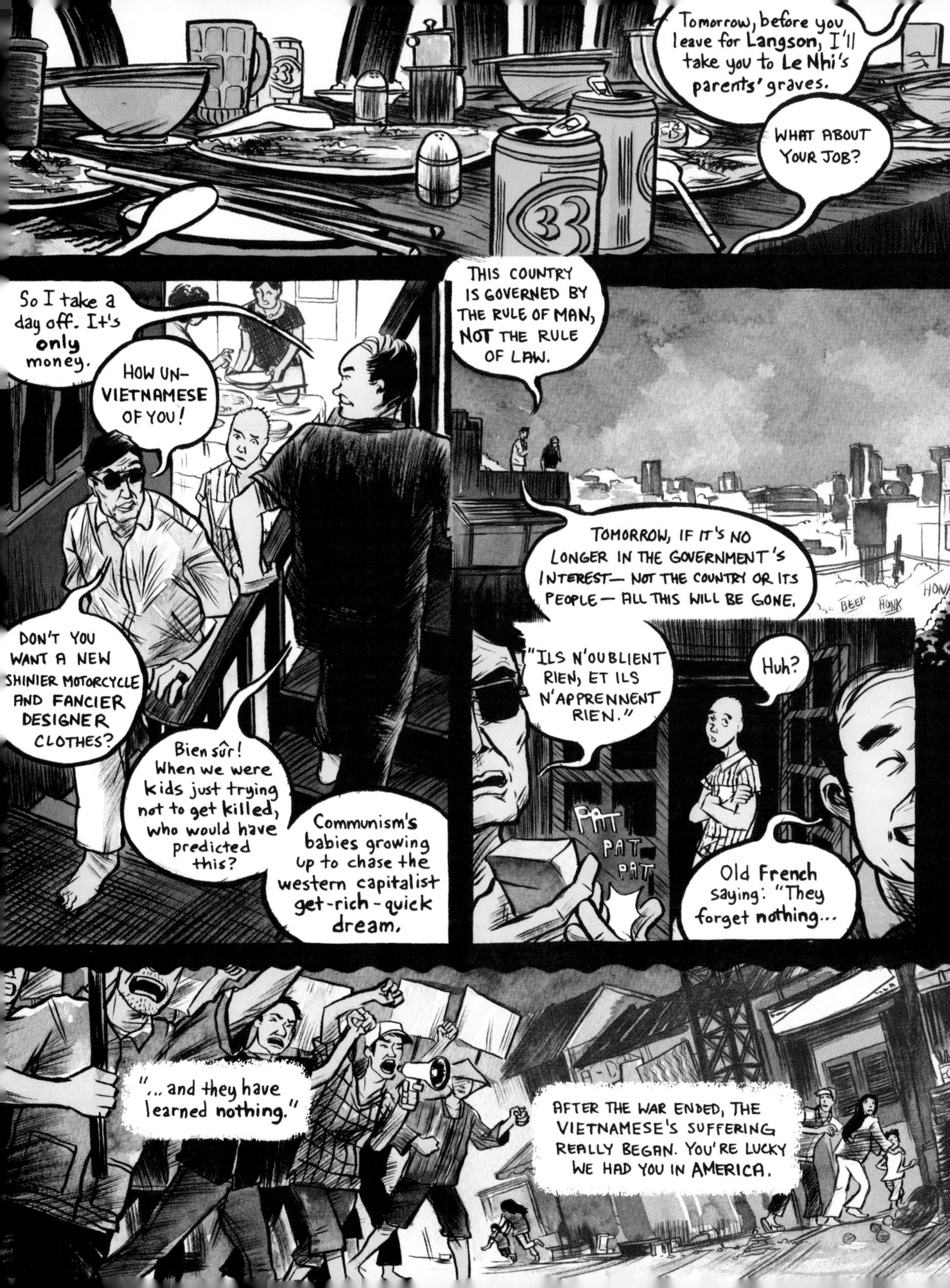

Tomorrow, before you leave for Langson, I'll take you to Le Nhi's parents' graves.
WHAT ABOUT YOUR JOB?
So I take a day off. It's only money.
HOW UN-VIETNAMESE OF YOU!
DON'T YOU WANT A NEW SHINIER MOTORCYCLE AND FANCIER DESIGNER CLOTHES?
Bien sûr! When we were kids just trying not to get killed, who would have predicted this?
Communism's babies growing up to chase the western capitalist get-rich-quick dream.
THIS COUNTRY IS GOVERNED BY THE RULE OF MAN, NOT THE RULE OF LAW.
TOMORROW, IF IT'S NO LONGER IN THE GOVERNMENT'S INTEREST— NOT THE COUNTRY OR ITS PEOPLE— ALL THIS WILL BE GONE.
BEEP HONK HONK
"ILS N'OUBLIENT RIEN, ET ILS N'APPRENNENT RIEN."
PAT PAT PAT
Huh?
Old French saying: "They forget nothing...
"... and they have learned nothing."
AFTER THE WAR ENDED, THE VIETNAMESE'S SUFFERING REALLY BEGAN. YOU'RE LUCKY WE HAD YOU IN AMERICA.

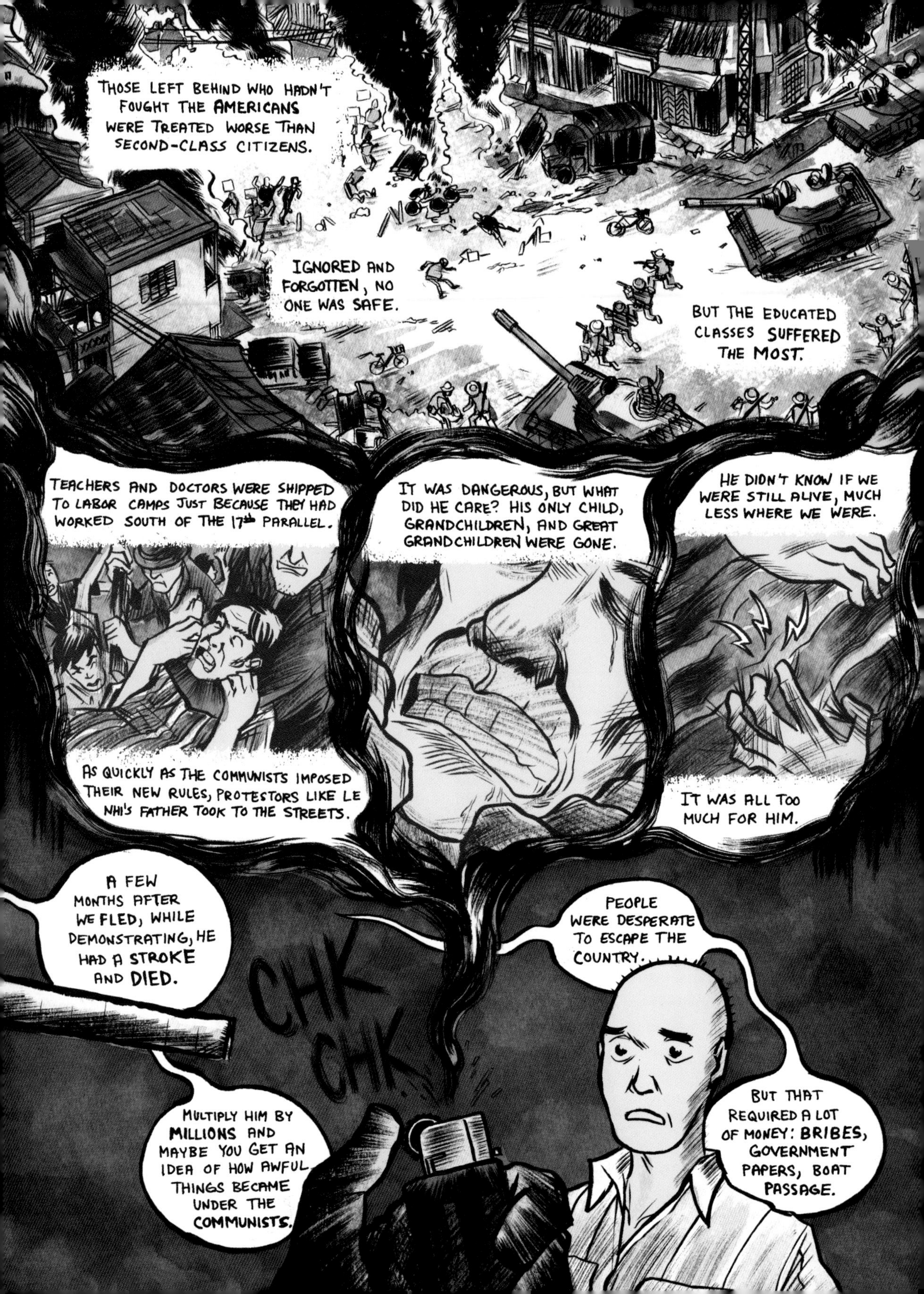
THOSE LEFT BEHIND WHO HADN'T FOUGHT THE AMERICANS WERE TREATED WORSE THAN SECOND-CLASS CITIZENS.
IGNORED AND FORGOTTEN, NO ONE WAS SAFE.
BUT THE EDUCATED CLASSES SUFFERED THE MOST.
TEACHERS AND DOCTORS WERE SHIPPED TO LABOR CAMPS JUST BECAUSE THEY HAD WORKED SOUTH OF THE 17th PARALLEL.
AS QUICKLY AS THE COMMUNISTS IMPOSED THEIR NEW RULES, PROTESTORS LIKE LE NHI'S FATHER TOOK TO THE STREETS.
IT WAS DANGEROUS, BUT WHAT DID HE CARE? HIS ONLY CHILD, GRANDCHILDREN, AND GREAT GRANDCHILDREN WERE GONE.
HE DIDN'T KNOW IF WE WERE STILL ALIVE, MUCH LESS WHERE WE WERE.
IT WAS ALL TOO MUCH FOR HIM.
A FEW MONTHS AFTER WE FLED, WHILE DEMONSTRATING, HE HAD A STROKE AND DIED.
CHK CHK
MULTIPLY HIM BY MILLIONS AND MAYBE YOU GET AN IDEA OF HOW AWFUL THINGS BECAME UNDER THE COMMUNISTS.
PEOPLE WERE DESPERATE TO ESCAPE THE COUNTRY.
BUT THAT REQUIRED A LOT OF MONEY: BRIBES, GOVERNMENT PAPERS, BOAT PASSAGE.

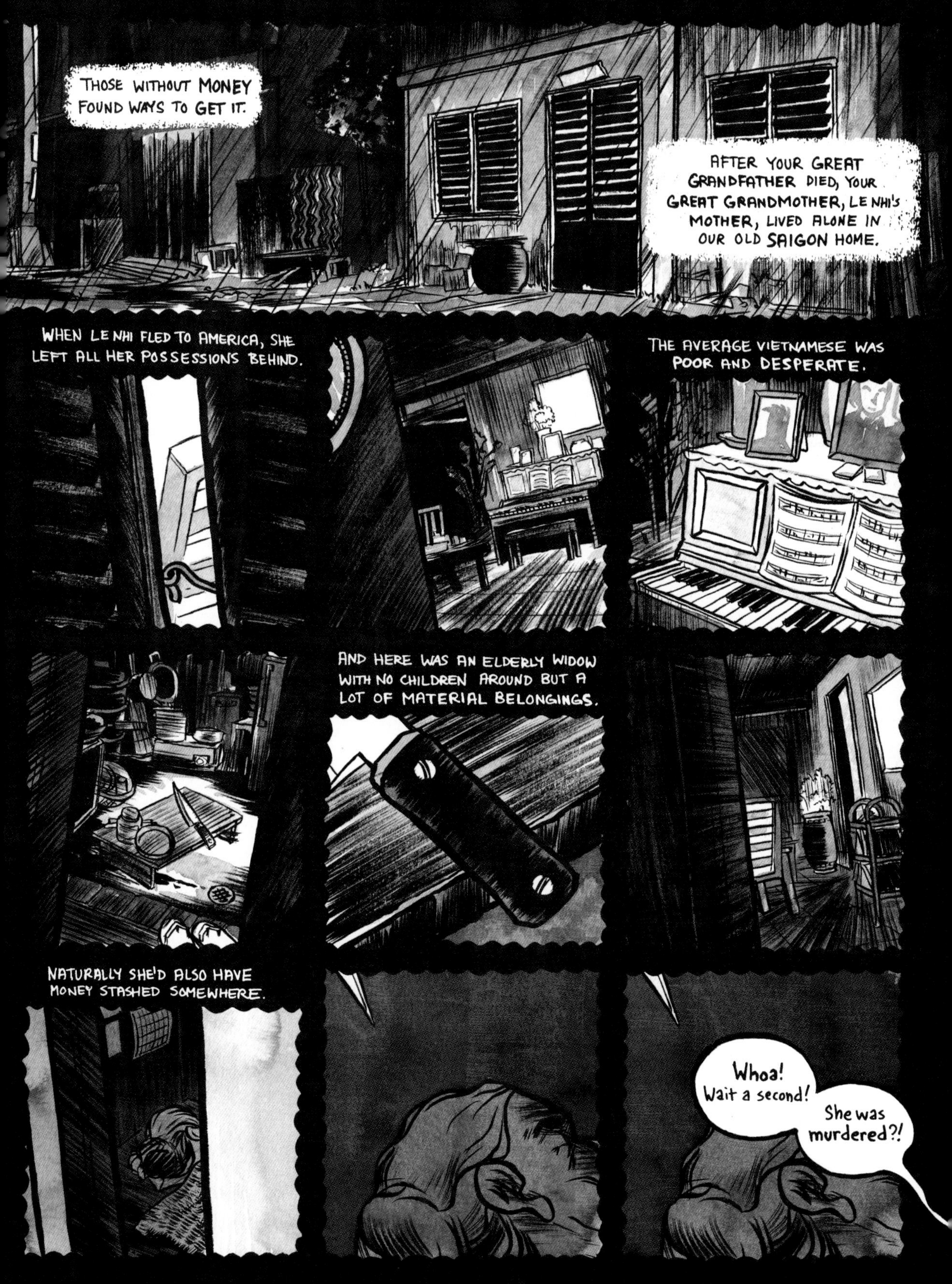
THOSE WITHOUT MONEY FOUND WAYS TO GET IT.
AFTER YOUR GREAT GRANDFATHER DIED, YOUR GREAT GRANDMOTHER, LE NHI'S MOTHER, LIVED ALONE IN OUR OLD SAIGON HOME.
WHEN LE NHI FLED TO AMERICA, SHE LEFT ALL HER POSSESSIONS BEHIND.
THE AVERAGE VIETNAMESE WAS POOR AND DESPERATE.
AND HERE WAS AN ELDERLY WIDOW WITH NO CHILDREN AROUND BUT A LOT OF MATERIAL BELONGINGS.
NATURALLY SHE'D ALSO HAVE MONEY STASHED SOMEWHERE.
Whoa! Wait a second!
She was murdered?!

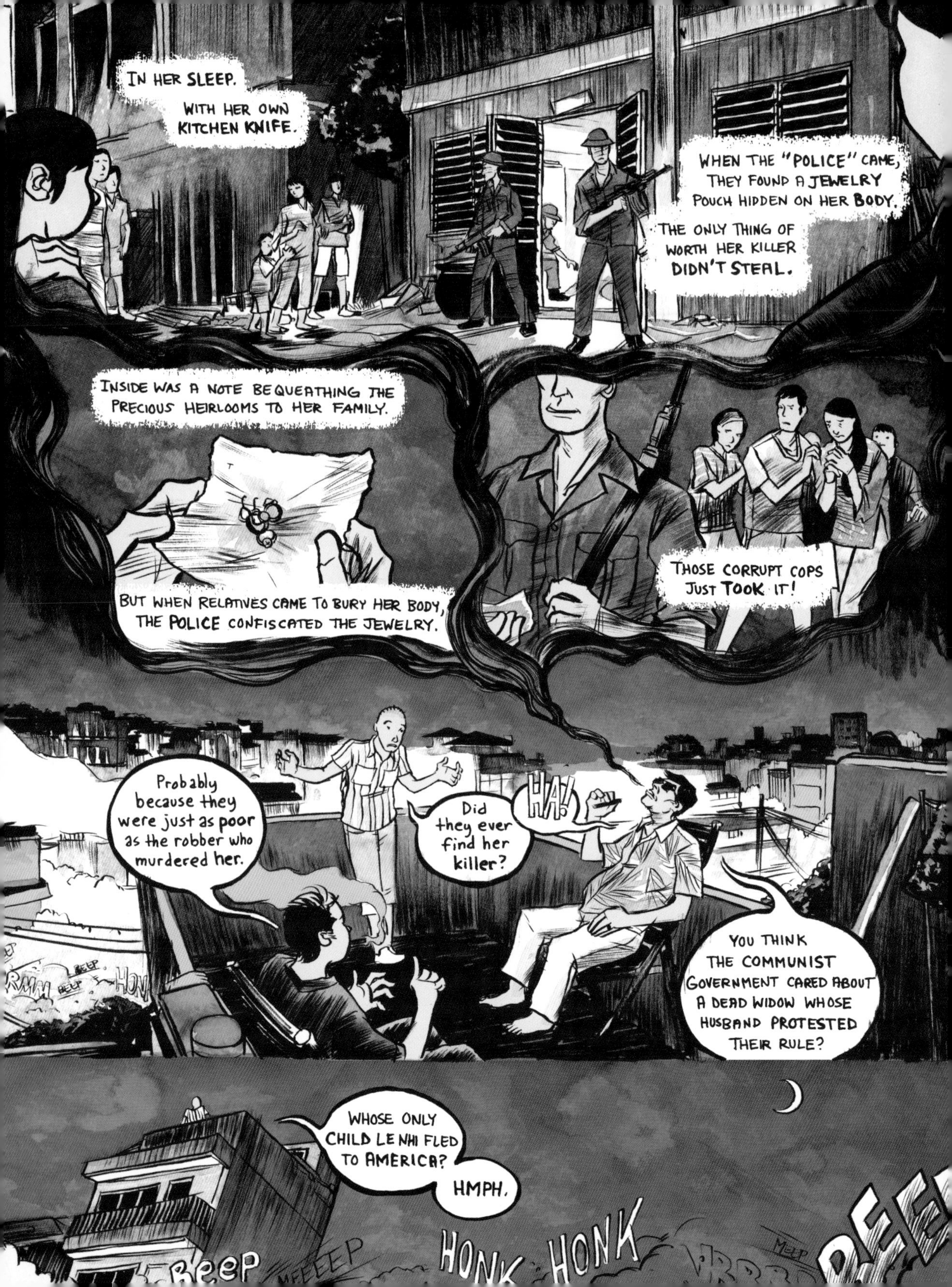

IN HER SLEEP.
WITH HER OWN KITCHEN KNIFE.
WHEN THE "POLICE" CAME, THEY FOUND A JEWELRY POUCH HIDDEN ON HER BODY.
THE ONLY THING OF WORTH HER KILLER DIDN'T STEAL.
INSIDE WAS A NOTE BEQUEATHING THE PRECIOUS HEIRLOOMS TO HER FAMILY.
BUT WHEN RELATIVES CAME TO BURY HER BODY, THE POLICE CONFISCATED THE JEWELRY.
THOSE CORRUPT COPS JUST TOOK IT!
Did they ever find her killer?
HA!
Probably because they were just as poor as the robber who murdered her.
YOU THINK THE COMMUNIST GOVERNMENT CARED ABOUT A DEAD WIDOW WHOSE HUSBAND PROTESTED THEIR RULE?
WHOSE ONLY CHILD LE NHI FLED TO AMERICA?
HMPH.
BEEP
MEEEEP
HONK HONK
MEEP

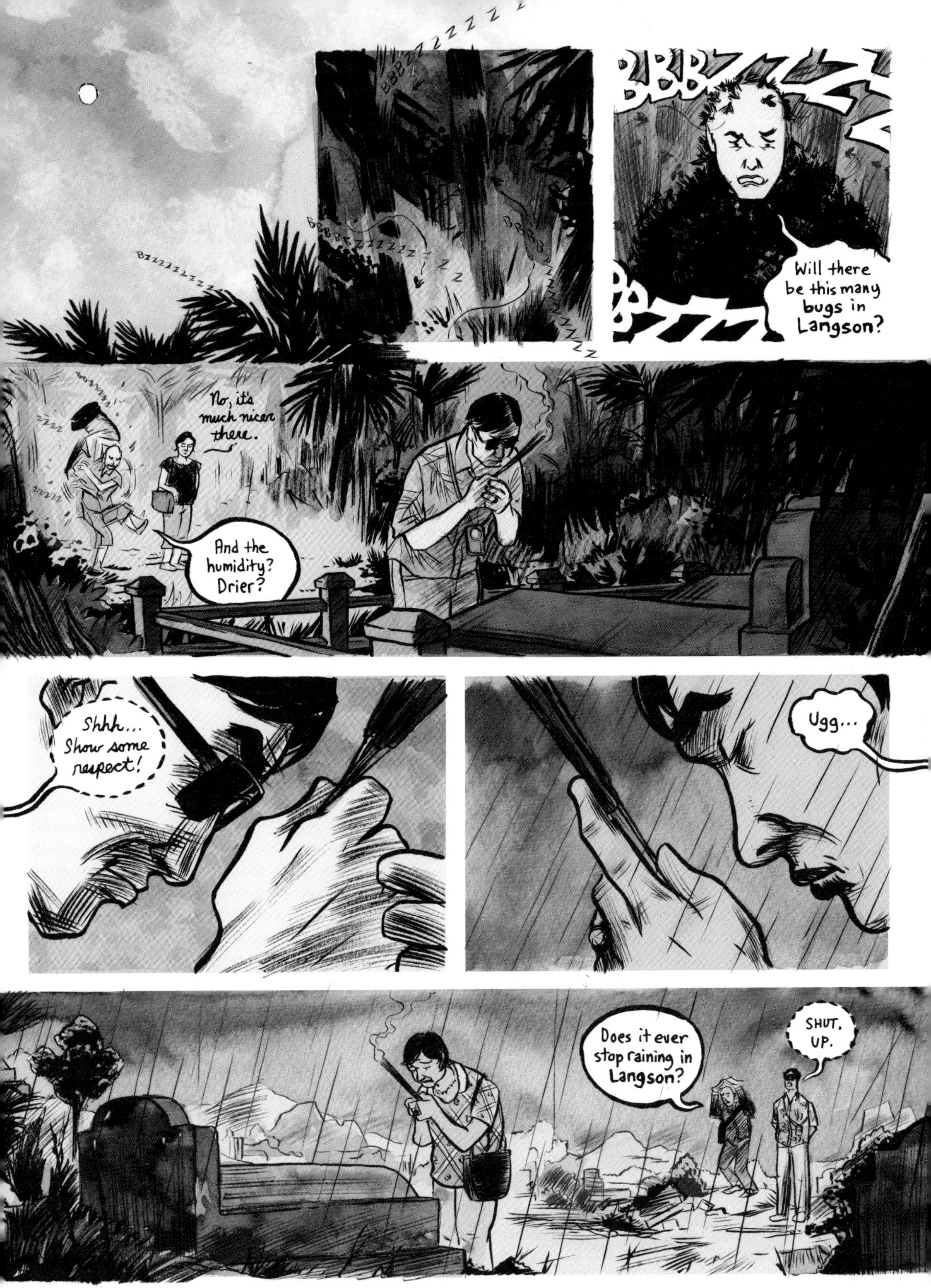
BBBZZZZZZZ
BZZZZZZZZZ
BBBBZZZZZZZZ
BBBZZZ
Will there be this many bugs in Langson?
No, it's much nicer there.
And the humidity? Drier?
Shhh... Show some respect!
Ugg...
Does it ever stop raining in Langson?
SHUT. UP.

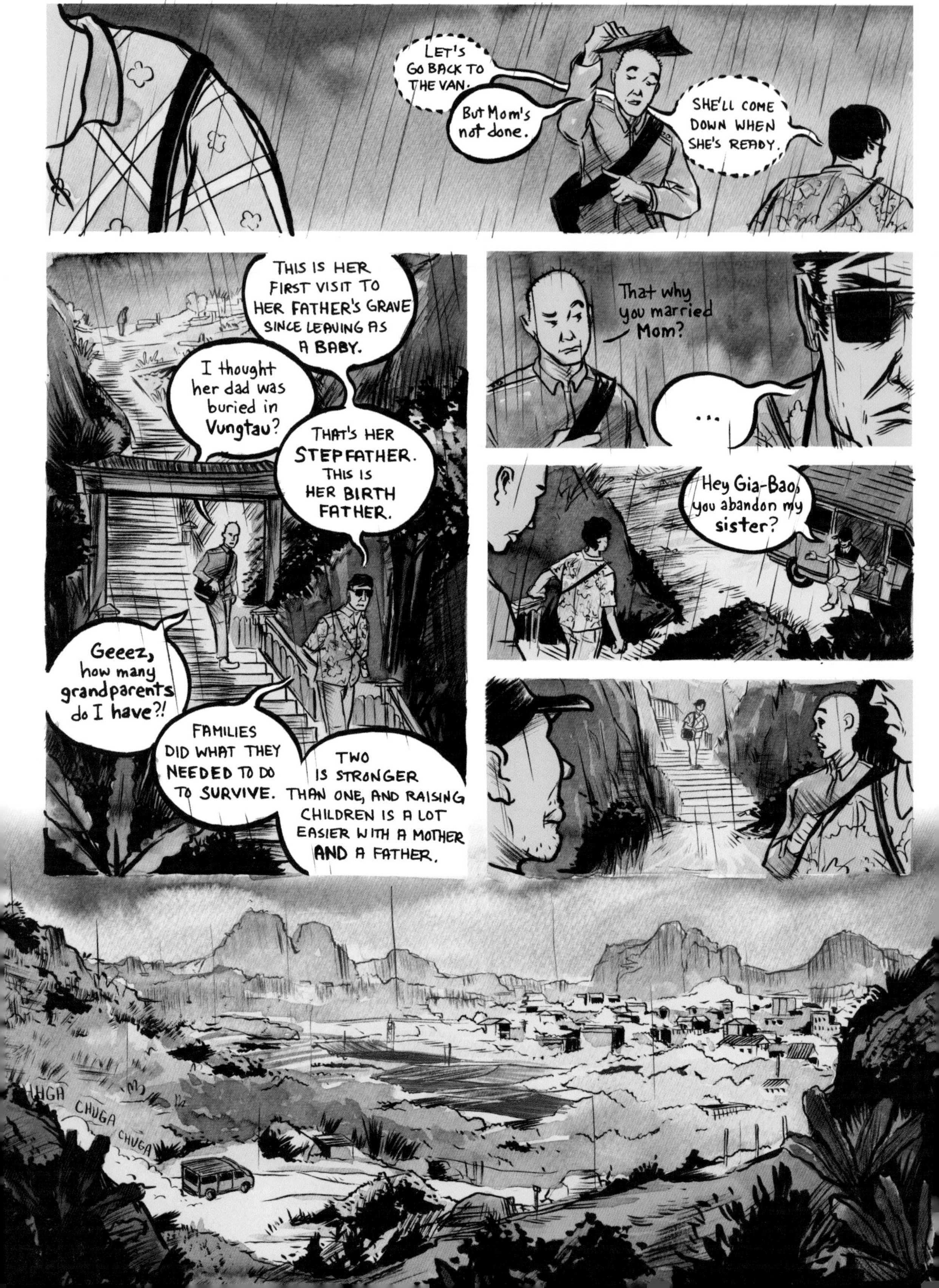

LET'S GO BACK TO THE VAN.
But Mom's not done.
SHE'LL COME DOWN WHEN SHE'S READY.
THIS IS HER FIRST VISIT TO HER FATHER'S GRAVE SINCE LEAVING AS A BABY.
I thought her dad was buried in Vungtau?
THAT'S HER STEPFATHER. THIS IS HER BIRTH FATHER.
Geeez, how many grandparents do I have?!
FAMILIES DID WHAT THEY NEEDED TO DO TO SURVIVE.
TWO IS STRONGER THAN ONE, AND RAISING CHILDREN IS A LOT EASIER WITH A MOTHER AND A FATHER.
That why you married Mom?
...
Hey Gia-Bao, you abandon my sister?
CHUGA
CHUGA
CHUGA

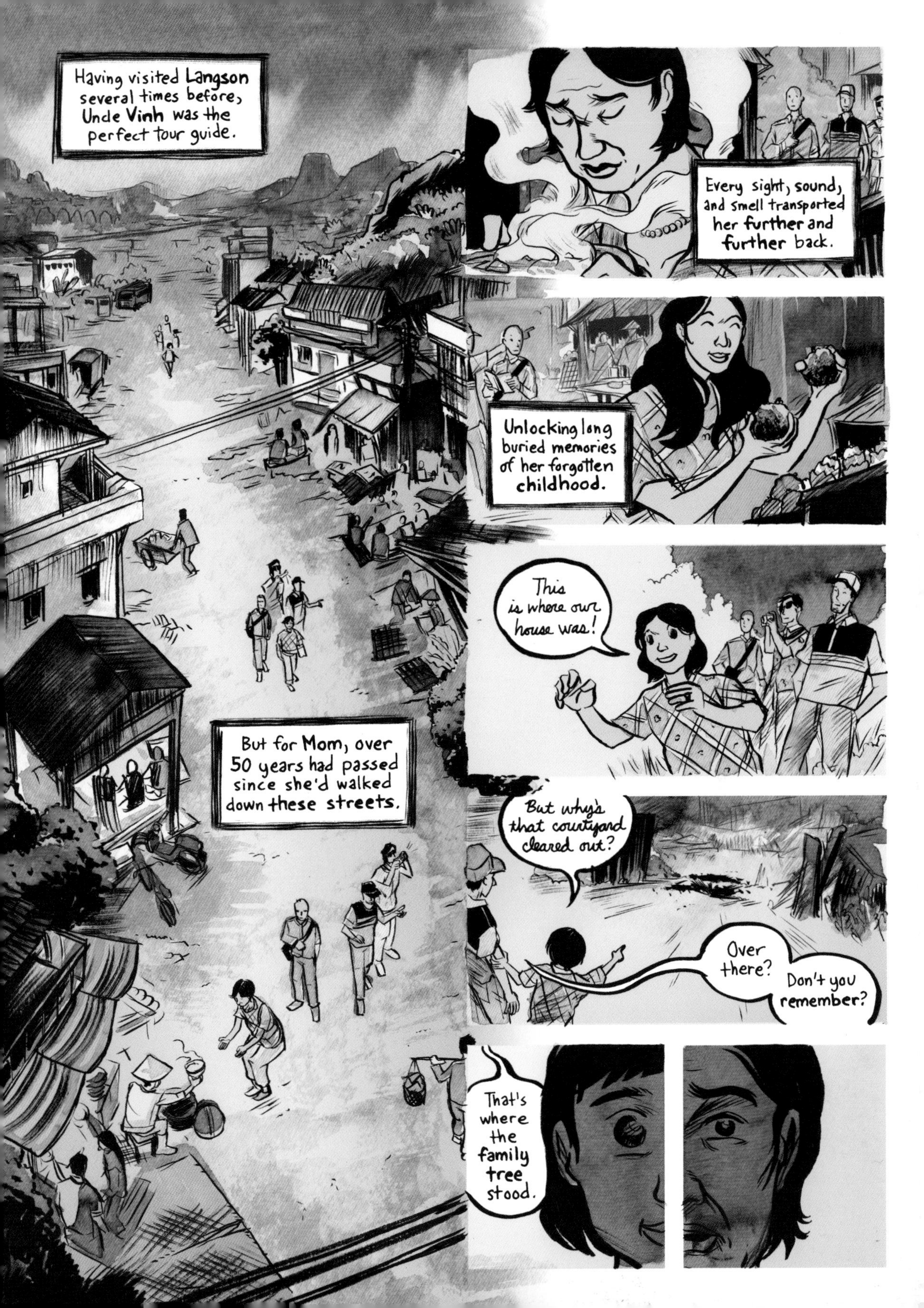

Having visited Langson several times before, Uncle Vinh was the perfect tour guide.
But for Mom, over 50 years had passed since she'd walked down these streets.
Every sight, sound, and smell transported her further and further back.
Unlocking long buried memories of her forgotten childhood.
This is where our house was!
But why's that courtyard cleared out?
Over there?
Don't you remember?
That's where the family tree stood.

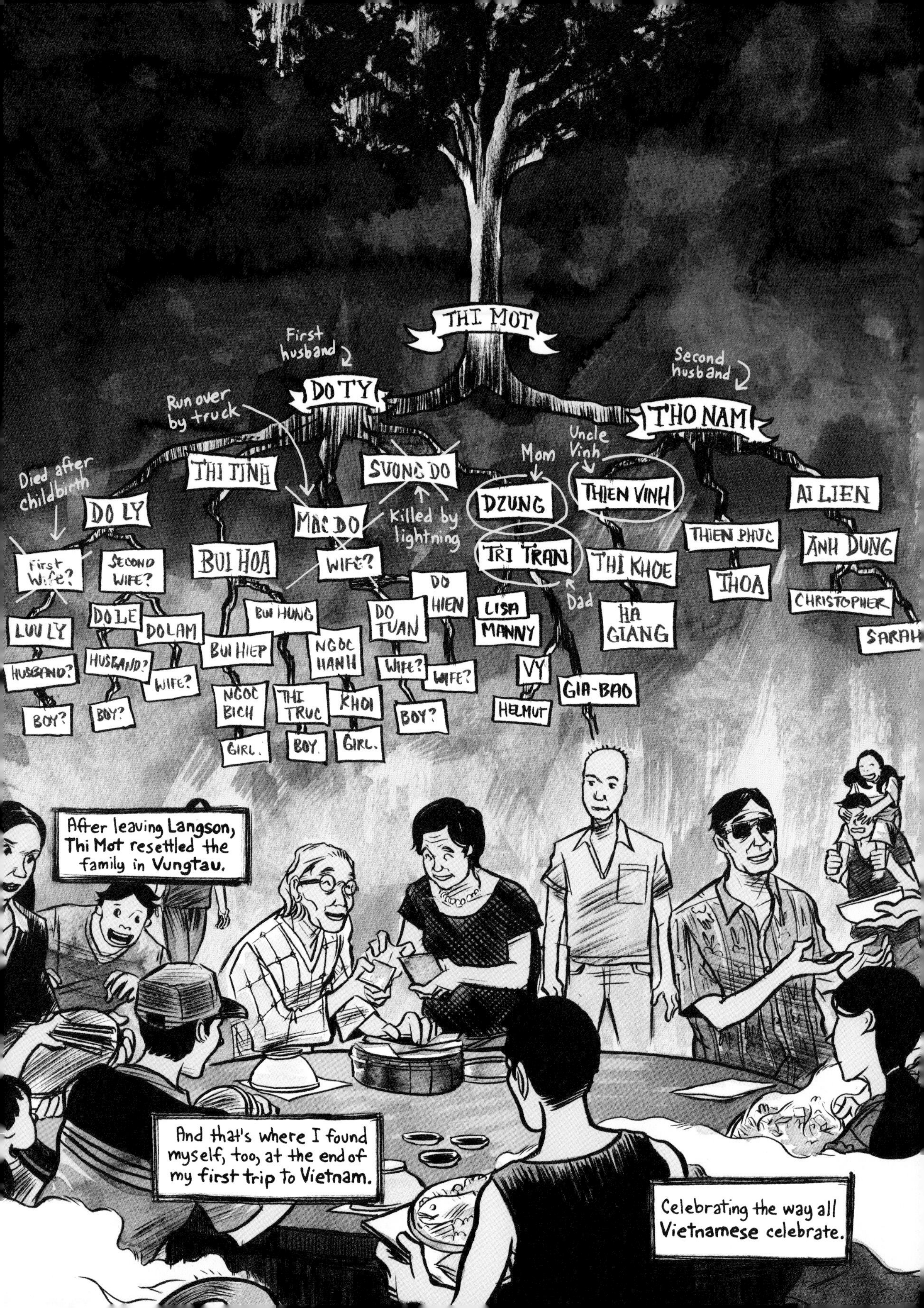

THI MOT
First husband
DO TY
Second husband
THO NAM
Run over by truck
Died after childbirth
THI TINH
SUONG DO
Mom
Uncle Vinh
DO LY
MAC DO
Killed by lightning
DZUNG
THIEN VINH
AI LIEN
First Wife?
SECOND WIFE?
BUI HOA
WIFE?
TRI TRAN
THI KHOE
THIEN PHUC
ANH DUNG
THOA
DO HIEN
Dad
LUU LY
DO LE
DO LAM
BUI HUNG
DO TUAN
LISA
MANNY
HA GIANG
CHRISTOPHER
SARAH
BUI HIEP
NGOC HANH
HUSBAND?
HUSBAND?
WIFE?
WIFE?
WIFE?
VY
GIA-BAO
NGOC BICH
THI TRUC
KHOI
BOY?
BOY?
BOY?
HELMUT
GIRL.
BOY.
GIRL.
After leaving Langson, Thi Mot resettled the family in Vungtau.
And that's where I found myself, too, at the end of my first trip to Vietnam.
Celebrating the way all Vietnamese celebrate.

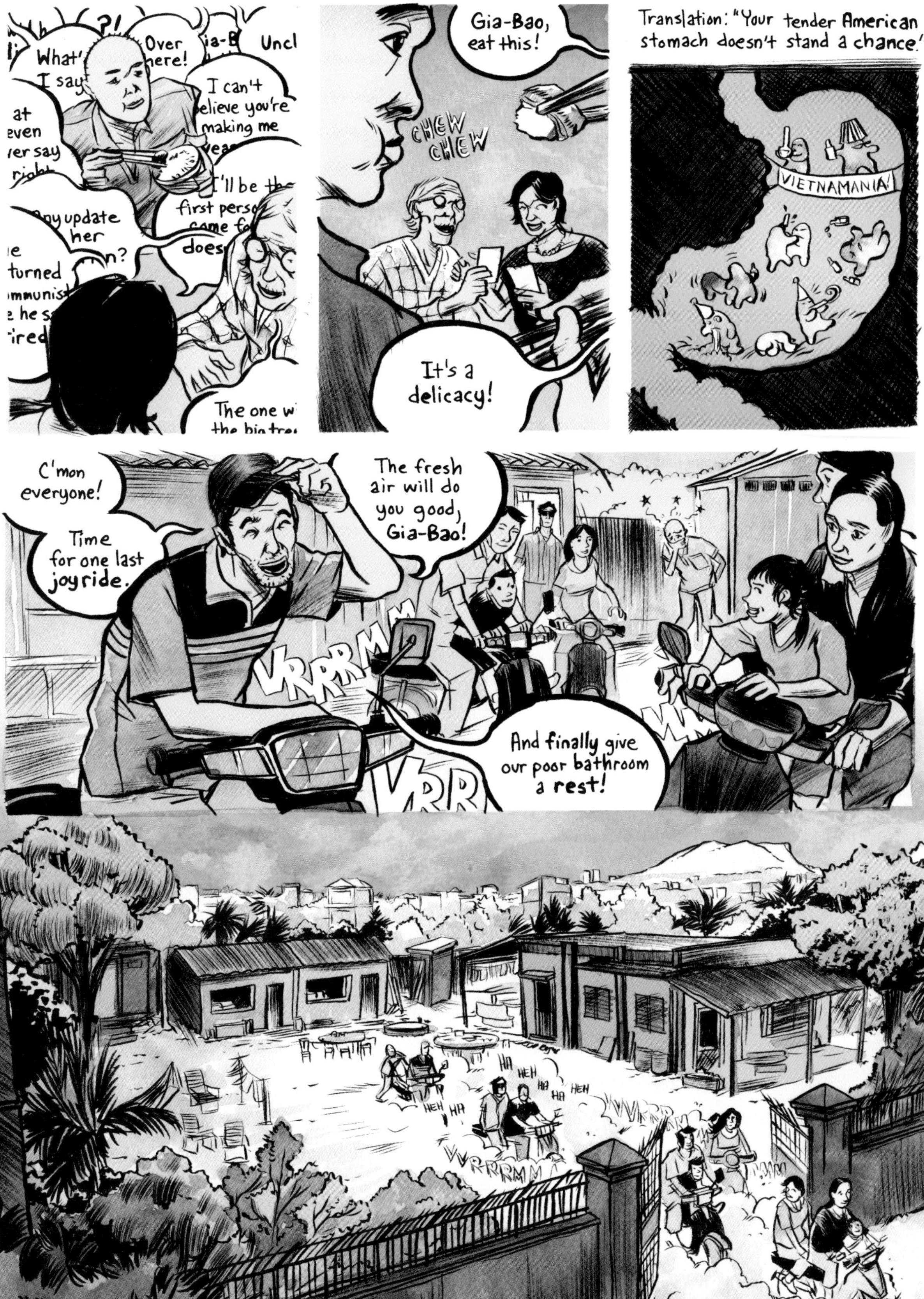

What'
I say
Over here!
Uncl
I can't elieve you're making me
I'll be th first perso
Any update her n?
turned
The one w
Gia-Bao, eat this!
CHEW CHEW
It's a delicacy!
Translation: "Your tender American stomach doesn't stand a chance."
VIETNAMANIA!
C'mon everyone!
Time for one last joyride.
The fresh air will do you good, Gia-Bao!
VRRRMM
VRR
And finally give our poor bathroom a rest!
HA
HEH
HA
HA
HEH
HEH
HA
VRRRMM

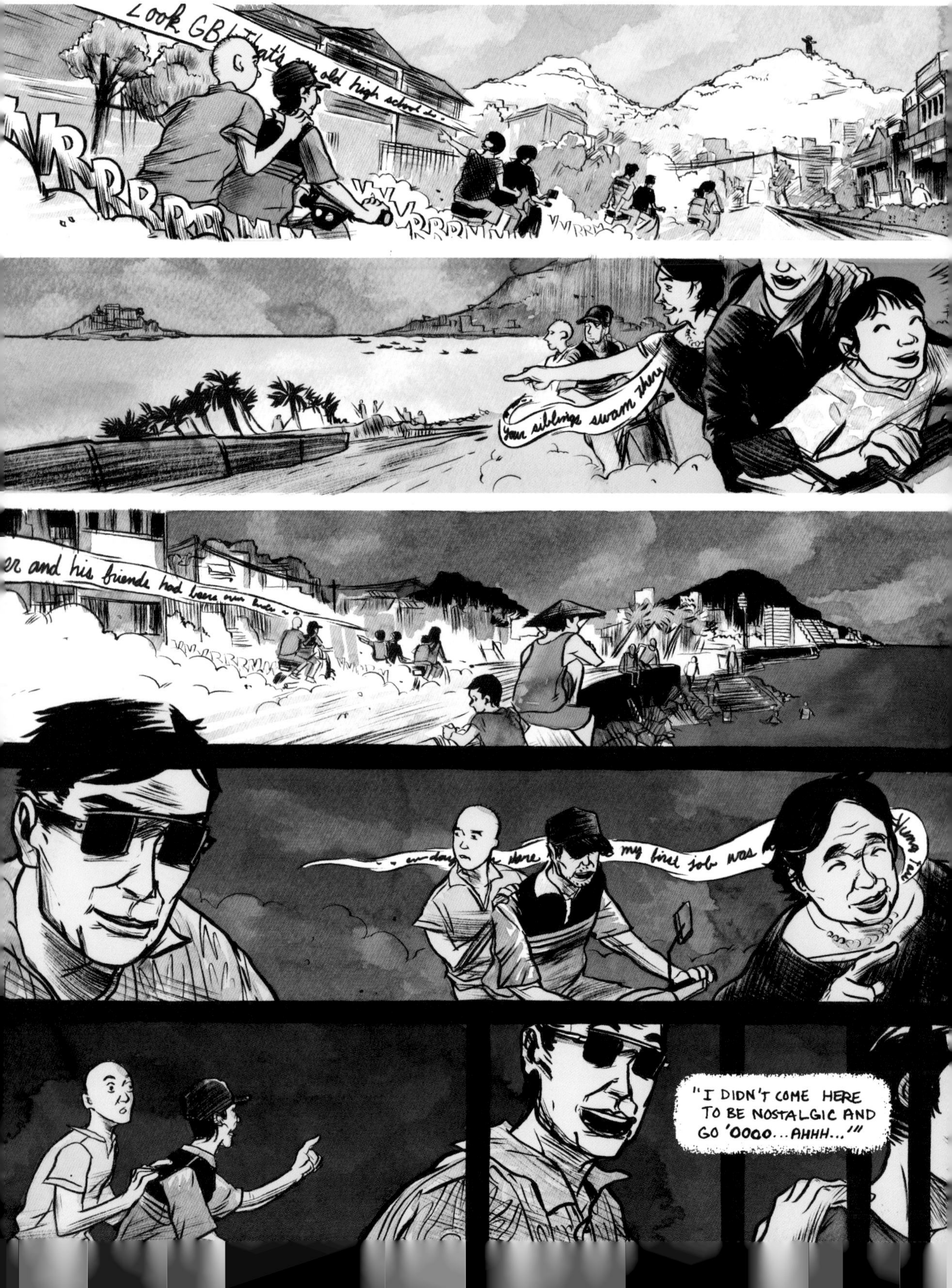
Look GB! That's my old high school . .
VRRRRMM
your siblings swam there
er and his friends had been . .
my first job was
"I DIDN'T COME HERE TO BE NOSTALGIC AND GO 'OOOO...AHHH...'"

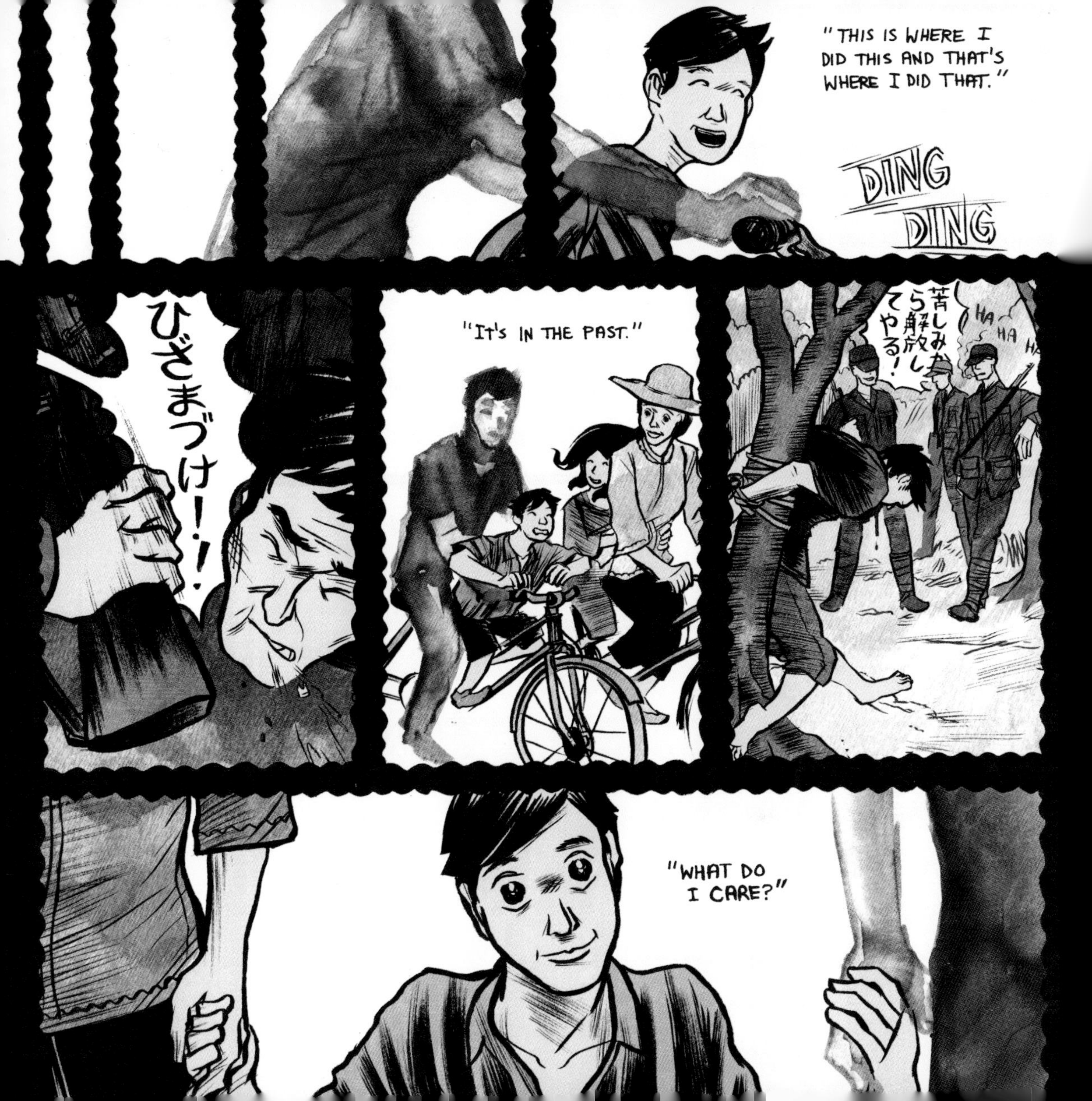
"THIS IS WHERE I DID THIS AND THAT'S WHERE I DID THAT."
DING DING
ひざまづけ!!
"IT'S IN THE PAST."
苦しみから解放してやる!
HA HA
"WHAT DO I CARE?"

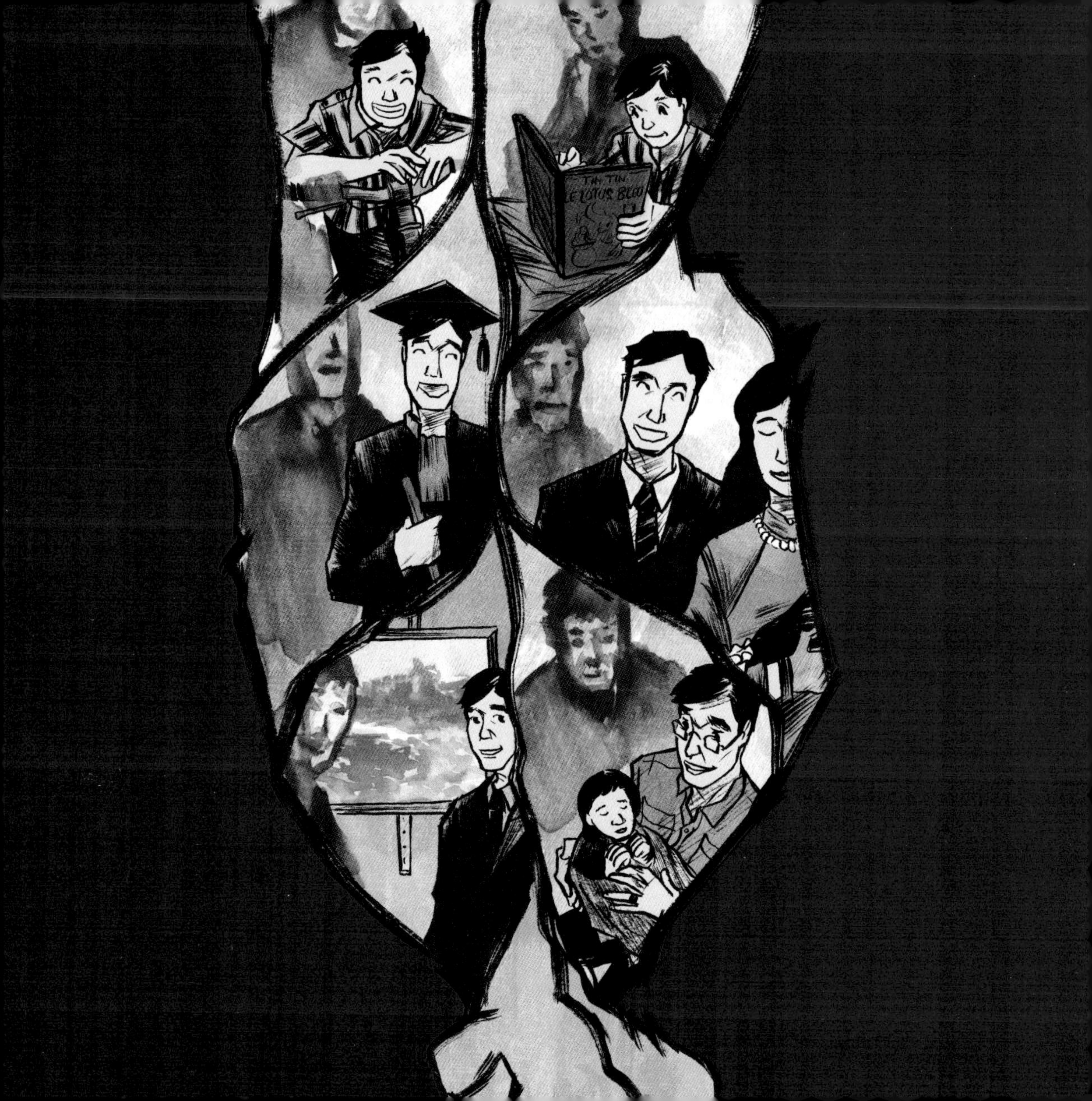
TIN TIN
LE LOTUS

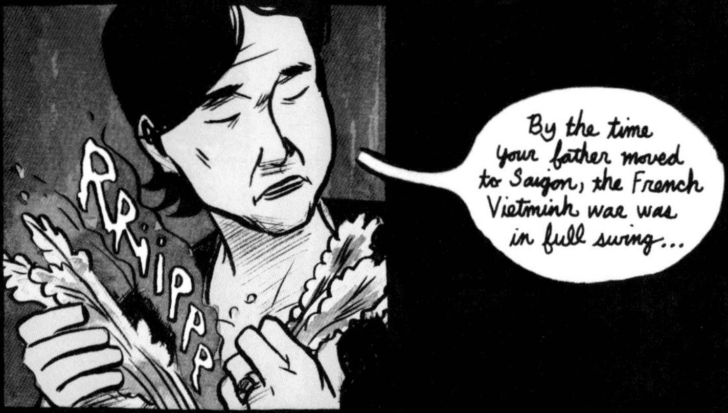
By the time your father moved to Saigon, the French Vietminh war was in full swing...

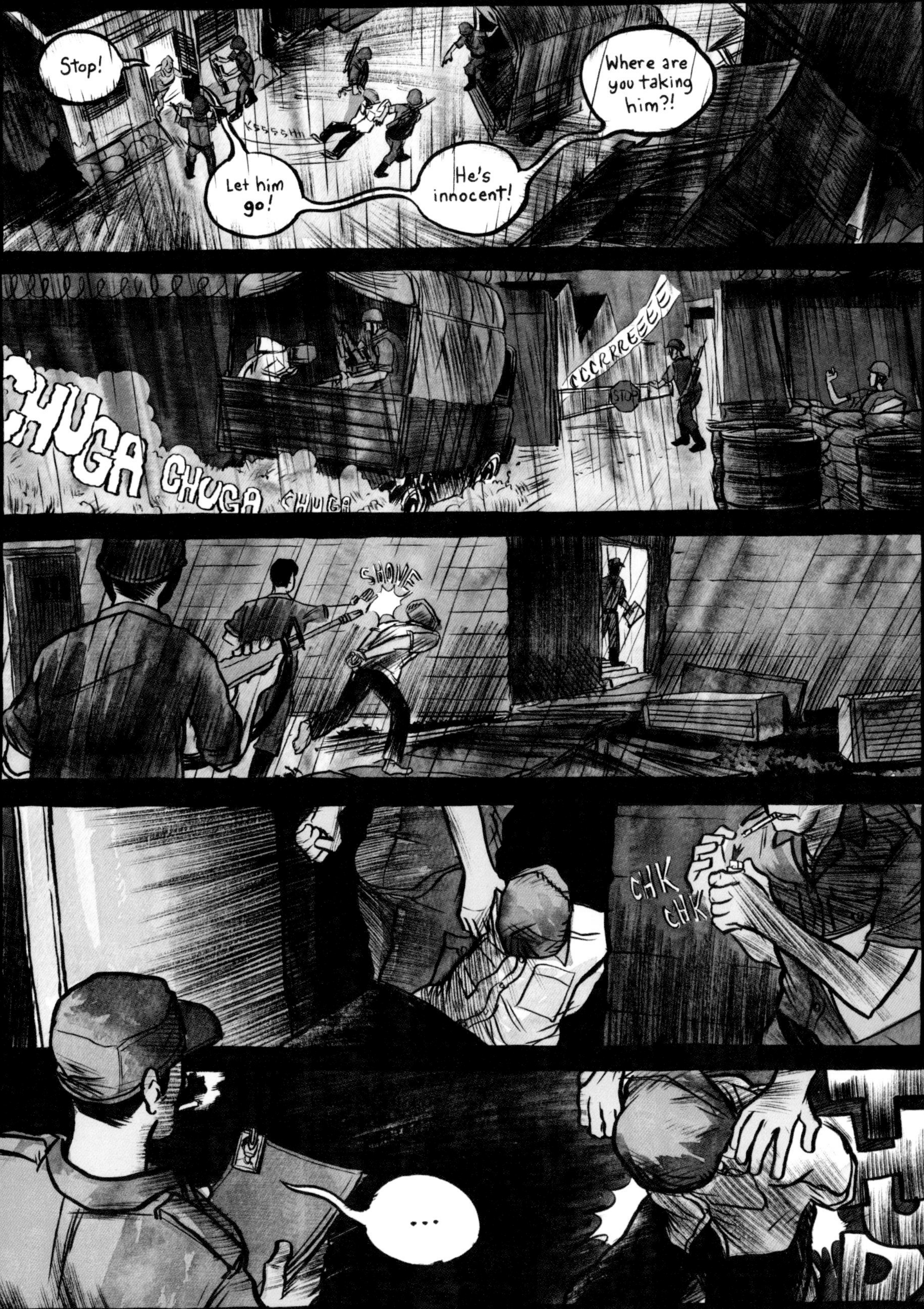

Stop!
Let him go!
He's innocent!
Where are you taking him?!
CCCRRREEEEE
STOP
CHUGA
CHUGA
CHUGA
SHOVE
CHK
CHK
...
THUD

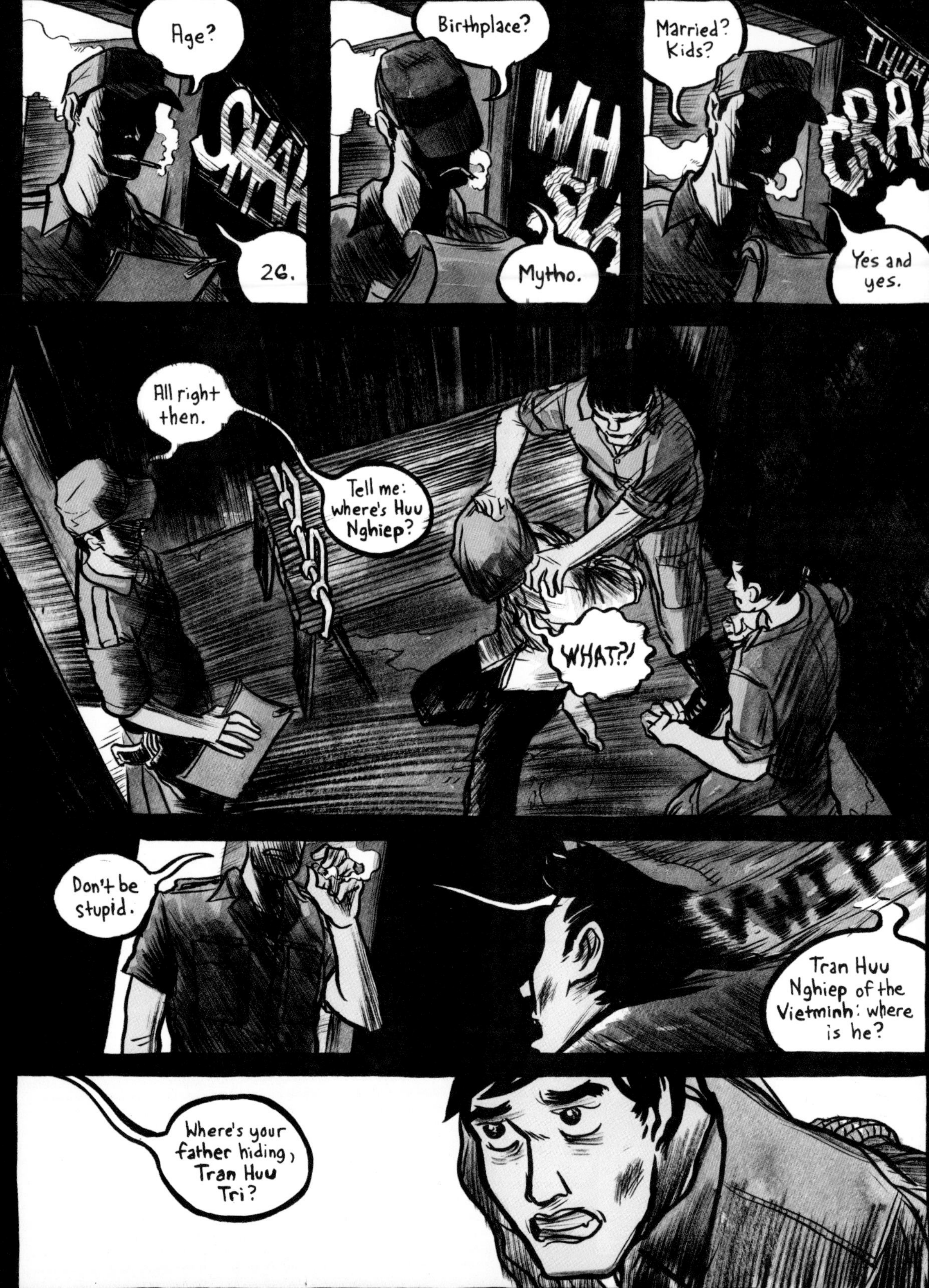

Age?
26.
Birthplace?
Mytho.
Married? Kids?
Yes and yes.
All right then.
Tell me: where's Huu Nghiep?
WHAT?!
Don't be stupid.
Tran Huu Nghiep of the Vietminh: where is he?
Where's your father hiding, Tran Huu Tri?

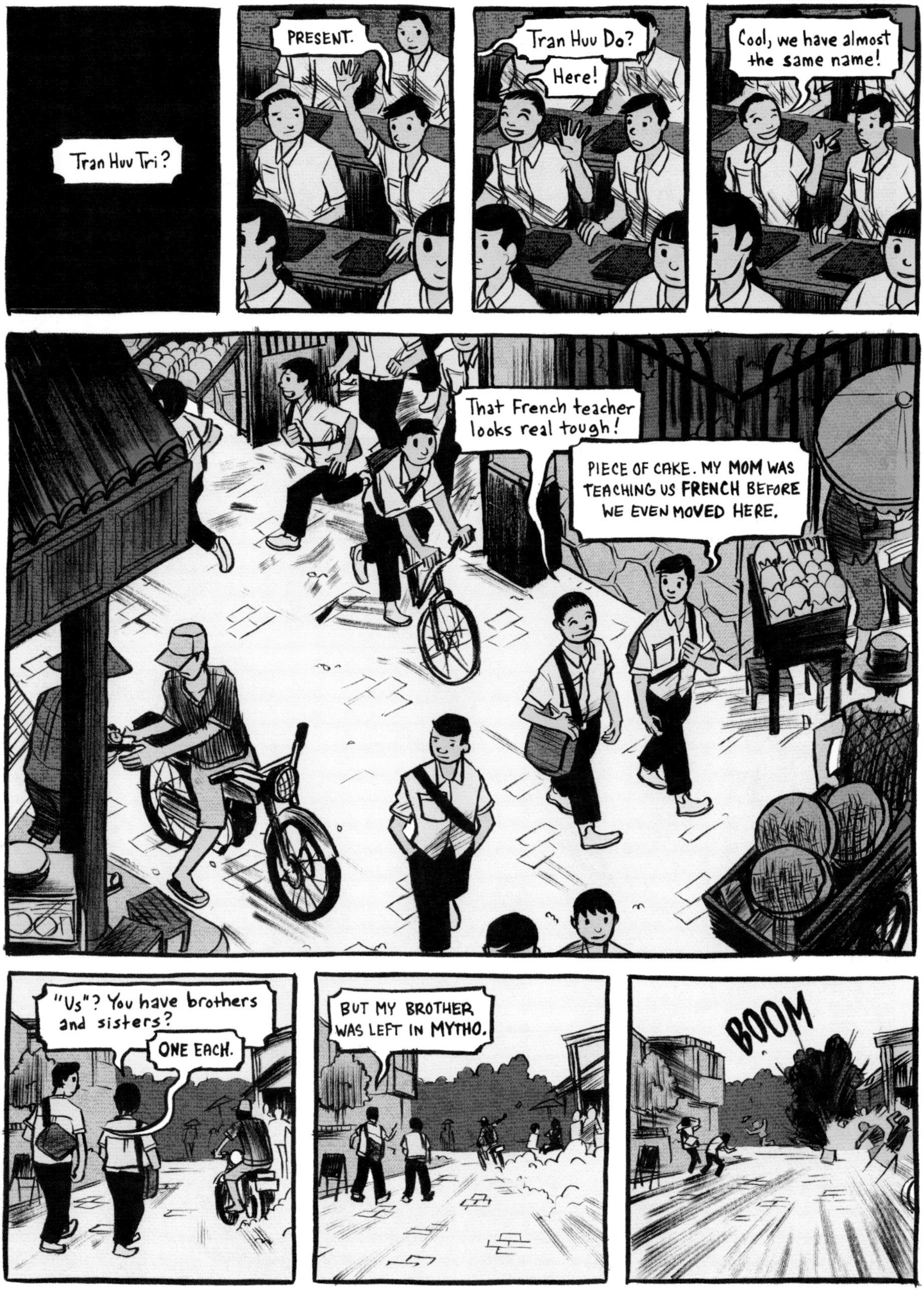
Tran Huu Tri?
PRESENT.
Tran Huu Do?
Here!
Cool, we have almost the same name!
That French teacher looks real tough!
PIECE OF CAKE. MY MOM WAS TEACHING US FRENCH BEFORE WE EVEN MOVED HERE.
"Us"? You have brothers and sisters?
ONE EACH.
BUT MY BROTHER WAS LEFT IN MYTHO.
BOOM

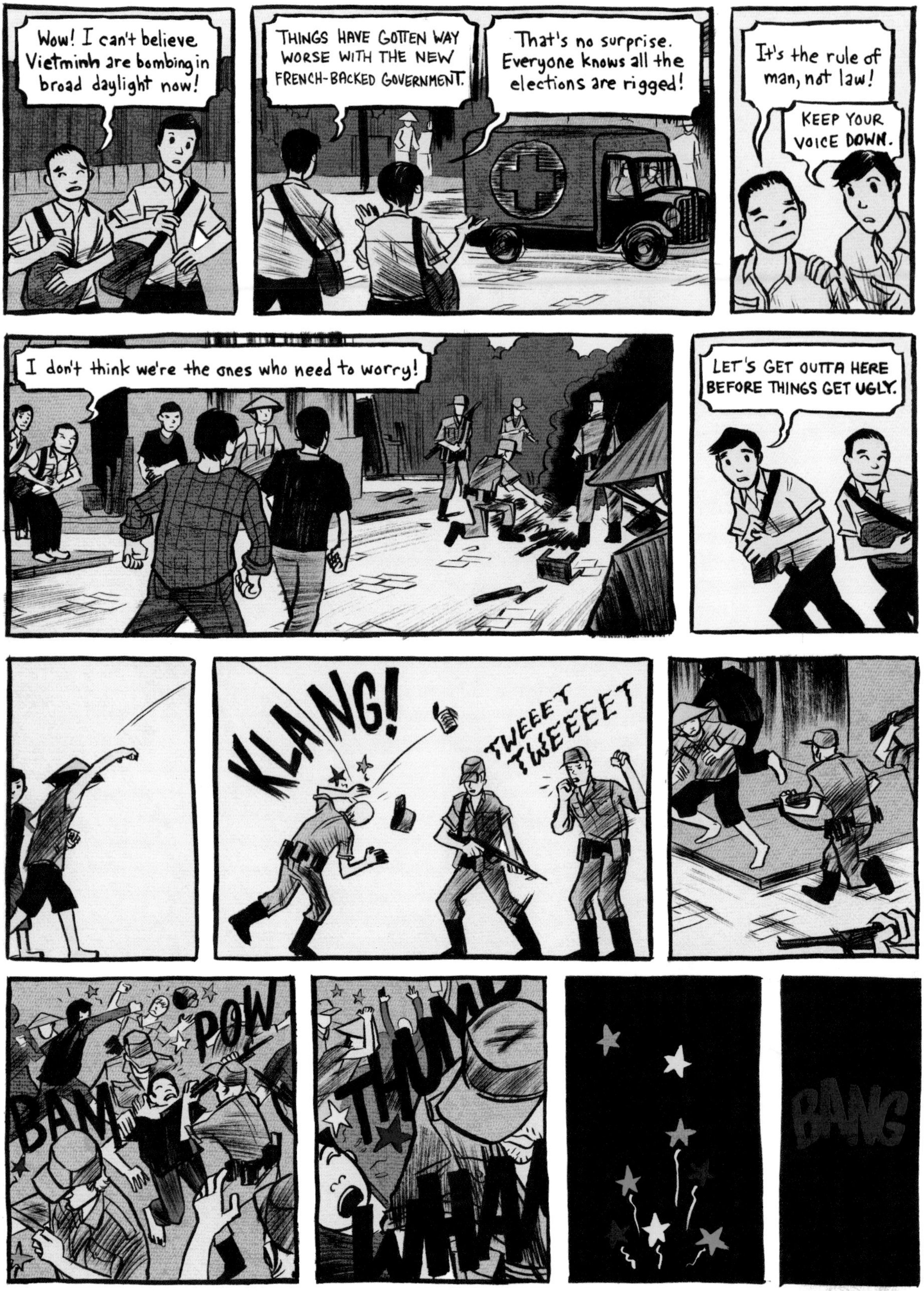
Wow! I can't believe Vietminh are bombing in broad daylight now!
THINGS HAVE GOTTEN WAY WORSE WITH THE NEW FRENCH-BACKED GOVERNMENT.
That's no surprise. Everyone knows all the elections are rigged!
It's the rule of man, not law!
KEEP YOUR VOICE DOWN.
I don't think we're the ones who need to worry!
LET'S GET OUTTA HERE BEFORE THINGS GET UGLY.
KLANG!
TWEEET
TWEEEEET
POW
BAM
THUMP
WHAM
BANG

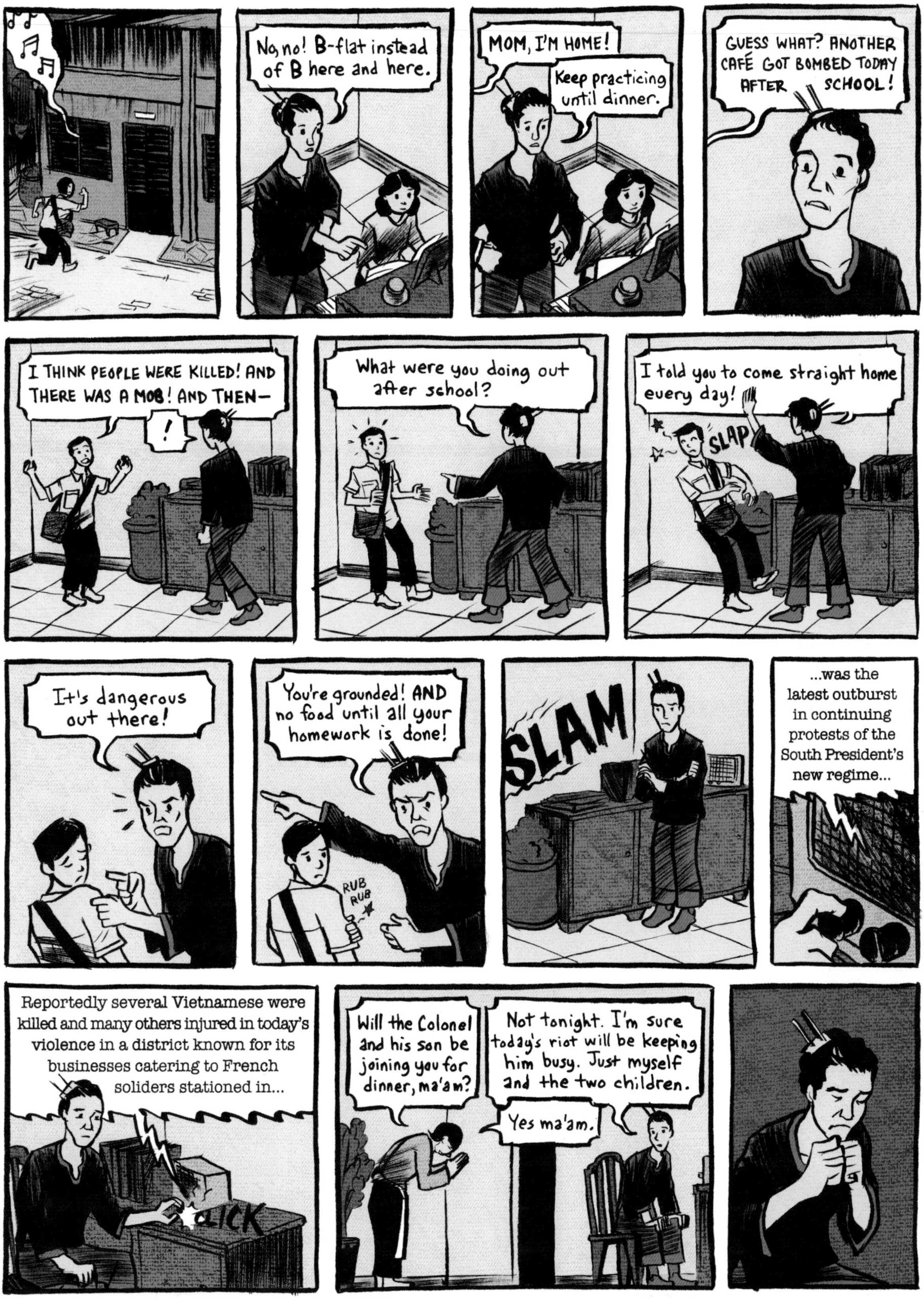
No, no! B-flat instead of B here and here.
MOM, I'M HOME!
Keep practicing until dinner.
GUESS WHAT? ANOTHER CAFÉ GOT BOMBED TODAY AFTER SCHOOL!
I THINK PEOPLE WERE KILLED! AND THERE WAS A MOB! AND THEN—
!
What were you doing out after school?
I told you to come straight home every day!
SLAP
It's dangerous out there!
You're grounded! AND no food until all your homework is done!
RUB RUB
SLAM
...was the latest outburst in continuing protests of the South President's new regime...
Reportedly several Vietnamese were killed and many others injured in today's violence in a district known for its businesses catering to French soliders stationed in...
CLICK
Will the Colonel and his son be joining you for dinner, ma'am?
Not tonight. I'm sure today's riot will be keeping him busy. Just myself and the two children.
Yes ma'am.

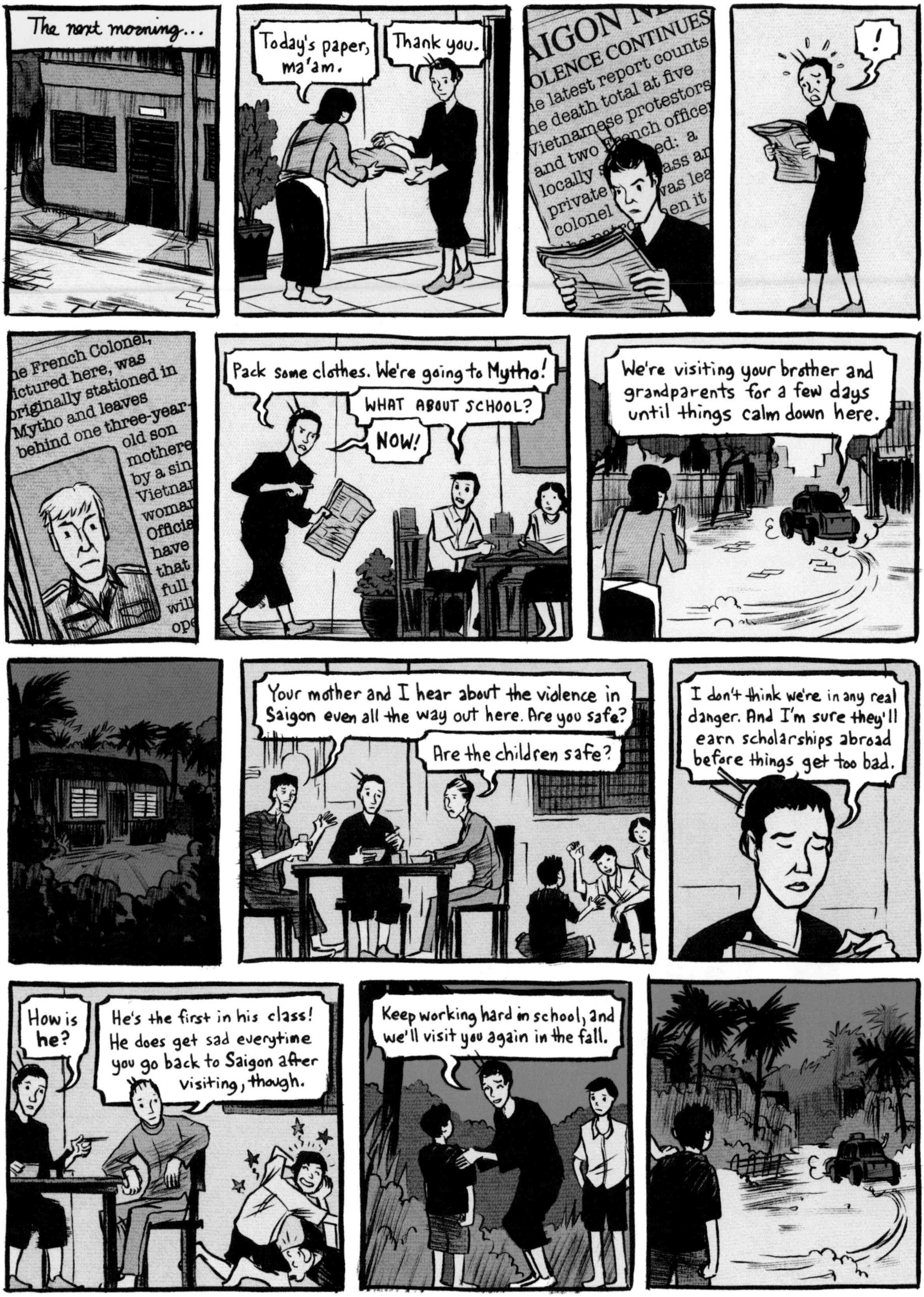
The next morning...
Today's paper, ma'am.
Thank you.
AIGON NE
OLENCE CONTINUES
he latest report counts
he death total at five
Vietnamese protestors
and two French officer
!
he French Colonel,
ictured here, was
originally stationed in
Mytho and leaves
behind one three-year-
old son
Pack some clothes. We're going to Mytho!
WHAT ABOUT SCHOOL?
NOW!
We're visiting your brother and grandparents for a few days until things calm down here.
Your mother and I hear about the violence in Saigon even all the way out here. Are you safe?
Are the children safe?
I don't think we're in any real danger. And I'm sure they'll earn scholarships abroad before things get too bad.
How is he?
He's the first in his class! He does get sad everytime you go back to Saigon after visiting, though.
Keep working hard in school, and we'll visit you again in the fall.

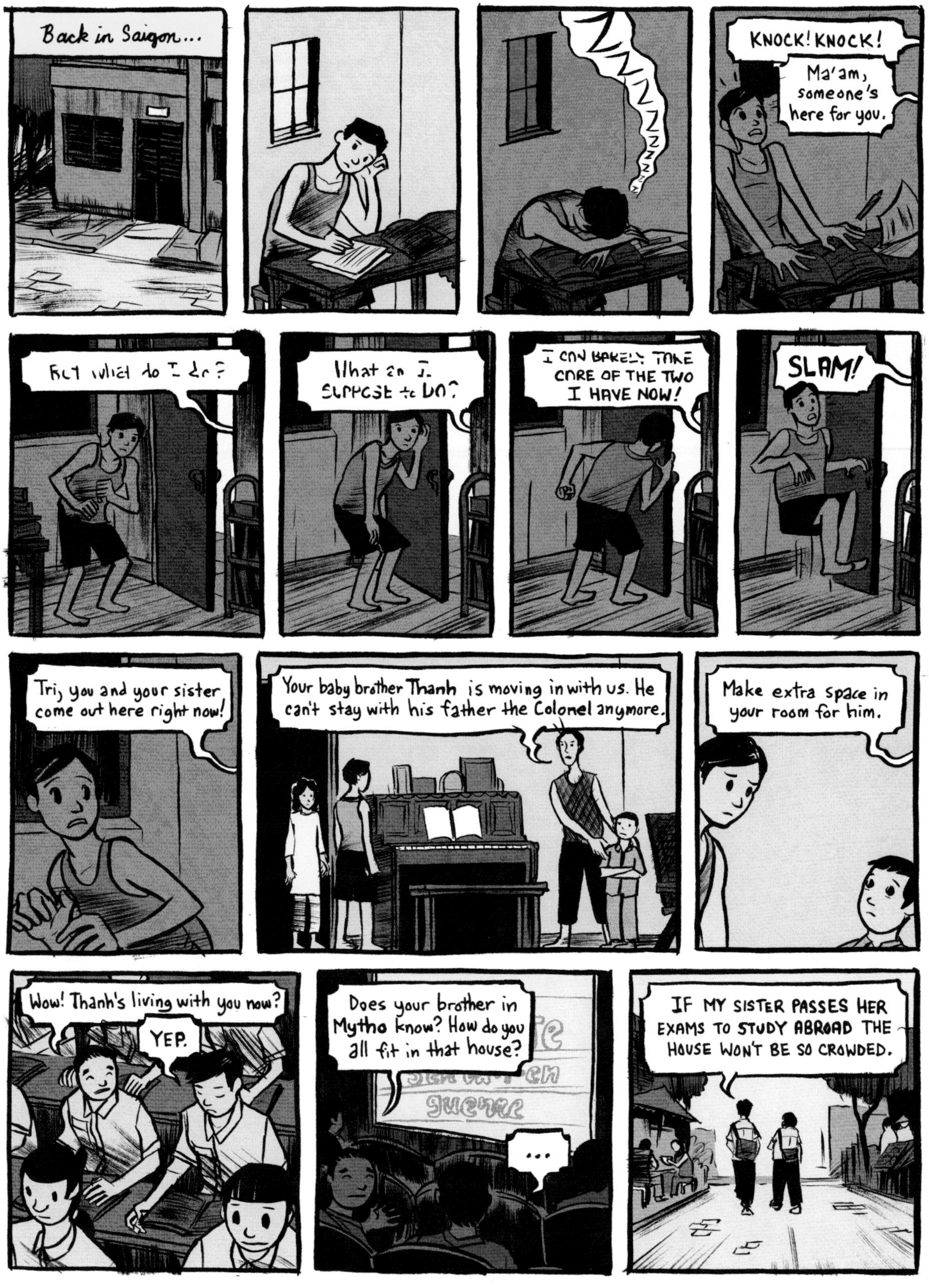
Back in Saigon...
ZZZZZZZZZ
KNOCK! KNOCK!
Ma'am, someone's here for you.
What am I suppose to do?
I CAN BARELY TAKE CARE OF THE TWO I HAVE NOW!
SLAM!
Tri, you and your sister come out here right now!
Your baby brother Thanh is moving in with us. He can't stay with his father the Colonel anymore.
Make extra space in your room for him.
Wow! Thanh's living with you now?
YEP.
Does your brother in Mytho know? How do you all fit in that house?
...
IF MY SISTER PASSES HER EXAMS TO STUDY ABROAD THE HOUSE WON'T BE SO CROWDED.

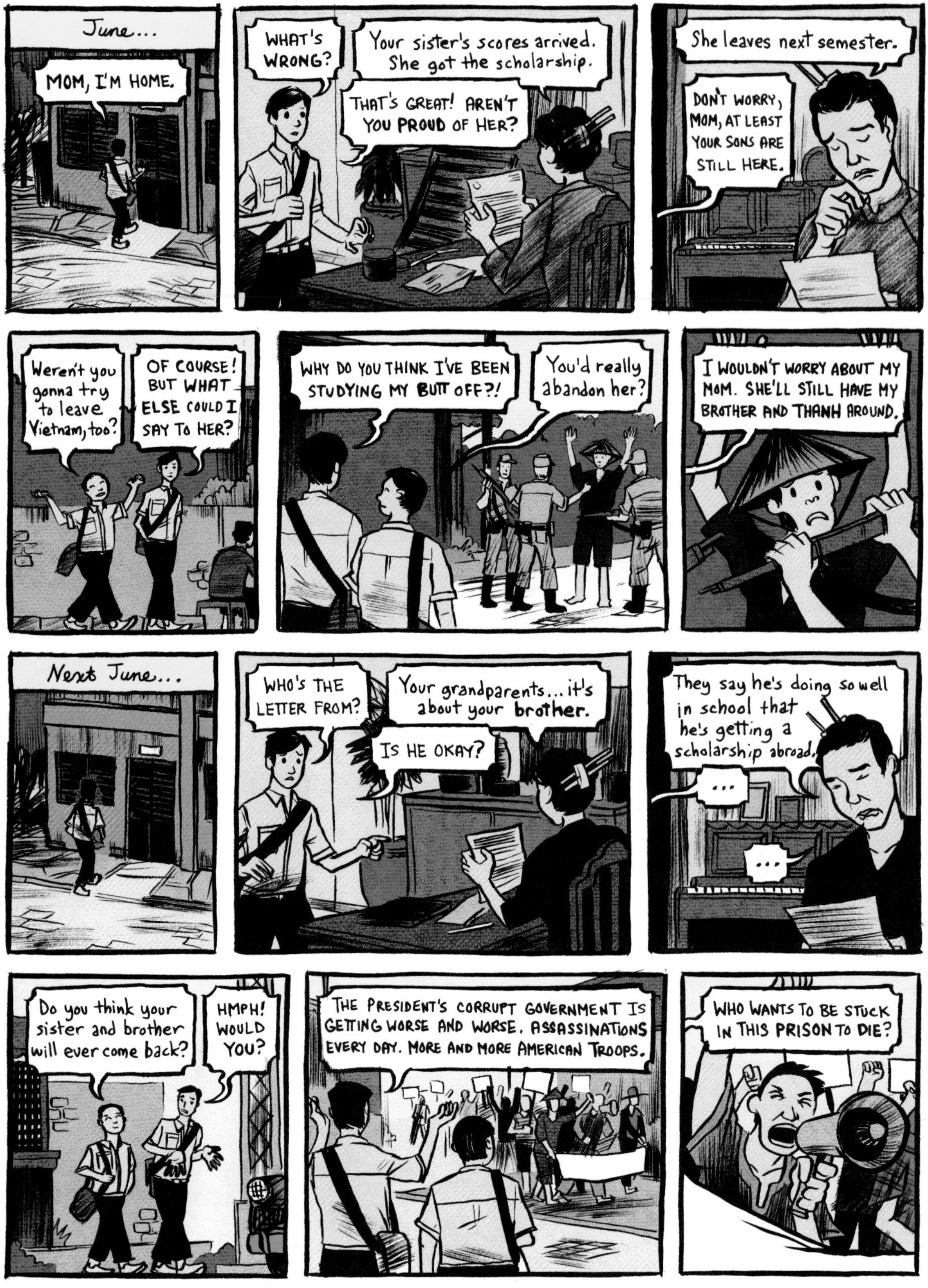
June...
MOM, I'M HOME.
WHAT'S WRONG?
Your sister's scores arrived. She got the scholarship.
THAT'S GREAT! AREN'T YOU PROUD OF HER?
She leaves next semester.
DON'T WORRY, MOM, AT LEAST YOUR SONS ARE STILL HERE.
Weren't you gonna try to leave Vietnam, too?
OF COURSE! BUT WHAT ELSE COULD I SAY TO HER?
WHY DO YOU THINK I'VE BEEN STUDYING MY BUTT OFF?!
You'd really abandon her?
I WOULDN'T WORRY ABOUT MY MOM. SHE'LL STILL HAVE MY BROTHER AND THANH AROUND.
Next June...
WHO'S THE LETTER FROM?
Your grandparents... it's about your brother.
IS HE OKAY?
They say he's doing so well in school that he's getting a scholarship abroad.
...
...
Do you think your sister and brother will ever come back?
HMPH! WOULD YOU?
THE PRESIDENT'S CORRUPT GOVERNMENT IS GETTING WORSE AND WORSE. ASSASSINATIONS EVERY DAY. MORE AND MORE AMERICAN TROOPS.
WHO WANTS TO BE STUCK IN THIS PRISON TO DIE?

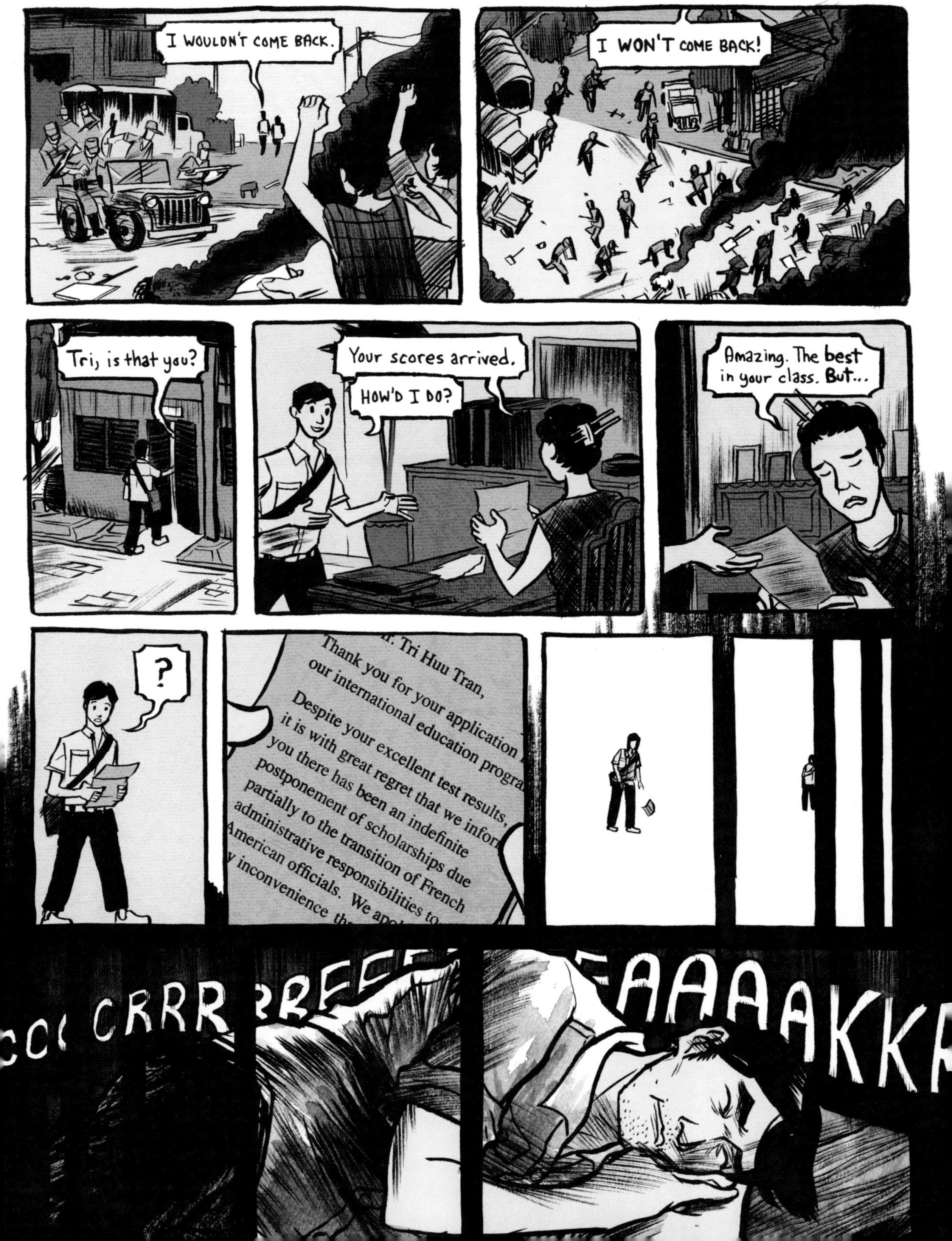

I WOULDN'T COME BACK.
I WON'T COME BACK!
Tri, is that you?
Your scores arrived.
HOW'D I DO?
Amazing. The best in your class. But...
?
Tri Huu Tran,
Thank you for your application
our international education
Despite your excellent test results,
it is with great regret that we
you there has been an indefinite
postponement of scholarships due
partially to the transition of French
administrative responsibilities to
American officials. We
inconvenience
CRRR
AAAAKK

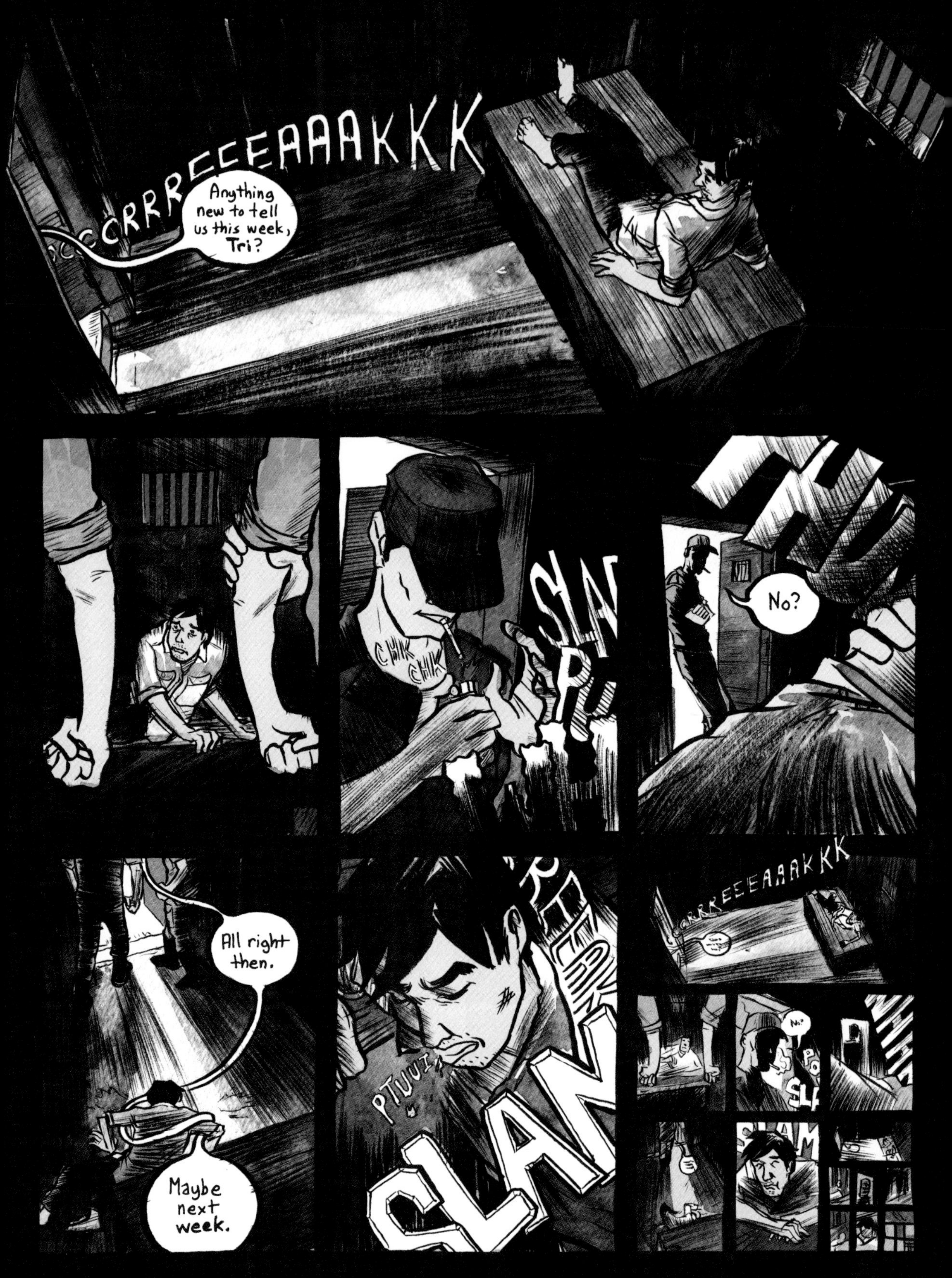

CRRREEEAAAKKK
Anything new to tell us this week, Tri?
CHK CHK
SLAP
No?
All right then.
Maybe next week.
PTUUI
SLAM
CRRREEEAAAKKK
No?
SLAM

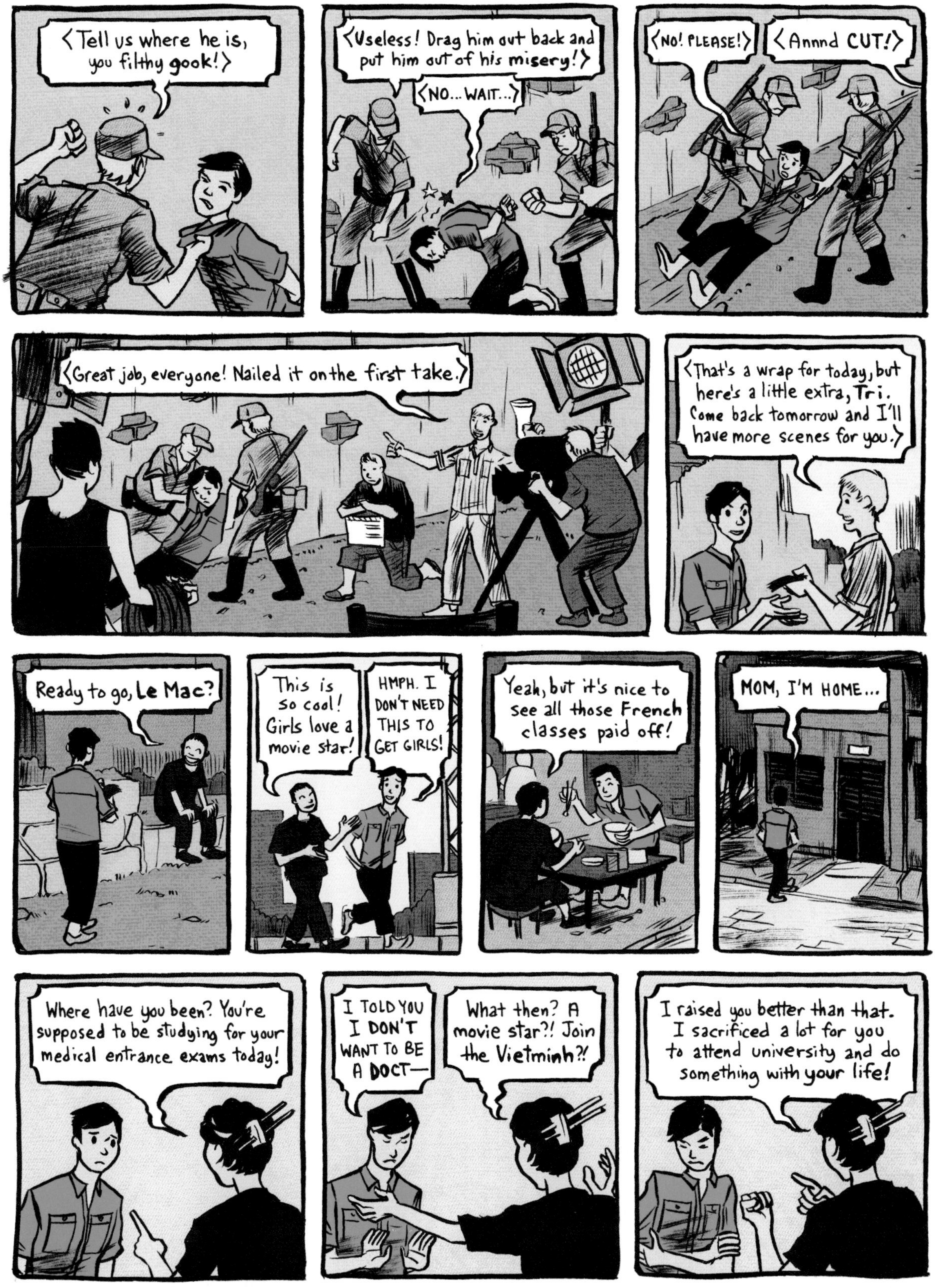
<Tell us where he is, you filthy gook!>
<Useless! Drag him out back and put him out of his misery!>
<NO... WAIT...>
<NO! PLEASE!>
<Annnd CUT!>
<Great job, everyone! Nailed it on the first take.>
<That's a wrap for today, but here's a little extra, Tri. Come back tomorrow and I'll have more scenes for you.>
Ready to go, Le Mac?
This is so cool! Girls love a movie star!
HMPH. I DON'T NEED THIS TO GET GIRLS!
Yeah, but it's nice to see all those French classes paid off!
MOM, I'M HOME...
Where have you been? You're supposed to be studying for your medical entrance exams today!
I TOLD YOU I DON'T WANT TO BE A DOCT—
What then? A movie star?! Join the Vietminh?!
I raised you better than that. I sacrificed a lot for you to attend university and do something with your life!

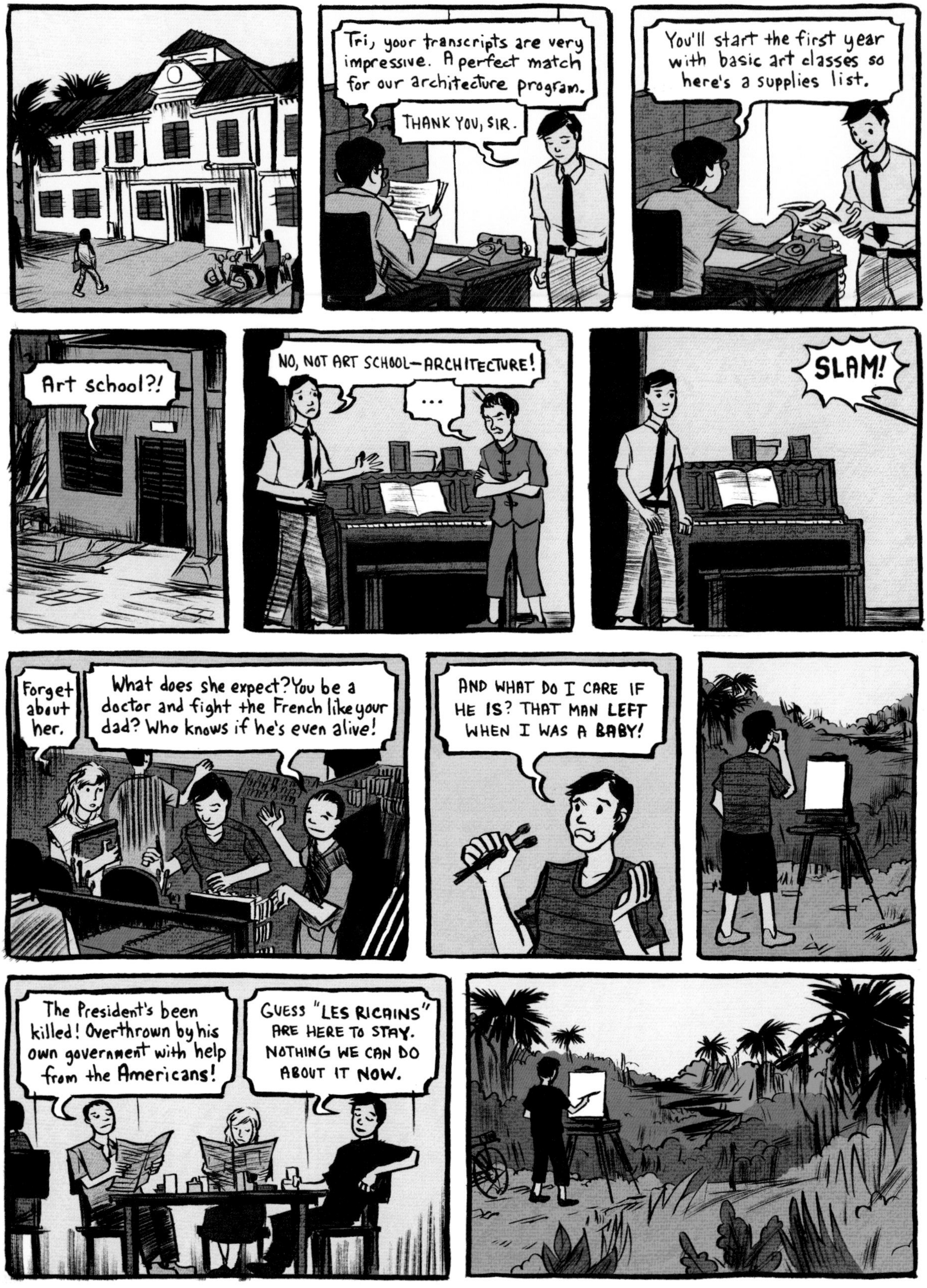
Tri, your transcripts are very impressive. A perfect match for our architecture program.
THANK YOU, SIR.
You'll start the first year with basic art classes so here's a supplies list.
Art school?!
NO, NOT ART SCHOOL—ARCHITECTURE!
...
SLAM!
Forget about her.
What does she expect? You be a doctor and fight the French like your dad? Who knows if he's even alive!
AND WHAT DO I CARE IF HE IS? THAT MAN LEFT WHEN I WAS A BABY!
The President's been killed! Overthrown by his own government with help from the Americans!
GUESS "LES RICAINS" ARE HERE TO STAY. NOTHING WE CAN DO ABOUT IT NOW.

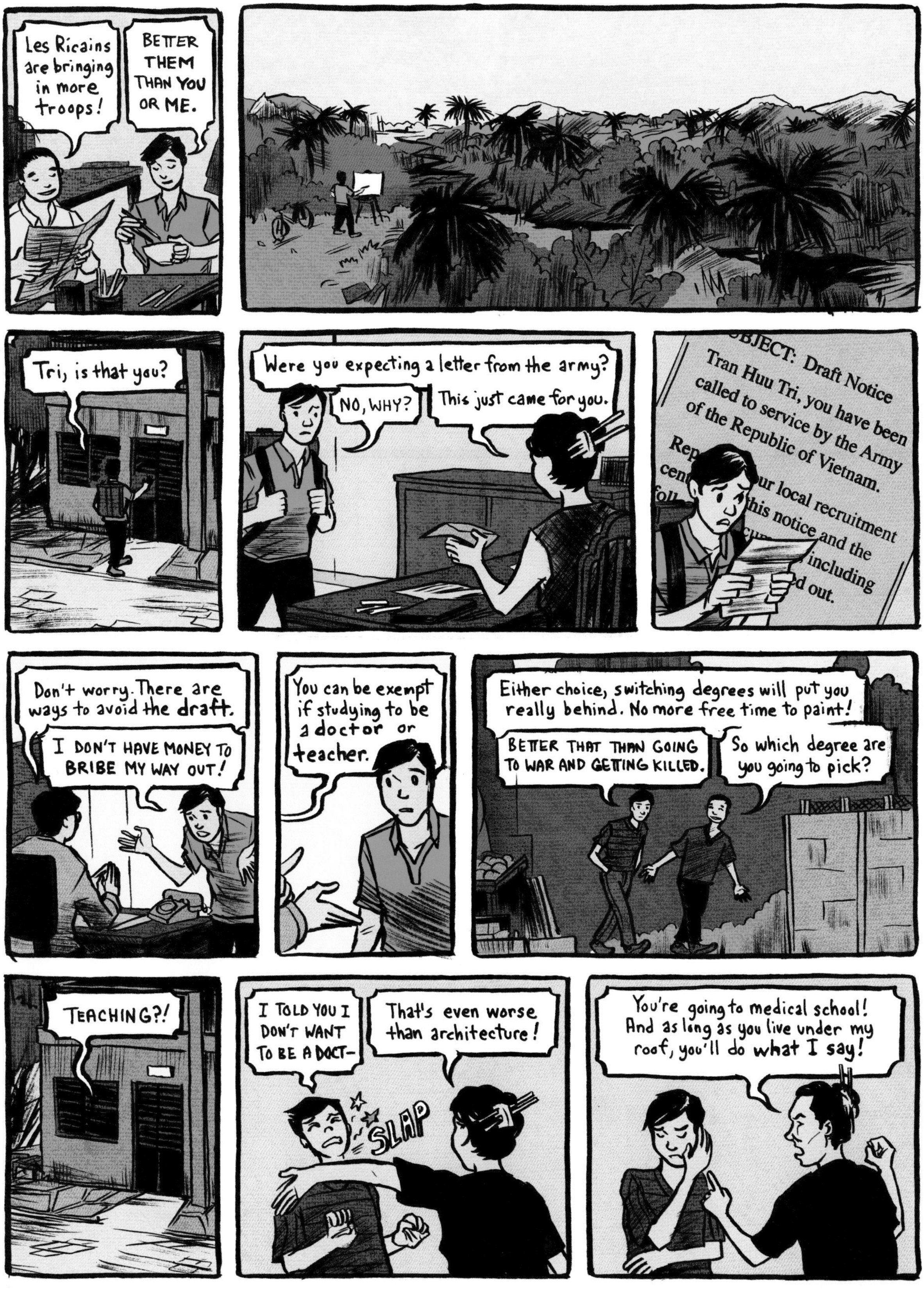
Les Ricains are bringing in more troops!
BETTER THEM THAN YOU OR ME.
Tri, is that you?
Were you expecting a letter from the army?
NO, WHY?
This just came for you.
SUBJECT: Draft Notice
Tran Huu Tri, you have been called to service by the Army of the Republic of Vietnam.
Don't worry. There are ways to avoid the draft.
I DON'T HAVE MONEY TO BRIBE MY WAY OUT!
You can be exempt if studying to be a doctor or teacher.
Either choice, switching degrees will put you really behind. No more free time to paint!
BETTER THAT THAN GOING TO WAR AND GETTING KILLED.
So which degree are you going to pick?
TEACHING?!
I TOLD YOU I DON'T WANT TO BE A DOCT-
SLAP
That's even worse than architecture!
You're going to medical school! And as long as you live under my roof, you'll do what I say!

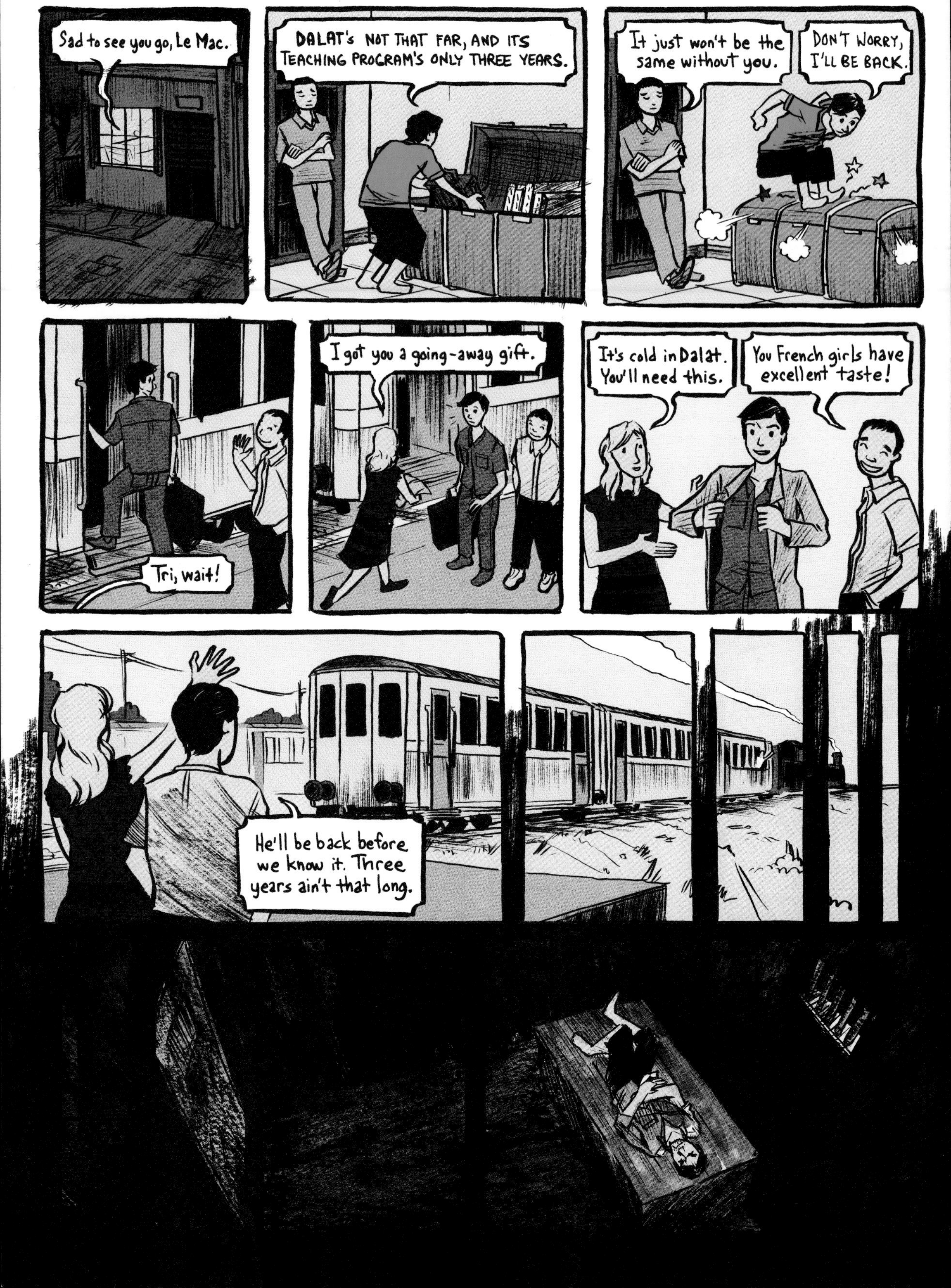
Sad to see you go, Le Mac.
DALAT's NOT THAT FAR, AND ITS TEACHING PROGRAM'S ONLY THREE YEARS.
It just won't be the same without you.
DON'T WORRY, I'LL BE BACK.
Tri, wait!
I got you a going-away gift.
It's cold in Dalat. You'll need this.
You French girls have excellent taste!
He'll be back before we know it. Three years ain't that long.

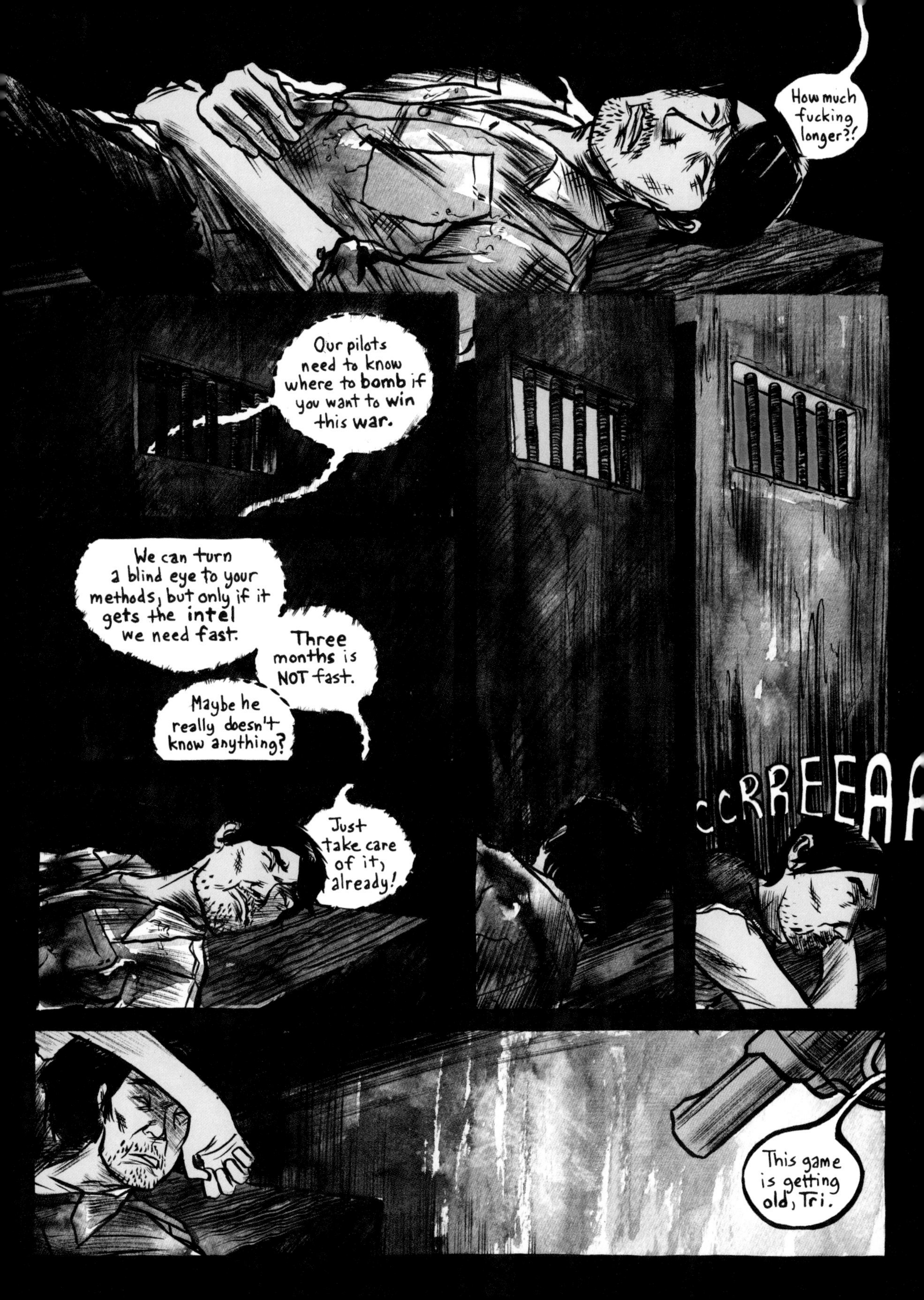
How much fucking longer?!
Our pilots need to know where to bomb if you want to win this war.
We can turn a blind eye to your methods, but only if it gets the intel we need fast.
Three months is NOT fast.
Maybe he really doesn't know anything?
Just take care of it, already!
CCRREEAA
This game is getting old, Tri.

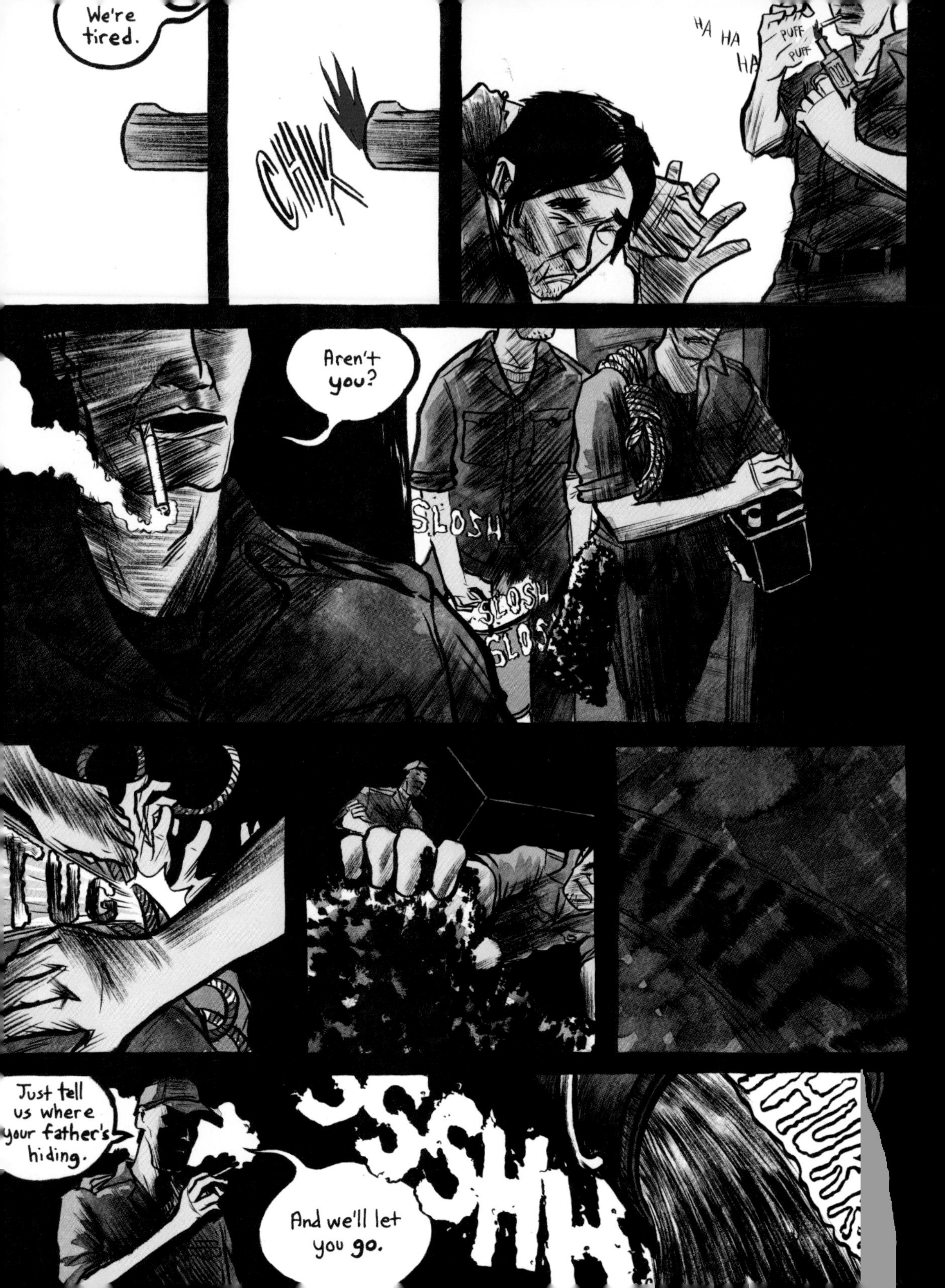
We're tired.
CHIK
HA HA HA
PUFF PUFF
Aren't you?
SLOSH SLOSH SLOSH
TUG
Just tell us where your father's hiding.
And we'll let you go.

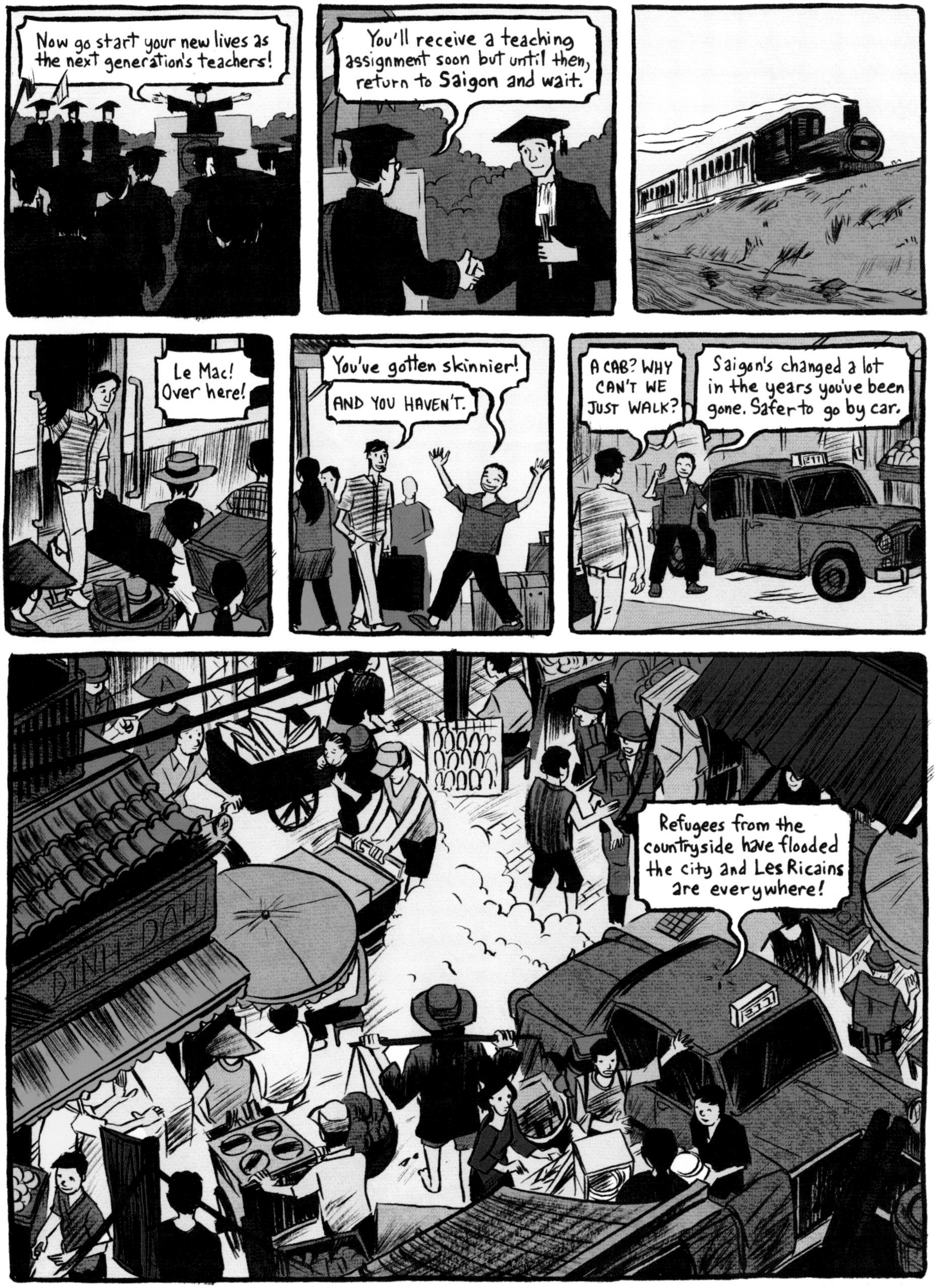
Now go start your new lives as the next generation's teachers!
You'll receive a teaching assignment soon but until then, return to Saigon and wait.
Le Mac! Over here!
You've gotten skinnier!
AND YOU HAVEN'T.
A CAB? WHY CAN'T WE JUST WALK?
Saigon's changed a lot in the years you've been gone. Safer to go by car.
Refugees from the countryside have flooded the city and Les Ricains are everywhere!

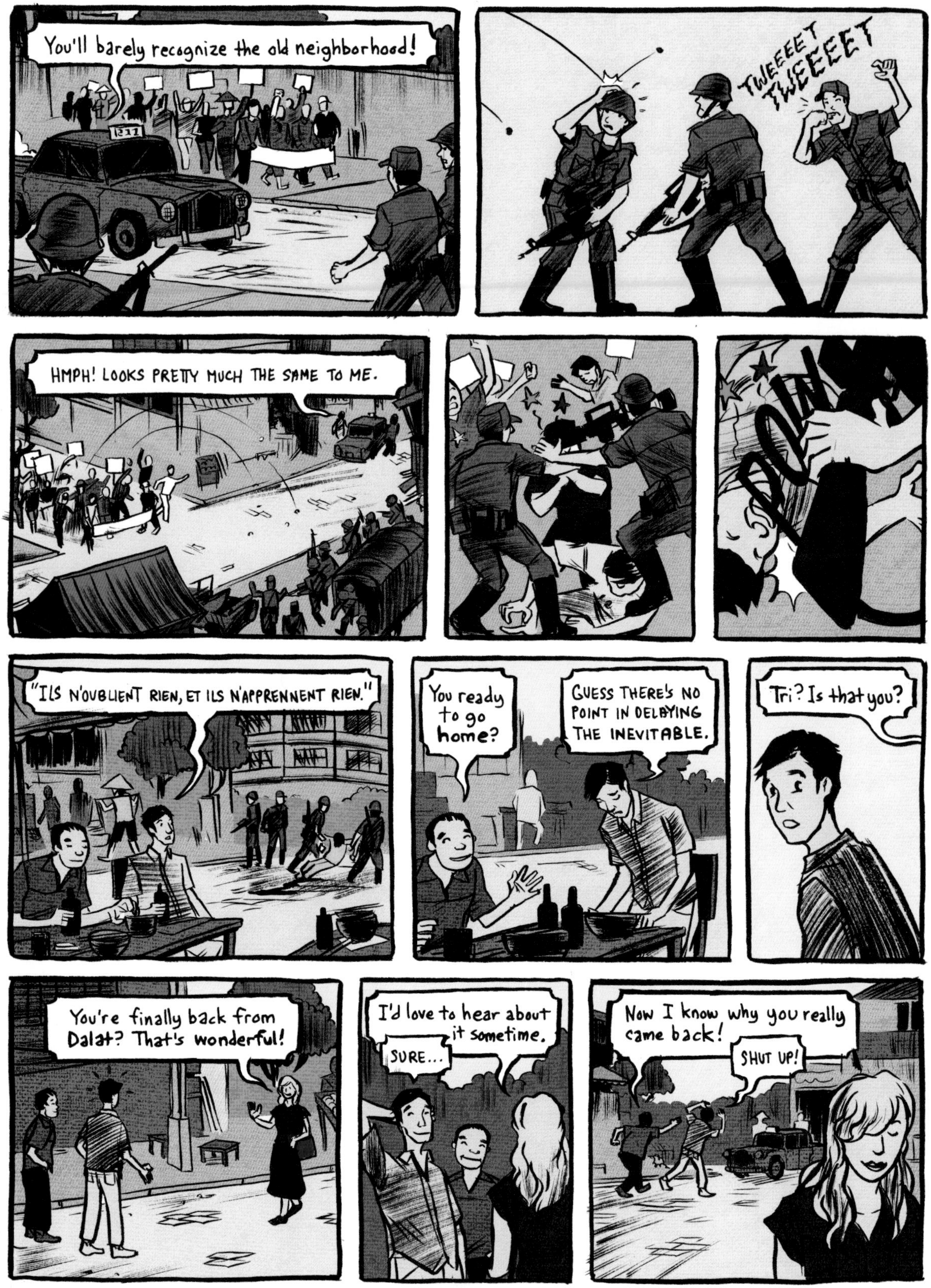

You'll barely recognize the old neighborhood!
TWEEEET TWEEEET
HMPH! LOOKS PRETTY MUCH THE SAME TO ME.
POW
"ILS N'OUBLIENT RIEN, ET ILS N'APPRENNENT RIEN."
You ready to go home?
GUESS THERE'S NO POINT IN DELAYING THE INEVITABLE.
Tri? Is that you?
You're finally back from Dalat? That's wonderful!
I'd love to hear about it sometime.
SURE...
Now I know why you really came back!
SHUT UP!

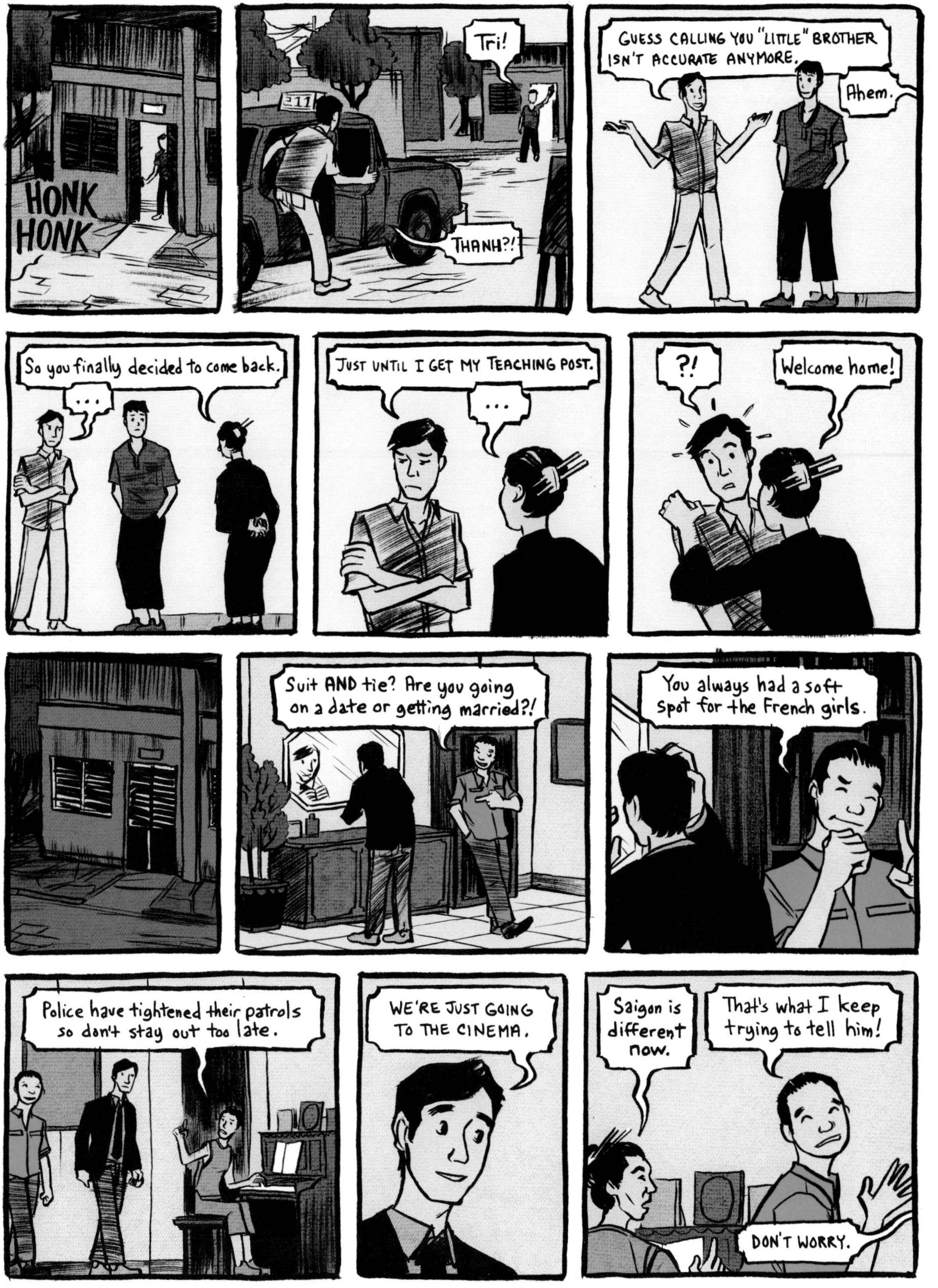
HONK
HONK
Tri!
THANH?!
GUESS CALLING YOU "LITTLE" BROTHER ISN'T ACCURATE ANYMORE.
Ahem.
So you finally decided to come back.
...
JUST UNTIL I GET MY TEACHING POST.
...
?!
Welcome home!
Suit AND tie? Are you going on a date or getting married?!
You always had a soft spot for the French girls.
Police have tightened their patrols so don't stay out too late.
WE'RE JUST GOING TO THE CINEMA.
Saigon is different now.
That's what I keep trying to tell him!
DON'T WORRY.

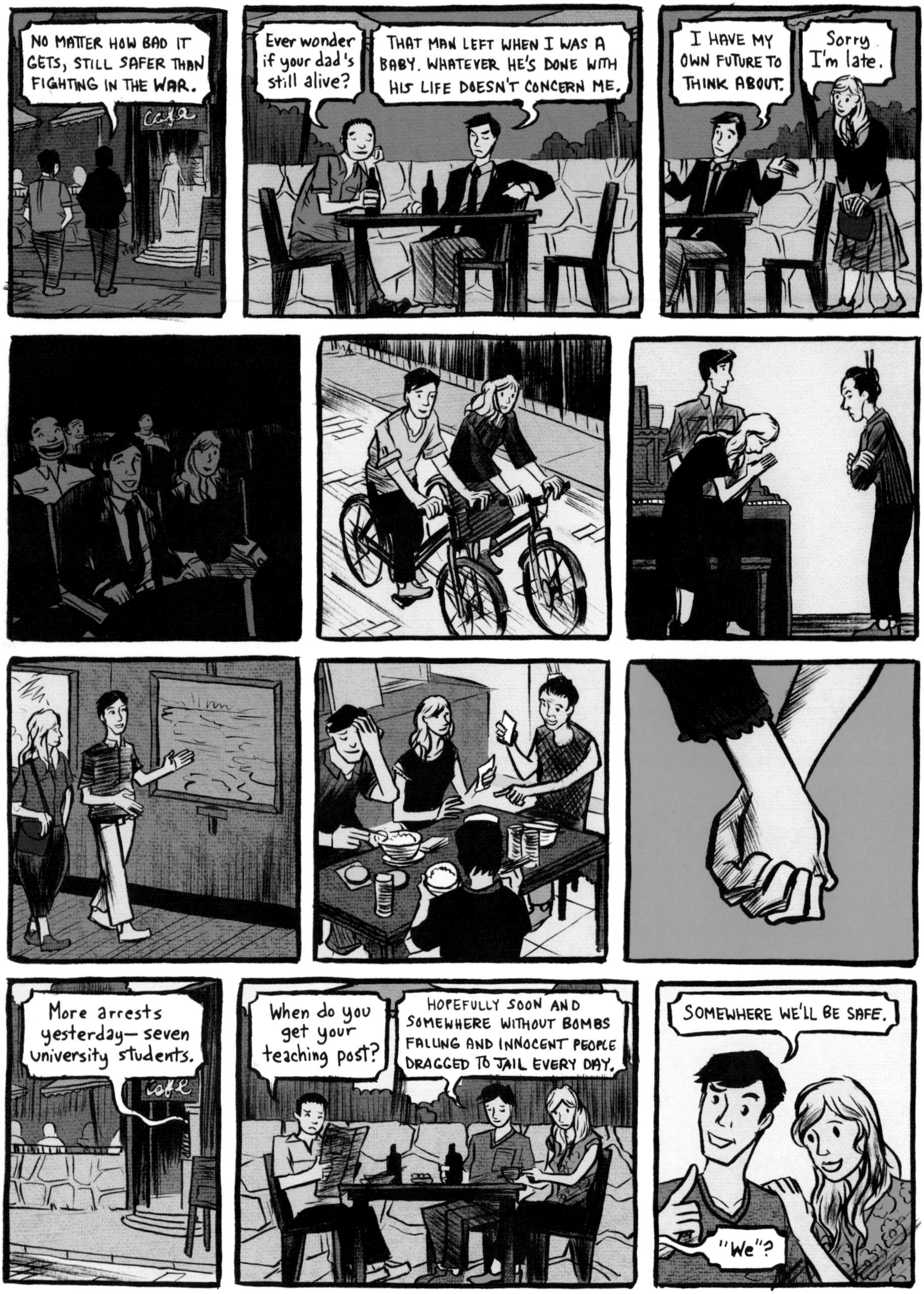
NO MATTER HOW BAD IT GETS, STILL SAFER THAN FIGHTING IN THE WAR.
Café
Ever wonder if your dad's still alive?
THAT MAN LEFT WHEN I WAS A BABY. WHATEVER HE'S DONE WITH HIS LIFE DOESN'T CONCERN ME.
I HAVE MY OWN FUTURE TO THINK ABOUT.
Sorry I'm late.
More arrests yesterday— seven university students.
Café
When do you get your teaching post?
HOPEFULLY SOON AND SOMEWHERE WITHOUT BOMBS FALLING AND INNOCENT PEOPLE DRAGGED TO JAIL EVERY DAY.
SOMEWHERE WE'LL BE SAFE.
"We"?

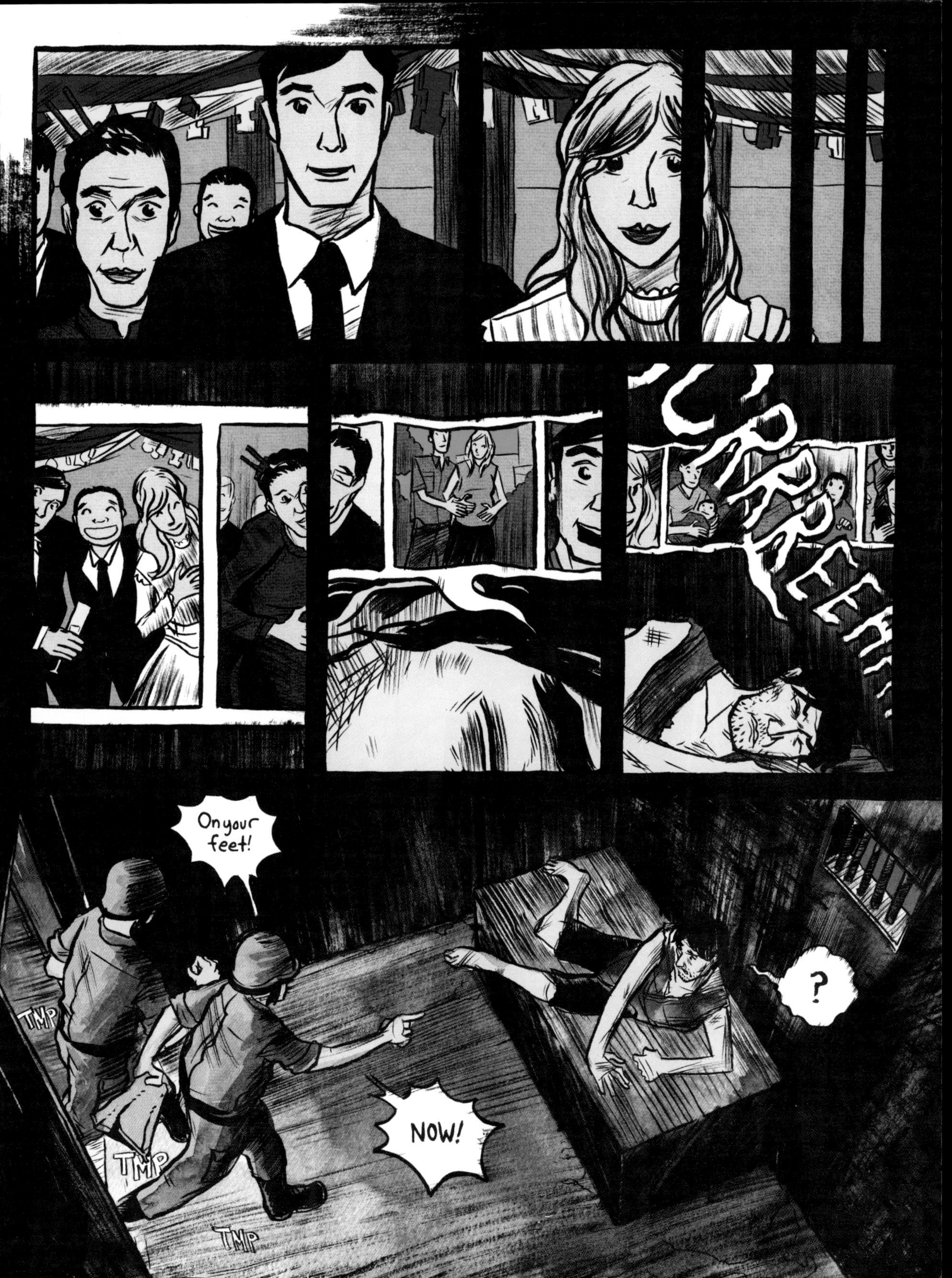

SCRREEEH!!
On your feet!
?
NOW!
TMP
TMP
TMP

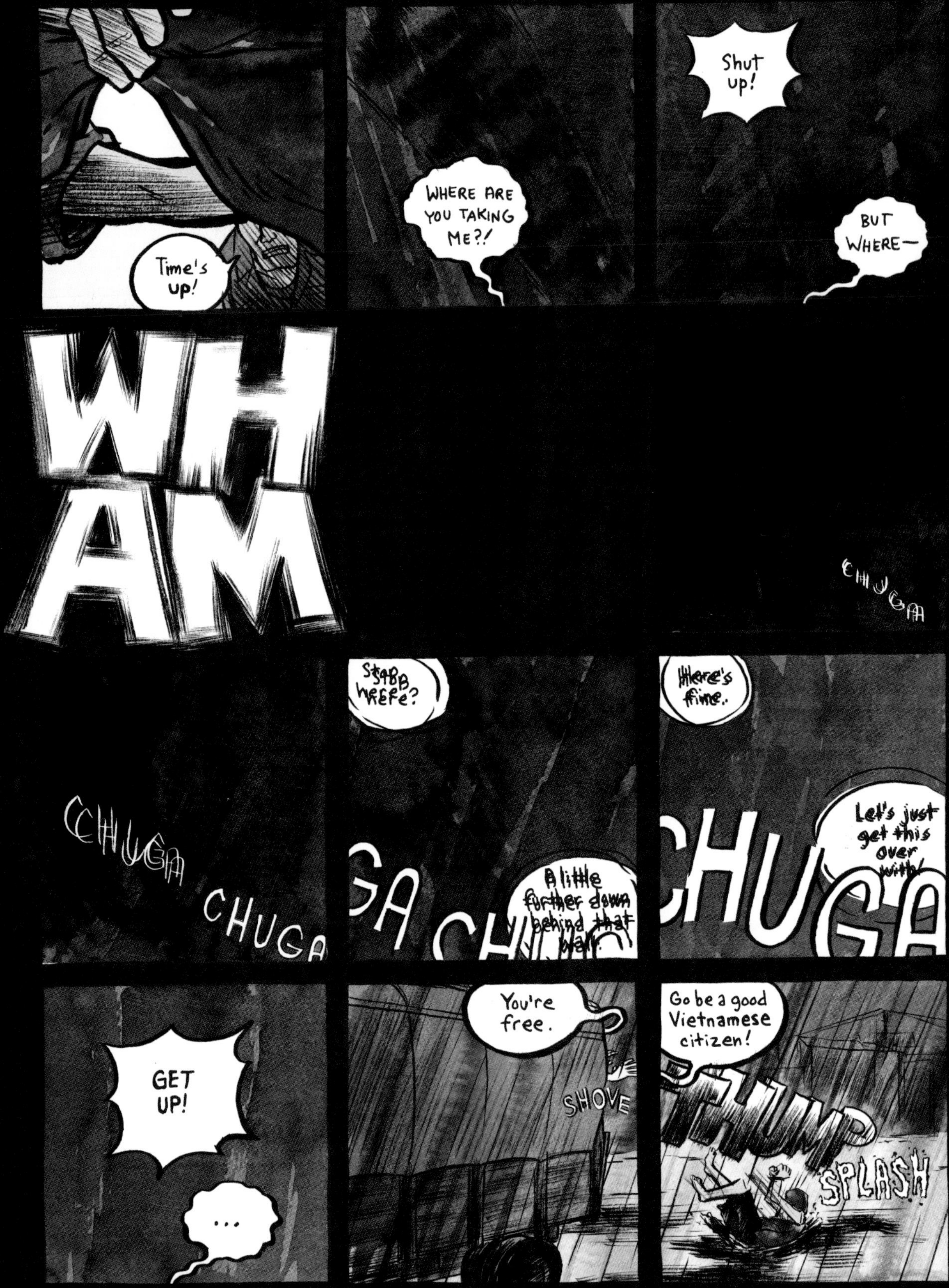

Time's up!
WHERE ARE YOU TAKING ME?!
Shut up!
BUT WHERE—
WHAM
CHUGA
CHUGA
CHUGA
Stop here?
A little further down behind that wall.
GA
Here's fine.
Let's just get this over with!
CHUGA
GET UP!
...
You're free.
SHOVE
Go be a good Vietnamese citizen!
THUMP
SPLASH

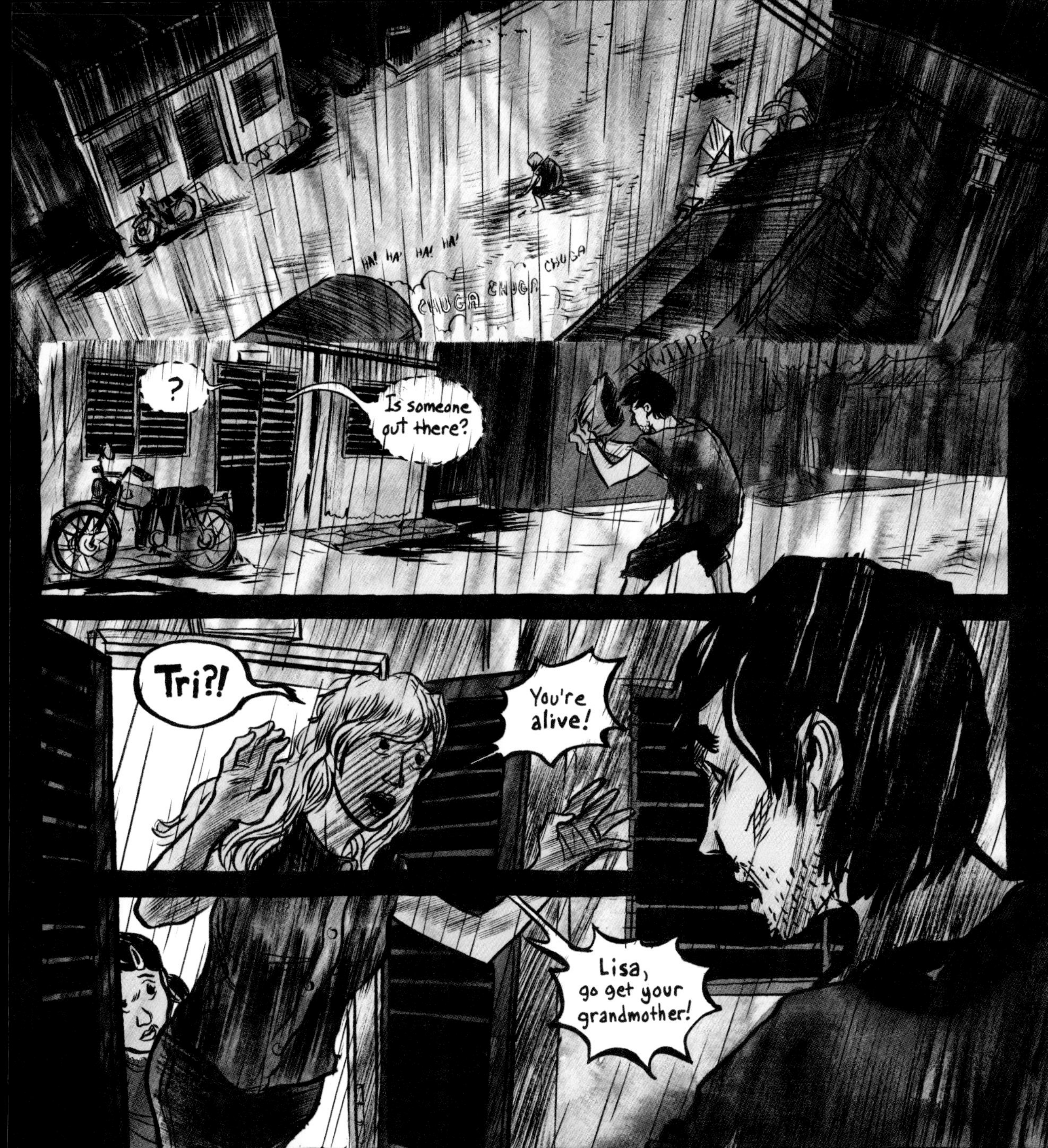
HA! HA! HA! HA!
CHUGA CHUGA CHUGA
WWTIPP
?
Is someone out there?
Tri?!
You're alive!
Lisa, go get your grandmother!

BEEP

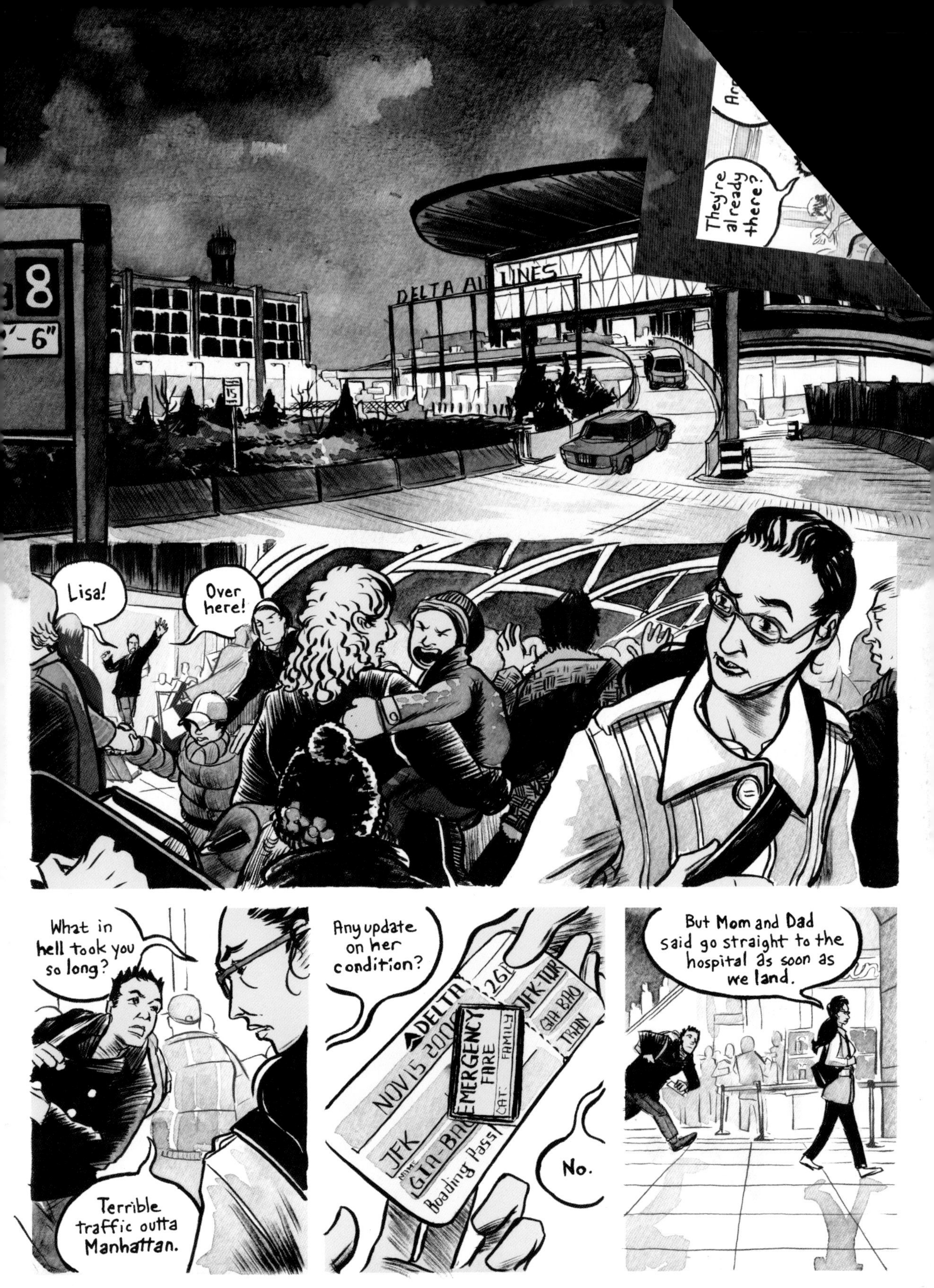

8
They're already there?
Lisa!
Over here!
What in hell took you so long?
Terrible traffic outta Manhattan.
Any update on her condition?
DELTA
NOV 15 2000
EMERGENCY FARE
FAMILY
JFK-TUP
GIA-BAO TRAN
JFK
Boarding Pass
No.
But Mom and Dad said go straight to the hospital as soon as we land.

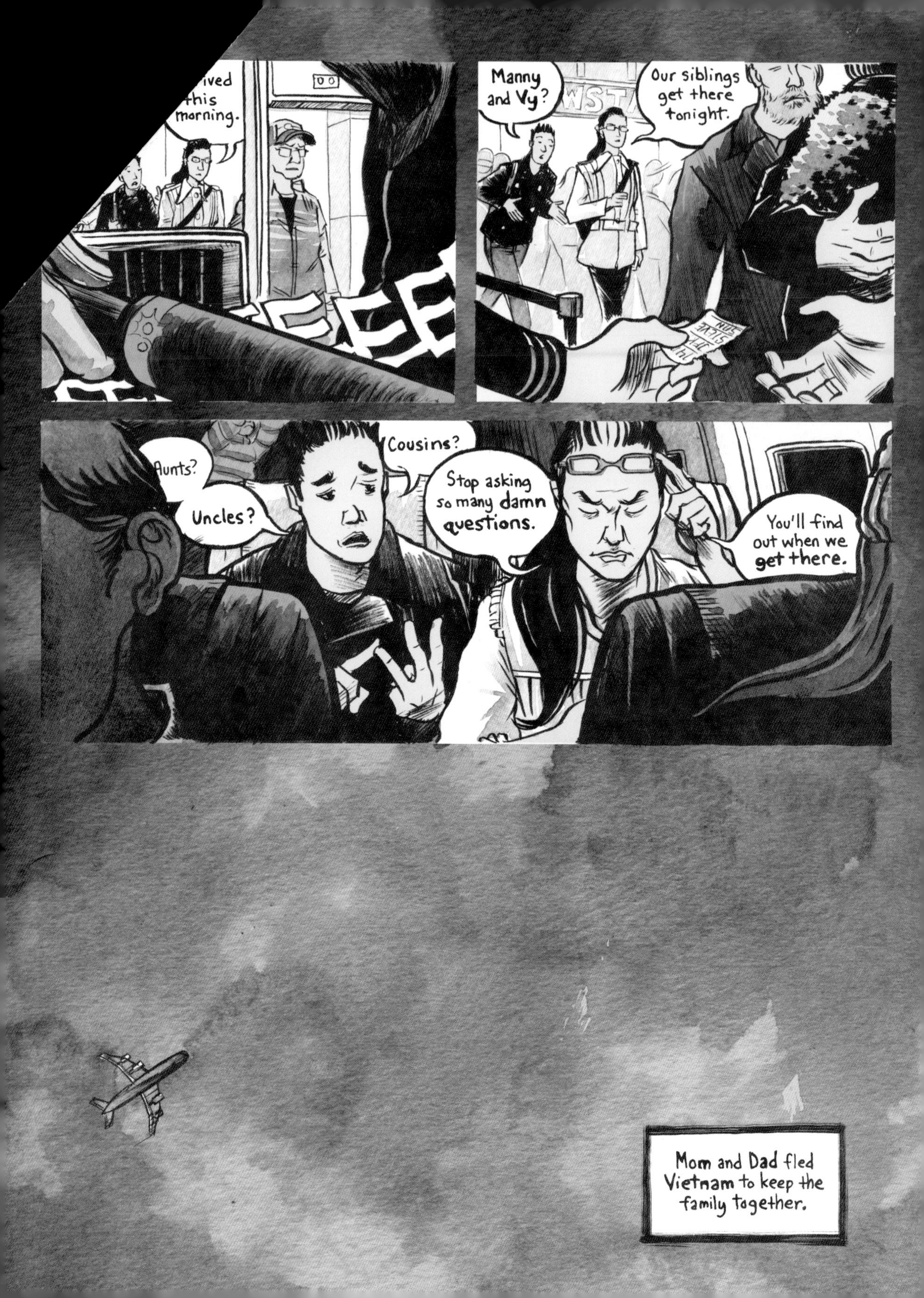

rived this morning.
Manny and Vy?
Our siblings get there tonight.
Aunts?
Uncles?
Cousins?
Stop asking so many damn questions.
You'll find out when we get there.
Mom and Dad fled Vietnam to keep the family together.

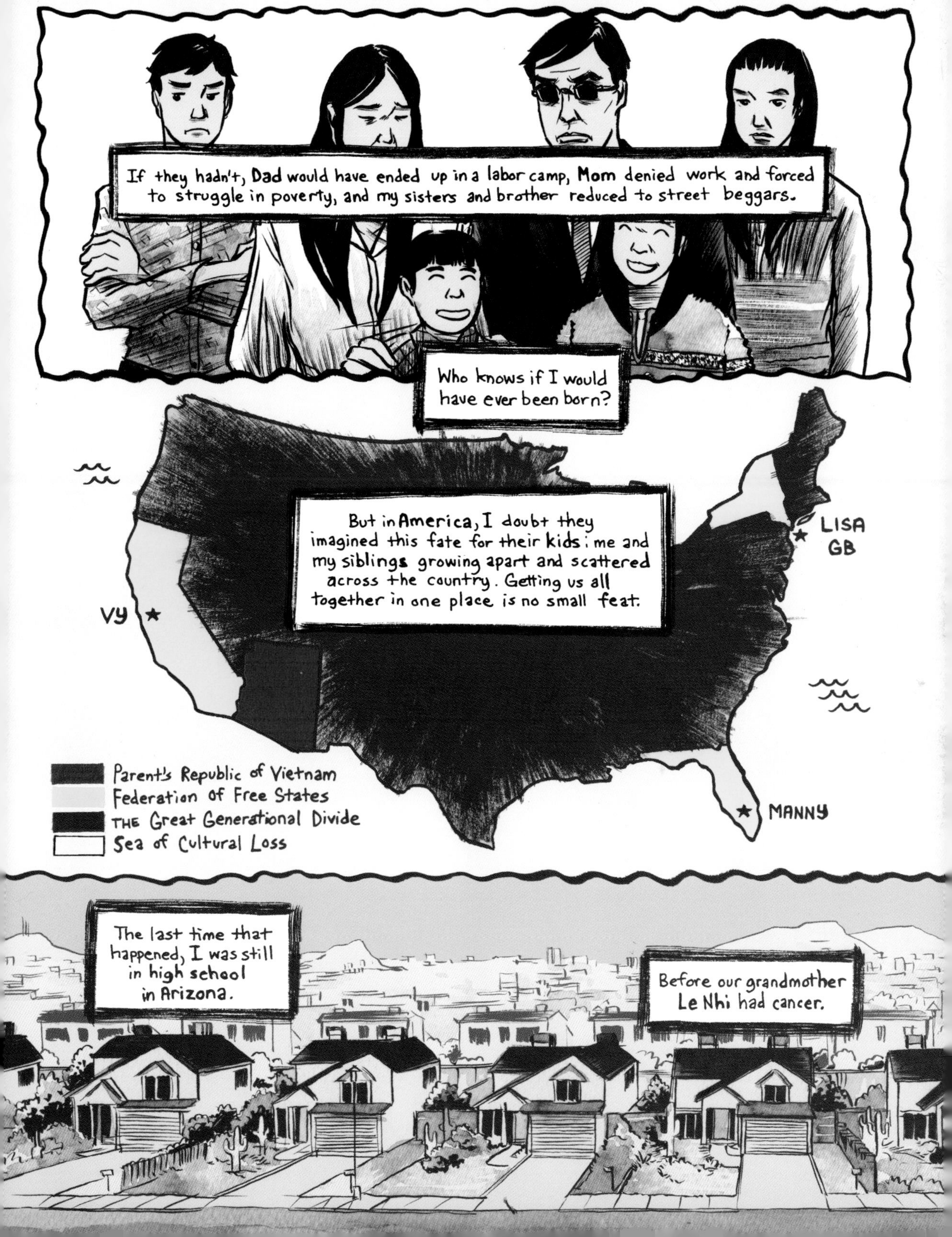

If they hadn't, Dad would have ended up in a labor camp, Mom denied work and forced to struggle in poverty, and my sisters and brother reduced to street beggars.
Who knows if I would have ever been born?
But in America, I doubt they imagined this fate for their kids: me and my siblings growing apart and scattered across the country. Getting us all together in one place is no small feat.
LISA
GB
VY
MANNY
Parent's Republic of Vietnam
Federation of Free States
THE Great Generational Divide
Sea of Cultural Loss
The last time that happened, I was still in high school in Arizona.
Before our grandmother Le Nhi had cancer.

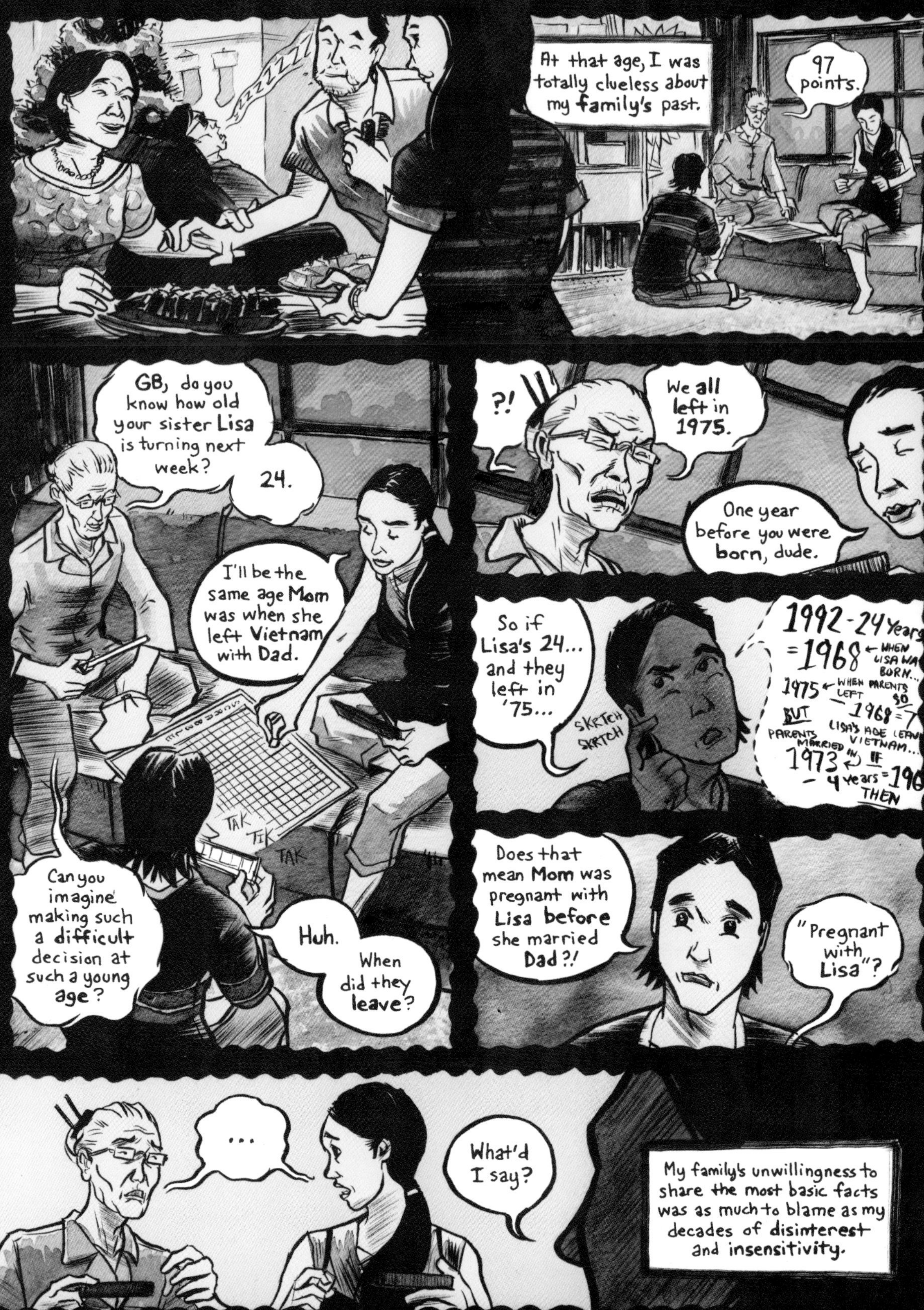

At that age, I was totally clueless about my family's past.
97 points.
GB, do you know how old your sister Lisa is turning next week?
24.
I'll be the same age Mom was when she left Vietnam with Dad.
TAK
TIK
TAK
Can you imagine making such a difficult decision at such a young age?
Huh.
When did they leave?
?!
We all left in 1975.
One year before you were born, dude.
So if Lisa's 24... and they left in '75...
SKRTCH
SKRTCH
1992 - 24 Years
= 1968 ← WHEN LISA WA BORN...
1975 ← WHEN PARENTS LEFT
SO
- 1968 = 7
BUT
LISA'S AGE LEAV VIETNAM...
PARENTS MARRIED IN 1973
IF
- 4 years = 196
THEN
Does that mean Mom was pregnant with Lisa before she married Dad?!
"Pregnant with Lisa"?
...
What'd I say?
My family's unwillingness to share the most basic facts was as much to blame as my decades of disinterest and insensitivity.

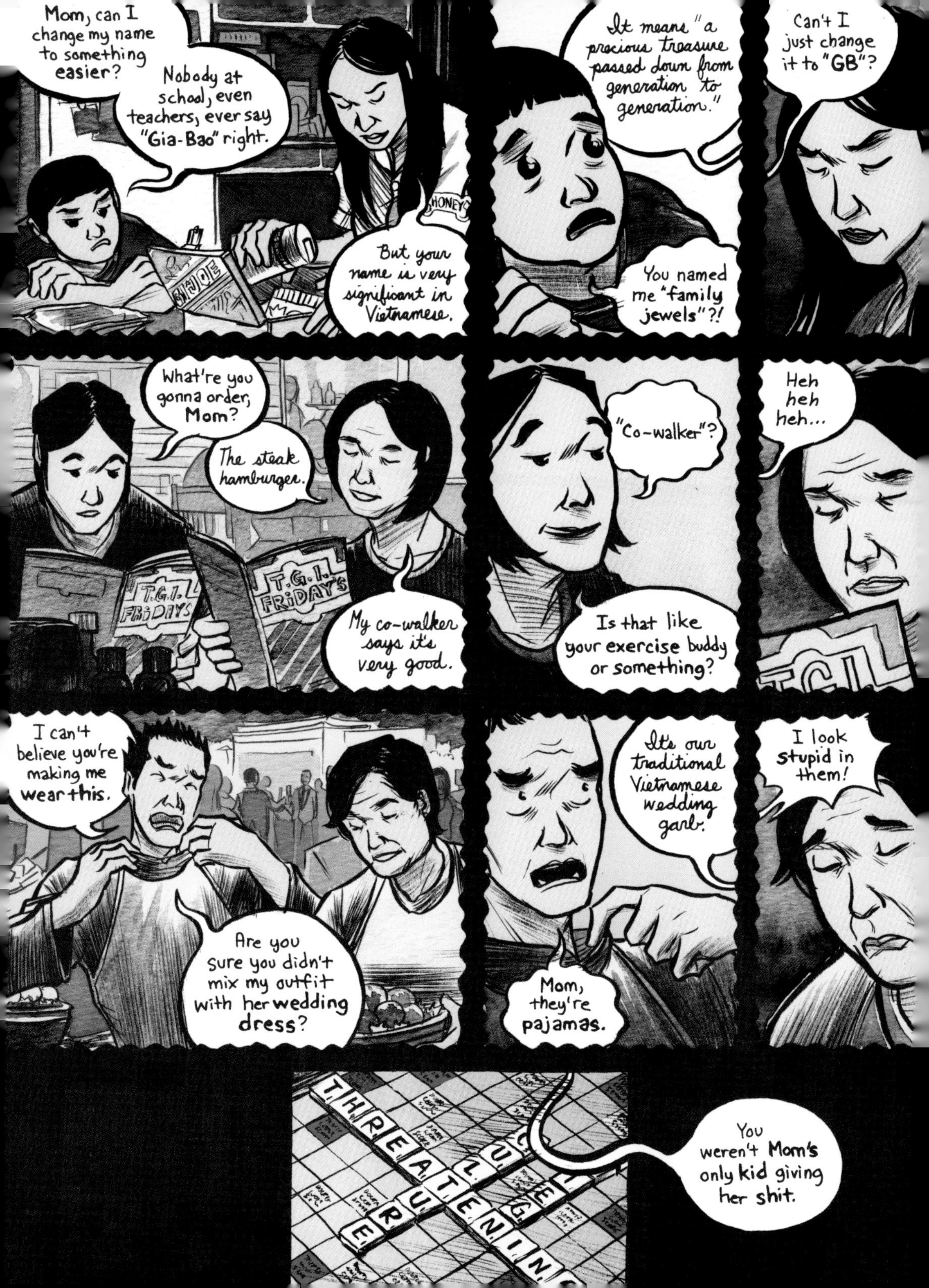

Mom, can I change my name to something easier?
Nobody at school, even teachers, ever say "Gia-Bao" right.
But your name is very significant in Vietnamese.
It means "a precious treasure passed down from generation to generation."
You named me "family jewels"?!
Can't I just change it to "GB"?
What're you gonna order, Mom?
The steak hamburger.
T.G.I. FRIDAY'S
T.G.I. FRIDAYS
My co-walker says it's very good.
"Co-walker"?
Is that like your exercise buddy or something?
Heh heh heh...
I can't believe you're making me wear this.
Are you sure you didn't mix my outfit with her wedding dress?
It's our traditional Vietnamese wedding garb.
Mom, they're pajamas.
I look stupid in them!
You weren't Mom's only kid giving her shit.

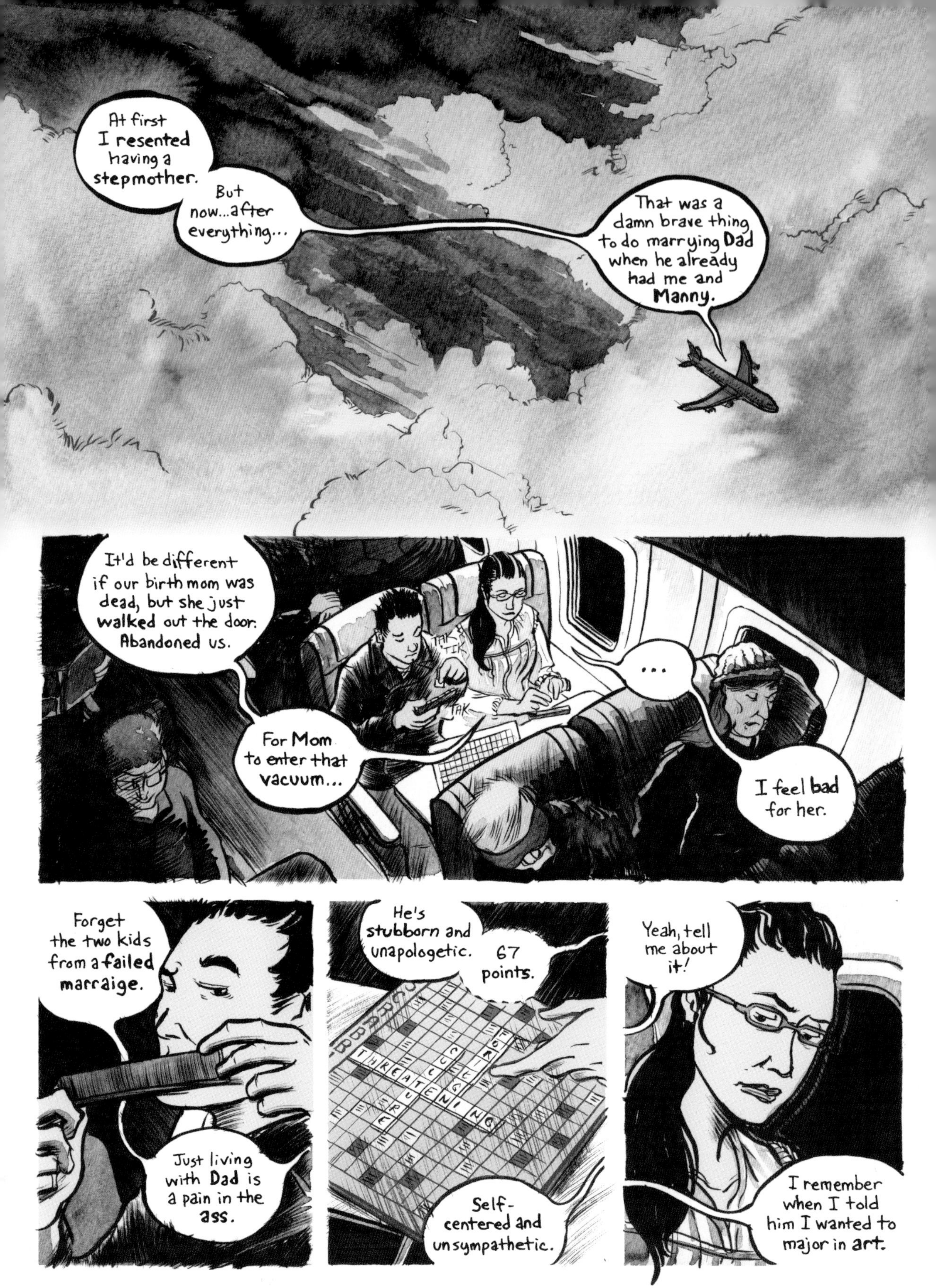
At first I resented having a stepmother.
But now...after everything...
That was a damn brave thing to do marrying Dad when he already had me and Manny.
It'd be different if our birth mom was dead, but she just walked out the door. Abandoned us.
TAK TIK
TAK
For Mom to enter that vacuum...
...
I feel bad for her.
Forget the two kids from a failed marraige.
Just living with Dad is a pain in the ass.
He's stubborn and unapologetic.
67 points.
Self-centered and unsympathetic.
Yeah, tell me about it!
I remember when I told him I wanted to major in art.

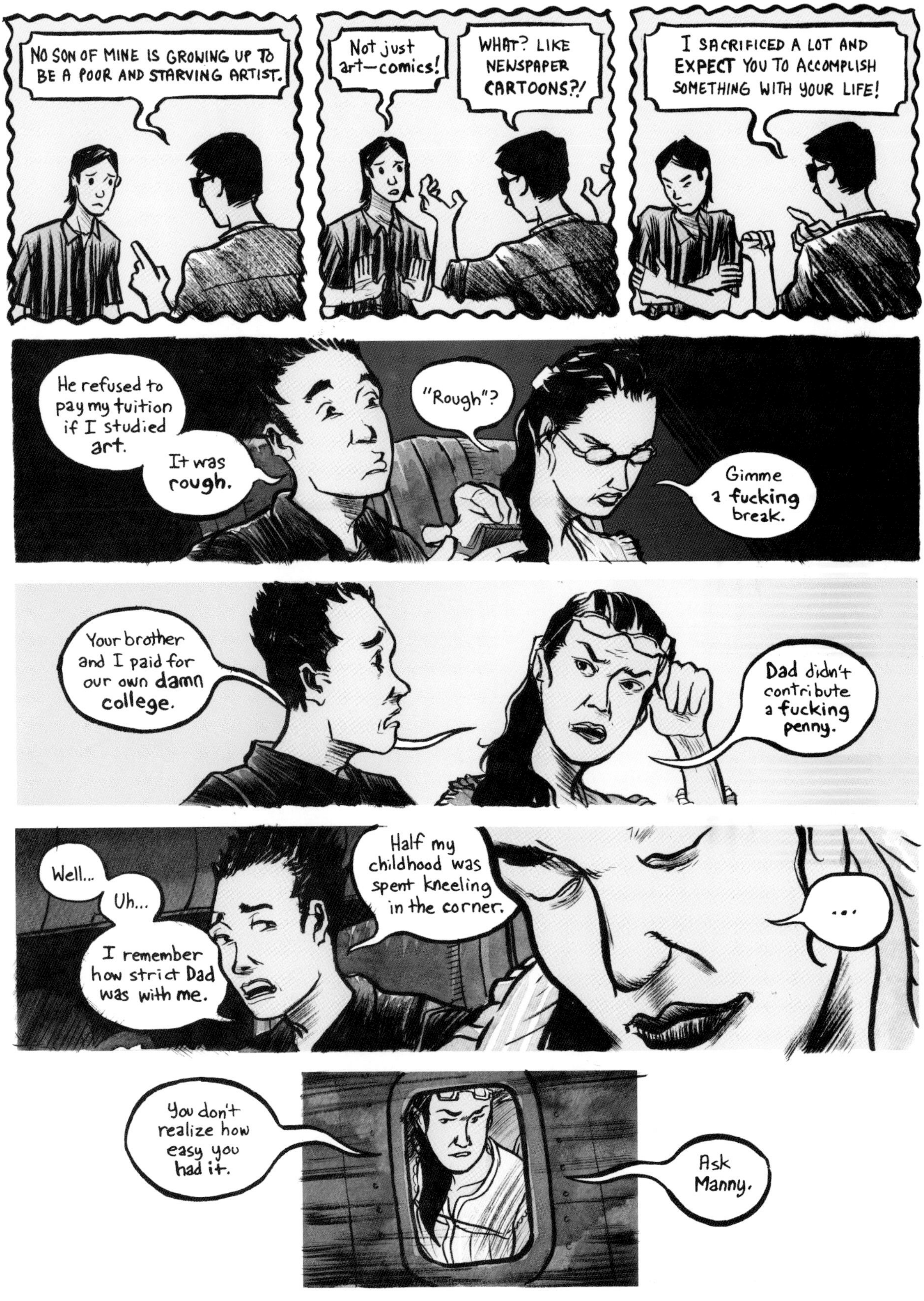

NO SON OF MINE IS GROWING UP TO BE A POOR AND STARVING ARTIST.
Not just art—comics!
WHAT? LIKE NEWSPAPER CARTOONS?!
I SACRIFICED A LOT AND EXPECT YOU TO ACCOMPLISH SOMETHING WITH YOUR LIFE!
He refused to pay my tuition if I studied art.
It was rough.
"Rough"?
Gimme a fucking break.
Your brother and I paid for our own damn college.
Dad didn't contribute a fucking penny.
Well...
Uh...
I remember how strict Dad was with me.
Half my childhood was spent kneeling in the corner.
...
You don't realize how easy you had it.
Ask Manny.

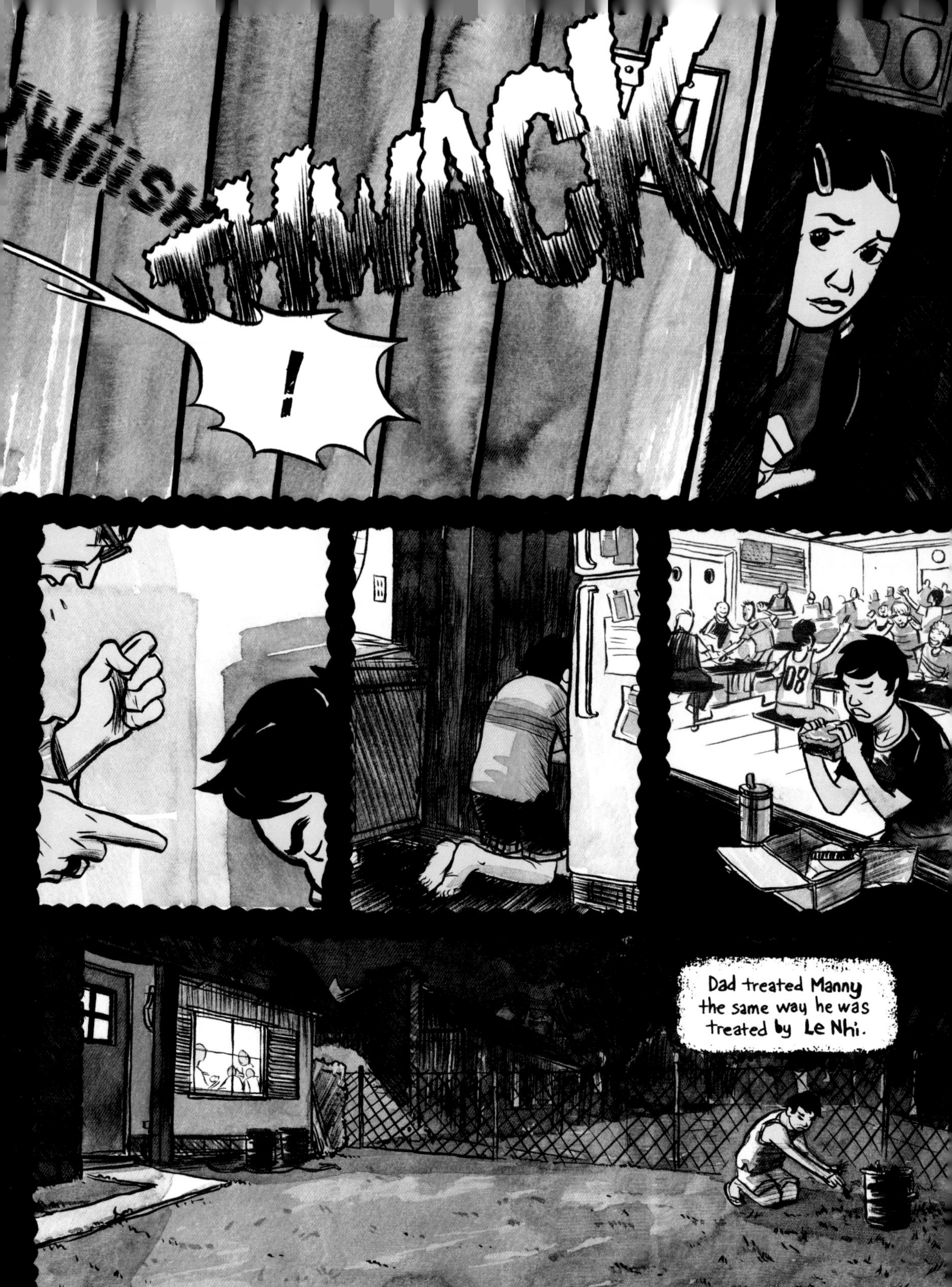
WHISH
THWACK
!
Dad treated Manny the same way he was treated by Le Nhi.
08

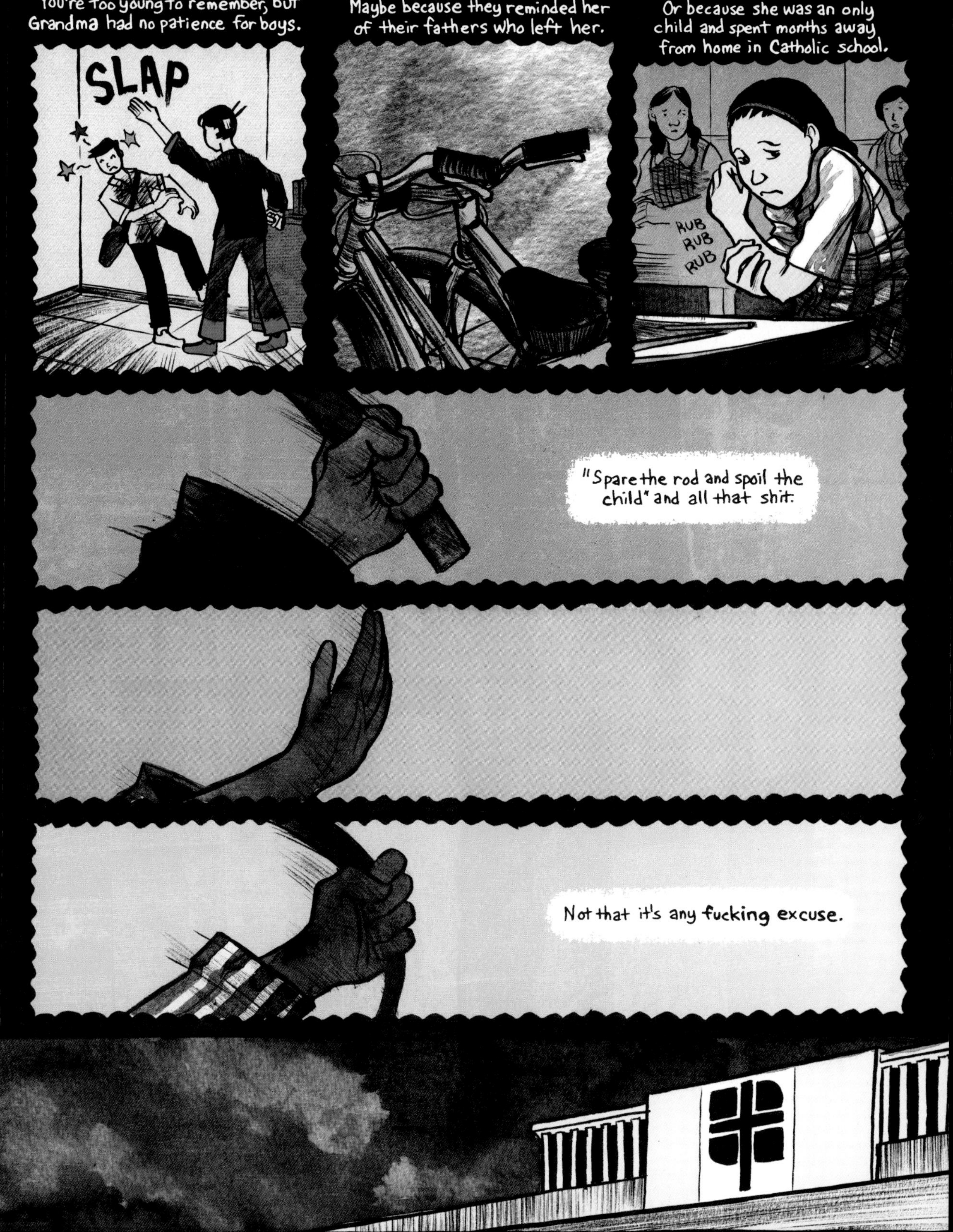
You're too young to remember, but Grandma had no patience for boys.
SLAP
Maybe because they reminded her of their fathers who left her.
Or because she was an only child and spent months away from home in Catholic school.
RUB
RUB
RUB
"Spare the rod and spoil the child" and all that shit.
Not that it's any fucking excuse.

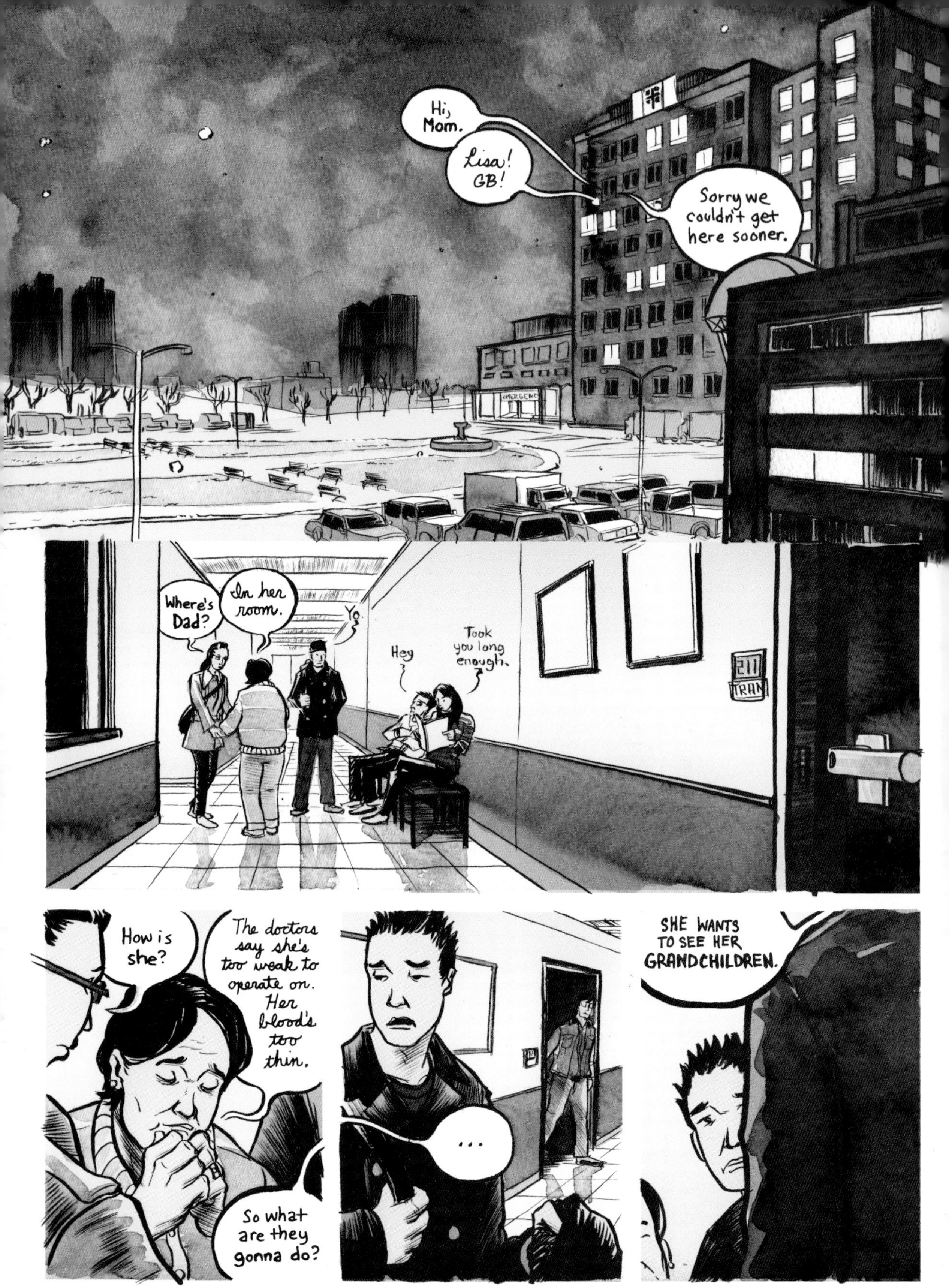
Hi, Mom.
Lisa! GB!
Sorry we couldn't get here sooner.
Where's Dad?
In her room.
Yo.
Hey
Took you long enough.
How is she?
The doctors say she's too weak to operate on. Her blood's too thin.
So what are they gonna do?
...
SHE WANTS TO SEE HER GRANDCHILDREN.

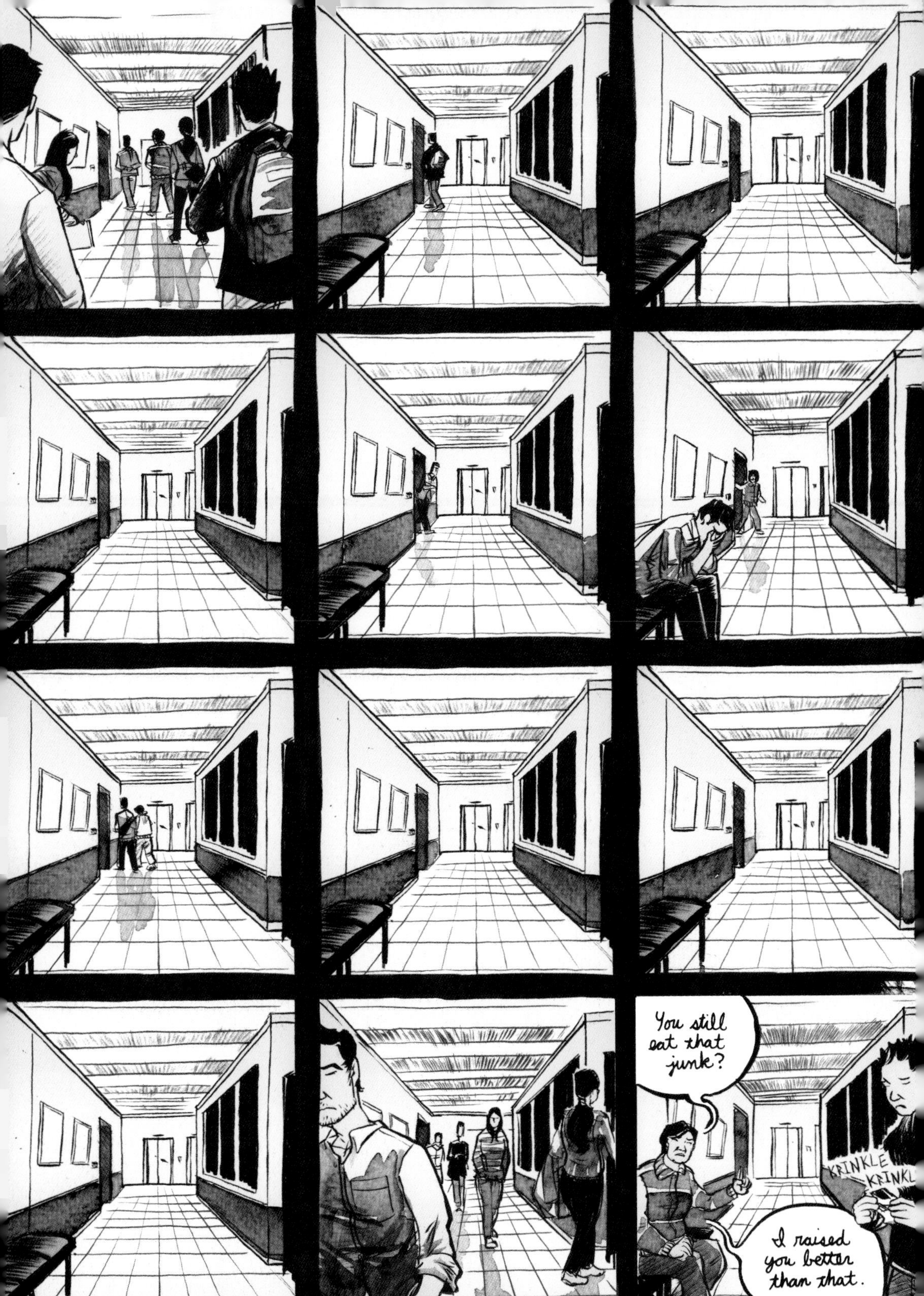
You still eat that junk?
KRINKLE
KRINKLE
I raised you better than that.

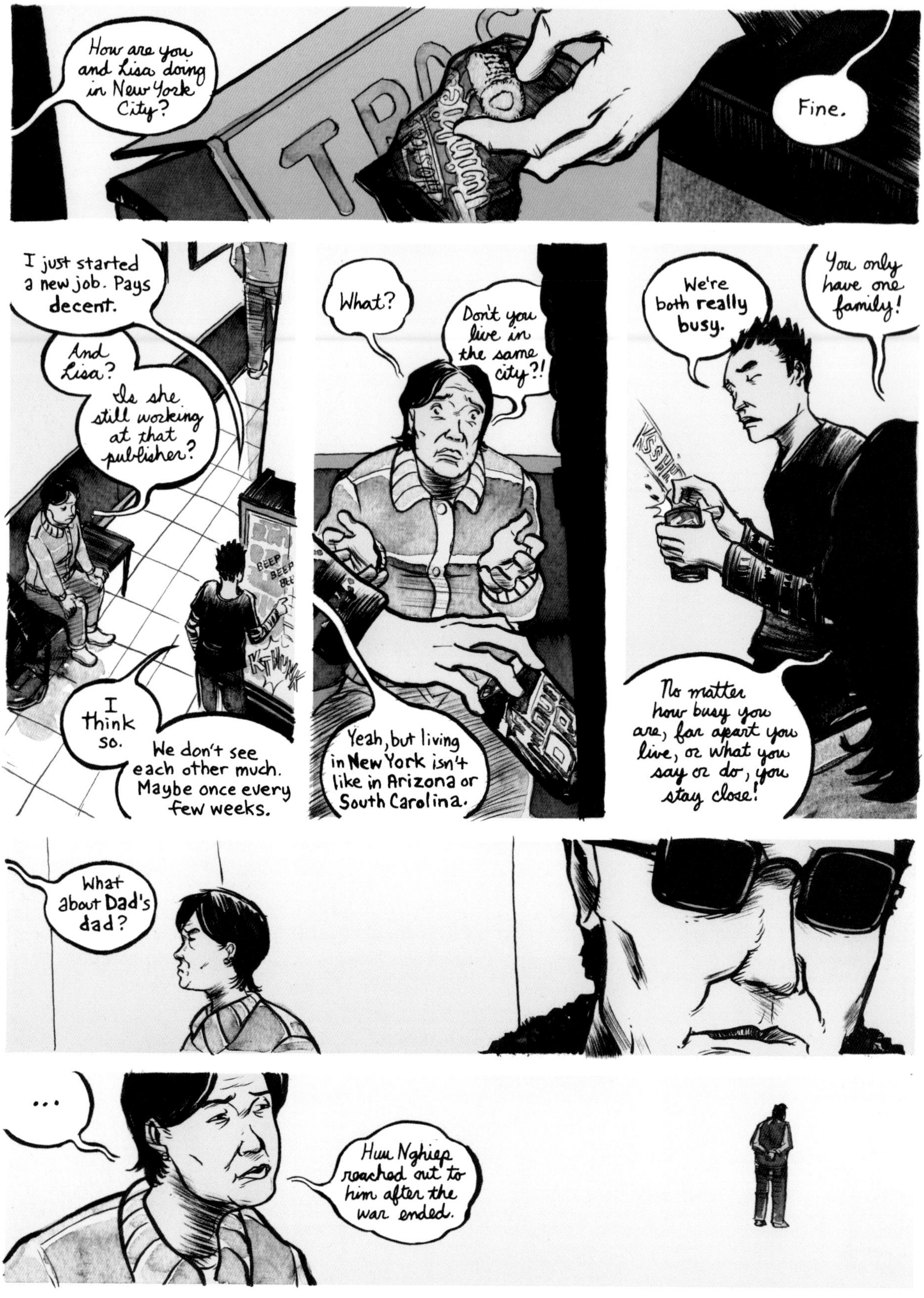
How are you and Lisa doing in New York City?
Fine.
I just started a new job. Pays decent.
And Lisa?
Is she still working at that publisher?
BEEP BEEP
KTHUNK
I think so.
We don't see each other much. Maybe once every few weeks.
What?
Don't you live in the same city?!
Yeah, but living in New York isn't like in Arizona or South Carolina.
We're both really busy.
You only have one family!
No matter how busy you are, far apart you live, or what you say or do, you stay close!
What about Dad's dad?
...
Huu Nghiep reached out to him after the war ended.

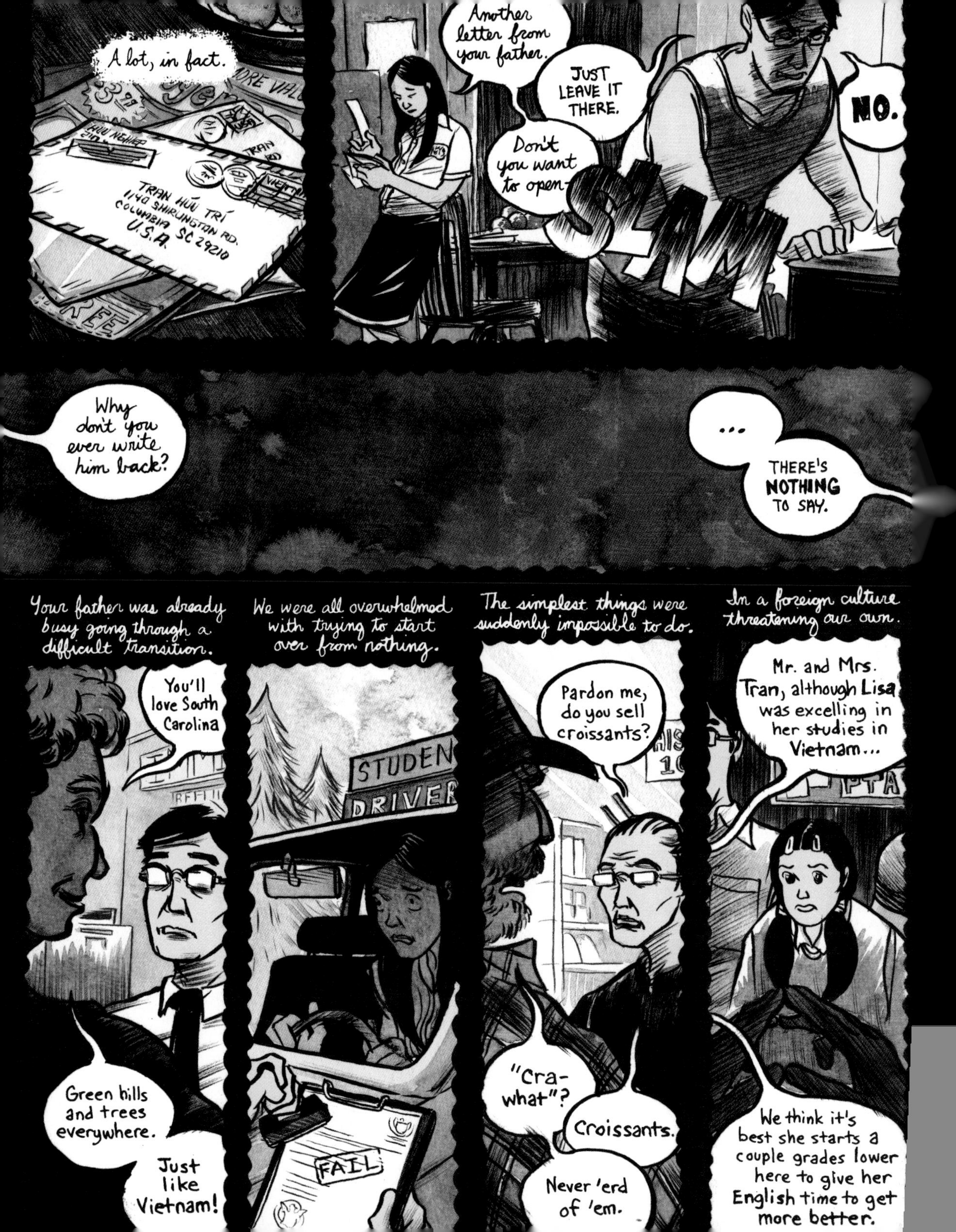
A lot, in fact.
TRAN HỮU TRÍ
1140 SHIRLINGTON RD.
COLUMBIA SC 29210
U.S.A.
Another letter from your father.
JUST LEAVE IT THERE.
Don't you want to open-
SLAM
NO.
Why don't you ever write him back?
...
THERE'S NOTHING TO SAY.
Your father was already busy going through a difficult transition.
You'll love South Carolina
Green hills and trees everywhere.
Just like Vietnam!
We were all overwhelmed with trying to start over from nothing.
STUDEN
DRIVER
FAIL
The simplest things were suddenly impossible to do.
Pardon me, do you sell croissants?
"Cra-what"?
Croissants.
Never 'erd of 'em.
In a foreign culture threatening our own.
Mr. and Mrs. Tran, although Lisa was excelling in her studies in Vietnam...
PTA
We think it's best she starts a couple grades lower here to give her English time to get more better.

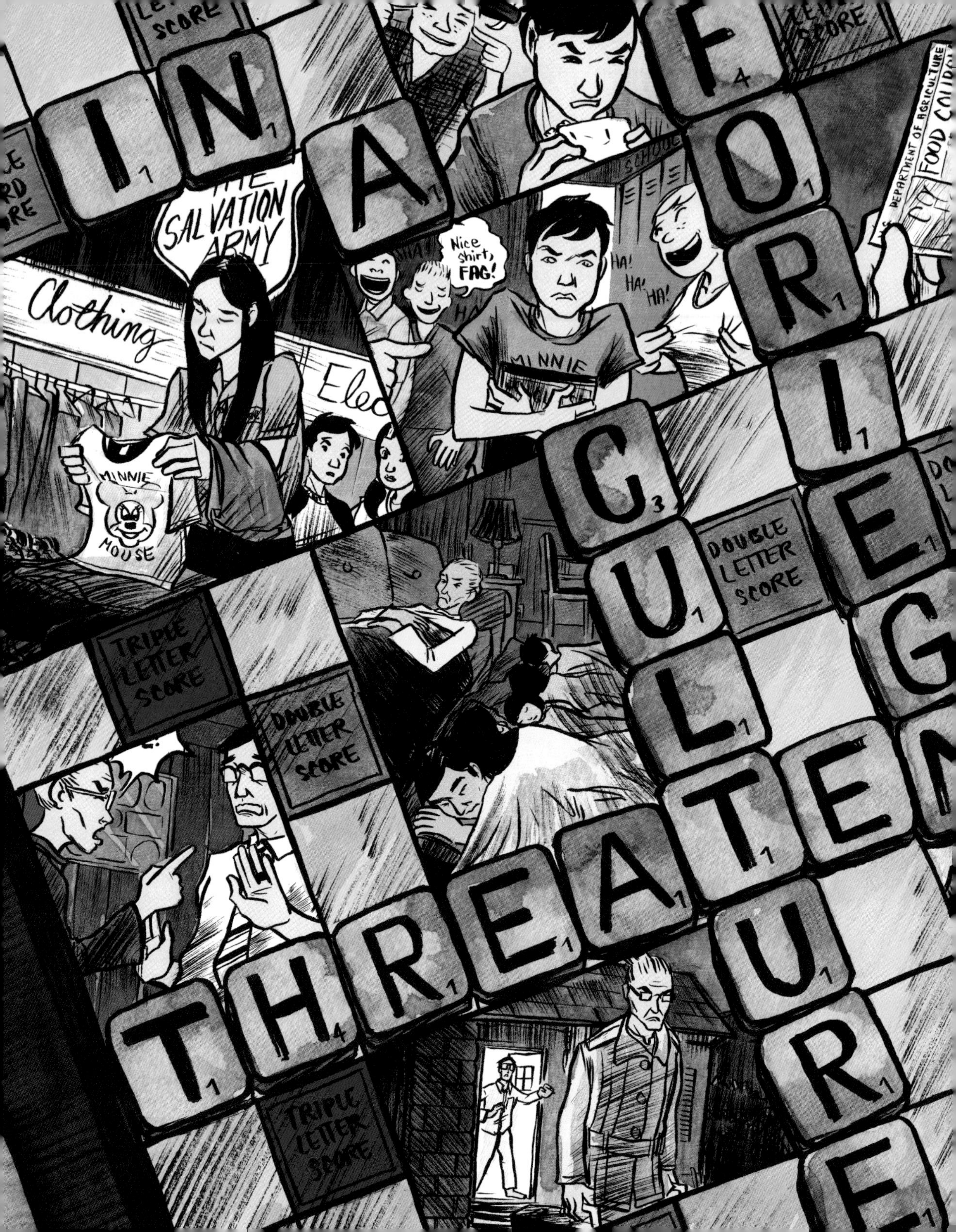
IN A FOREIGN CULTURE THREATE
SALVATION ARMY
Clothing
MINNIE MOUSE
Nice shirt, FAG!
HA! HA! HA!
MINNIE
DEPARTMENT OF AGRICULTURE
DOUBLE LETTER SCORE
TRIPLE LETTER SCORE
DOUBLE LETTER SCORE
TRIPLE LETTER SCORE

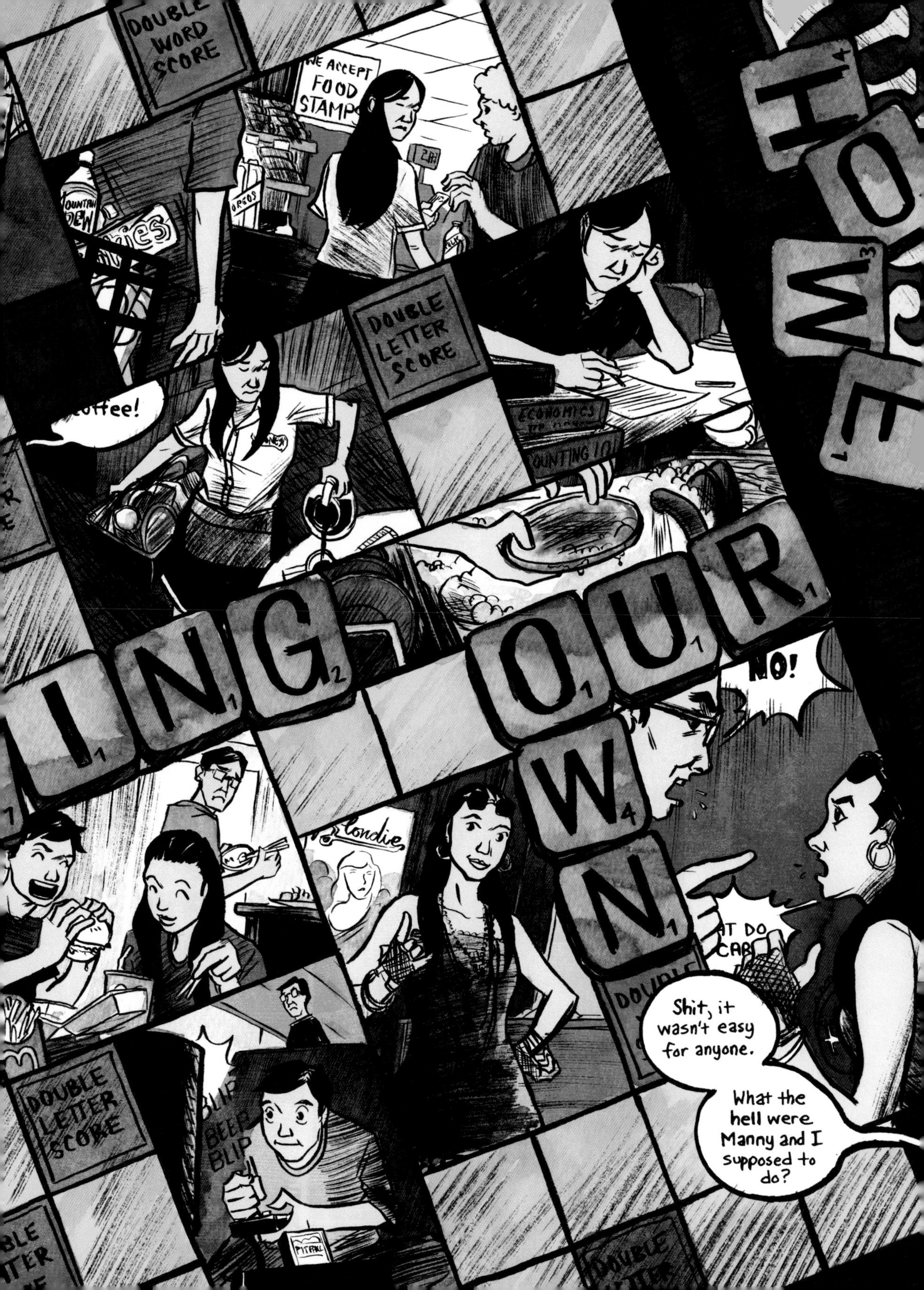
DOUBLE WORD SCORE
WE ACCEPT FOOD STAMPS
OREOS
DOUBLE LETTER SCORE
ECONOMICS
COUNTING 101
coffee!
HOWE
ING OUR OWN
NO!
AT DO CAR
Shit, it wasn't easy for anyone.
What the hell were Manny and I supposed to do?
DOUBLE LETTER SCORE
BLIP BEEP BLIP

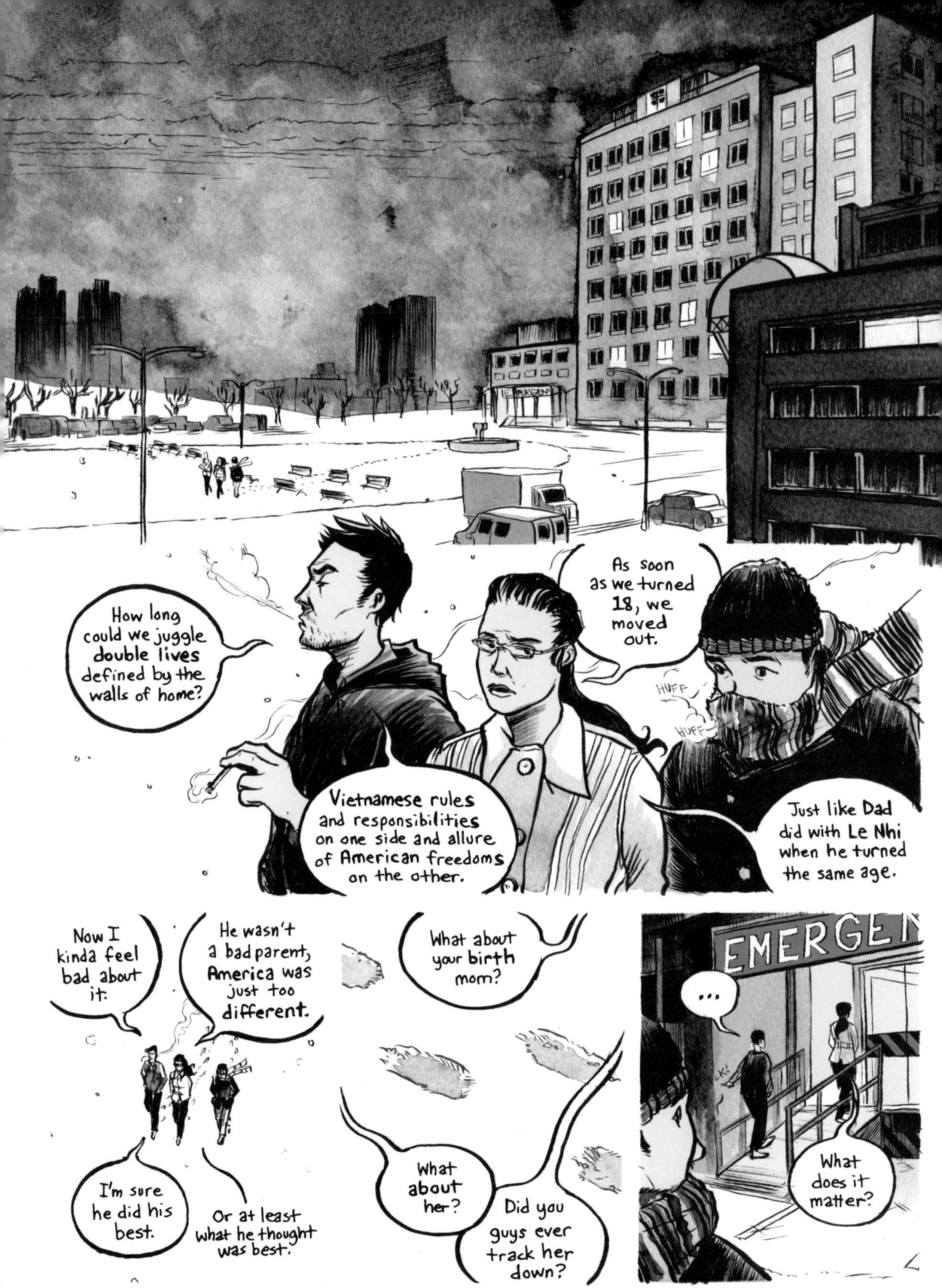

How long could we juggle double lives defined by the walls of home?
As soon as we turned 18, we moved out.
HUFF
HUFF
Vietnamese rules and responsibilities on one side and allure of American freedoms on the other.
Just like Dad did with Le Nhi when he turned the same age.
Now I kinda feel bad about it.
He wasn't a bad parent, America was just too different.
I'm sure he did his best.
Or at least what he thought was best.
What about your birth mom?
What about her?
Did you guys ever track her down?
EMERGEN
...
What does it matter?

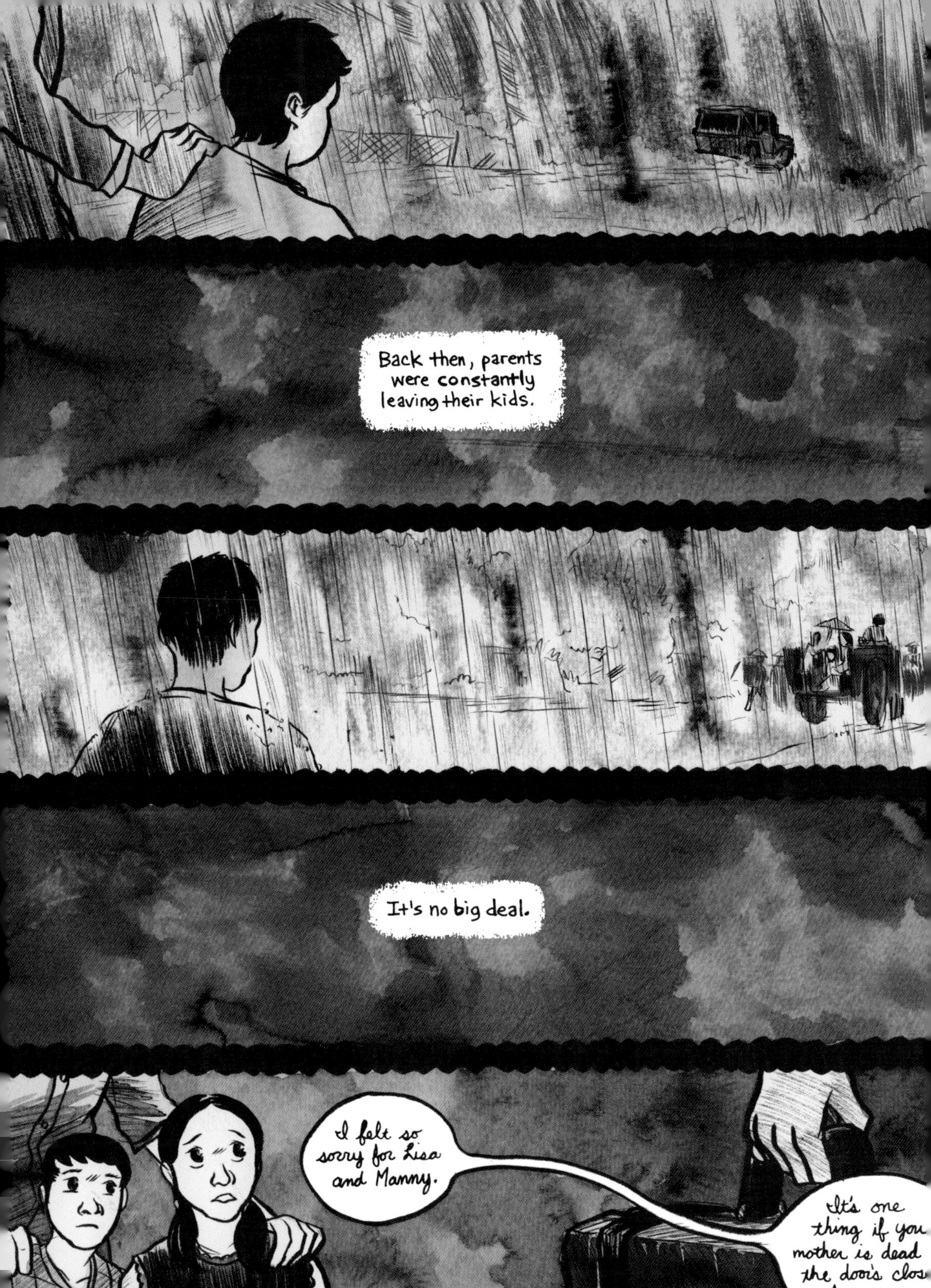
Back then, parents were constantly leaving their kids.
It's no big deal.
I felt so sorry for Lisa and Manny.
It's one thing if you mother is dead the door's clos

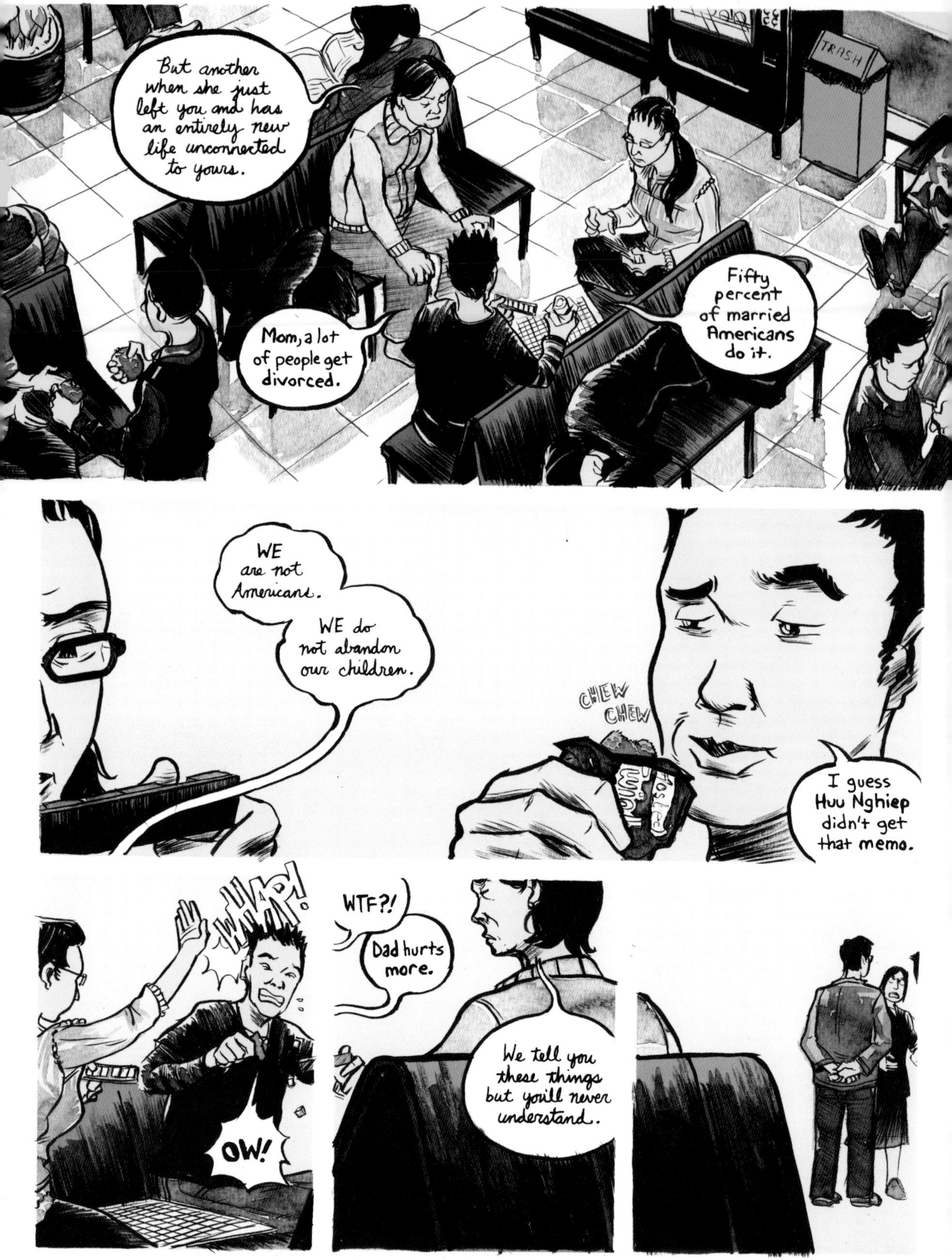
TRASH
But another when she just left you and has an entirely new life unconnected to yours.
Mom, a lot of people get divorced.
Fifty percent of married Americans do it.
WE are not Americans.
WE do not abandon our children.
CHEW CHEW
I guess Huu Nghiep didn't get that memo.
WHAP!
OW!
WTF?!
Dad hurts more.
We tell you these things but you'll never understand.

Mom and Dad fled Vietnam to keep our family together.

But I doubt they ever imagined things turning out the way they have in America.

Sons and daughters, brothers and sisters, customs and shared history lost within the span of a single generation.

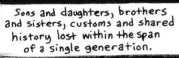

A sterile hospital deathbed the unlikely place for our reunion.

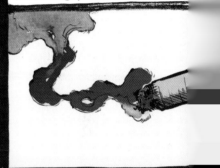

Tri It's time.

Do you want us to go with you?

NO.

JUST HER CHILDREN.

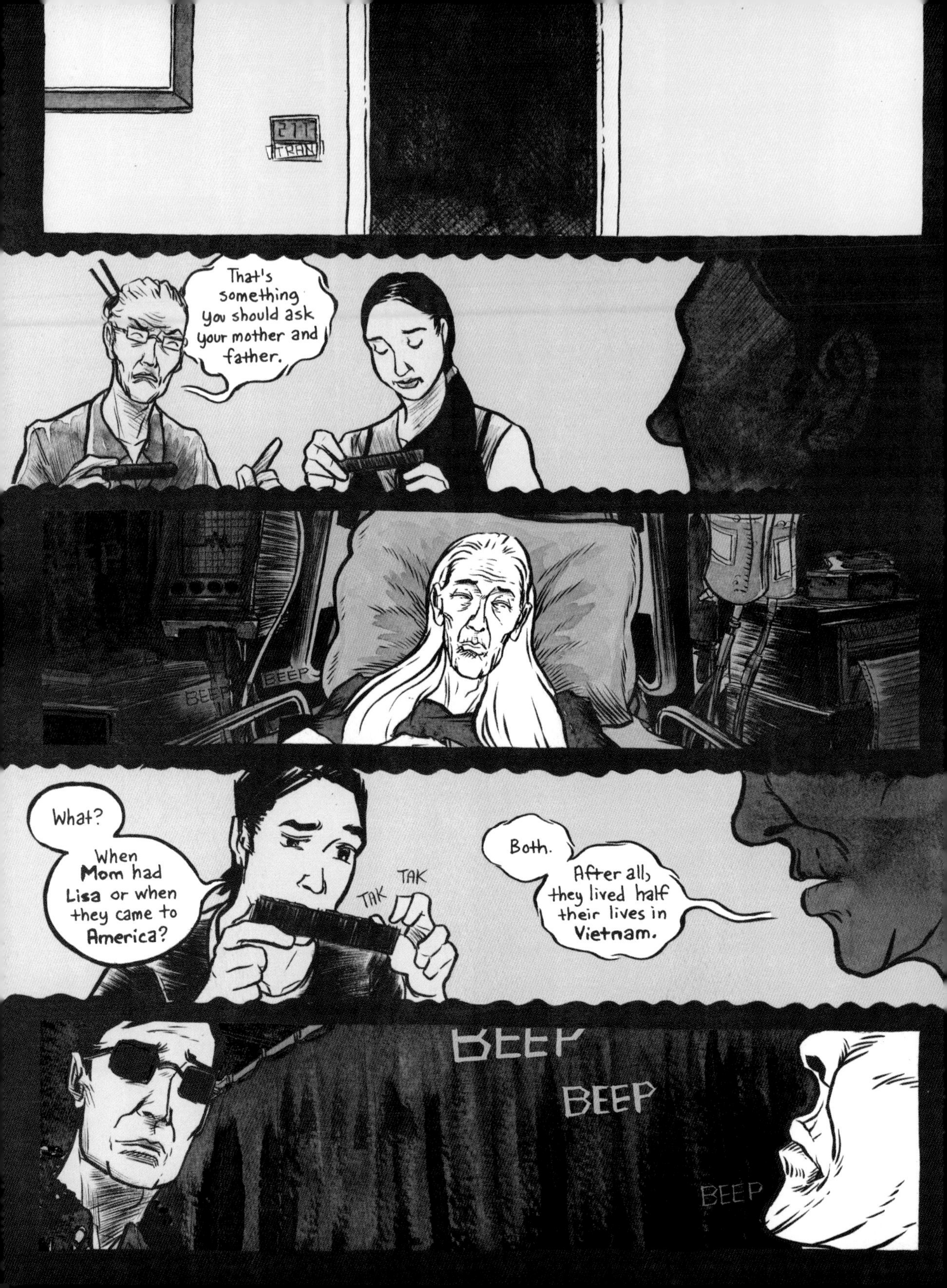

27
TRAN
That's something you should ask your mother and father.
BEEP
BEEP
What?
When Mom had Lisa or when they came to America?
TAK
TAK
Both.
After all, they lived half their lives in Vietnam.
BEEP
BEEP
BEEP

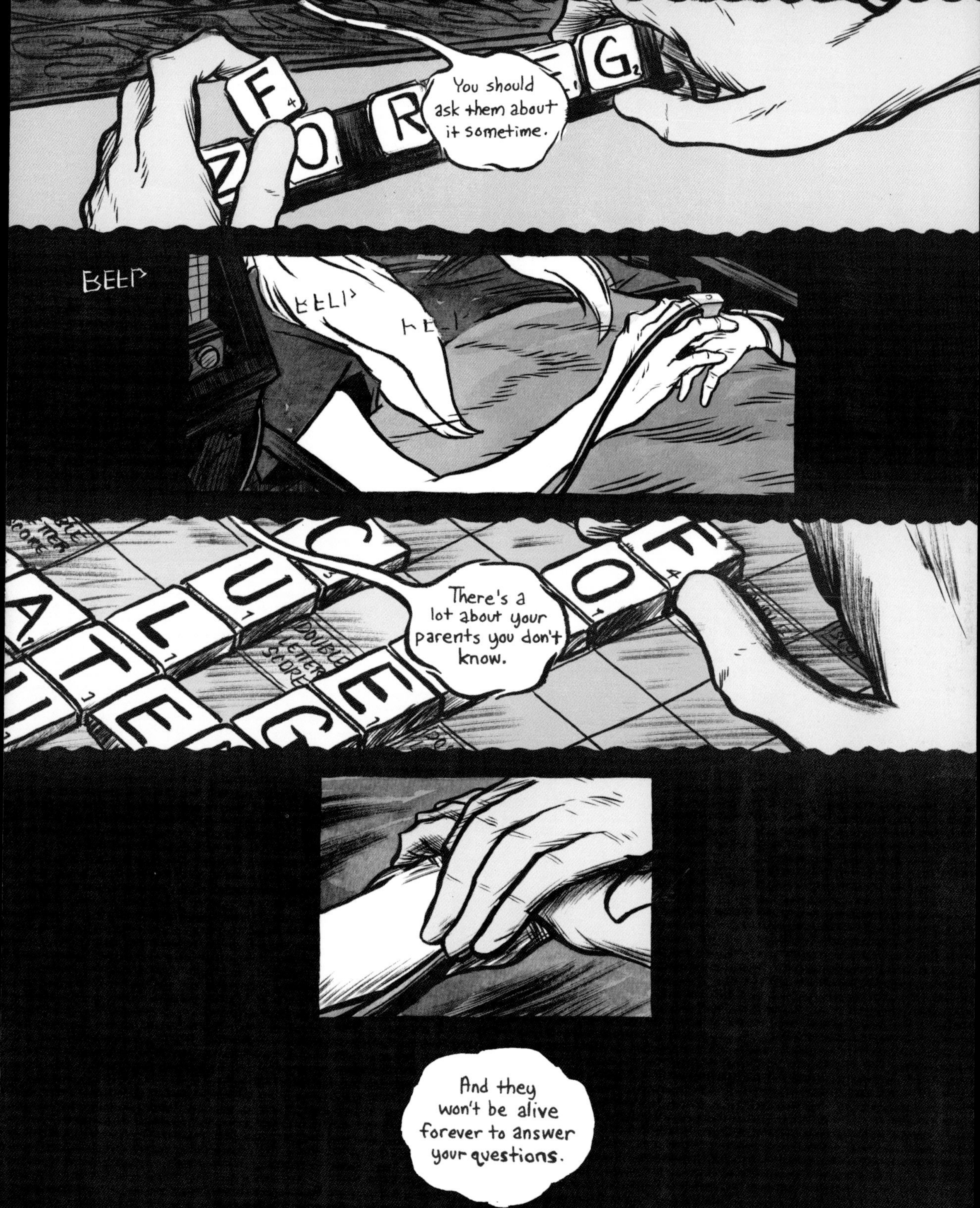
You should ask them about it sometime.
BEEP
There's a lot about your parents you don't know.
And they won't be alive forever to answer your questions.

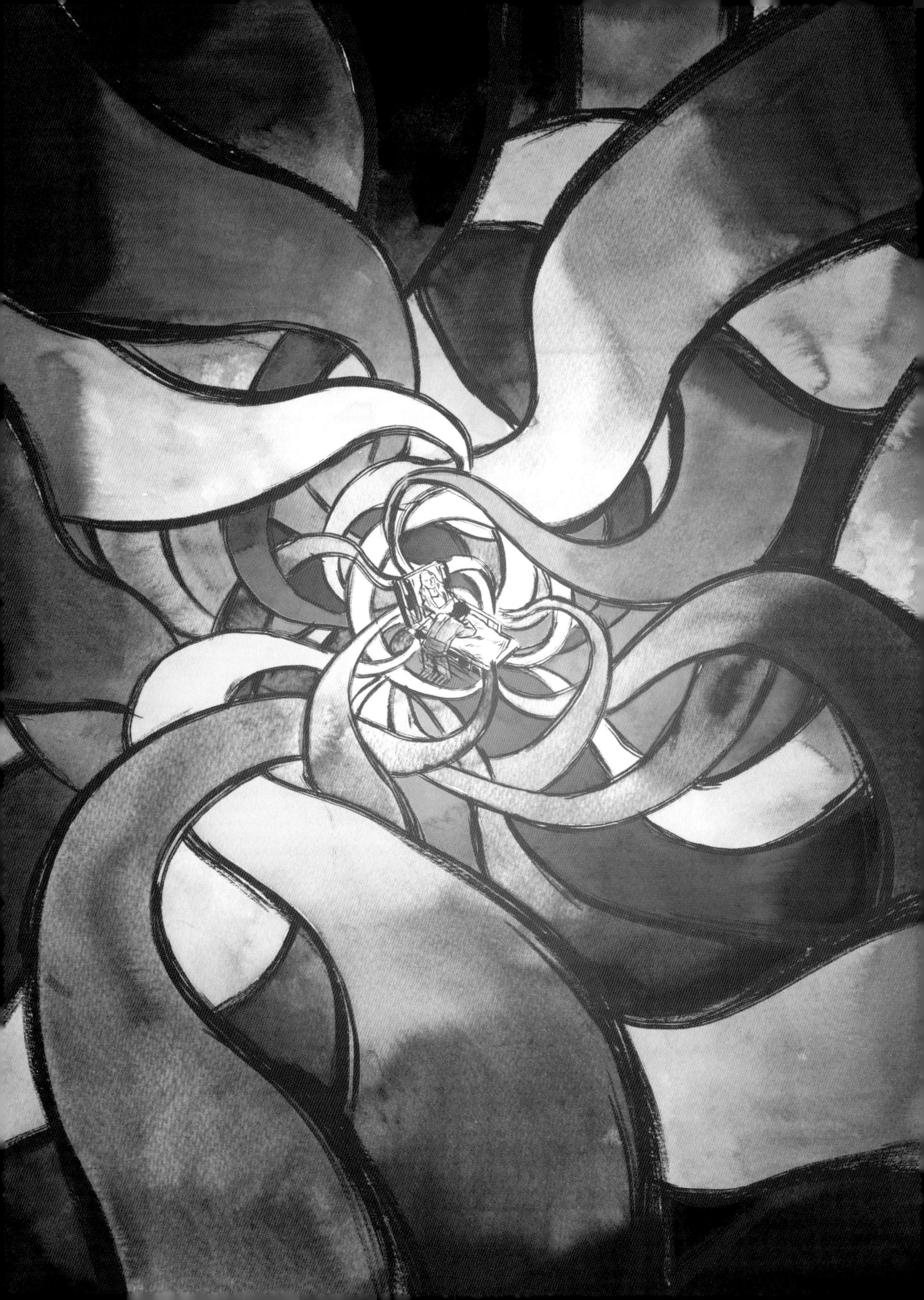

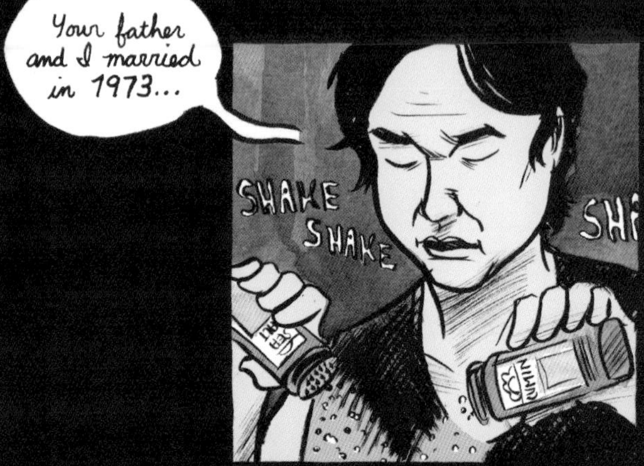
Your father and I married in 1973...
SHAKE
SHAKE

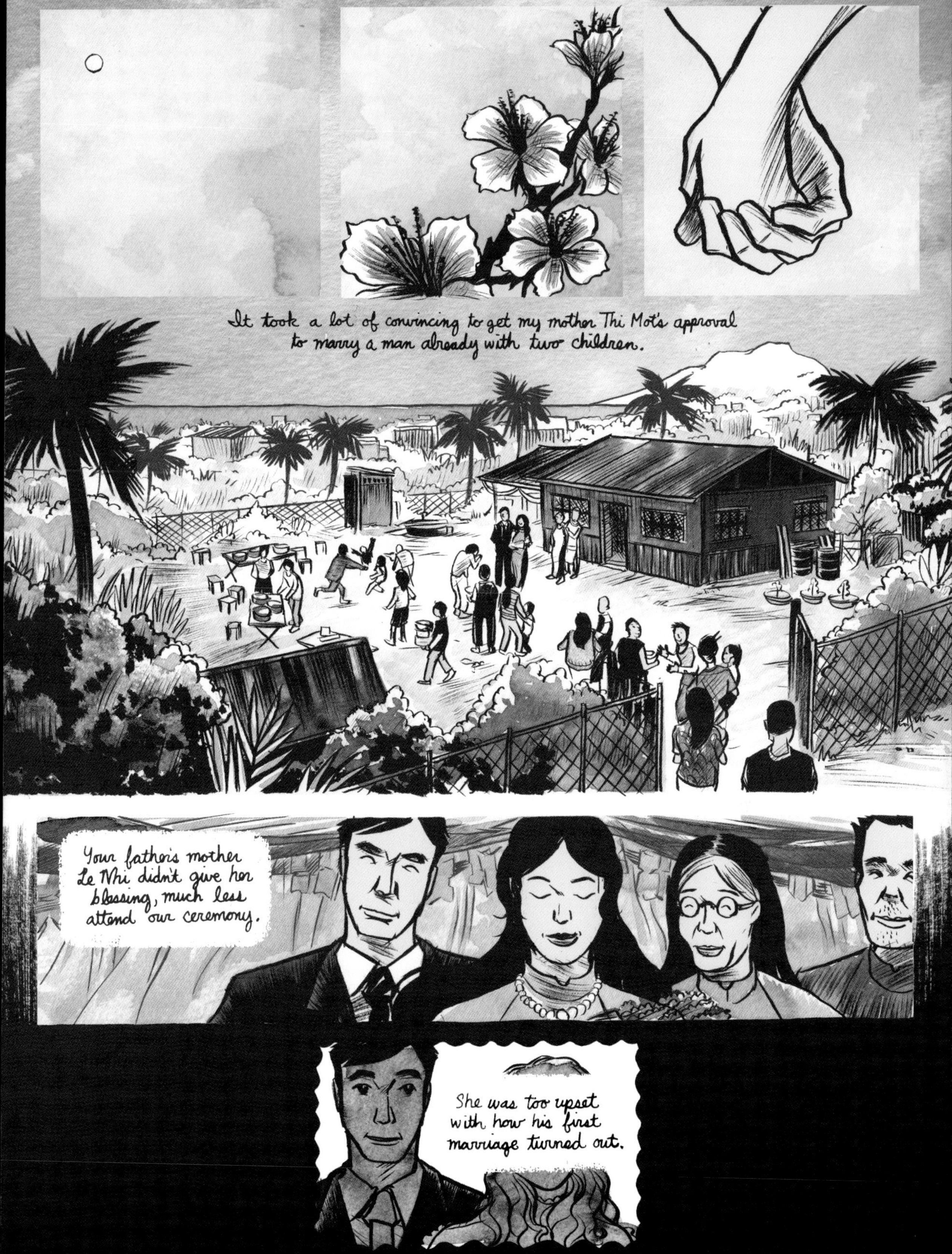
It took a lot of convincing to get my mother Thi Mot's approval to marry a man already with two children.
Your father's mother Le Nhi didn't give her blessing, much less attend our ceremony.
She was too upset with how his first marriage turned out.

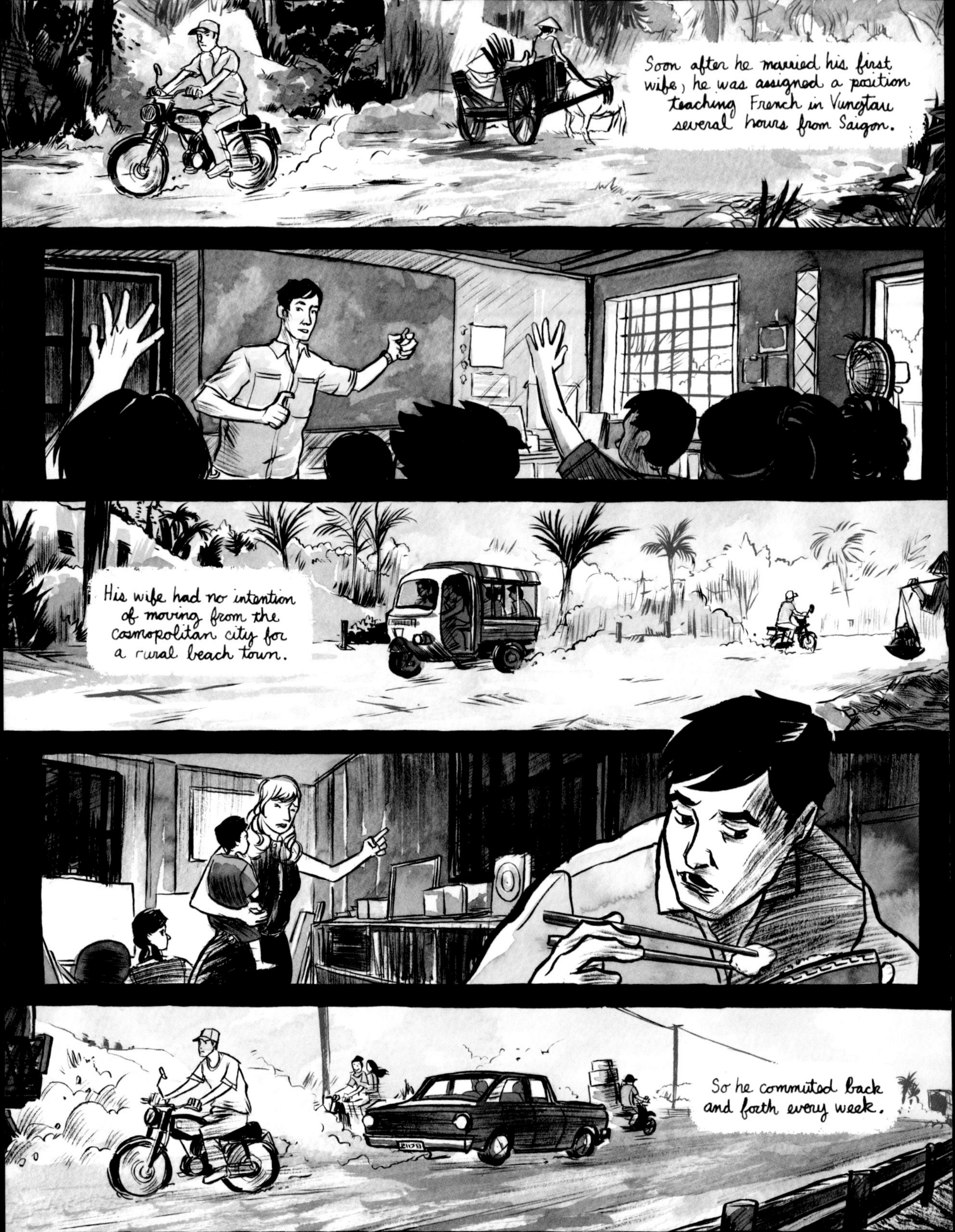
Soon after he married his first wife, he was assigned a position teaching French in Vungtau several hours from Saigon.
His wife had no intention of moving from the cosmopolitan city for a rural beach town.
So he commuted back and forth every week.

Whenever he was home, she'd go out with her friends leaving him with Lisa and Manny.

Instead, Do and his wife babysat him.

Your father and his wife were both too stubborn to adapt to each other.

She was a typical Frenchwoman and he a typical Vietnamese man.

She didn't have enough patience to understand your father's actions.

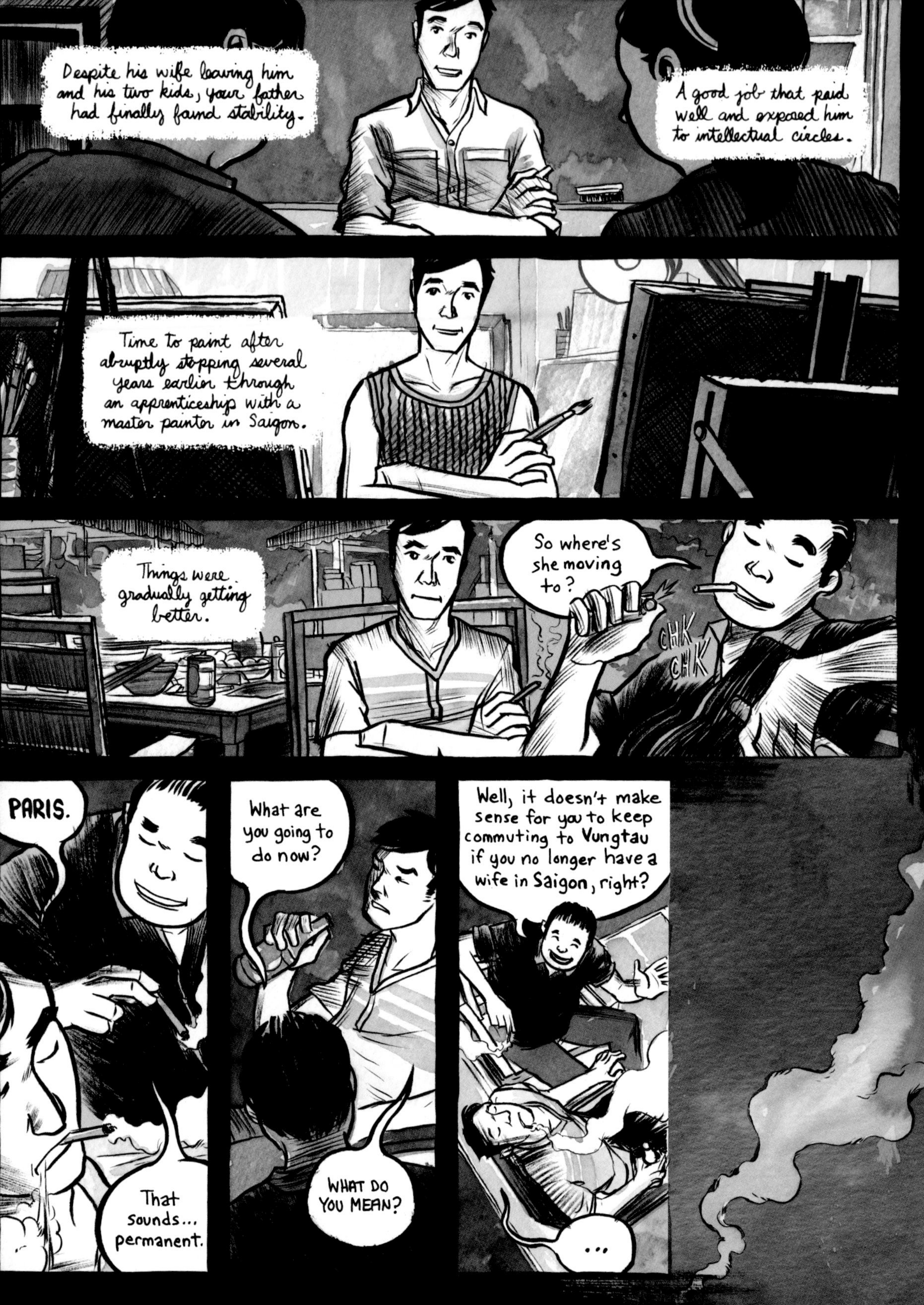

Despite his wife leaving him and his two kids, your father had finally found stability.
A good job that paid well and exposed him to intellectual circles.
Time to paint after abruptly stopping several years earlier through an apprenticeship with a master painter in Saigon.
Things were gradually getting better.
So where's she moving to?
CHK CHK
PARIS.
That sounds... permanent.
What are you going to do now?
WHAT DO YOU MEAN?
Well, it doesn't make sense for you to keep commuting to Vungtau if you no longer have a wife in Saigon, right?
...

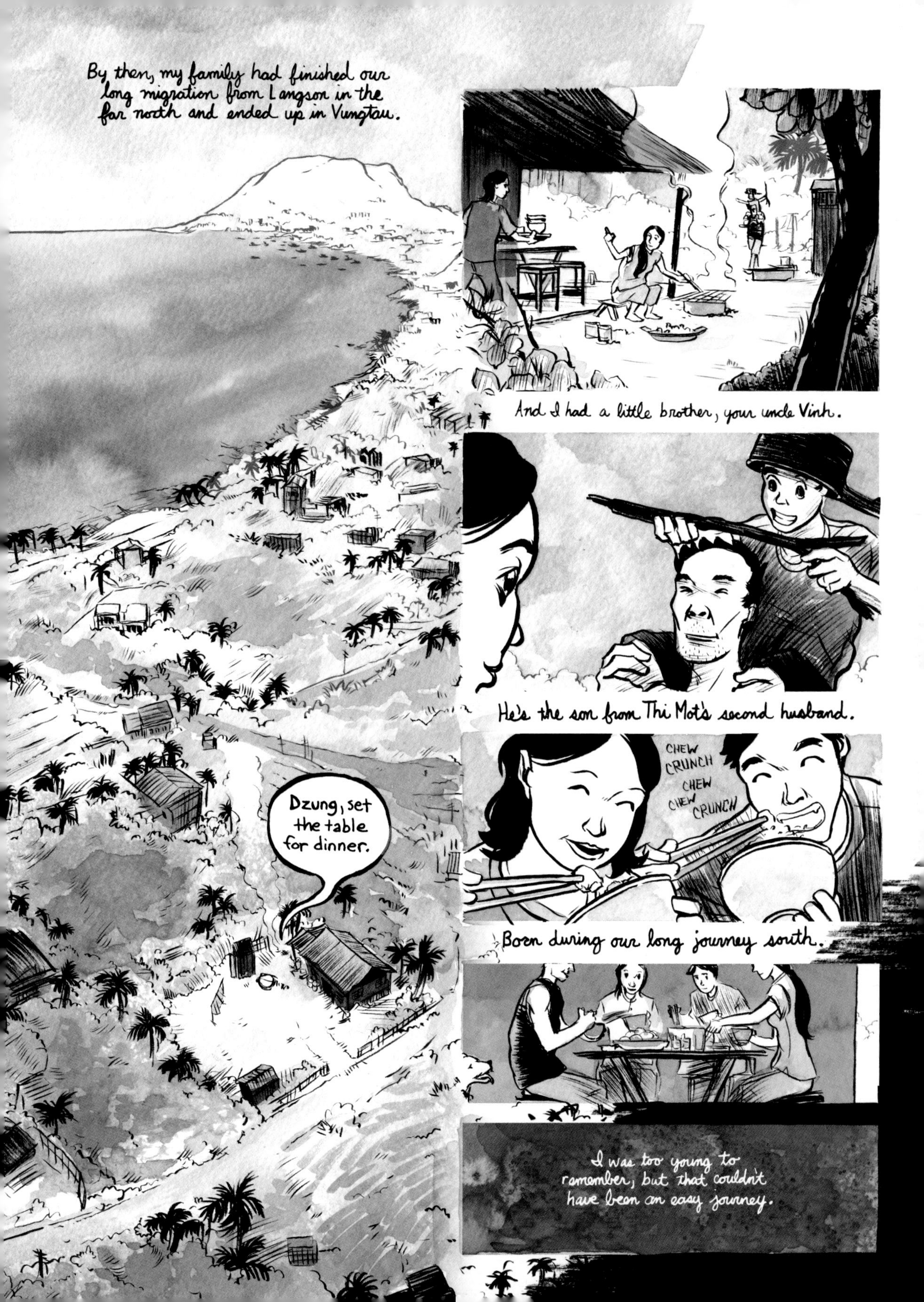
By then, my family had finished our long migration from Langson in the far north and ended up in Vungtau.
Dzung, set the table for dinner.
And I had a little brother, your uncle Vinh.
He's the son from Thi Mot's second husband.
CHEW
CRUNCH
CHEW
CHEW
CRUNCH
Born during our long journey south.
I was too young to remember, but that couldn't have been an easy journey.

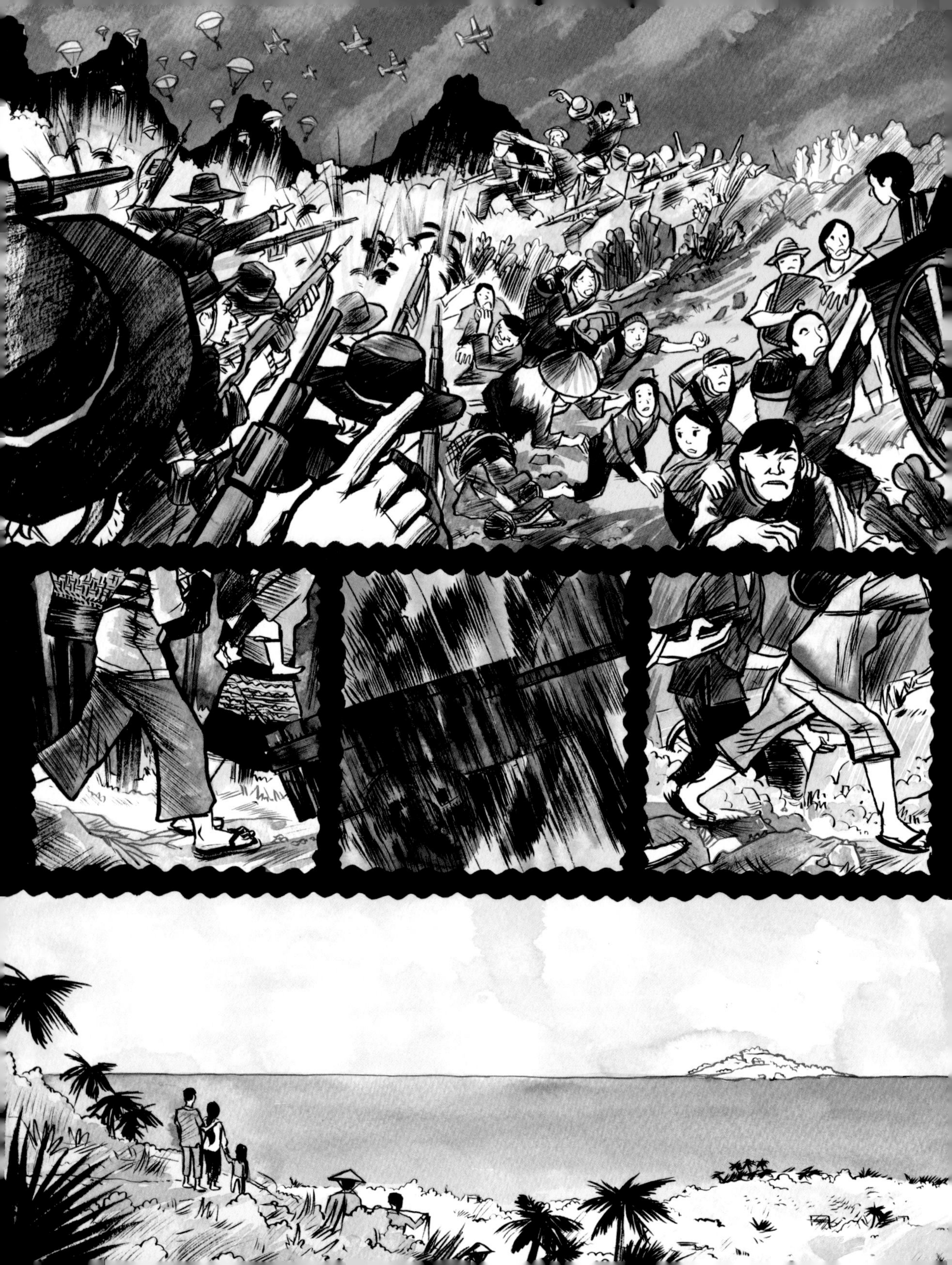

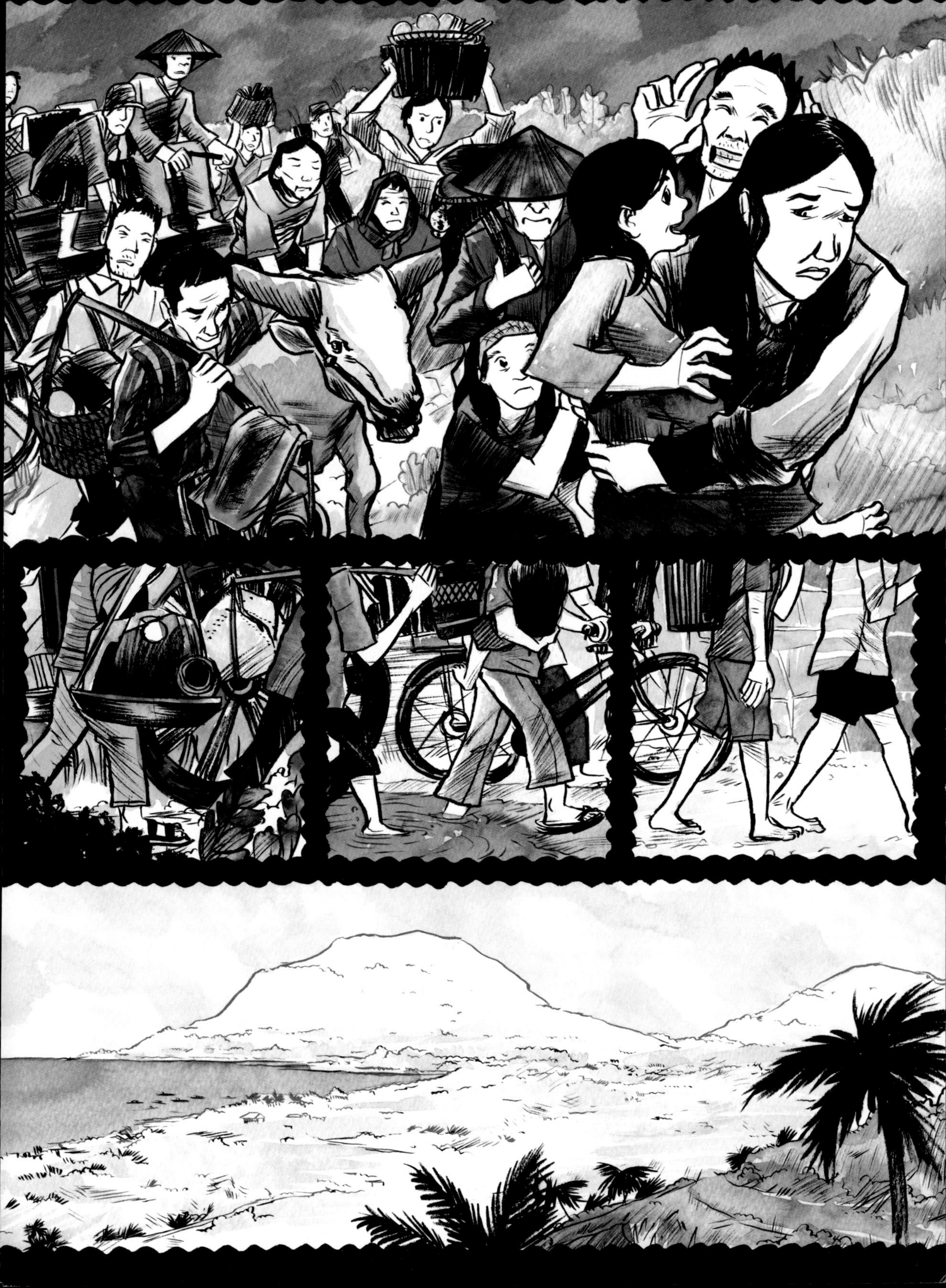

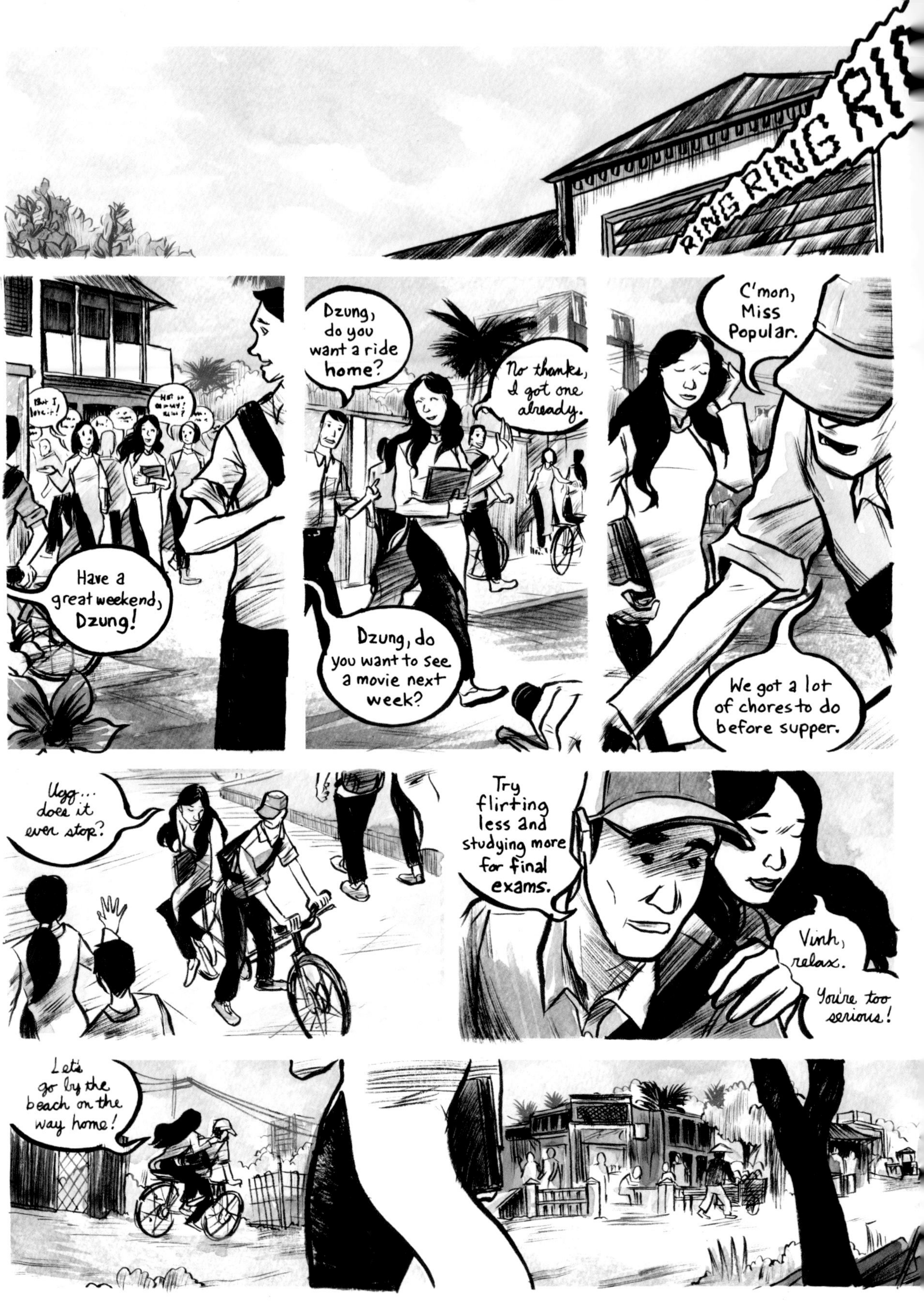
RING RING RI
Have a great weekend, Dzung!
Dzung, do you want a ride home?
No thanks, I got one already.
Dzung, do you want to see a movie next week?
C'mon, Miss Popular.
We got a lot of chores to do before supper.
Ugg... does it ever stop?
Try flirting less and studying more for final exams.
Vinh, relax.
You're too serious!
Let's go by the beach on the way home!

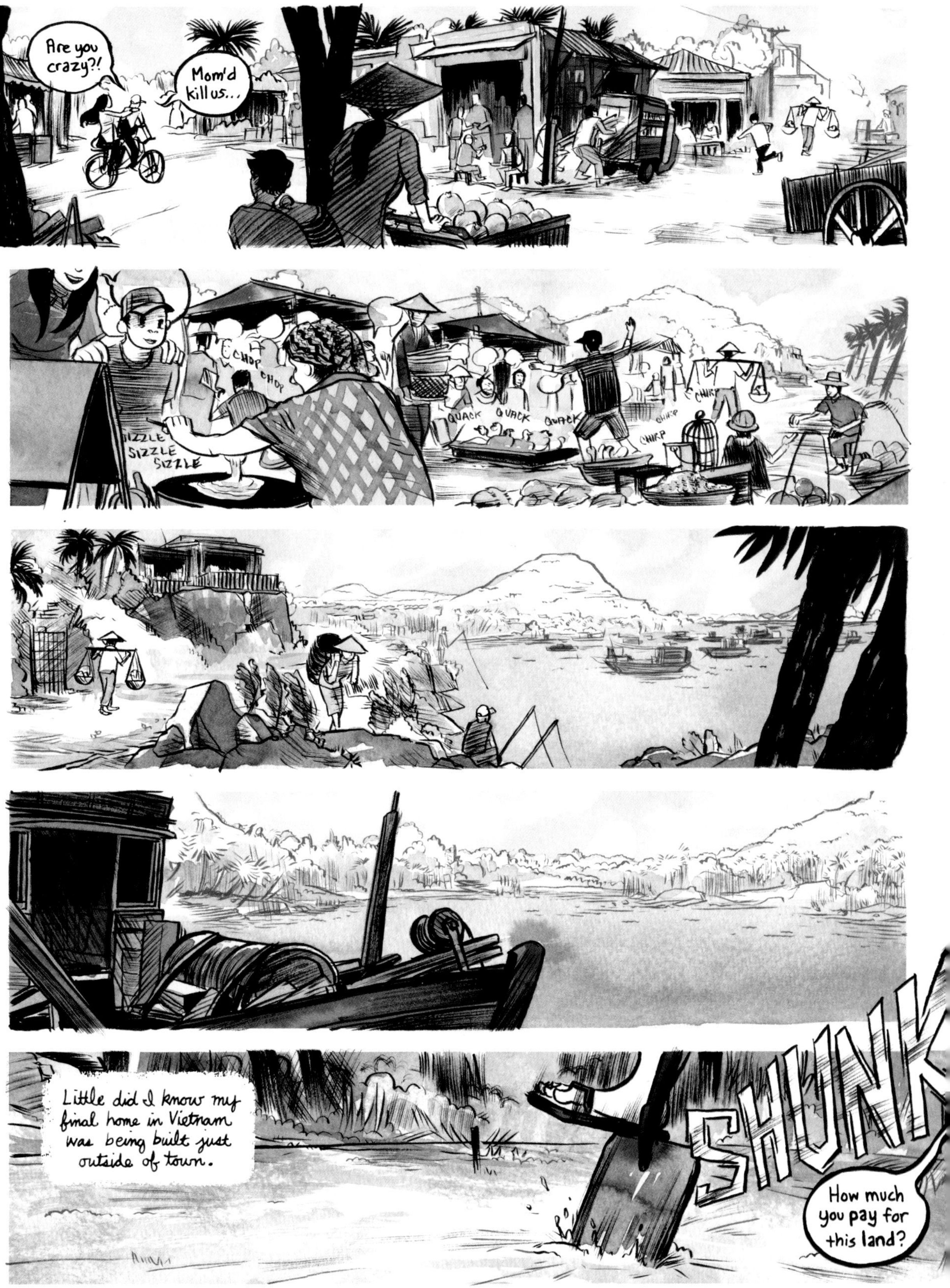
Are you crazy?!
Mom'd kill us...
CHOP CHOP
SIZZLE SIZZLE SIZZLE
QUACK QUACK QUACK
CHIRP
CHIRP
Little did I know my final home in Vietnam was being built just outside of town.
SHUNK
How much you pay for this land?

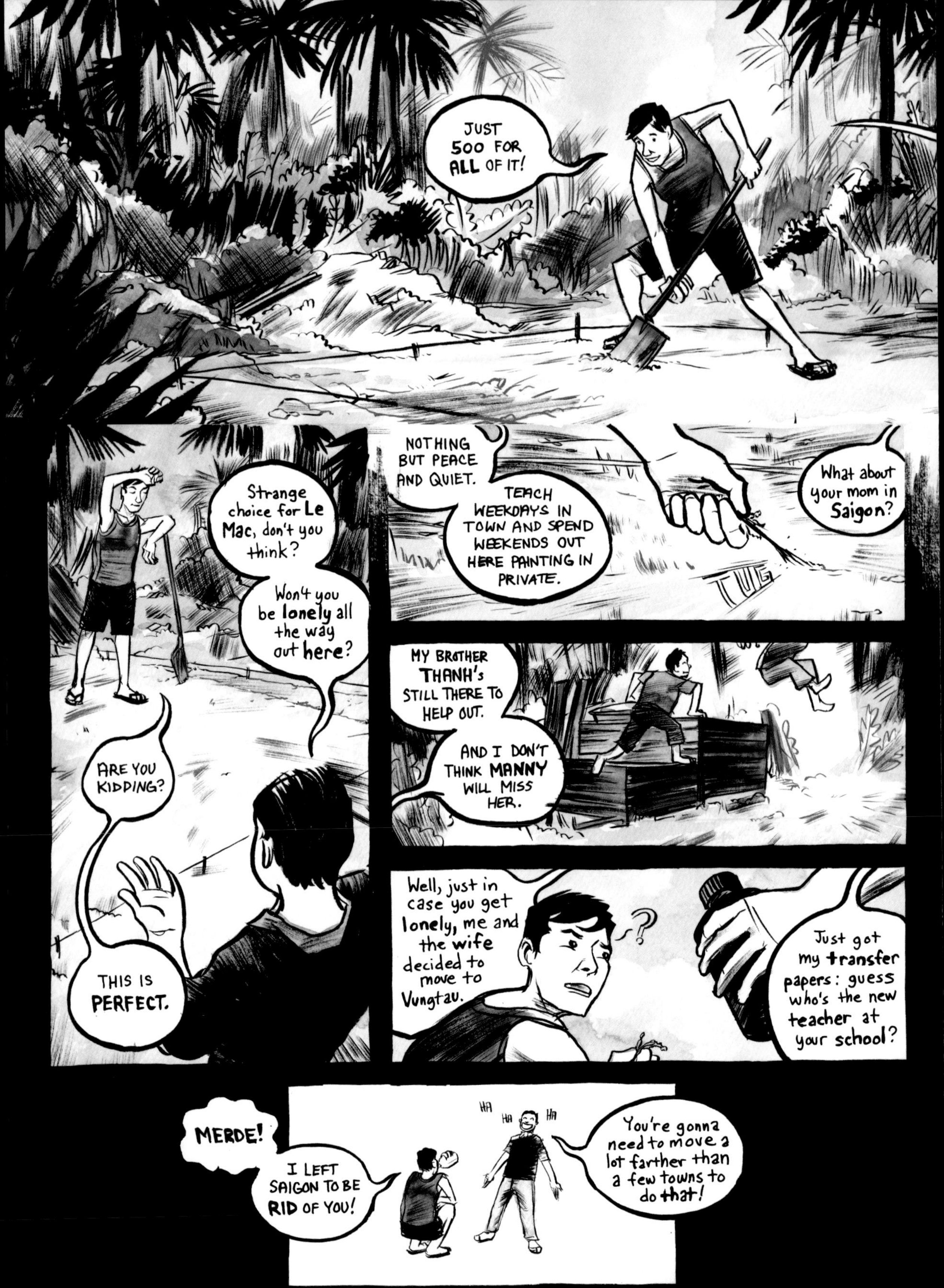

JUST 500 FOR ALL OF IT!
Strange choice for Le Mac, don't you think?
Won't you be lonely all the way out here?
ARE YOU KIDDING?
THIS IS PERFECT.
NOTHING BUT PEACE AND QUIET.
TEACH WEEKDAYS IN TOWN AND SPEND WEEKENDS OUT HERE PAINTING IN PRIVATE.
What about your mom in Saigon?
MY BROTHER THANH's STILL THERE TO HELP OUT.
AND I DON'T THINK MANNY WILL MISS HER.
Well, just in case you get lonely, me and the wife decided to move to Vungtau.
?
Just got my transfer papers: guess who's the new teacher at your school?
MERDE!
I LEFT SAIGON TO BE RID OF YOU!
HA HA HA
You're gonna need to move a lot farther than a few towns to do that!

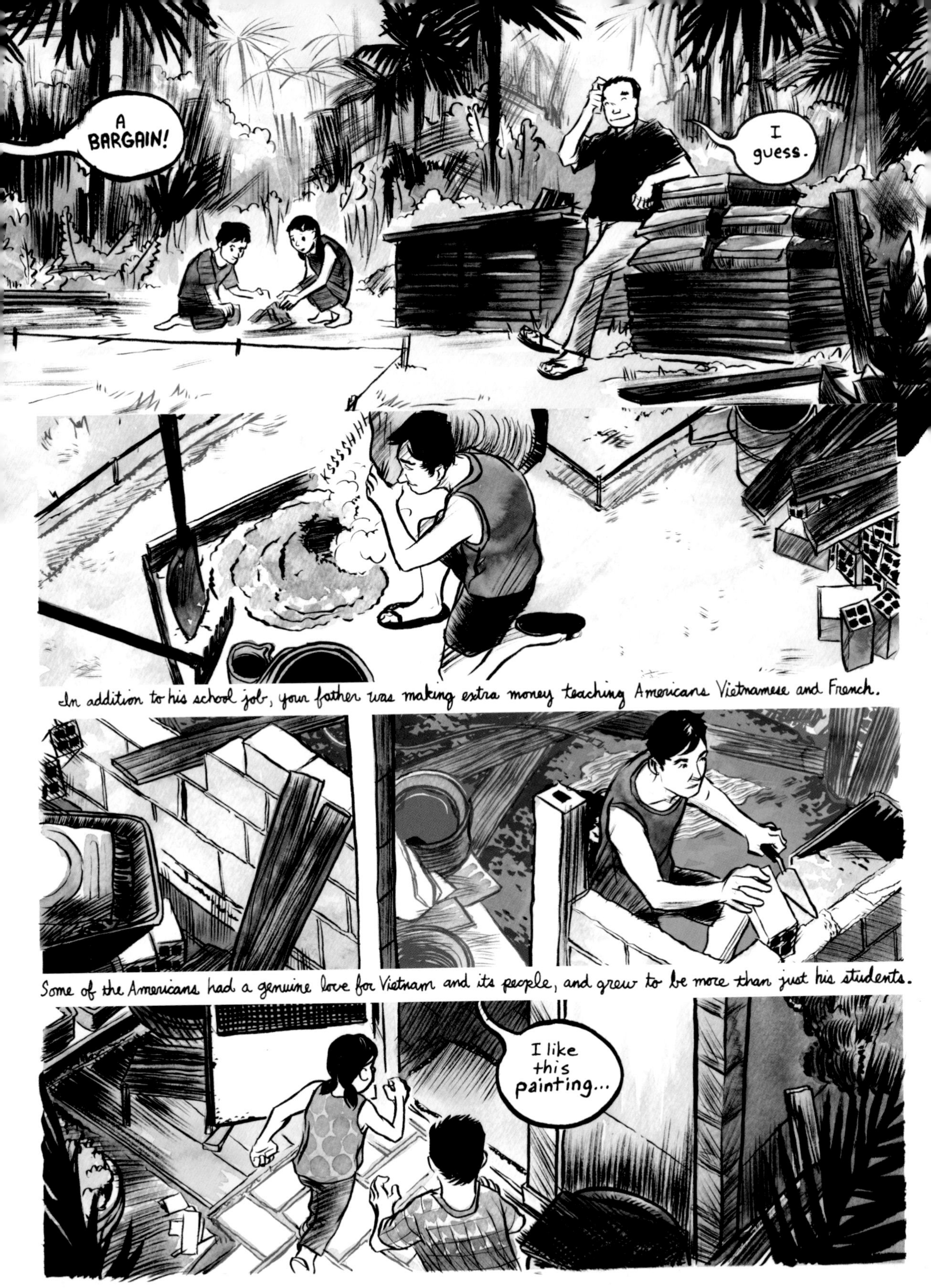
A BARGAIN!
I guess.
KSSSSHH
In addition to his school job, your father was making extra money teaching Americans Vietnamese and French.
Some of the Americans had a genuine love for Vietnam and its people, and grew to be more than just his students.
I like this painting...

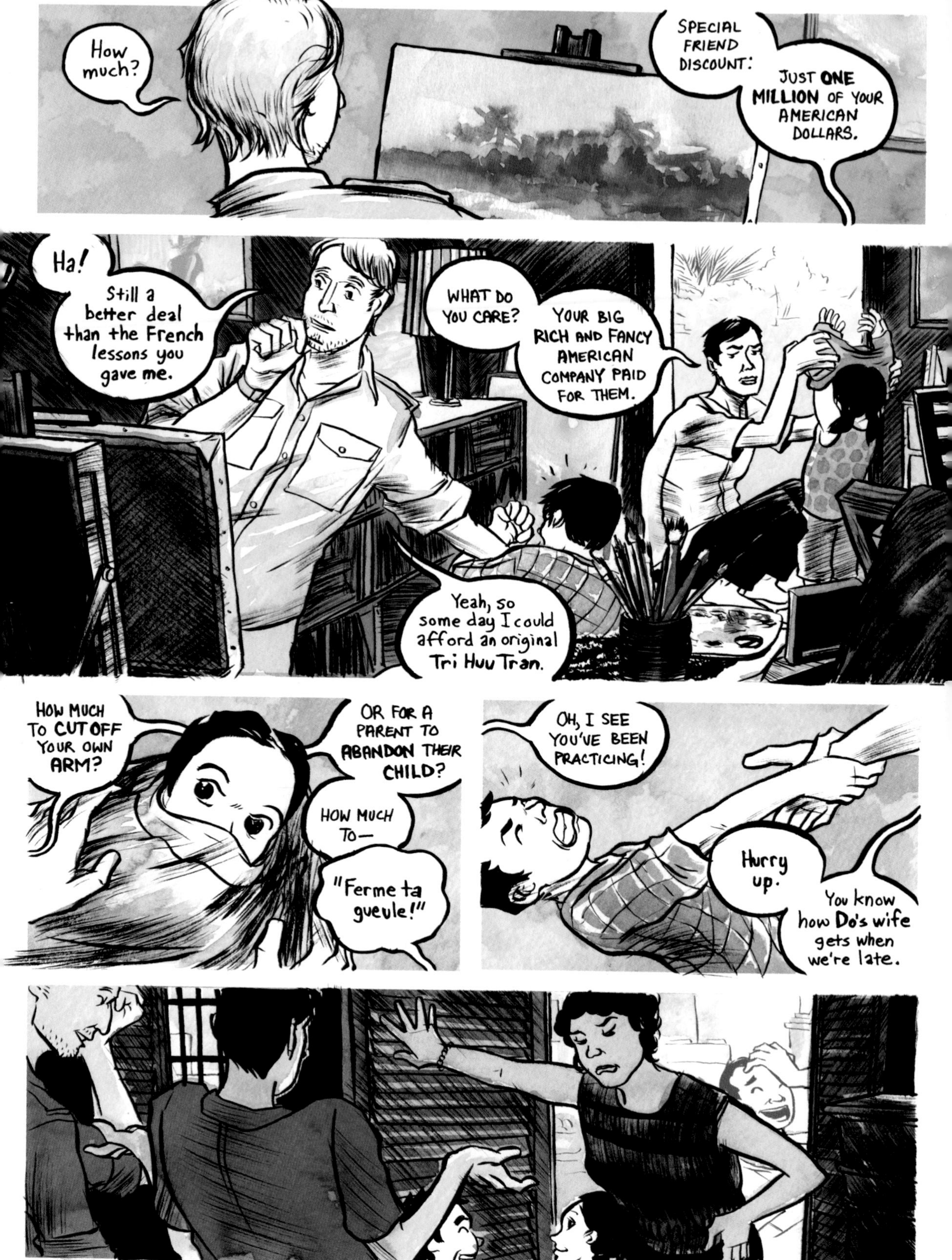
How much?
SPECIAL FRIEND DISCOUNT:
JUST ONE MILLION OF YOUR AMERICAN DOLLARS.
Ha!
Still a better deal than the French lessons you gave me.
WHAT DO YOU CARE?
YOUR BIG RICH AND FANCY AMERICAN COMPANY PAID FOR THEM.
Yeah, so some day I could afford an original Tri Huu Tran.
HOW MUCH TO CUT OFF YOUR OWN ARM?
OR FOR A PARENT TO ABANDON THEIR CHILD?
HOW MUCH TO—
"Ferme ta gueule!"
OH, I SEE YOU'VE BEEN PRACTICING!
Hurry up.
You know how Do's wife gets when we're late.

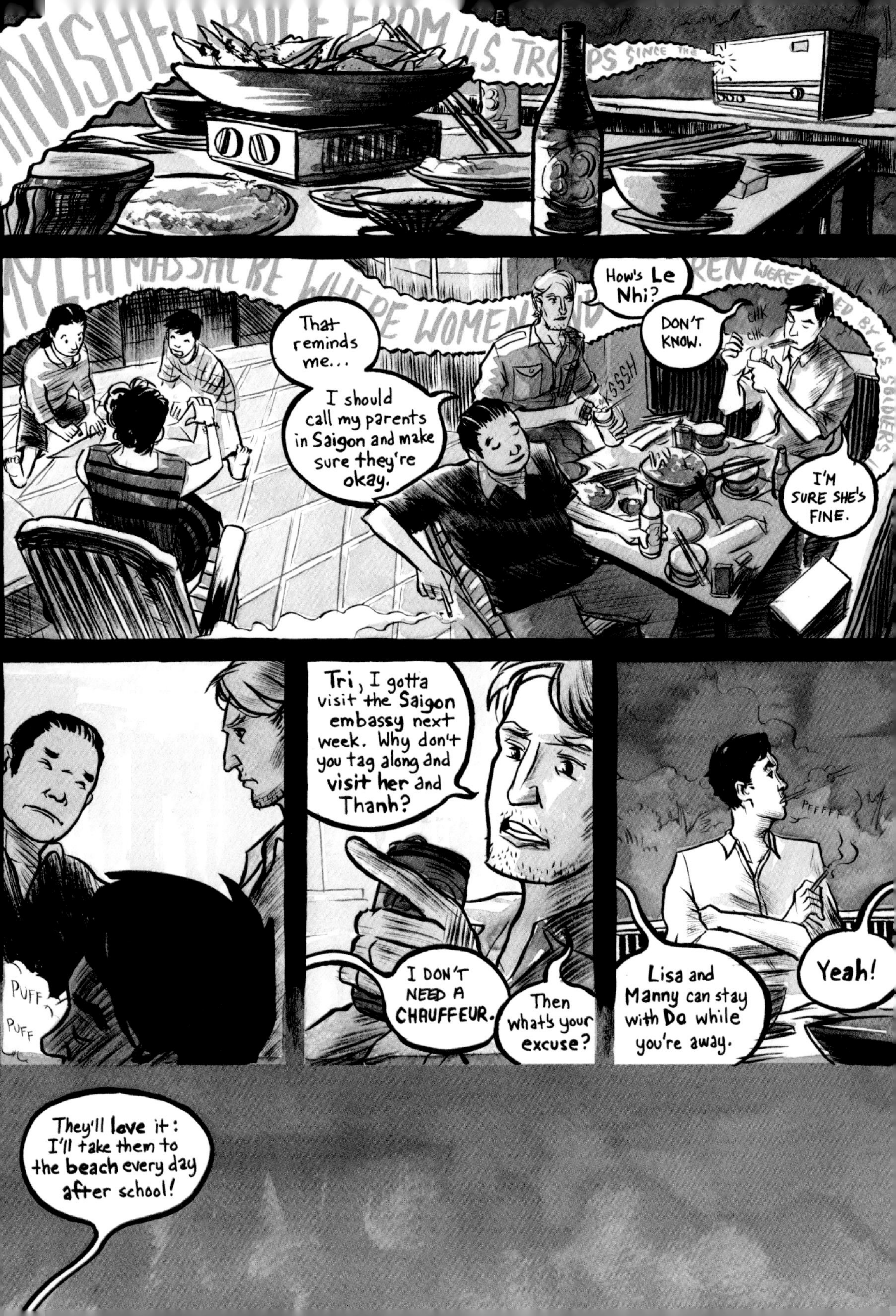
U.S. TROOPS SINCE THE
WOMEN
WERE
BY U.S. SOLDIERS
That reminds me...
I should call my parents in Saigon and make sure they're okay.
How's Le Nhi?
DON'T KNOW.
CHK
CHK
KSSSH
I'M SURE SHE'S FINE.
PUFF
PUFF
Tri, I gotta visit the Saigon embassy next week. Why don't you tag along and visit her and Thanh?
I DON'T NEED A CHAUFFEUR.
Then what's your excuse?
PFFFFF
Lisa and Manny can stay with Do while you're away.
Yeah!
They'll love it: I'll take them to the beach every day after school!

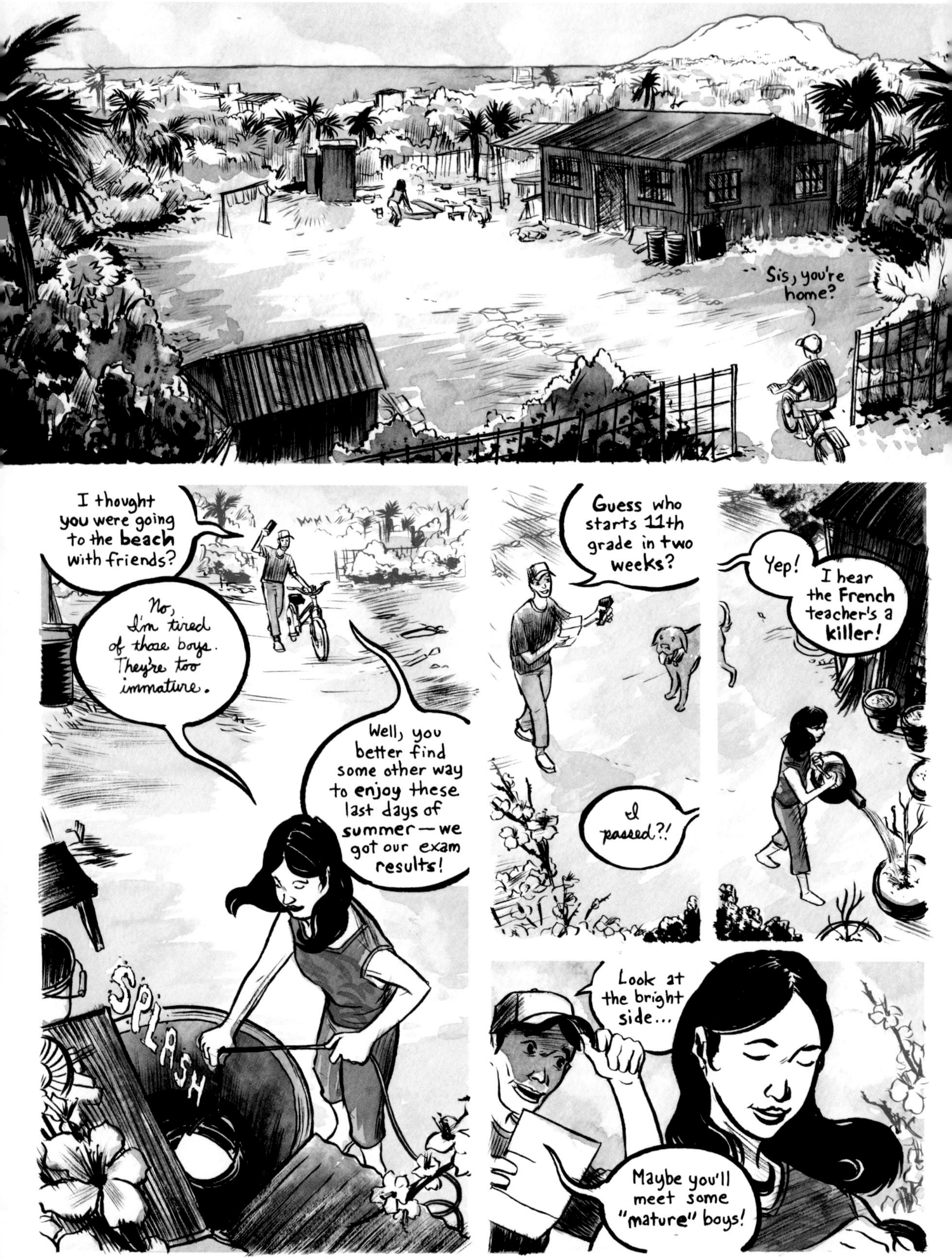

Sis, you're home?
I thought you were going to the beach with friends?
No, I'm tired of those boys. They're too immature.
Well, you better find some other way to enjoy these last days of summer—we got our exam results!
SPLASH
Guess who starts 11th grade in two weeks?
I passed?!
Yep!
I hear the French teacher's a killer!
Look at the bright side...
Maybe you'll meet some "mature" boys!

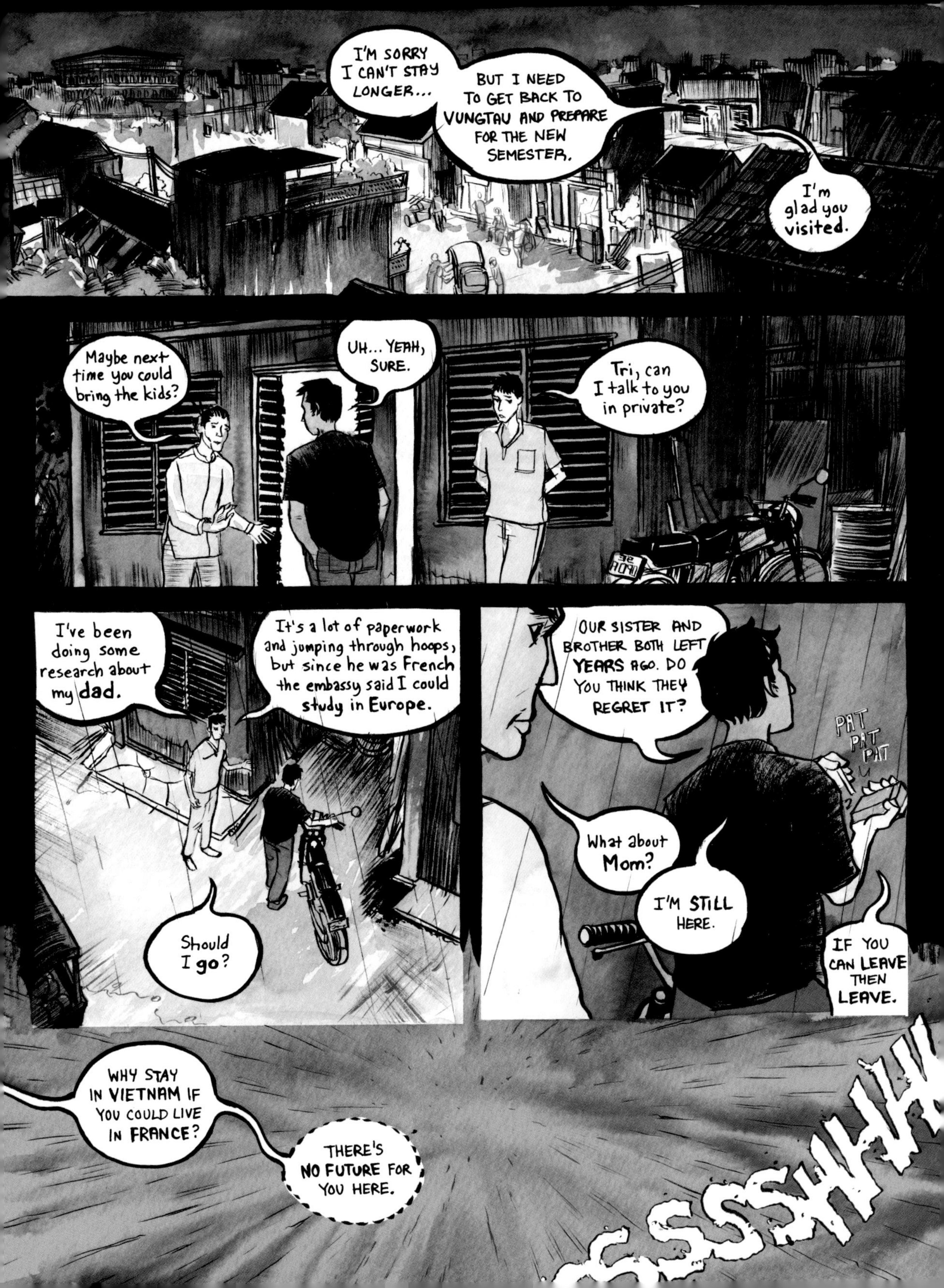
I'M SORRY I CAN'T STAY LONGER...
BUT I NEED TO GET BACK TO VUNGTAU AND PREPARE FOR THE NEW SEMESTER.
I'm glad you visited.
Maybe next time you could bring the kids?
UH... YEAH, SURE.
Tri, can I talk to you in private?
I've been doing some research about my dad.
It's a lot of paperwork and jumping through hoops, but since he was French the embassy said I could study in Europe.
Should I go?
OUR SISTER AND BROTHER BOTH LEFT YEARS AGO. DO YOU THINK THEY REGRET IT?
PAT PAT PAT
What about Mom?
I'M STILL HERE.
IF YOU CAN LEAVE THEN LEAVE.
WHY STAY IN VIETNAM IF YOU COULD LIVE IN FRANCE?
THERE'S NO FUTURE FOR YOU HERE.
SSSSHHHH

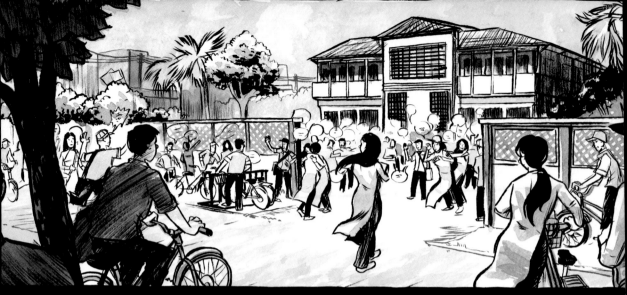

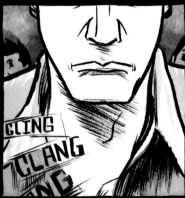

CLING
CLANG
You know what students nicknamed your father?
CLANG
CLING
CLANG
CLING
The WARDEN.
CLING
CLANG
CLING
He carried so many keys everywhere, but none of them locked any doors.
It was just his way of warning us, "I'm coming so if you're screwing around, knock it off!"

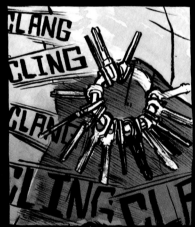

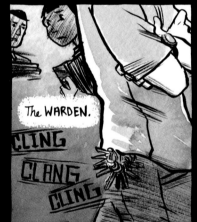

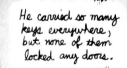

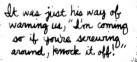

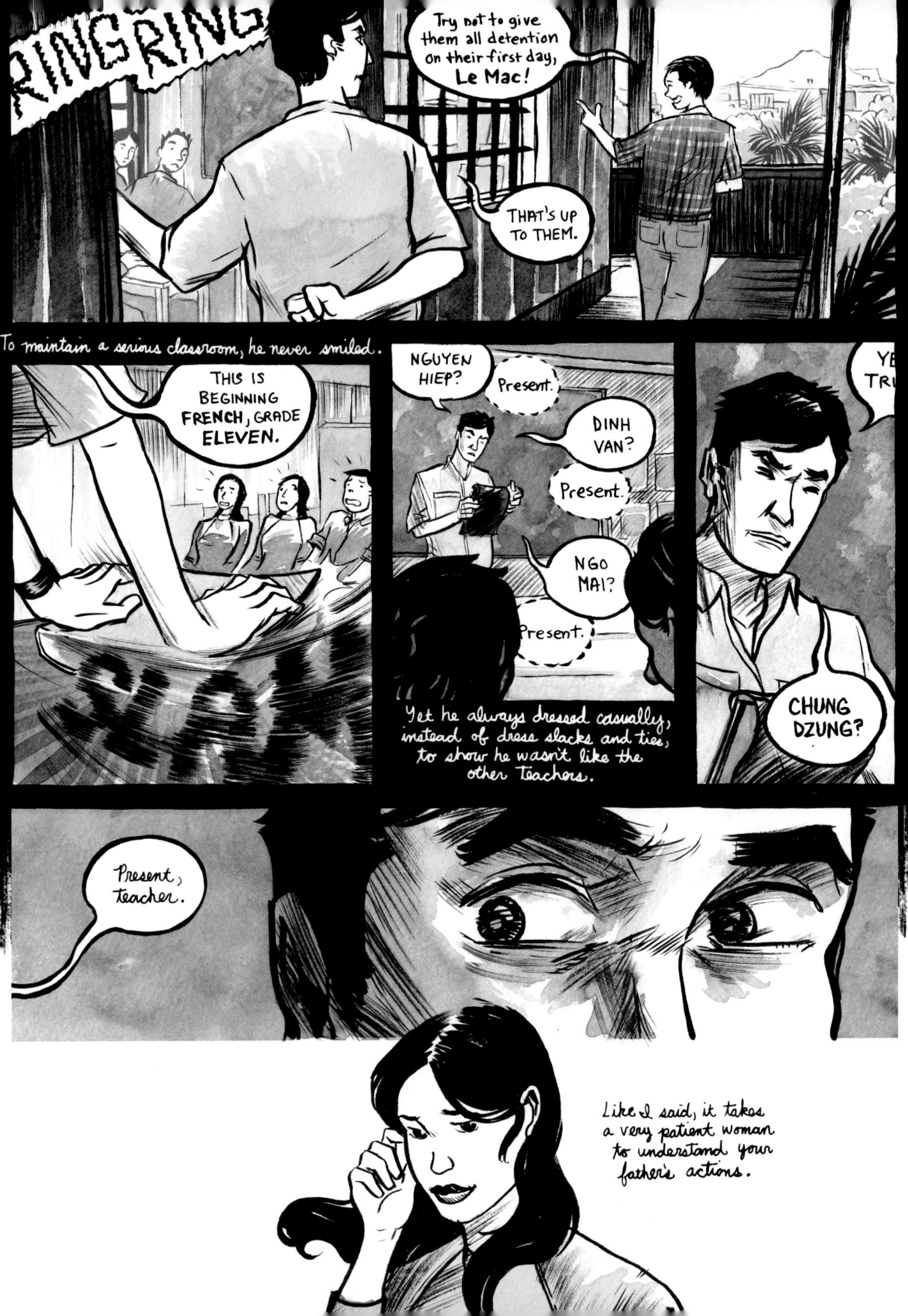
RINGRING
Try not to give them all detention on their first day, Le Mac!
THAT'S UP TO THEM.
To maintain a serious classroom, he never smiled.
THIS IS BEGINNING FRENCH, GRADE ELEVEN.
NGUYEN HIEP?
Present.
DINH VAN?
Present.
NGO MAI?
Present.
Yet he always dressed casually, instead of dress slacks and ties, to show he wasn't like the other teachers.
CHUNG DZUNG?
Present, teacher.
Like I said, it takes a very patient woman to understand your father's actions.

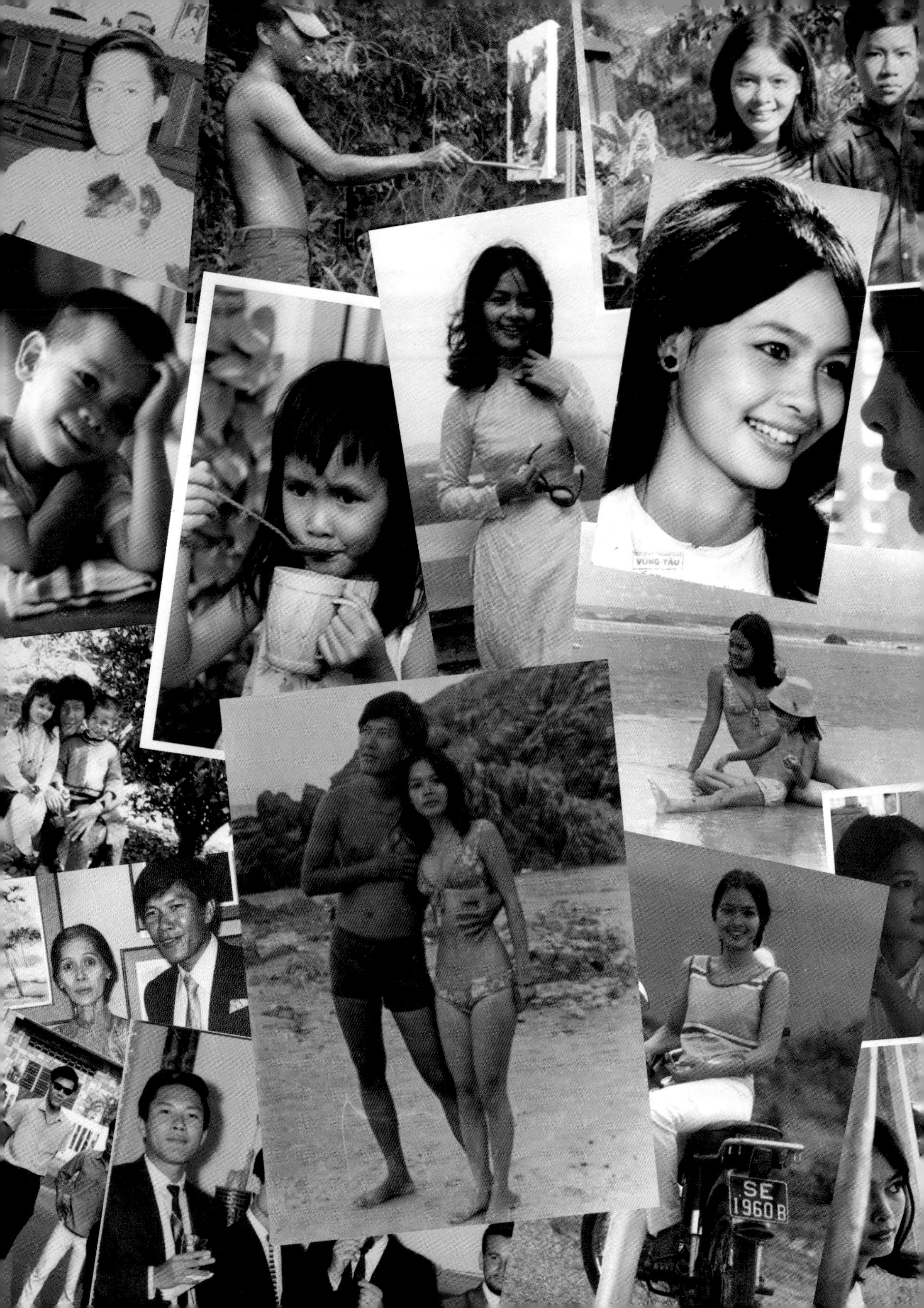
VŨNG TÀU
SE 1960 B

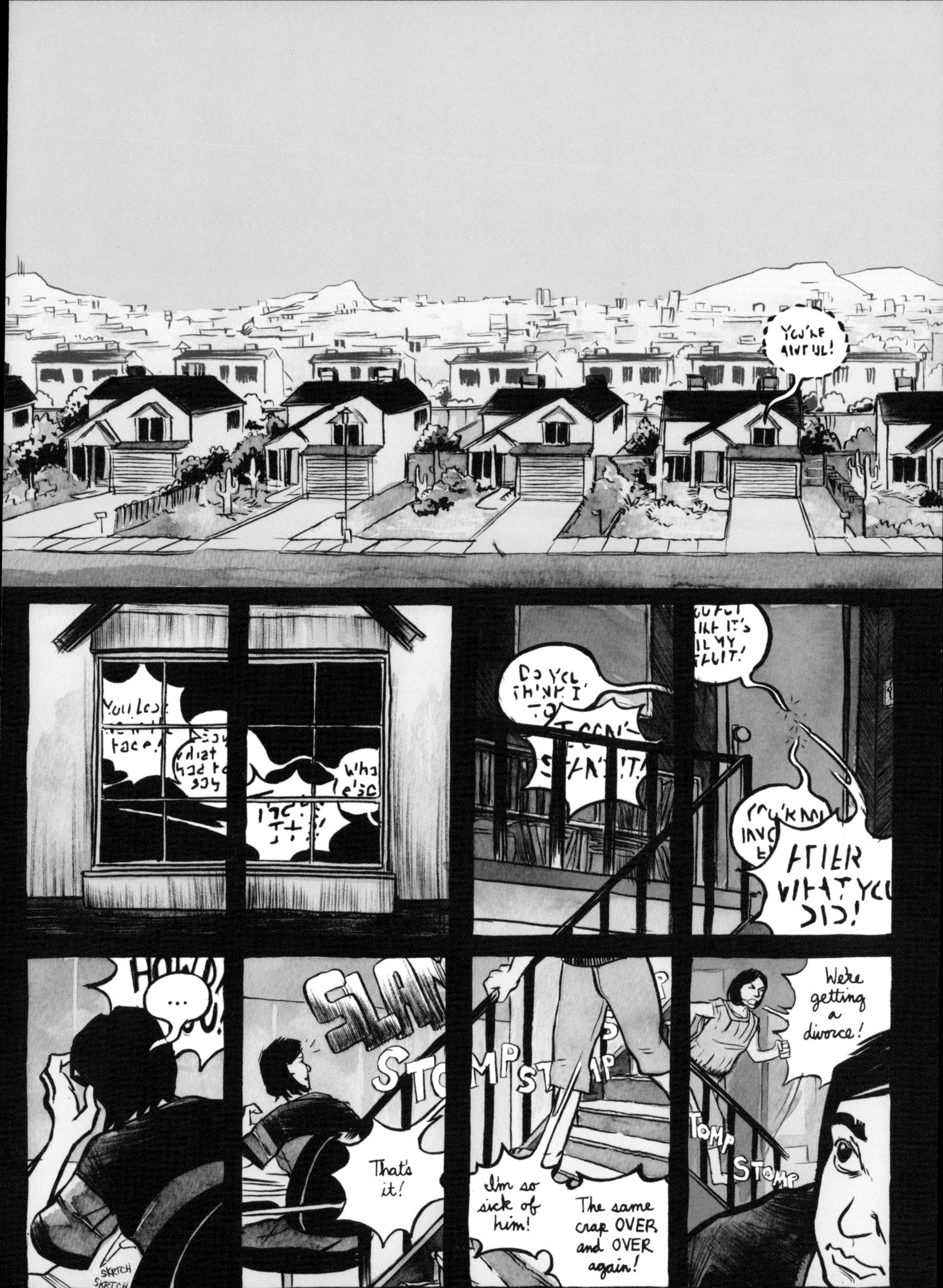

YOU'RE AWFUL!
...
AFTER WHAT YOU DID!
SKRTCH
SKRTCH
STOMP
That's it!
I'm so sick of him!
The same crap OVER and OVER again!
STOMP
STOMP
We're getting a divorce!

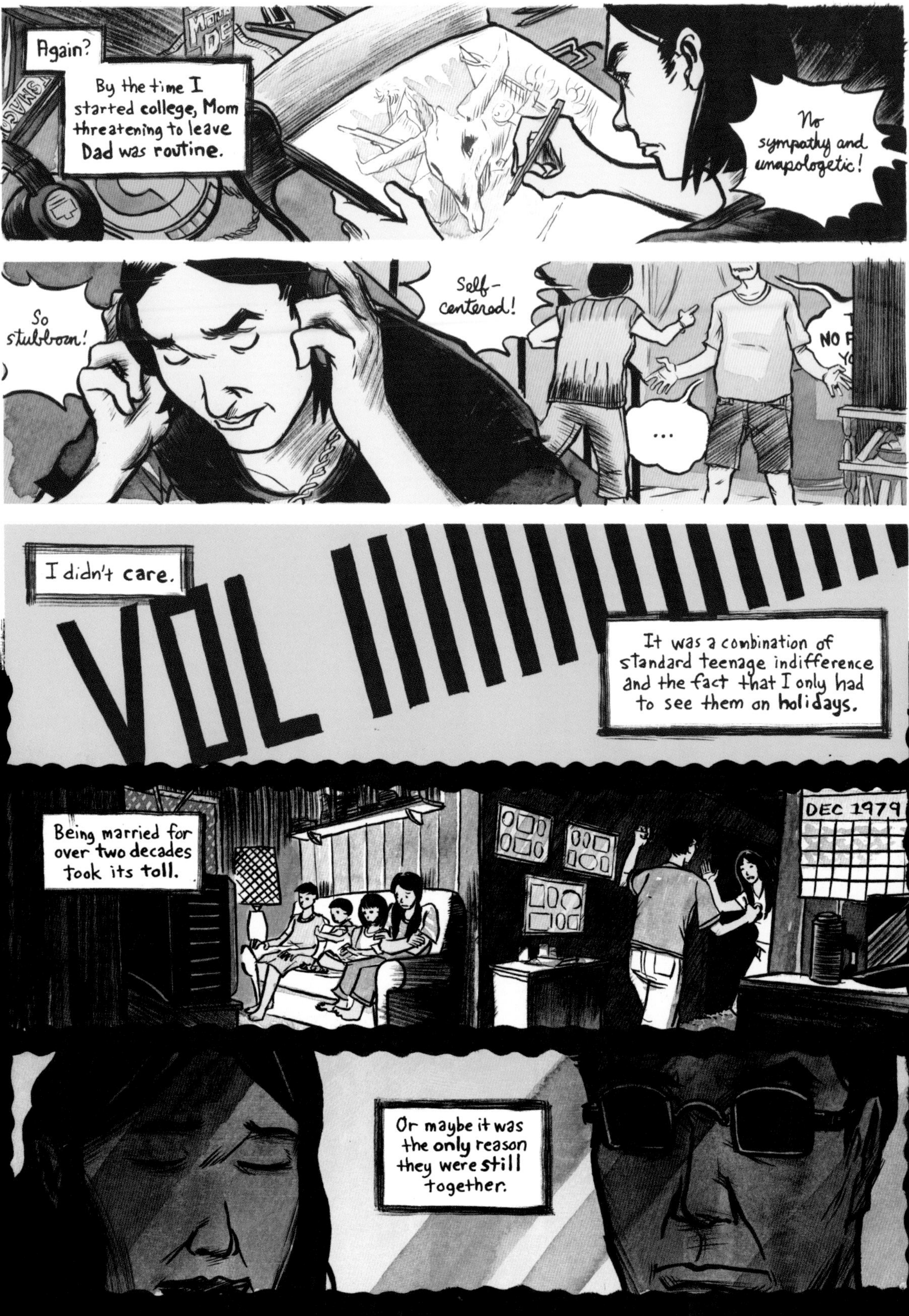
Again?
By the time I started college, Mom threatening to leave Dad was routine.
No sympathy and unapologetic!
So stubborn!
Self-centered!
...
I didn't care.
VOL
It was a combination of standard teenage indifference and the fact that I only had to see them on holidays.
Being married for over two decades took its toll.
DEC 1979
Or maybe it was the only reason they were still together.

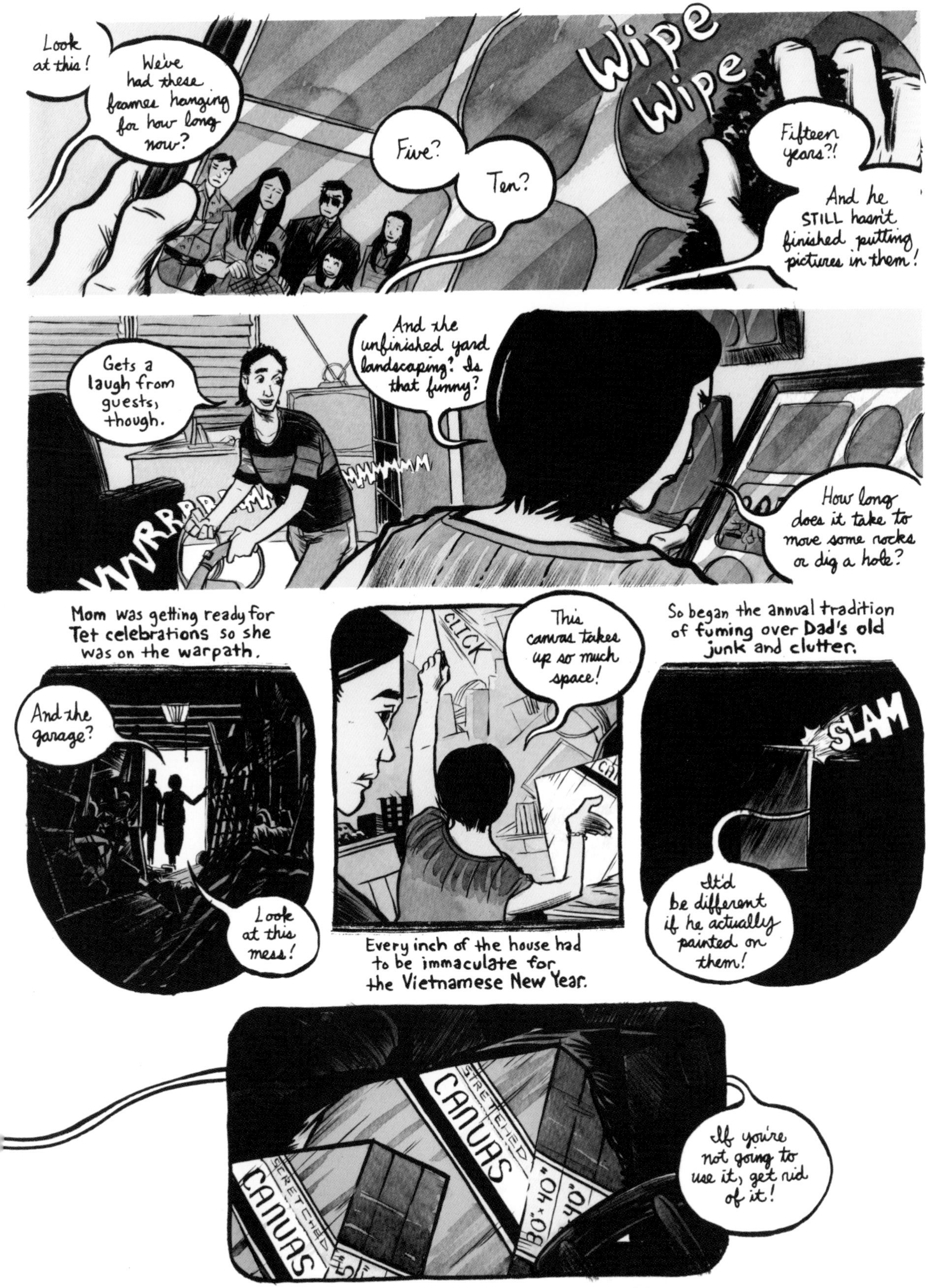

Look at this!
We've had these frames hanging for how long now?
Wipe
Wipe
Five?
Ten?
Fifteen years?!
And he STILL hasn't finished putting pictures in them!
Gets a laugh from guests, though.
And the unfinished yard landscaping? Is that funny?
VVVRRRRMMMMMMM
How long does it take to move some rocks or dig a hole?
Mom was getting ready for Tet celebrations so she was on the warpath.
And the garage?
Look at this mess!
CLICK
This canvas takes up so much space!
Every inch of the house had to be immaculate for the Vietnamese New Year.
So began the annual tradition of fuming over Dad's old junk and clutter.
SLAM
It'd be different if he actually painted on them!
STRETCHED CANVAS
30"×40"
STRETCHED CANVAS
If you're not going to use it, get rid of it!

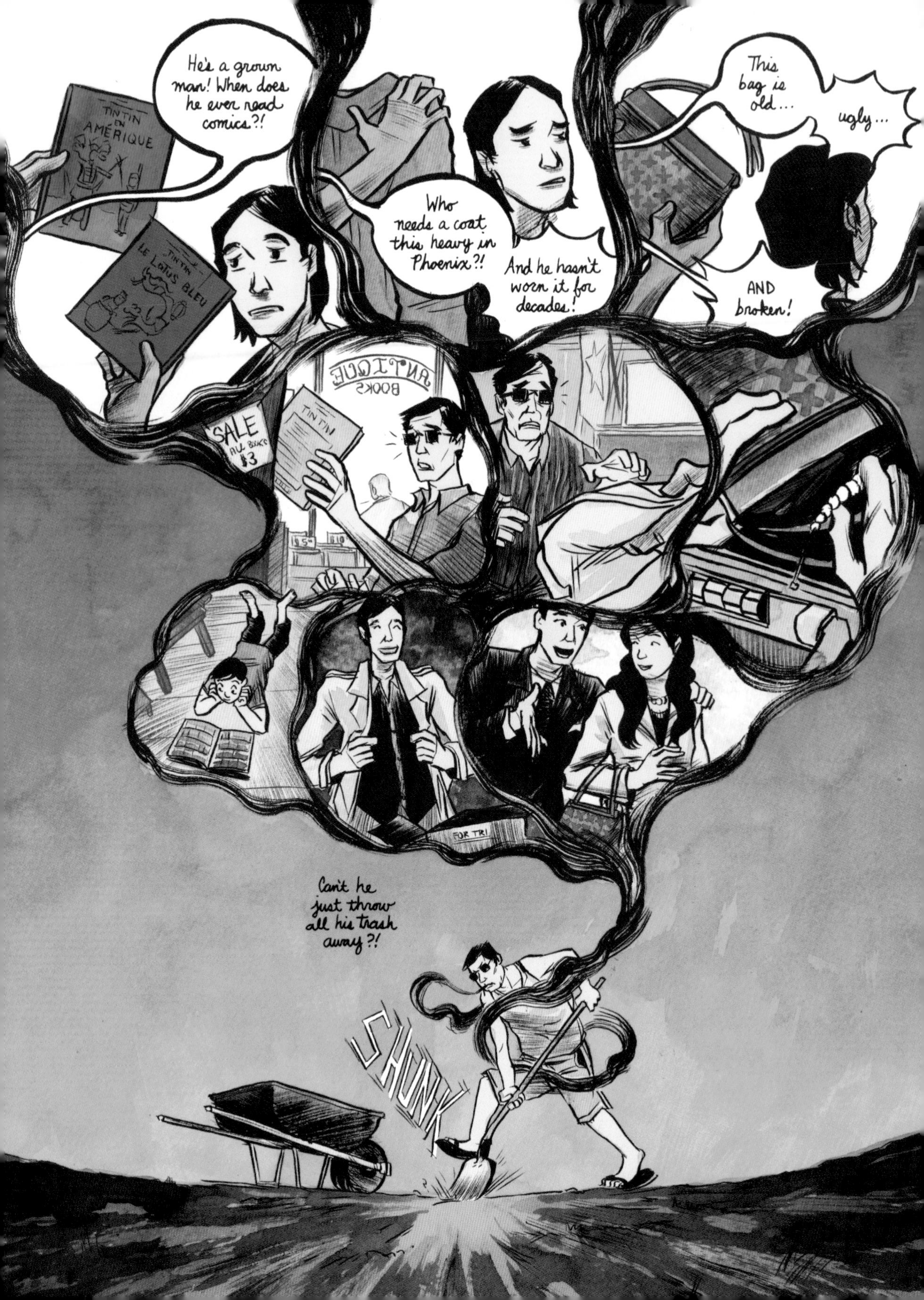
He's a grown man! When does he ever read comics?!
TINTIN EN AMÉRIQUE
TINTIN LE LOTUS BLEU
Who needs a coat this heavy in Phoenix?!
And he hasn't worn it for decades!
This bag is old...
ugly...
AND broken!
ANTIQUE BOOKS
SALE ALL BOOKS $3
TINTIN
FOR TRI
Can't he just throw all his trash away?!
SHUNK

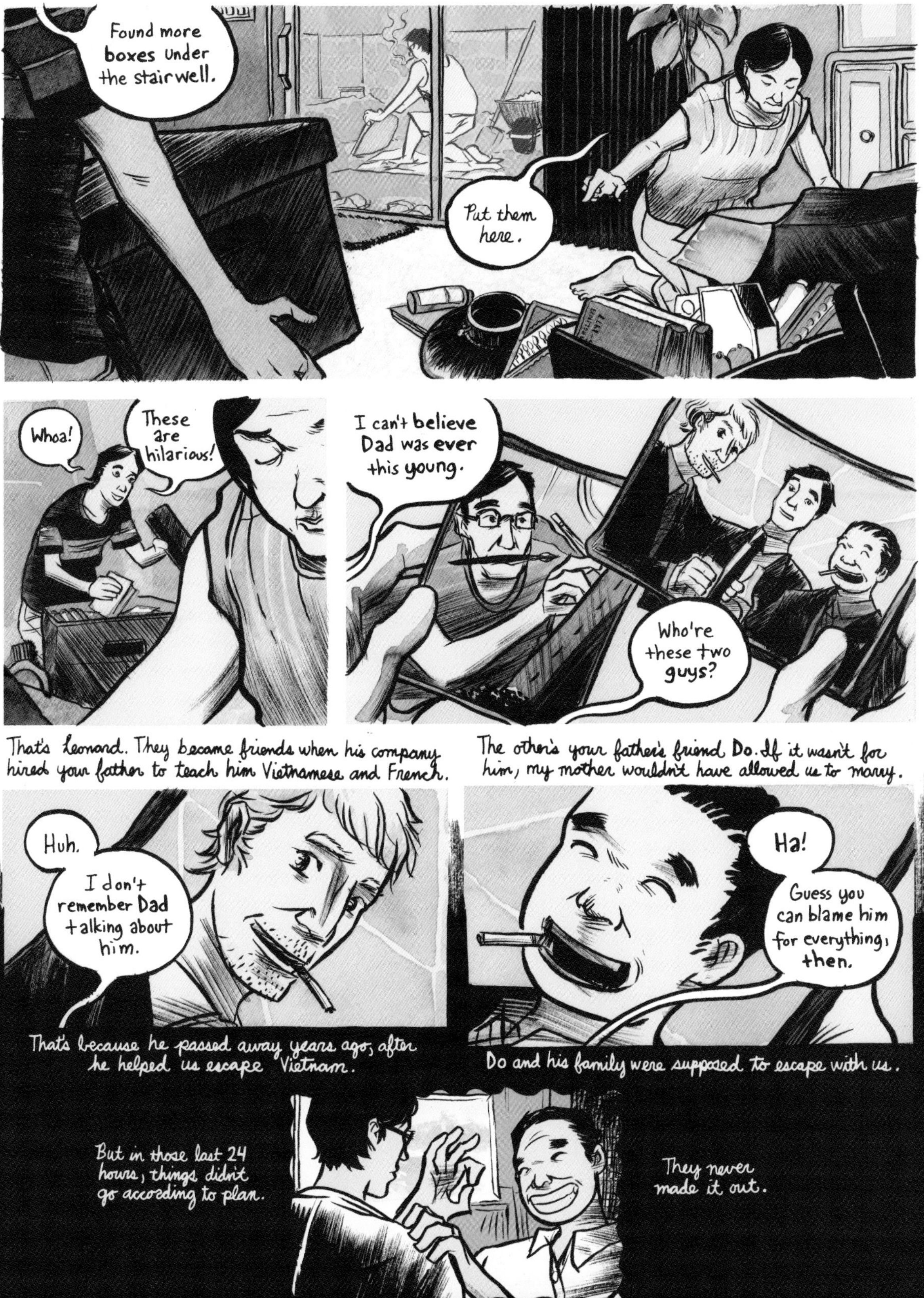
Found more boxes under the stairwell.
Put them here.
Whoa!
These are hilarious!
I can't believe Dad was ever this young.
Who're these two guys?
That's Leonard. They became friends when his company hired your father to teach him Vietnamese and French.
The other's your father's friend Do. If it wasn't for him, my mother wouldn't have allowed us to marry.
Huh.
I don't remember Dad talking about him.
Ha!
Guess you can blame him for everything, then.
That's because he passed away years ago, after he helped us escape Vietnam.
Do and his family were supposed to escape with us.
But in those last 24 hours, things didn't go according to plan.
They never made it out.

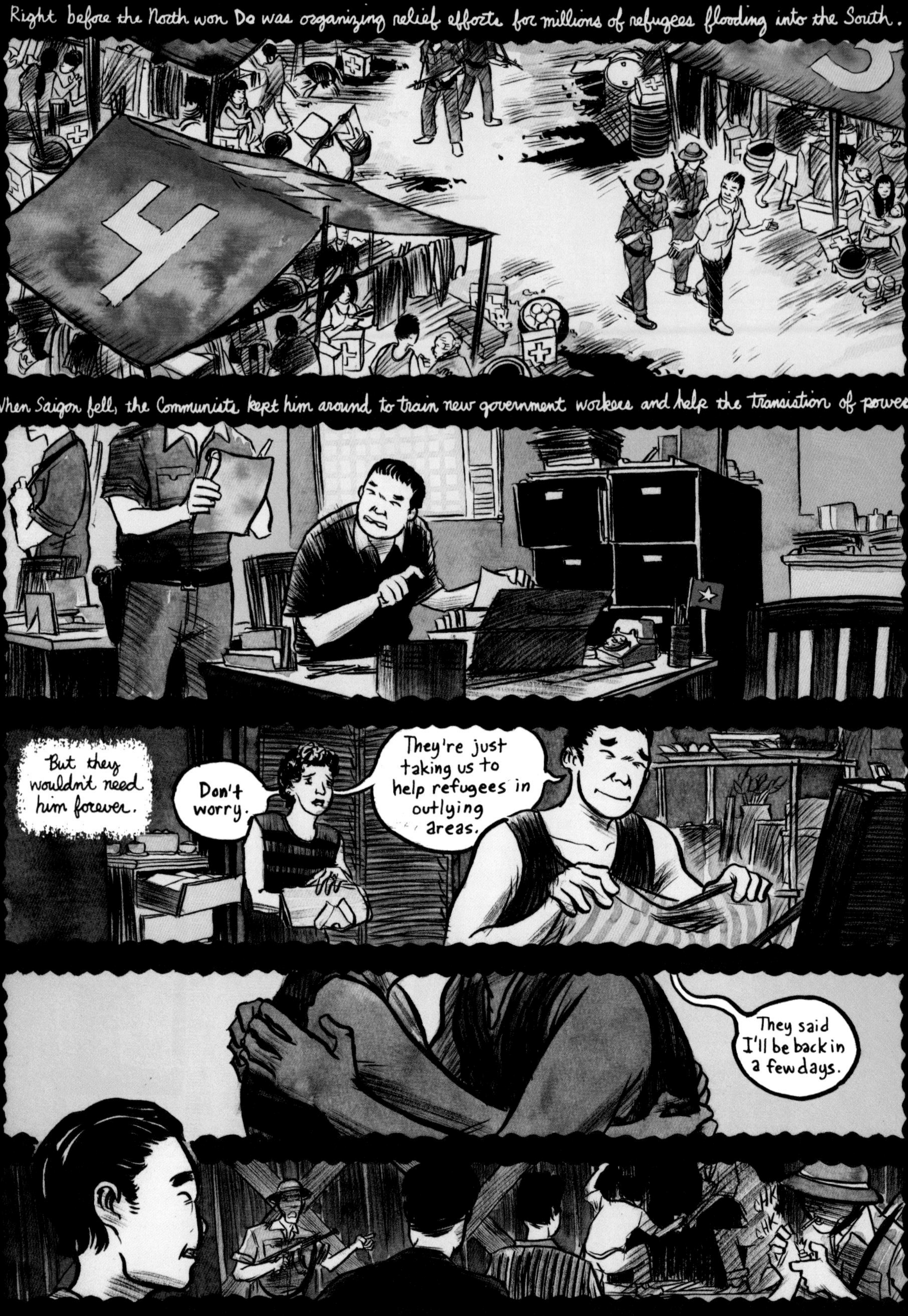

Right before the North won Do was organizing relief efforts for millions of refugees flooding into the South.
When Saigon fell, the Communists kept him around to train new government workers and help the transistion of power.
But they wouldn't need him forever.
Don't worry.
They're just taking us to help refugees in outlying areas.
They said I'll be back in a few days.
CHK
CHK

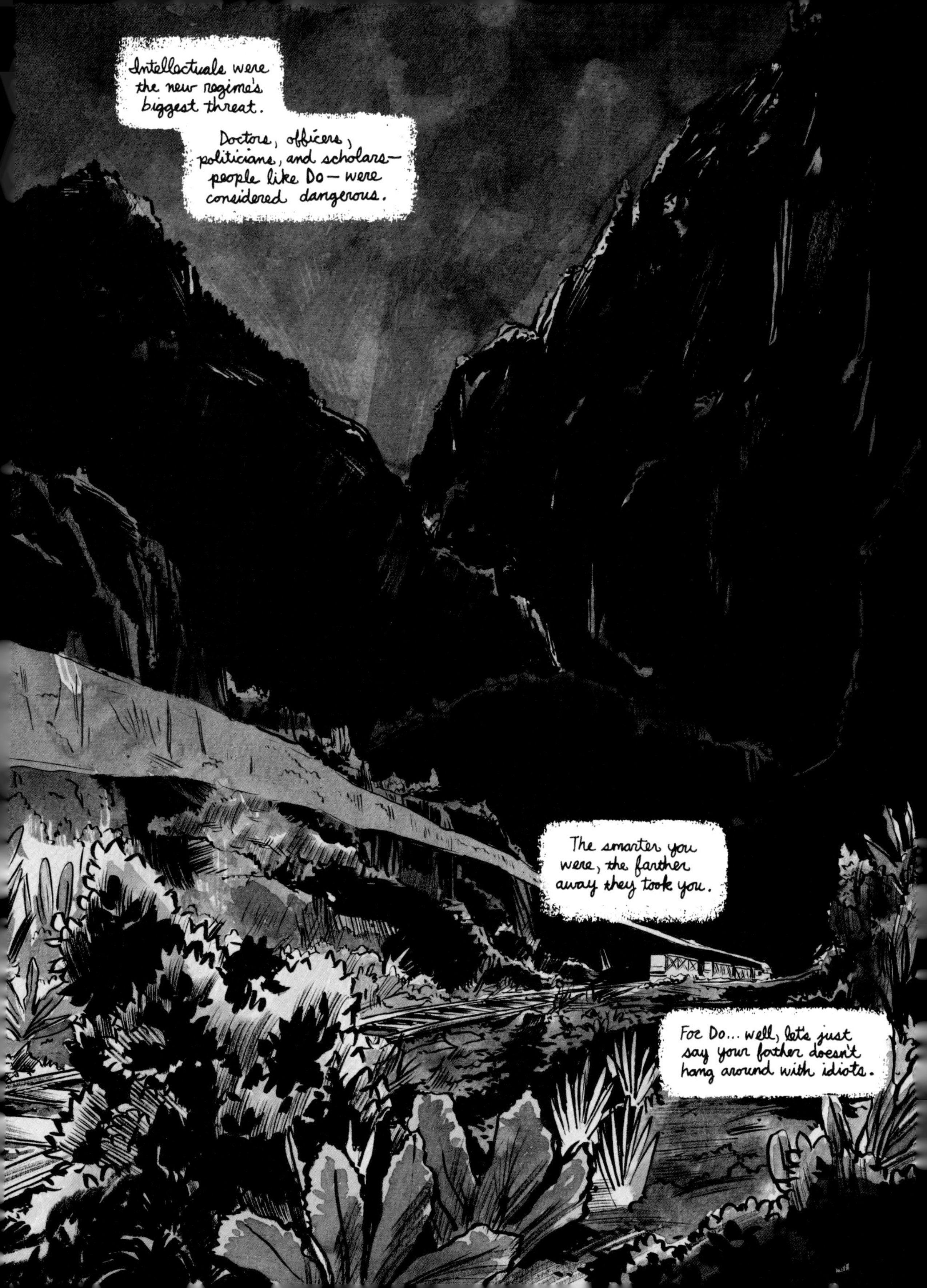
Intellectuals were the new regime's biggest threat.
Doctors, officers, politicians, and scholars—people like Do—were considered dangerous.
The smarter you were, the farther away they took you.
For Do... well, let's just say your father doesn't hang around with idiots.

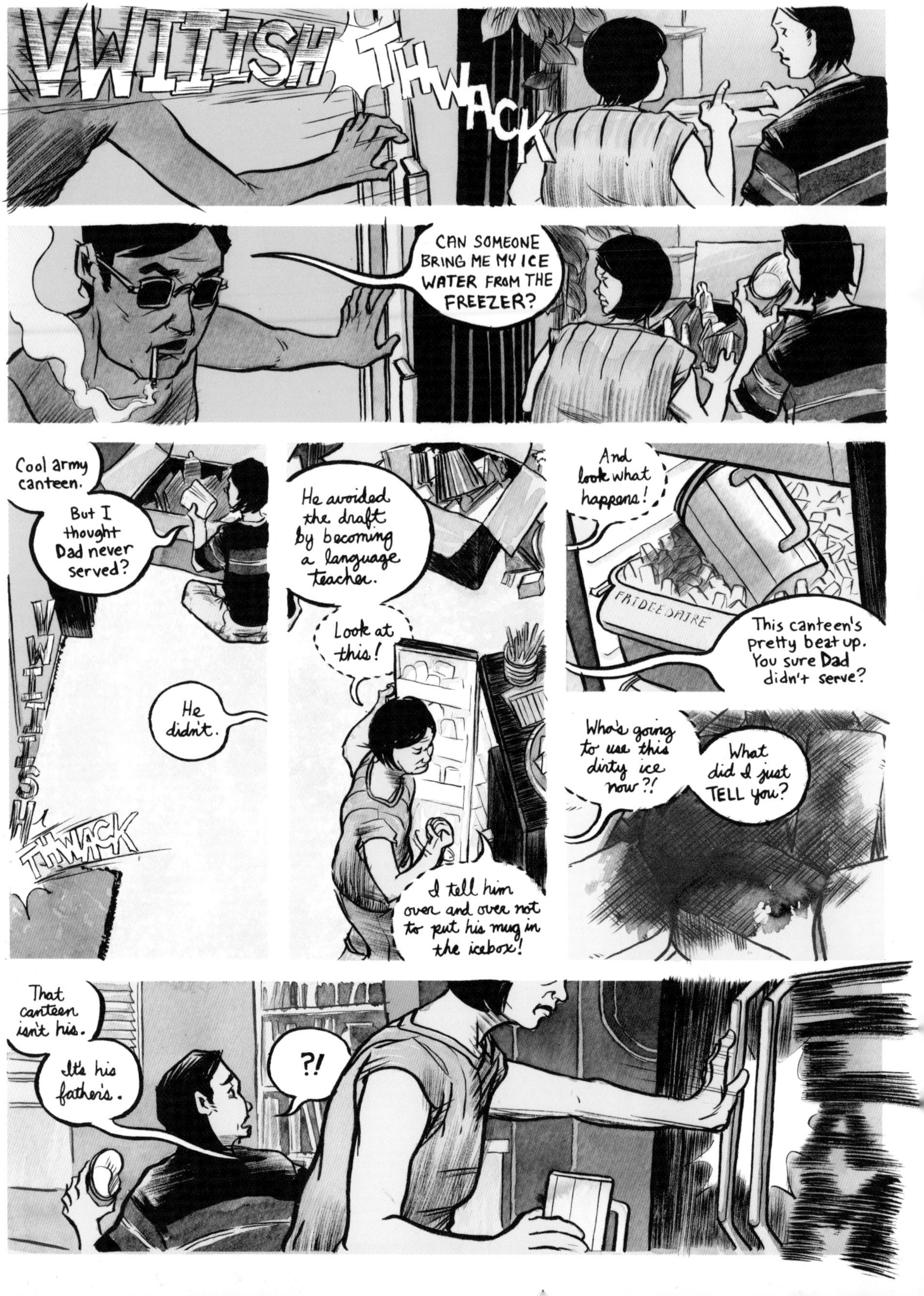
VWIIISH
THWACK
CAN SOMEONE BRING ME MY ICE WATER FROM THE FREEZER?
Cool army canteen.
But I thought Dad never served?
He didn't.
VWIIISH
THWACK
He avoided the draft by becoming a language teacher.
Look at this!
I tell him over and over not to put his mug in the icebox!
And look what happens!
FRIGIDAIRE
This canteen's pretty beat up. You sure Dad didn't serve?
Who's going to use this dirty ice now?!
What did I just TELL you?
That canteen isn't his.
It's his father's.
?!

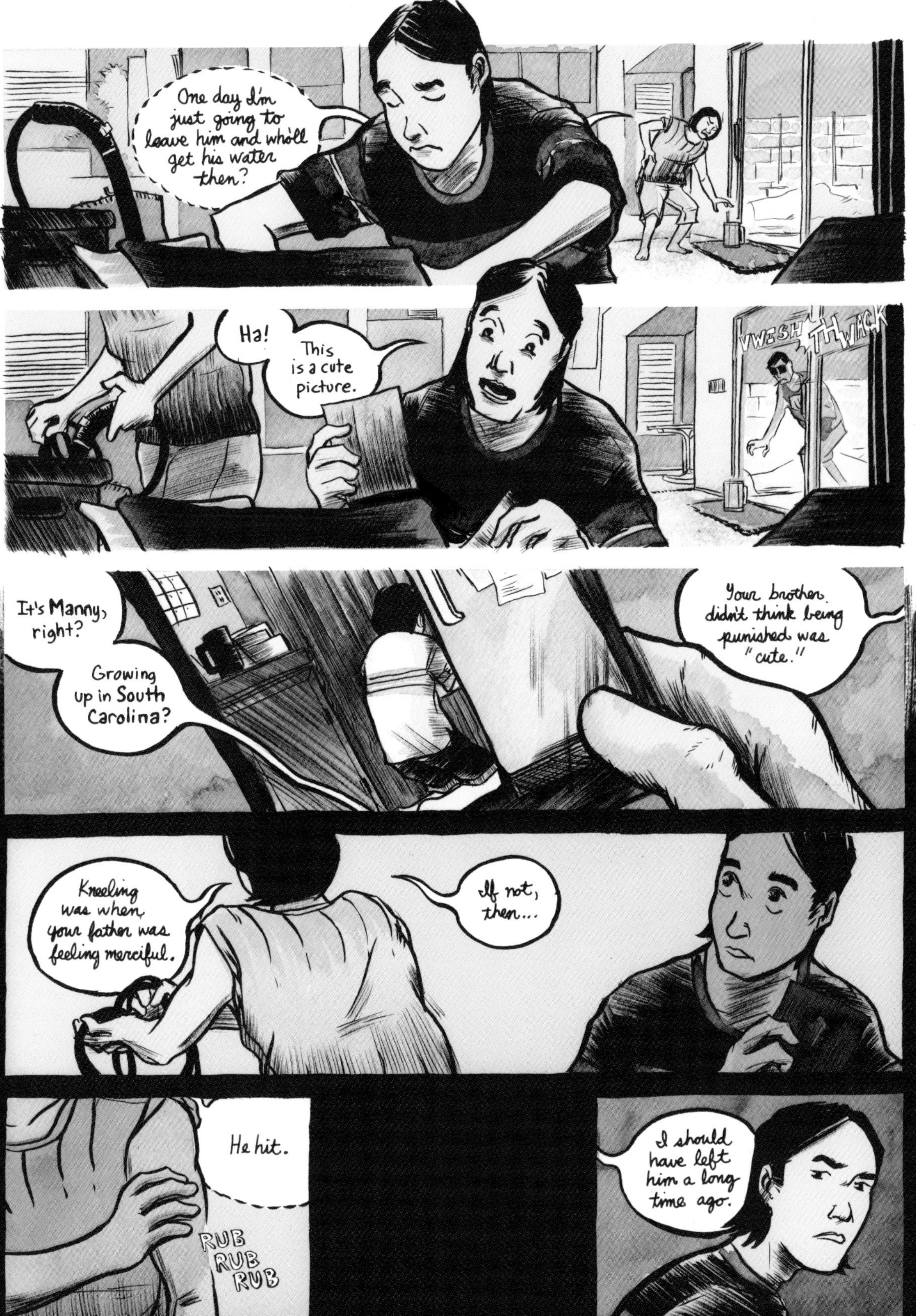
One day I'm just going to leave him and who'll get his water then?
Ha!
This is a cute picture.
VWISH
THWACK
It's Manny, right?
Growing up in South Carolina?
Your brother didn't think being punished was "cute."
Kneeling was when your father was feeling merciful.
If not, then...
He hit.
RUB RUB RUB
I should have left him a long time ago.

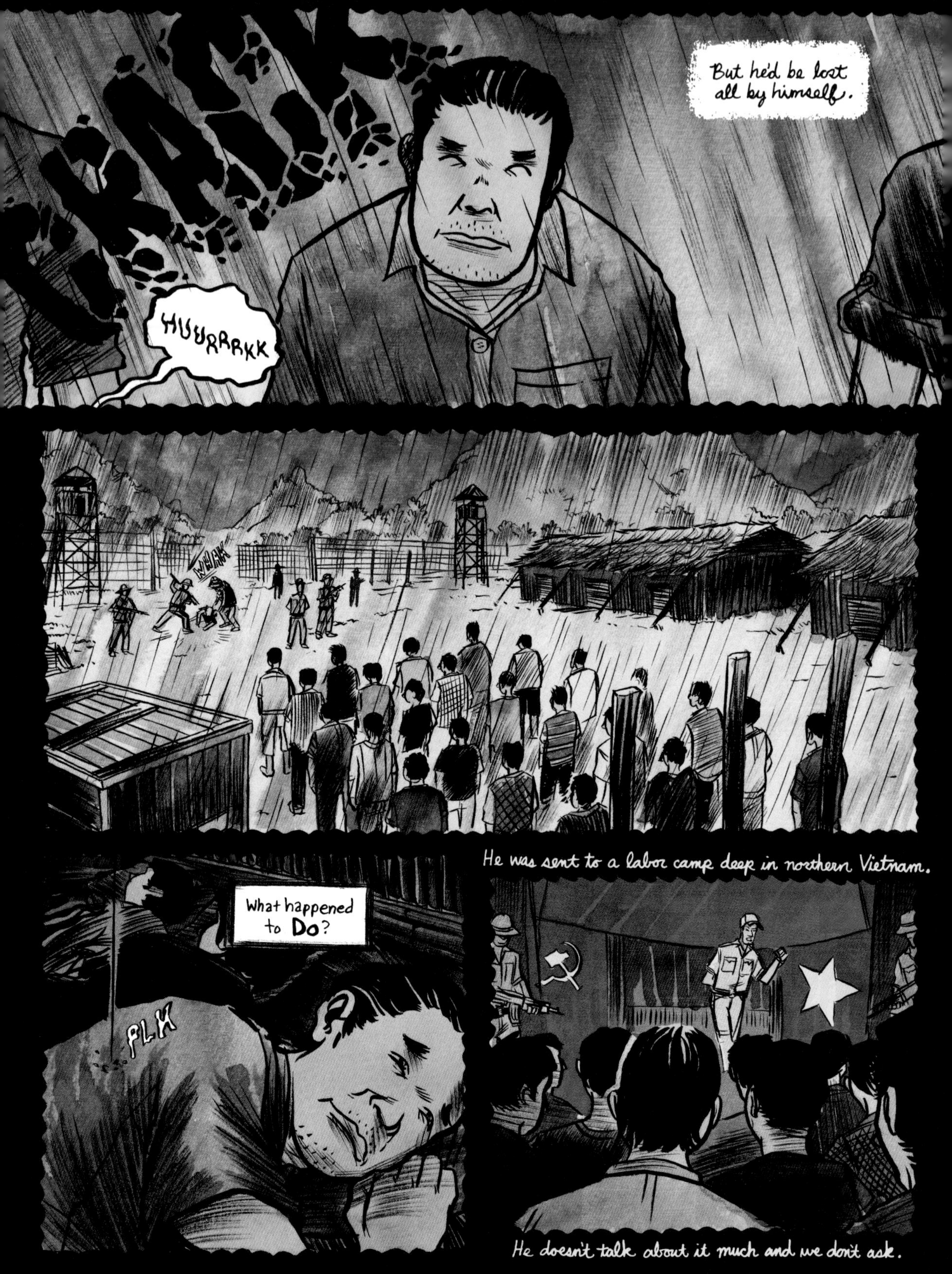

But he'd be lost all by himself.
HUURRRKK
WHAK
What happened to **Do**?
PLH
He was sent to a labor camp deep in northern Vietnam.
He doesn't talk about it much and we don't ask.

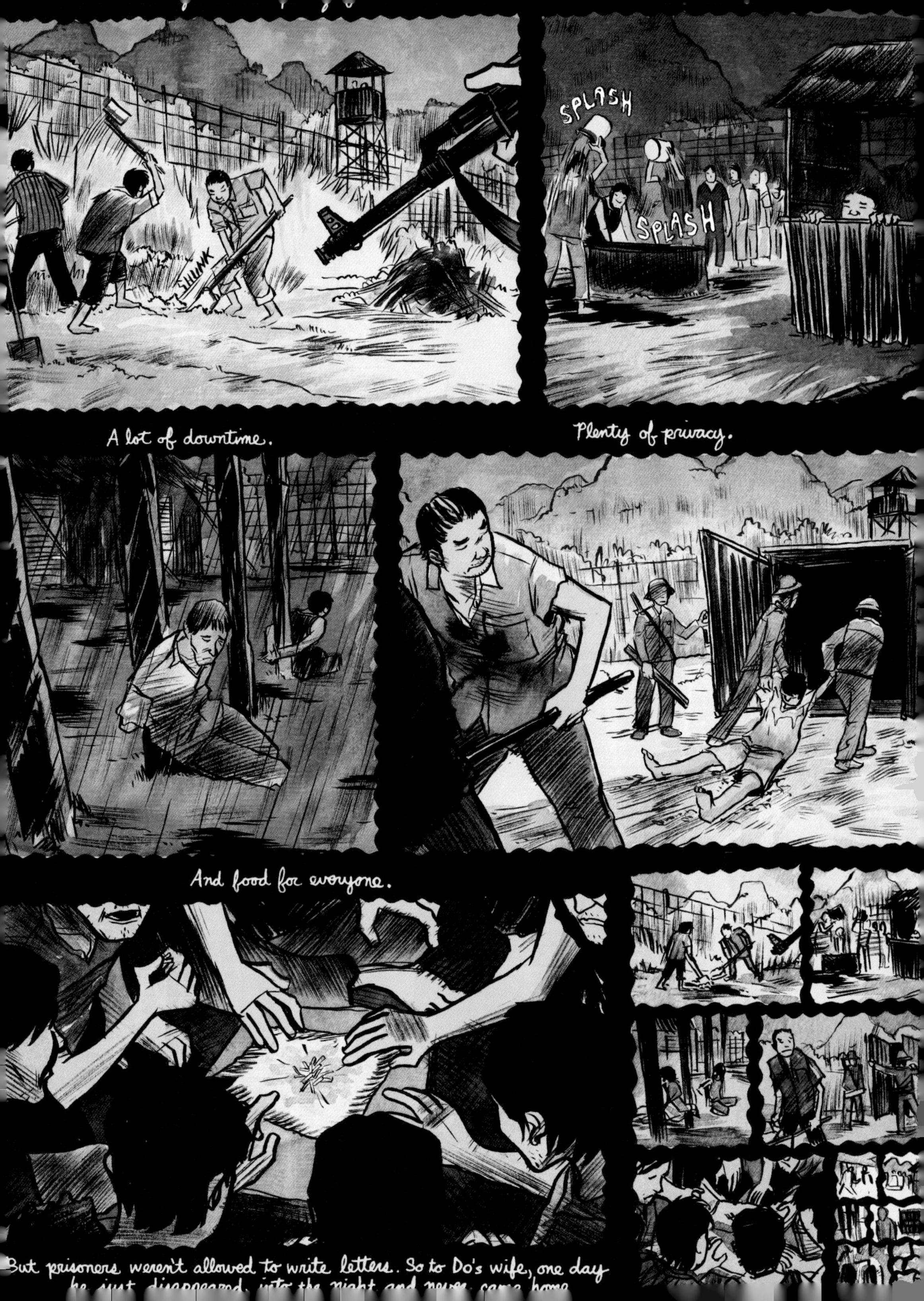
SHUNK
SPLASH
SPLASH
A lot of downtime.
Plenty of privacy.
And food for everyone.
But prisoners weren't allowed to write letters. So to Do's wife, one day
he just disappeared, into the night and never came home

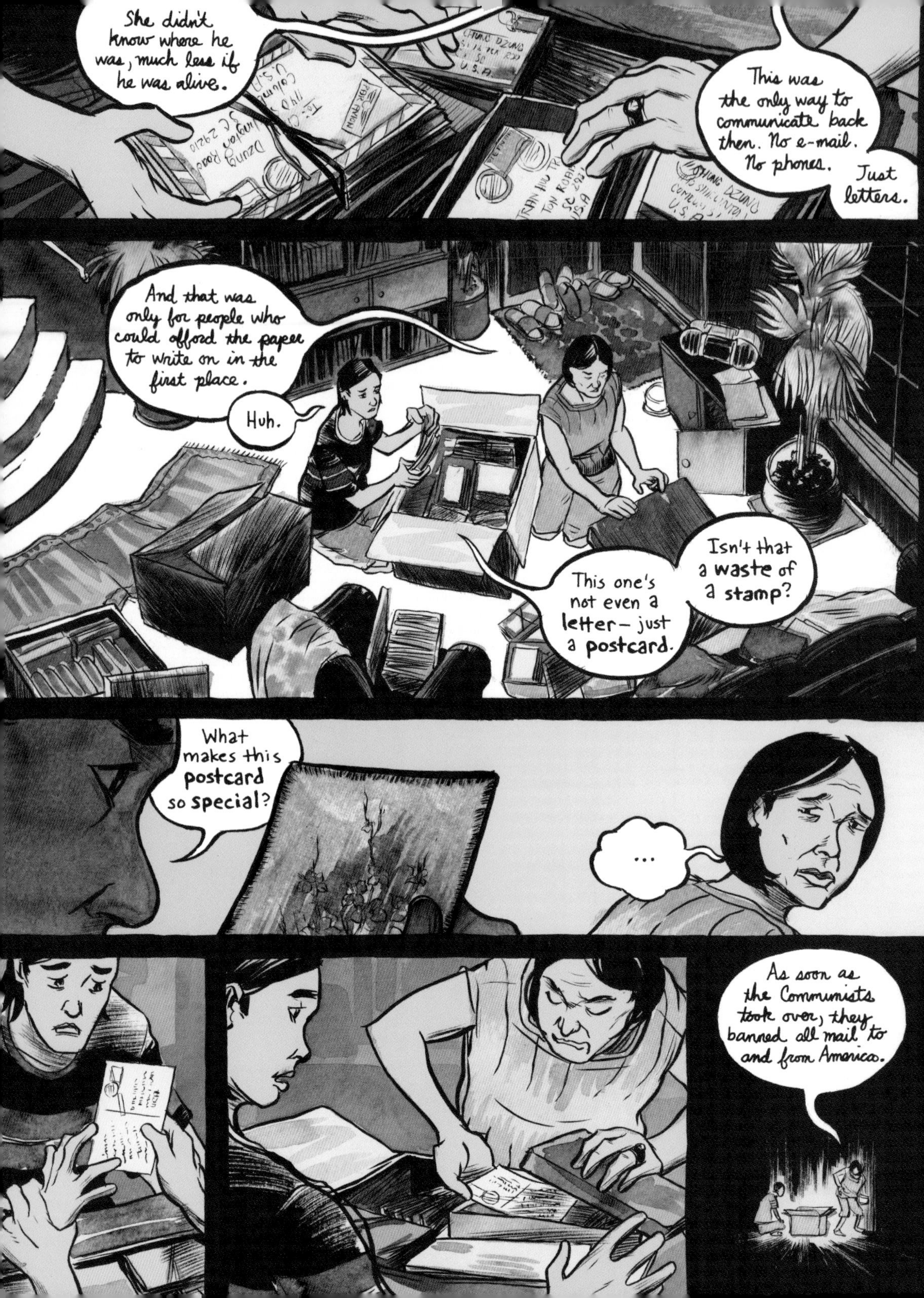
She didn't know where he was, much less if he was alive.
This was the only way to communicate back then. No e-mail. No phones.
Just letters.
And that was only for people who could afford the paper to write on in the first place.
Huh.
This one's not even a letter– just a postcard.
Isn't that a waste of a stamp?
What makes this postcard so special?
...
As soon as the Communists took over, they banned all mail to and from America.

We had to sneak letters through friends and family living in other countries like France and New Caledonia.

They took over six months to get to Vietnam, if they even made it at all.

Peace is what the Communists promised.

Peace in which everyone had enough to eat, clothes to wear, and a government free from corruption.

FRRRRRRRRRP!

RRi:p

But their "peace" wasn't for the masses — only for those who had power.

I tell you these things, but you'll never understand.

How could you?

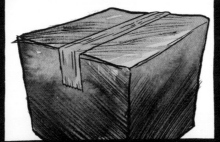

We left Vietnam so you would NEVER have to know what it's like.

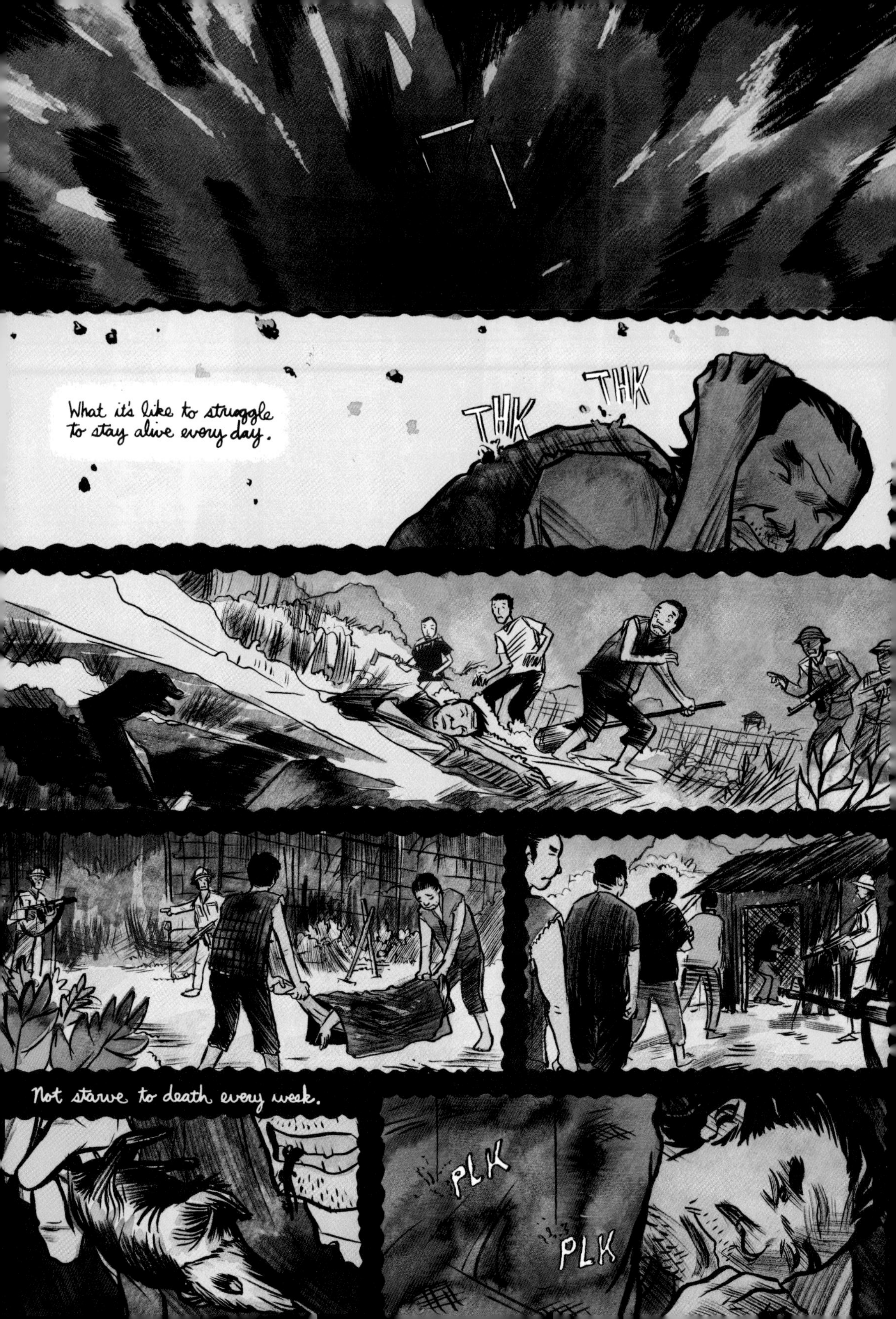
What it's like to struggle to stay alive every day.
THK
THK
Not starve to death every week.
PLK
PLK

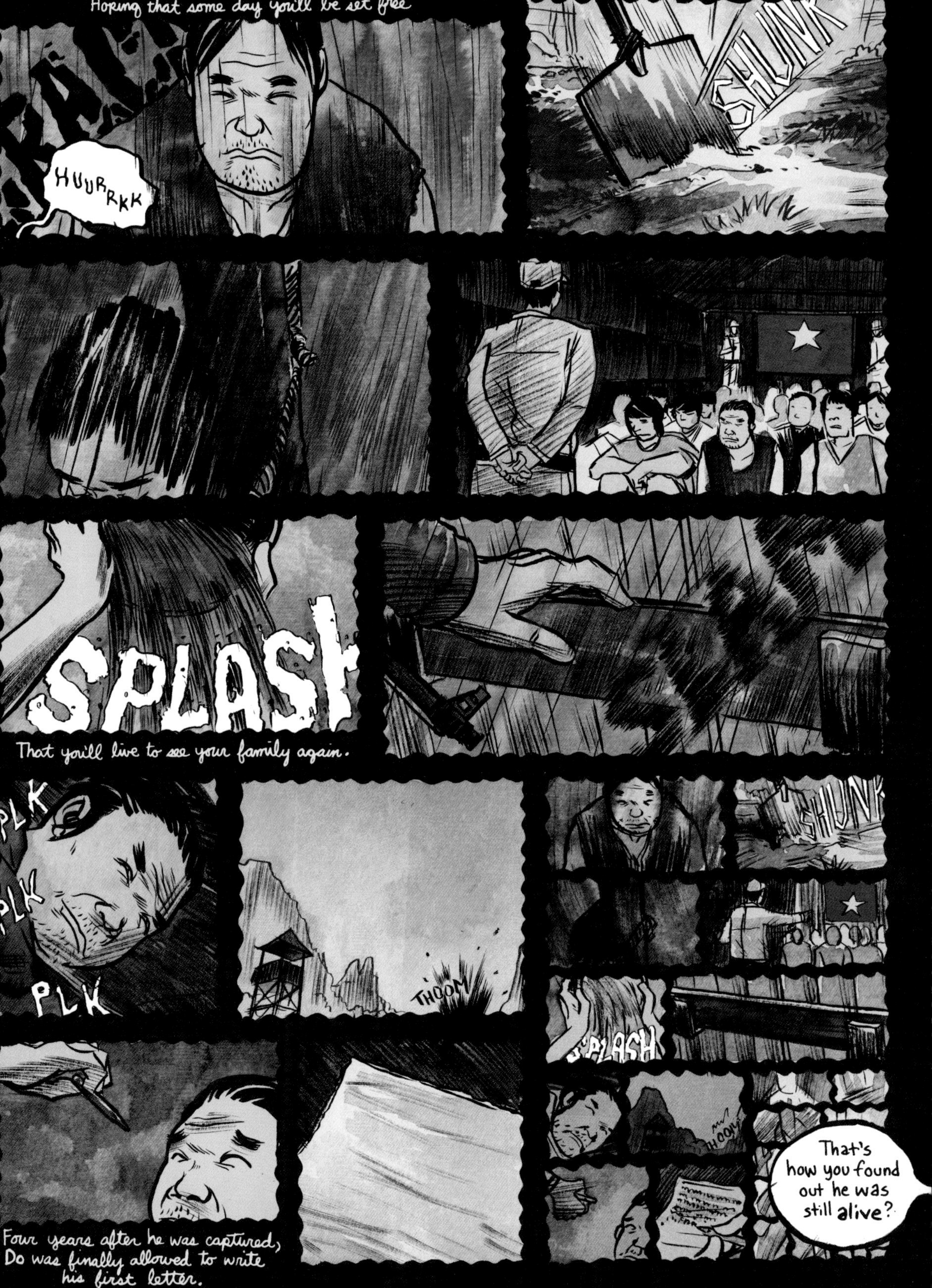

Hoping that some day you'll be set free
HUURRKK
SHUNK
SPLASH
That you'll live to see your family again.
PLK
PLK
PLK
THOOM
SHUNK
SPLASH
THOOM
Four years after he was captured, Do was finally allowed to write his first letter.
That's how you found out he was still alive?

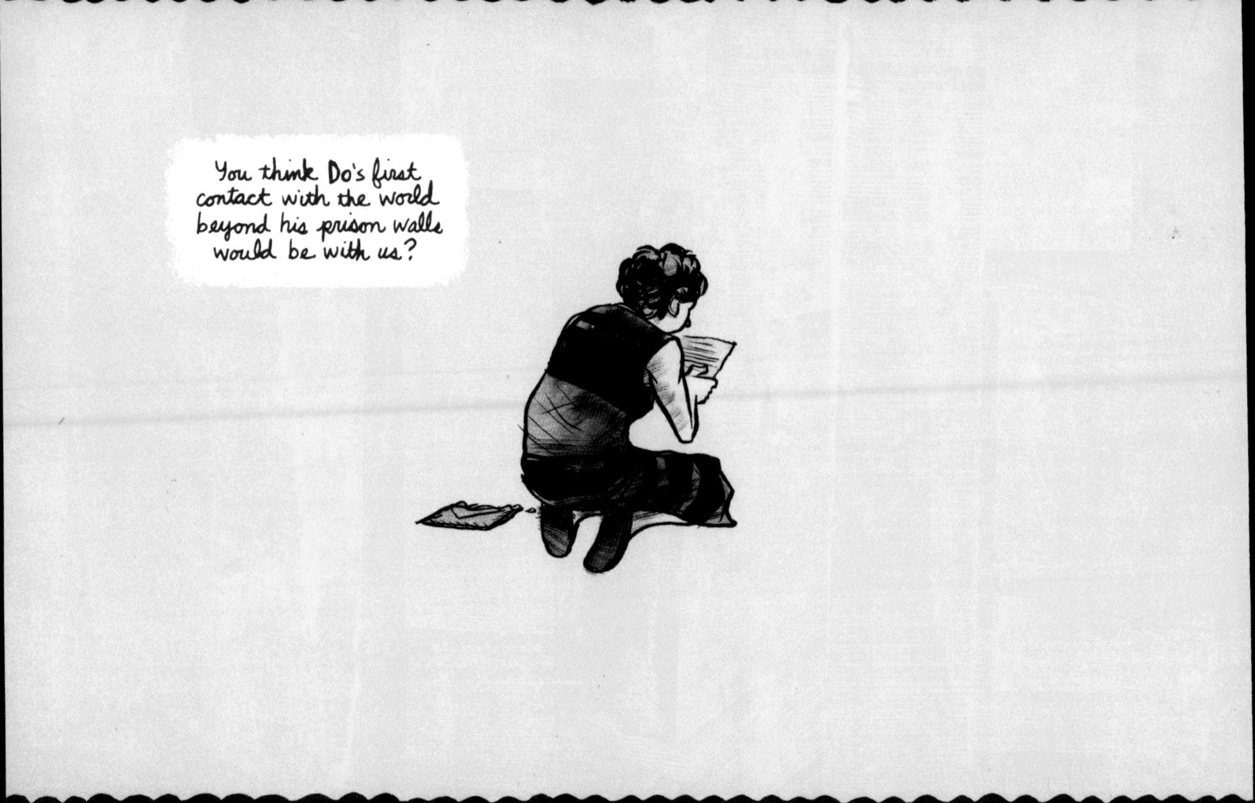
You think Do's first contact with the world beyond his prison walls would be with us?

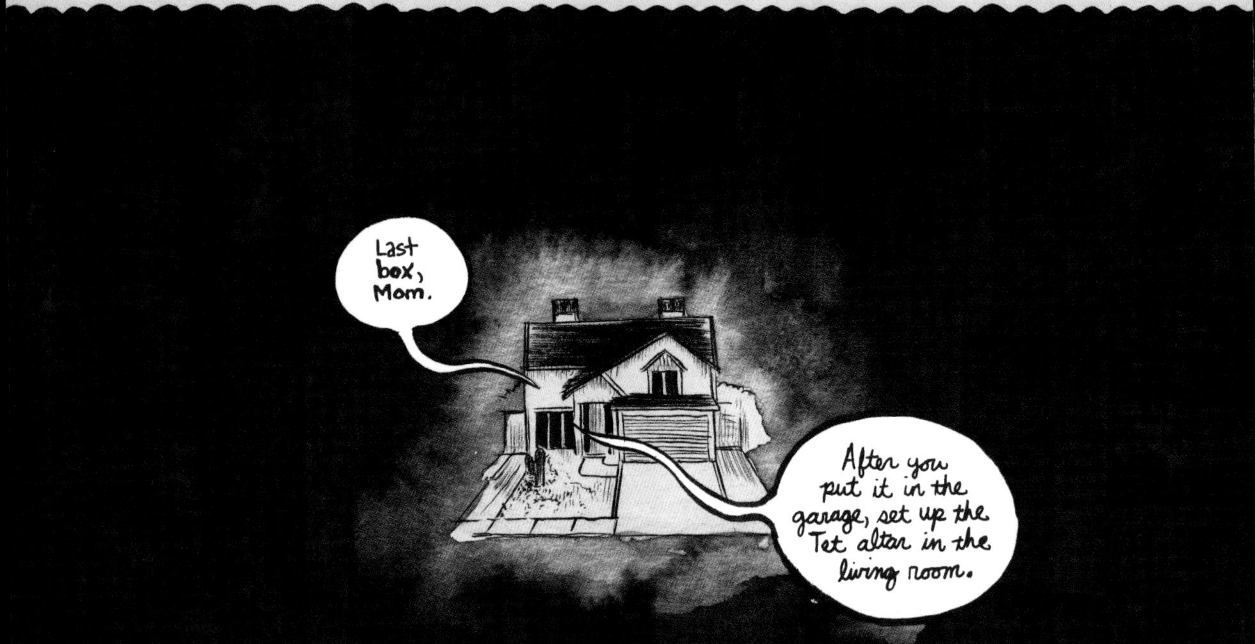
Last box, Mom.
After you put it in the garage, set up the Tet altar in the living room.

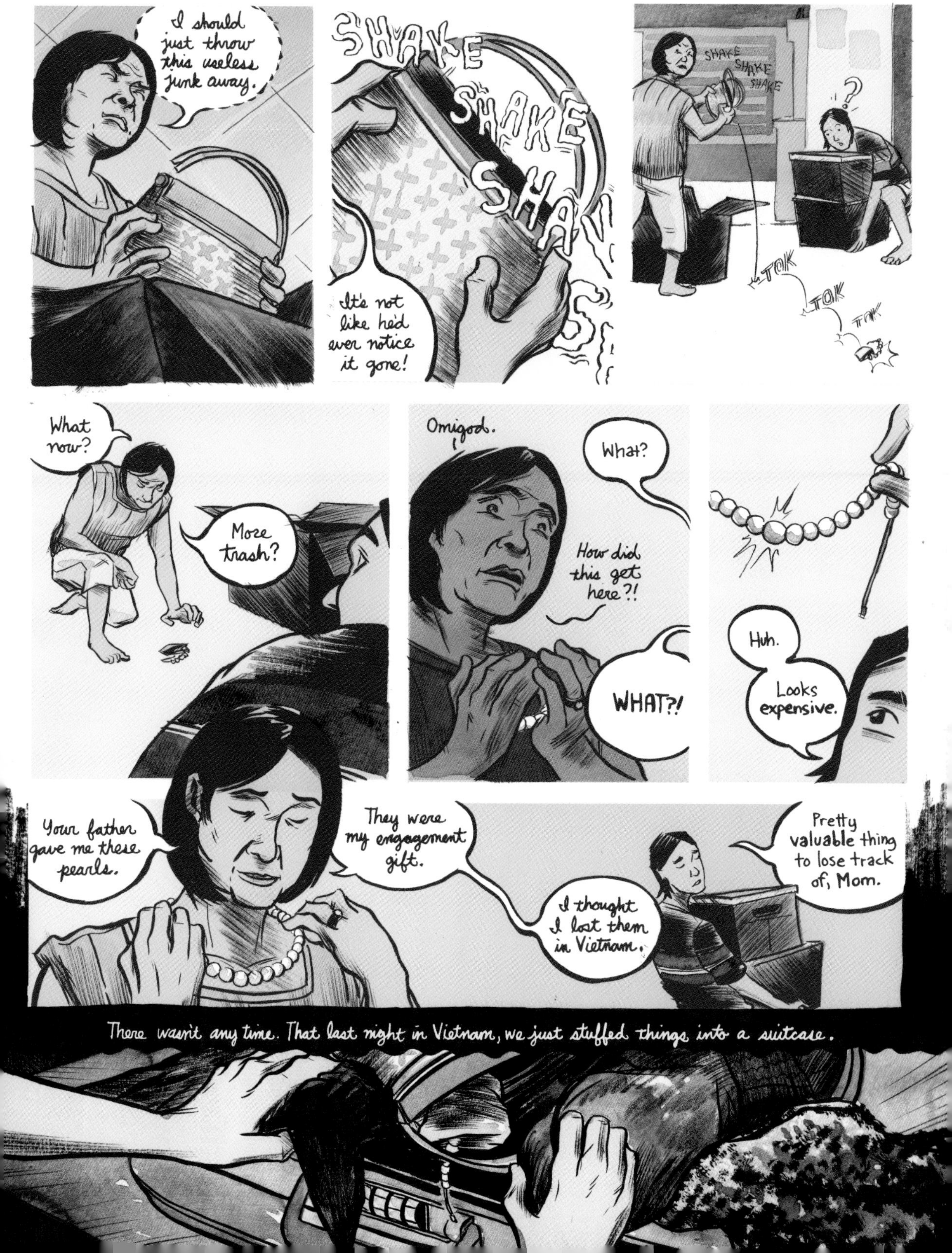
I should just throw this useless junk away.
SHAKE SHAKE SHAKE
It's not like he'd ever notice it gone!
SHAKE SHAKE SHAKE
?
TOK TOK TOK
What now?
More trash?
Omigod.
What?
How did this get here?!
WHAT?!
Huh.
Looks expensive.
Your father gave me these pearls.
They were my engagement gift.
I thought I lost them in Vietnam.
Pretty valuable thing to lose track of, Mom.
There wasn't any time. That last night in Vietnam, we just stuffed things into a suitcase.

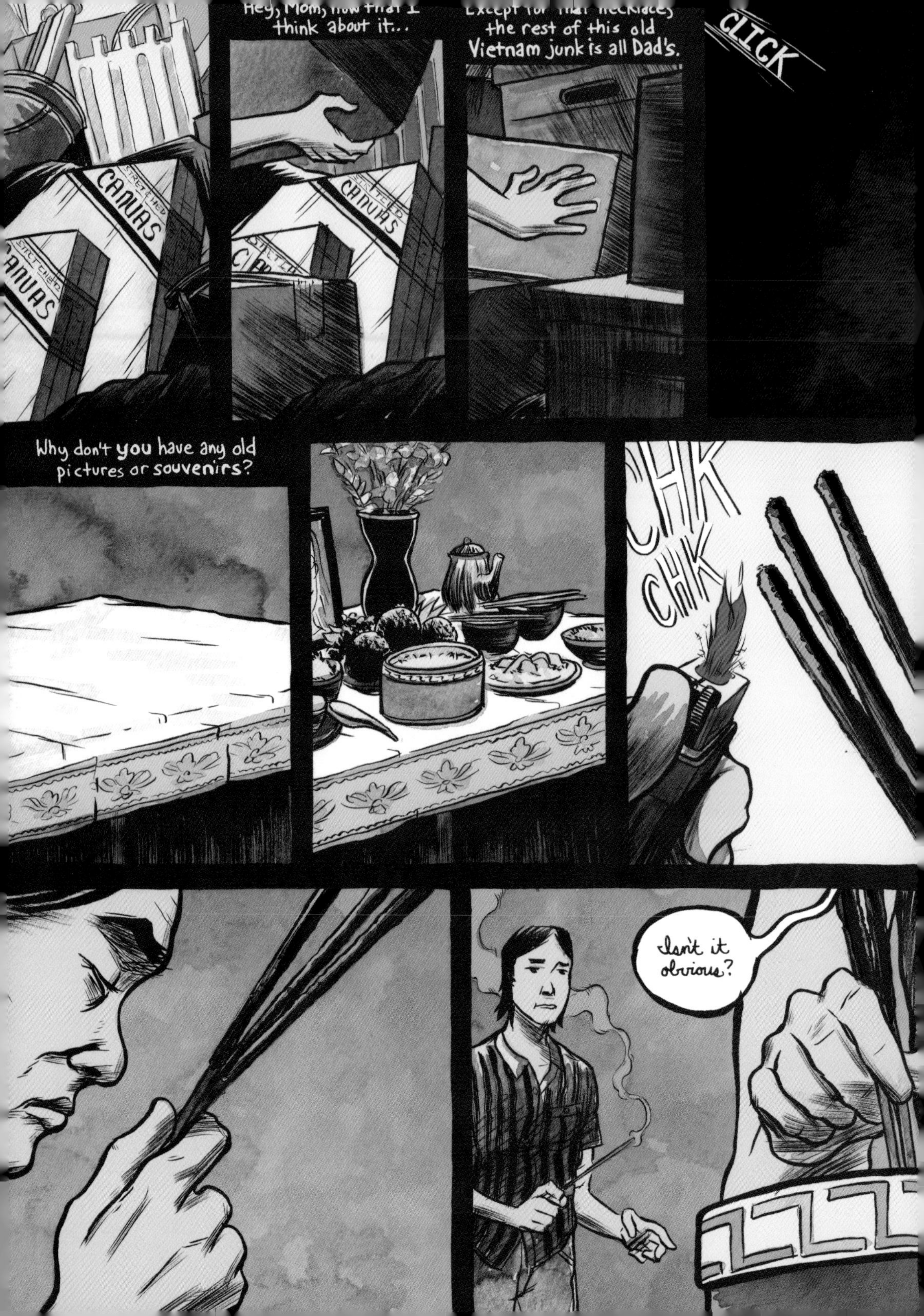

Hey, Mom, now that I think about it...
Except for that necklace, the rest of this old Vietnam junk is all Dad's.
CLICK
CANVAS
Why don't you have any old pictures or souvenirs?
CHK CHK
Isn't it obvious?

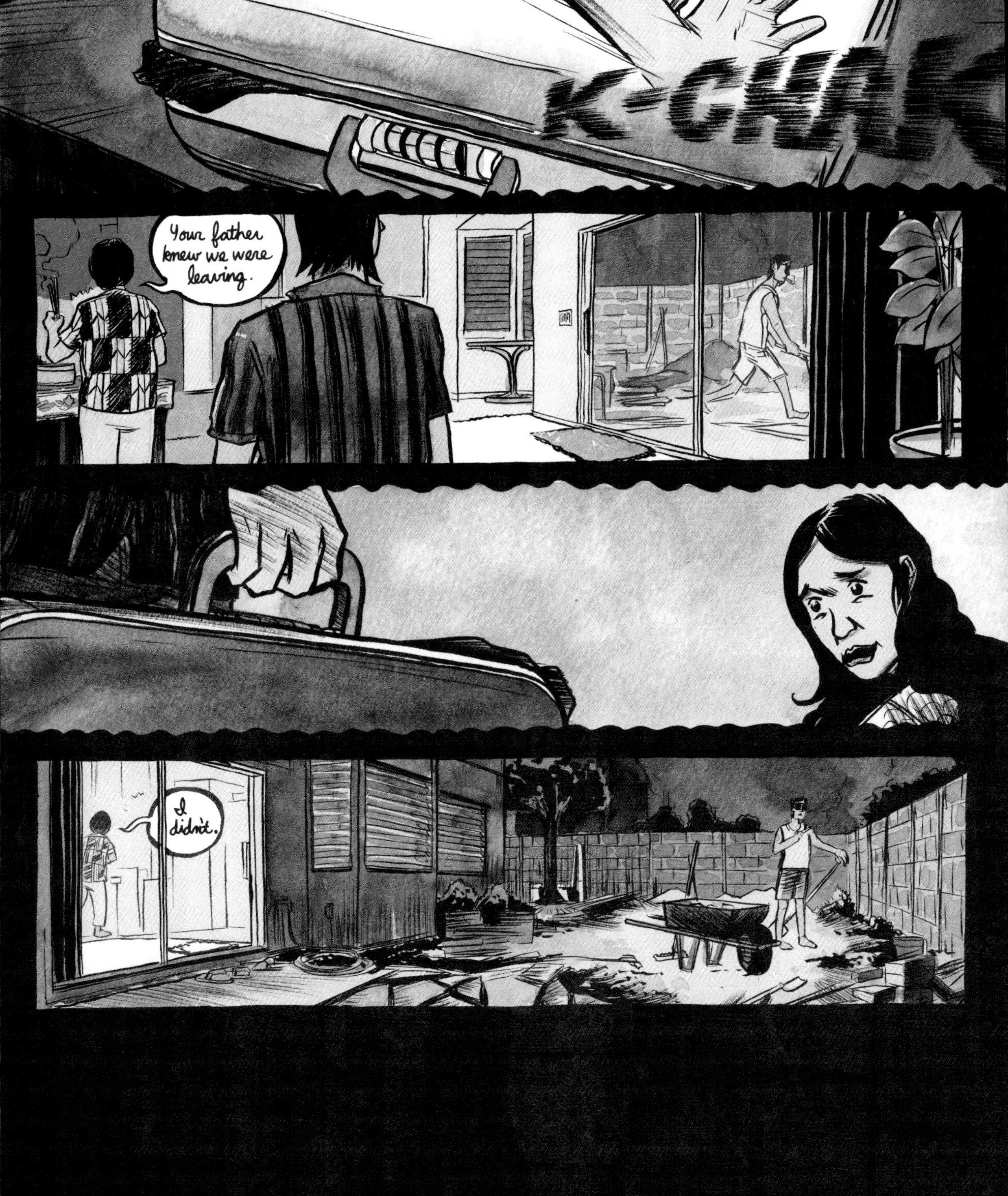
K-CHA
Your father knew we were leaving.
I didn't.

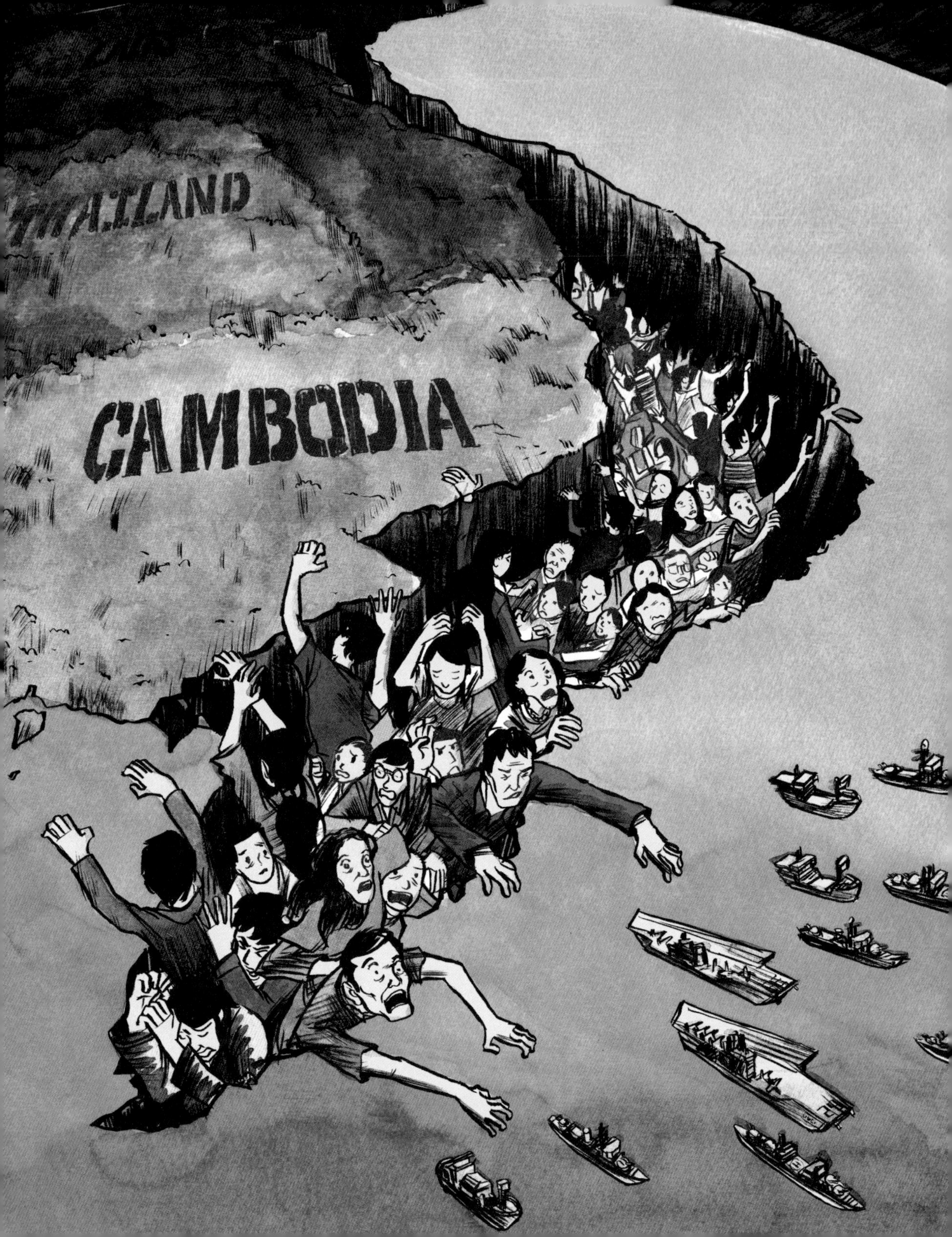
THAILAND
CAMBODIA

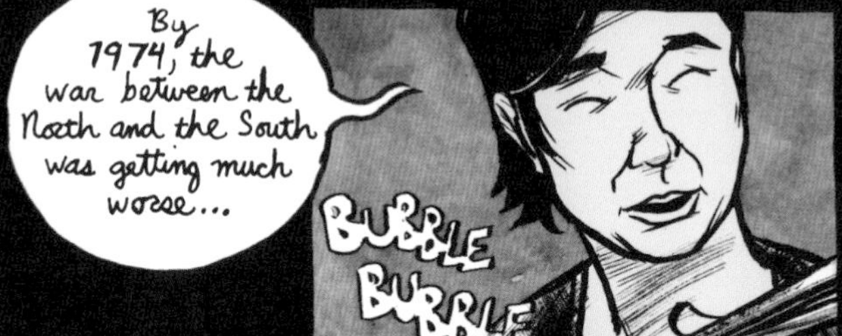
By 1974, the war between the North and the South was getting much worse...
BUBBLE BUBBLE

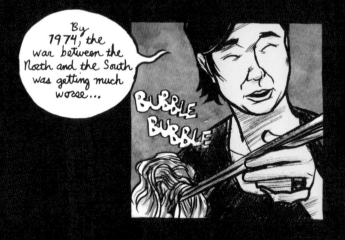

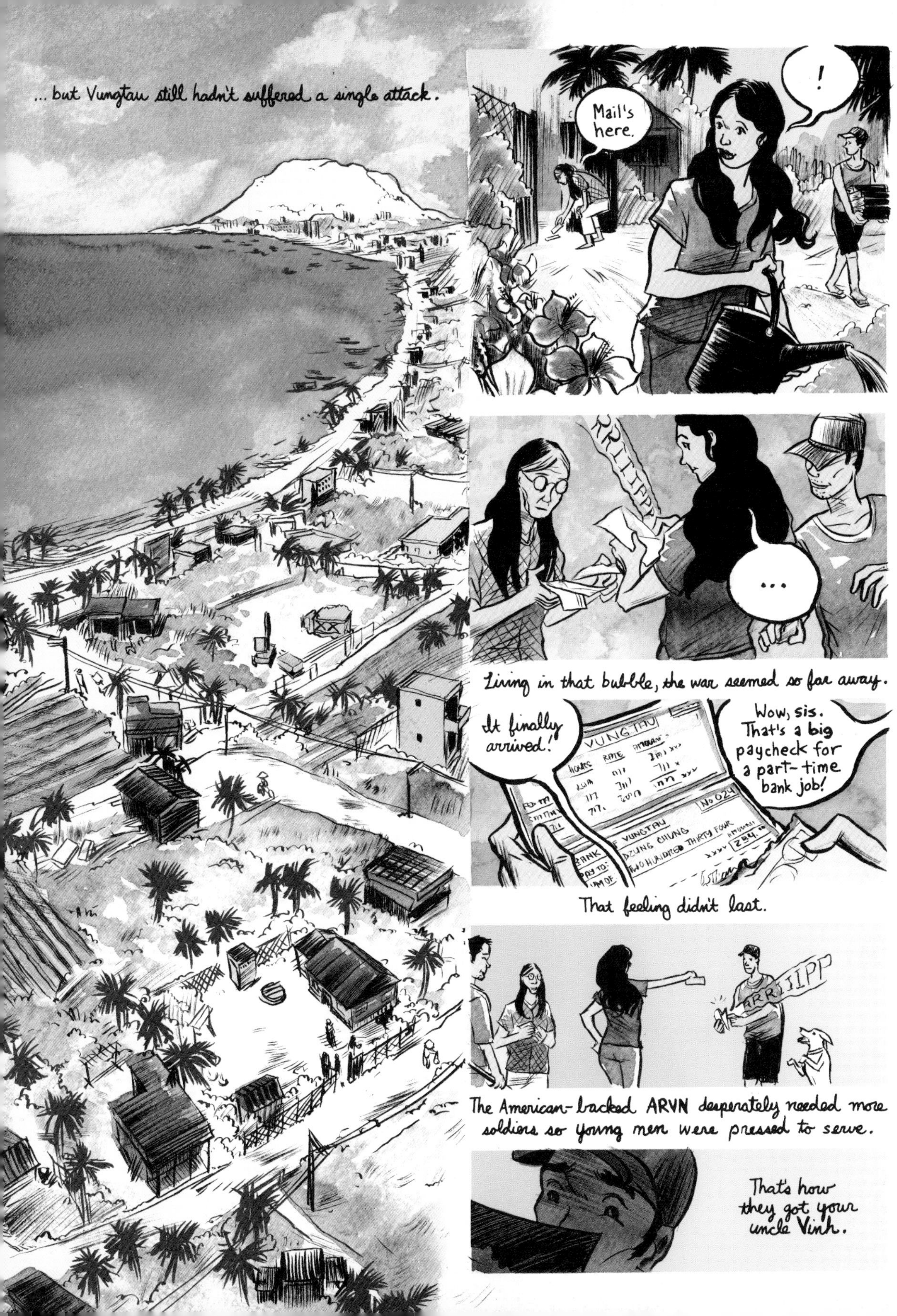
... but Vungtau still hadn't suffered a single attack.
Mail's here.
!
...
Living in that bubble, the war seemed so far away.
It finally arrived!
VUNGTAU
No 024
DZUNG CHUNG
TWO HUNDRED THIRTY FOUR
Wow, sis. That's a big paycheck for a part-time bank job!
That feeling didn't last.
RRIIIPP
The American-backed ARVN desperately needed more soldiers so young men were pressed to serve.
That's how they got your uncle Vinh.

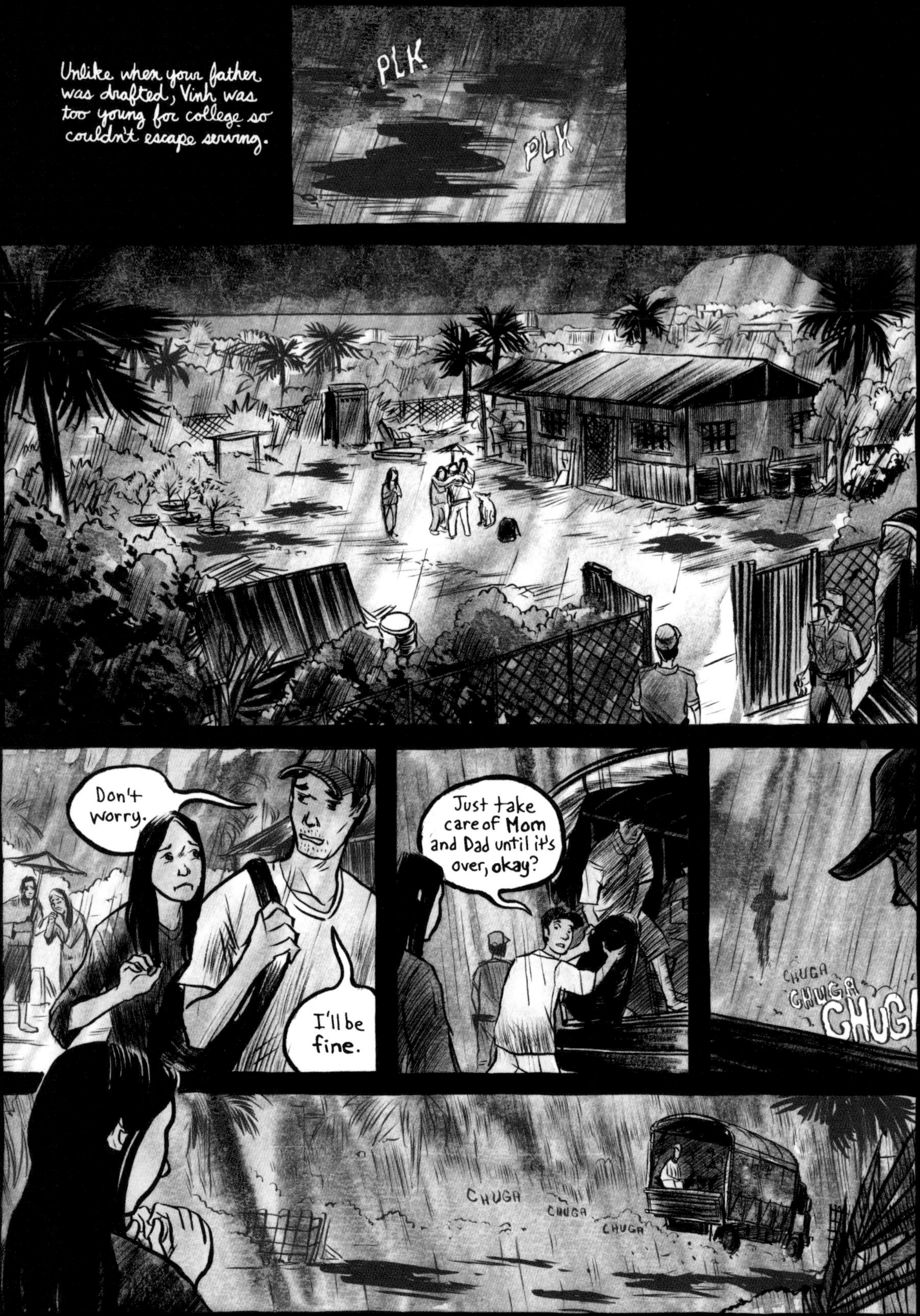
Unlike when your father was drafted, Vinh was too young for college so couldn't escape serving.
PLK!
PLK
Don't worry.
I'll be fine.
Just take care of Mom and Dad until it's over, okay?
CHUGA
CHUGA
CHUG
CHUGA
CHUGA
CHUGA

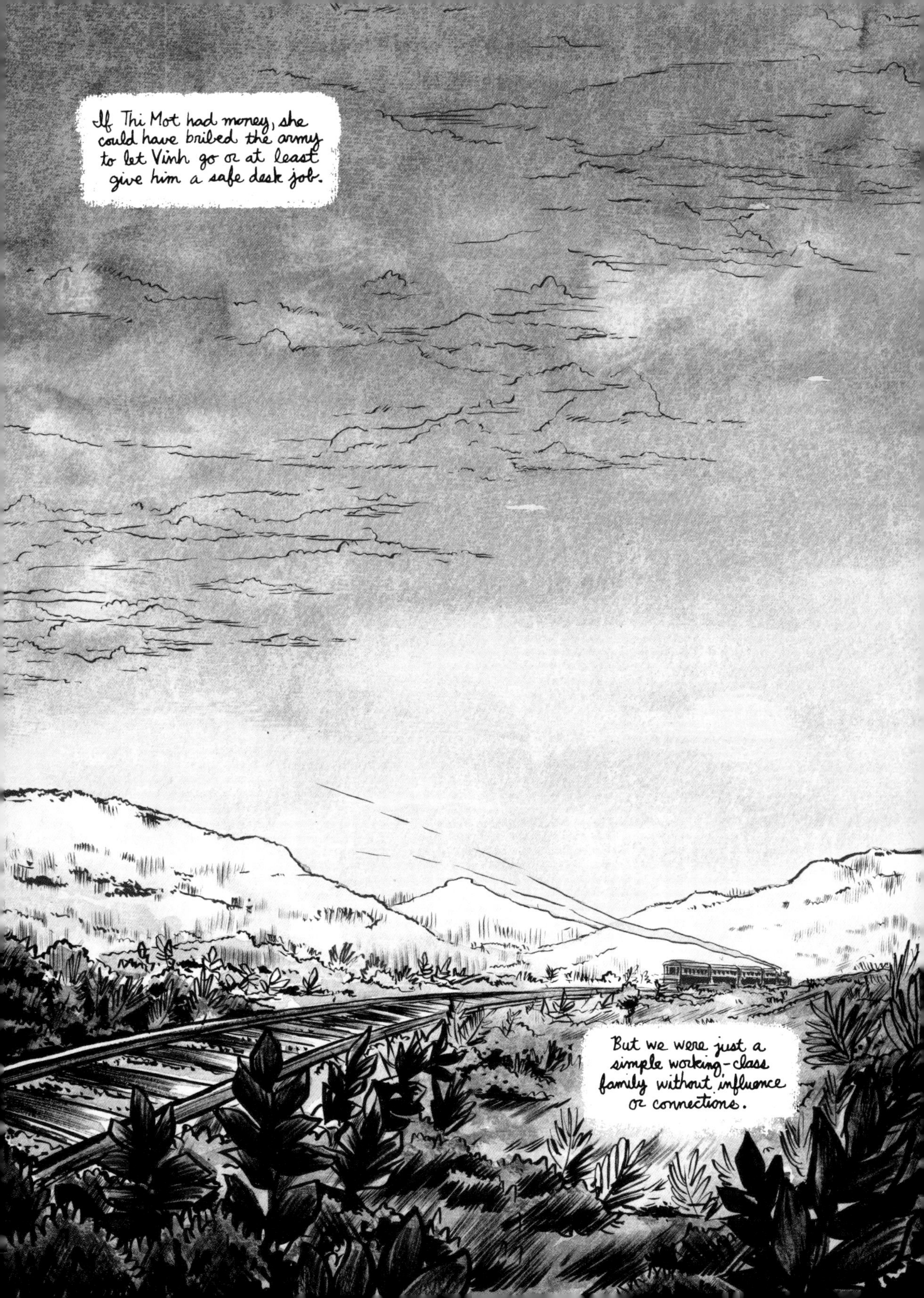
If Thi Mot had money, she could have bribed the army to let Vinh go or at least give him a safe desk job.
But we were just a simple working-class family without influence or connections.

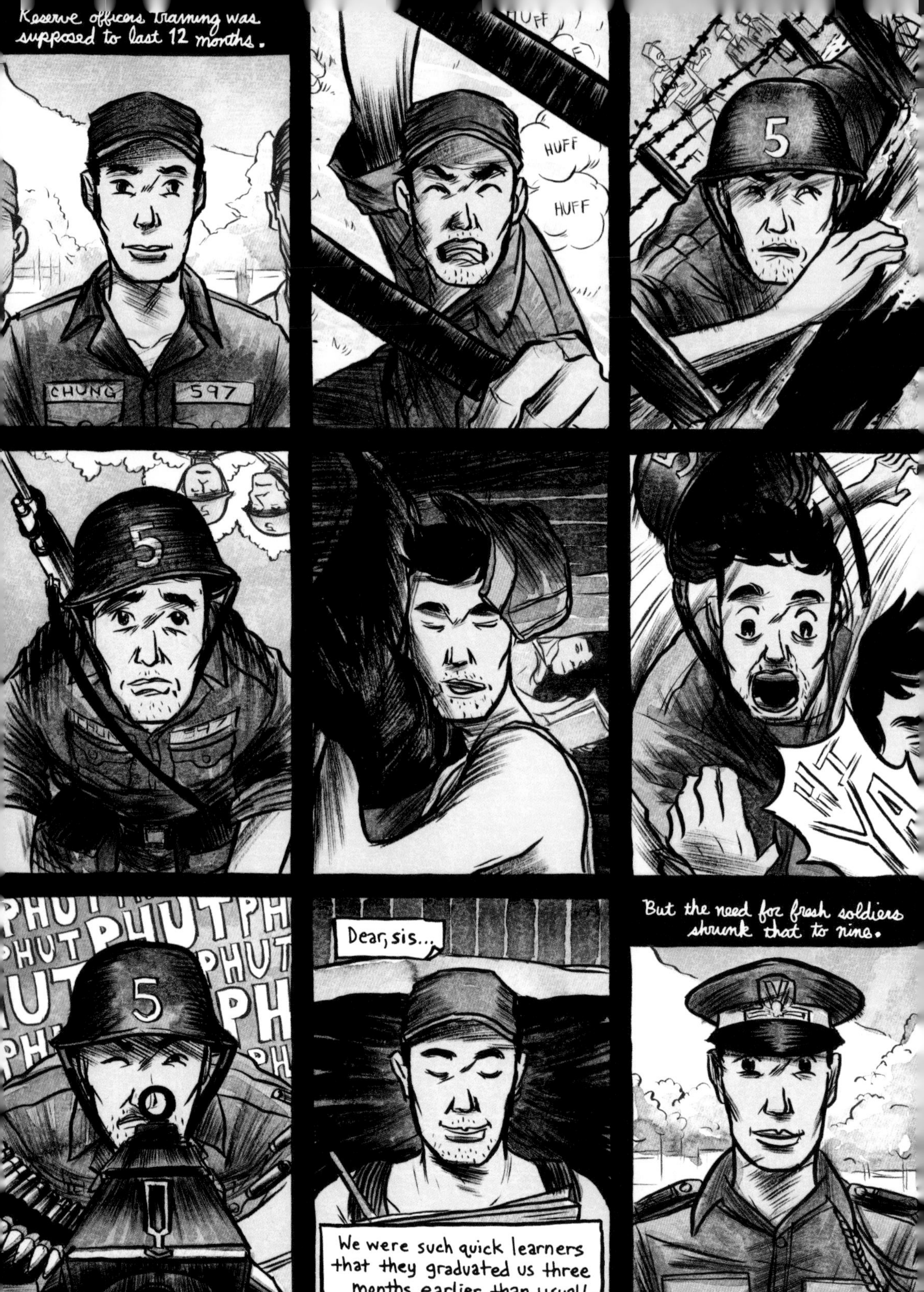
Reserve officers training was supposed to last 12 months.
CHUNG
597
HUFF
HUFF
HUFF
5
5
5
PHUT PHUT PHUT PHUT
Dear, sis...
We were such quick learners that they graduated us three months earlier than usual!
But the need for fresh soldiers shrunk that to nine.

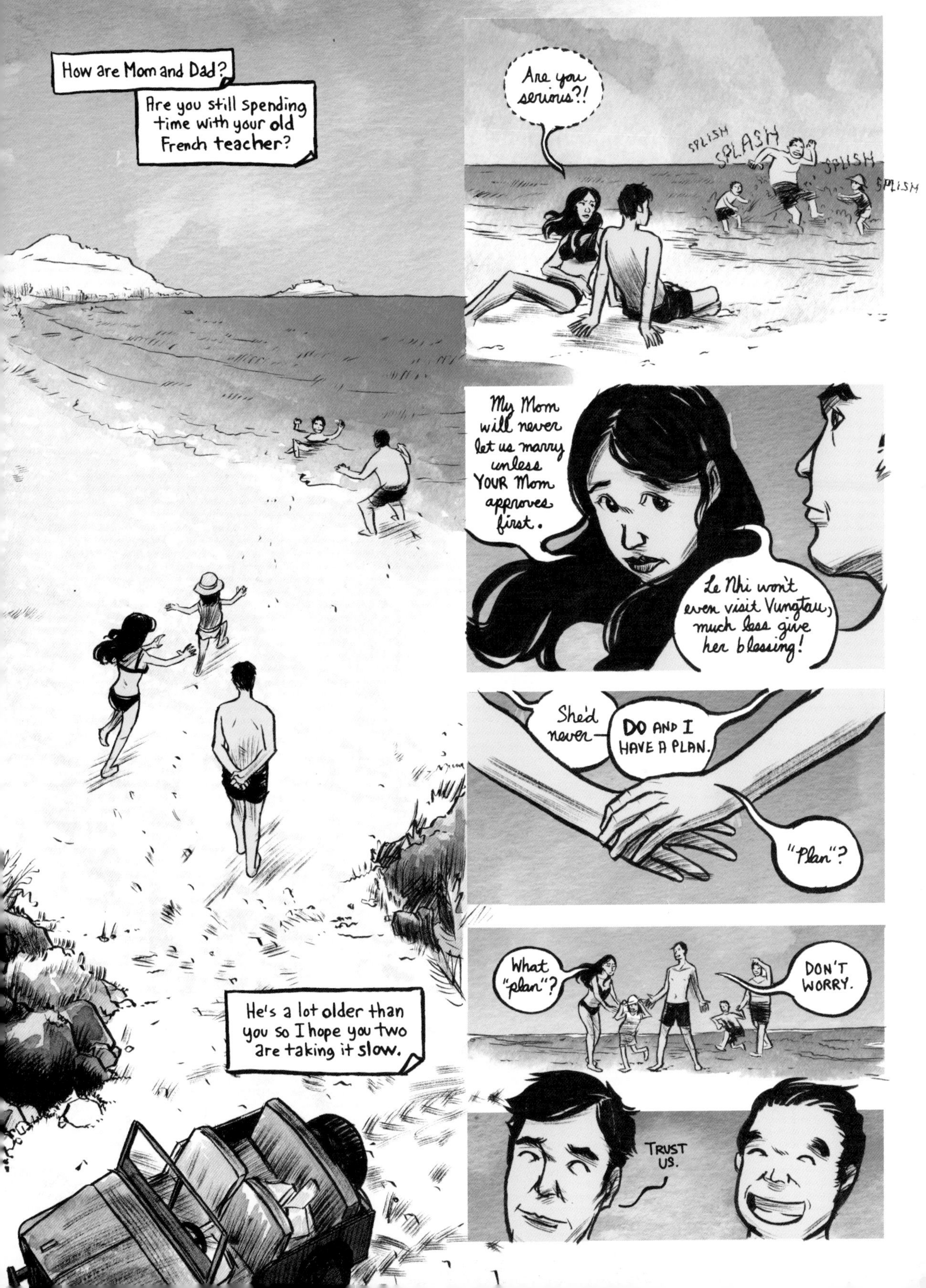
How are Mom and Dad?
Are you still spending time with your old French teacher?
He's a lot older than you so I hope you two are taking it slow.
Are you serious?!
SPLISH
SPLASH
SPLISH
SPLISH
My Mom will never let us marry unless YOUR Mom approves first.
Le Nhi won't even visit Vungtau, much less give her blessing!
She'd never—
DO AND I HAVE A PLAN.
"Plan"?
What "plan"?
DON'T WORRY.
TRUST US.

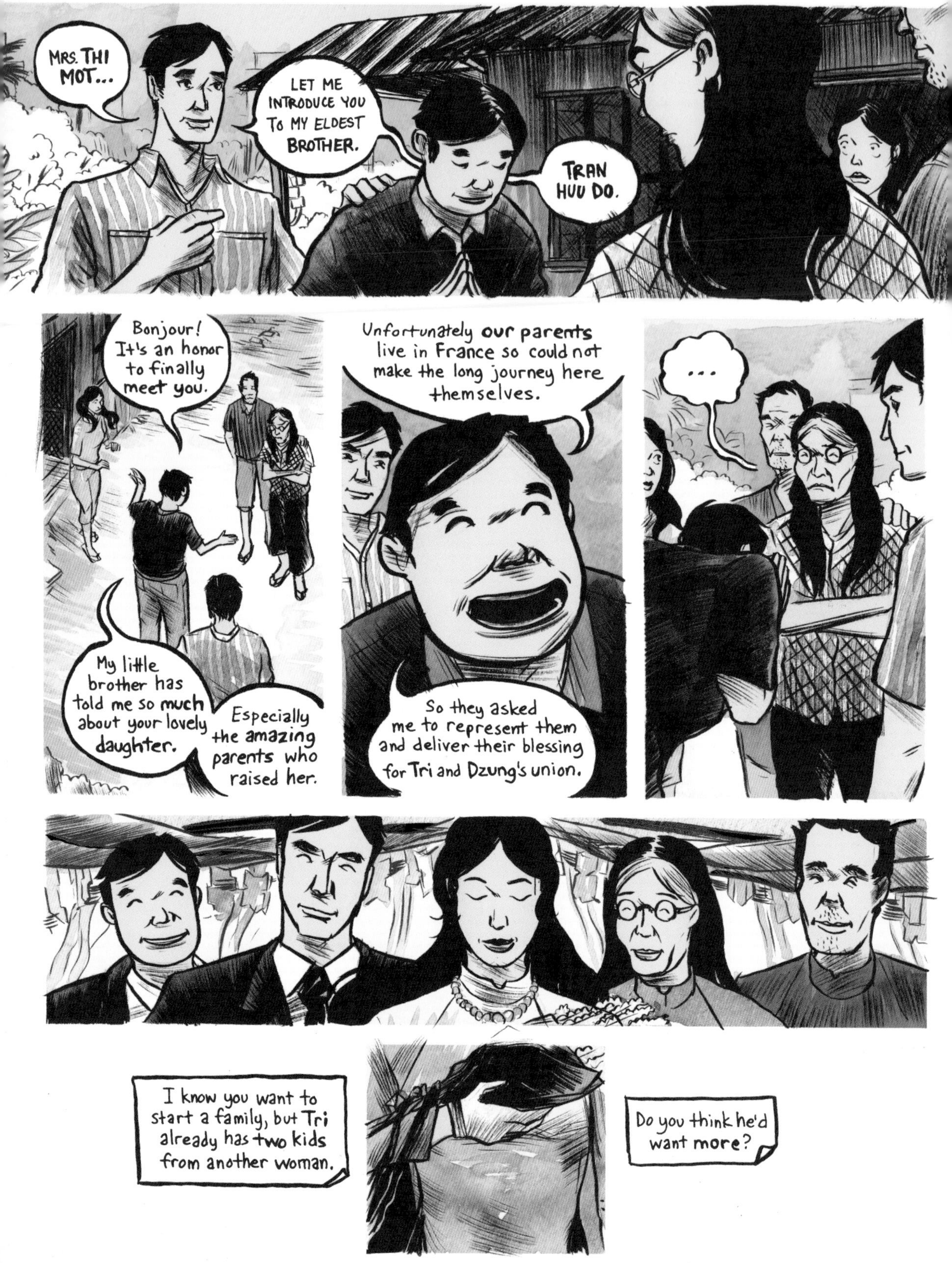

MRS. THI MOT...
LET ME INTRODUCE YOU TO MY ELDEST BROTHER.
TRAN HUU DO.
Bonjour! It's an honor to finally meet you.
My little brother has told me so much about your lovely daughter.
Especially the amazing parents who raised her.
Unfortunately our parents live in France so could not make the long journey here themselves.
So they asked me to represent them and deliver their blessing for Tri and Dzung's union.
...
I know you want to start a family, but Tri already has two kids from another woman.
Do you think he'd want more?

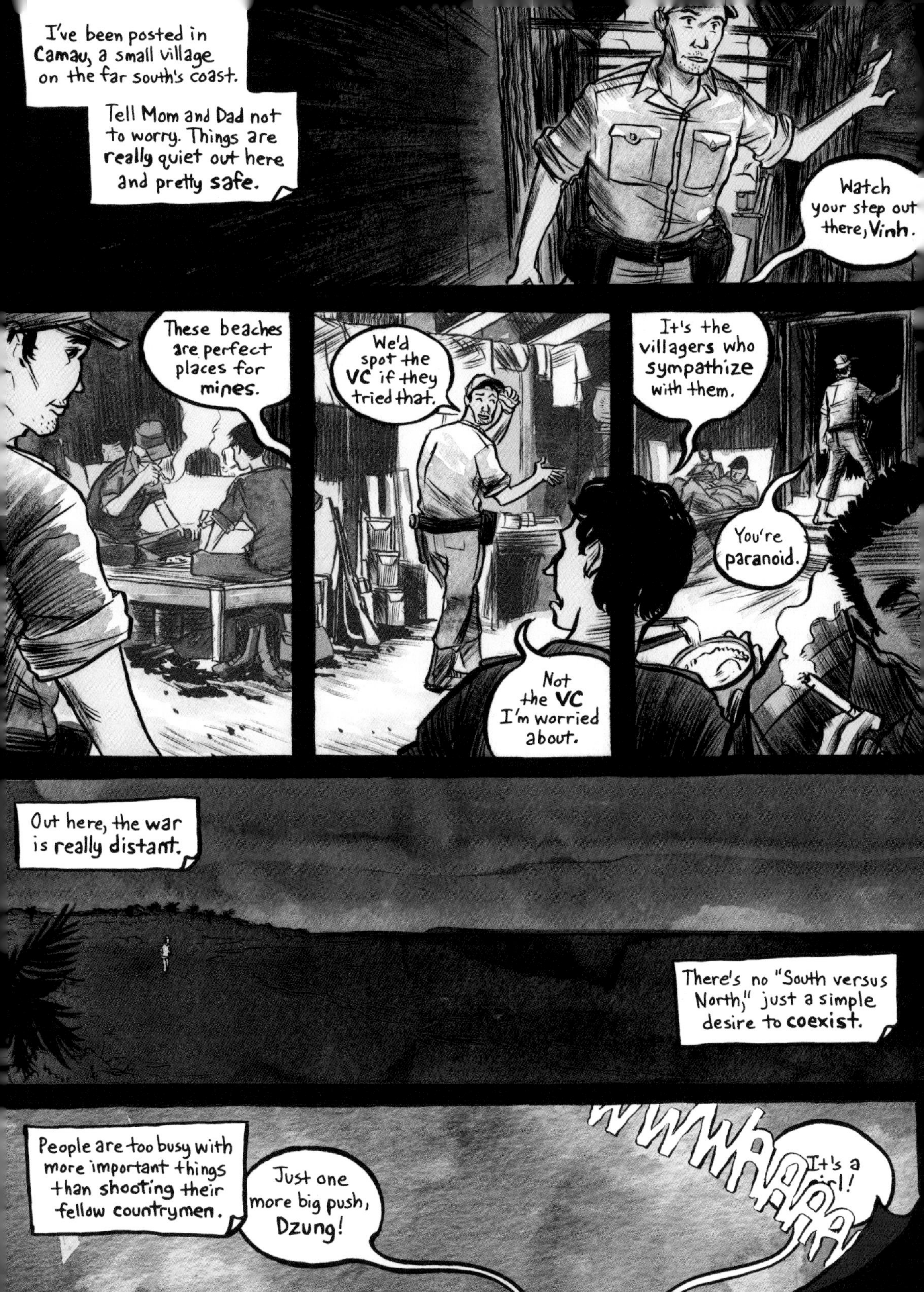

I've been posted in Camau, a small village on the far south's coast.
Tell Mom and Dad not to worry. Things are really quiet out here and pretty safe.
Watch your step out there, Vinh.
These beaches are perfect places for mines.
We'd spot the VC if they tried that.
It's the villagers who sympathize with them.
You're paranoid.
Not the VC I'm worried about.
Out here, the war is really distant.
There's no "South versus North," just a simple desire to coexist.
People are too busy with more important things than shooting their fellow countrymen.
Just one more big push, Dzung!
WWWAAAA
It's a girl!

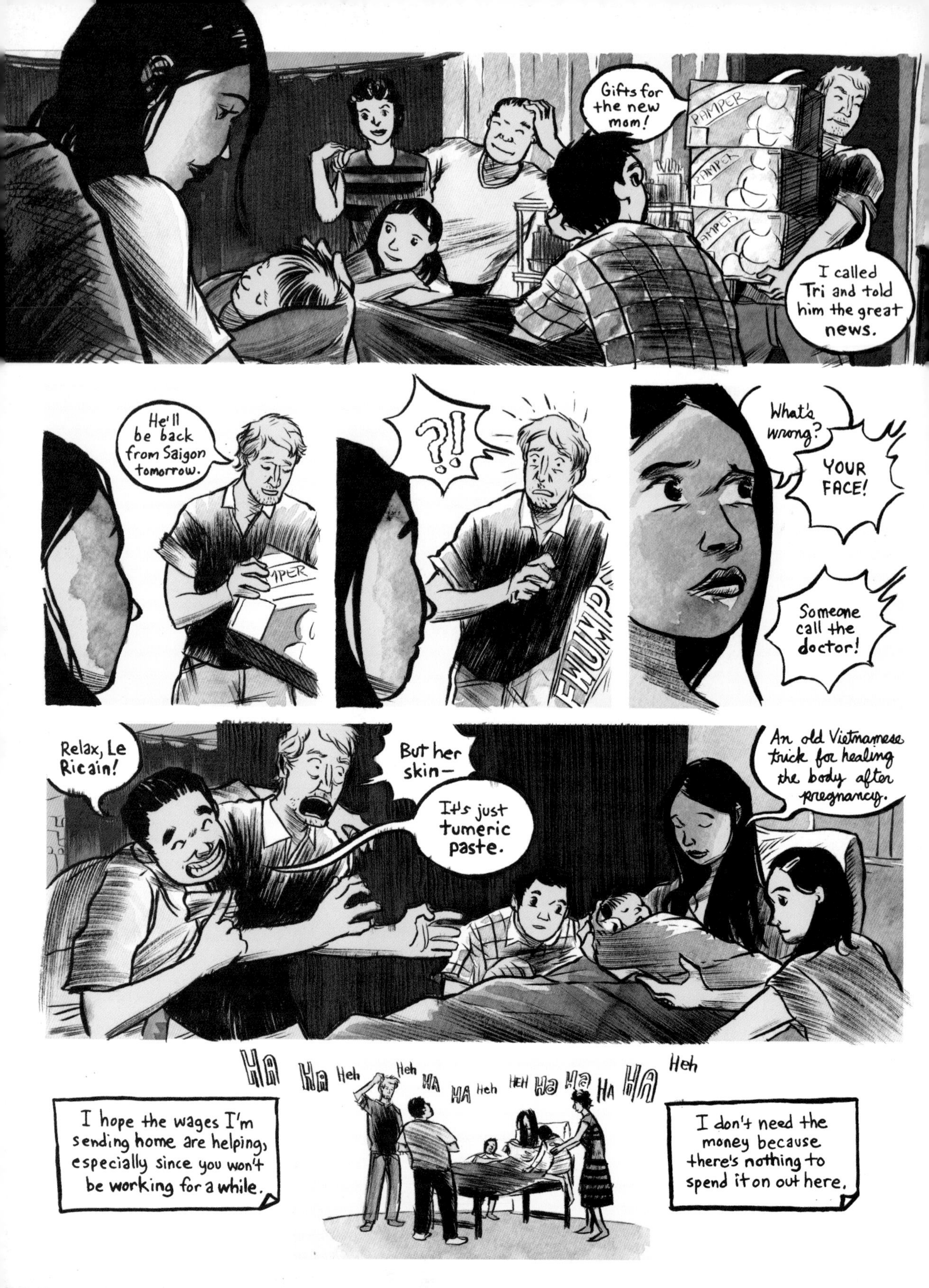
Gifts for the new mom!
I called Tri and told him the great news.
He'll be back from Saigon tomorrow.
?!
THUMP
What's wrong?
YOUR FACE!
Someone call the doctor!
Relax, Le Ricain!
But her skin—
It's just tumeric paste.
An old Vietnamese trick for healing the body after pregnancy.
HA Ha Heh Heh HA HA Heh HEH Ha Ha HA HA Heh
I hope the wages I'm sending home are helping, especially since you won't be working for a while.
I don't need the money because there's nothing to spend it on out here.

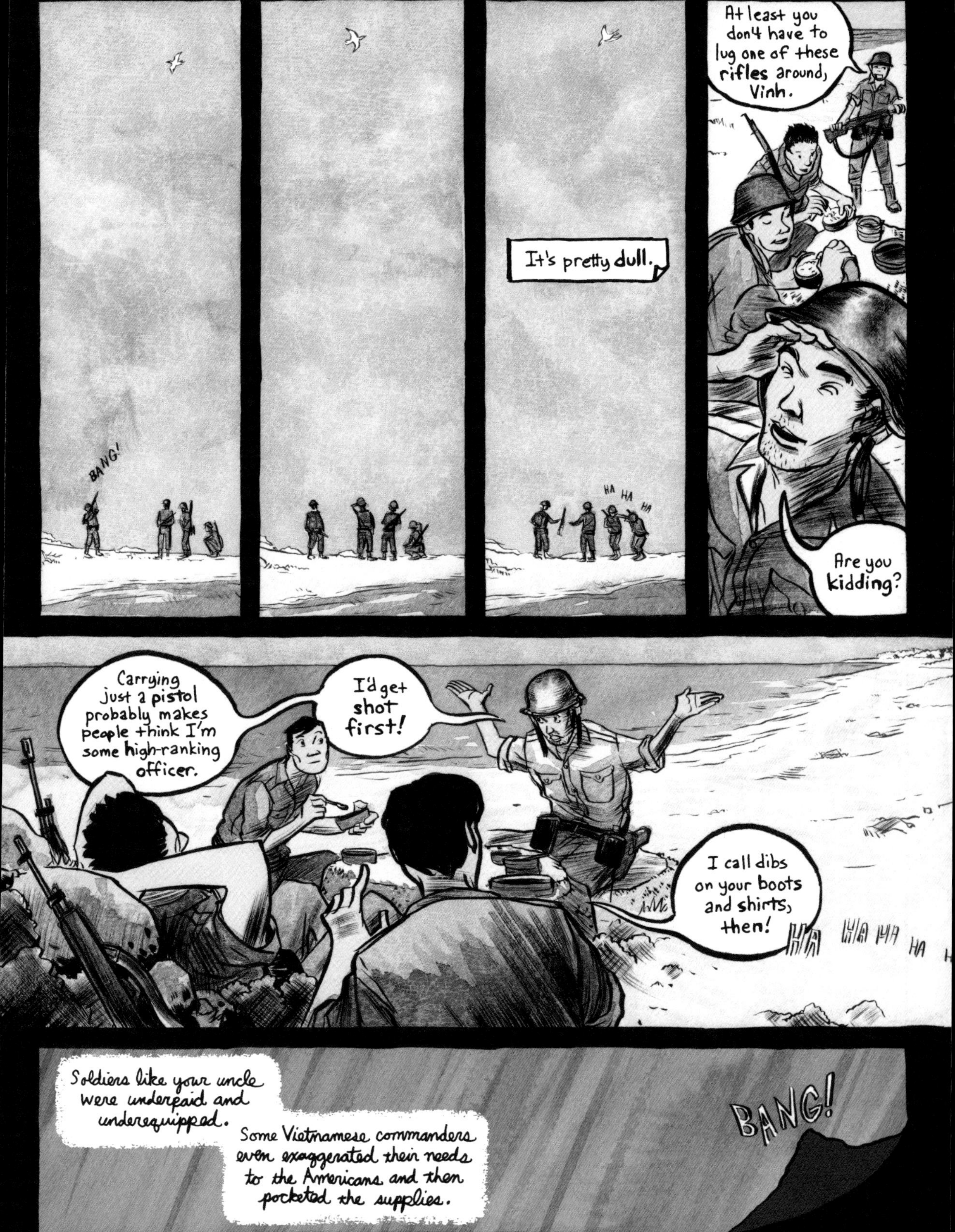
BANG!
It's pretty dull.
HA HA HA
At least you don't have to lug one of these rifles around, Vinh.
Are you kidding?
Carrying just a pistol probably makes people think I'm some high-ranking officer.
I'd get shot first!
I call dibs on your boots and shirts, then!
HA HA HA HA HA
Soldiers like your uncle were underpaid and underequipped.
Some Vietnamese commanders even exaggerated their needs to the Americans and then pocketed the supplies.
BANG!

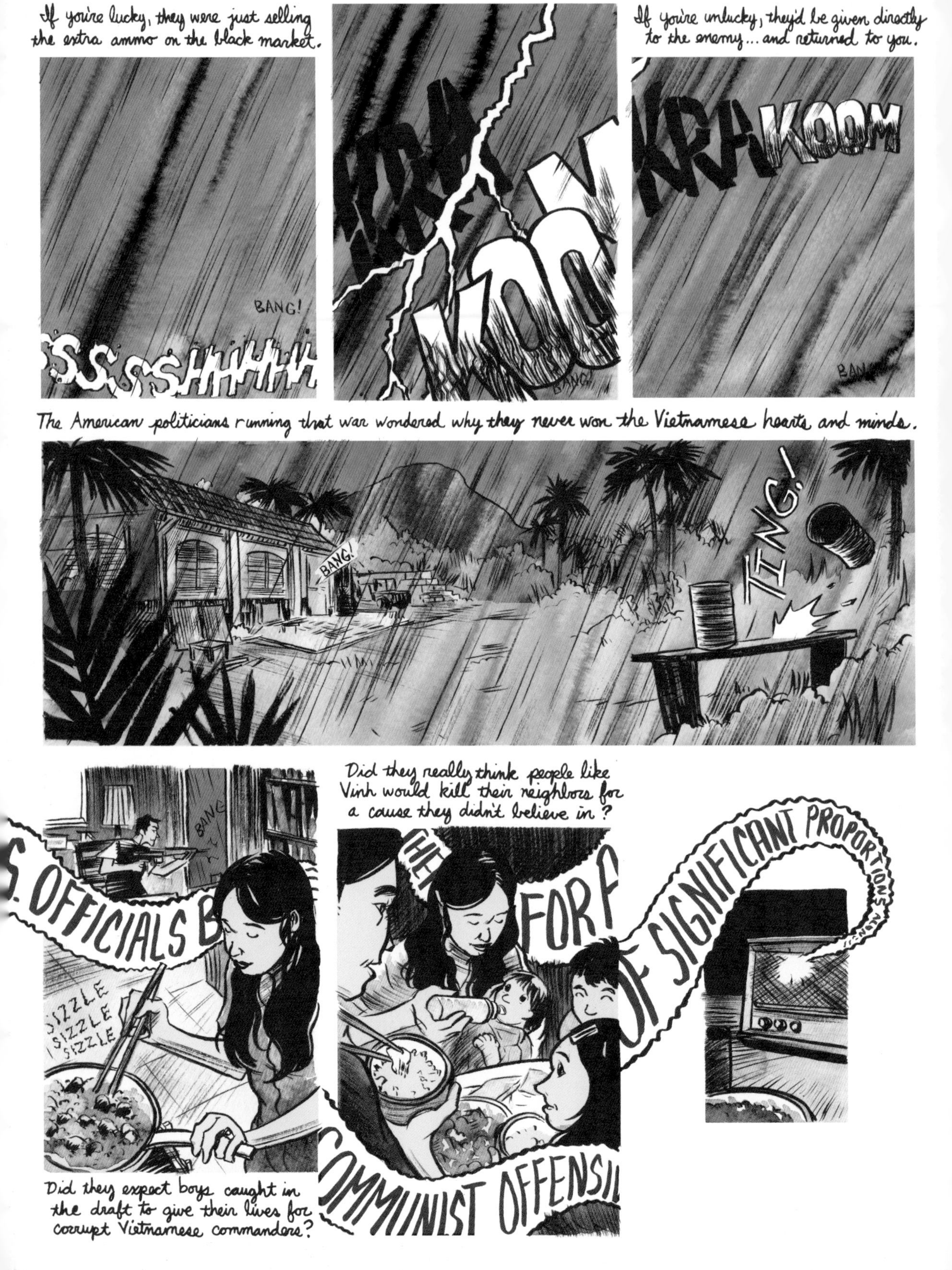
If you're lucky, they were just selling the extra ammo on the black market.
BANG!
If you're unlucky, they'd be given directly to the enemy... and returned to you.
KRAKOOM
The American politicians running that war wondered why they never won the Vietnamese hearts and minds.
BANG!
TING!
S. OFFICIALS B
SIZZLE
SIZZLE
SIZZLE
Did they expect boys caught in the draft to give their lives for corrupt Vietnamese commanders?
Did they really think people like Vinh would kill their neighbors for a cause they didn't believe in?
THEY
FOR
COMMUNIST OFFENSI
OF SIGNIFICANT PROPORTIONS

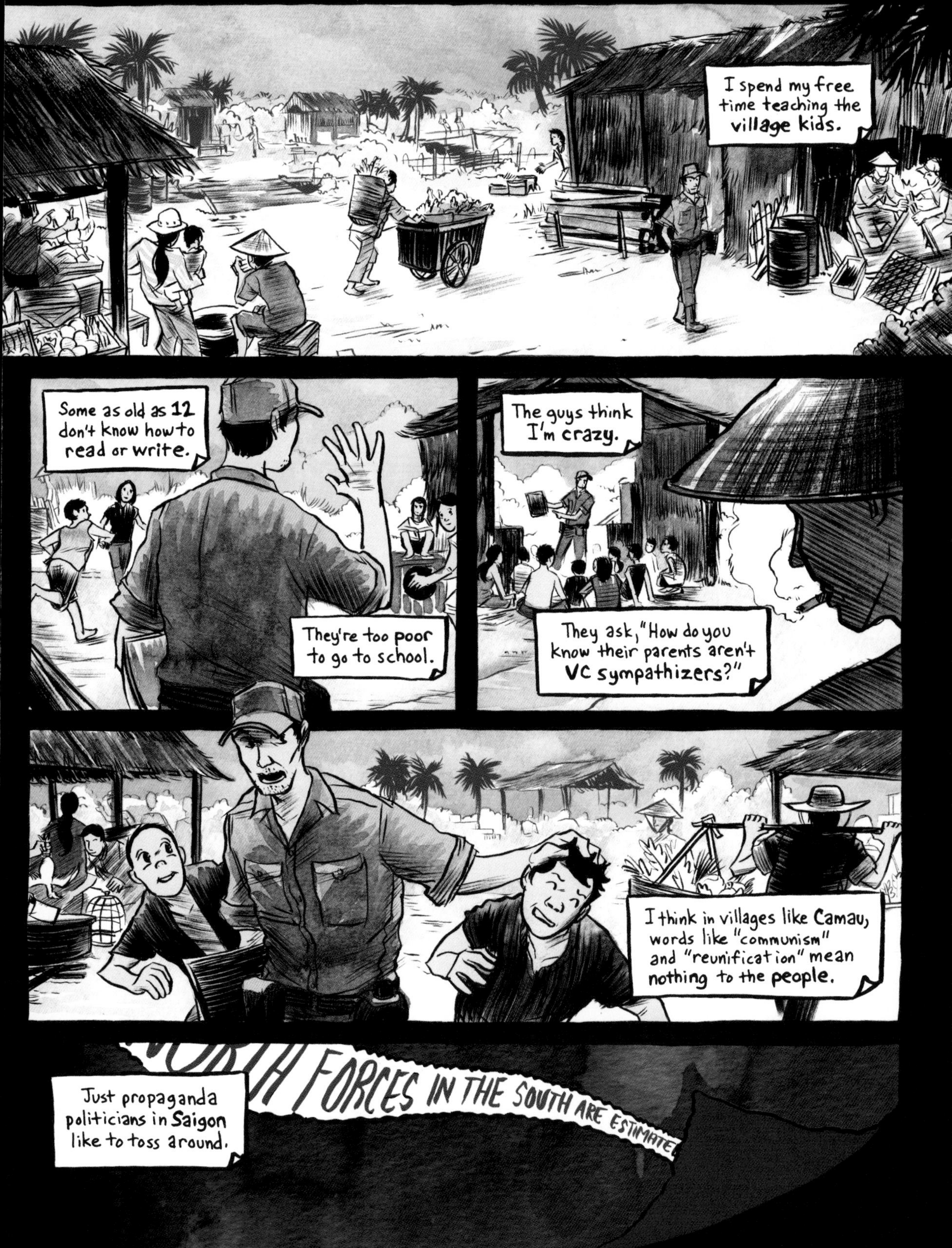
I spend my free time teaching the village kids.
Some as old as 12 don't know how to read or write.
They're too poor to go to school.
The guys think I'm crazy.
They ask, "How do you know their parents aren't VC sympathizers?"
I think in villages like Camau, words like "communism" and "reunification" mean nothing to the people.
Just propaganda politicians in Saigon like to toss around.
FORCES IN THE SOUTH ARE ESTIMATE

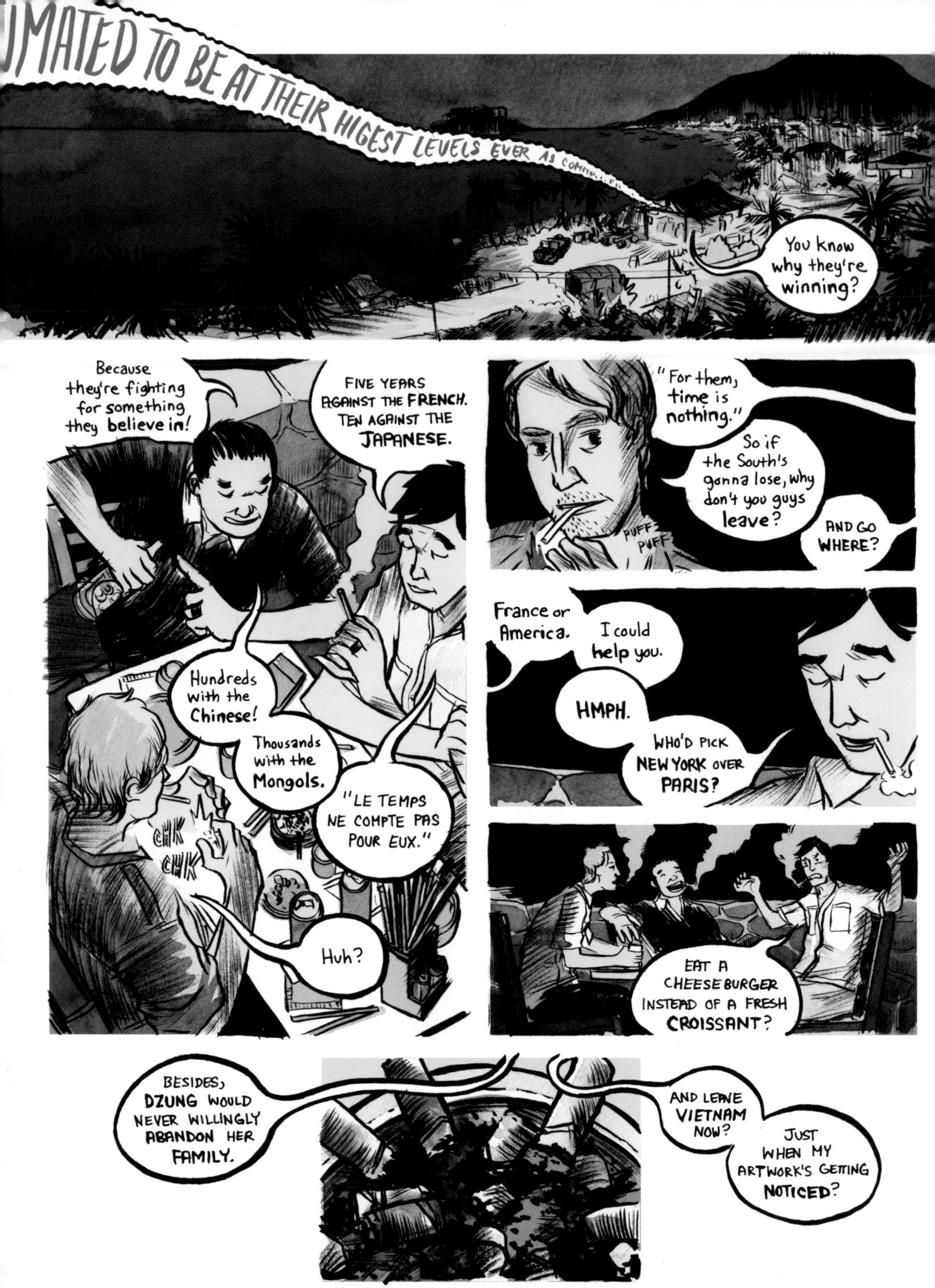
MATED TO BE AT THEIR HIGEST LEVELS EVER AS
You know why they're winning?
Because they're fighting for something they believe in!
FIVE YEARS AGAINST THE FRENCH. TEN AGAINST THE JAPANESE.
Hundreds with the Chinese!
Thousands with the Mongols.
"LE TEMPS NE COMPTE PAS POUR EUX."
CHK CHK
Huh?
"For them, time is nothing."
PUFF PUFF
So if the South's gonna lose, why don't you guys leave?
AND GO WHERE?
France or America.
I could help you.
HMPH.
WHO'D PICK NEW YORK OVER PARIS?
EAT A CHEESEBURGER INSTEAD OF A FRESH CROISSANT?
BESIDES, DZUNG WOULD NEVER WILLINGLY ABANDON HER FAMILY.
AND LEAVE VIETNAM NOW?
JUST WHEN MY ARTWORK'S GETTING NOTICED?

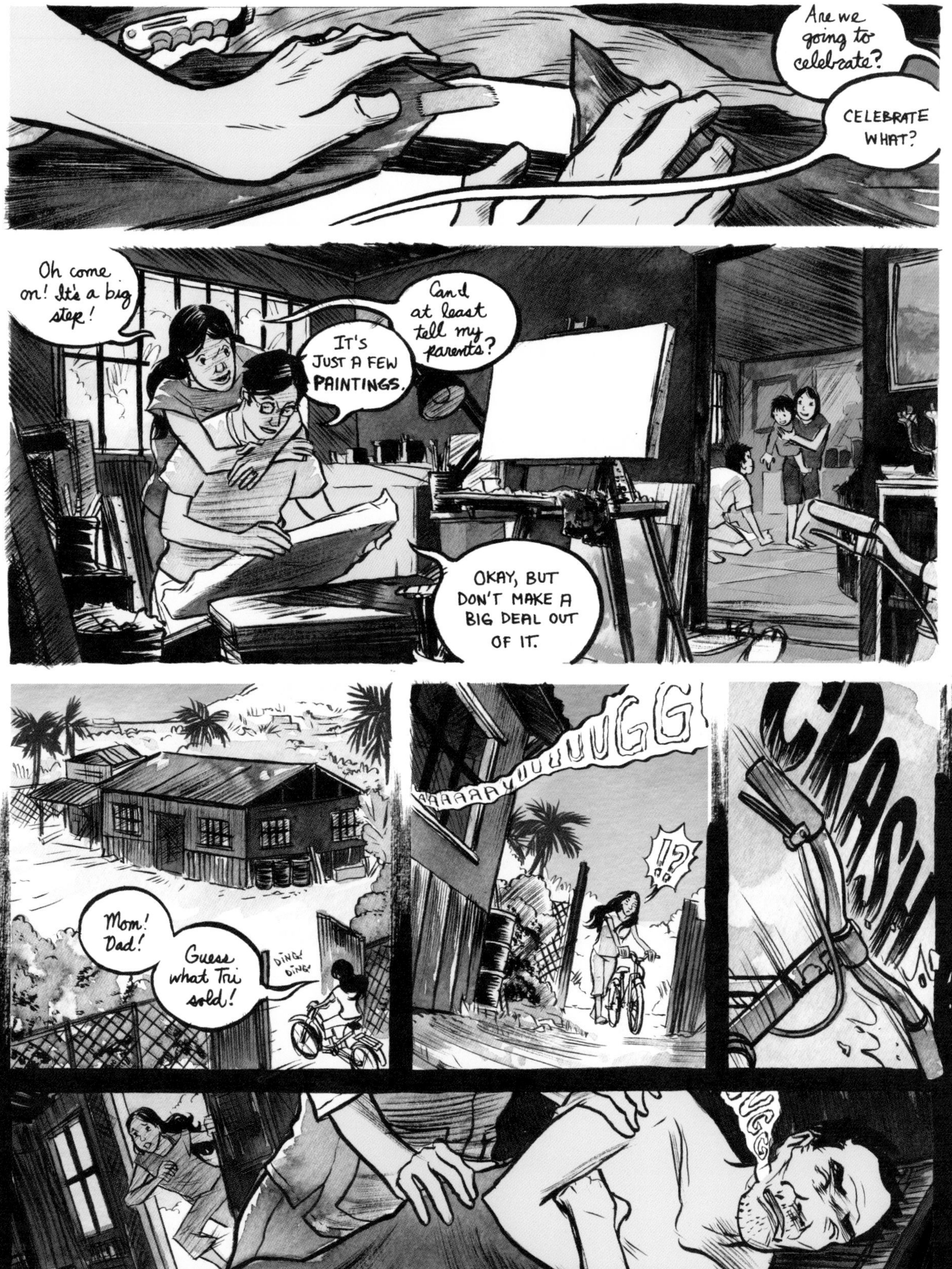

Are we going to celebrate?
CELEBRATE WHAT?
Oh come on! It's a big step!
It's JUST A FEW PAINTINGS.
Can I at least tell my parents?
OKAY, BUT DON'T MAKE A BIG DEAL OUT OF IT.
Mom! Dad!
Guess what Tri sold!
DING! DING!
AAAAAAAUUUUUUUGG
!?
CRASH

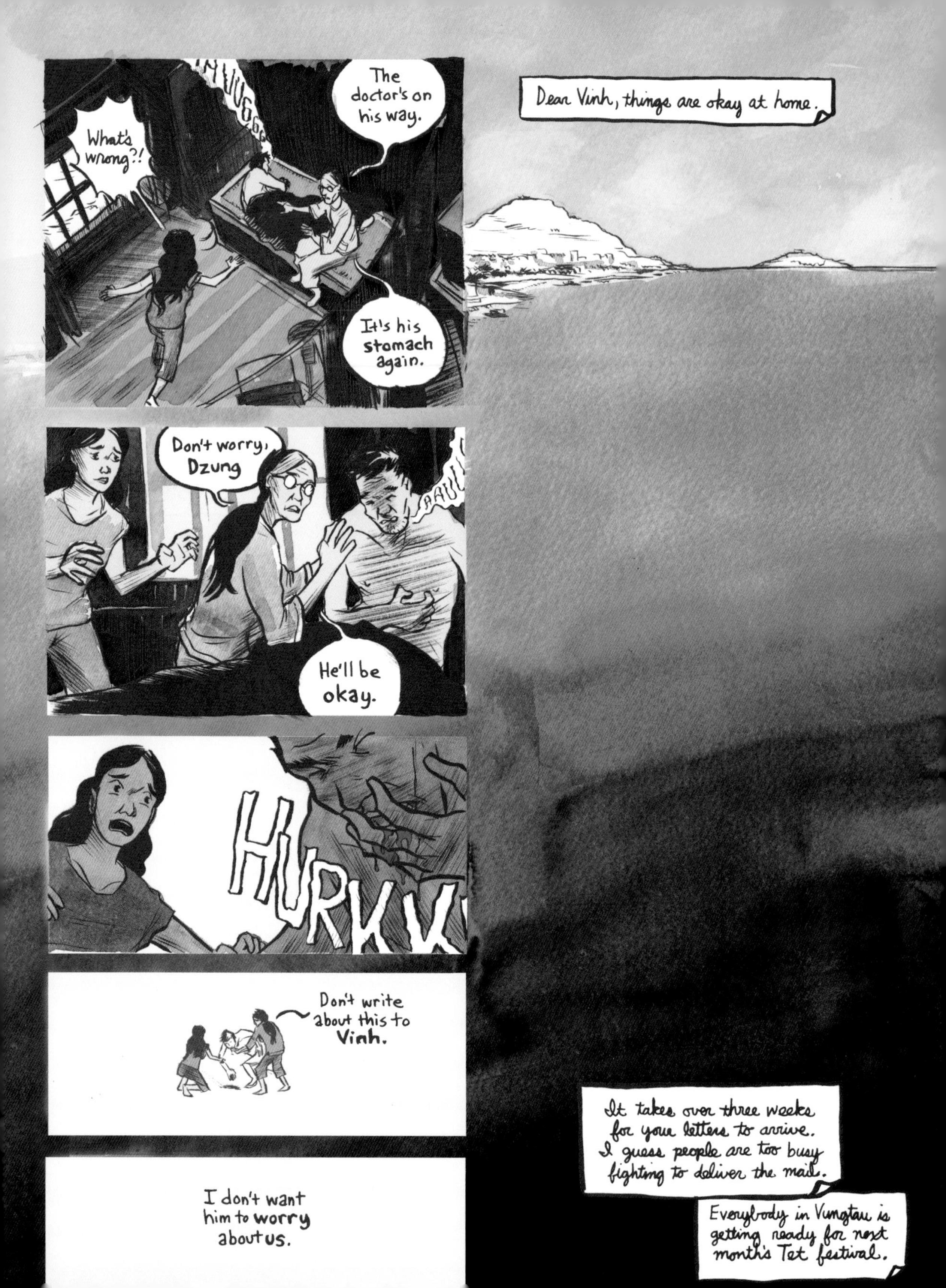
Dear Vinh, things are okay at home.
What's wrong?!
The doctor's on his way.
It's his stomach again.
Don't worry, Dzung
He'll be okay.
HURKK
Don't write about this to Vinh.
I don't want him to worry about us.
It takes over three weeks for your letters to arrive. I guess people are too busy fighting to deliver the mail.
Everybody in Vungtau is getting ready for next month's Tet festival.

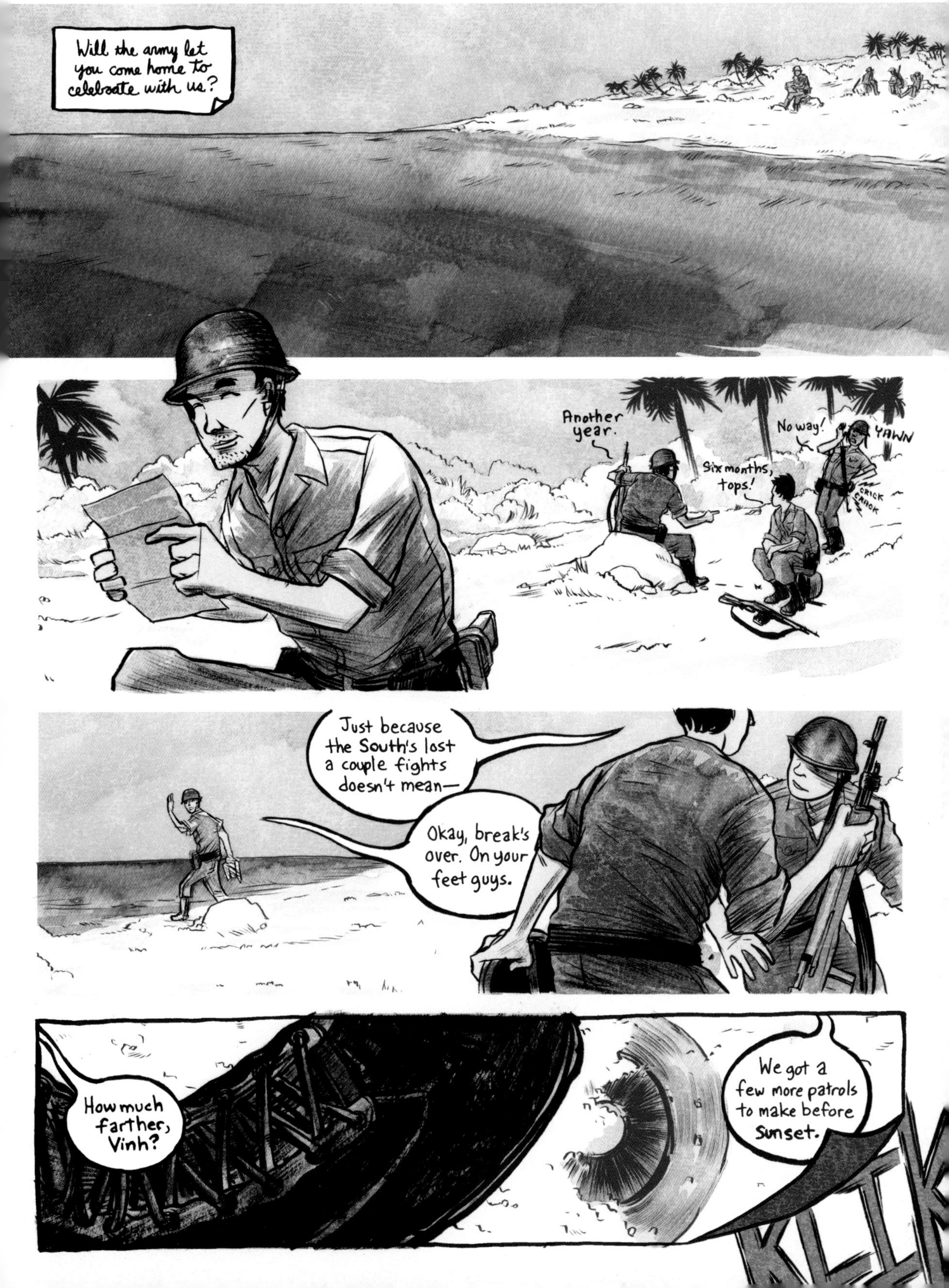
Will the army let you come home to celebrate with us?
Another year.
Six months, tops!
No way!
YAWN
CRICK CRACK
Just because the South's lost a couple fights doesn't mean—
Okay, break's over. On your feet guys.
How much farther, Vinh?
We got a few more patrols to make before sunset.
KLIK

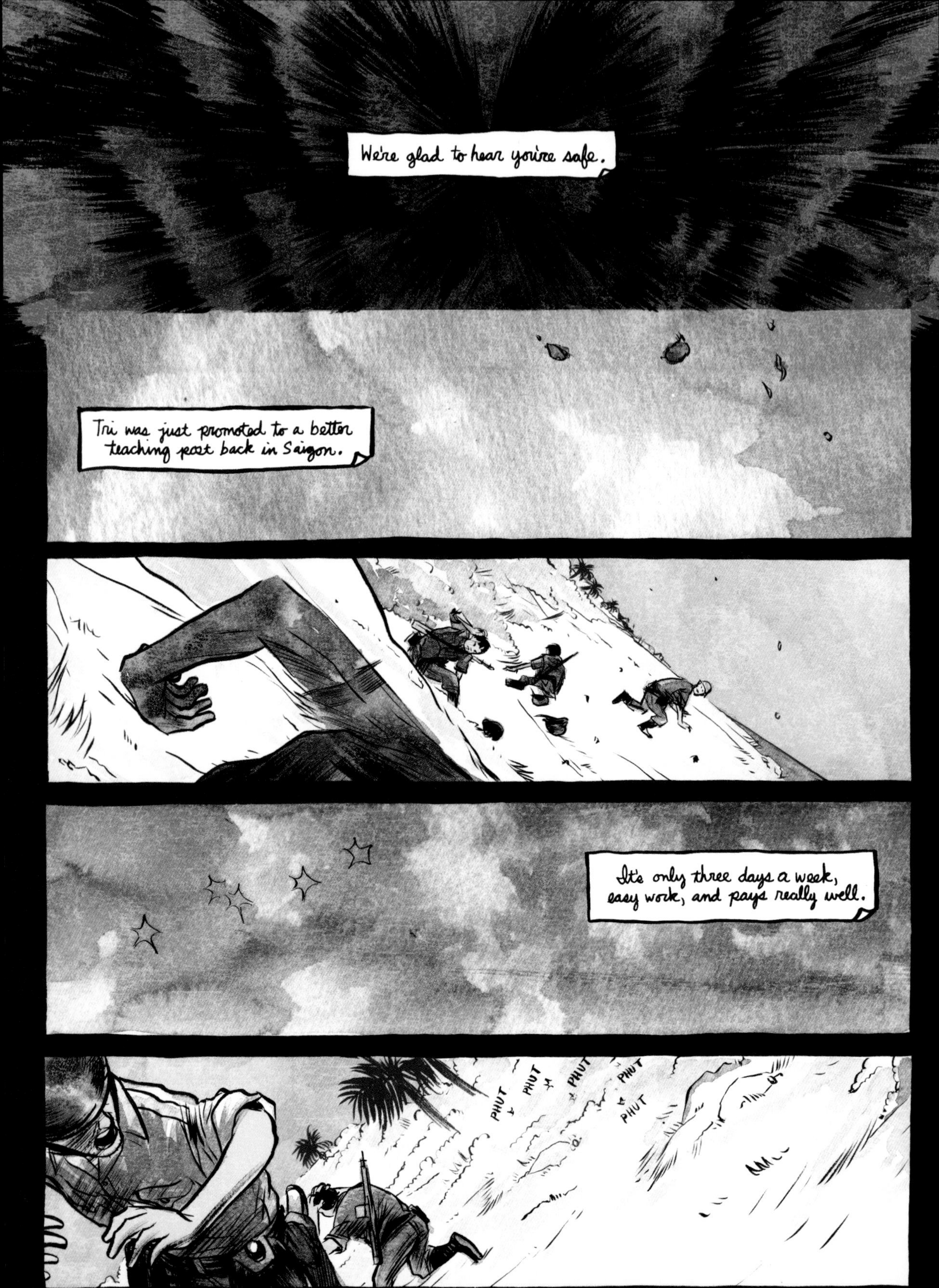
We're glad to hear you're safe.
Tri was just promoted to a better teaching post back in Saigon.
It's only three days a week, easy work, and pays really well.
PHUT
PHUT
PHUT
PHUT
PHUT

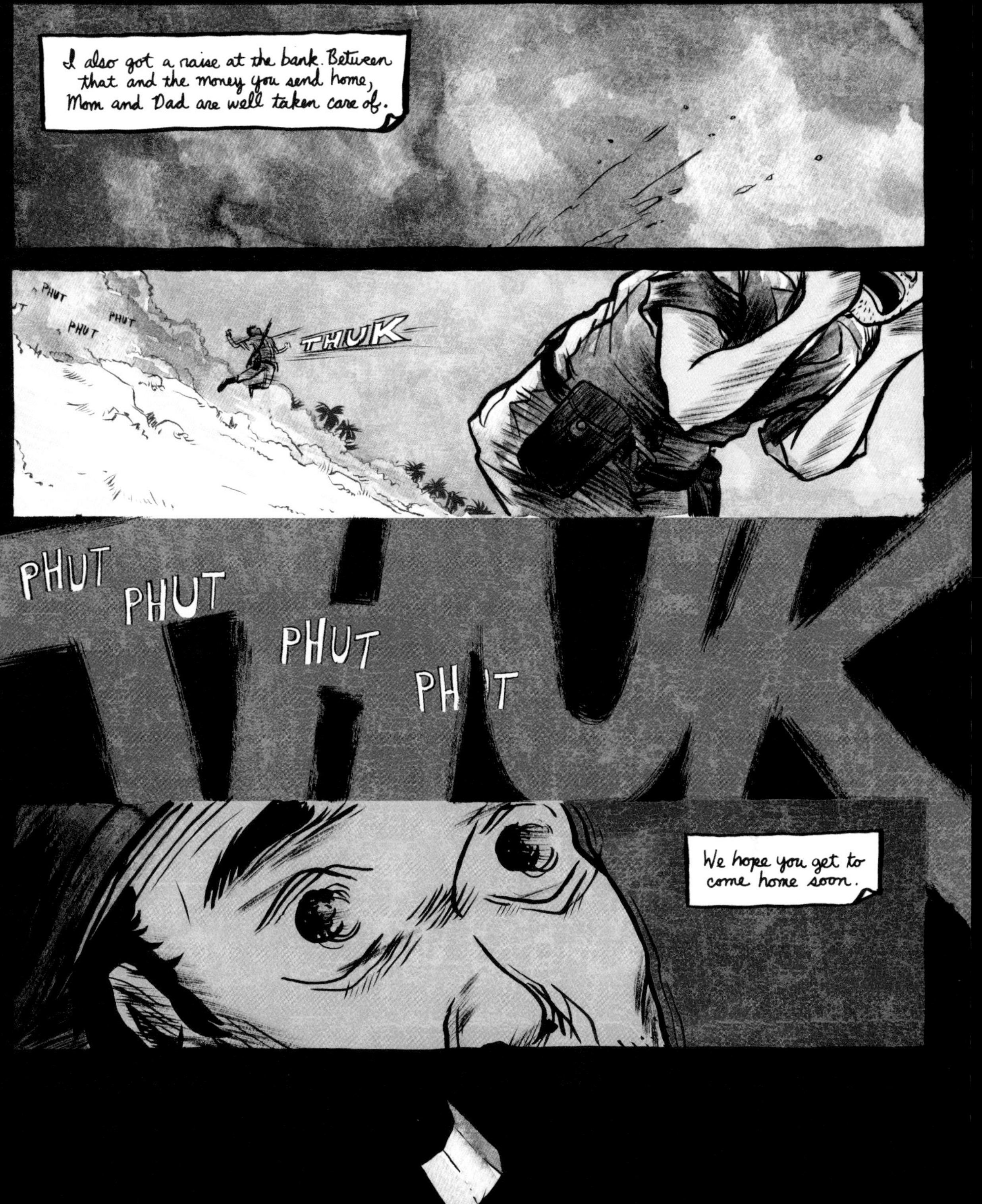
I also got a raise at the bank. Between that and the money you send home, Mom and Dad are well taken care of.
PHUT
PHUT
PHUT
THUK
PHUT
PHUT
PHUT
We hope you get to come home soon.

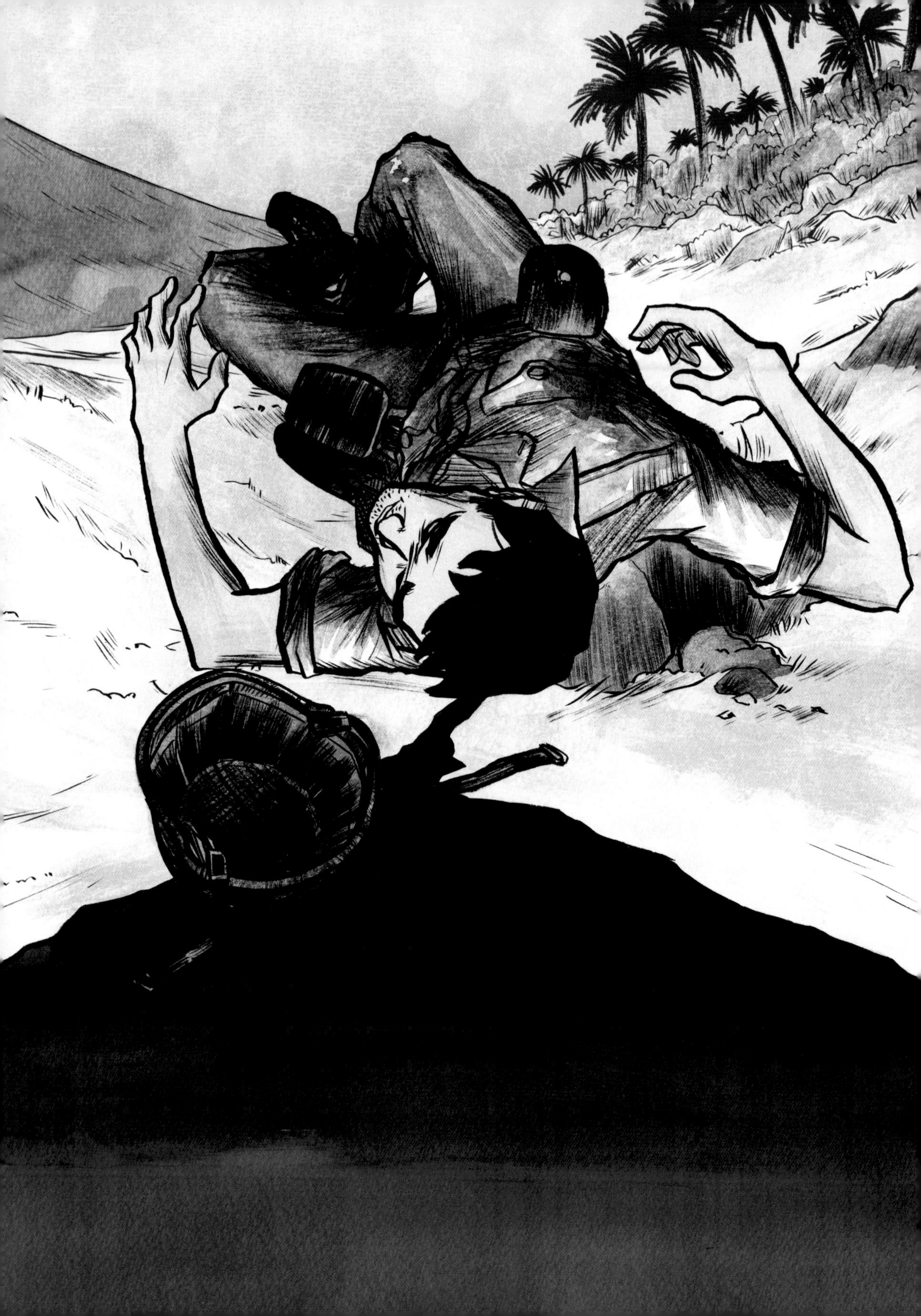

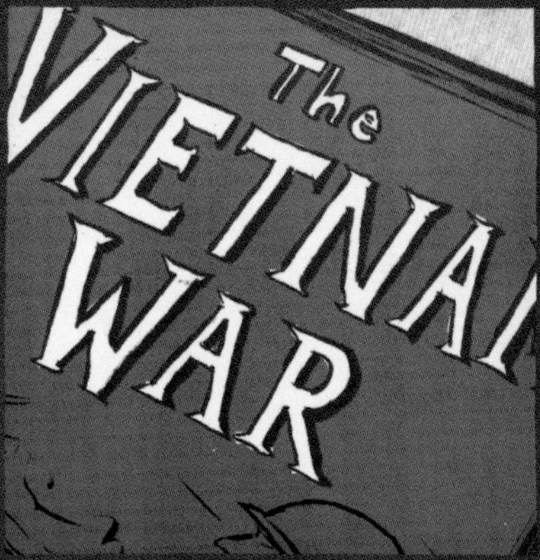
The
VIETNA
WAR

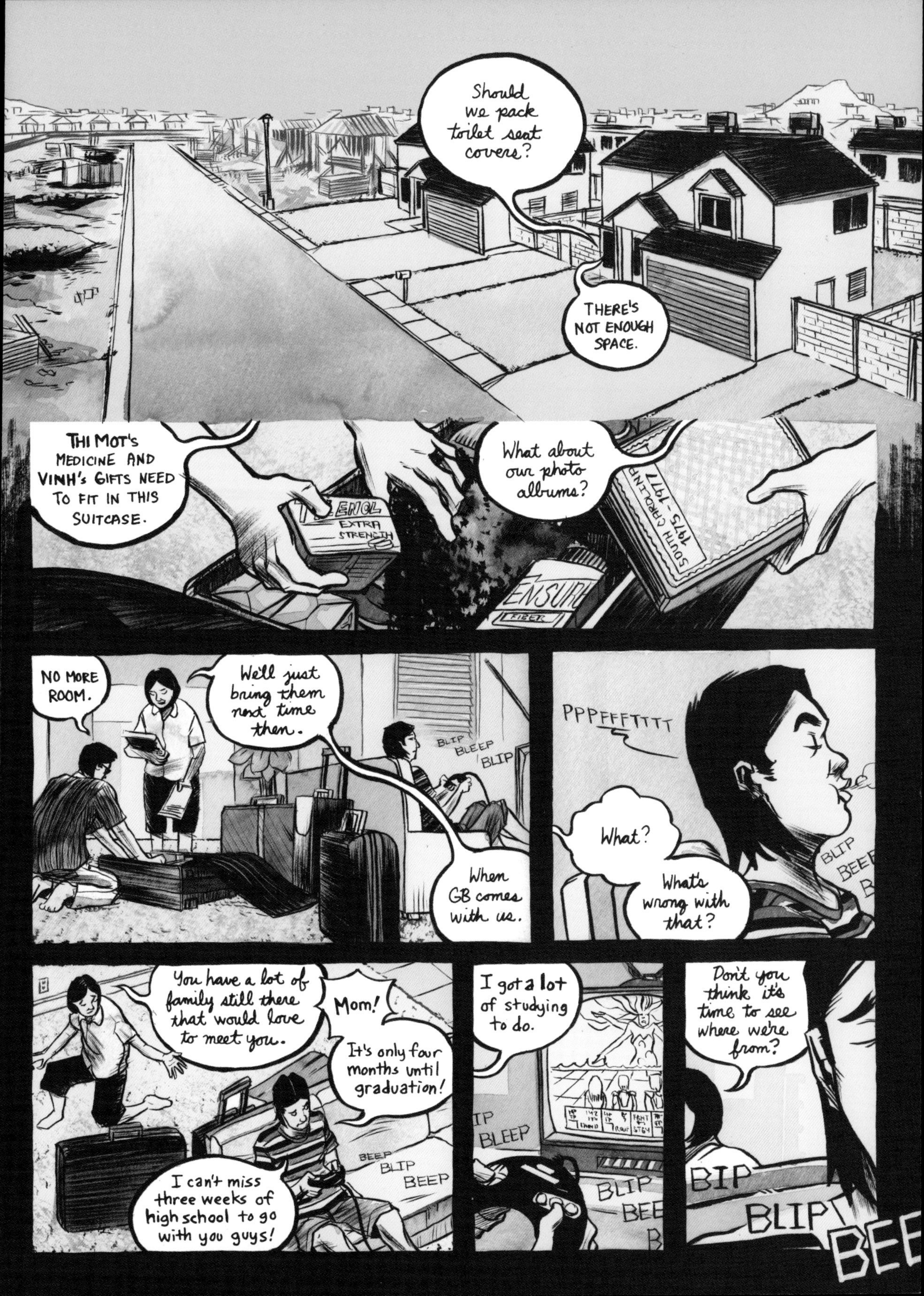
Should we pack toilet seat covers?
THERE'S NOT ENOUGH SPACE.
THI MOT'S MEDICINE AND VINH'S GIFTS NEED TO FIT IN THIS SUITCASE.
EXTRA STRENGTH
What about our photo albums?
SOUTH CAROLINA 1975 - 1977
ENSURE
FIBER
NO MORE ROOM.
We'll just bring them next time then.
BLIP BLEEP BLIP
When GB comes with us.
PPPFFFTTTT
What?
What's wrong with that?
You have a lot of family still there that would love to meet you.
Mom!
It's only four months until graduation!
BEEP BLIP BEEP
I can't miss three weeks of high school to go with you guys!
I got a lot of studying to do.
BLEEP
BLIP
Don't you think it's time to see where we're from?
BLIP
BLIP

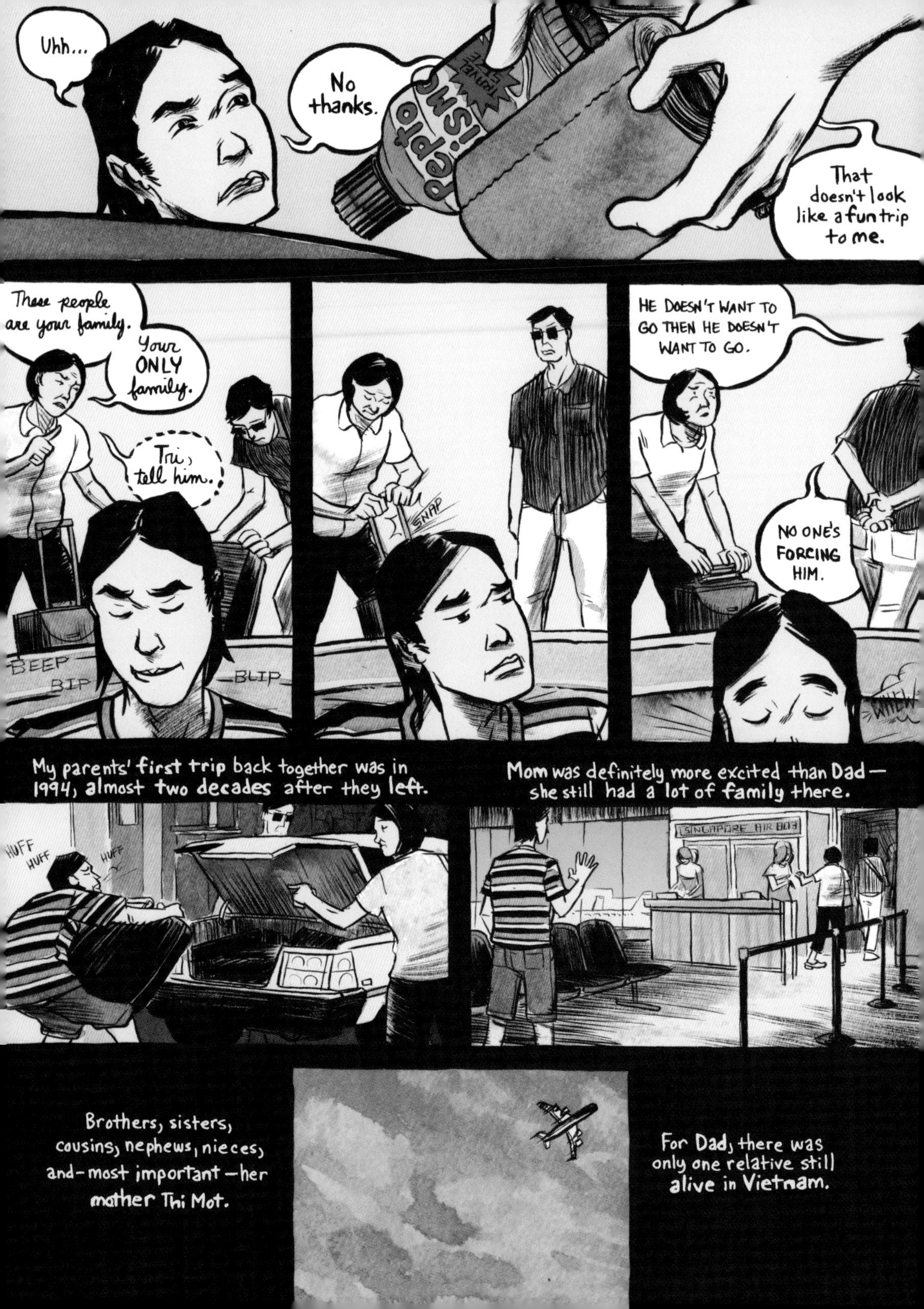

Uhh...
No thanks.
PEPTO BISMOL
TRAVEL SIZE
That doesn't look like a fun trip to me.
These people are your family.
Your ONLY family.
Tri, tell him.
BEEP
BIP
BLIP
SNAP
HE DOESN'T WANT TO GO THEN HE DOESN'T WANT TO GO.
NO ONE'S FORCING HIM.
WHEW
My parents' first trip back together was in 1994, almost two decades after they left.
Mom was definitely more excited than Dad—she still had a lot of family there.
HUFF
HUFF
HUFF
SINGAPORE AIR
Brothers, sisters, cousins, nephews, nieces, and—most important—her mother Thi Mot.
For Dad, there was only one relative still alive in Vietnam.

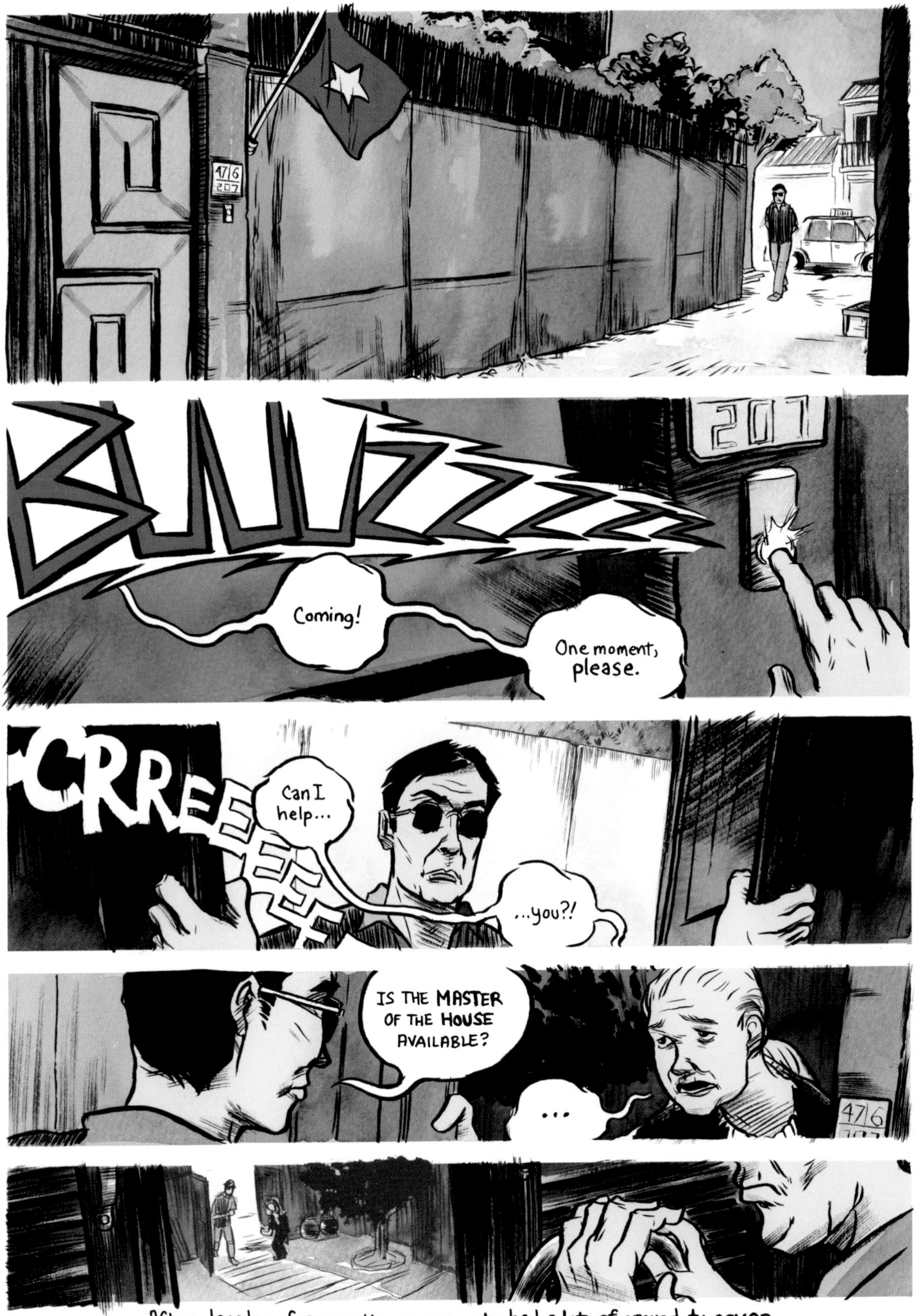
47/6
207
Coming!
One moment, please.
Can I help...
...you?!
IS THE MASTER OF THE HOUSE AVAILABLE?
...

After decades of seperation, my parents had a lot of ground to cover.

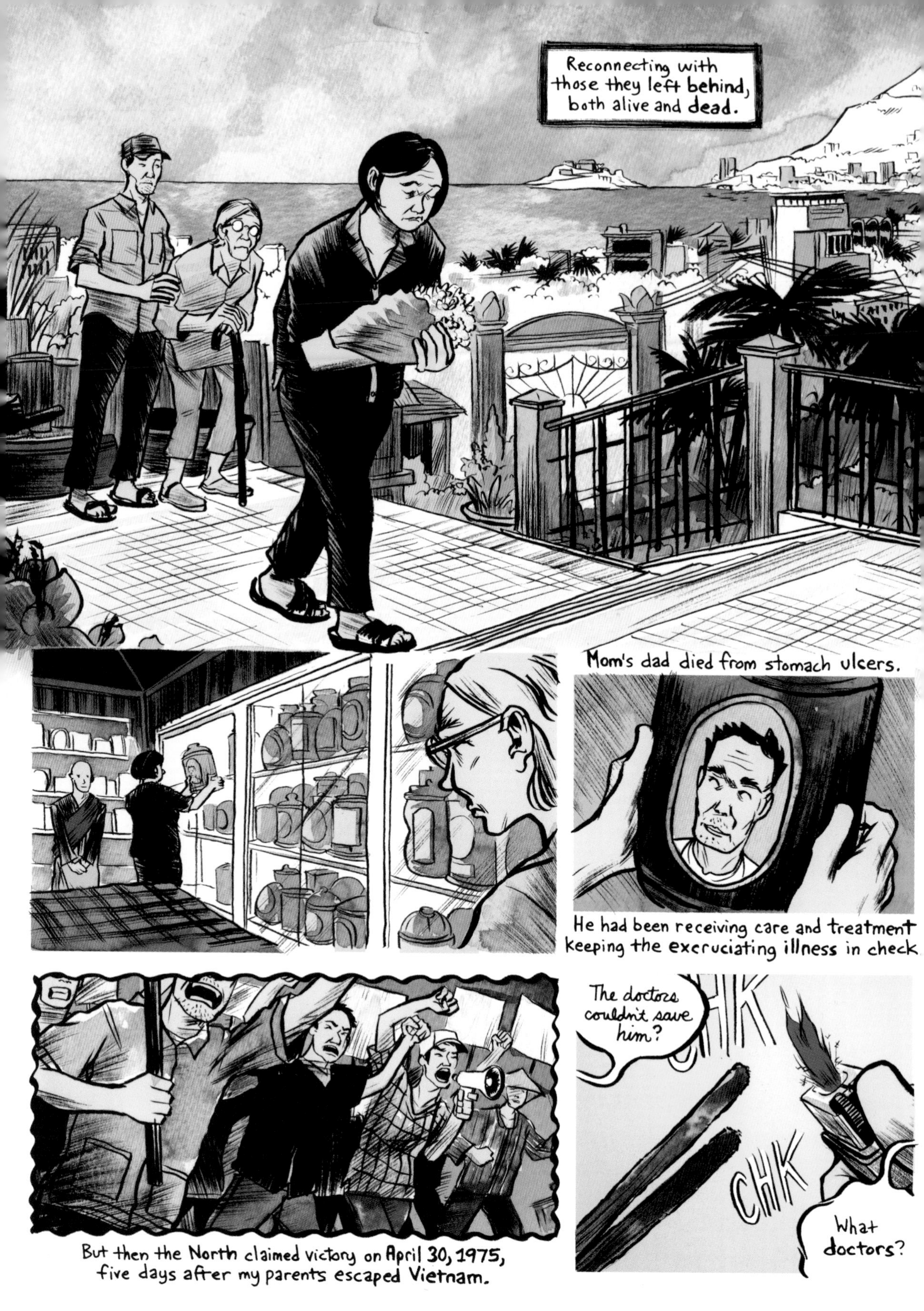
Reconnecting with those they left behind, both alive and dead.
Mom's dad died from stomach ulcers.
He had been receiving care and treatment keeping the excruciating illness in check.
But then the North claimed victory on April 30, 1975, five days after my parents escaped Vietnam.
The doctors couldn't save him?
CHK
CHK
What doctors?

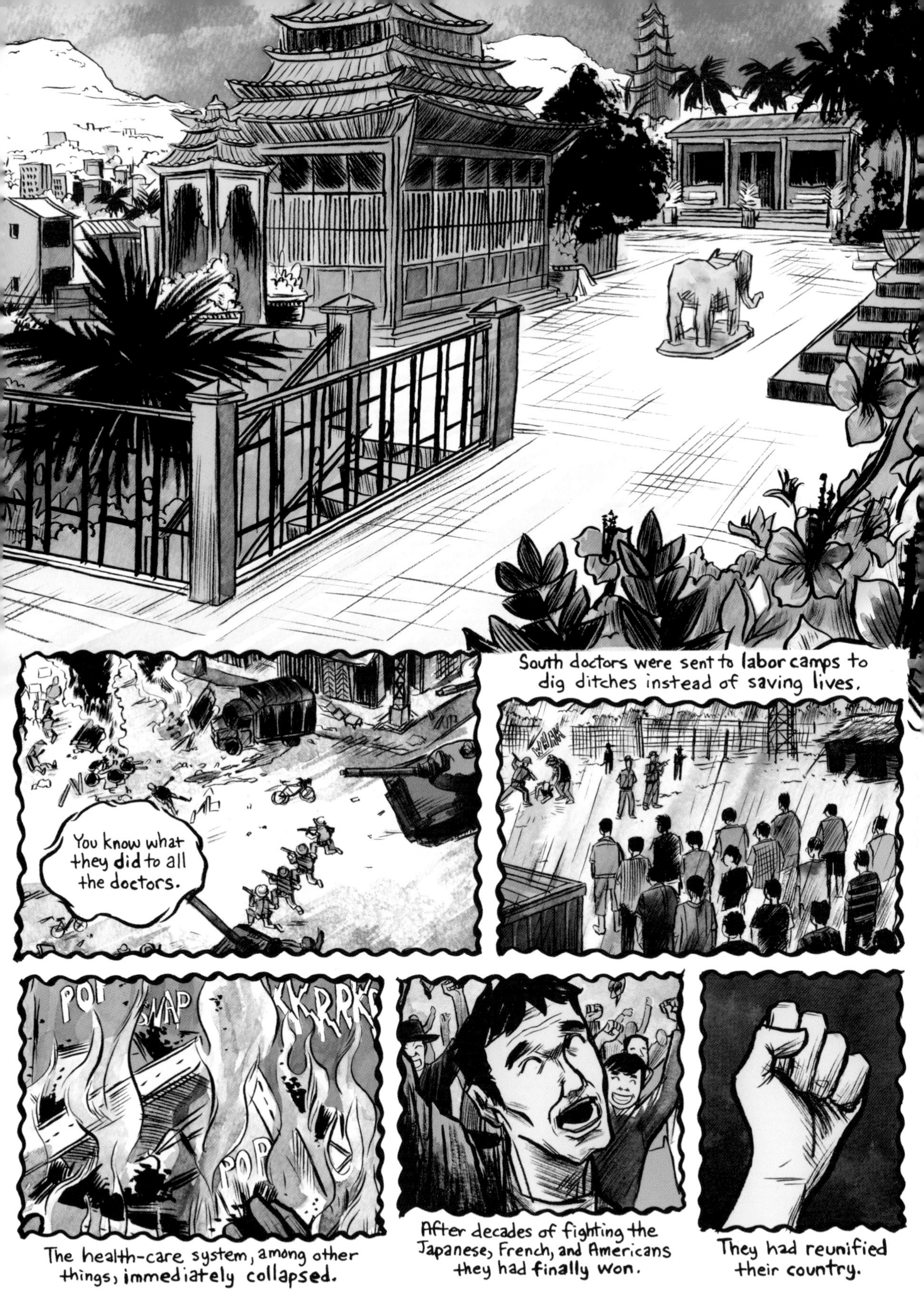
You know what they did to all the doctors.
South doctors were sent to labor camps to dig ditches instead of saving lives.
WHAK
POP
SNAP
KKRRK!
POP
The health-care system, among other things, immediately collapsed.
After decades of fighting the Japanese, French, and Americans they had finally won.
They had reunified their country.

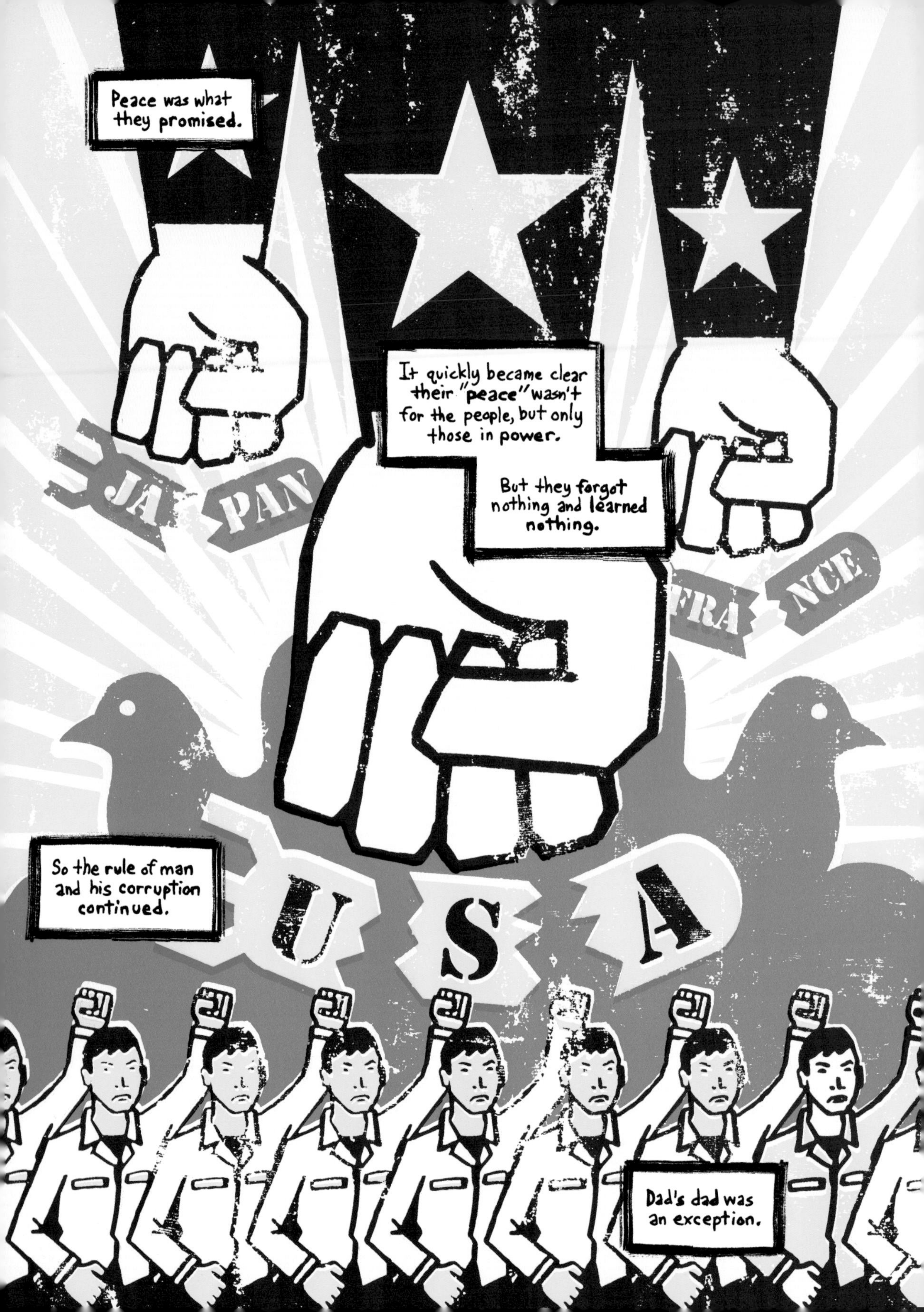
Peace was what they promised.
It quickly became clear their "peace" wasn't for the people, but only those in power.
But they forgot nothing and learned nothing.
JA PAN
FRA NCE
So the rule of man and his corruption continued.
U S A
Dad's dad was an exception.

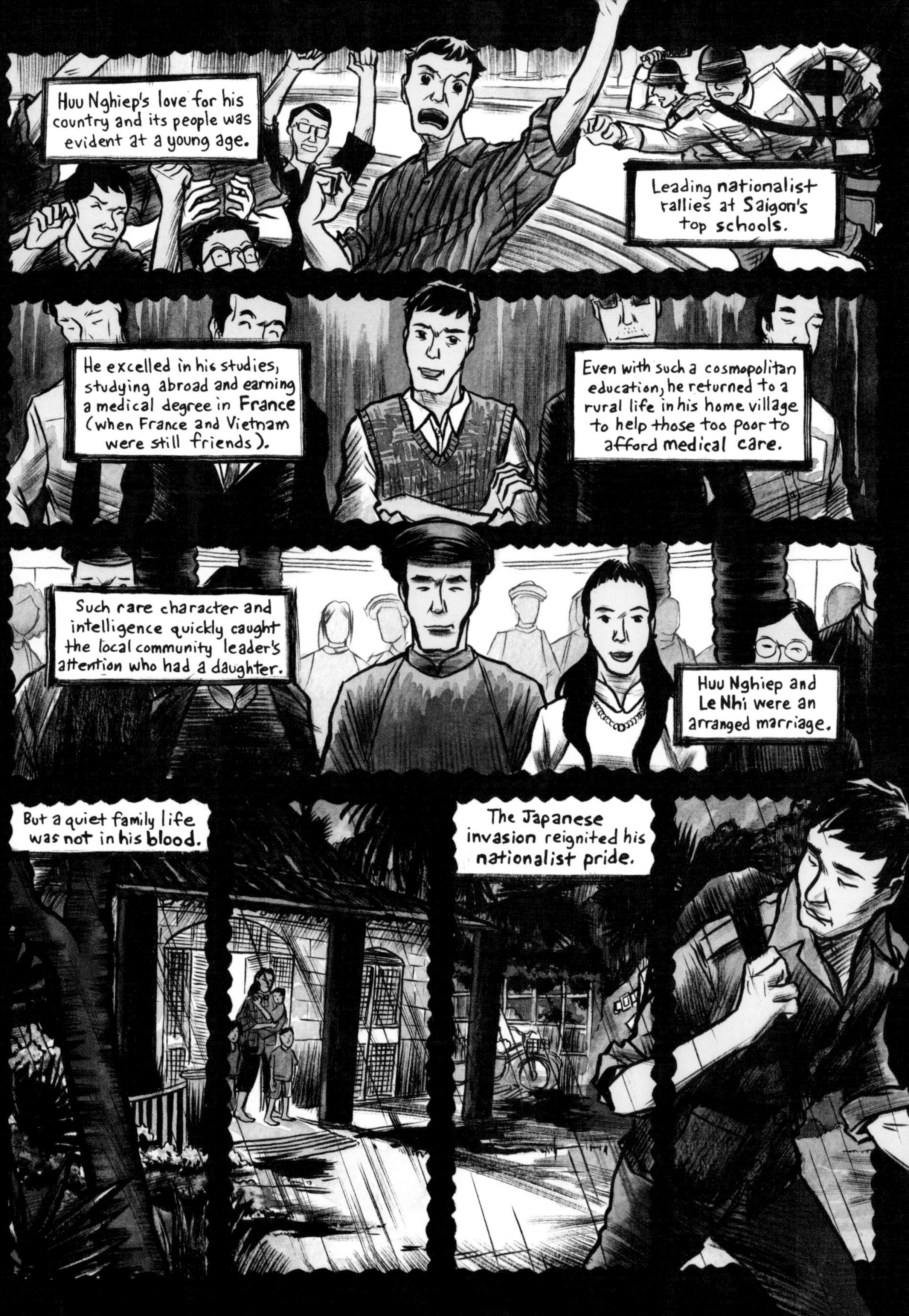

Huu Nghiep's love for his country and its people was evident at a young age.
Leading nationalist rallies at Saigon's top schools.
He excelled in his studies, studying abroad and earning a medical degree in France (when France and Vietnam were still friends).
Even with such a cosmopolitan education, he returned to a rural life in his home village to help those too poor to afford medical care.
Such rare character and intelligence quickly caught the local community leader's attention who had a daughter.
Huu Nghiep and Le Nhi were an arranged marriage.
But a quiet family life was not in his blood.
The Japanese invasion reignited his nationalist pride.

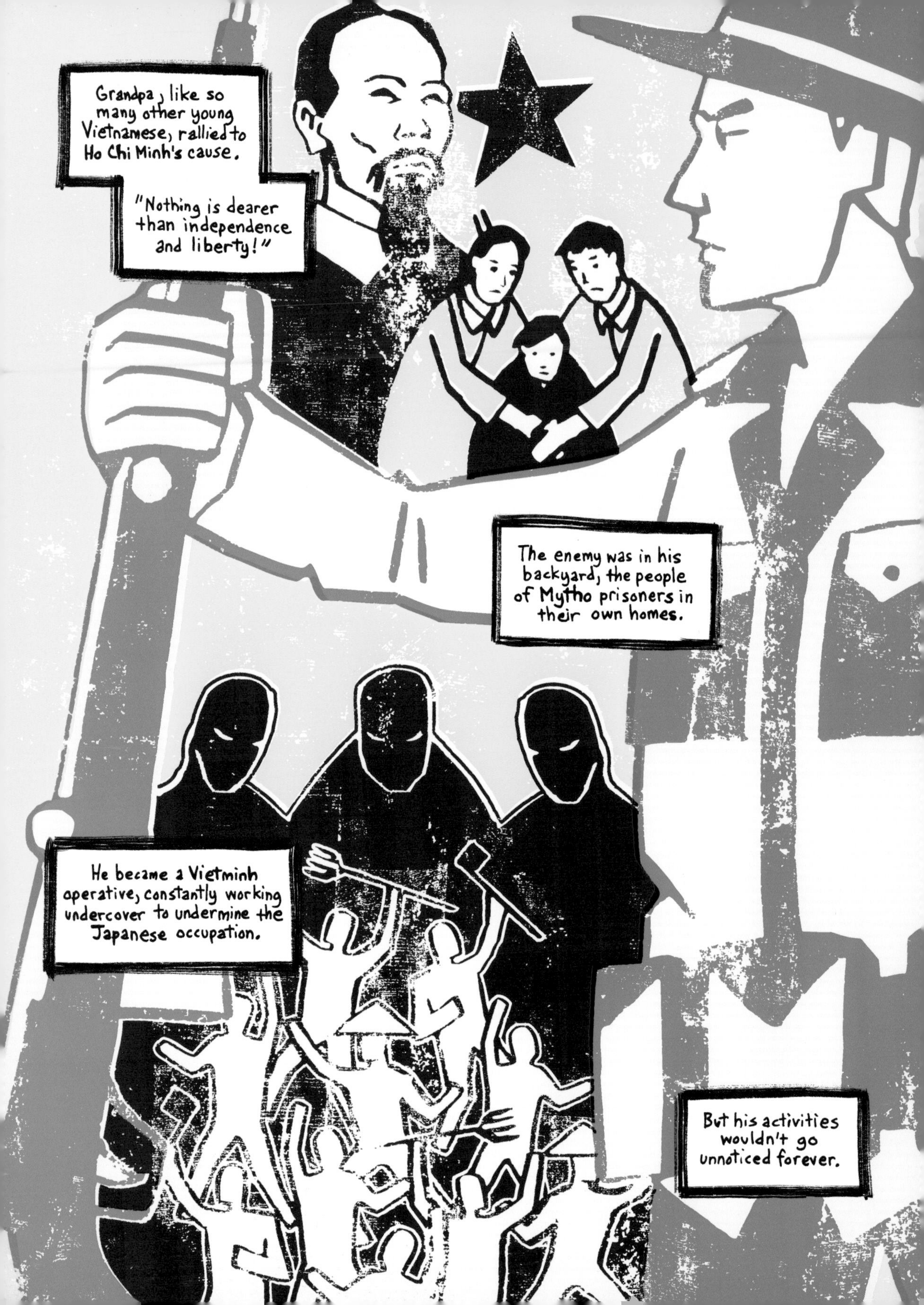
Grandpa, like so many other young Vietnamese, rallied to Ho Chi Minh's cause.
"Nothing is dearer than independence and liberty!"
The enemy was in his backyard, the people of Mytho prisoners in their own homes.
He became a Vietminh operative, constantly working undercover to undermine the Japanese occupation.
But his activities wouldn't go unnoticed forever.

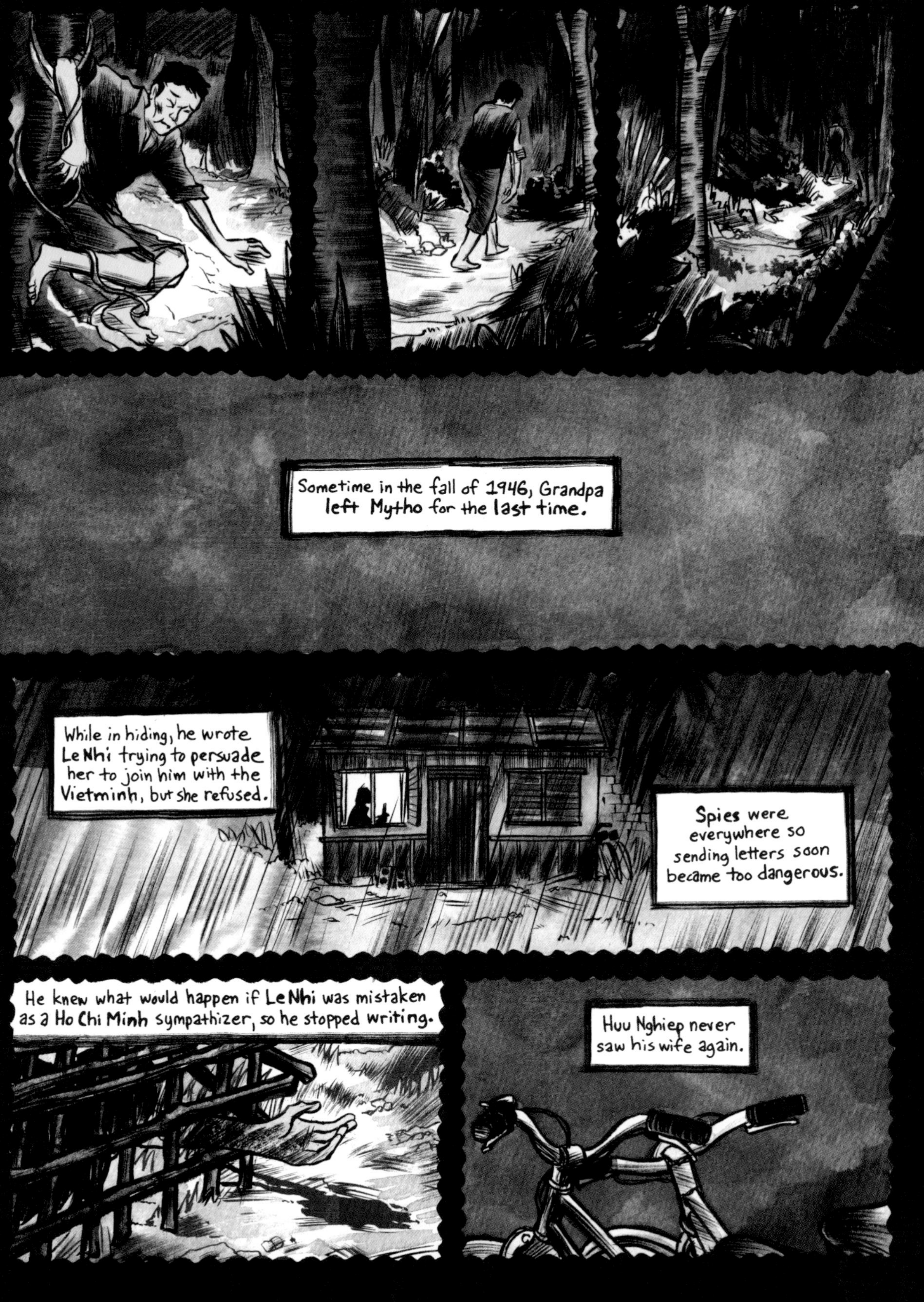
Sometime in the fall of 1946, Grandpa left Mytho for the last time.
While in hiding, he wrote Le Nhi trying to persuade her to join him with the Vietminh, but she refused.
Spies were everywhere so sending letters soon became too dangerous.
He knew what would happen if Le Nhi was mistaken as a Ho Chi Minh sympathizer, so he stopped writing.
Huu Nghiep never saw his wife again.

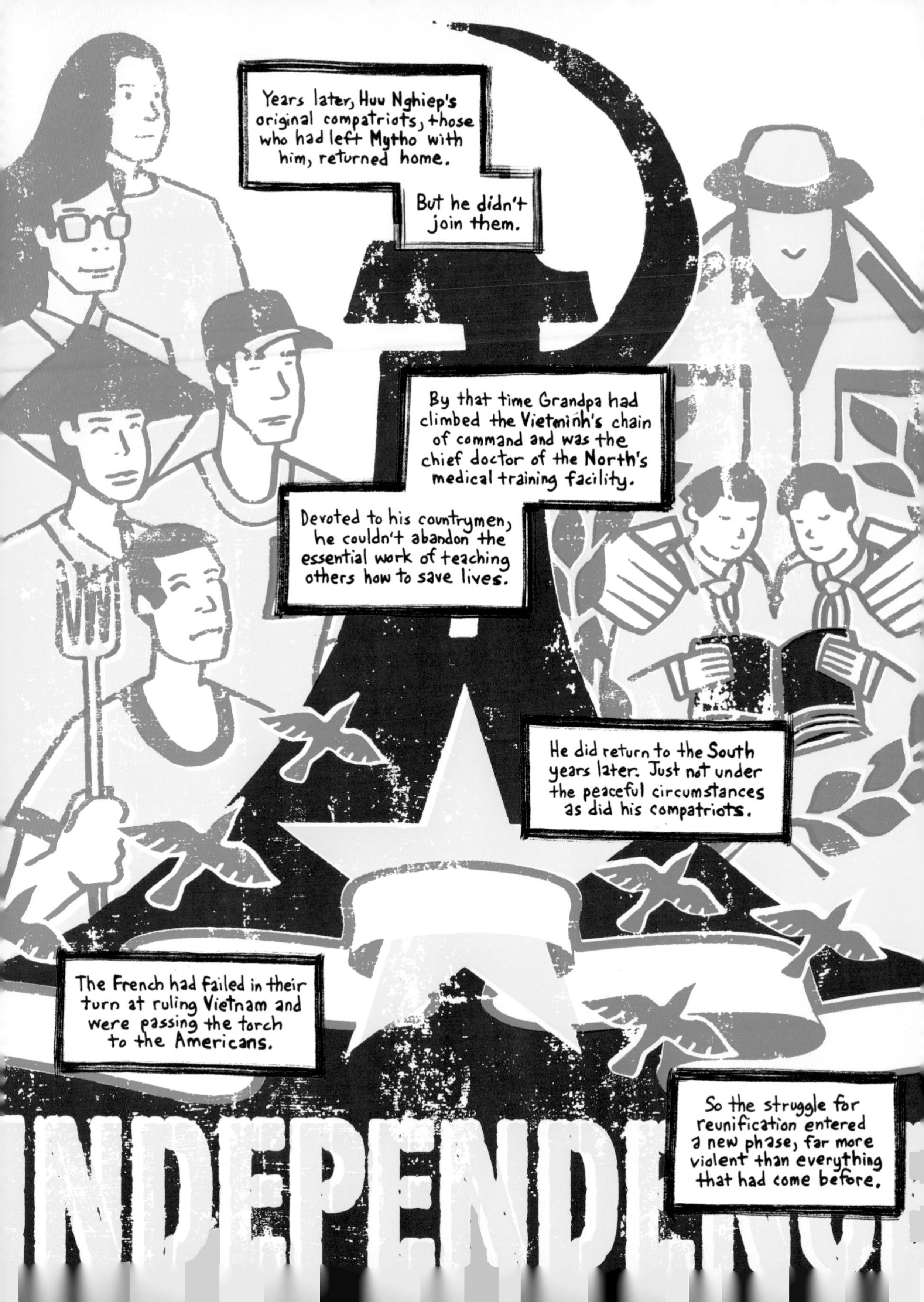
Years later, Huu Nghiep's original compatriots, those who had left Mytho with him, returned home.
But he didn't join them.
By that time Grandpa had climbed the Vietminh's chain of command and was the chief doctor of the North's medical training facility.
Devoted to his countrymen, he couldn't abandon the essential work of teaching others how to save lives.
He did return to the South years later. Just not under the peaceful circumstances as did his compatriots.
The French had failed in their turn at ruling Vietnam and were passing the torch to the Americans.
So the struggle for reunification entered a new phase, far more violent than everything that had come before.
INDEPENDENCE

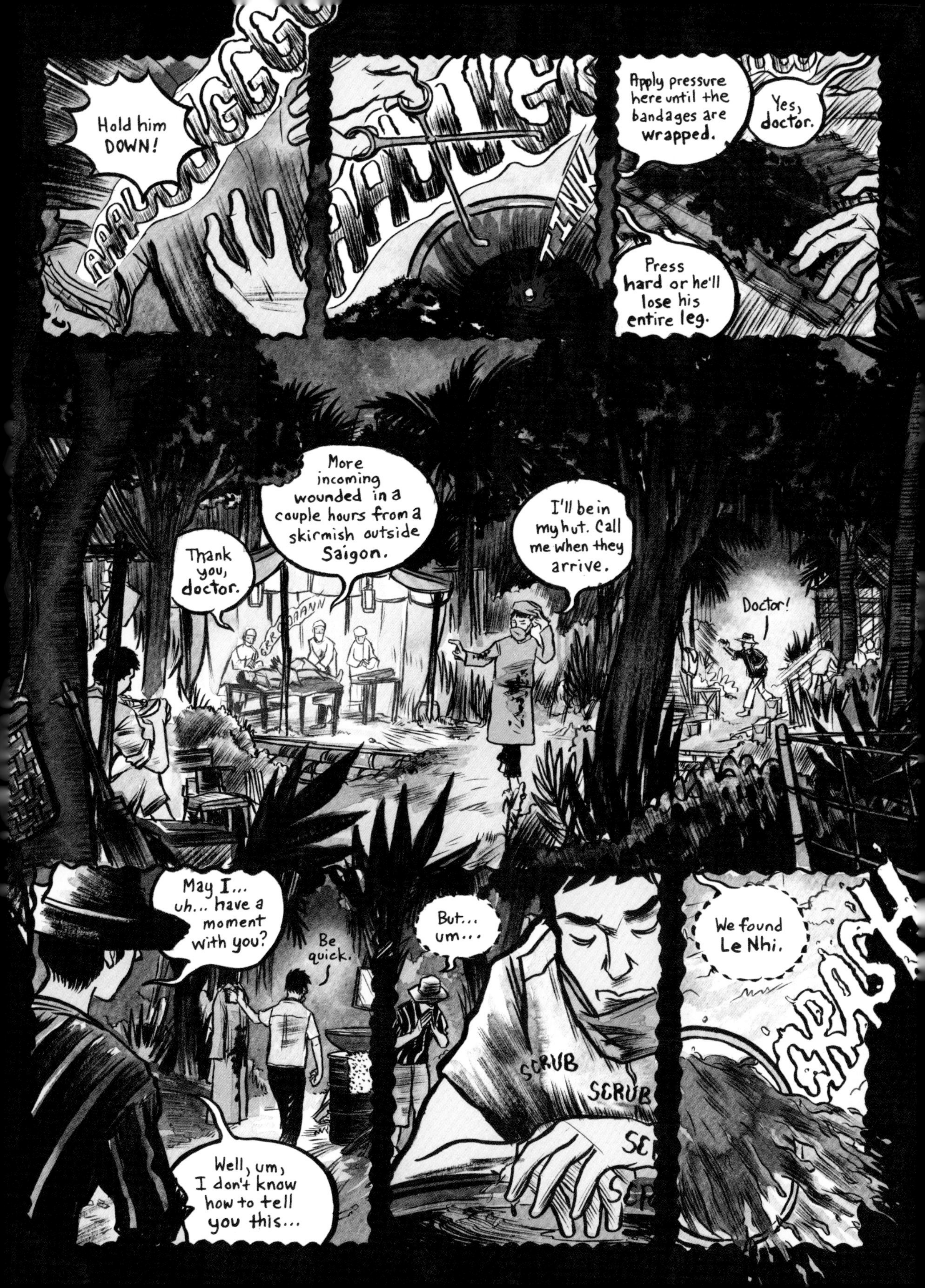
Hold him DOWN!
Apply pressure here until the bandages are wrapped.
Yes, doctor.
Press hard or he'll lose his entire leg.
Thank you, doctor.
More incoming wounded in a couple hours from a skirmish outside Saigon.
I'll be in my hut. Call me when they arrive.
Doctor!
May I... uh... have a moment with you?
Be quick.
Well, um, I don't know how to tell you this...
But... um...
SCRUB
SCRUB
We found Le Nhi.

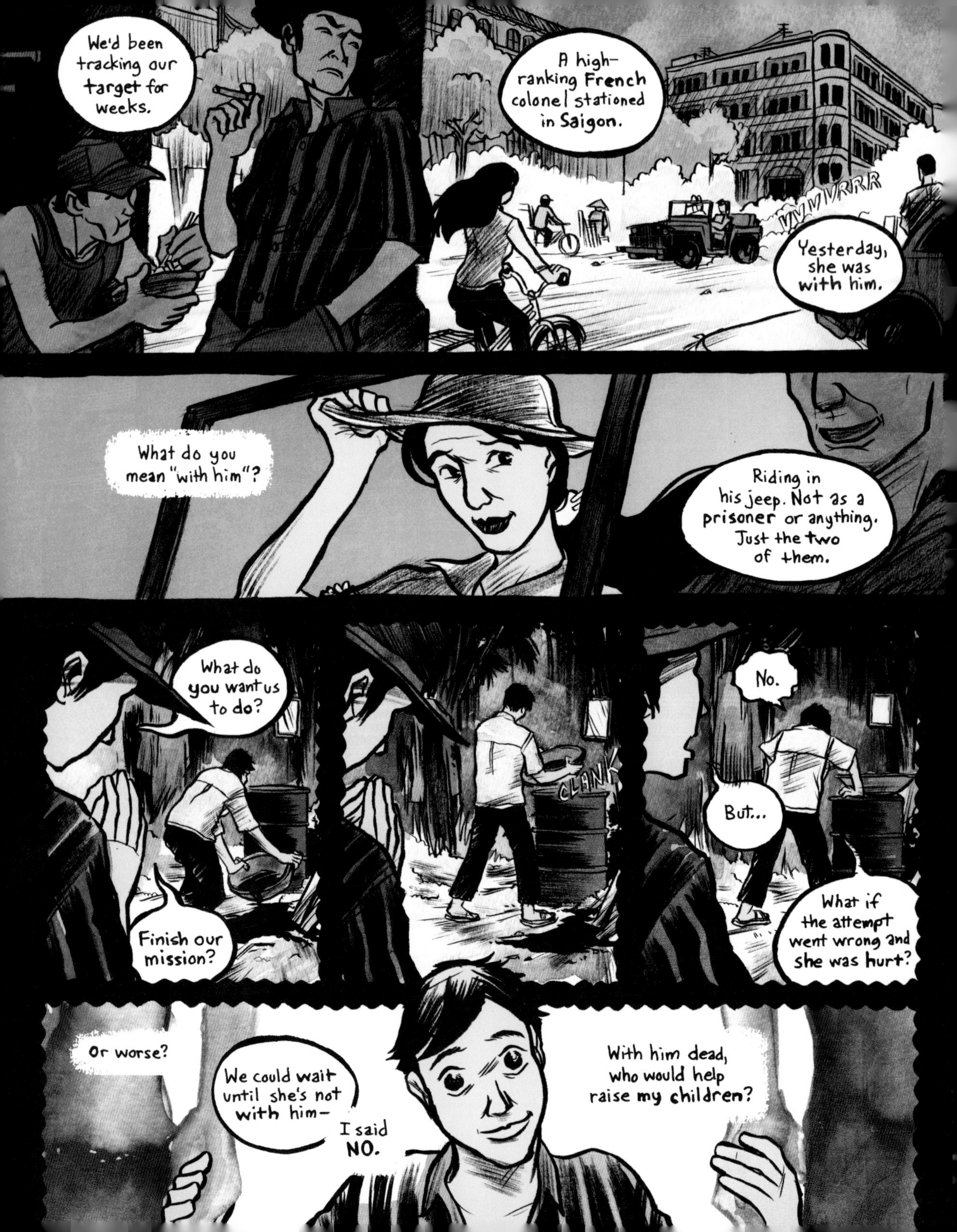
We'd been tracking our target for weeks.
A high-ranking French colonel stationed in Saigon.
VVVVVRRR
Yesterday, she was with him.
What do you mean "with him"?
Riding in his jeep. Not as a prisoner or anything. Just the two of them.
What do you want us to do?
Finish our mission?
CLANK
No.
But...
What if the attempt went wrong and she was hurt?
Or worse?
We could wait until she's not with him—
I said NO.
With him dead, who would help raise my children?

My commander's dissuaded me. It was too dangerous. They knew she was being secretly watched by the South government.

The South wanted to capture me and assumed she knew where I was.

As soon as I learned Le Nhi was so close to me in Saigon, I wanted to contact her!

And by then, she and you weren't my only family that I needed to protect.

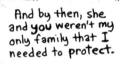

PAT
PA
PAT
PAT

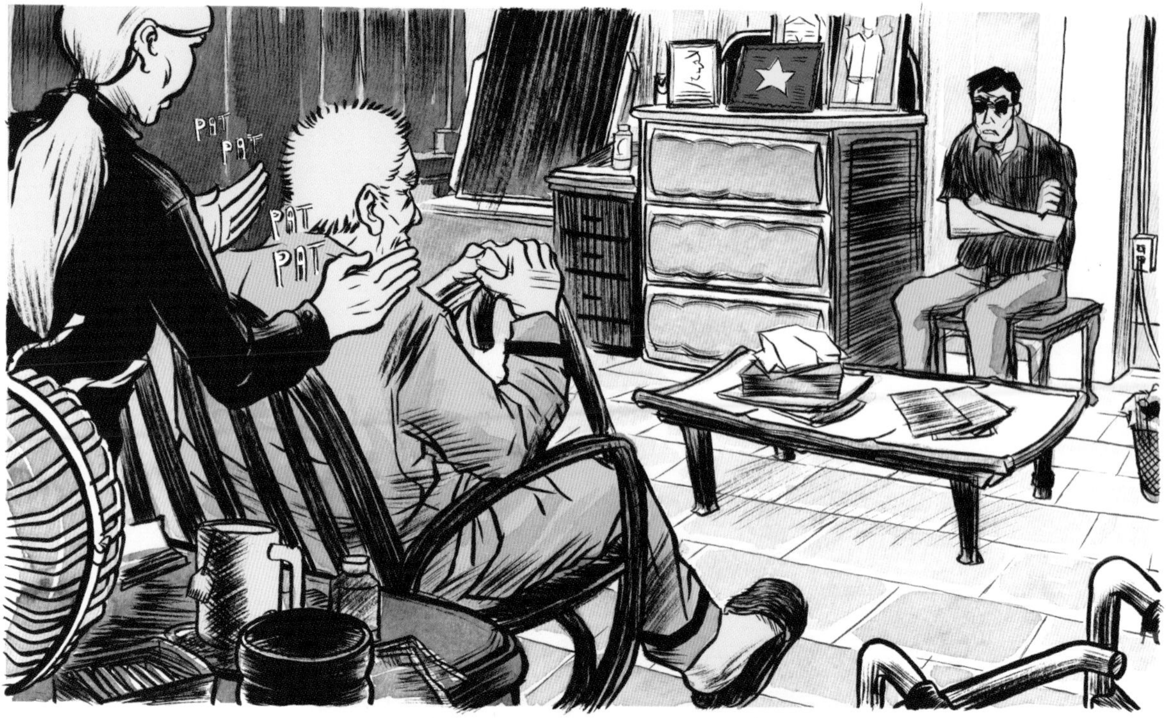
PAT PAT
PAT PAT

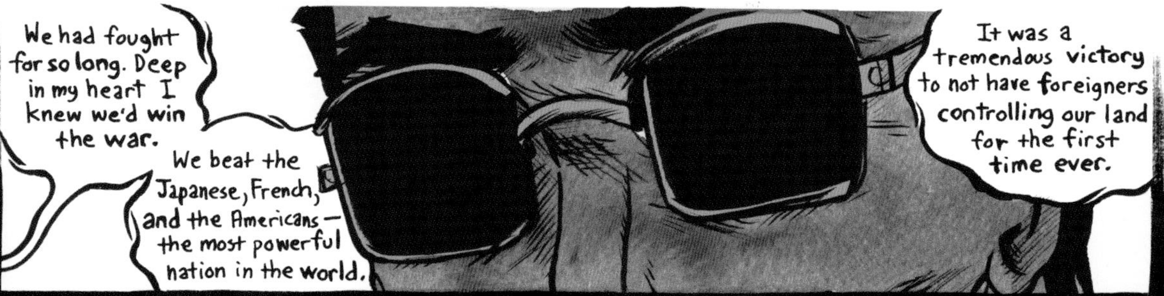
We had fought for so long. Deep in my heart I knew we'd win the war.
We beat the Japanese, French, and the Americans— the most powerful nation in the world.
It was a tremendous victory to not have foreigners controlling our land for the first time ever.

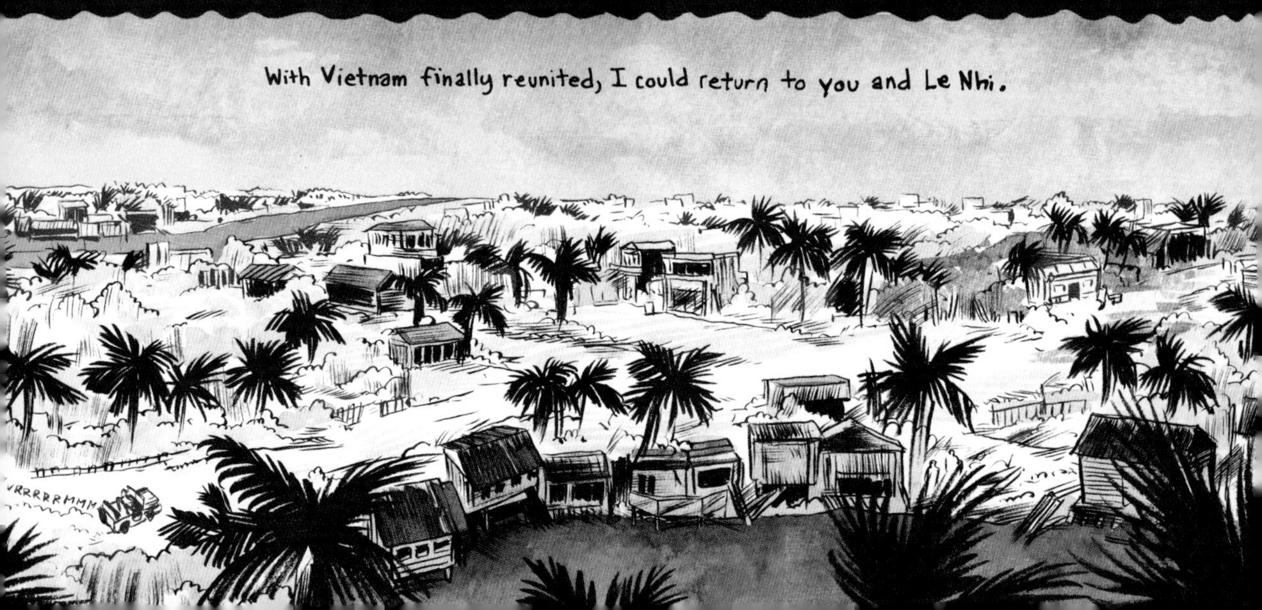
With Vietnam finally reunited, I could return to you and Le Nhi.
VRRRRRMMM

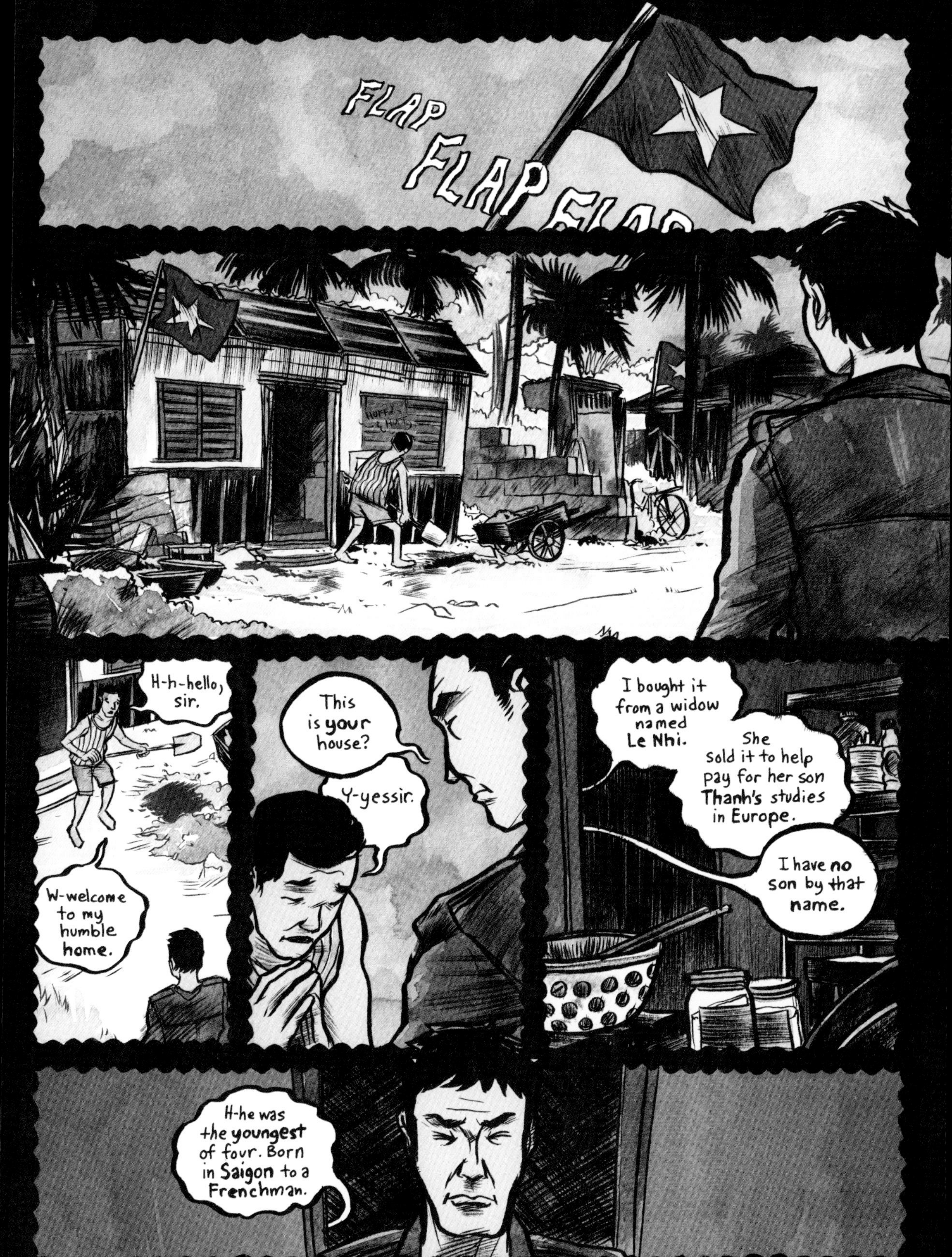
FLAP FLAP FLAP
H-h-hello, sir.
W-welcome to my humble home.
This is your house?
Y-yessir.
I bought it from a widow named Le Nhi.
She sold it to help pay for her son Thanh's studies in Europe.
I have no son by that name.
H-he was the youngest of four. Born in Saigon to a Frenchman.

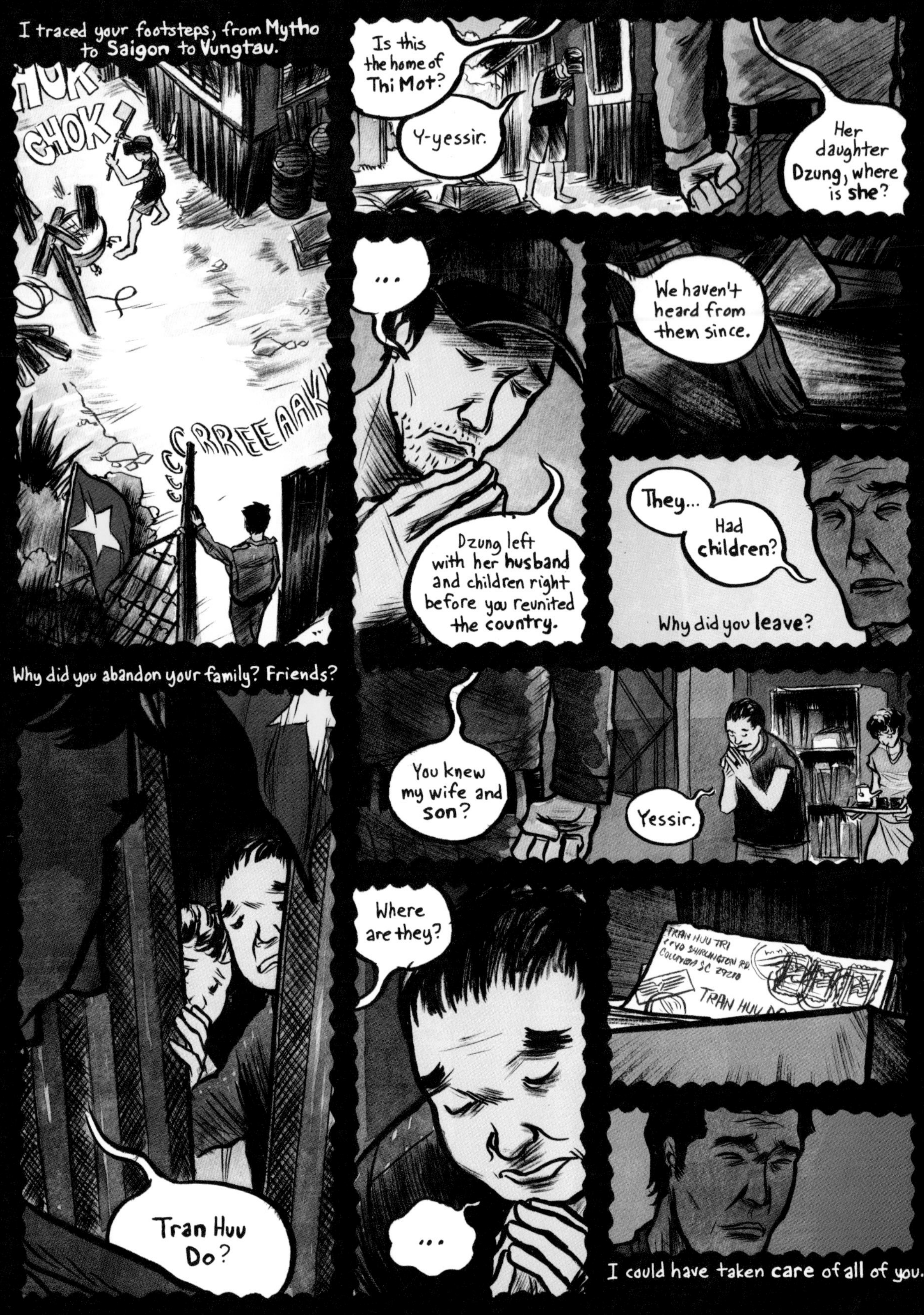
I traced your footsteps, from Mytho to Saigon to Vungtau.
CHOK
CRRREEAAK
Is this the home of Thi Mot?
Y-yessir.
Her daughter Dzung, where is she?
...
Dzung left with her husband and children right before you reunited the country.
We haven't heard from them since.
They... Had children?
Why did you leave?
Why did you abandon your family? Friends?
Tran Huu Do?
You knew my wife and son?
Yessir.
Where are they?
...
TRAN HUU TRI
I could have taken care of all of you.

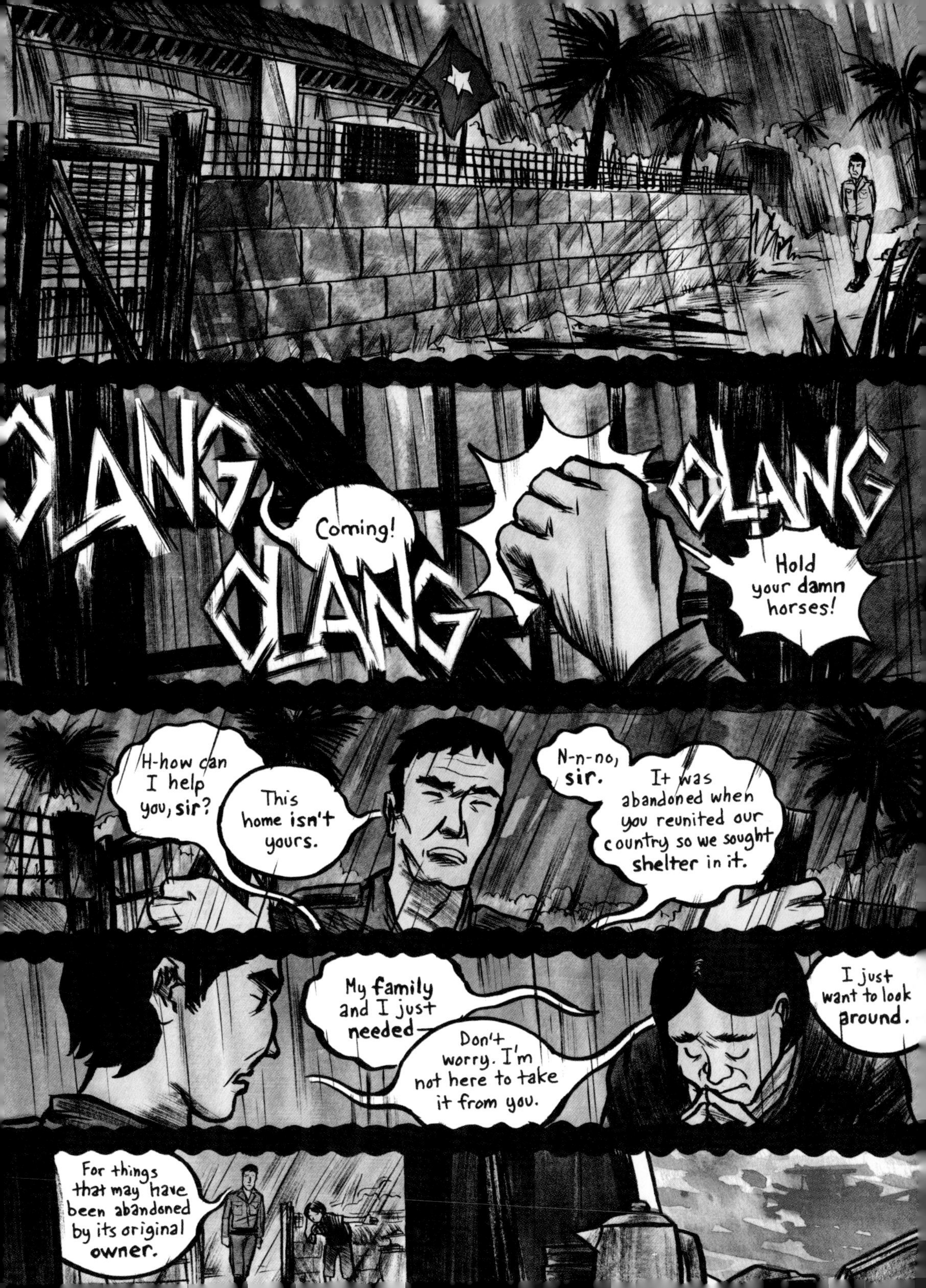
CLANG
CLANG
Coming!
CLANG
Hold your damn horses!
H-how can I help you, sir?
This home isn't yours.
N-n-no, sir.
It was abandoned when you reunited our country so we sought shelter in it.
My family and I just needed—
Don't worry. I'm not here to take it from you.
I just want to look around.
For things that may have been abandoned by its original owner.

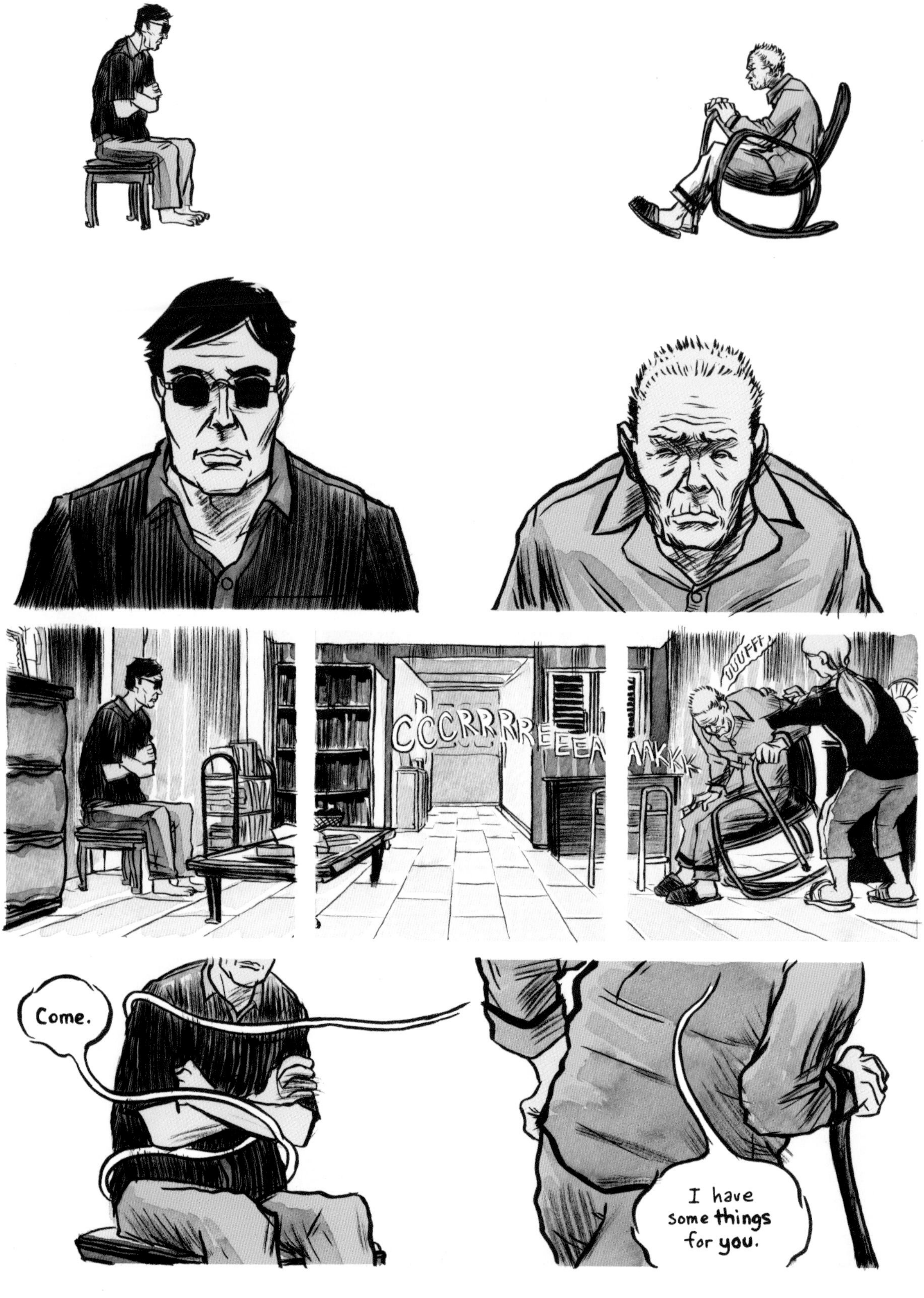
CCCRRRRREEEEAAAKKK
UUUFFF
Come.
I have some things for you.

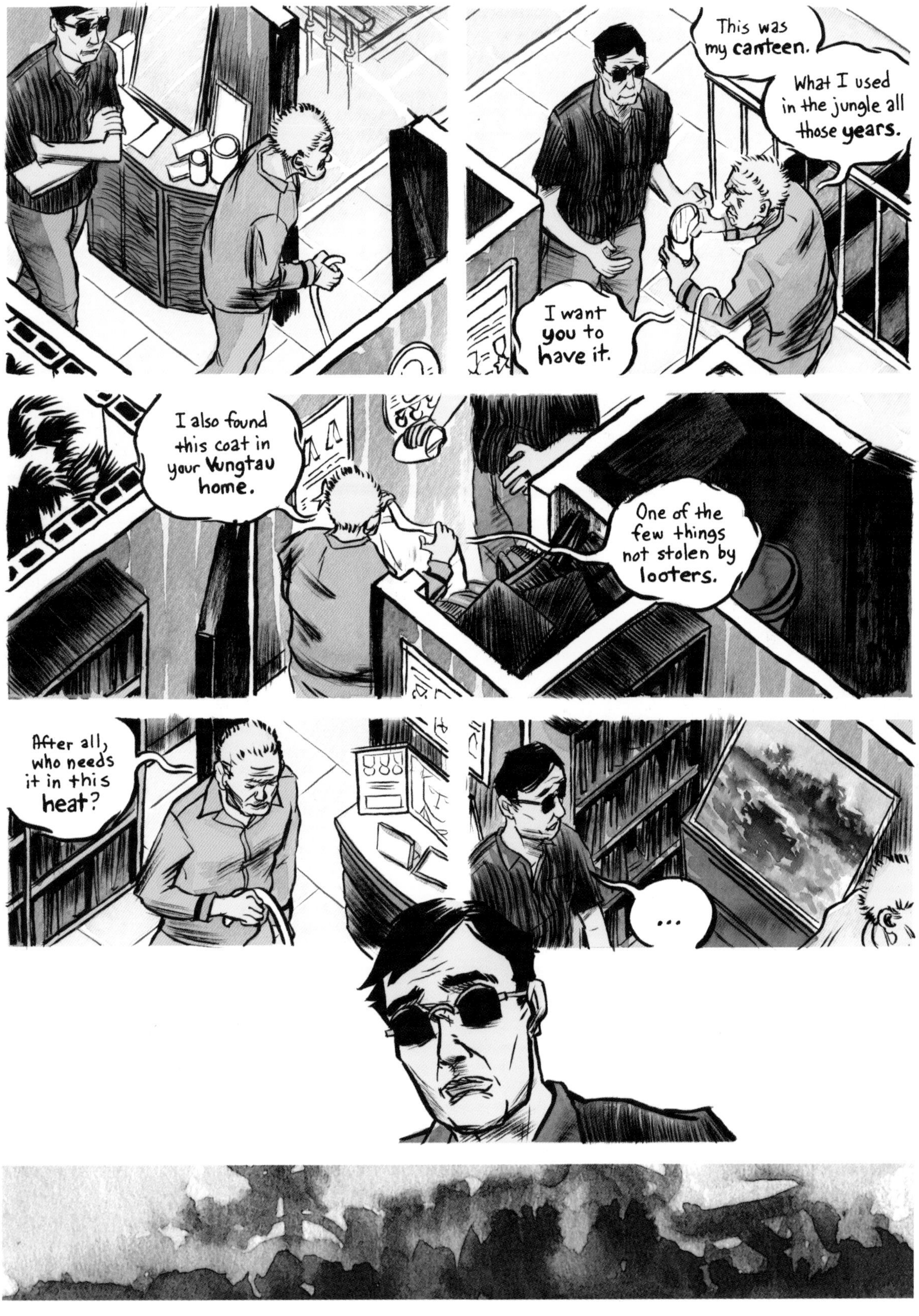
This was my canteen.
What I used in the jungle all those years.
I want you to have it.
I also found this coat in your Vungtau home.
One of the few things not stolen by looters.
After all, who needs it in this heat?
...

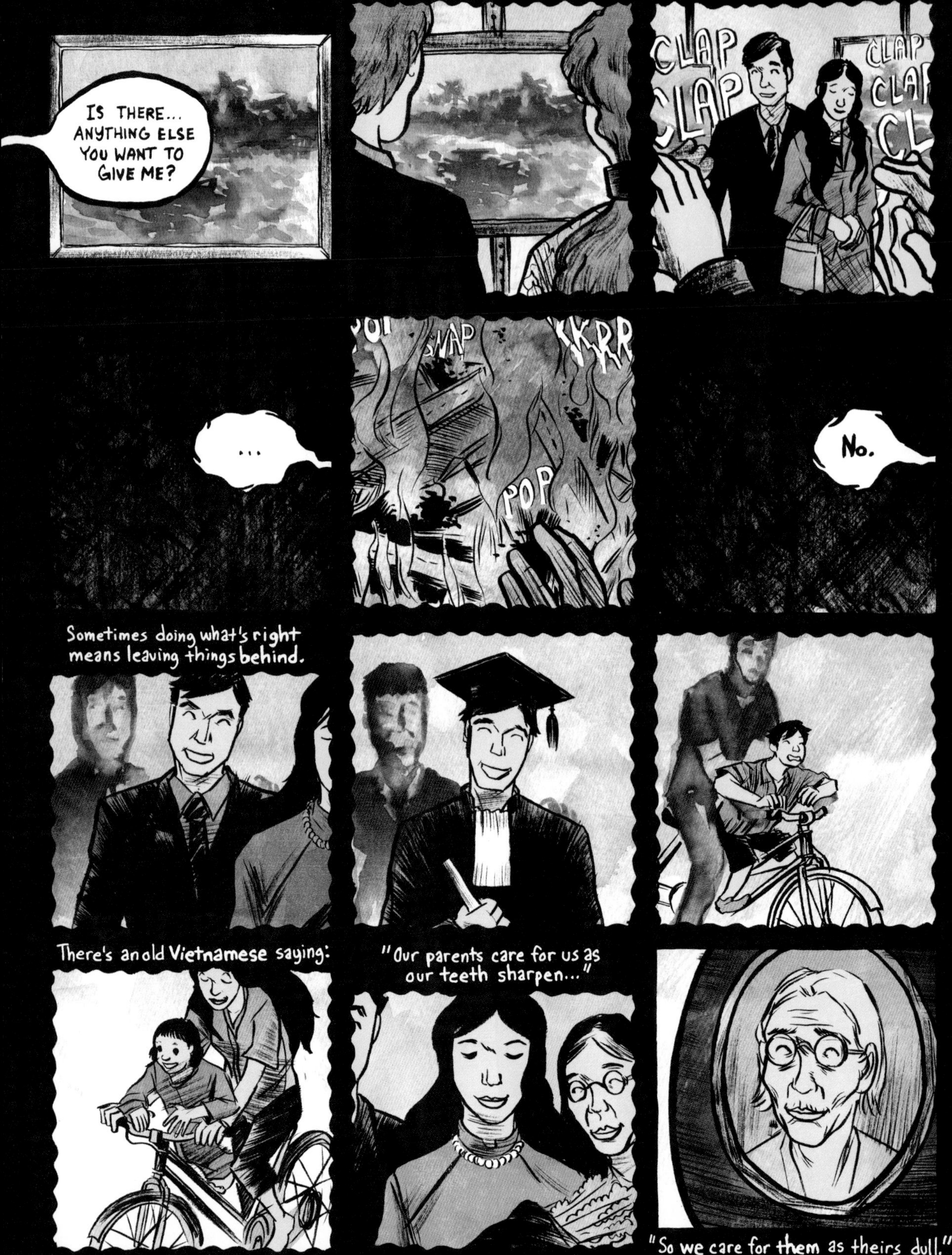
IS THERE... ANYTHING ELSE YOU WANT TO GIVE ME?
CLAP CLAP CLAP
CLAP CLAP CL
...
SNAP
KRR
POP
No.
Sometimes doing what's right means leaving things behind.
There's an old Vietnamese saying:
"Our parents care for us as our teeth sharpen..."
"So we care for them as theirs dull."

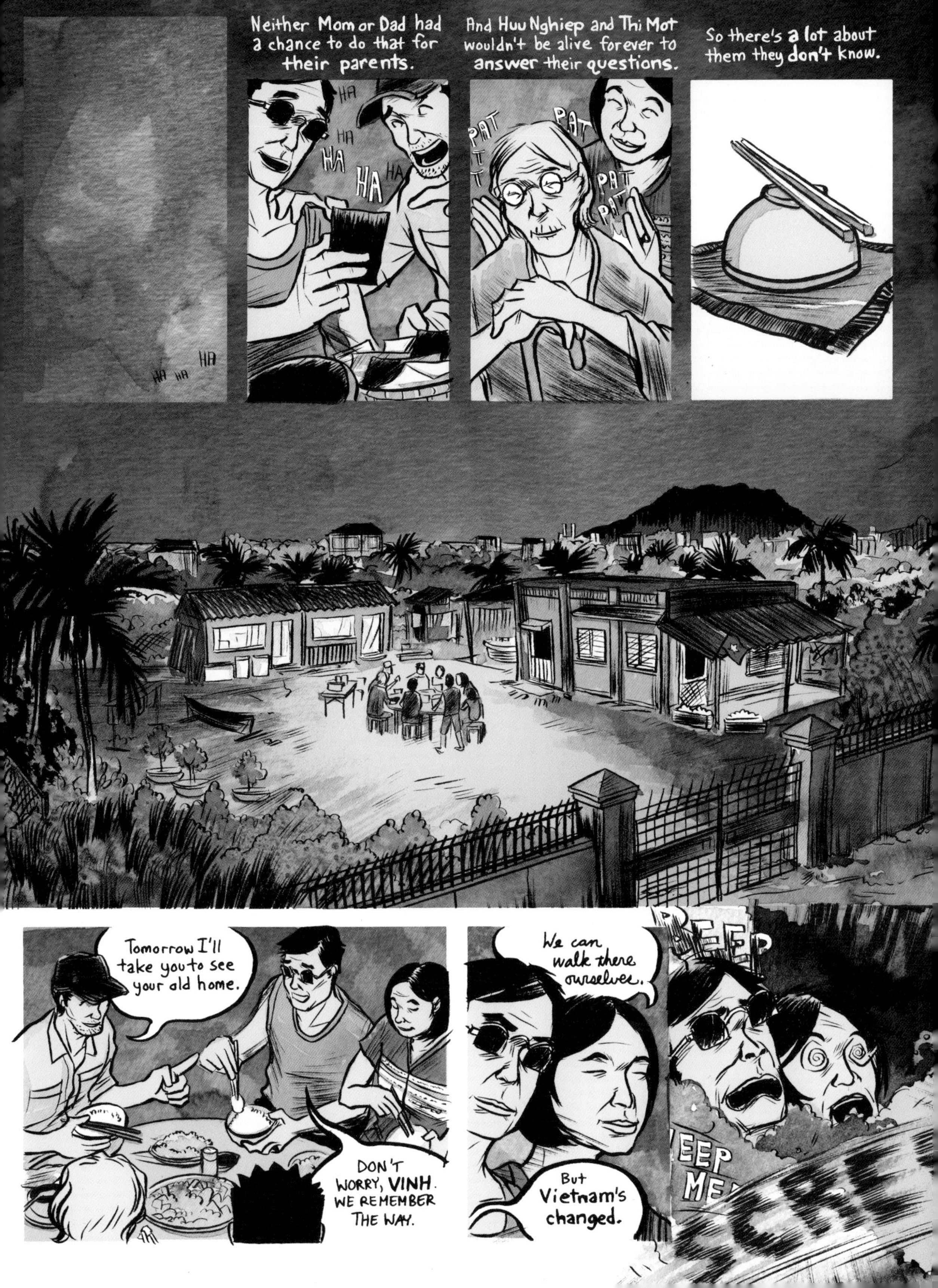

HA HA HA
Neither Mom or Dad had a chance to do that for their parents.
HA HA HA HA HA
And Huu Nghiep and Thi Mot wouldn't be alive forever to answer their questions.
PAT PAT PAT PAT
So there's a lot about them they don't know.
Tomorrow I'll take you to see your old home.
DON'T WORRY, VINH. WE REMEMBER THE WAY.
We can walk there ourselves.
But Vietnam's changed.

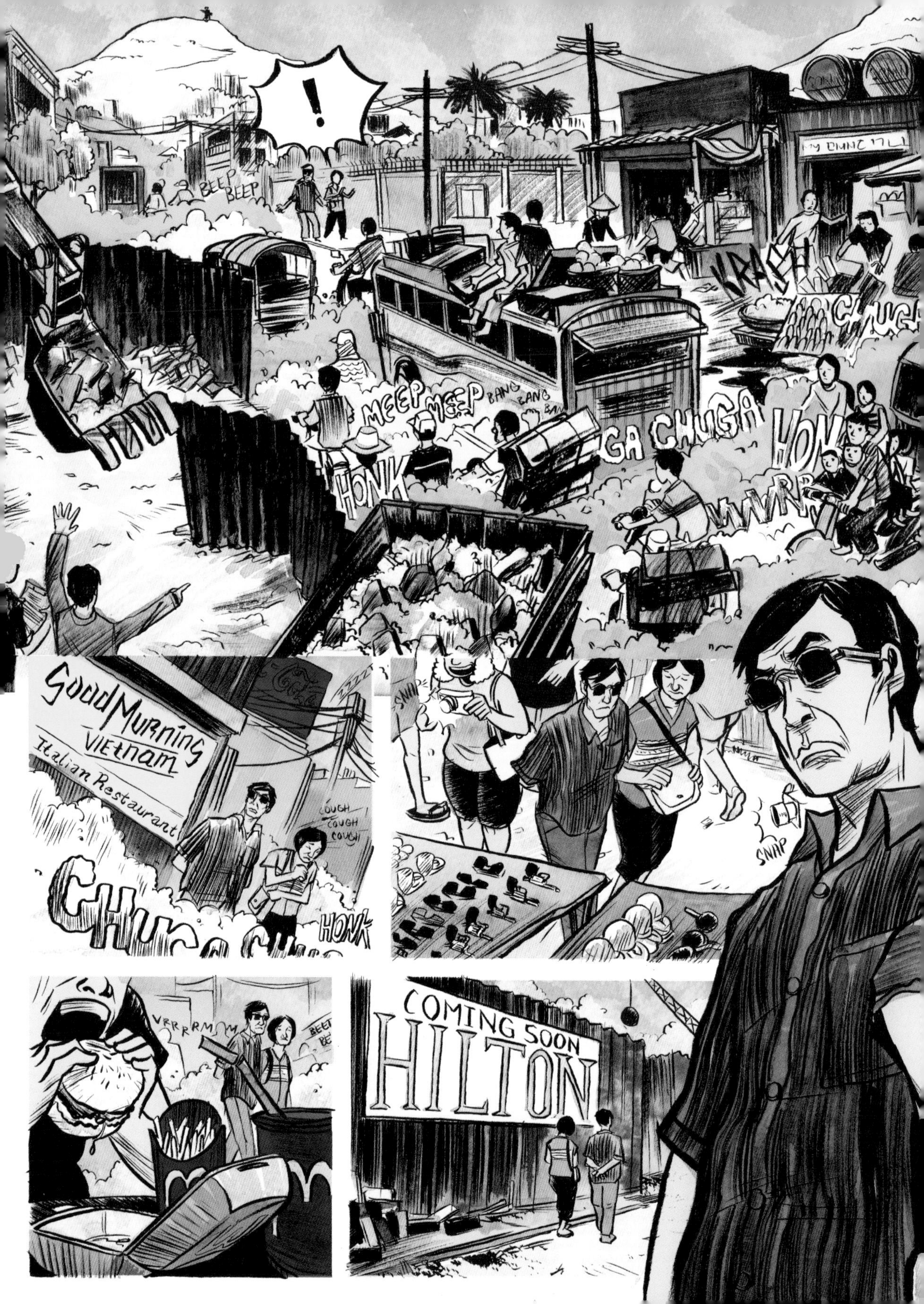
!
BEEP BEEP
MEEP MEEP
BANG BANG BANG
GA CHUGA
HONK
CRASH
CHUGA
HON
VVVVRR
Good Murning Vietnam
Italian Restaurant
COUGH COUGH COUGH
CHUGA CHUG
HONK
SNAP
SNAP
VRRRRM
COMING SOON
HILTON

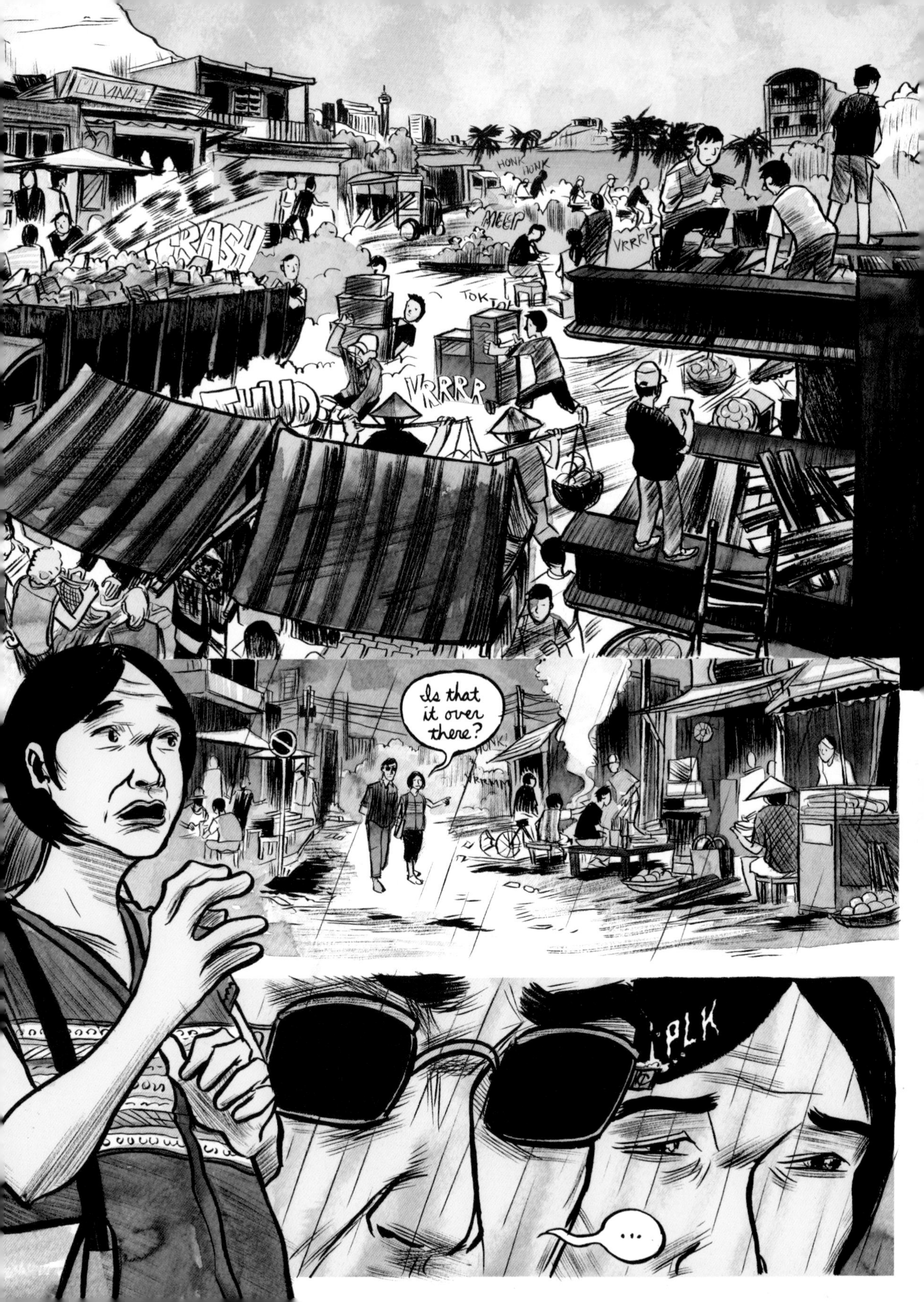

HONK
HONK
MEEP
VRRR
TOK TOK
THUD
VRRRR
CRASH
Is that it over there?
HONK
...

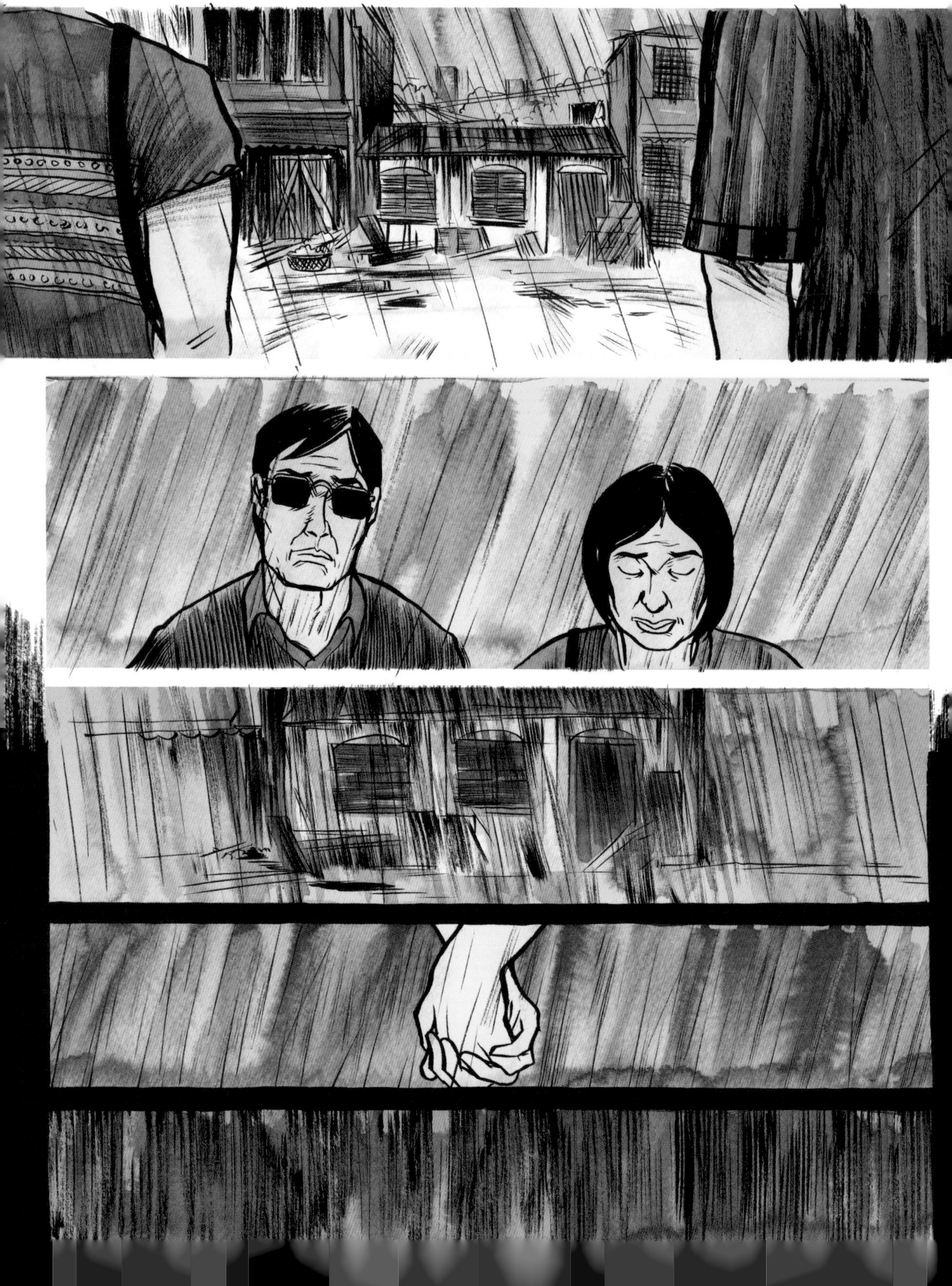

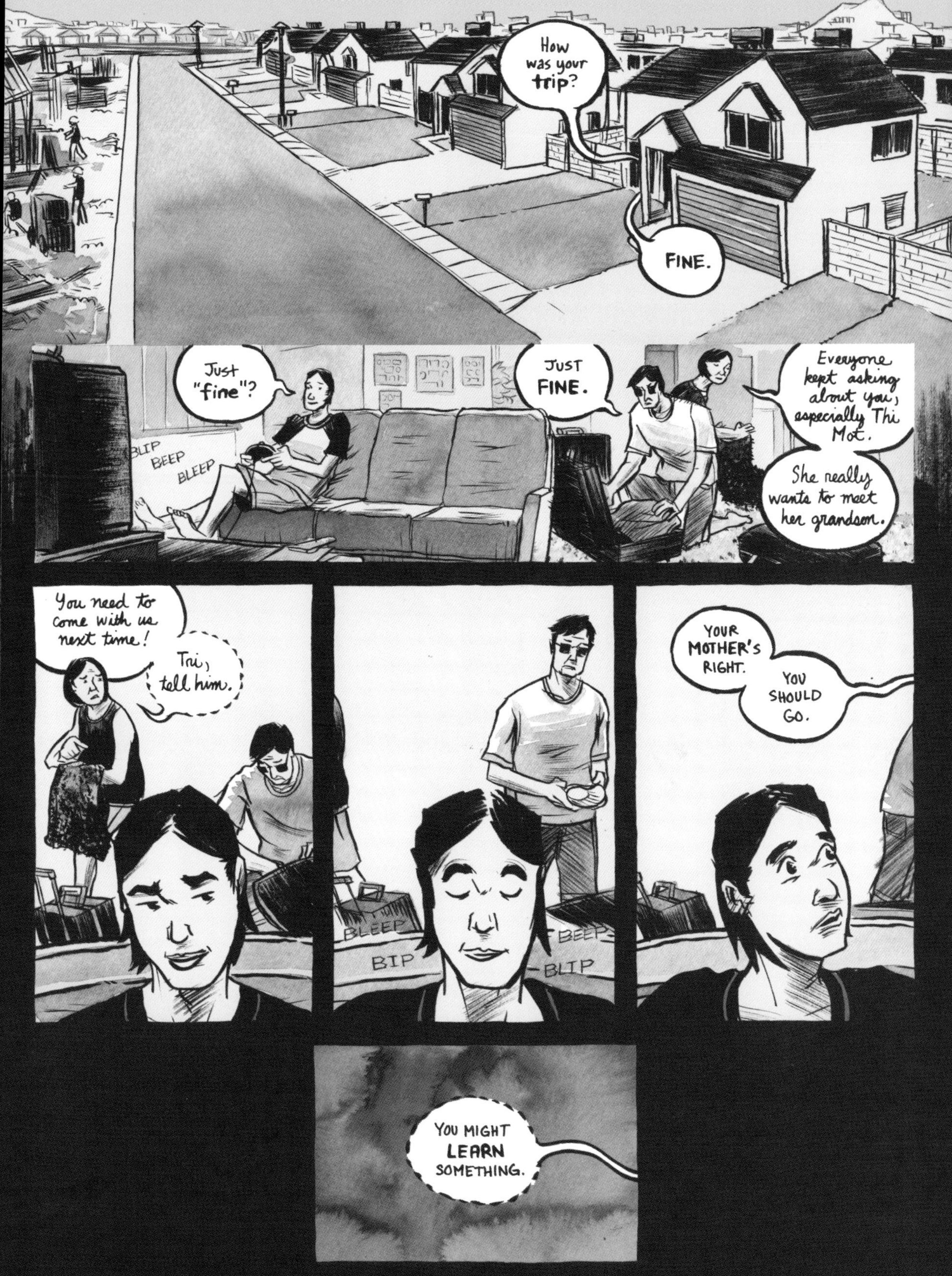
How was your trip?
FINE.
Just "fine"?
BLIP
BEEP
BLEEP
JUST FINE.
Everyone kept asking about you, especially Thi Mot.
She really wants to meet her grandson.
You need to come with us next time!
Tri, tell him.
BLEEP
BEEP
BIP
BLIP
YOUR MOTHER'S RIGHT.
YOU SHOULD GO.
YOU MIGHT LEARN SOMETHING.

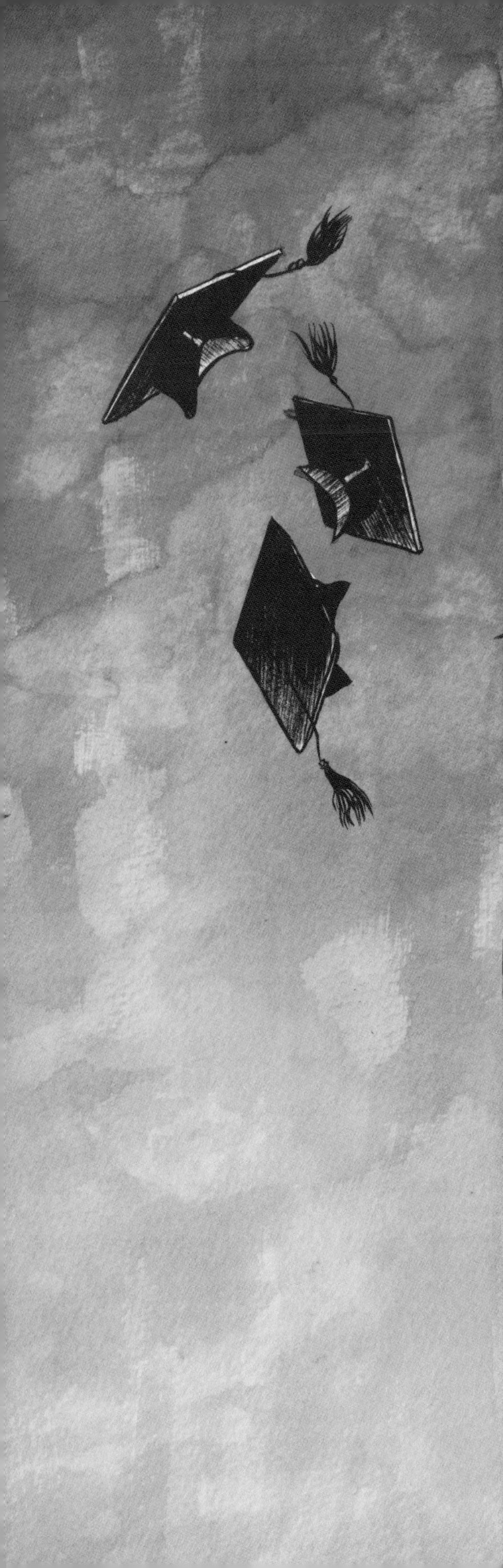

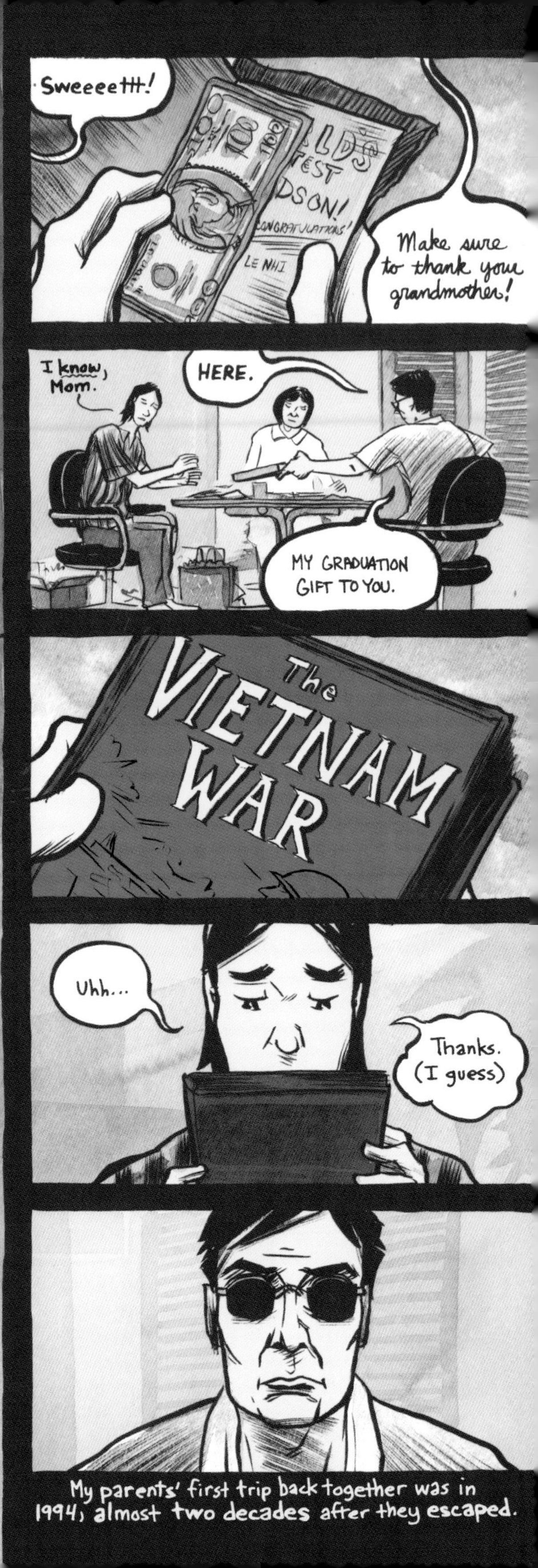

Sweeeettt!
CONGRATULATIONS!
LE NHI
Make sure to thank your grandmother!
I know, Mom.
HERE.
MY GRADUATION GIFT TO YOU.
The VIETNAM WAR
Uhh...
Thanks. (I guess)
My parents' first trip back together was in 1994, almost two decades after they escaped.

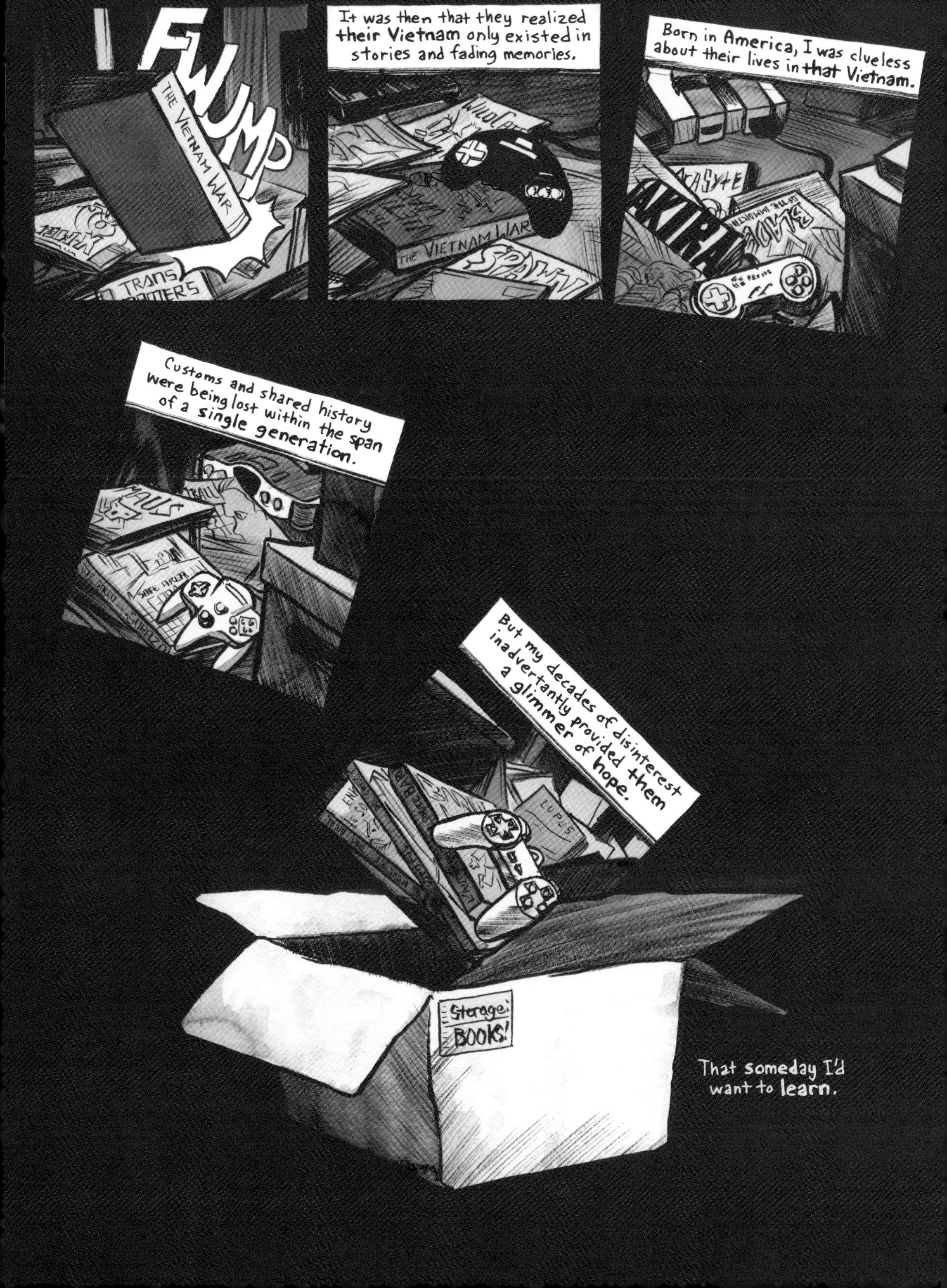
FWUMP
THE VIETNAM WAR
TRANSFORMERS
It was then that they realized their Vietnam only existed in stories and fading memories.
THE VIETNAM WAR
Born in America, I was clueless about their lives in that Vietnam.
AKIRA
Customs and shared history were being lost within the span of a single generation.
MAUS
But my decades of disinterest inadvertently provided them a glimmer of hope.
LUPUS
Storage BOOKS!
That someday I'd want to learn.

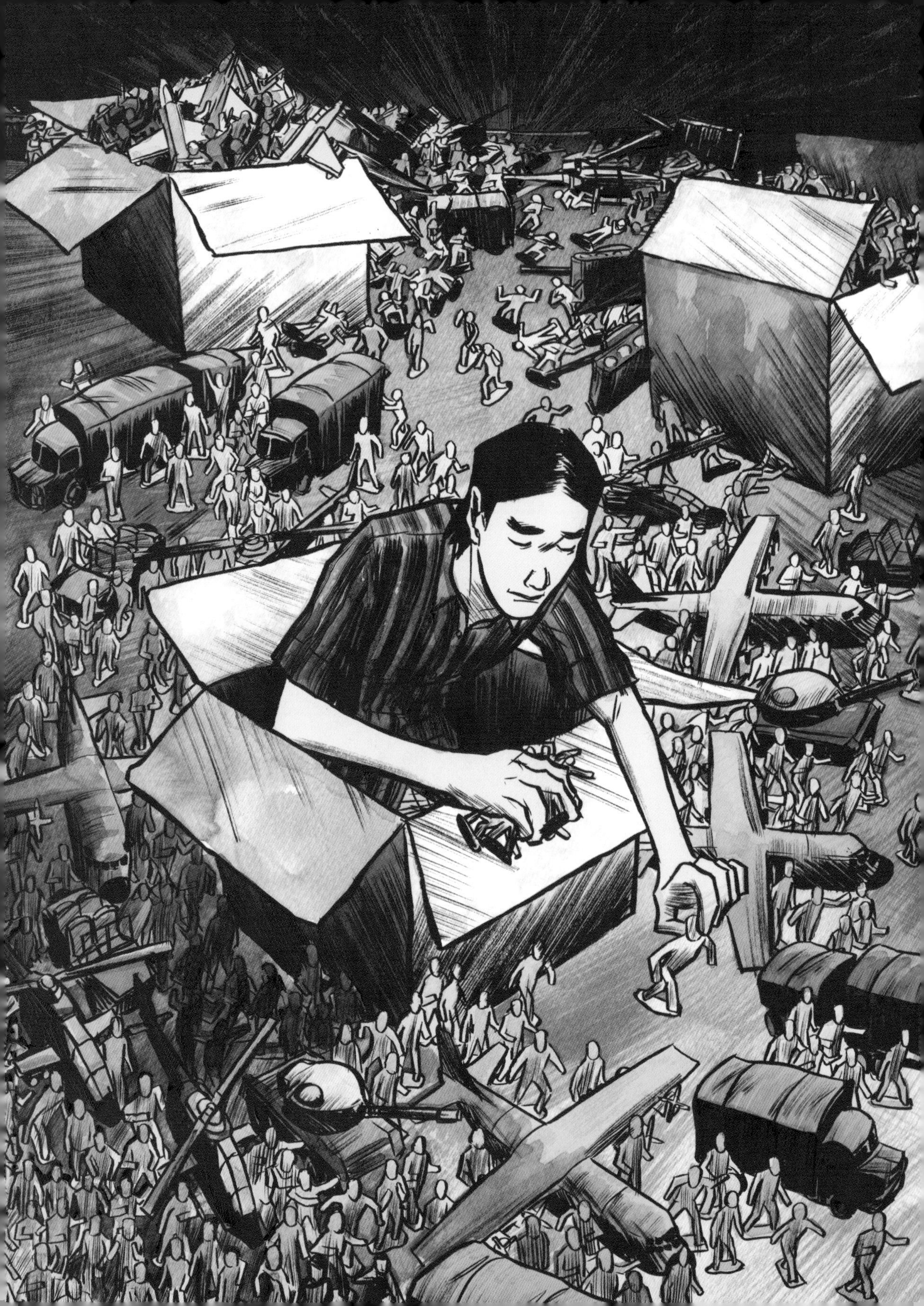

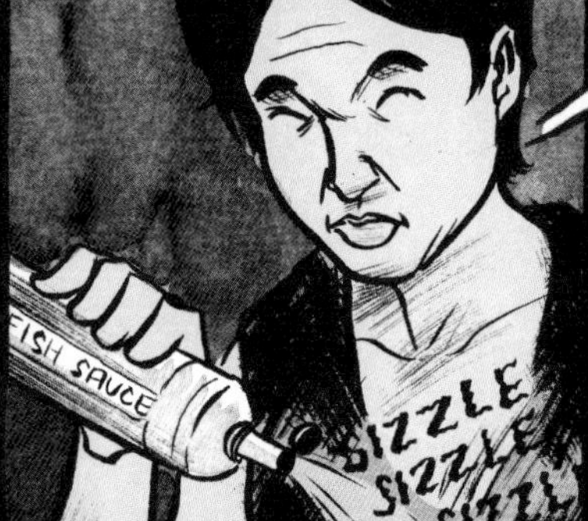
FISH SAUCE
SIZZLE
SIZZLE
SIZZLE

The 1975 Tet celebrations marked a very special time for us...

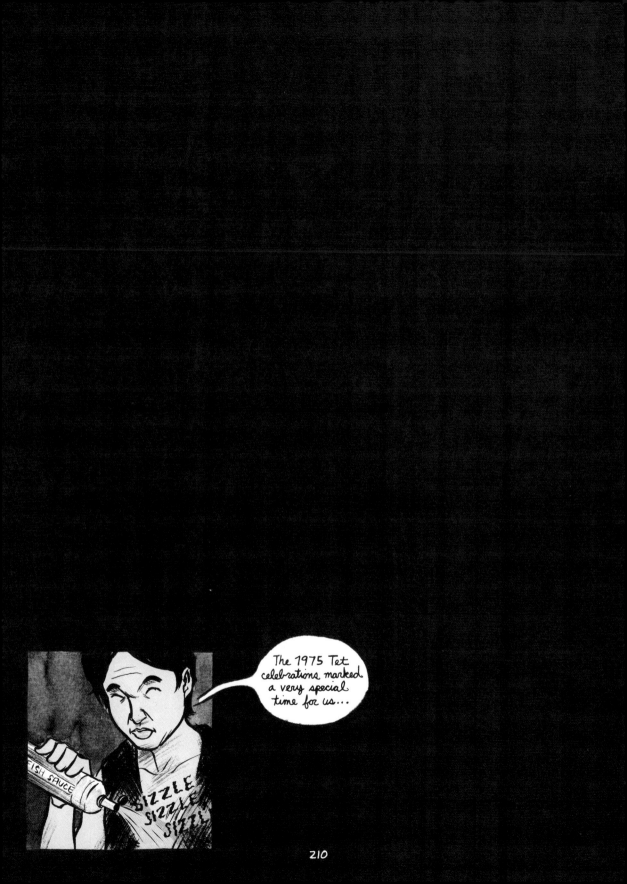

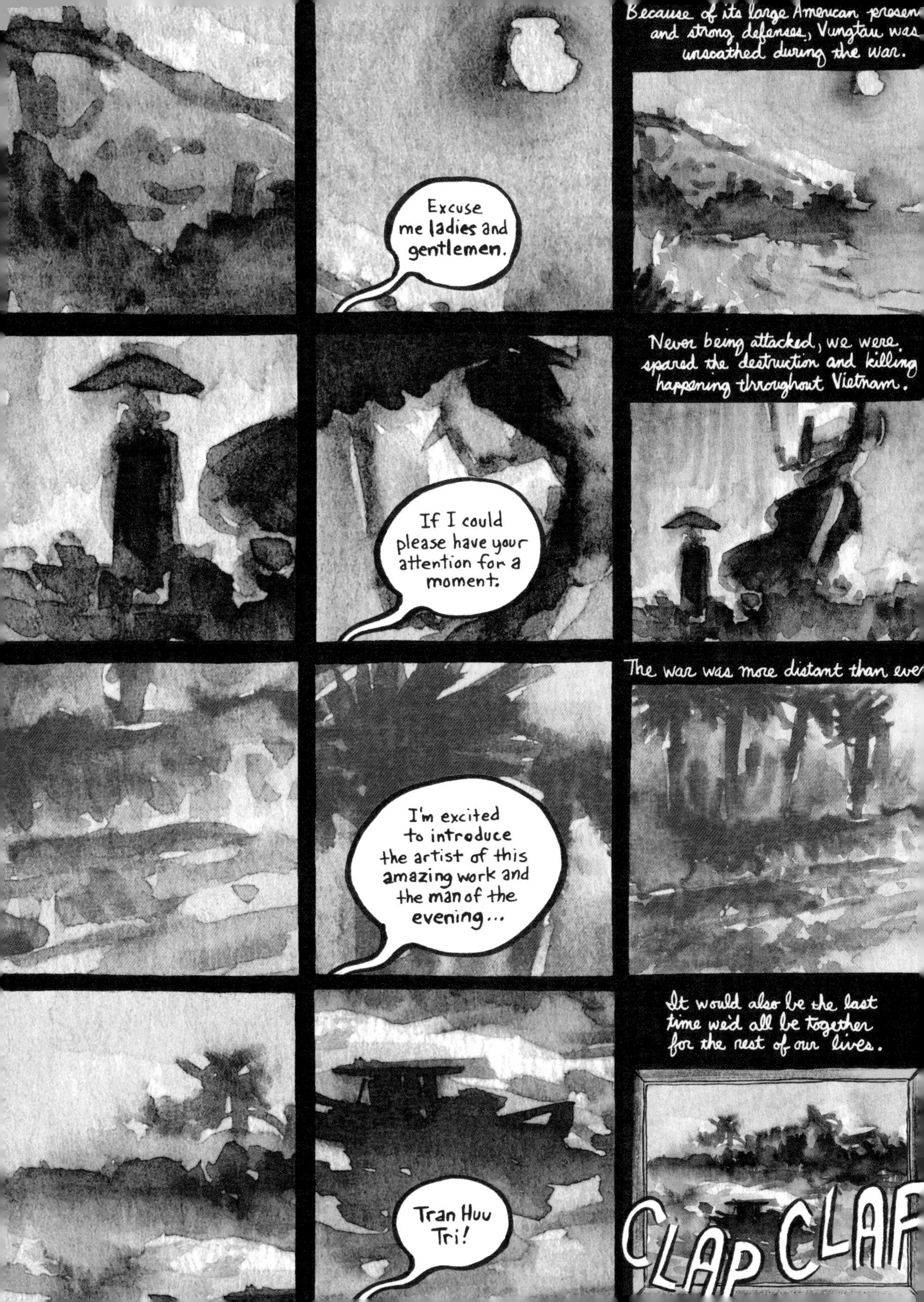
Excuse me ladies and gentlemen.
Because of its large American presen
and strong defenses, Vungtau was unscathed during the war.
If I could please have your attention for a moment.
Never being attacked, we were spared the destruction and killing happening throughout Vietnam.
I'm excited to introduce the artist of this amazing work and the man of the evening...
The war was more distant than eve
Tran Huu Tri!
It would also be the last time we'd all be together for the rest of our lives.
CLAP CLAP

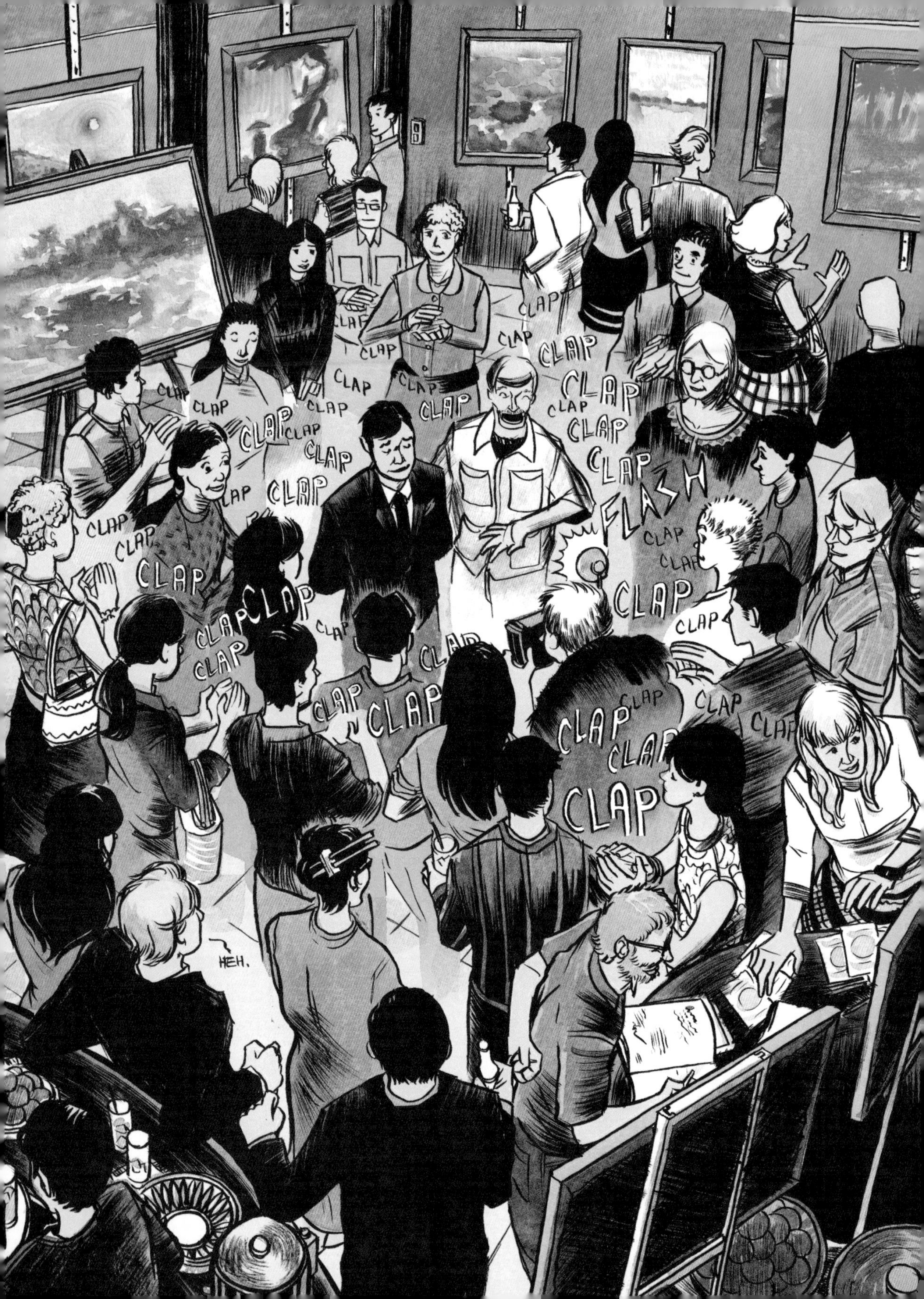

CLAP
CLAP
CLAP
CLAP
CLAP
CLAP
CLAP
CLAP
CLAP
CLAP
CLAP
CLAP
CLAP
CLAP
CLAP
CLAP
FLASH
CLAP
CLAP
CLAP
CLAP
CLAP
CLAP
CLAP
CLAP
CLAP
CLAP
CLAP
CLAP
CLAP
CLAP
CLAP
CLAP
CLAP
CLAP
HEH.

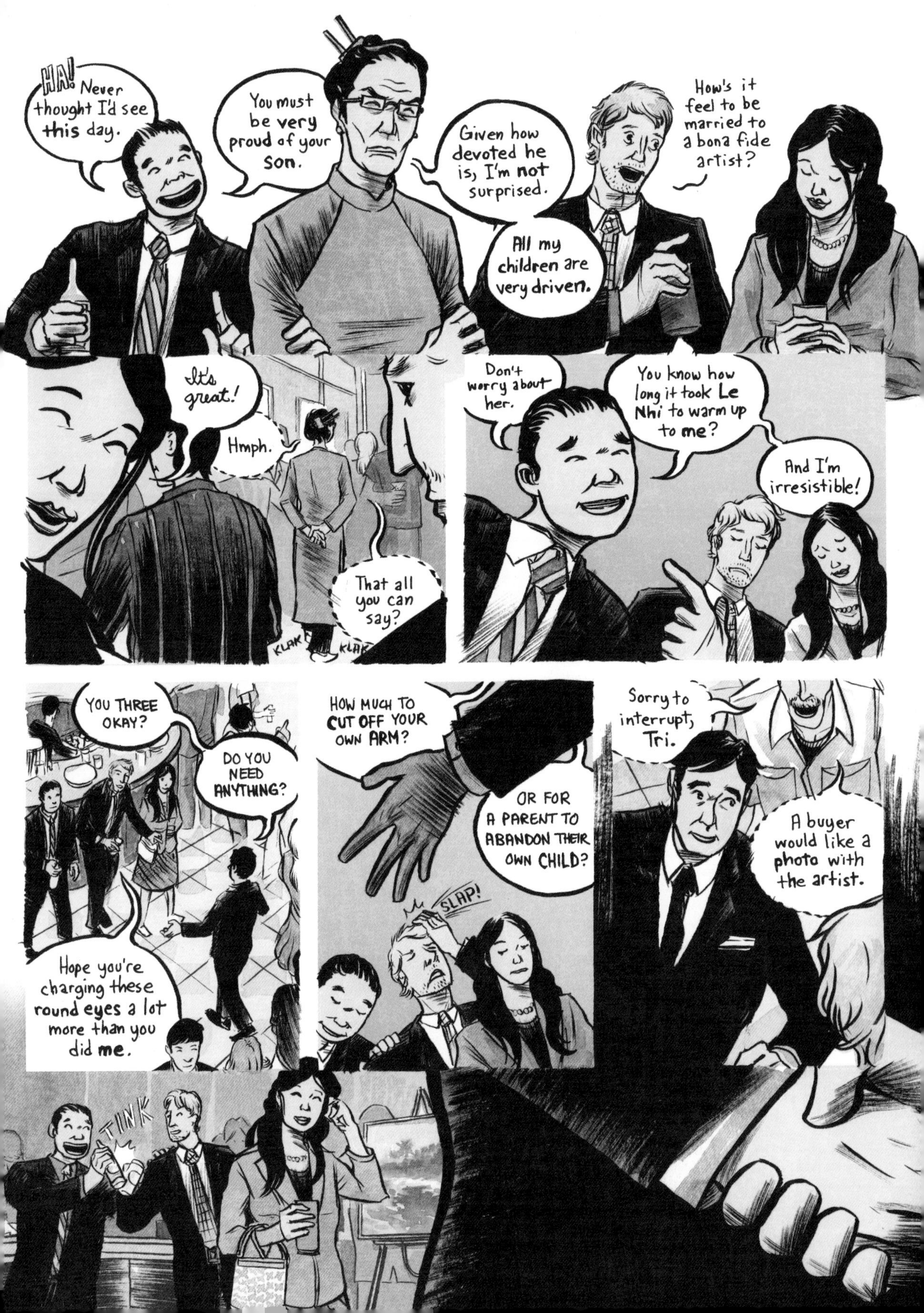
HA! Never thought I'd see this day.
You must be very proud of your son.
Given how devoted he is, I'm not surprised.
All my children are very driven.
How's it feel to be married to a bona fide artist?
It's great!
Hmph.
That all you can say?
KLAK KLAK
Don't worry about her.
You know how long it took Le Nhi to warm up to me?
And I'm irresistible!
YOU THREE OKAY?
DO YOU NEED ANYTHING?
Hope you're charging these round eyes a lot more than you did me.
HOW MUCH TO CUT OFF YOUR OWN ARM?
OR FOR A PARENT TO ABANDON THEIR OWN CHILD?
SLAP!
Sorry to interrupt, Tri.
A buyer would like a photo with the artist.
TINK

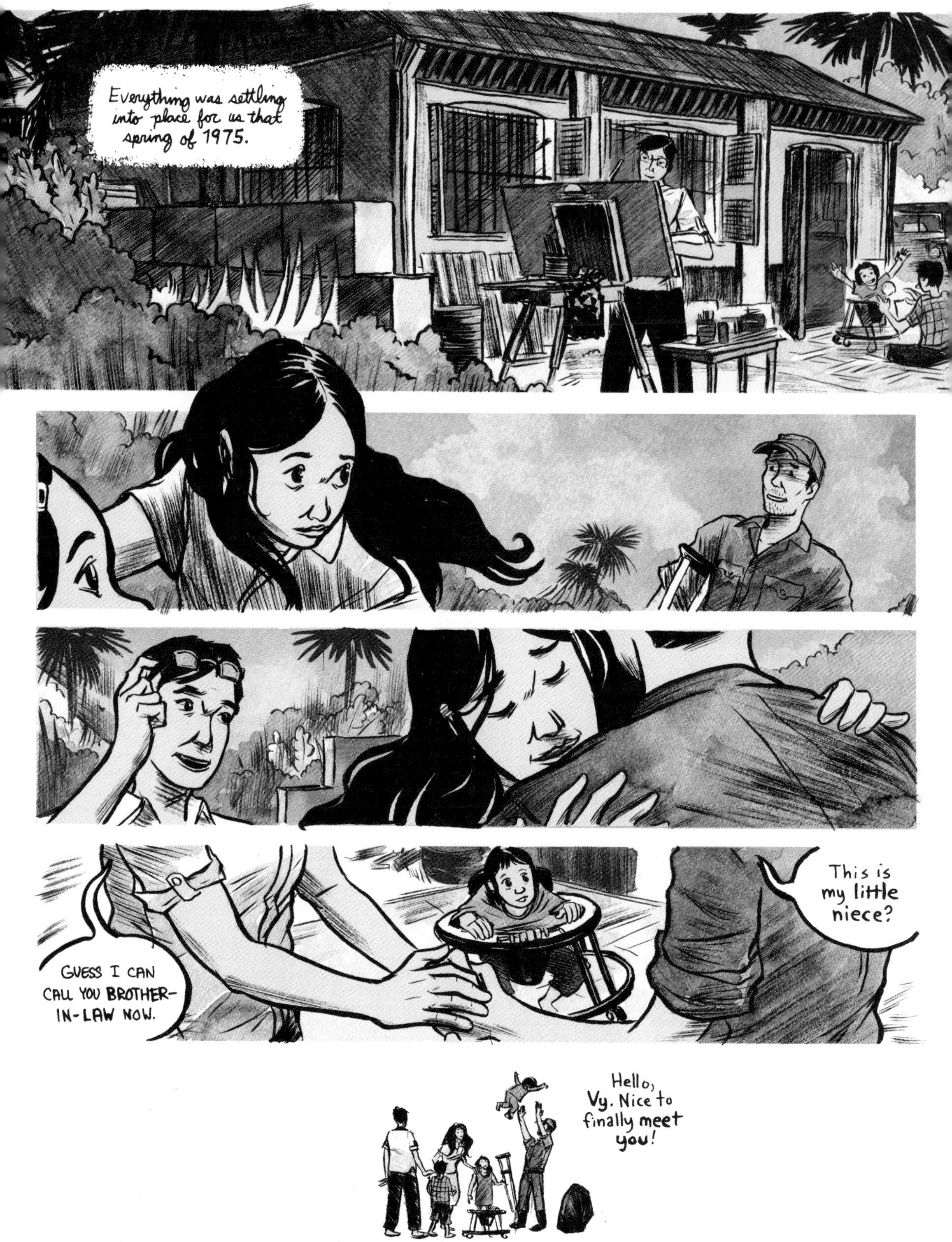
Everything was settling into place for us that spring of 1975.
GUESS I CAN CALL YOU BROTHER-IN-LAW NOW.
This is my little niece?
Hello, Vy. Nice to finally meet you!

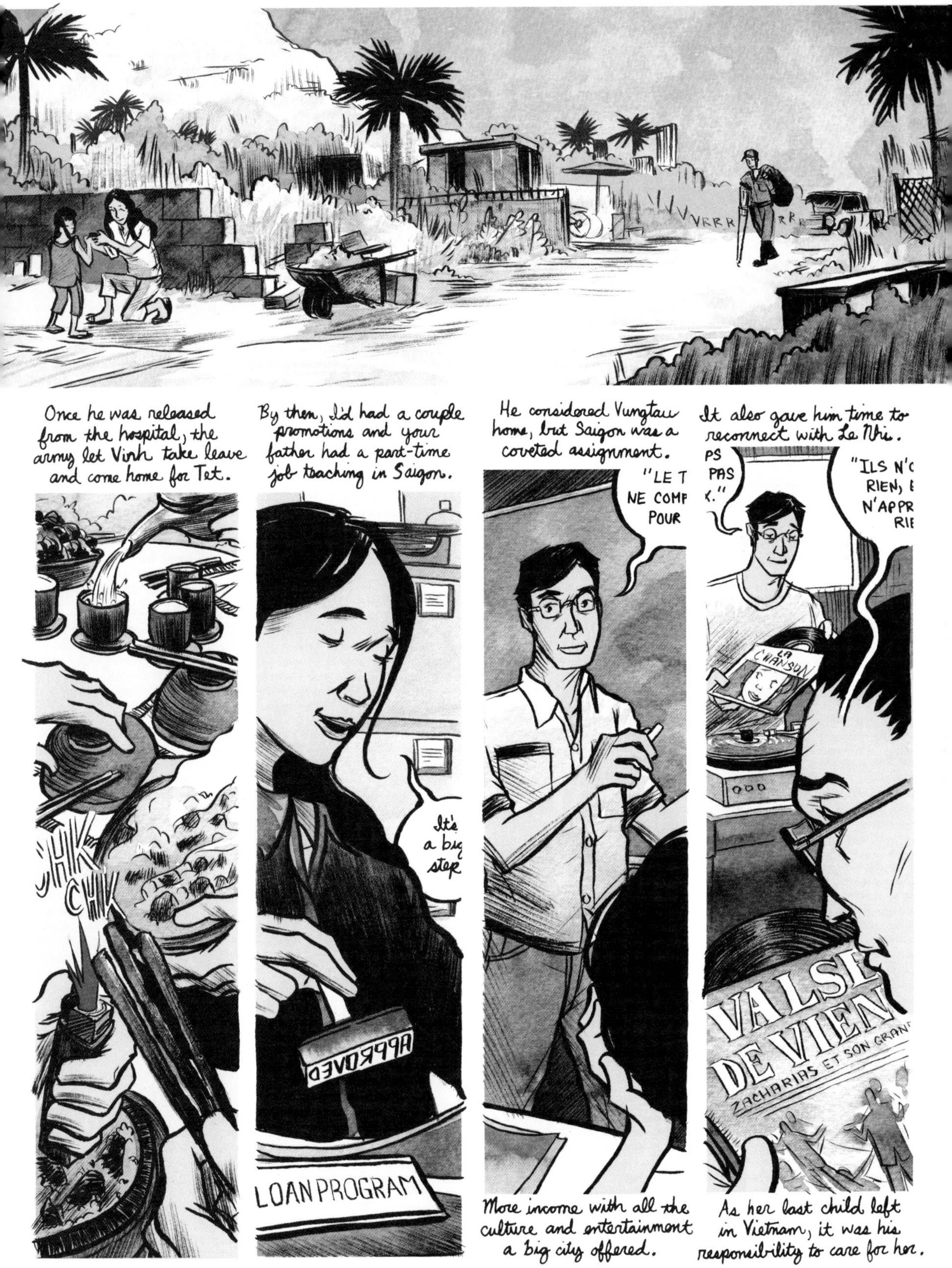

Once he was released from the hospital, the army let Vinh take leave and come home for Tet.
By then, I'd had a couple promotions and your father had a part-time job teaching in Saigon.
It's a big step
LOAN PROGRAM
He considered Vungtau home, but Saigon was a coveted assignment.
"LE T
NE COMP
POUR
More income with all the culture and entertainment a big city offered.
It also gave him time to reconnect with Le Nhi.
PS
PAS
X."
"ILS N'C
RIEN, E
N'APPR
RIE
LA CHANSON
VALSE
DE VIEN
ZACHARIAS ET SON GRAN
As her last child left in Vietnam, it was his responsibility to care for her.

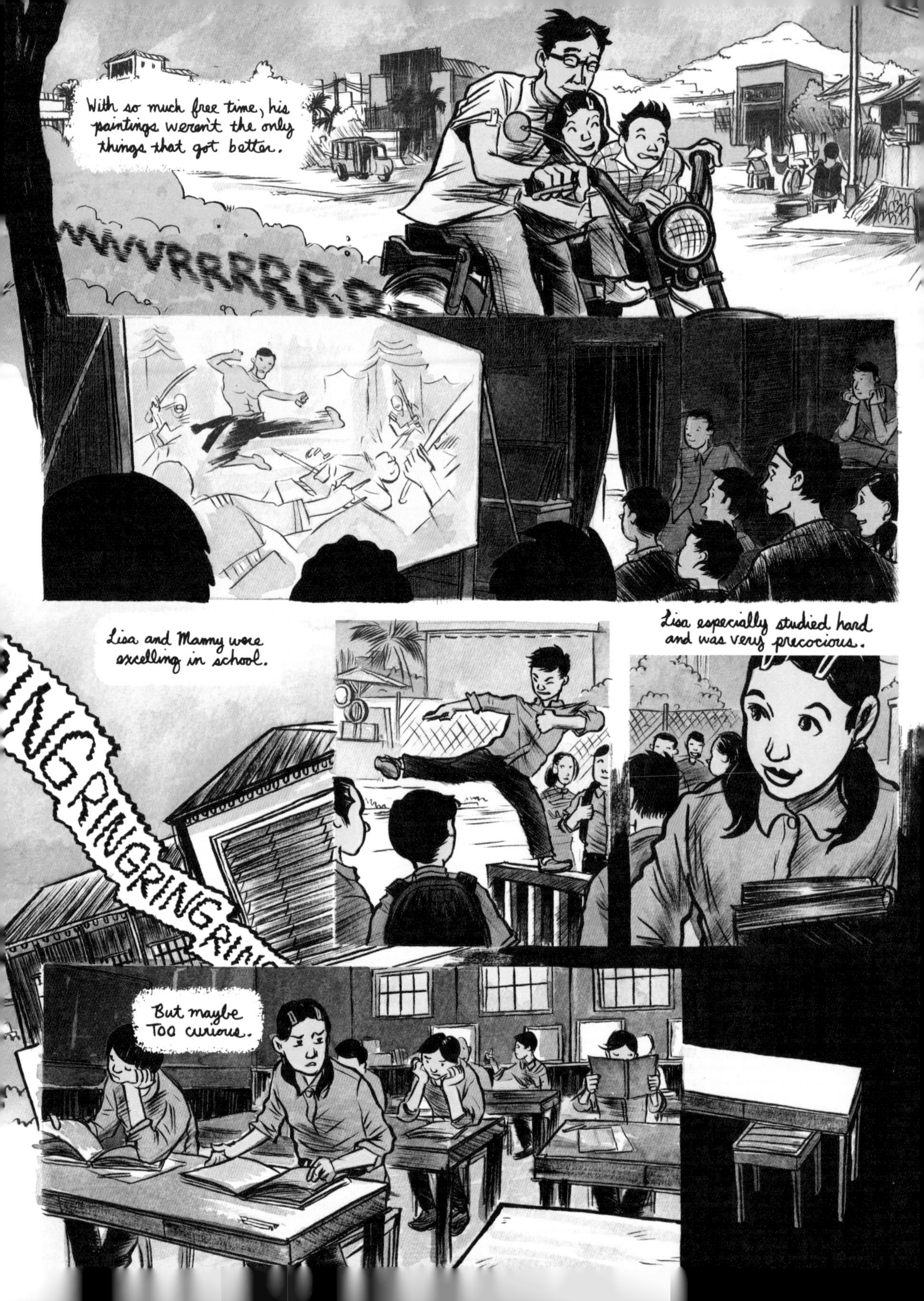
With so much free time, his paintings weren't the only things that got better.
WVVVRRRRRRO
Lisa and Manny were excelling in school.
Lisa especially studied hard and was very precocious.
RINGRINGRINGRI
But maybe TOO curious.

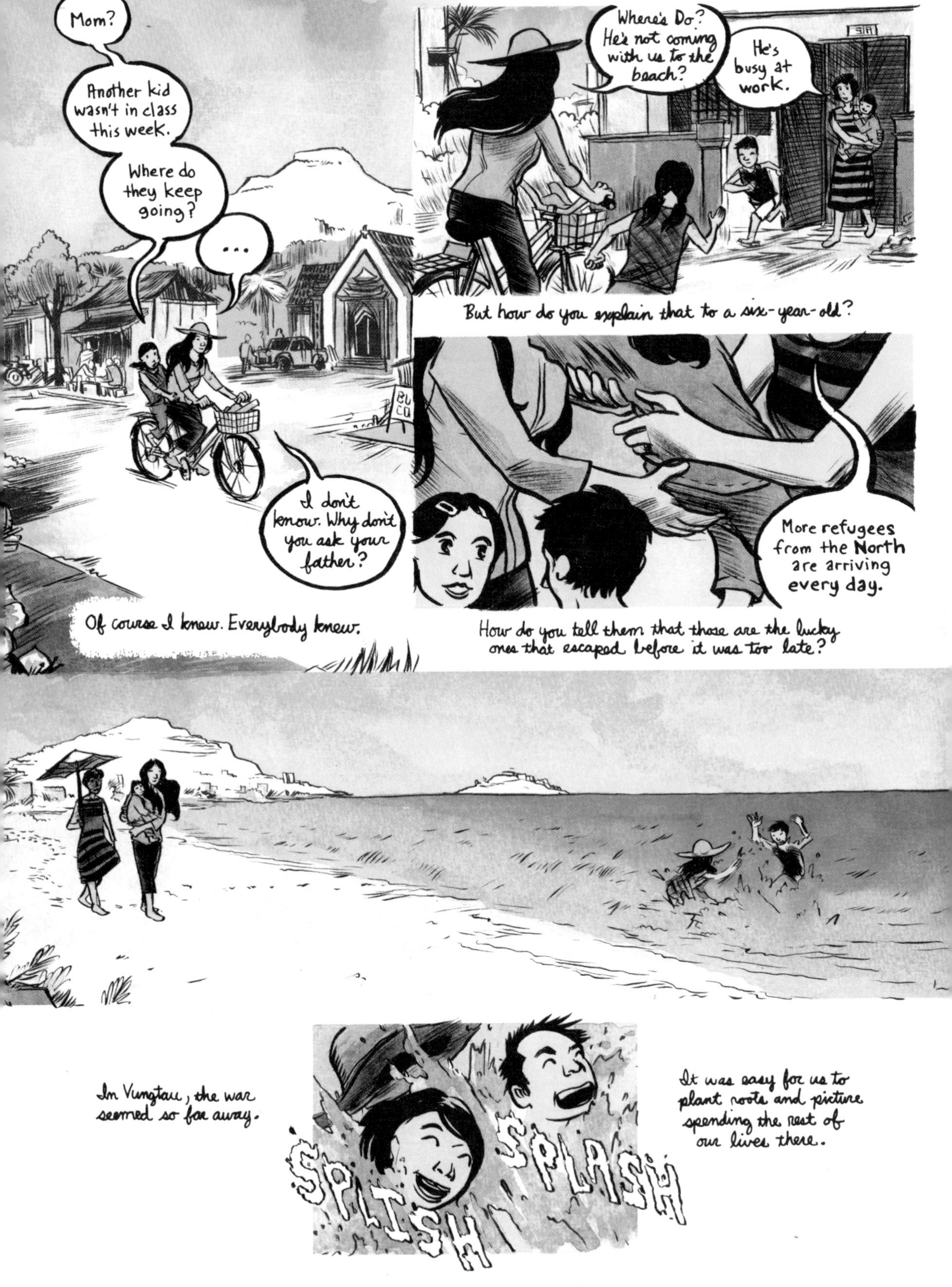
Mom?
Another kid wasn't in class this week.
Where do they keep going?
...
I don't know. Why don't you ask your father?
Of course I knew. Everybody knew.
Where's Do? He's not coming with us to the beach?
He's busy at work.
But how do you explain that to a six-year-old?
More refugees from the North are arriving every day.
How do you tell them that those are the lucky ones that escaped before it was too late?
In Vungtau, the war seemed so far away.
SPLISH
SPLASH
It was easy for us to plant roots and picture spending the rest of our lives there.

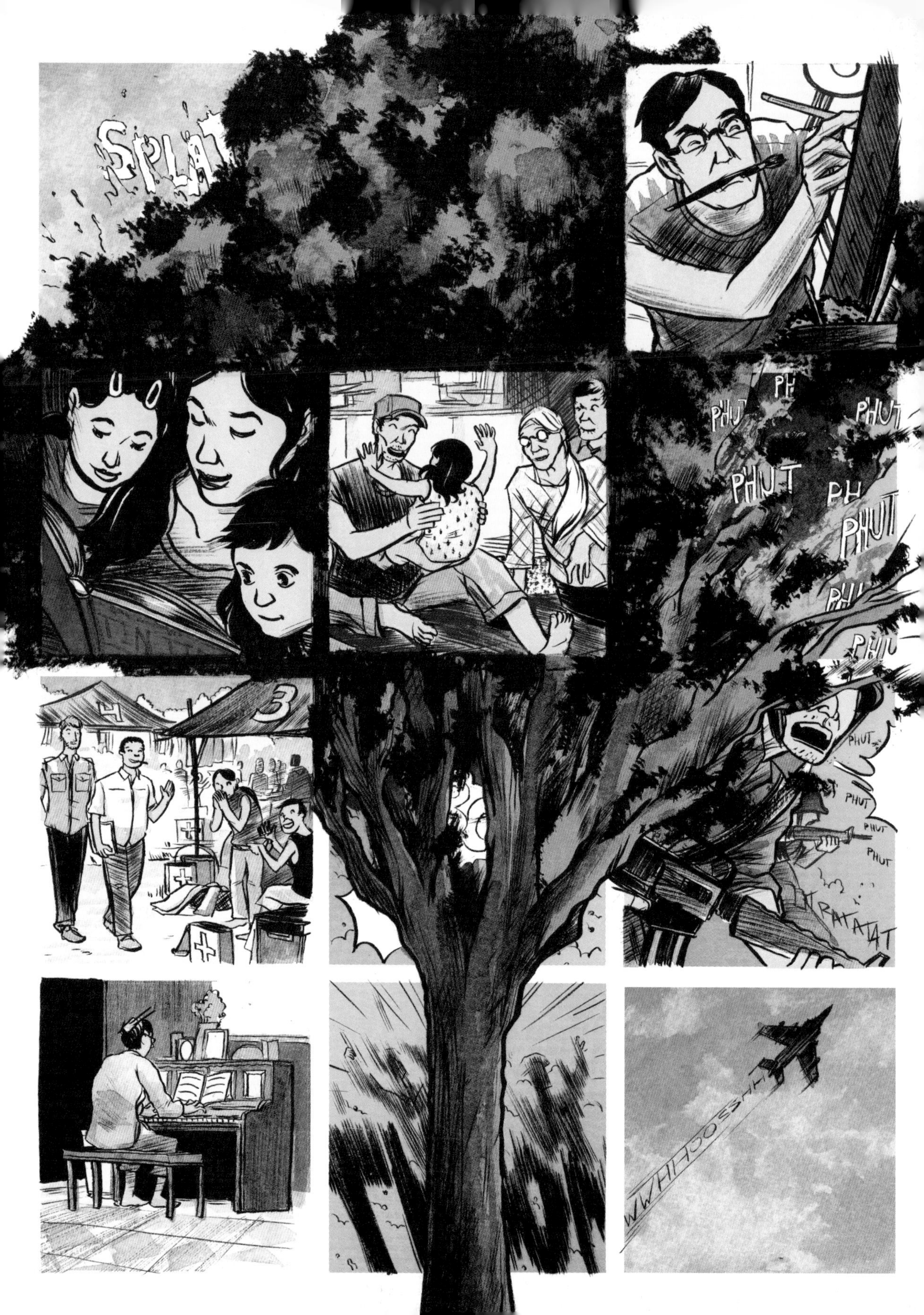
SPLAT
PH
PHUT
PHUT
PHUT
PH
PHUT
PHUT
PHUT
PHUT
PHUT
PHUT
RATATAT
WWHHOOSHH

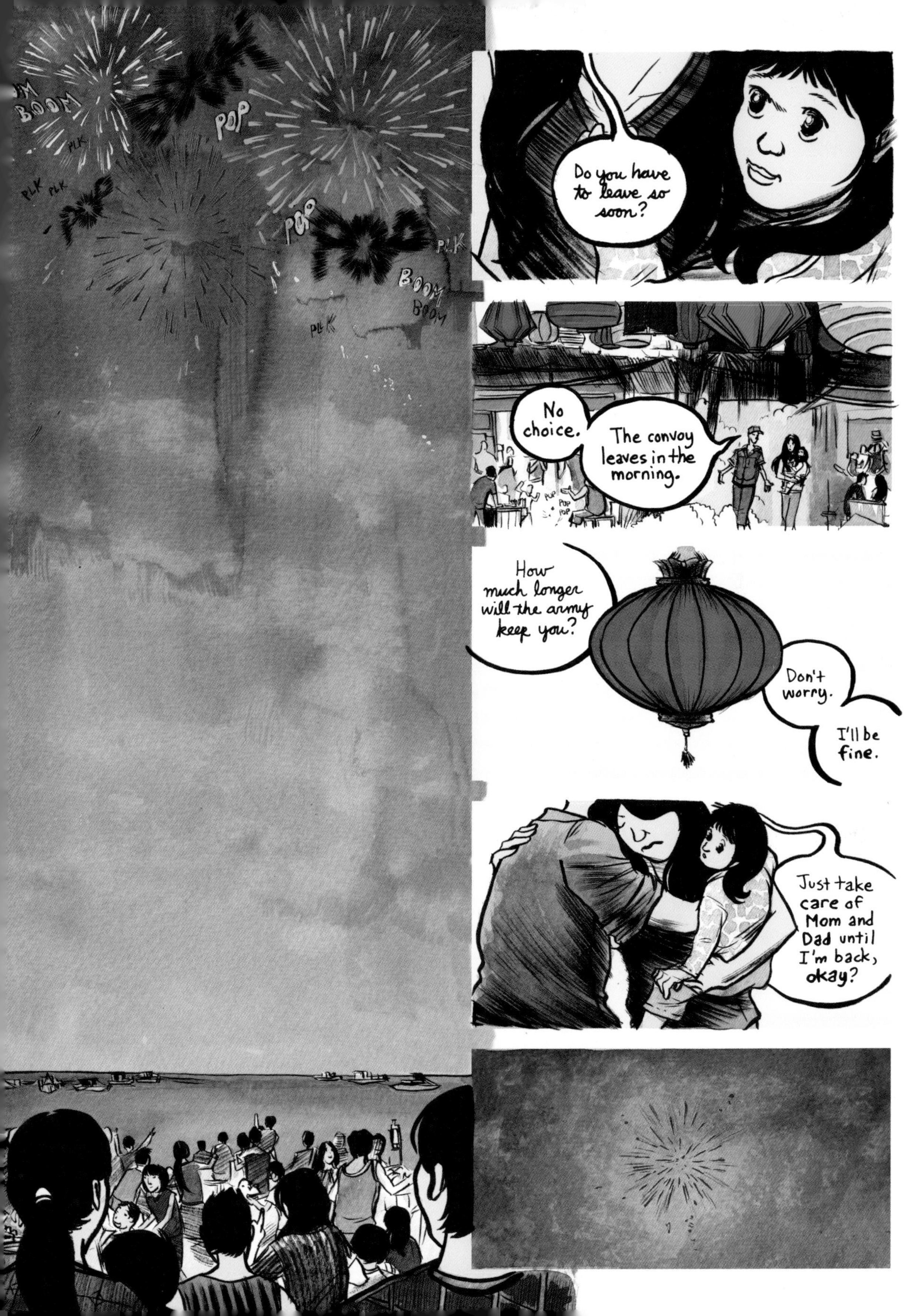
BOOM
PLK
POP
PLK PLK
POP
PLK
BOOM
BOOM
PLK
Do you have to leave so soon?
No choice.
The convoy leaves in the morning.
POP POP POP
How much longer will the army keep you?
Don't worry.
I'll be fine.
Just take care of Mom and Dad until I'm back, okay?

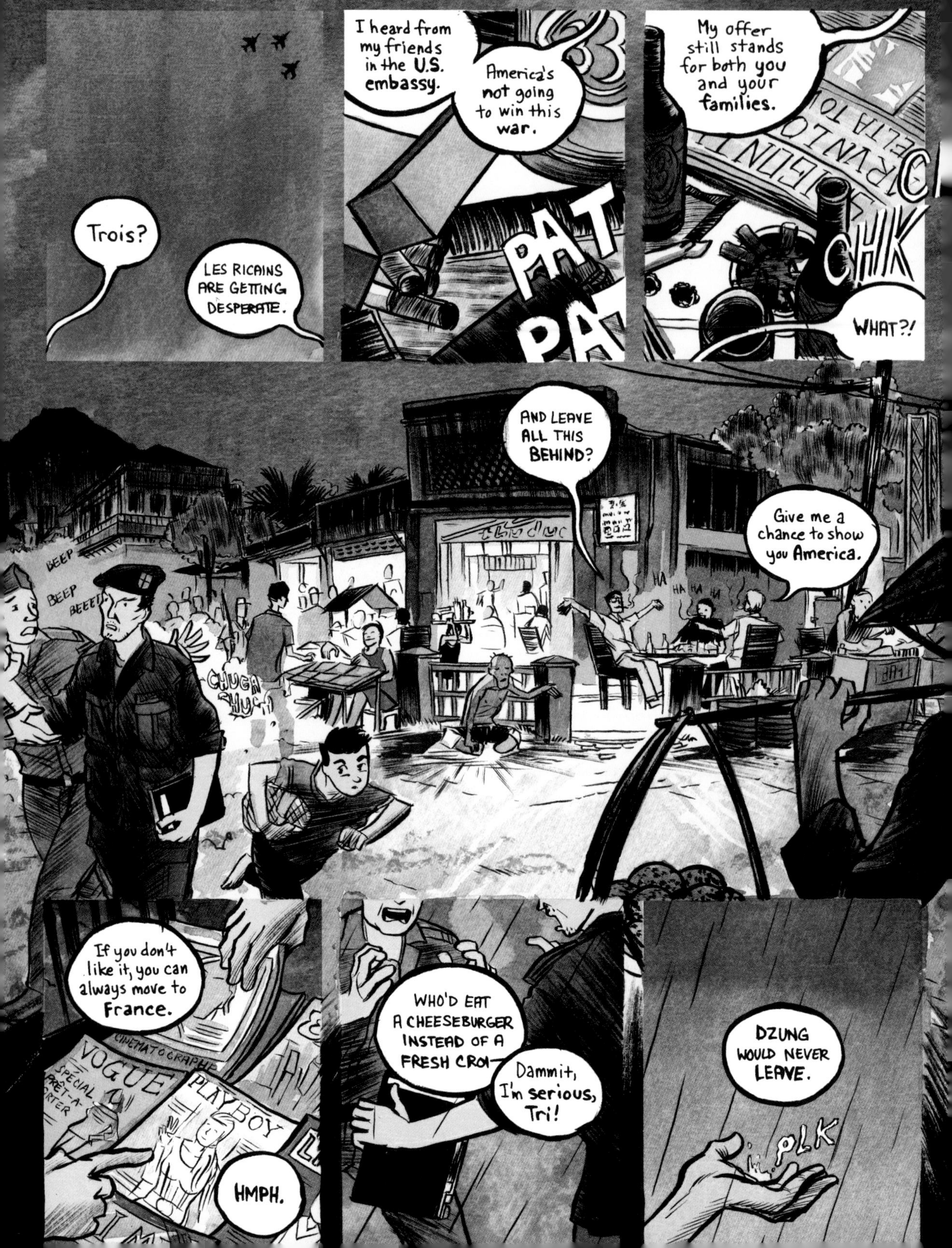
Trois?
LES RICAINS ARE GETTING DESPERATE.
I heard from my friends in the U.S. embassy.
America's not going to win this war.
PAT
PAT
My offer still stands for both you and your families.
CHK
WHAT?!
AND LEAVE ALL THIS BEHIND?
Give me a chance to show you America.
BEEP
BEEP
BEEEP
CHUGA CHUG
HA HA HA HA
If you don't like it, you can always move to France.
VOGUE
CINEMATOGRAPHE
PLAYBOY
HMPH.
WHO'D EAT A CHEESEBURGER INSTEAD OF A FRESH CROI—
Dammit, I'm serious, Tri!
DZUNG WOULD NEVER LEAVE.
PLK

Have you tried **asking her**?

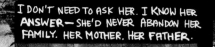
I DON'T NEED TO ASK HER. I KNOW HER ANSWER — SHE'D NEVER ABANDON HER FAMILY. HER MOTHER. HER FATHER.

I can get them **all out**, too.

SSHH...

ANNOUNCEMEN...

...RICAN...

...SIDENT GERALD FORD...

TODAY FROM THE U.S.

Tri, you have a family to protect.

AS FAR AS THE U.S. IS CONCERNED...

You **can't** stay here any longer.

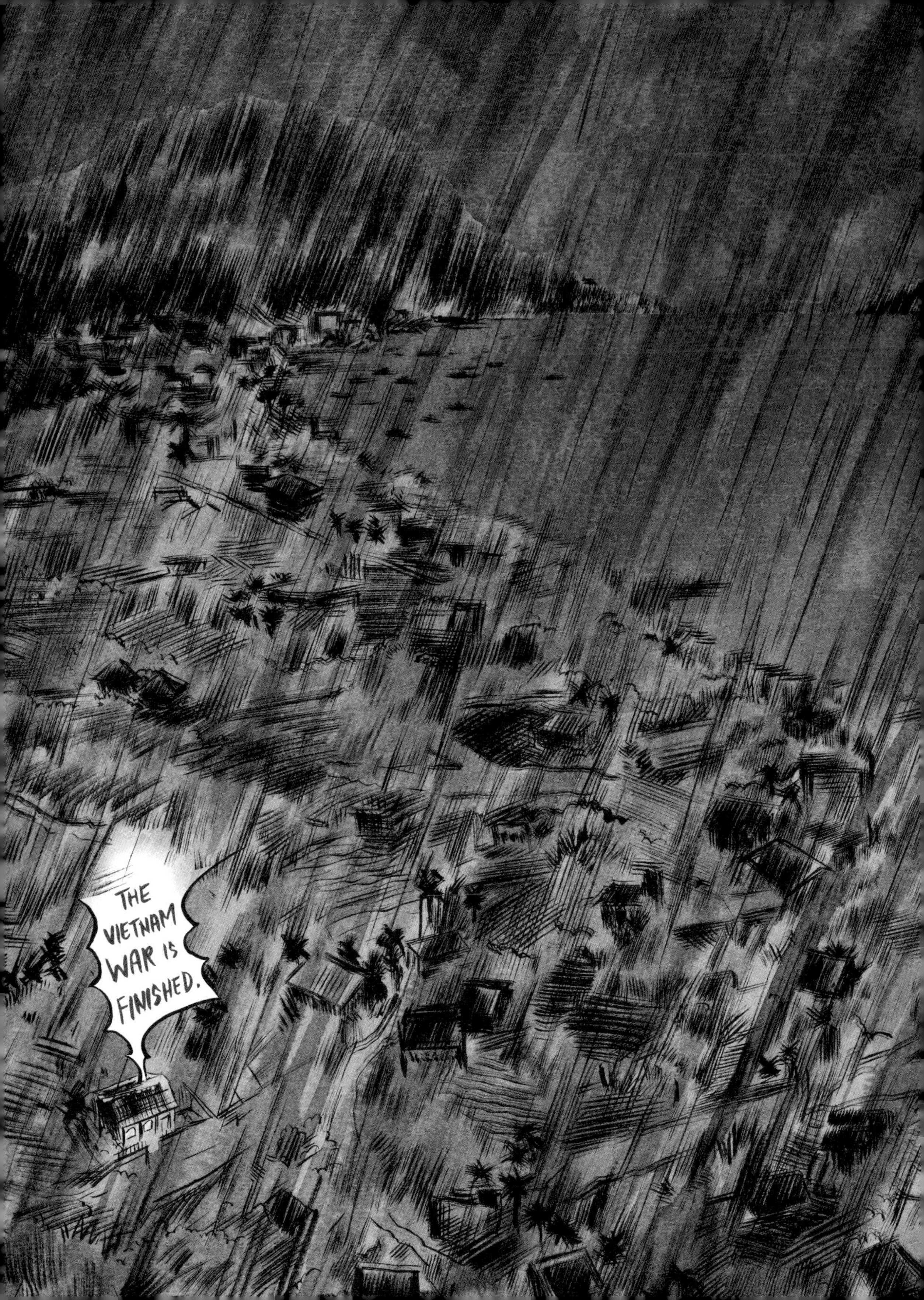
THE VIETNAM WAR IS FINISHED.

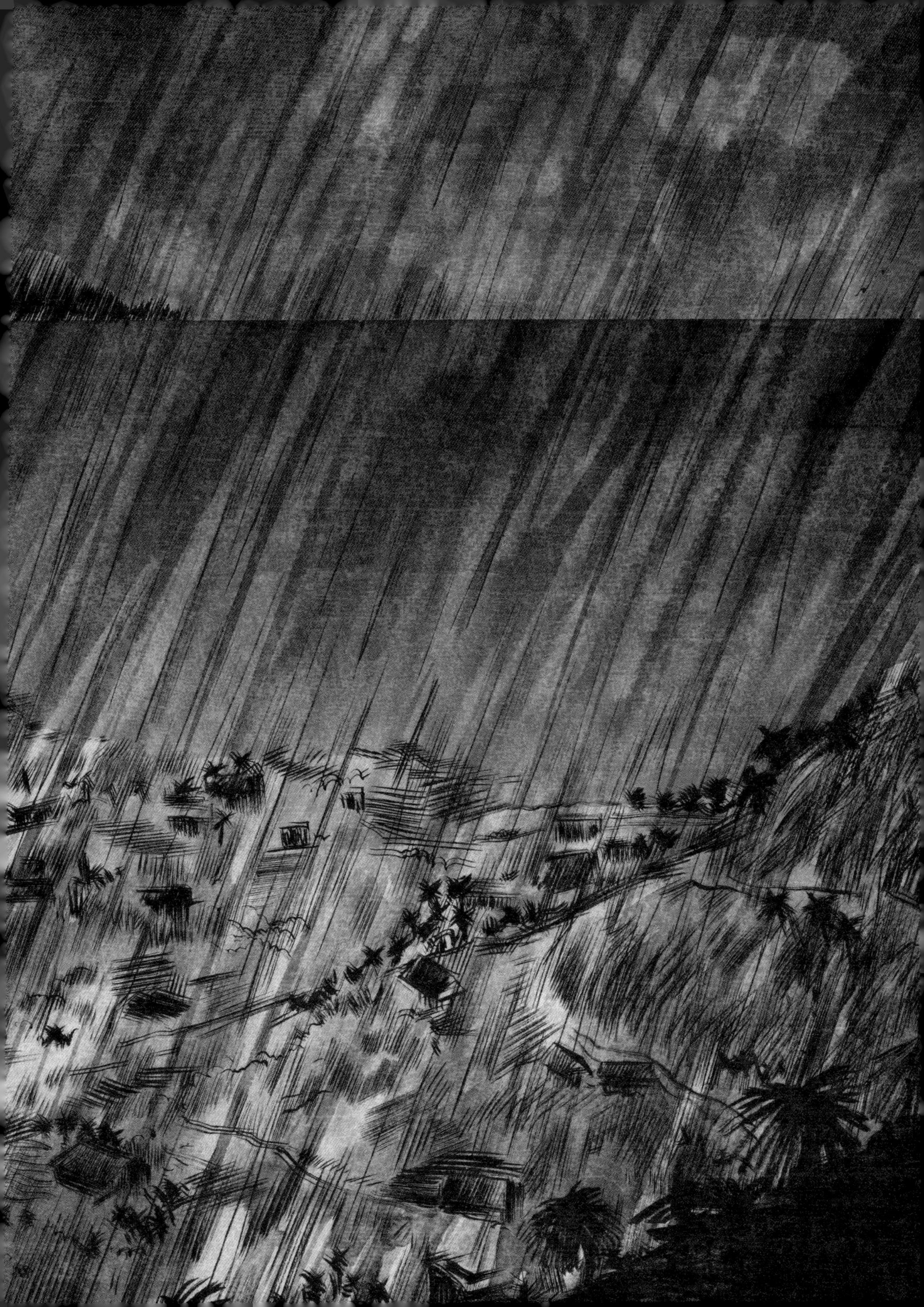

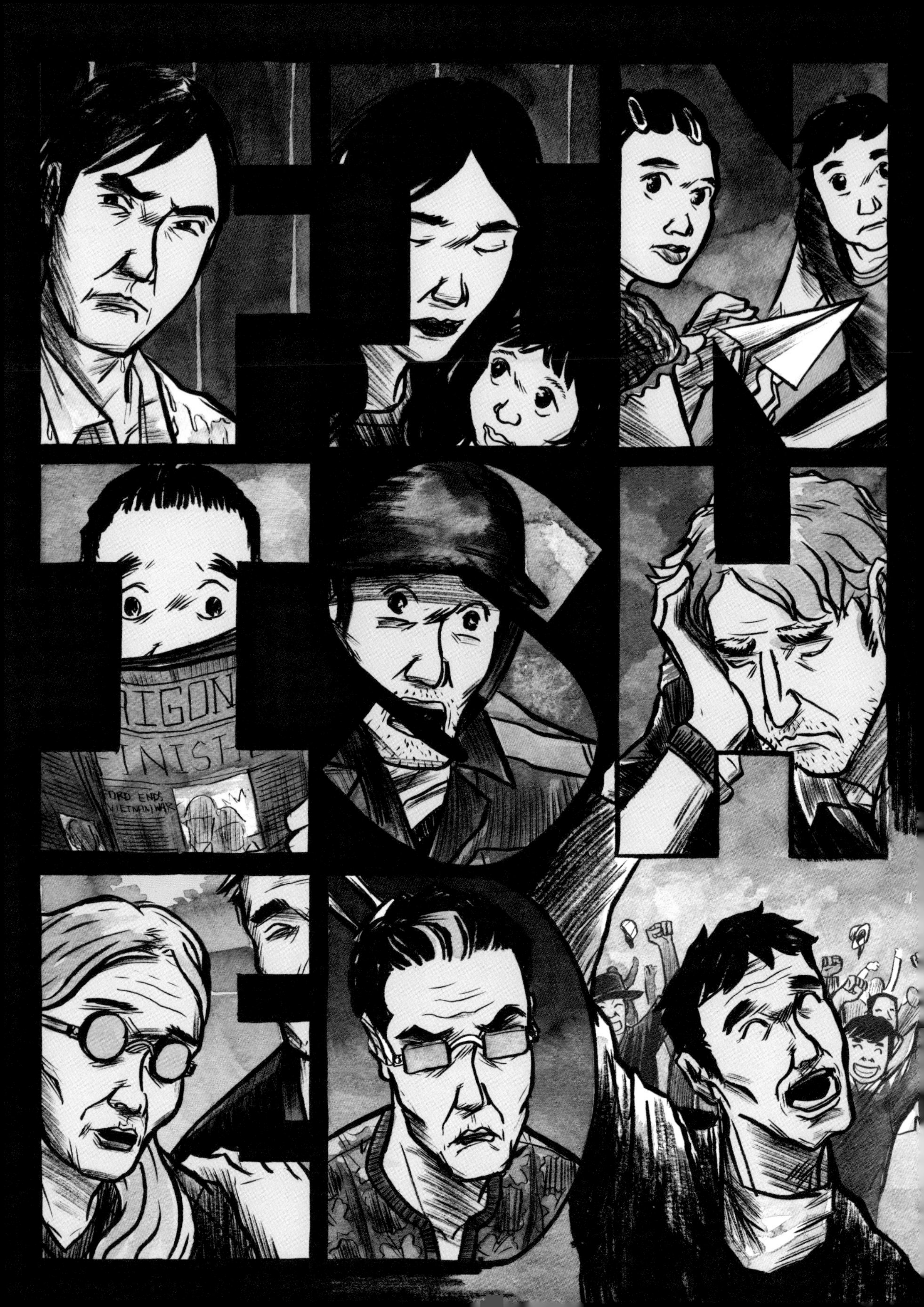
FINISHED
FORD ENDS VIETNAM WAR

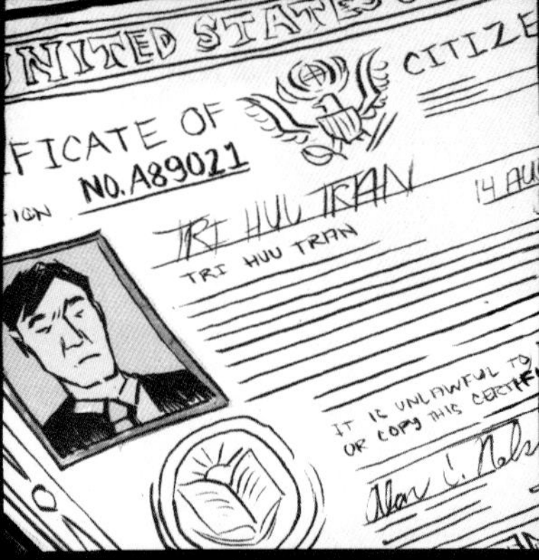
NITED STATES
CITIZE
FICATE OF
NO. A89021
TRI HUU TRAN
IT IS UNLAWFUL TO
OR COPY THIS CERTIF

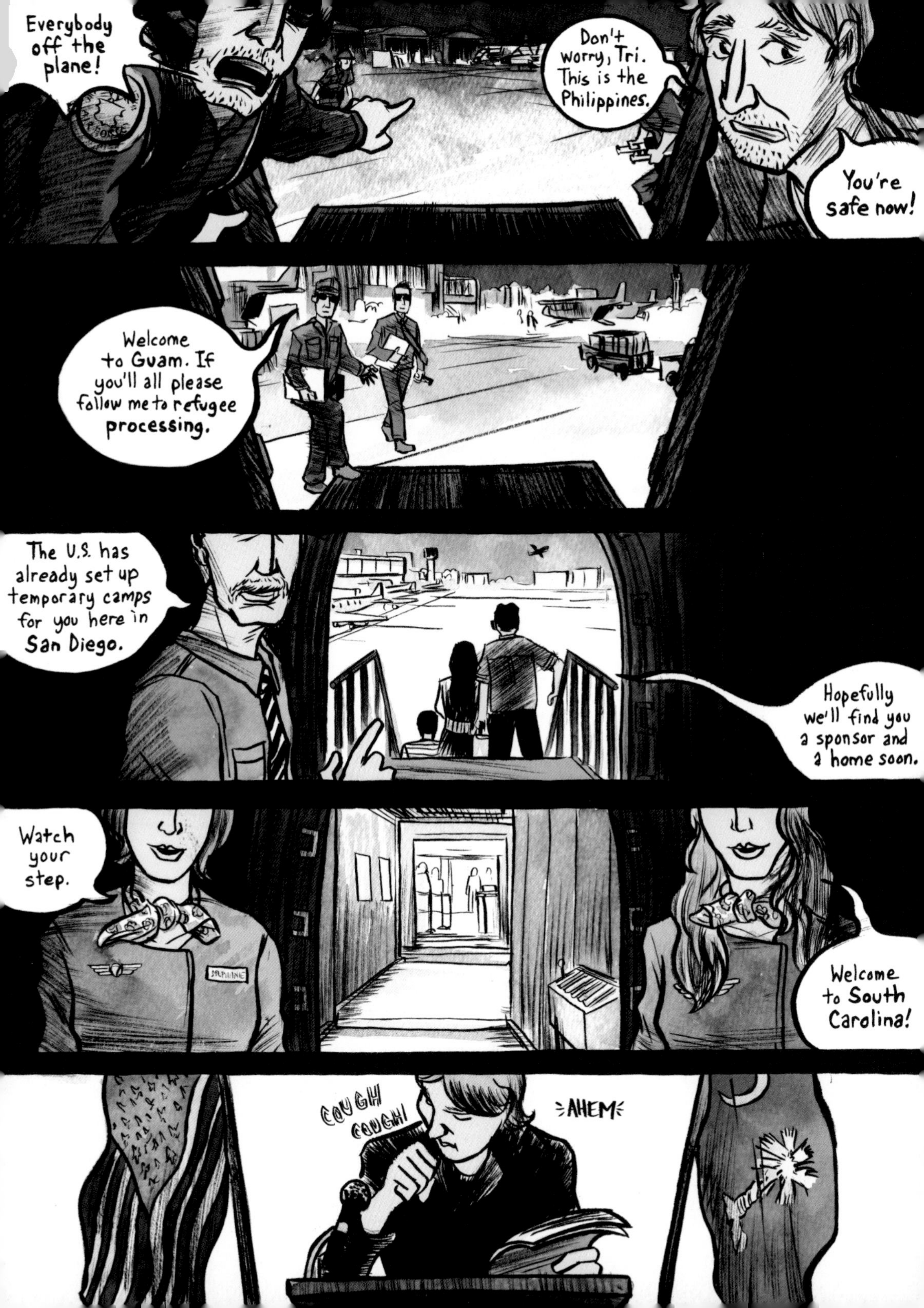
Everybody off the plane!
Don't worry, Tri. This is the Philippines.
You're safe now!
Welcome to Guam. If you'll all please follow me to refugee processing.
The U.S. has already set up temporary camps for you here in San Diego.
Hopefully we'll find you a sponsor and a home soon.
Watch your step.
Welcome to South Carolina!
COUGH COUGH!
AHEM

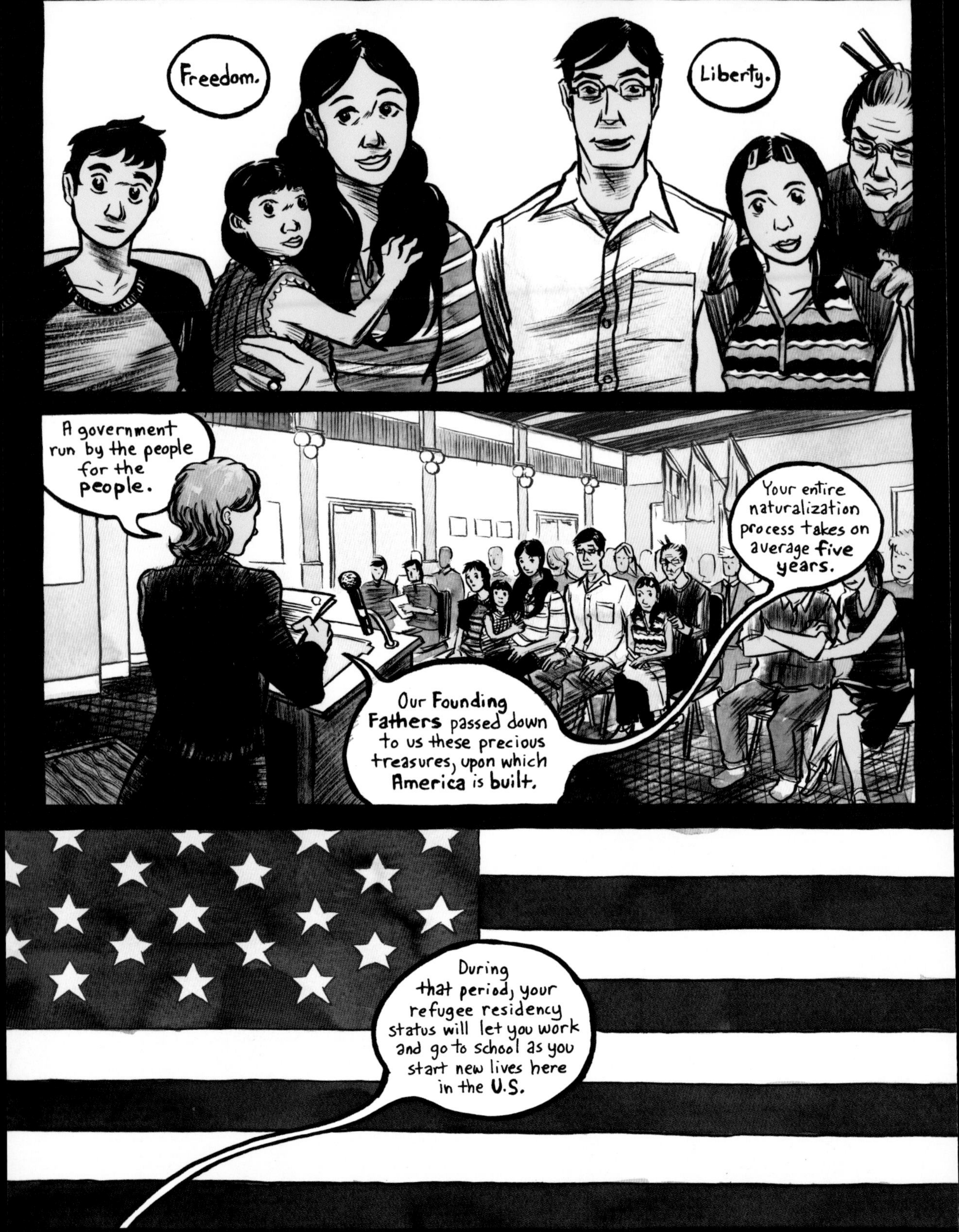
Freedom.
Liberty.
A government run by the people for the people.
Our Founding Fathers passed down to us these precious treasures, upon which America is built.
Your entire naturalization process takes on average five years.
During that period, your refugee residency status will let you work and go to school as you start new lives here in the U.S.

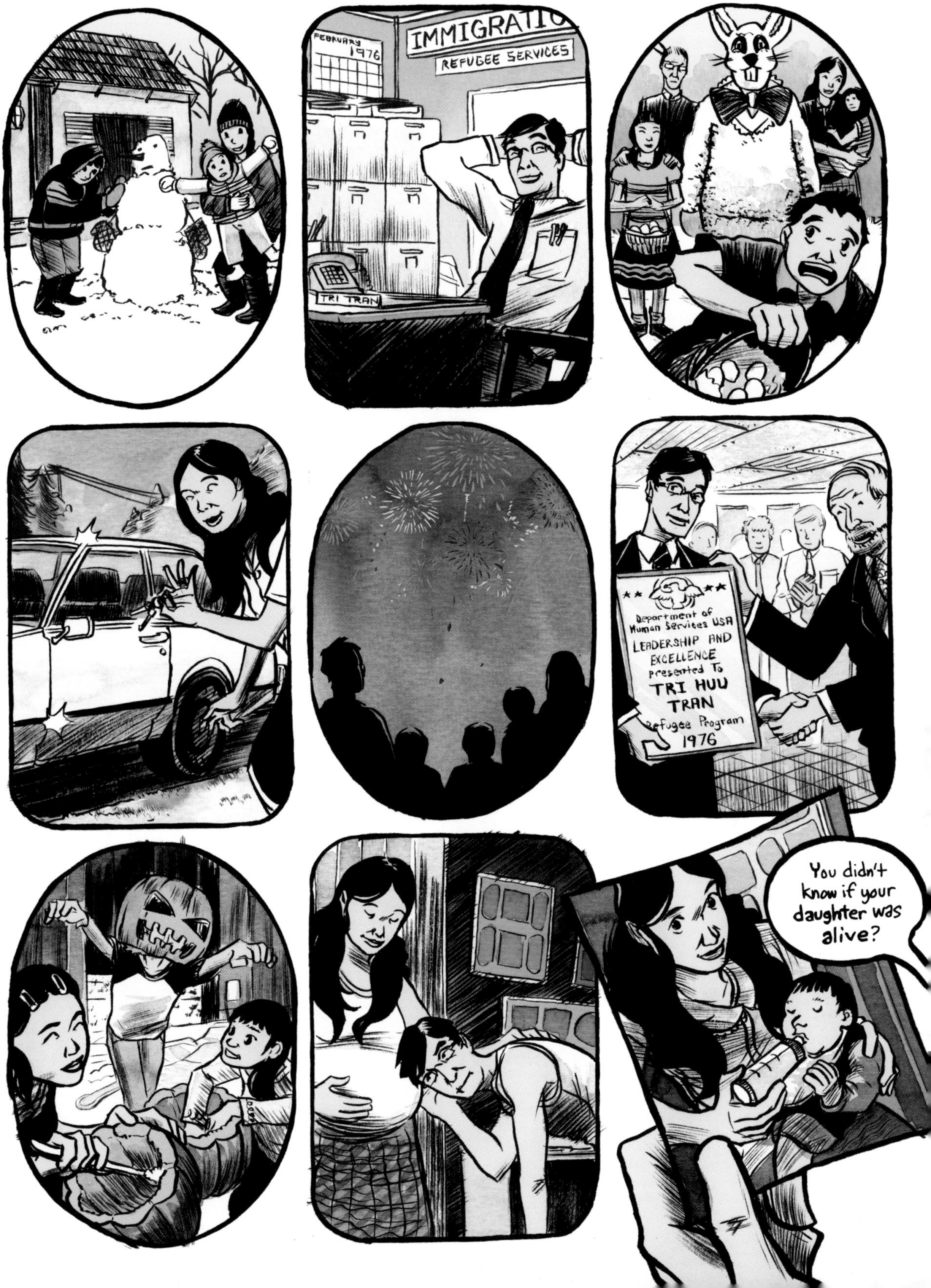
FEBRUARY
1976
IMMIGRATIO
REFUGEE SERVICES
TRI TRAN
Department of
Human Services USA
LEADERSHIP AND
EXCELLENCE
presented To
TRI HUU
TRAN
Refugee Program
1976
You didn't know if your daughter was alive?

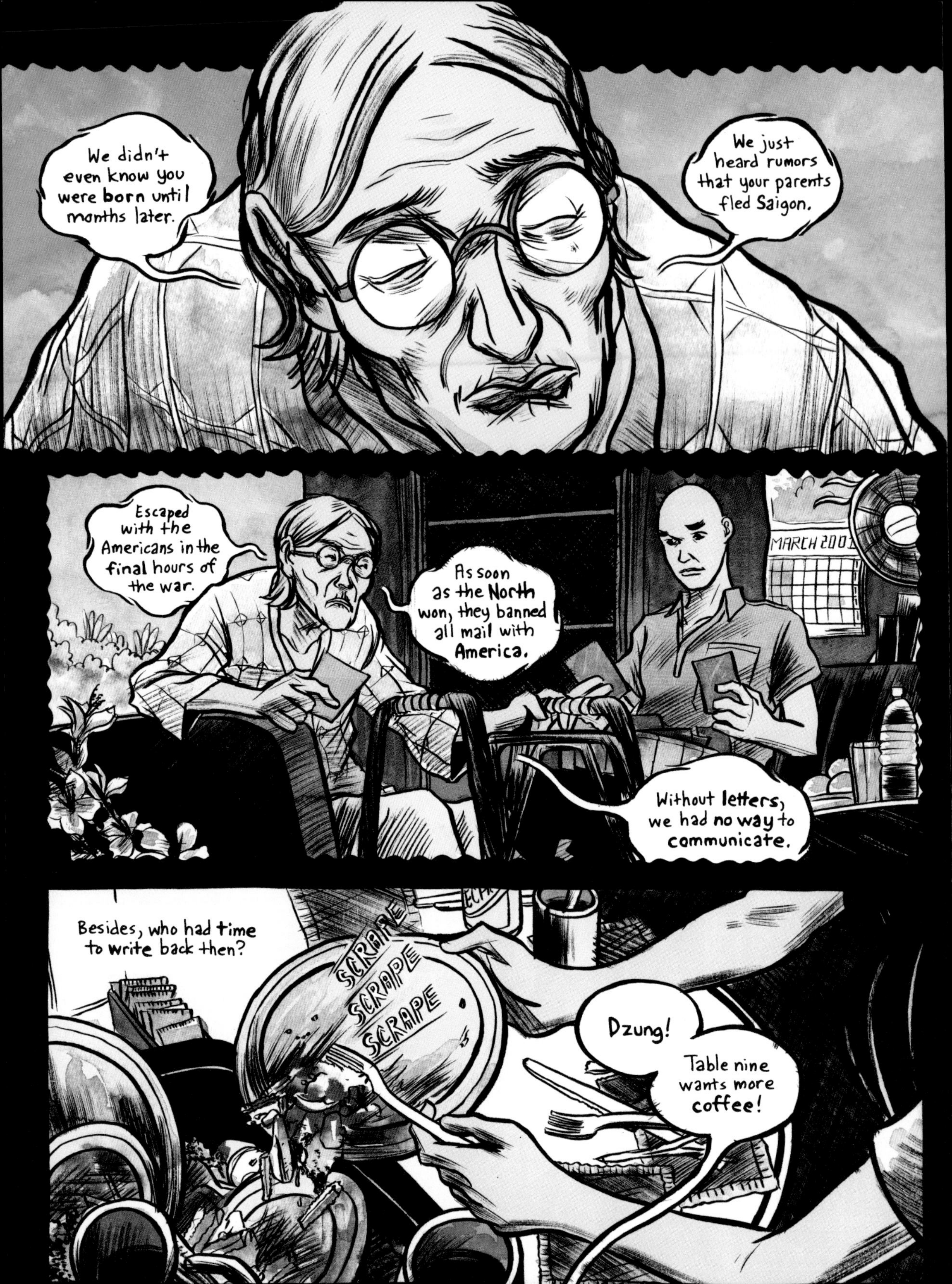
We didn't even know you were born until months later.
We just heard rumors that your parents fled Saigon.
Escaped with the Americans in the final hours of the war.
As soon as the North won, they banned all mail with America.
MARCH 2001
Without letters, we had no way to communicate.
Besides, who had time to write back then?
SCRAPE
SCRAPE
SCRAPE
Dzung!
Table nine wants more coffee!

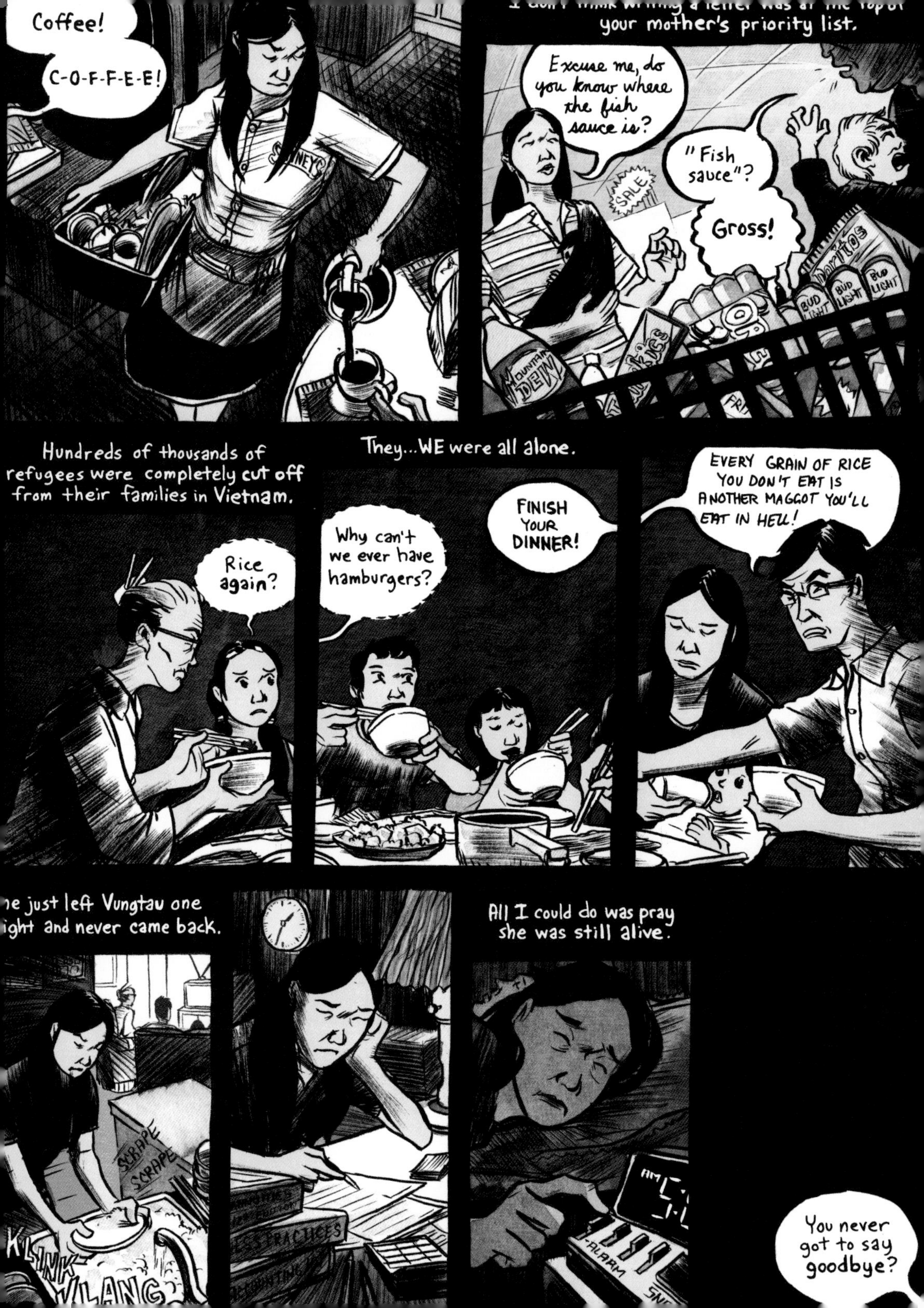
Coffee!
C-O-F-F-E-E!
your mother's priority list.
Excuse me, do you know where the fish sauce is?
SALE
"Fish sauce"?
Gross!
Doritos
BUD LIGHT
MOUNTAIN DEW
Hundreds of thousands of refugees were completely cut off from their families in Vietnam.
They...WE were all alone.
Rice again?
Why can't we ever have hamburgers?
FINISH YOUR DINNER!
EVERY GRAIN OF RICE YOU DON'T EAT IS ANOTHER MAGGOT YOU'LL EAT IN HELL!
ne just left Vungtau one
ight and never came back.
All I could do was pray she was still alive.
SCRAPE
SCRAPE
KLINK
LANG
AM
ALARM
You never got to say goodbye?

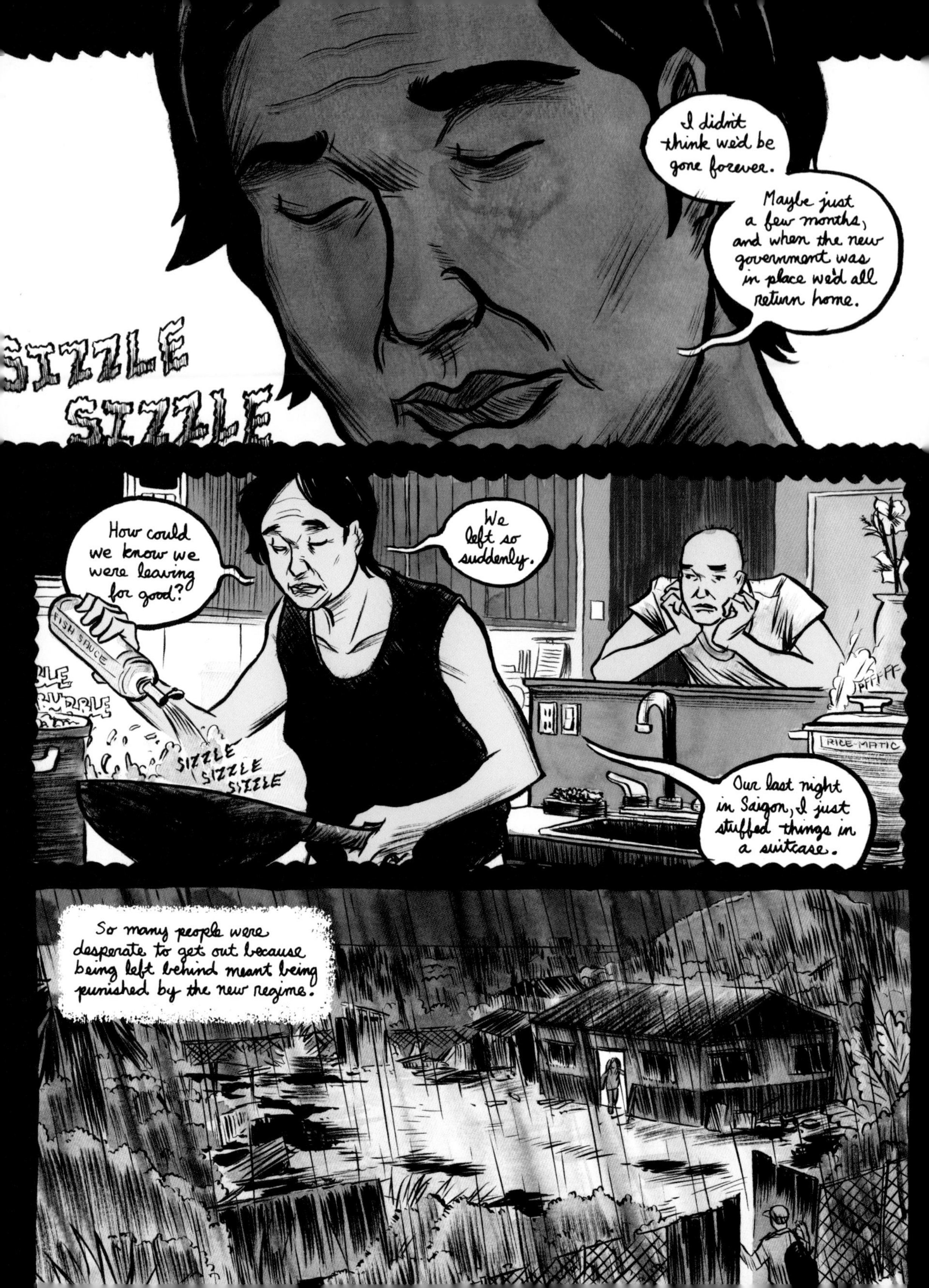
I didn't think we'd be gone forever.
Maybe just a few months, and when the new government was in place we'd all return home.
SIZZLE
SIZZLE
How could we know we were leaving for good?
We left so suddenly.
FISH SAUCE
SIZZLE
SIZZLE
SIZZLE
PFFFFF
RICE-MATIC
Our last night in Saigon, I just stuffed things in a suitcase.
So many people were desperate to get out because being left behind meant being punished by the new regime.

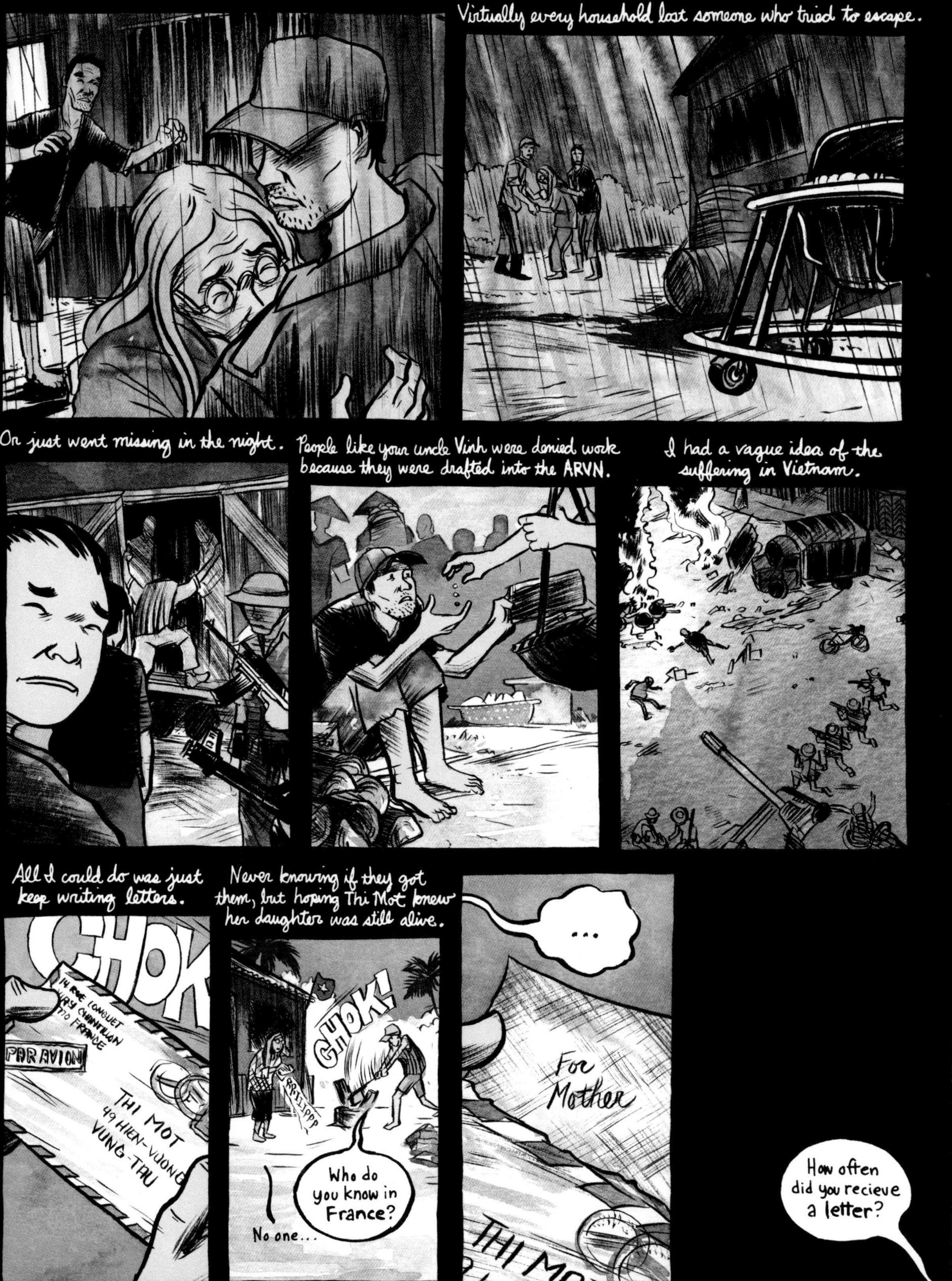

Virtually every household lost someone who tried to escape.
Or just went missing in the night.
People like your uncle Vinh were denied work because they were drafted into the ARVN.
I had a vague idea of the suffering in Vietnam.
All I could do was just keep writing letters.
CHOK
PAR AVION
THI MOT
49 HIEN-VUONG
VUNG-TAU
Never knowing if they got them, but hoping Thi Mot knew her daughter was still alive.
CHOK!
Who do you know in France?
No one...
...
For Mother
THI MOT
How often did you recieve a letter?

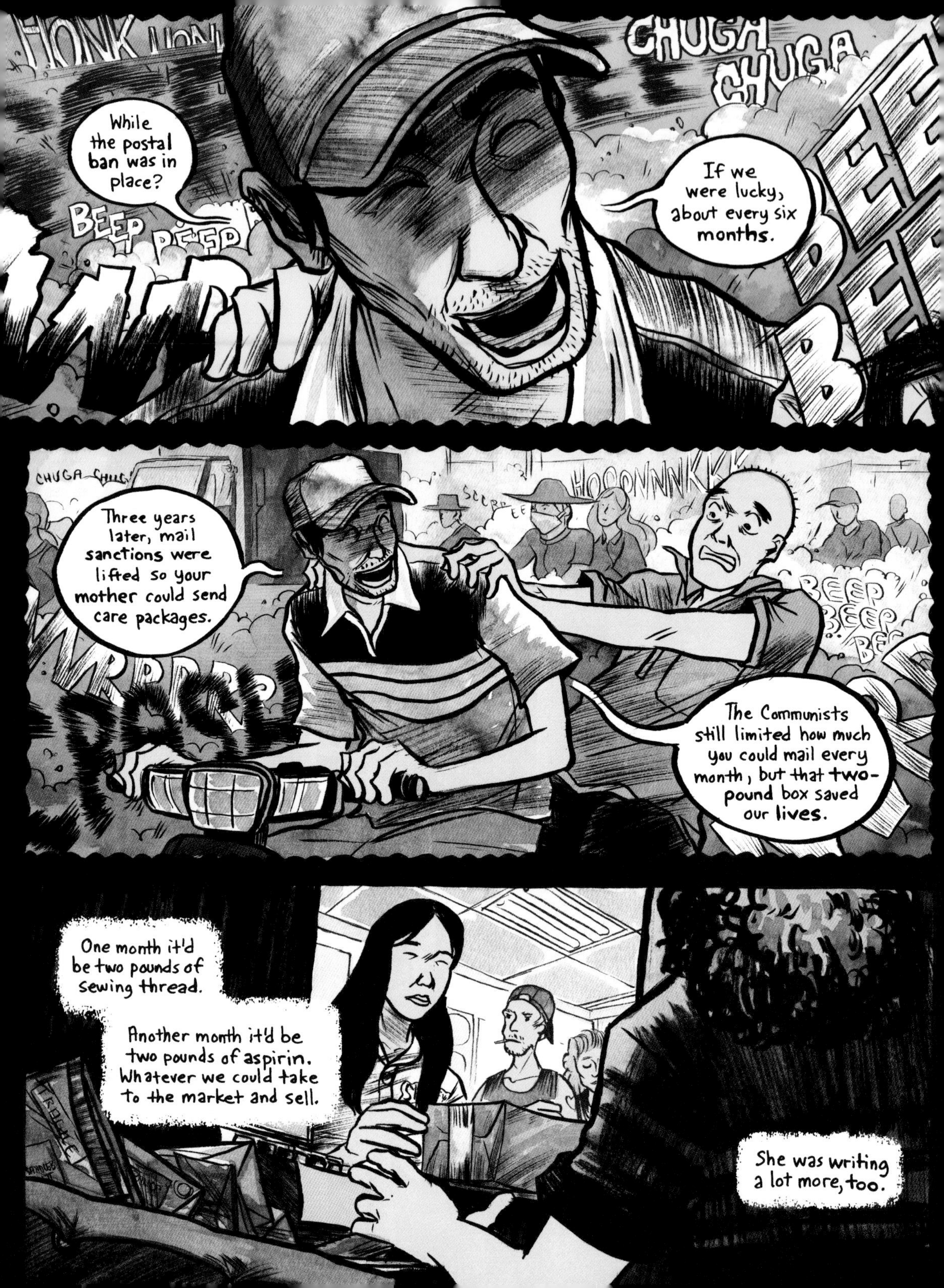
HONK HONK
CHUGA CHUGA
While the postal ban was in place?
BEEP BEEP
If we were lucky, about every six months.
CHUGA CHUG
HOOONNNKK
Three years later, mail sanctions were lifted so your mother could send care packages.
BEEP BEEP
The Communists still limited how much you could mail every month, but that two-pound box saved our lives.
One month it'd be two pounds of sewing thread.
Another month it'd be two pounds of aspirin. Whatever we could take to the market and sell.
She was writing a lot more, too.

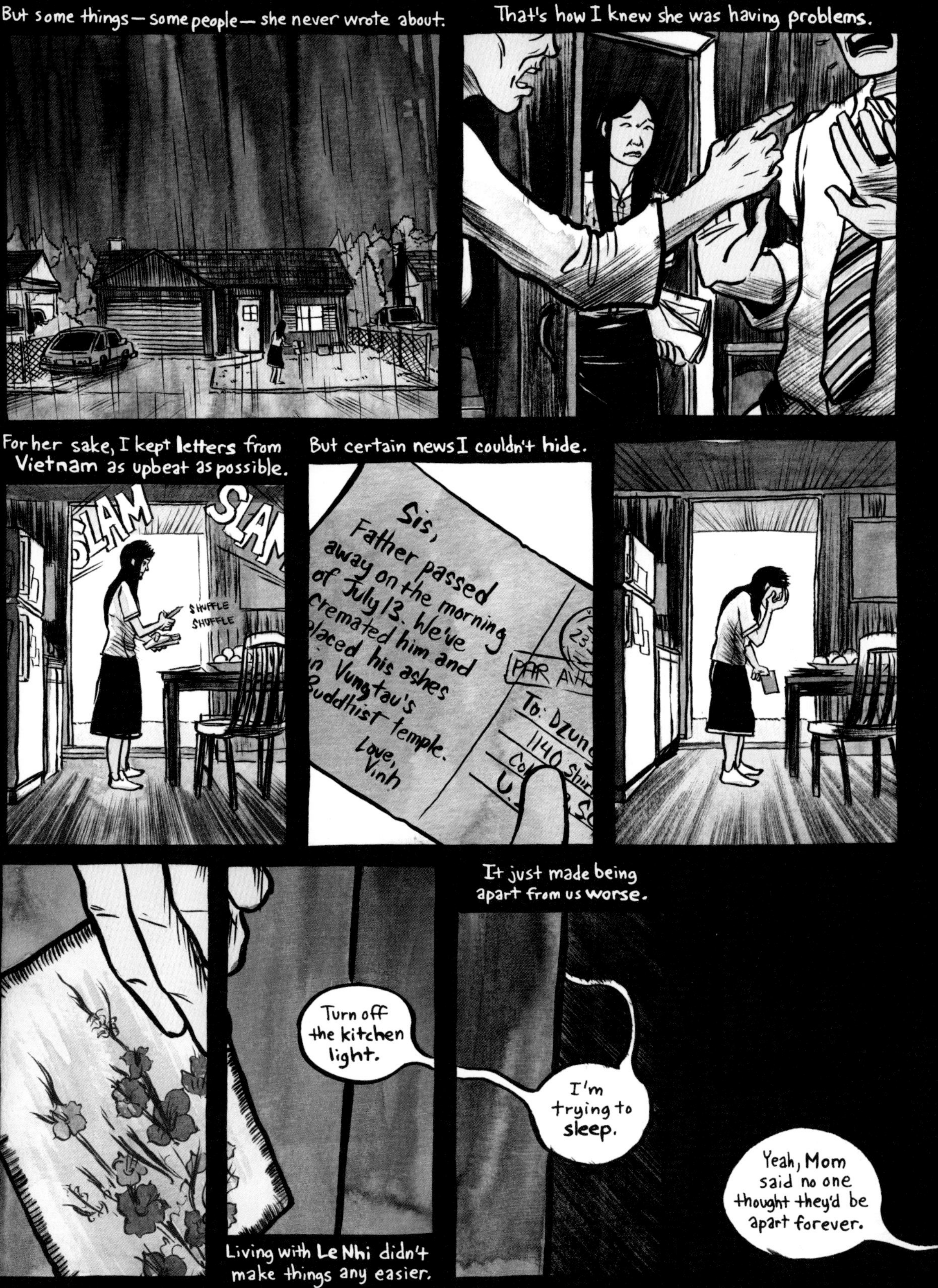
But some things—some people—she never wrote about.
That's how I knew she was having problems.
For her sake, I kept letters from Vietnam as upbeat as possible.
SLAM
SLAM
SHUFFLE
SHUFFLE
But certain news I couldn't hide.
Sis,
Father passed away on the morning of July 13. We've cremated him and placed his ashes in Vungtau's Buddhist temple.
Love,
Vinh
PAR AVI
To: Dzun
1140 Shir
It just made being apart from us worse.
Turn off the kitchen light.
I'm trying to sleep.
Living with Le Nhi didn't make things any easier.
Yeah, Mom said no one thought they'd be apart forever.

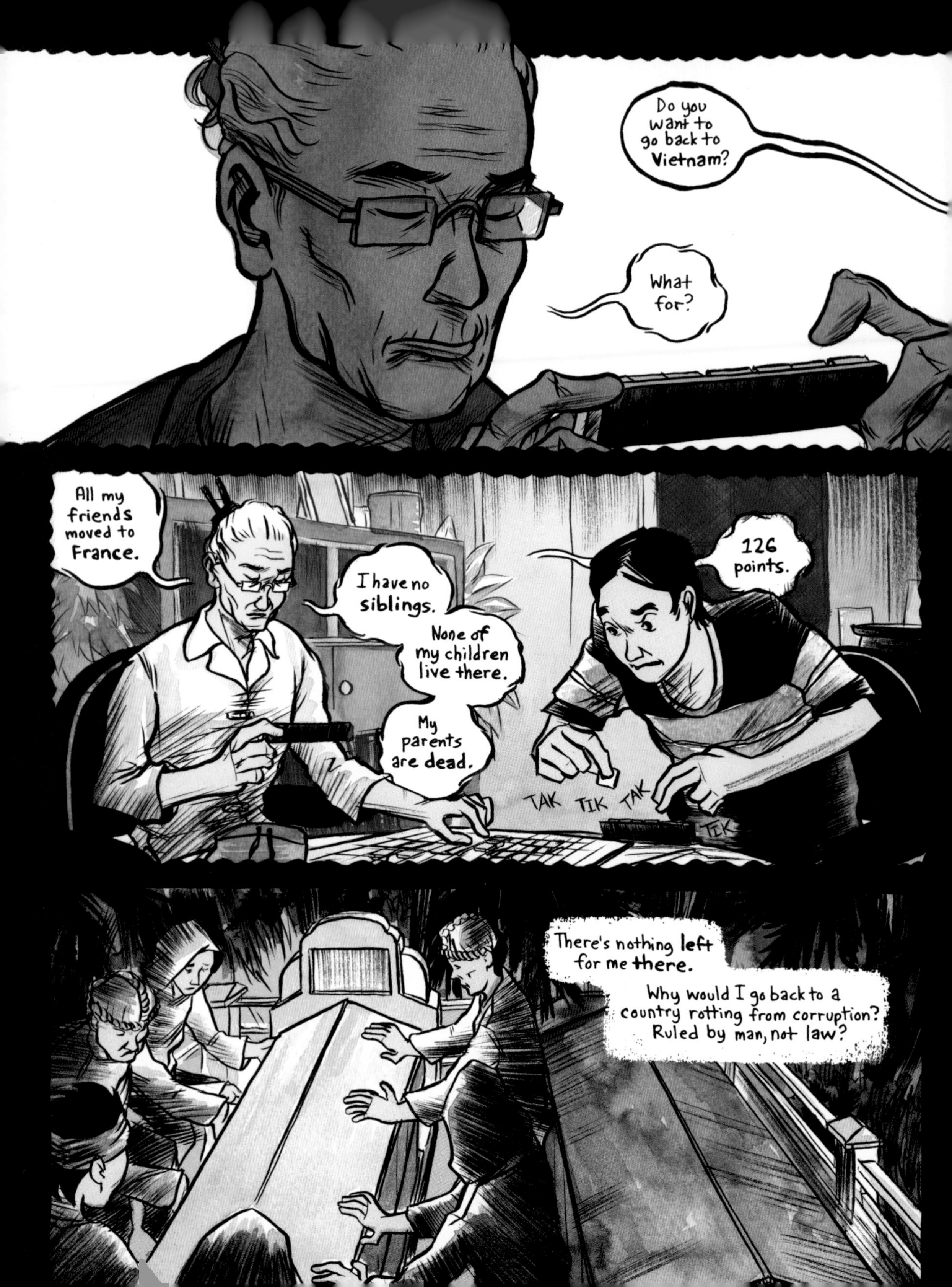
Do you want to go back to Vietnam?
What for?
All my friends moved to France.
I have no siblings.
None of my children live there.
My parents are dead.
126 points.
TAK TIK TAK TIK
There's nothing left for me there.
Why would I go back to a country rotting from corruption? Ruled by man, not law?

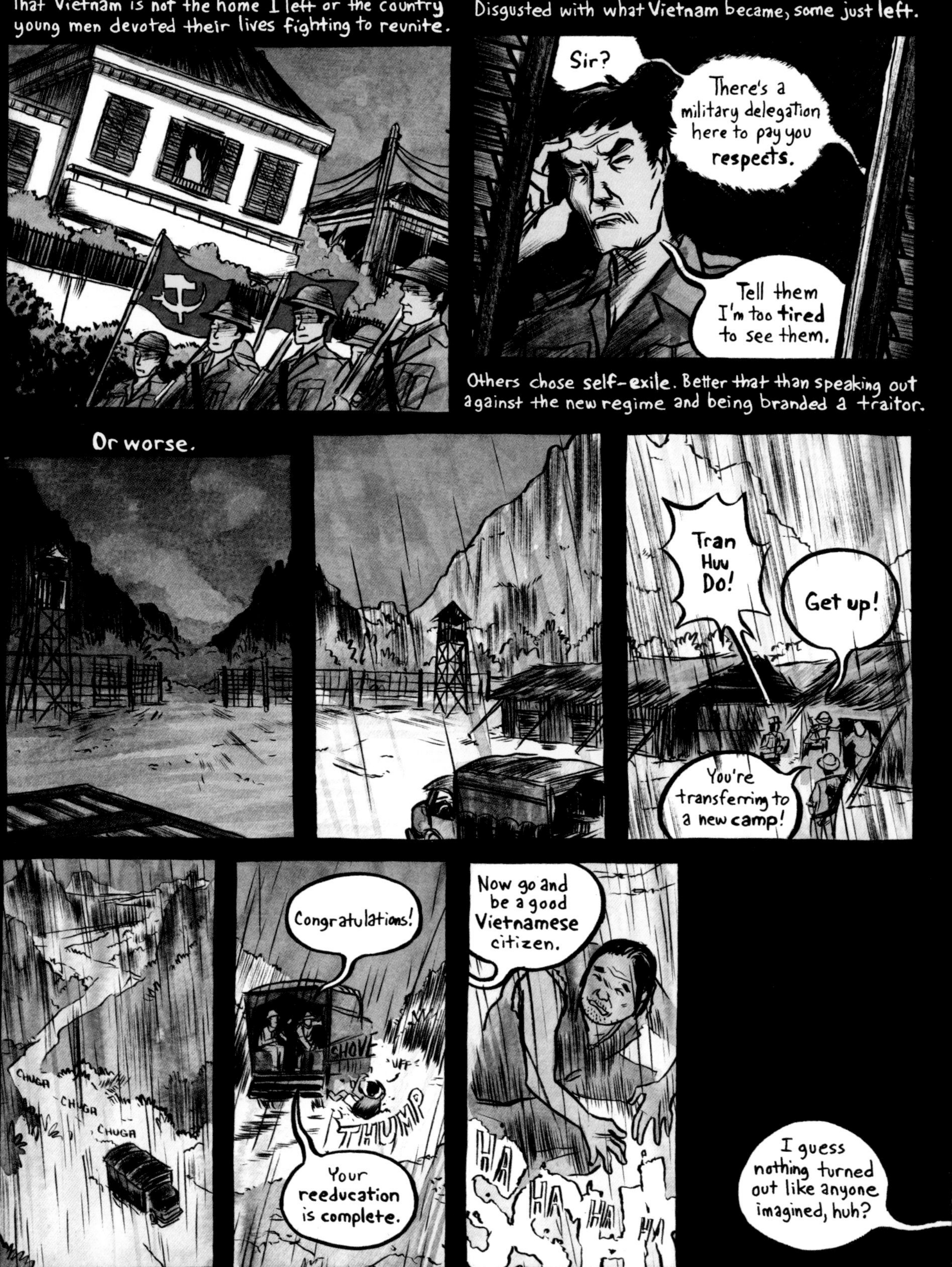

That Vietnam is not the home I left or the country young men devoted their lives fighting to reunite.
Disgusted with what Vietnam became, some just left.
Sir?
There's a military delegation here to pay you respects.
Tell them I'm too tired to see them.
Others chose self-exile. Better that than speaking out against the new regime and being branded a traitor.
Or worse.
Tran Huu Do!
Get up!
You're transferring to a new camp!
CHUGA
CHUGA
CHUGA
Congratulations!
SHOVE
UFF
THUMP
Your reeducation is complete.
Now go and be a good Vietnamese citizen.
HA
HA
HA
HA
I guess nothing turned out like anyone imagined, huh?

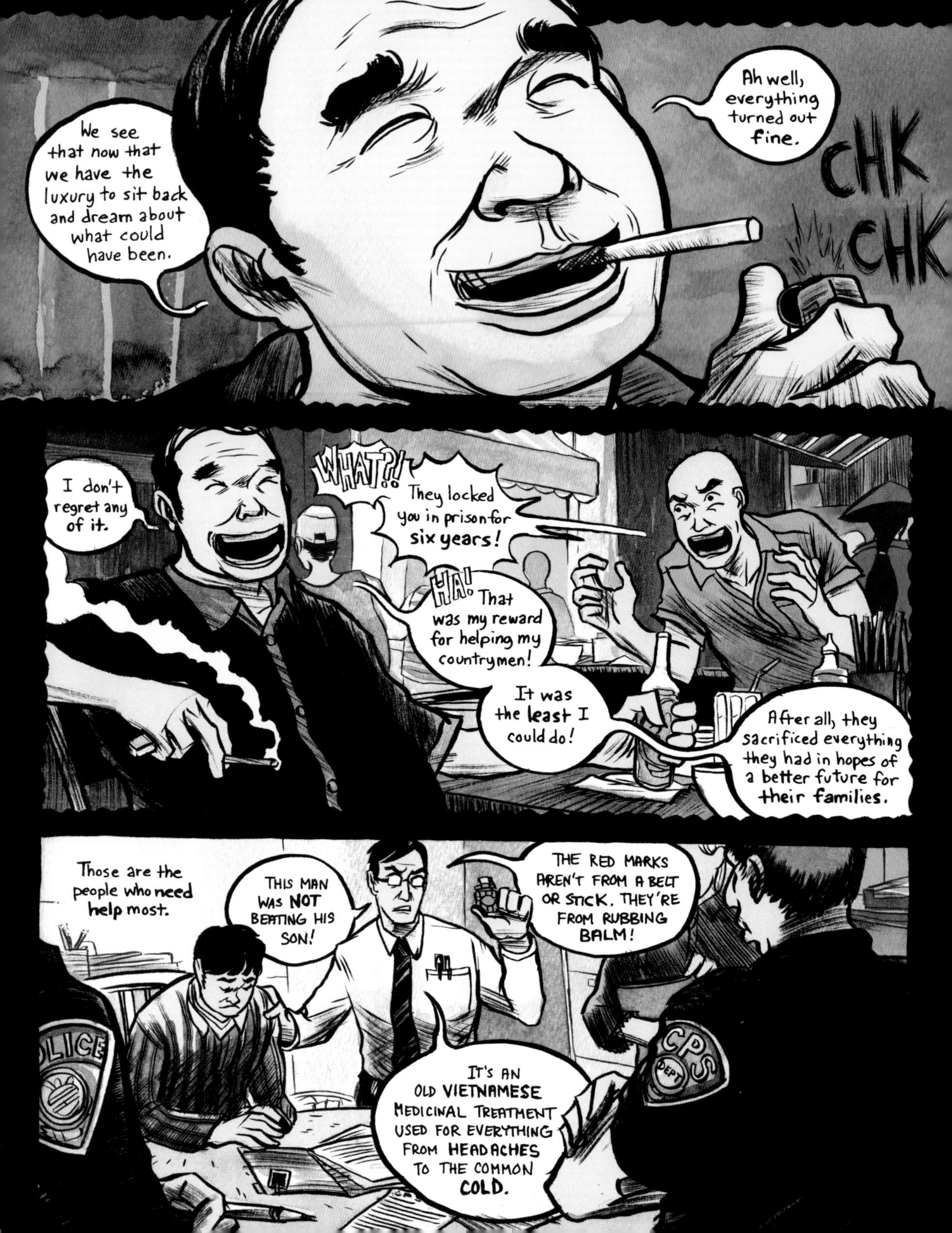

We see that now that we have the luxury to sit back and dream about what could have been.
Ah well, everything turned out fine.
CHK CHK
I don't regret any of it.
WHAT?!
They locked you in prison for six years!
HA! That was my reward for helping my countrymen!
It was the least I could do!
After all, they sacrificed everything they had in hopes of a better future for their families.
Those are the people who need help most.
THIS MAN WAS NOT BEATING HIS SON!
THE RED MARKS AREN'T FROM A BELT OR STICK. THEY'RE FROM RUBBING BALM!
IT'S AN OLD VIETNAMESE MEDICINAL TREATMENT USED FOR EVERYTHING FROM HEADACHES TO THE COMMON COLD.
POLICE
CPS
DEPT

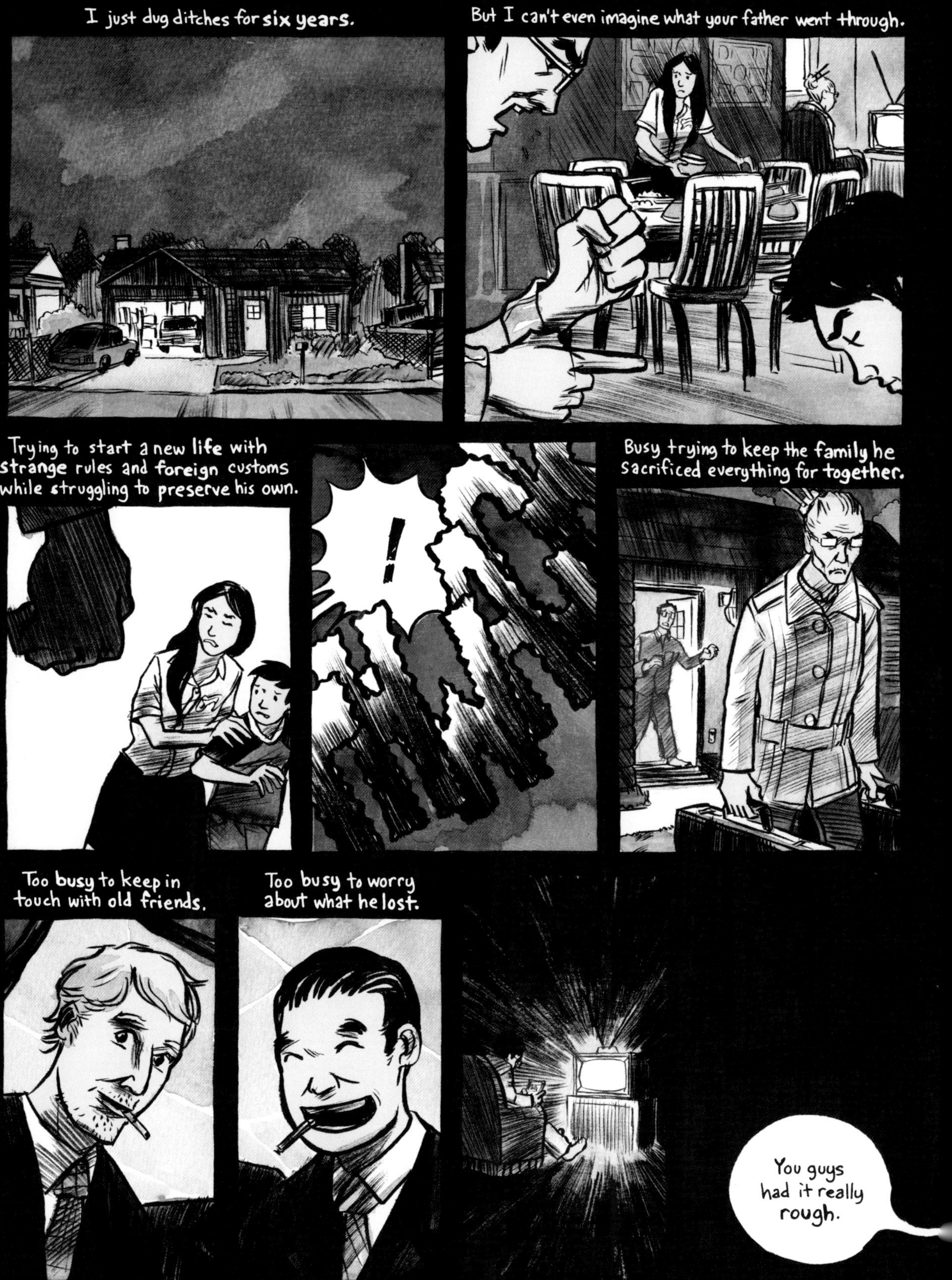
I just dug ditches for six years.
But I can't even imagine what your father went through.
Trying to start a new life with strange rules and foreign customs while struggling to preserve his own.
!
Busy trying to keep the family he sacrificed everything for together.
Too busy to keep in touch with old friends.
Too busy to worry about what he lost.
You guys had it really rough.

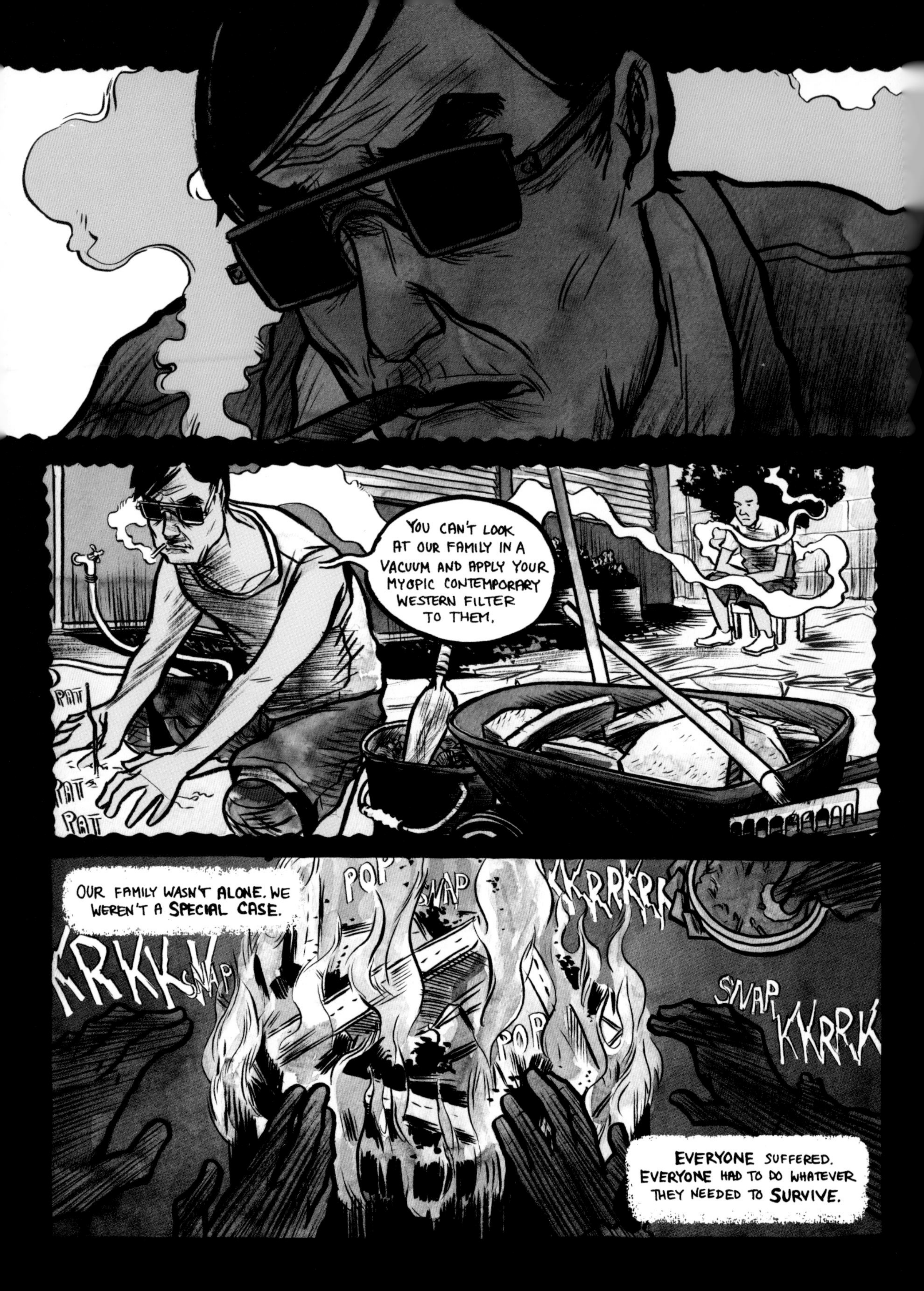
YOU CAN'T LOOK AT OUR FAMILY IN A VACUUM AND APPLY YOUR MYOPIC CONTEMPORARY WESTERN FILTER TO THEM.
PAT
PAT
PAT
OUR FAMILY WASN'T ALONE. WE WEREN'T A SPECIAL CASE.
POP
SNAP
KKRRKRR
KRKK
SNAP
SNAP
KKRRK
POP
EVERYONE SUFFERED. EVERYONE HAD TO DO WHATEVER THEY NEEDED TO SURVIVE.

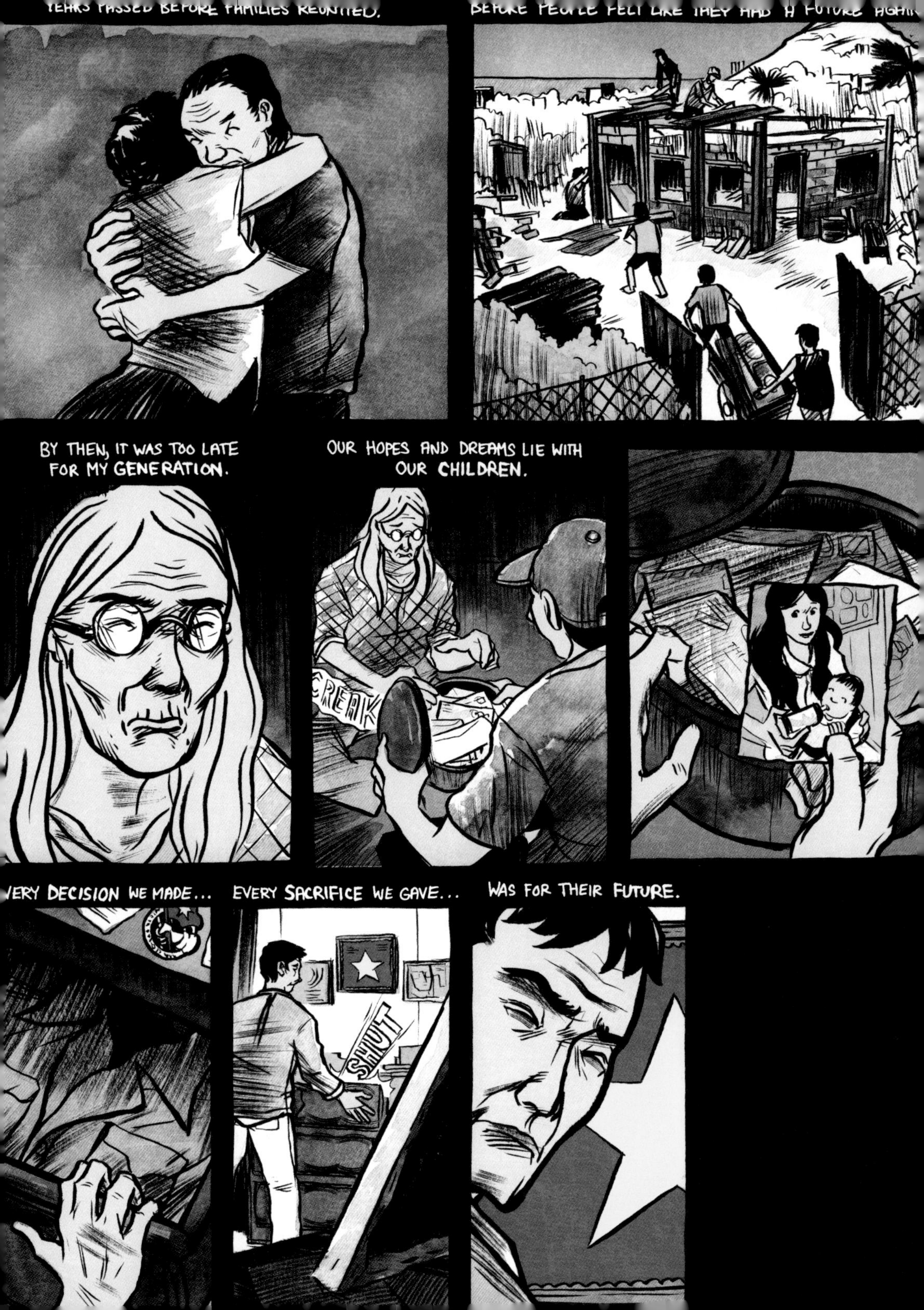
YEARS PASSED BEFORE FAMILIES REUNITED.
BEFORE PEOPLE FELT LIKE THEY HAD A FUTURE AGAI
BY THEN, IT WAS TOO LATE FOR MY GENERATION.
OUR HOPES AND DREAMS LIE WITH OUR CHILDREN.
CREAK
VERY DECISION WE MADE...
EVERY SACRIFICE WE GAVE...
SHUT
WAS FOR THEIR FUTURE.

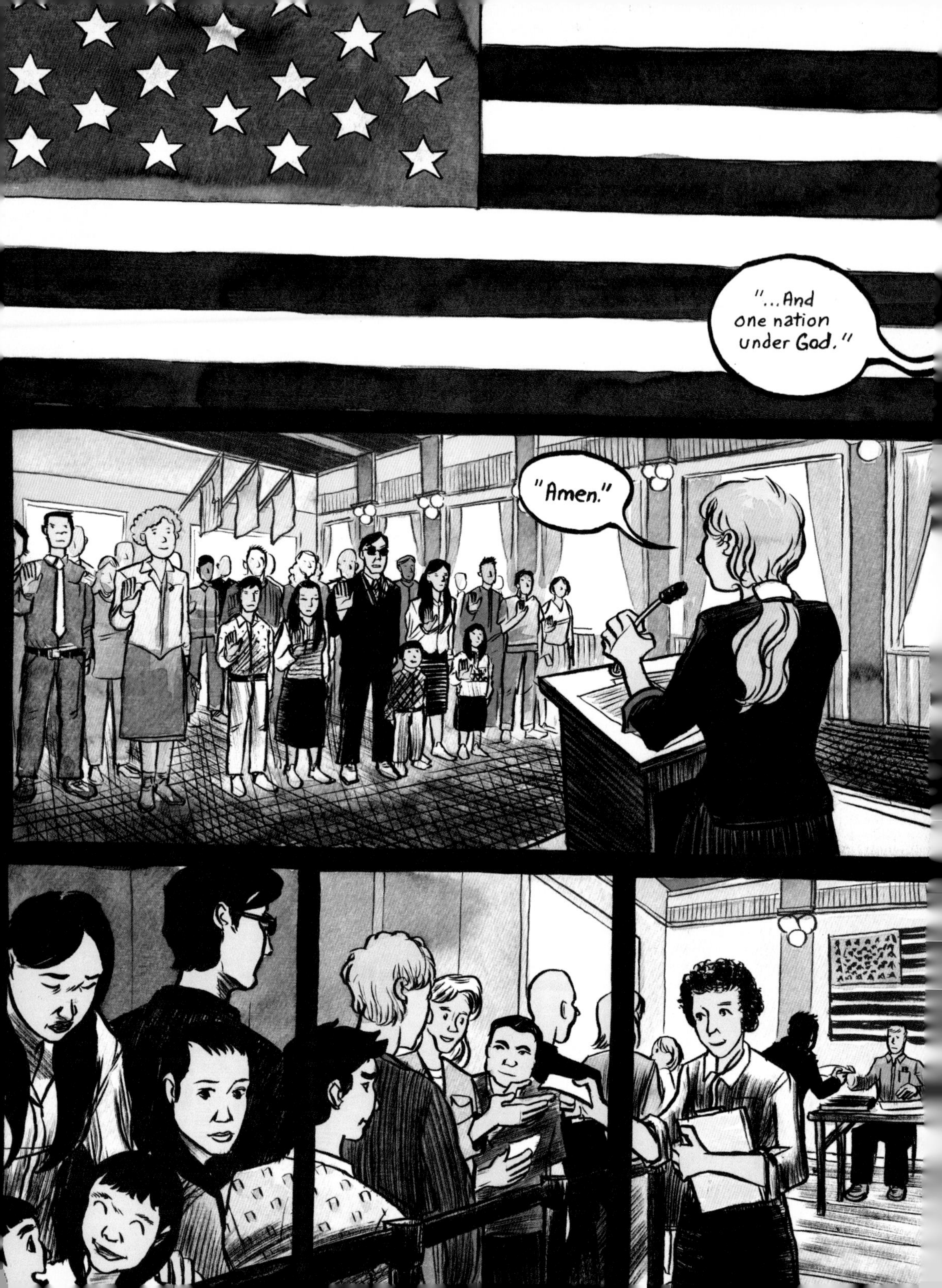
"...And
one nation
under God."
"Amen."

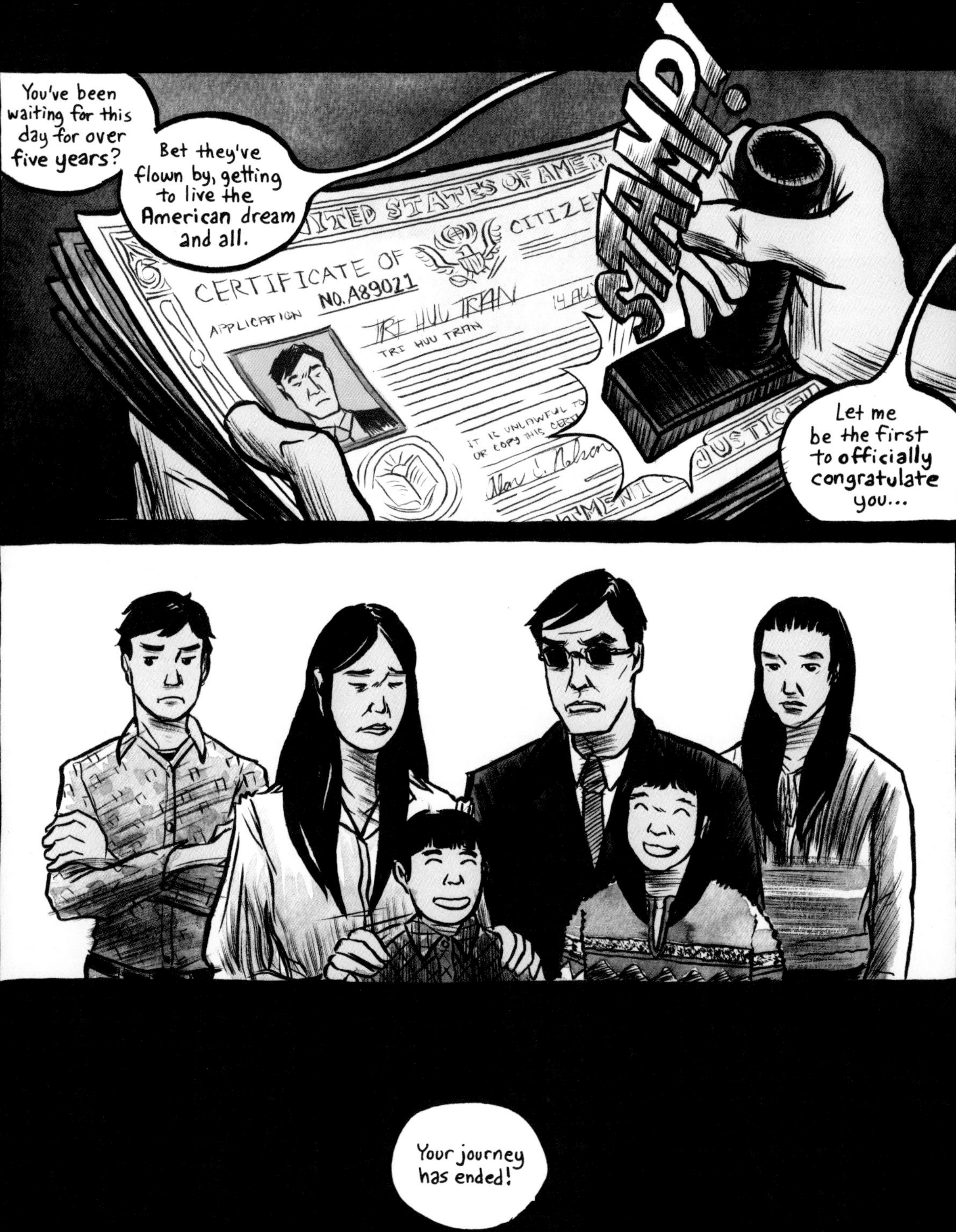
You've been waiting for this day for over five years?
Bet they've flown by, getting to live the American dream and all.
STAMP!
ITED STATES OF AMER
CITIZE
CERTIFICATE OF
NO. A89021
APPLICATION
TRI HUU TRAN
Let me be the first to officially congratulate you...
Your journey has ended!

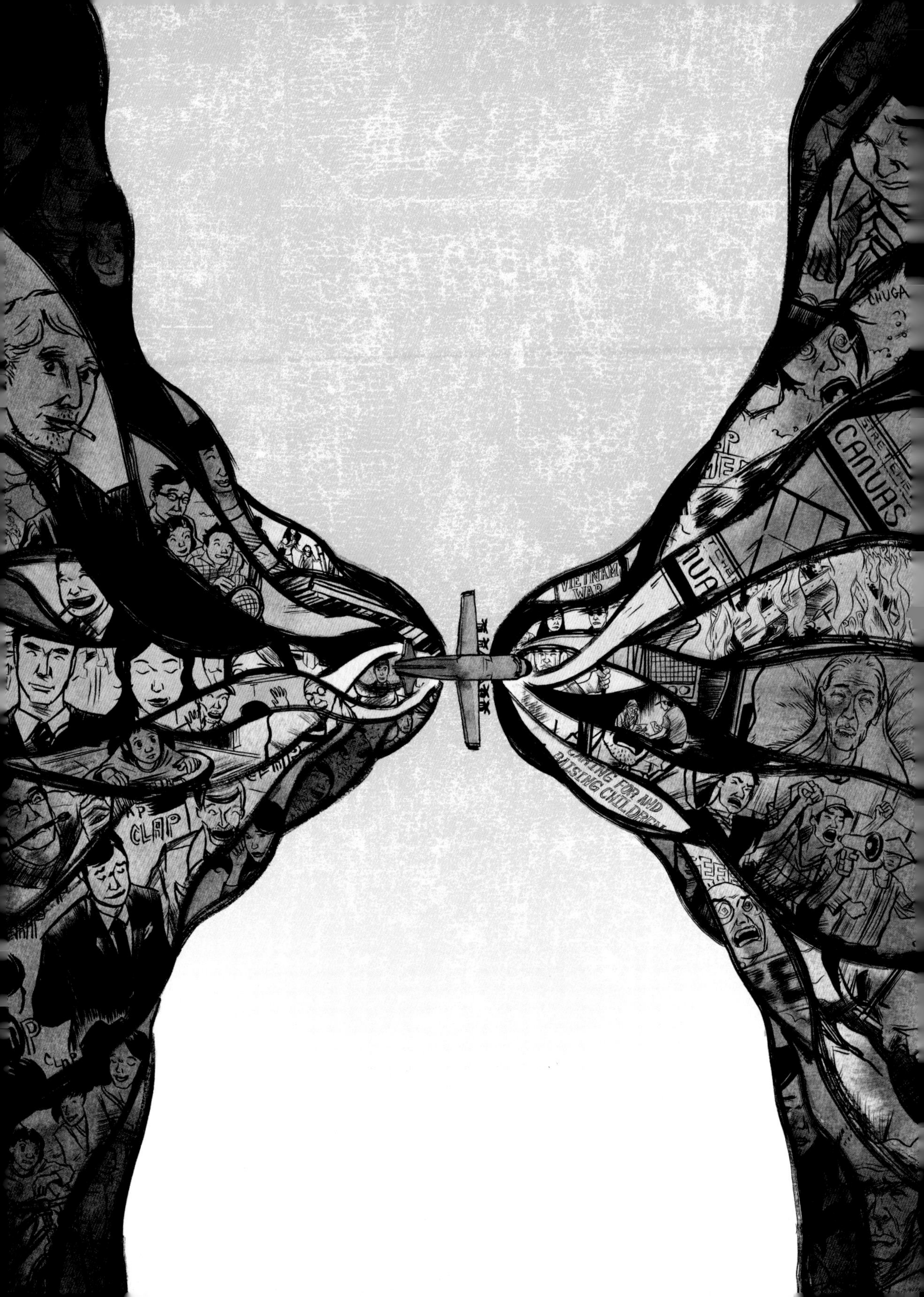

CHUGA
CANVAS
VIETNAM WAR
CARING FOR AND RAISING CHILDREN
CLAP

We fled Vietnam on April 25, 1975, five days before the North's tanks rolled into Saigon and claimed victory...
Wipe
Wipe
Wipe

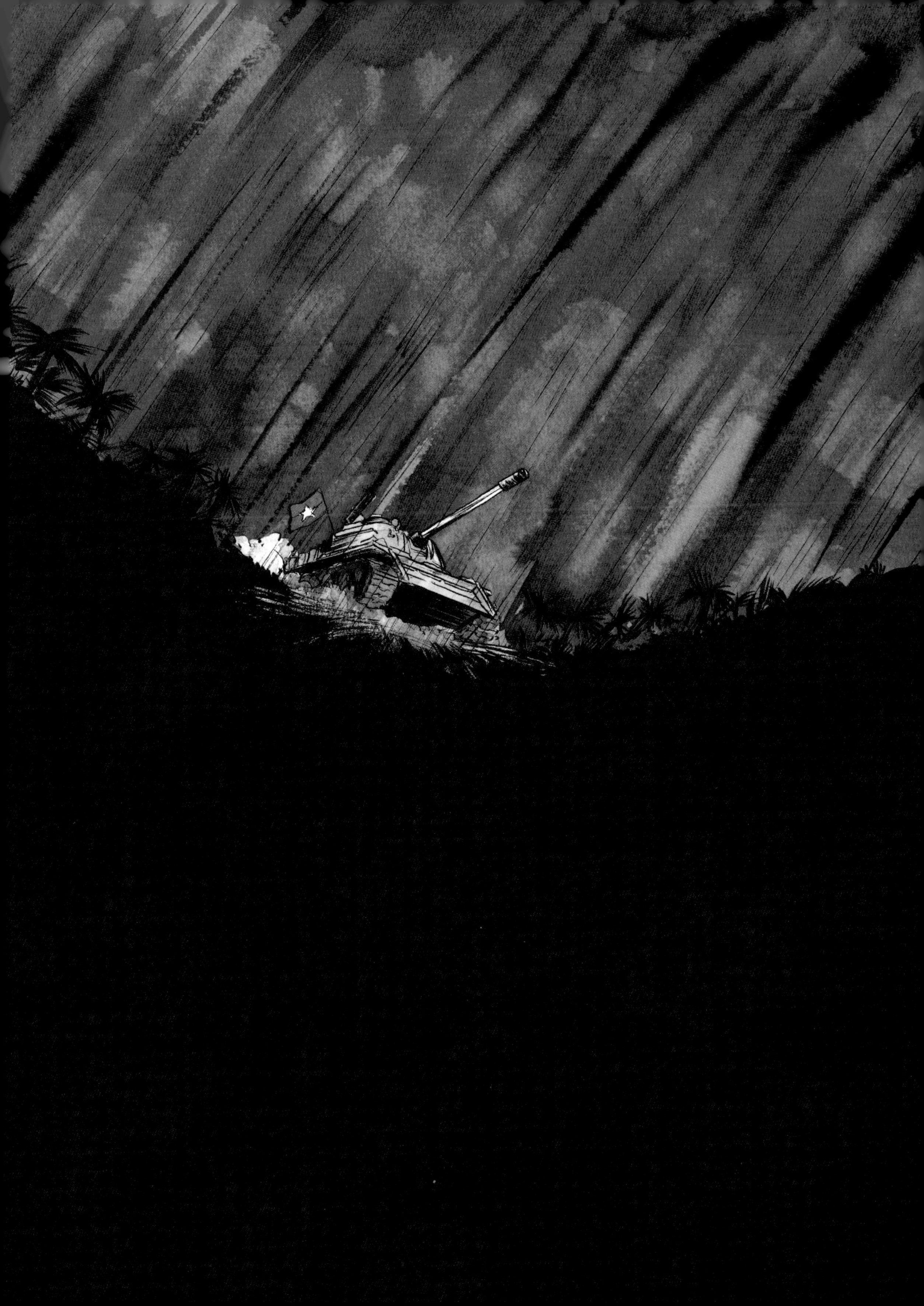

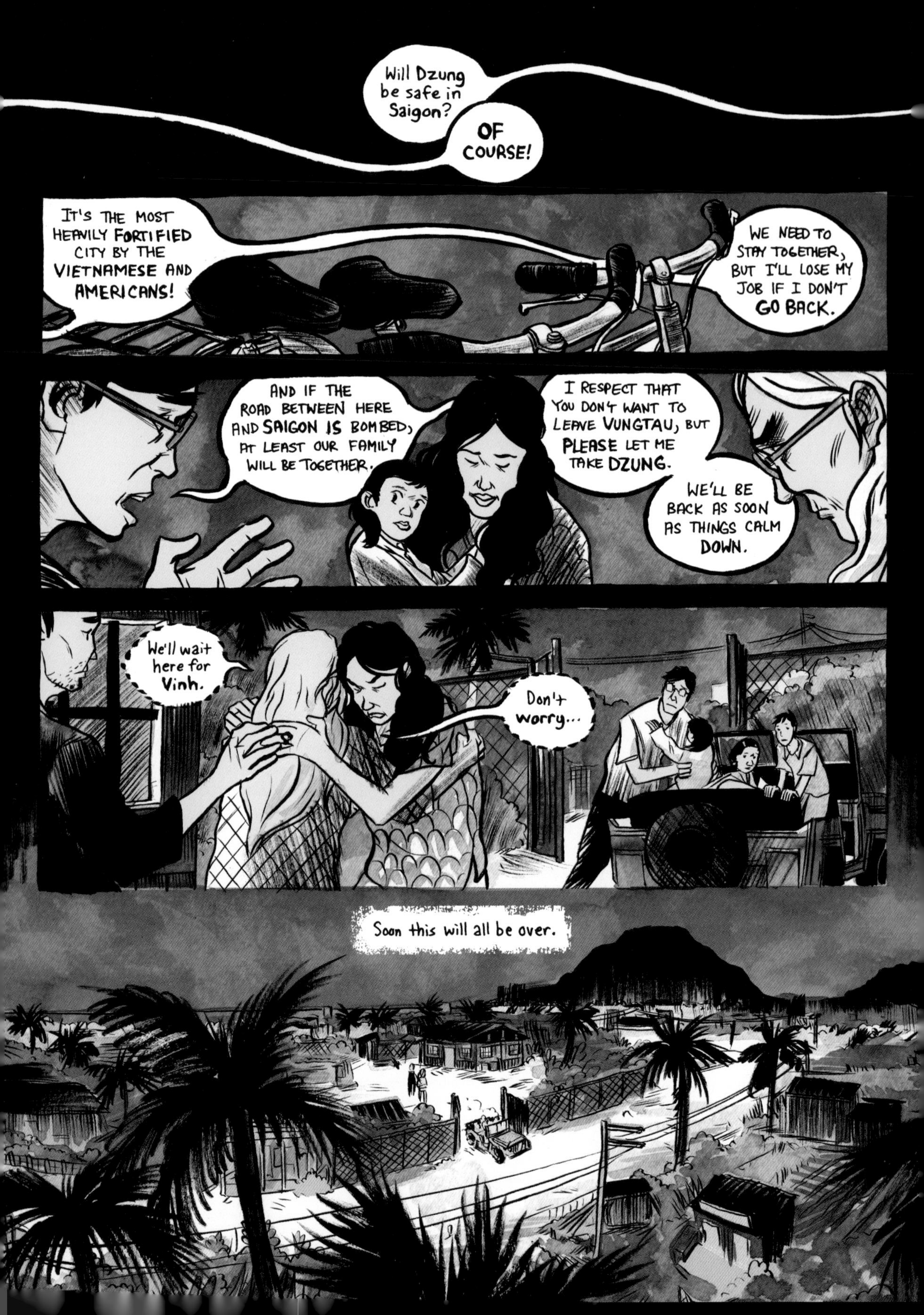
Will Dzung be safe in Saigon?
OF COURSE!
IT'S THE MOST HEAVILY FORTIFIED CITY BY THE VIETNAMESE AND AMERICANS!
WE NEED TO STAY TOGETHER, BUT I'LL LOSE MY JOB IF I DON'T GO BACK.
AND IF THE ROAD BETWEEN HERE AND SAIGON IS BOMBED, AT LEAST OUR FAMILY WILL BE TOGETHER.
I RESPECT THAT YOU DON'T WANT TO LEAVE VUNGTAU, BUT PLEASE LET ME TAKE DZUNG.
WE'LL BE BACK AS SOON AS THINGS CALM DOWN.
We'll wait here for Vinh.
Don't worry...
Soon this will all be over.

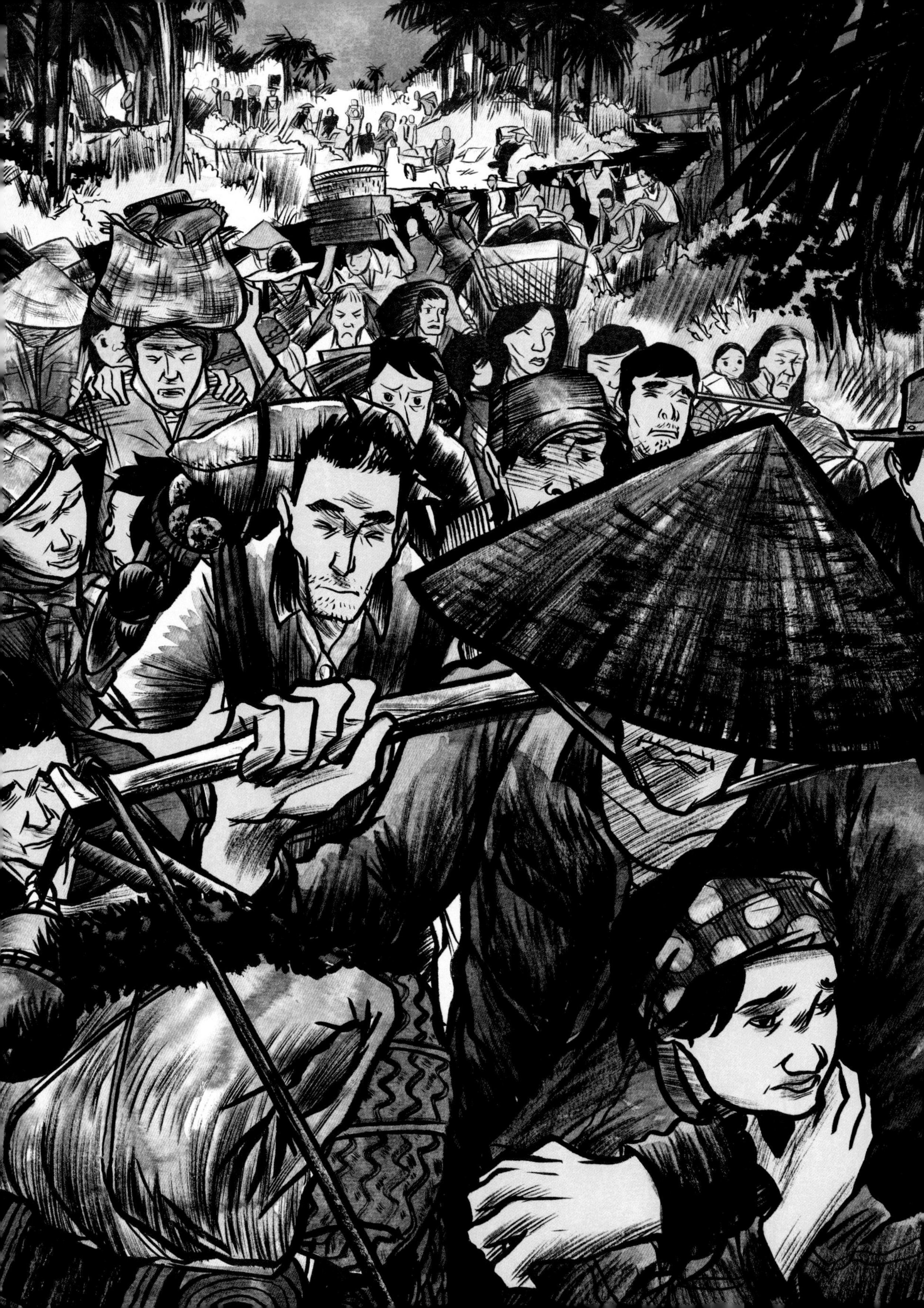

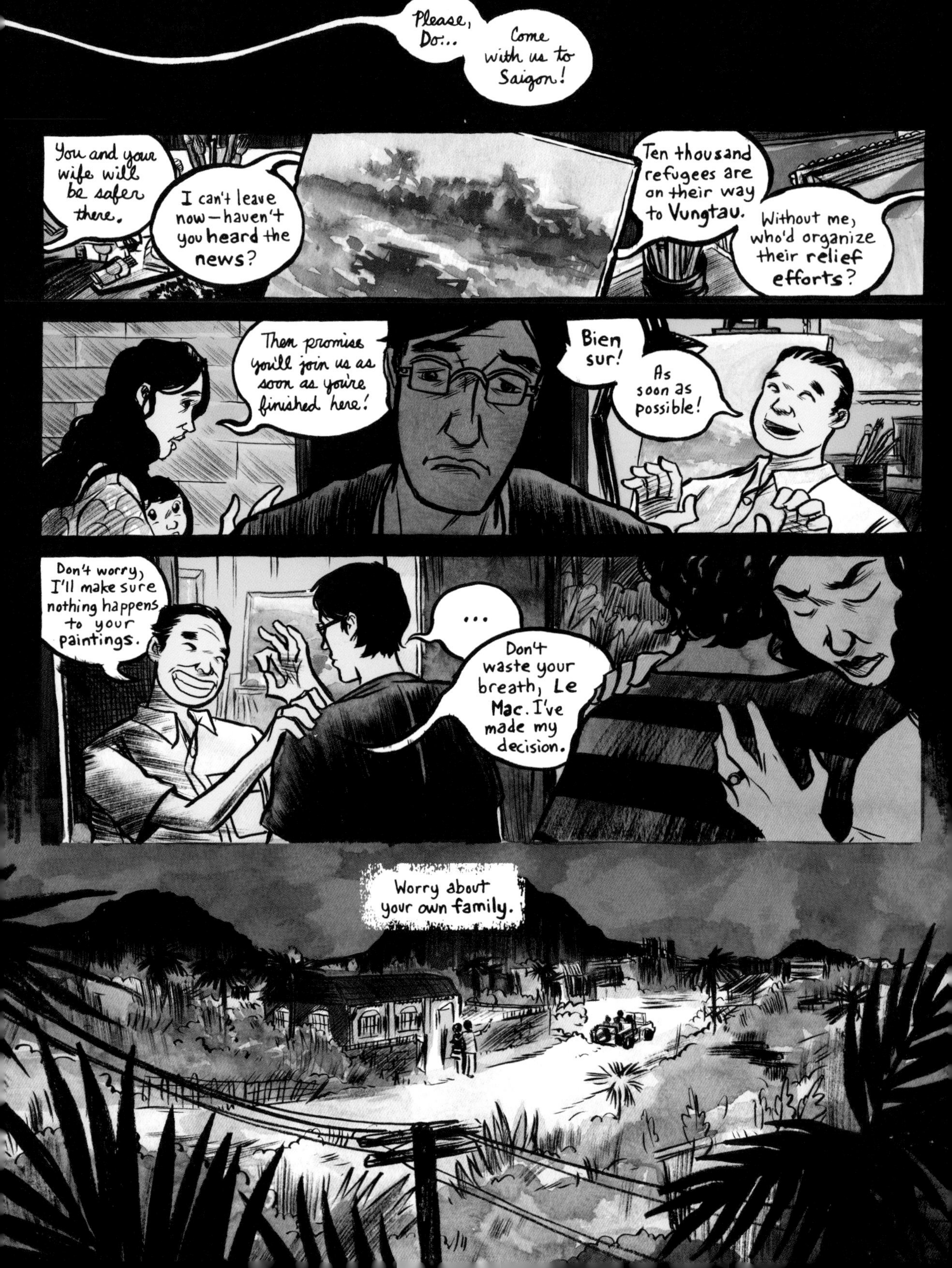
Please, Do...
Come with us to Saigon!
You and your wife will be safer there.
I can't leave now—haven't you heard the news?
Ten thousand refugees are on their way to Vungtau.
Without me, who'd organize their relief efforts?
Then promise you'll join us as soon as you're finished here!
Bien sur!
As soon as possible!
Don't worry, I'll make sure nothing happens to your paintings.
...
Don't waste your breath, Le Mac. I've made my decision.
Worry about your own family.

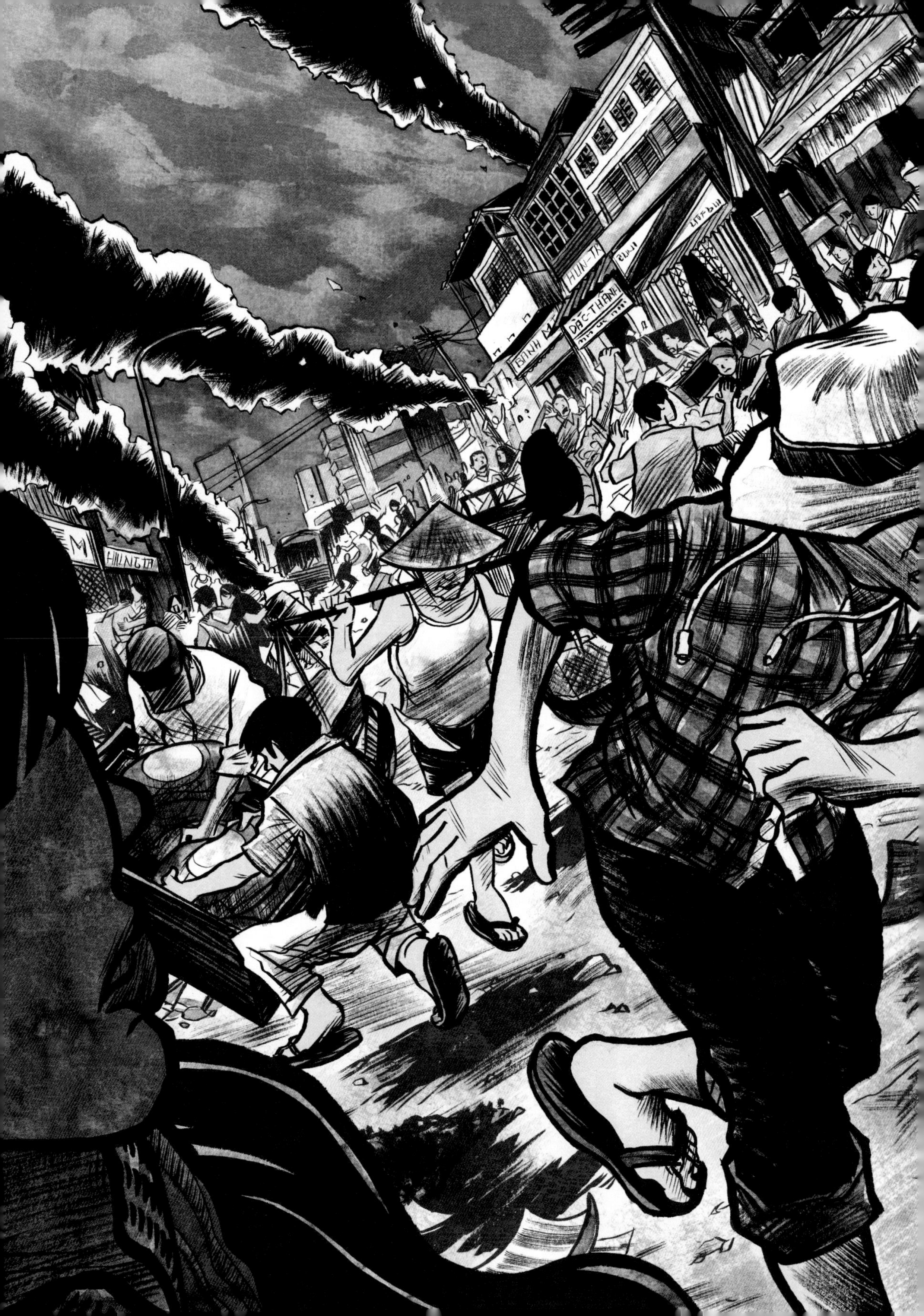

BANH M
HUN-TR
DAC-THANH

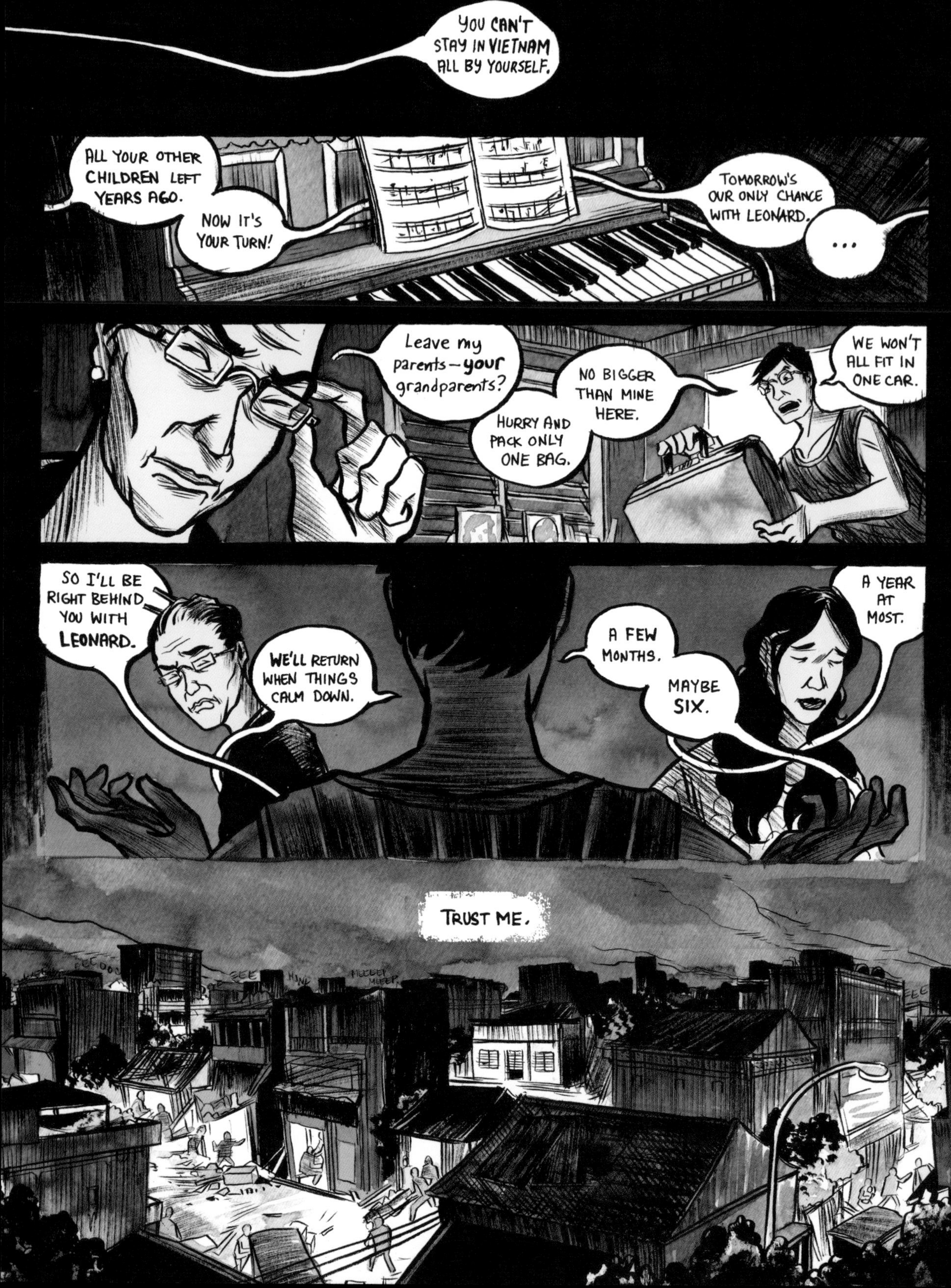
YOU CAN'T STAY IN VIETNAM ALL BY YOURSELF.
ALL YOUR OTHER CHILDREN LEFT YEARS AGO.
NOW IT'S YOUR TURN!
TOMORROW'S OUR ONLY CHANCE WITH LEONARD.
...
Leave my parents—your grandparents?
NO BIGGER THAN MINE HERE.
HURRY AND PACK ONLY ONE BAG.
WE WON'T ALL FIT IN ONE CAR.
SO I'LL BE RIGHT BEHIND YOU WITH LEONARD.
WE'LL RETURN WHEN THINGS CALM DOWN.
A FEW MONTHS.
MAYBE SIX.
A YEAR AT MOST.
TRUST ME.

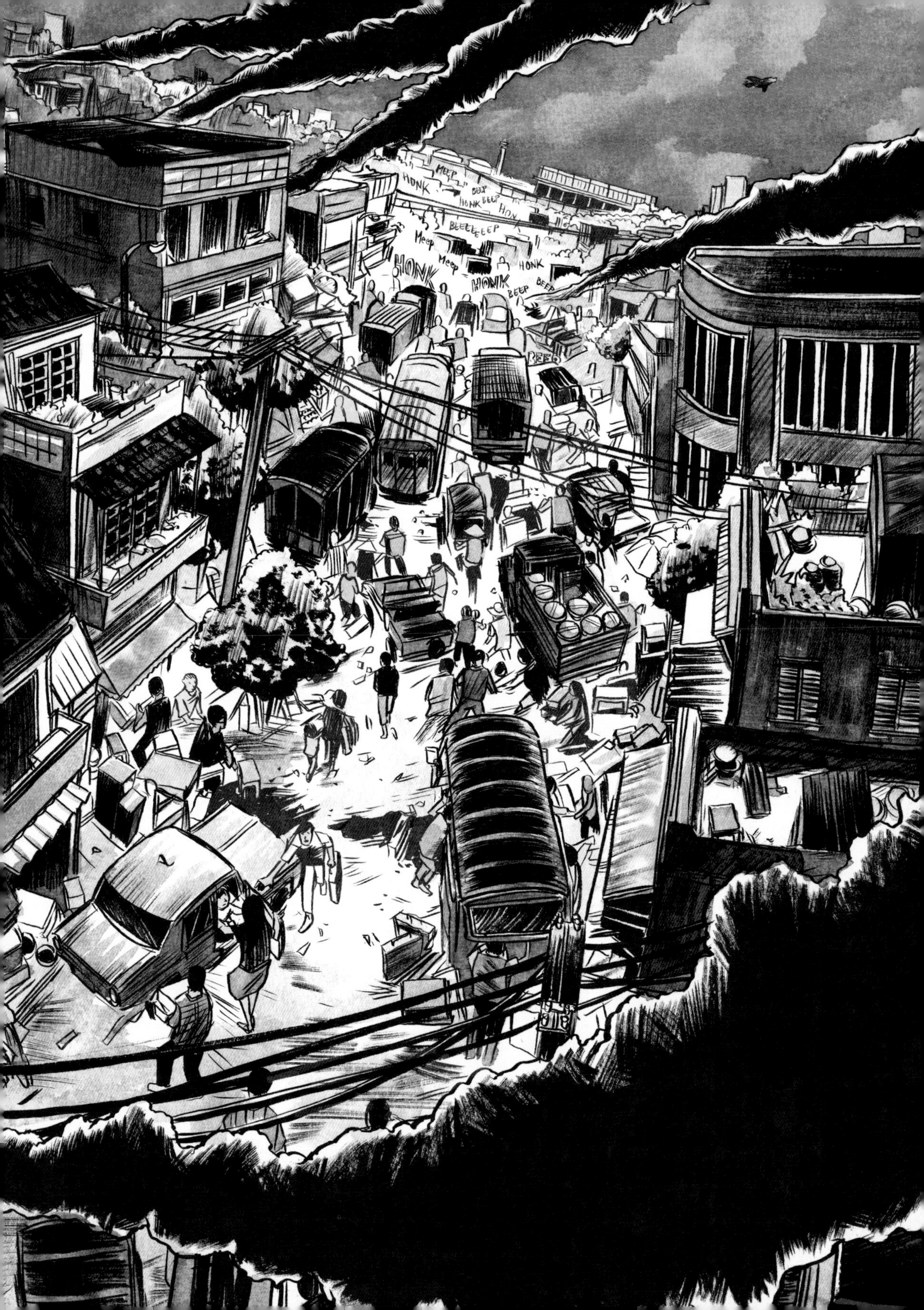
MEEP
HONK
HONK
BEEP
HON
BEEEEEEEP
Meep
HONK
Meep
HONK
HONK
BEEP
BEEP

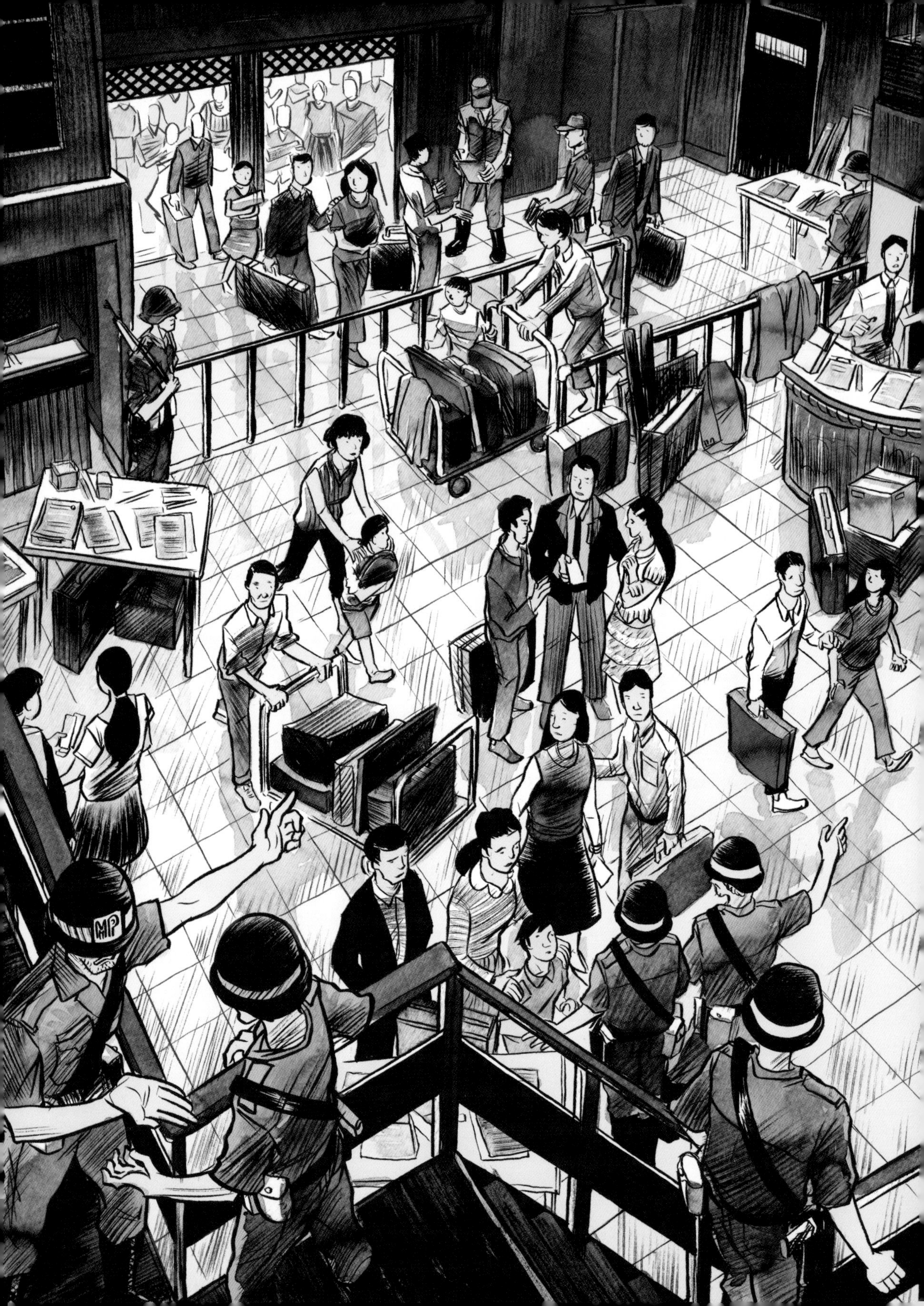
MP

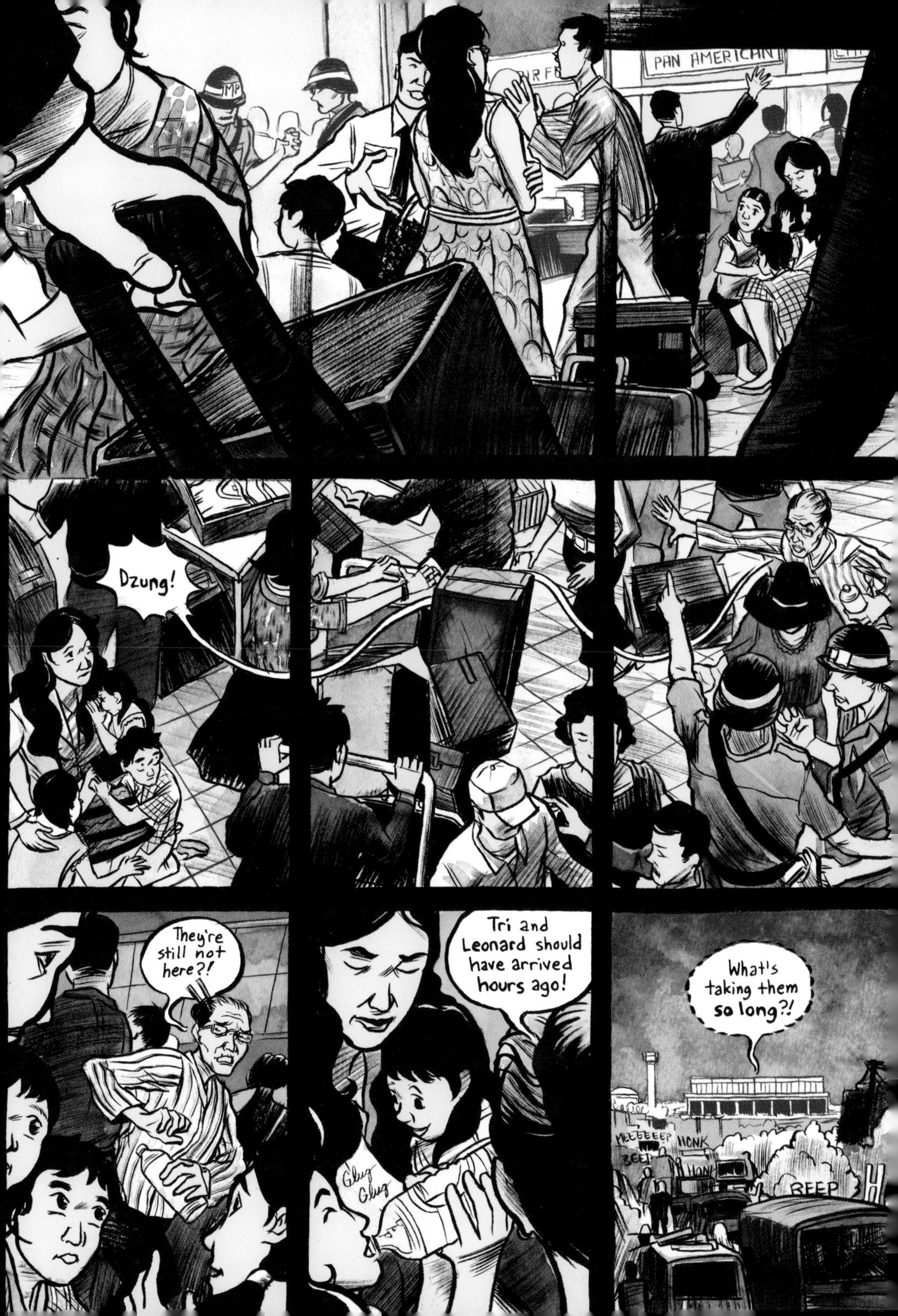
PAN AMERICAN
MP
Dzung!
They're still not here?!
Tri and Leonard should have arrived hours ago!
Glug Glug
What's taking them so long?!
MEEEEEEP
HONK
BEEP
BEEP

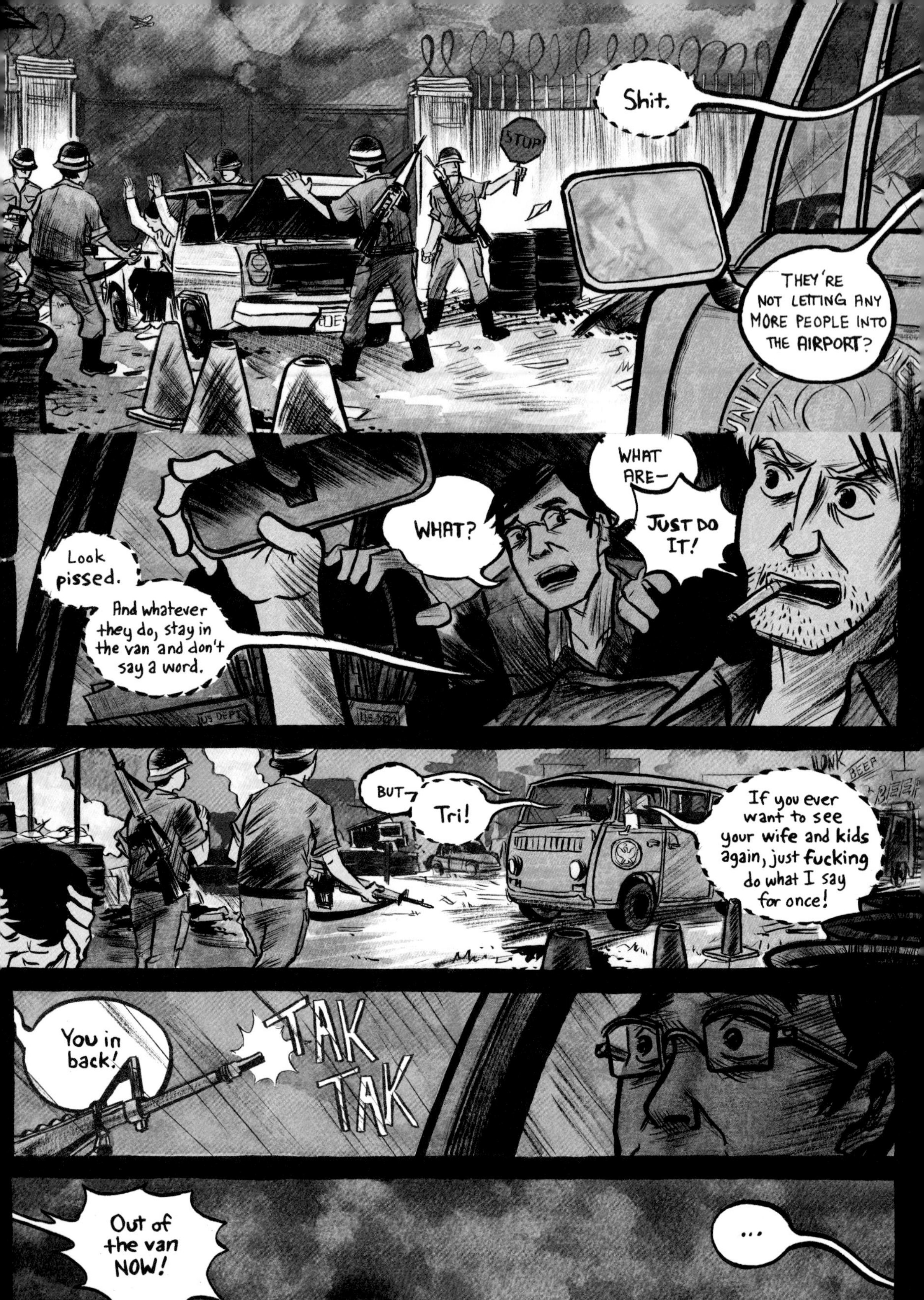
STOP
Shit.
THEY'RE NOT LETTING ANY MORE PEOPLE INTO THE AIRPORT?
Look pissed.
And whatever they do, stay in the van and don't say a word.
WHAT?
WHAT ARE—
JUST DO IT!
BUT—
Tri!
If you ever want to see your wife and kids again, just fucking do what I say for once!
HONK
BEEP
BEEP
You in back!
TAK TAK
Out of the van NOW!
...

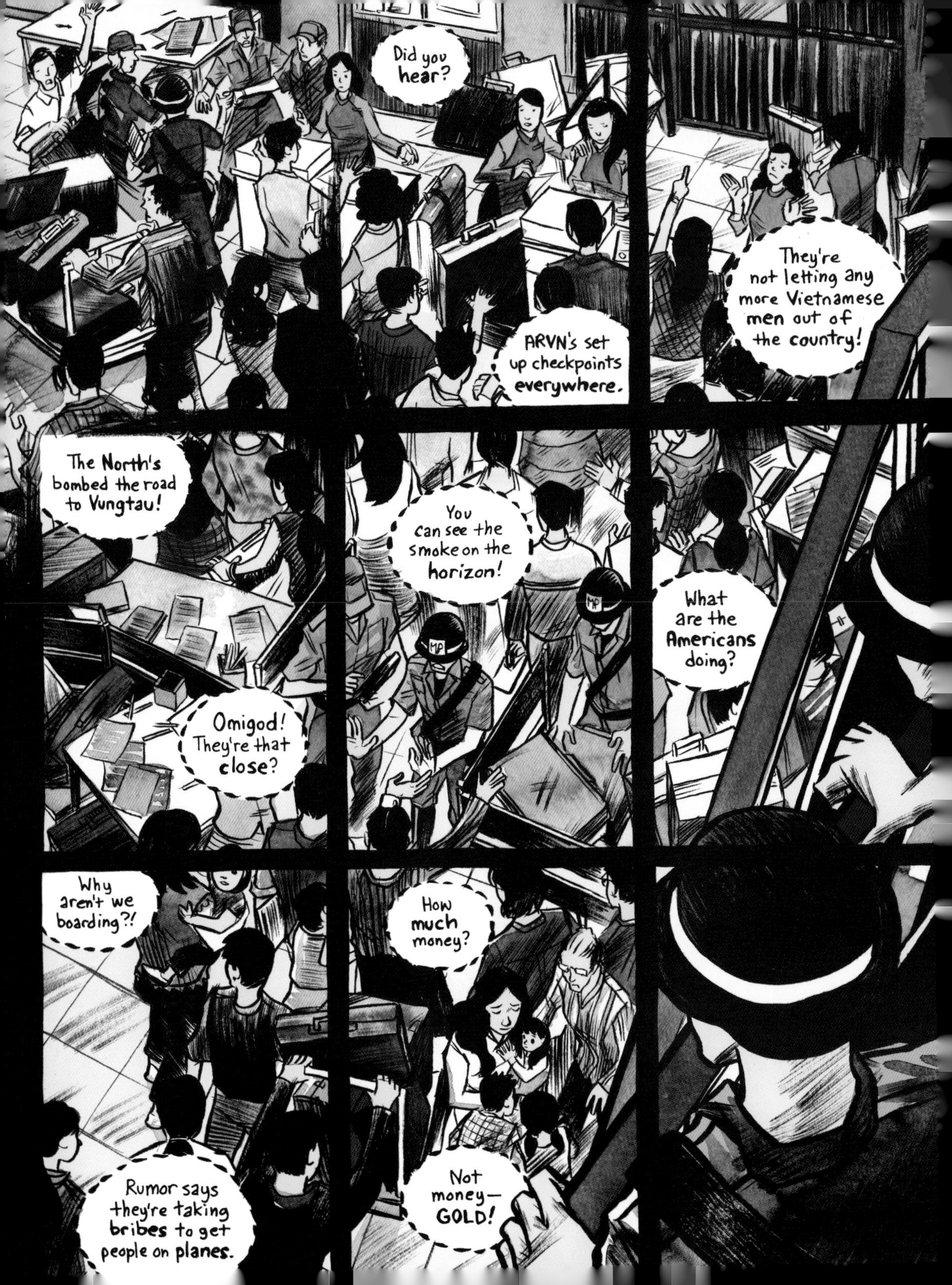
Did you hear?
ARVN's set up checkpoints everywhere.
They're not letting any more Vietnamese men out of the country!
The North's bombed the road to Vungtau!
You can see the smoke on the horizon!
Omigod! They're that close?
What are the Americans doing?
Why aren't we boarding?!
Rumor says they're taking bribes to get people on planes.
How much money?
Not money— GOLD!

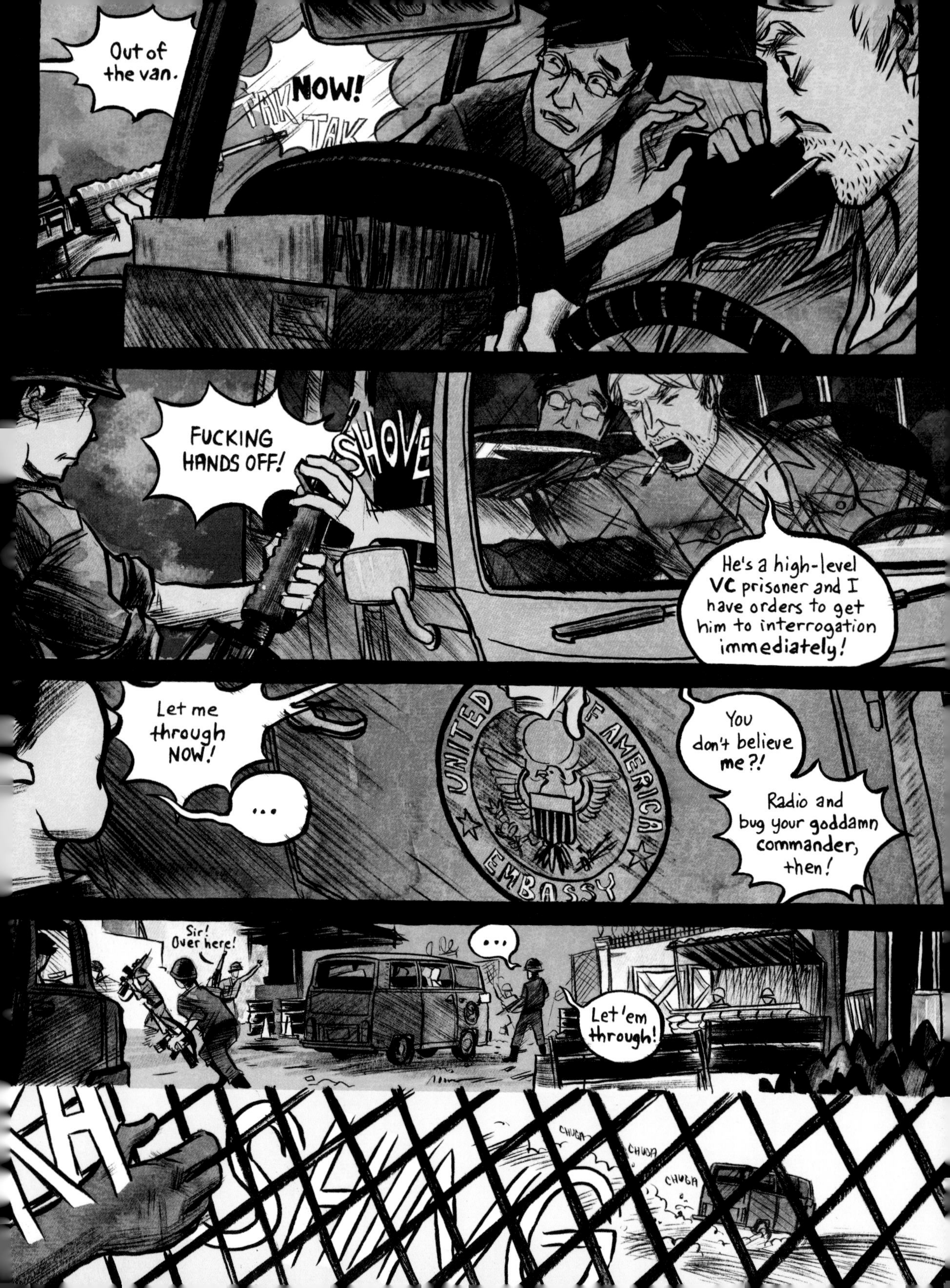
Out of the van.
NOW!
TAK TAK
FUCKING HANDS OFF!
SHOVE
He's a high-level VC prisoner and I have orders to get him to interrogation immediately!
UNITED STATES OF AMERICA EMBASSY
Let me through NOW!
...
You don't believe me?!
Radio and bug your goddamn commander, then!
Sir! Over here!
...
Let'em through!
CHUGA
CHUGA
CHUGA

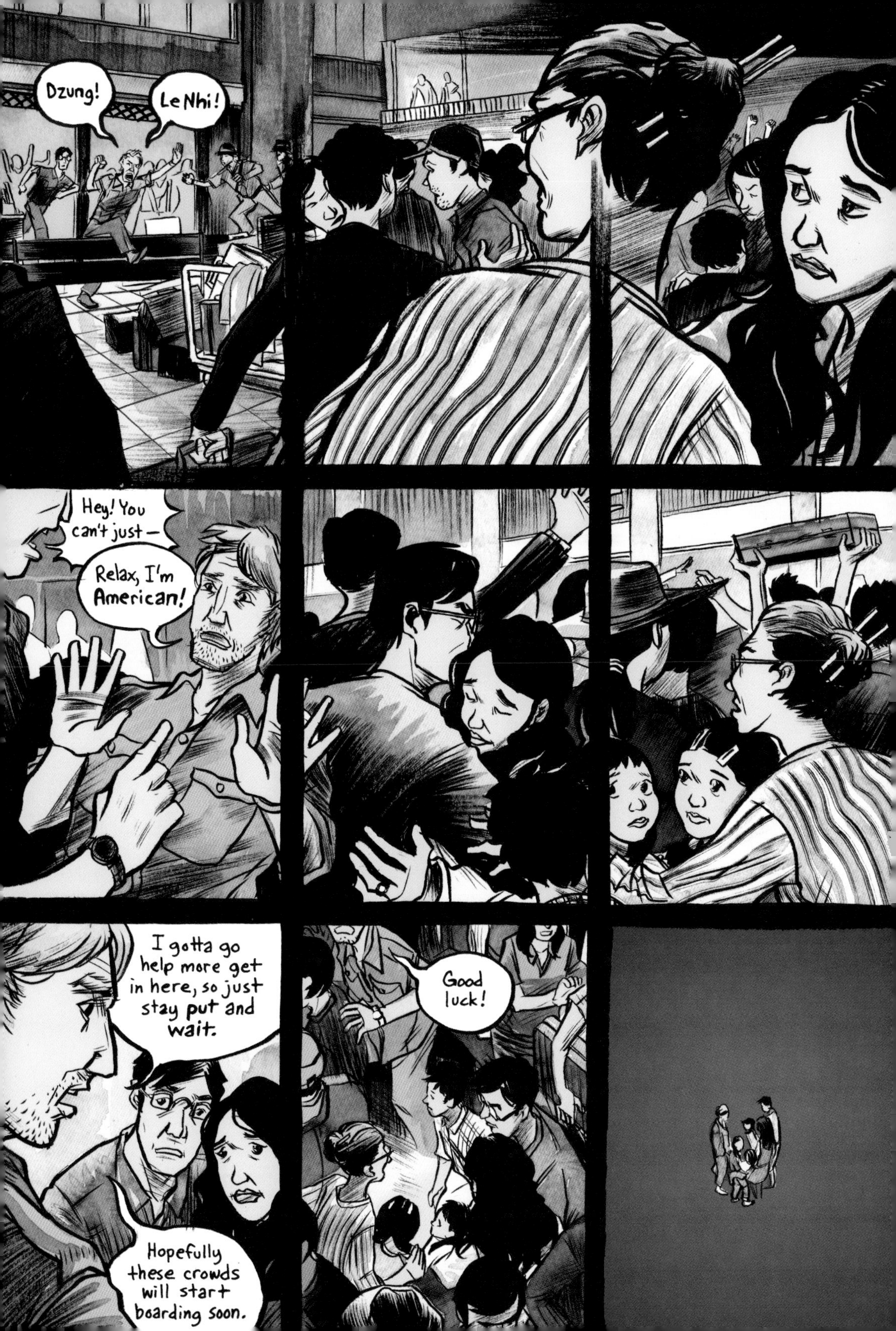
Dzung!
Le Nhi!
Hey! You can't just—
Relax, I'm American!
I gotta go help more get in here, so just stay put and wait.
Hopefully these crowds will start boarding soon.
Good luck!

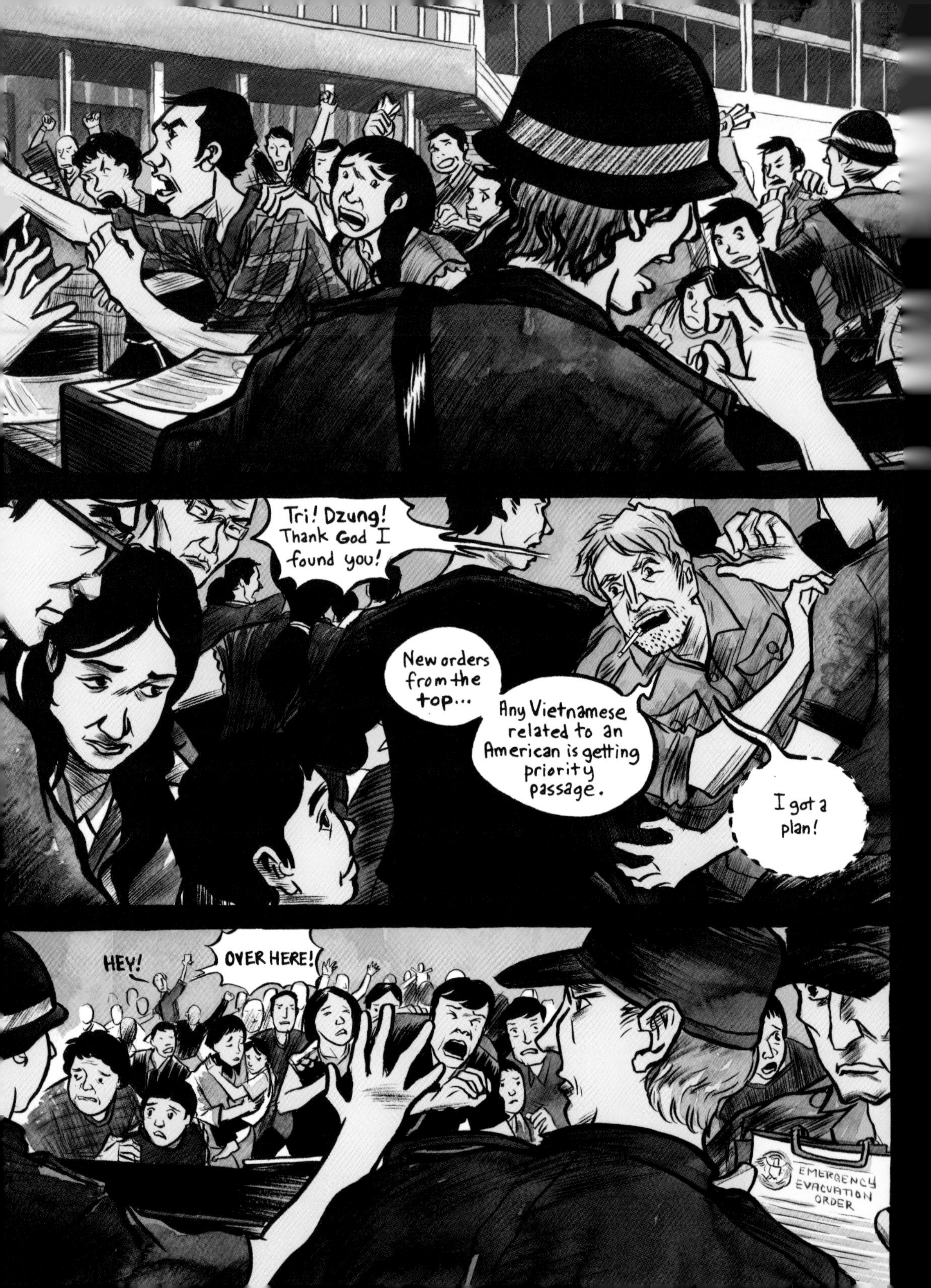

Tri! Dzung! Thank God I found you!
New orders from the top...
Any Vietnamese related to an American is getting priority passage.
I got a plan!
HEY!
OVER HERE!
EMERGENCY EVACUATION ORDER

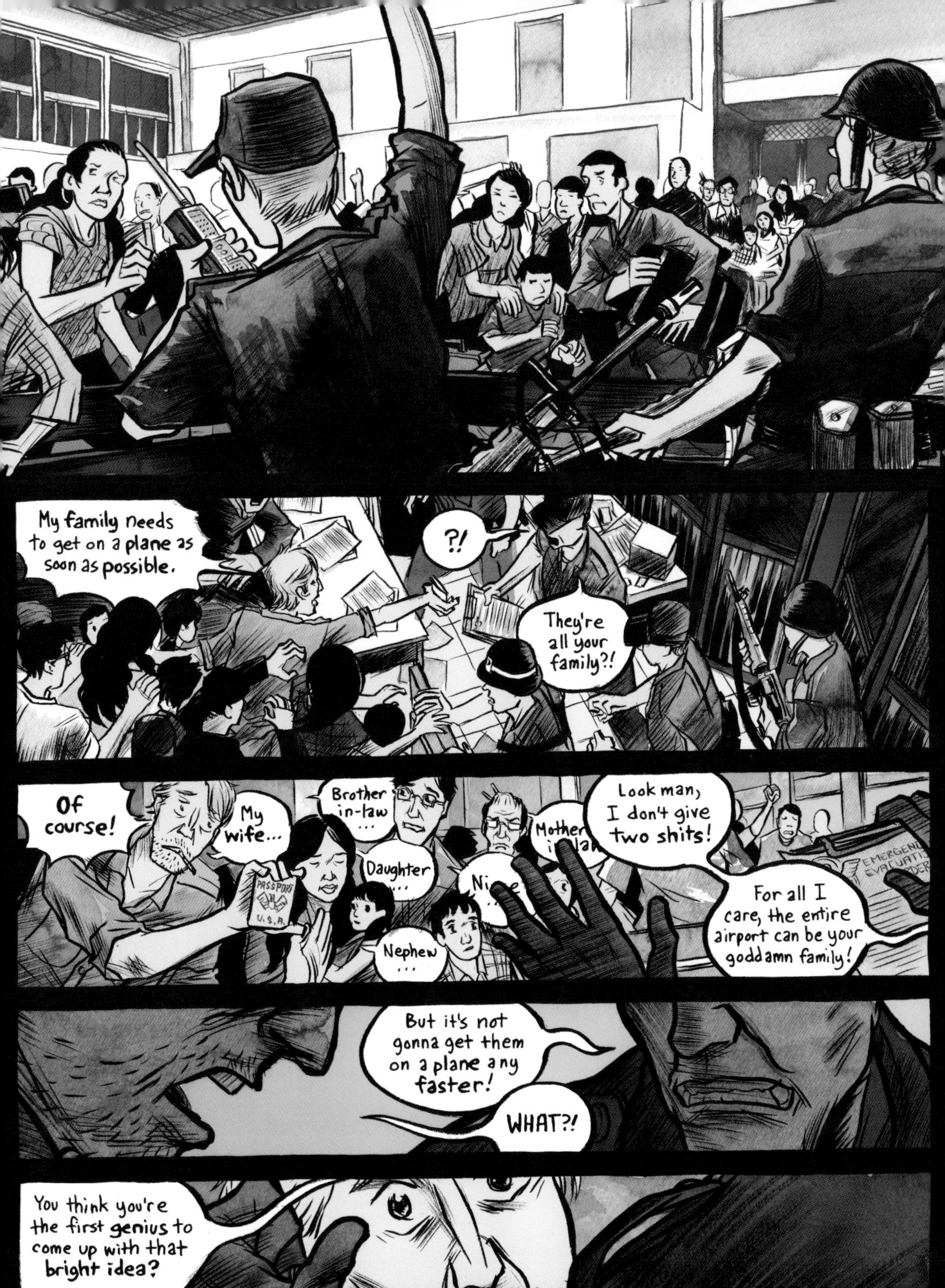
My family needs to get on a plane as soon as possible.
?!
They're all your family?!
Of course!
My wife...
Brother in-law ...
Daughter ...
Nephew ...
Mother in-law
Look man, I don't give two shits!
For all I care, the entire airport can be your goddamn family!
PASSPORT U.S.A.
But it's not gonna get them on a plane any faster!
WHAT?!
You think you're the first genius to come up with that bright idea?

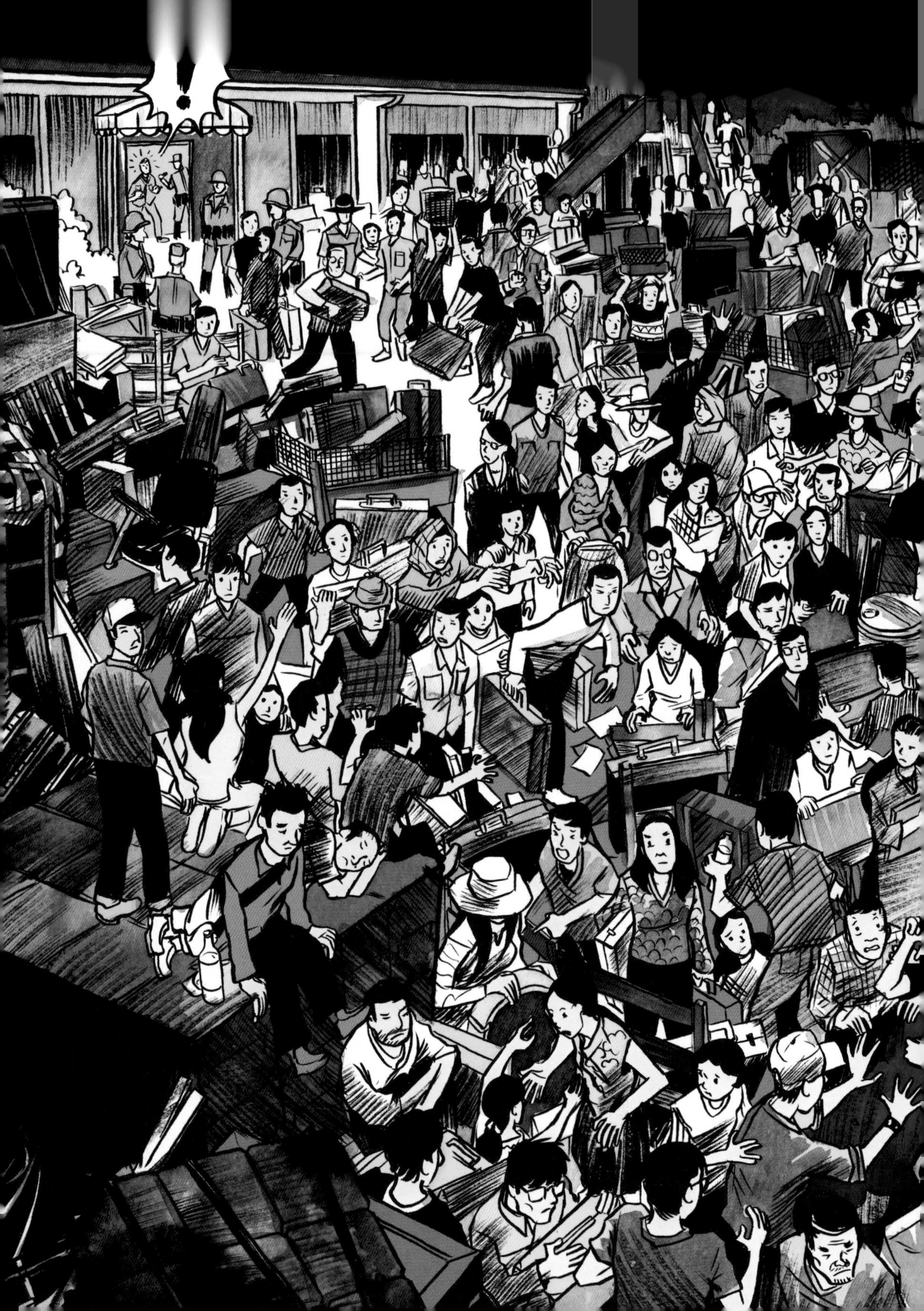
!

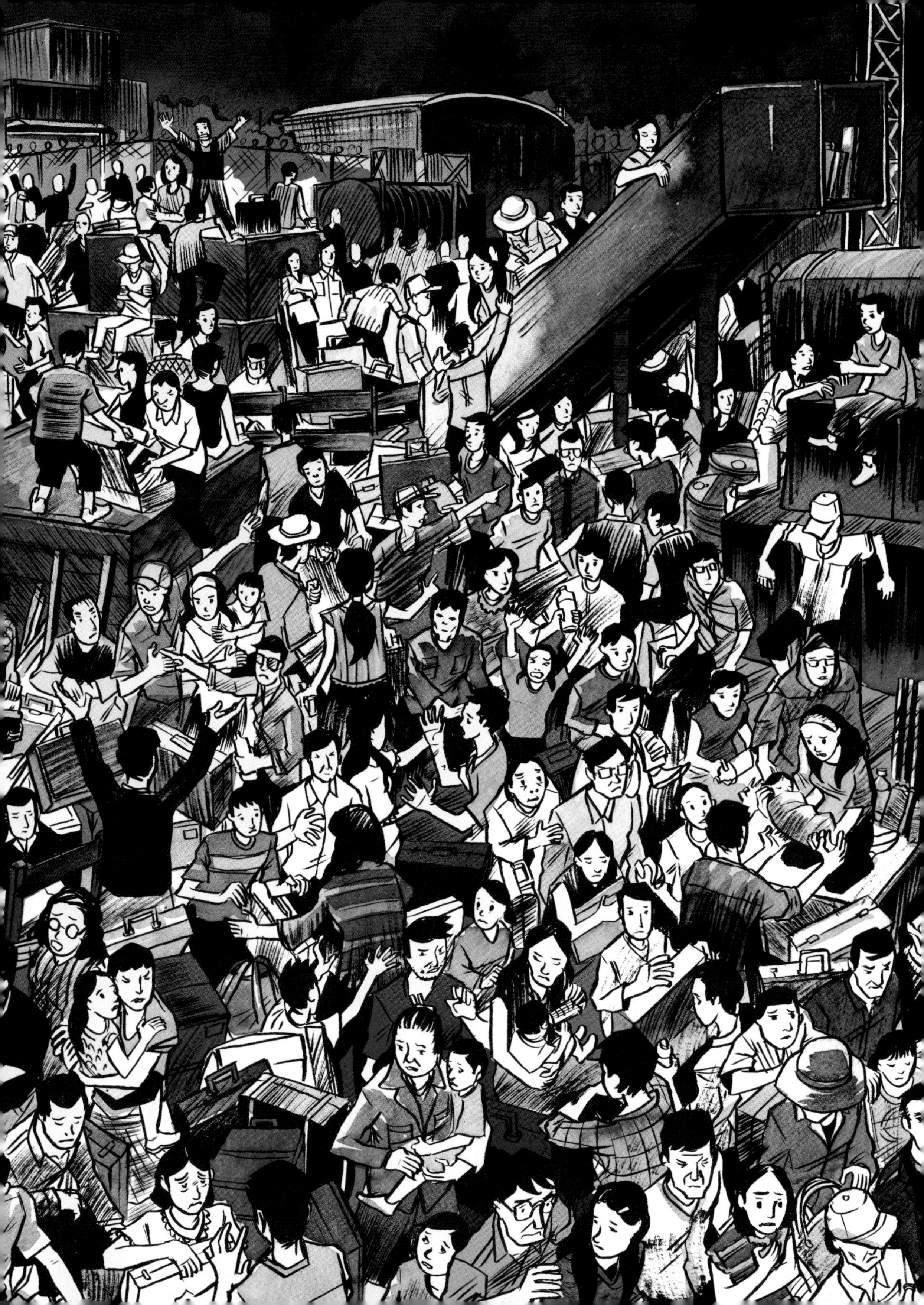

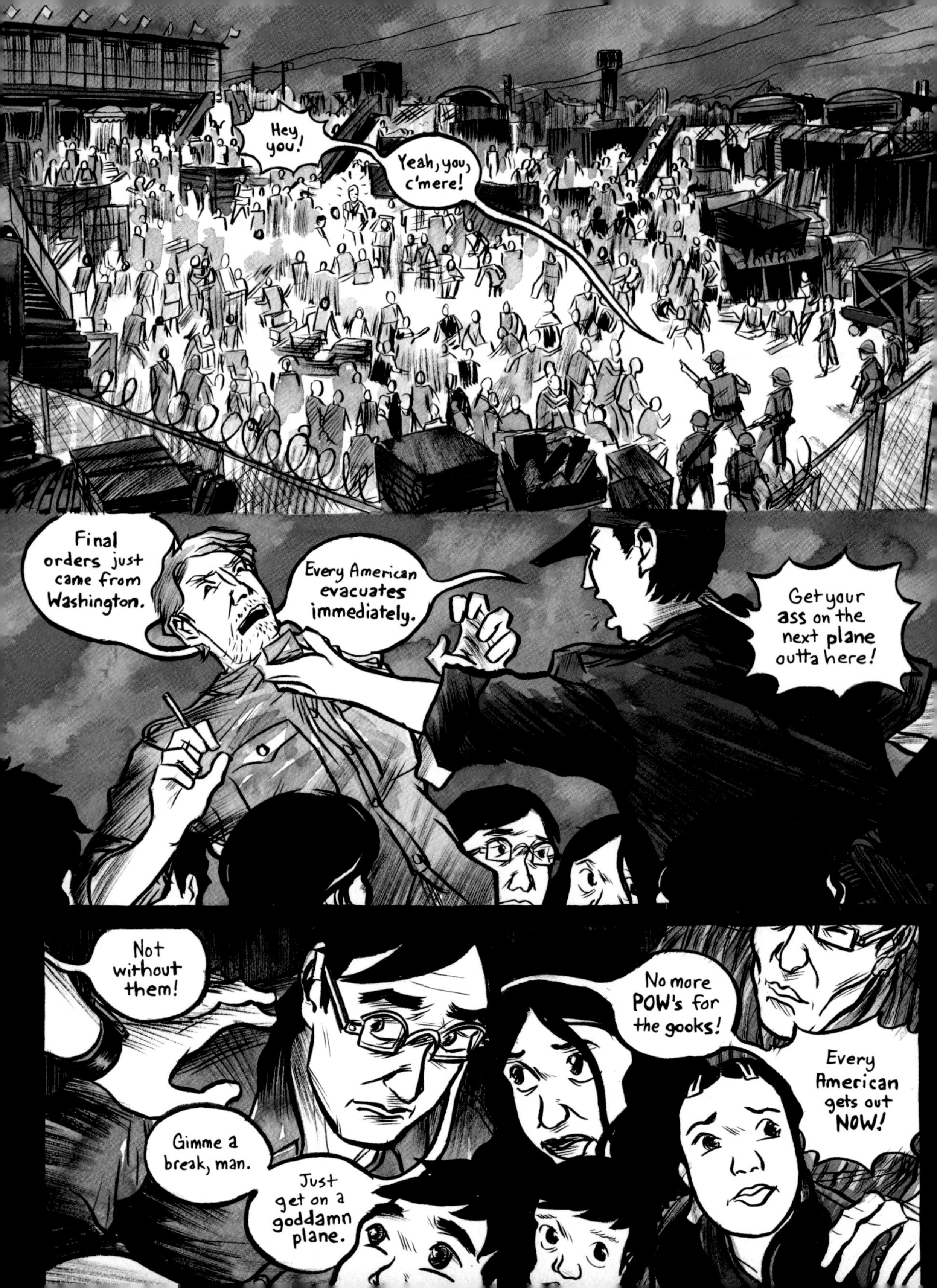
Hey you!
Yeah, you, c'mere!
Final orders just came from Washington.
Every American evacuates immediately.
Get your ass on the next plane outta here!
Not without them!
No more POW's for the gooks!
Every American gets out NOW!
Gimme a break, man.
Just get on a goddamn plane.

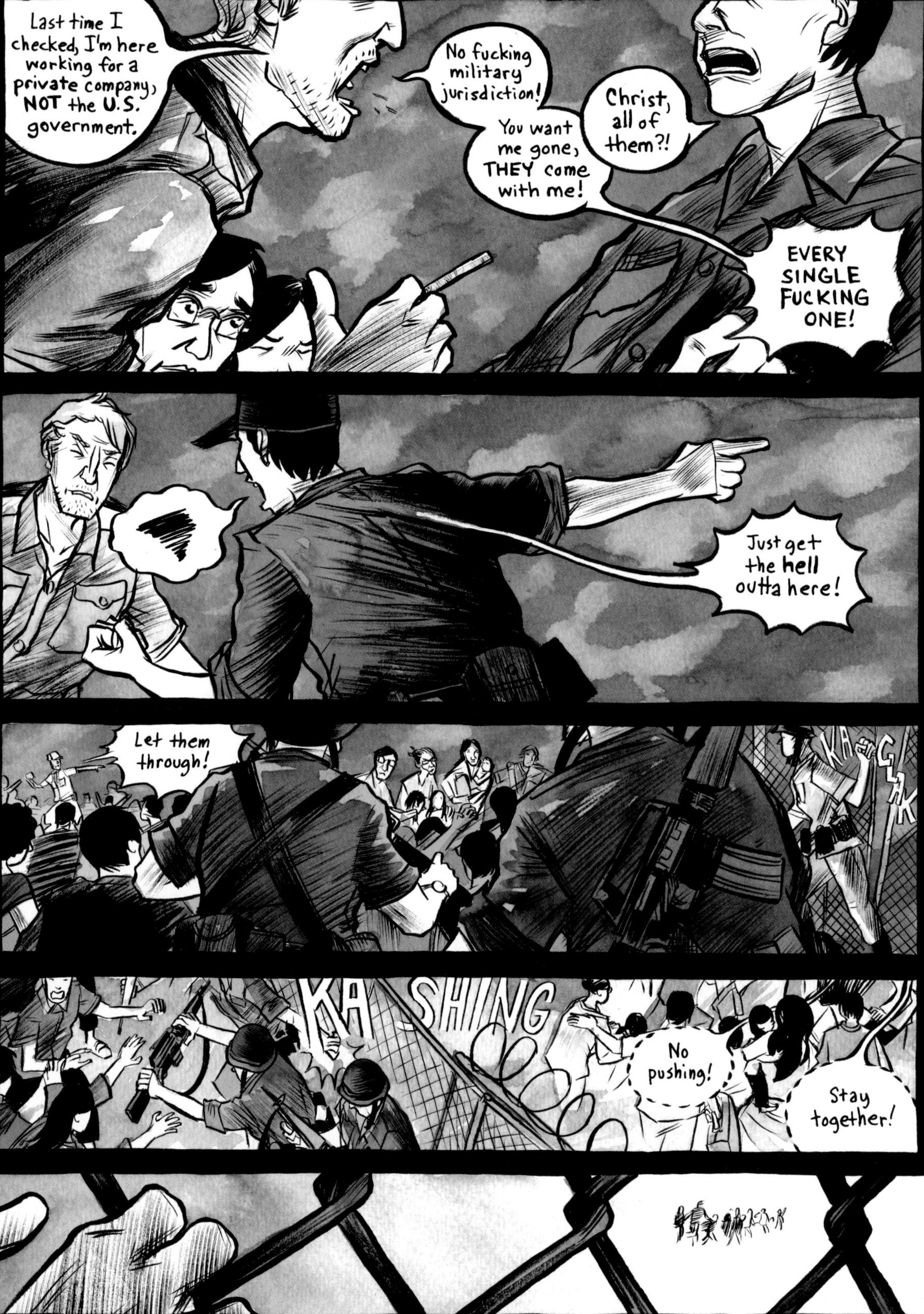
Last time I checked, I'm here working for a private company, NOT the U.S. government.
No fucking military jurisdiction!
You want me gone, THEY come with me!
Christ, all of them?!
EVERY SINGLE FUCKING ONE!
Just get the hell outta here!
Let them through!
KA GLAK
KA SHING
No pushing!
Stay together!

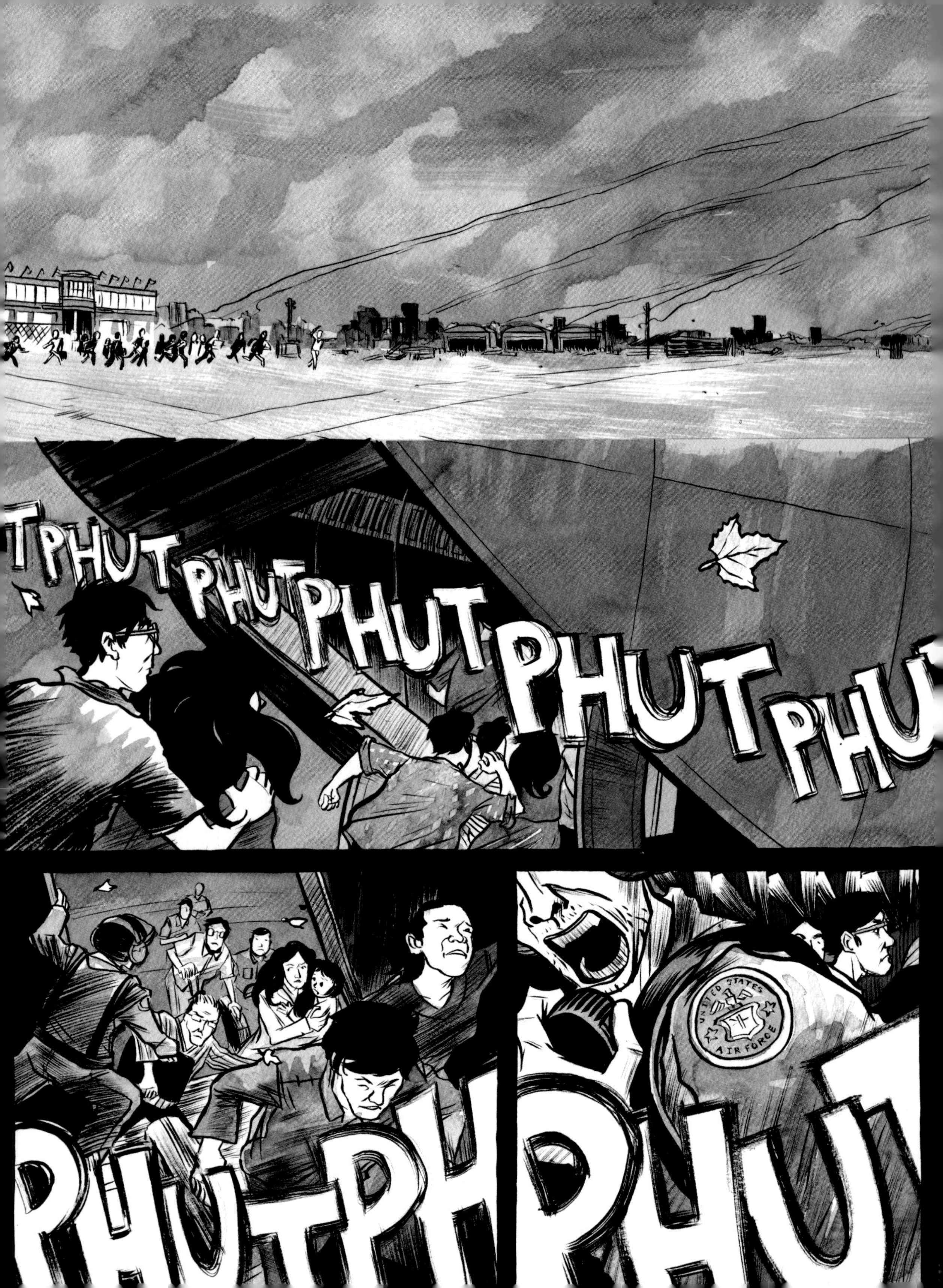
PHUT PHUT PHUT PHUT PHU
PHUT PH
UNITED STATES AIR FORCE
PHU

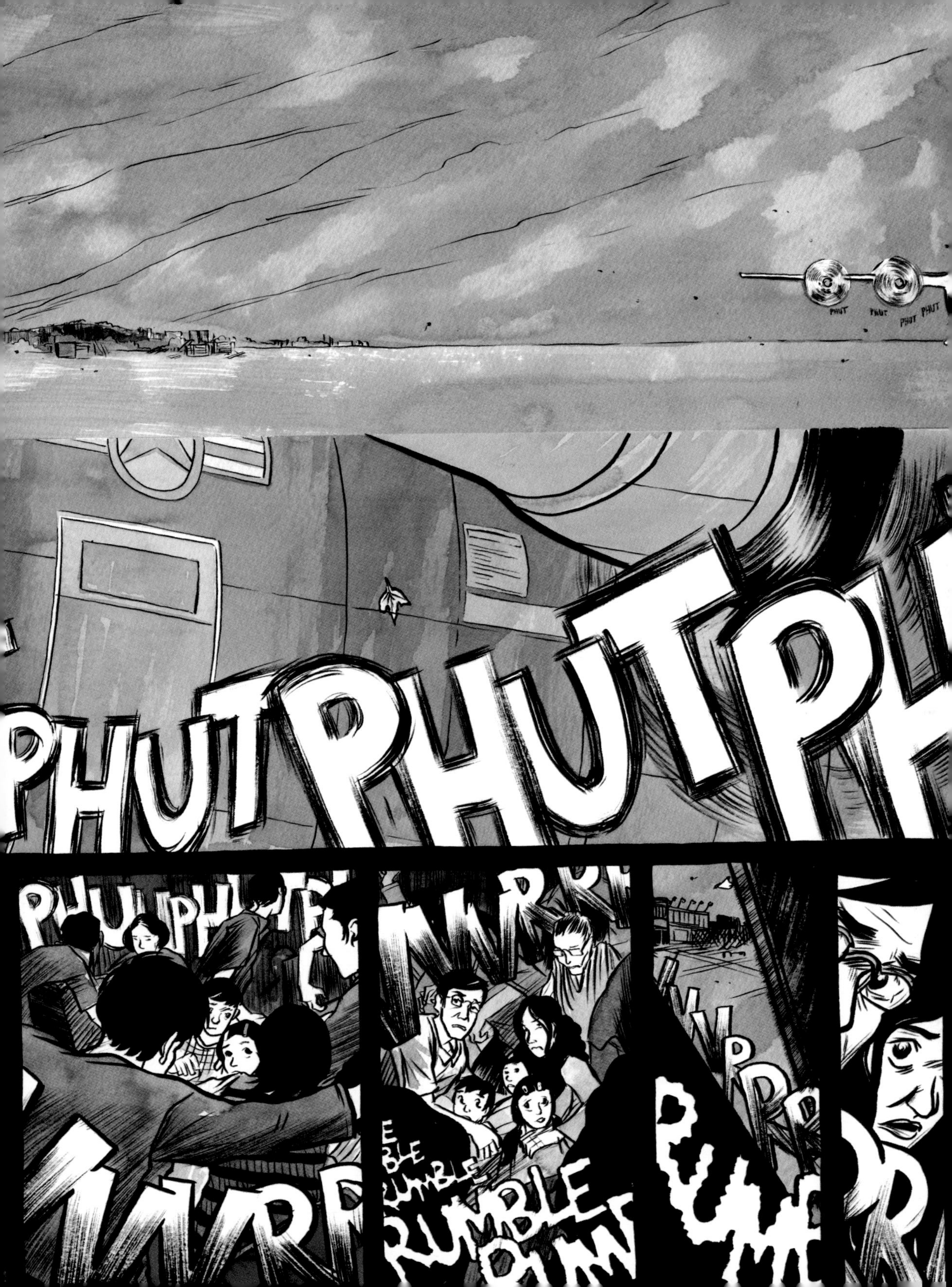
PHUT PHUT PHUT PHUT
PHUT
PHUT
RUMBLE
RUMBLE

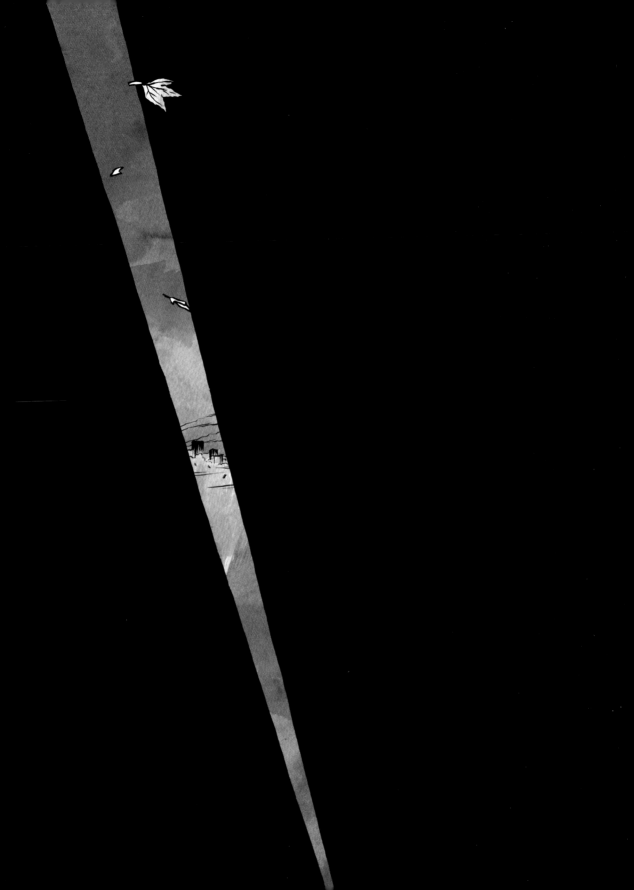

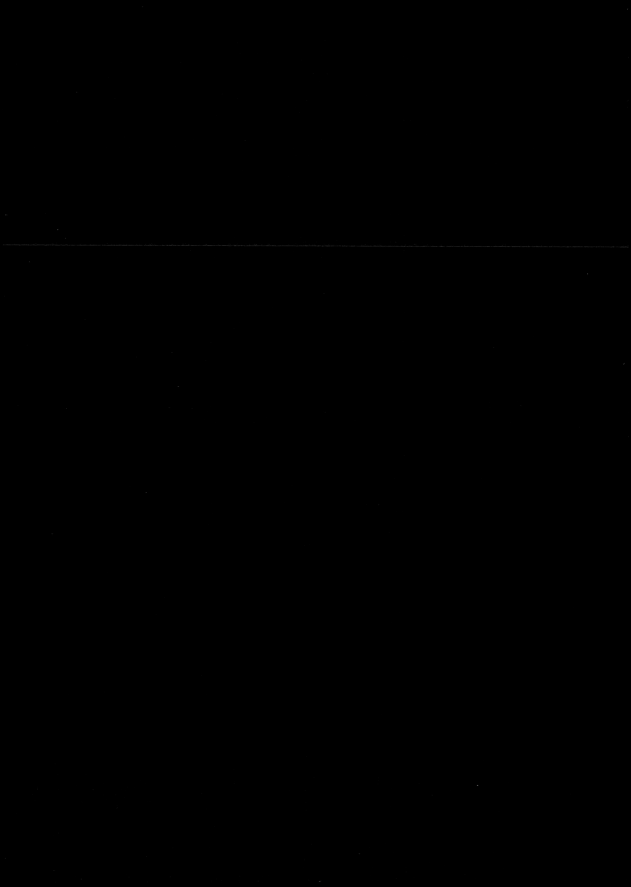

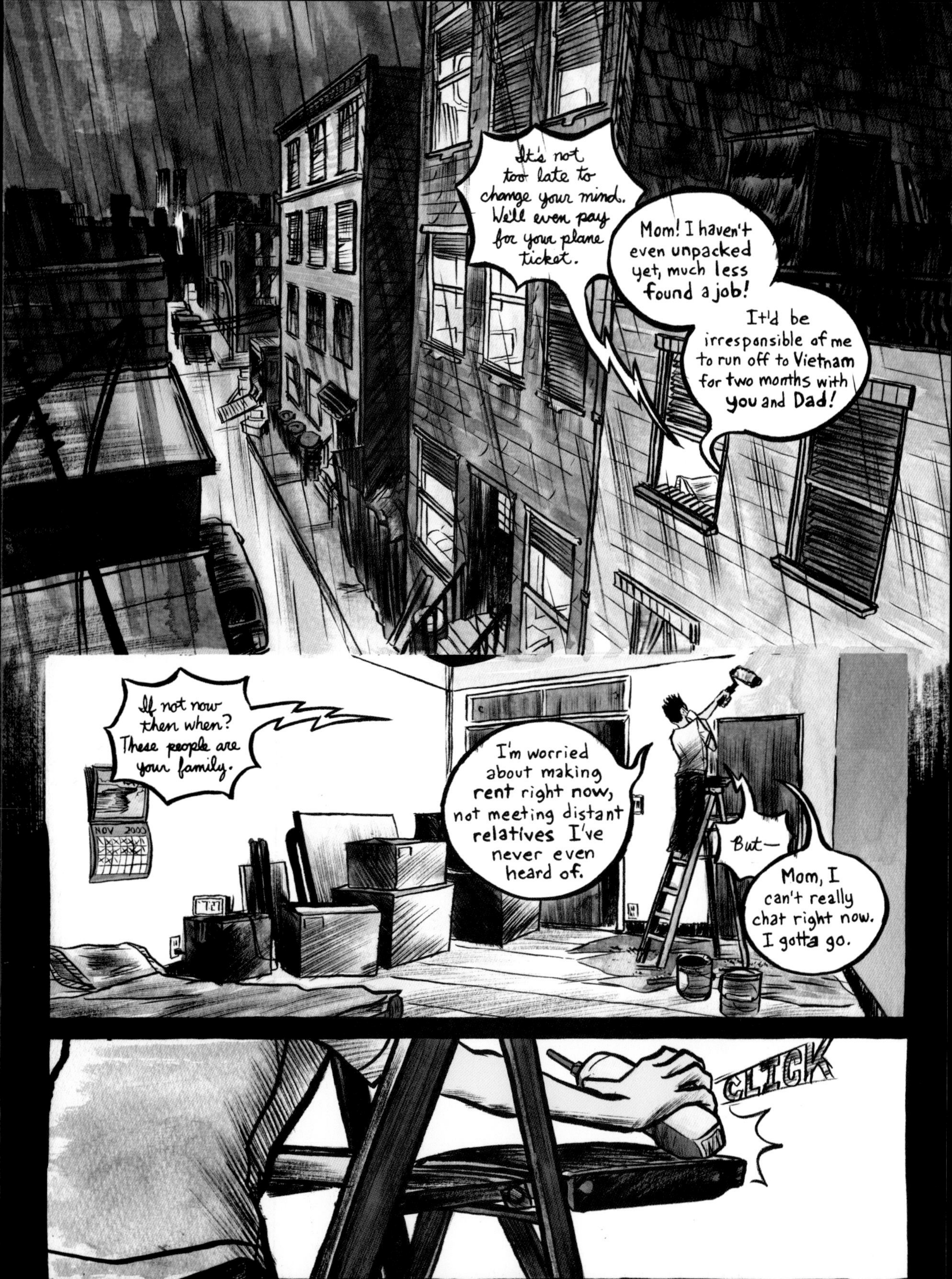
It's not too late to change your mind. We'll even pay for your plane ticket.
Mom! I haven't even unpacked yet, much less found a job!
It'd be irresponsible of me to run off to Vietnam for two months with you and Dad!
If not now then when? These people are your family.
NOV 2000
7:27
I'm worried about making rent right now, not meeting distant relatives I've never even heard of.
But—
Mom, I can't really chat right now. I gotta go.
CLICK

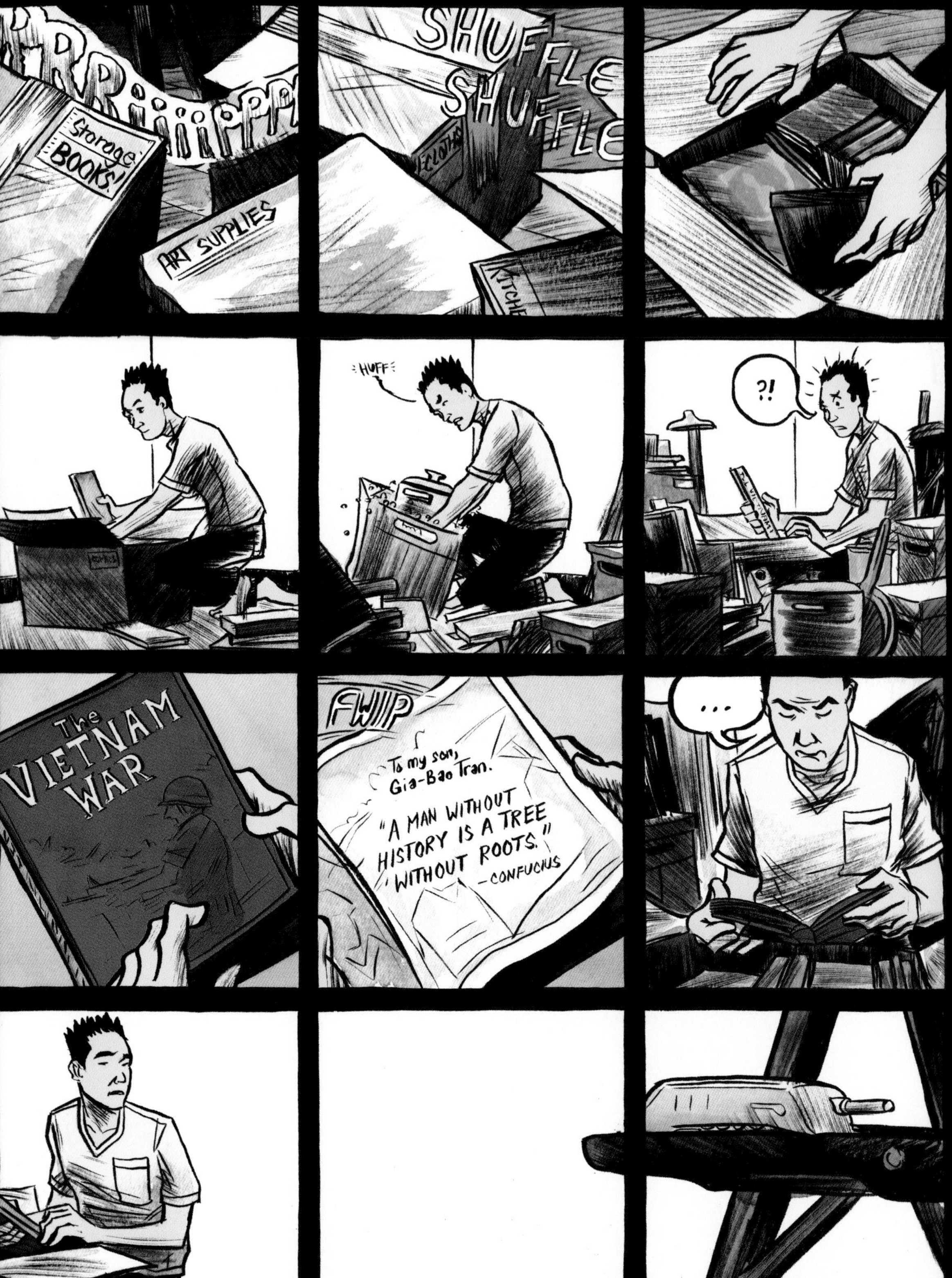

RRRiiiiiPPP
Storage BOOKS!
ART SUPPLIES
SHUFFLE SHUFFLE
CLOTH
KITCHE
HUFF
?!
The VIETNAM WAR
FWIP
To my son, Gia-Bao Tran.
"A MAN WITHOUT HISTORY IS A TREE WITHOUT ROOTS."
-CONFUCIUS
...

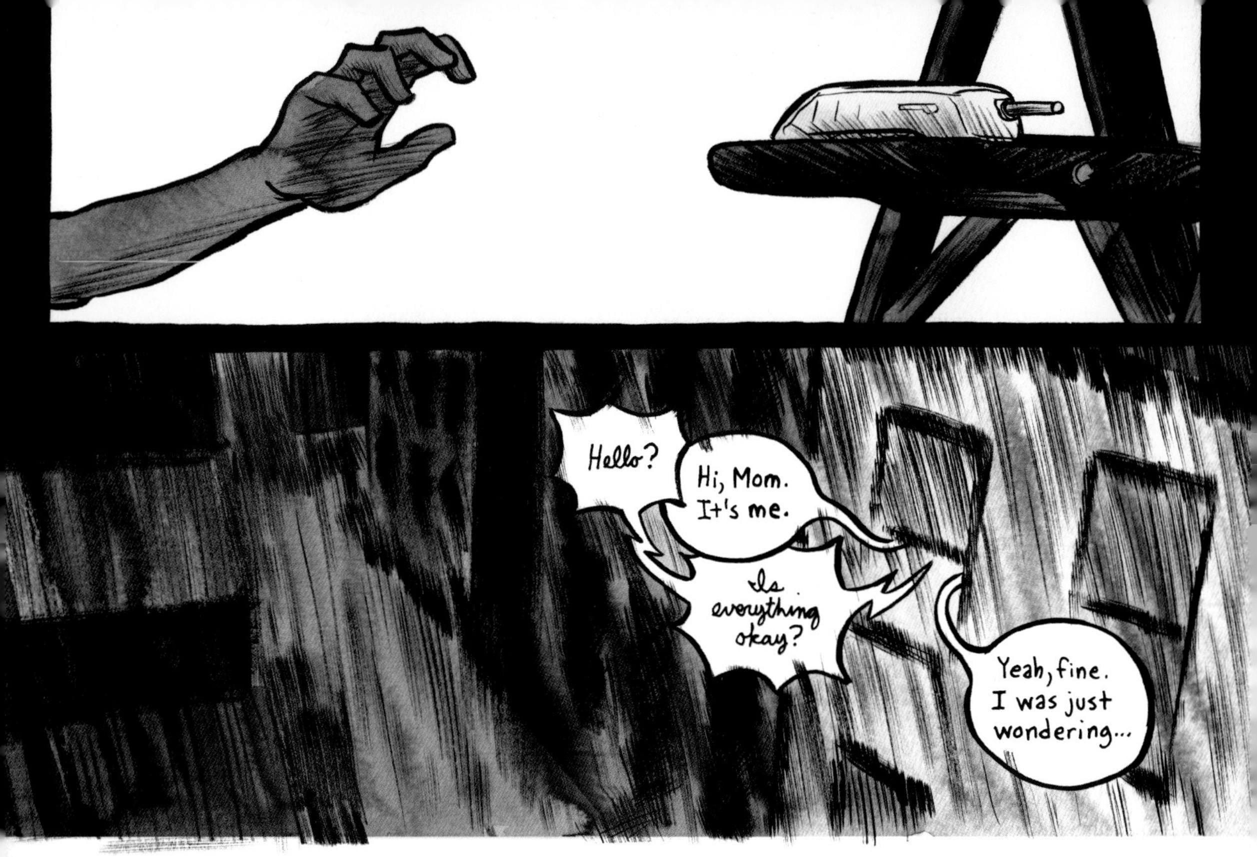
Hello?
Hi, Mom. It's me.
Is everything okay?
Yeah, fine. I was just wondering...

Can I still go to Vietnam with you?

This
book
was
written
and drawn
from April
2008 to April
2010, guided and
edited by Tricia
Pasternak every step
of the way. Thanks also to the critical eye and transformative input of Hanvey
Hsiung, vision and cheerleading of Bob Mecoy, unwavering support of
Dallas Middaugh, buff 'n' polish of Phil Jackson and Leland
Purvis, efficiency training of Josh Blaker, two cents
of Matt Madden, and technical support of Casey
Stock, Alex Meyer, Neil Swaab, and Sarah
Niersbach. Trying to build a single
history from a collective memory
is prone to imperfections and flaws
so thanks to all the cousins, aunts,
uncles, and family and friends who
shared their stories and helped me
puzzle together   my family's past
before it was   too late.
Thanks to   my parents
and siblings   for being
part   of it.

Making this book broke my heart — my deepest gratitude
to Stephanie for putting it all back together.

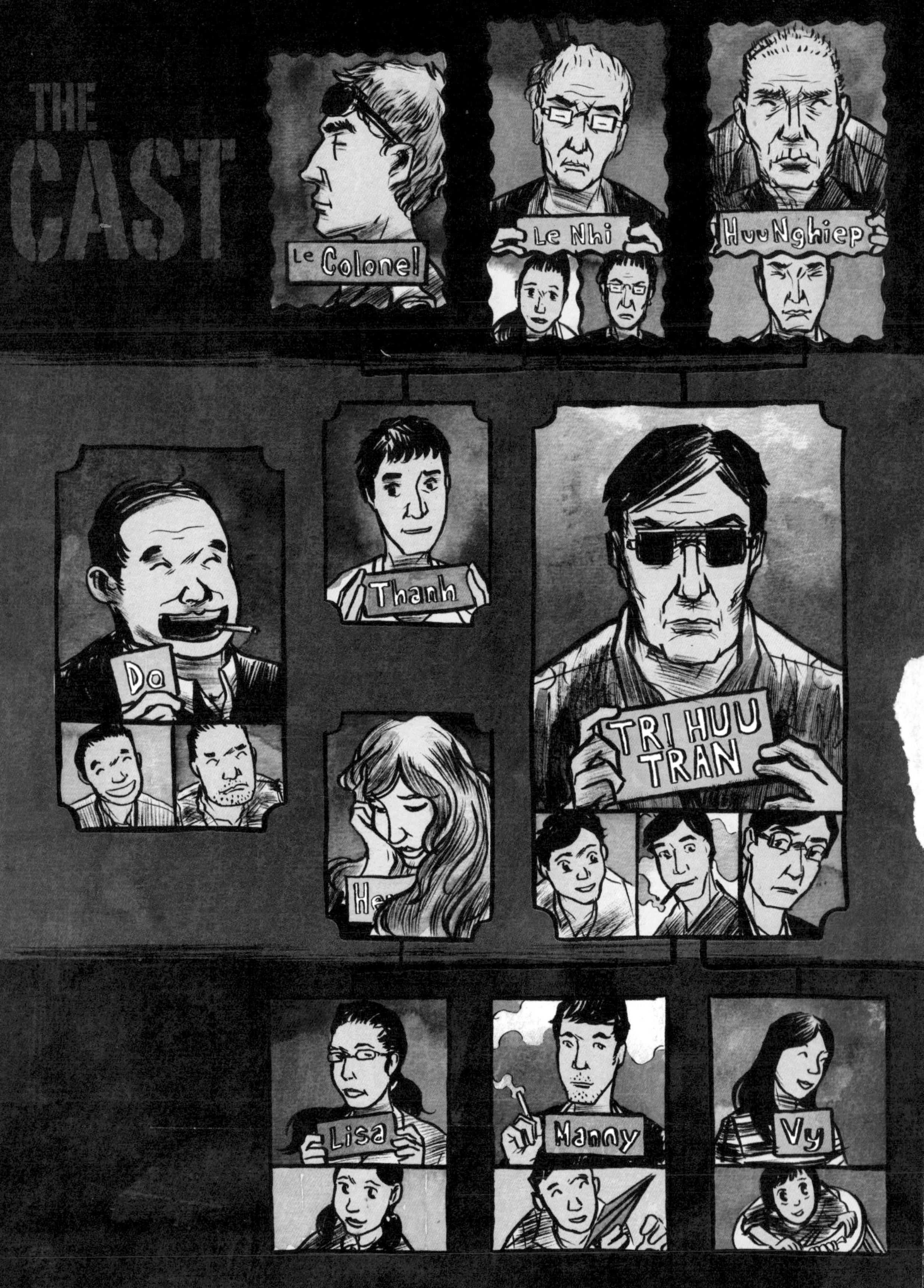
THE CAST
Le Colonel
Le Nhi
HuuNghiep
Do
Thanh
TRI HUU TRAN
Lisa
Manny
Vy